MW00685198

Routes to Language

Routes to Language

Studies in Honor of Melissa Bowerman

Edited by
Virginia C. Mueller Gathercole

New York London

The front cover features a quilt, titled Canopy, made by Gloria Loughman of Clifton Springs in Australia. A contemporary quilt maker, author and teacher, she has spent many years working with students with special needs in the secondary setting. The photo of the quilt is by Tony Loughman. www.glorialoughman.com <outbind://42/www.glorialoughman.com>

Psychology Press
Taylor & Francis Group
270 Madison Avenue
New York, NY 10016

Psychology Press
Taylor & Francis Group
27 Church Road
Hove, East Sussex BN3 2FA

Printed in the United States of America on acid-free paper
10 9 8 7 6 5 4 3 2 1

International Standard Book Number-13: 978-1-84169-716-1 (Hardcover)

Visit the Taylor & Francis Web site at
http://www.taylorandfrancis.com

and the Psychology Press Web site at
http://www.psypress.com

DEDICATION

To Melissa, inspiring teacher, colleague, mentor, scientist, friend

Contents

PART III CROSSLINGUISTIC PATTERNING AND EVENTS, PATHS, AND CAUSES

PART IV INFLUENCES ON DEVELOPMENT

Preface

This volume has been prepared with the utmost dedication and care in honor of one of the lights of the field of child language. Melissa Bowerman has had a profound, widespread, and enduring influence on research conducted for nearly 40 years in our field. Her influence has been both direct—as was the case for, among others, every contributor to this volume—and indirect—the case for every contributor to this volume and every other researcher and student of child language. Her direct influence has taken the form of acting variously as mentor, PhD director, collaborator, and colleague. Her direct and indirect influence have consisted of meticulous, thought-provoking, and insightful examinations of theoretical and empirical claims of key thinkers in the field over the course of her research life; of challenging yet noncombative discussions with collaborators, colleagues, and students; and of precise, careful, and helpful commentaries on written work not only of her own students but also of every manuscript she has reviewed, every paper she has provided comments on. Melissa's work has been wide-ranging, and it has had a major impact on many of the primary theoretical issues that have been of concern across the field.

One would have to look very far indeed to find another researcher with such an optimal mix of qualities as Melissa, either in our field or in any other area of science, for that matter. It is no accident that the authors of the works included here have come back again and again to a multitude of positive labels to describe Melissa: She approaches data and theories with "respect" and "honesty," "seriously," "carefully," and "thoughtfully." In all of her endeavors, she has been "open-minded," "unprejudiced," "noncombative," and "noncontentious," a "model scientist." Her interactions with colleagues and students have been "modest," "patient," "supportive," "warm," and "caring," and, at the same time, "challenging," "firm," "insistent," and "persuasive." The "richness" of her work has inspired many of the authors here, as others, to reevaluate their positions, to change the way they think, and to seek the "truth," both in terms of the "big picture" and the "small details." Her students uniformly consider themselves "blessed," "fortunate," and permanently touched by the "Melissa magic" (Schaefer's term). Her colleagues uniformly report that Melissa "greatly influenced" and "forced them to refine" their thinking.

Melissa Bowerman has applied these qualities to a wealth of areas of inquiry within the field of child language, and in each case, her work, through its precision, its thoughtfulness, and its meticulousness, has opened new avenues of thinking and set new challenges for research in child language. Her early work set her on two important paths that she has continued to pursue throughout her career: focus on crosslinguistic evidence and the mysteries it can help to resolve, and careful examination of theoretical issues concerning the semantic and syntactic structures children are using, based on close consideration of the data. The former began with her work on the acquisition of Finnish (Bowerman, 1973a), the latter with her work on deciphering psychologically real grammars of children's two-word utterances (Bowerman, 1973b, 1975a, 1976a, 1978c).

Melissa's work on Finnish did not just examine the acquisition of a language—and a language type—largely unexplored in the child language literature, although that alone would have been a tremendous gift to a field dominated at the time by English. She also took advantage of the differences between Finnish and English to focus on some of the major theoretical issues of the time: Do children always follow a consistent word order in the early two-word period (as was largely being reported for English)? Did consistency in word order depend on consistency in the input? How do children acquire language in the face of wide variation across languages, and even within a single language, in how meaning gets encoded (Bowerman, 1981b, 1989)?

At the same time, Melissa drew on her work with Roger Brown and colleagues at Harvard and jumped right into the thorniest theoretical debates of the time concerning the syntactic or semantic basis of children's psychologically real grammars in the two-word period (Bowerman, 1971, 1975a, 1976a, 1976b) and the universal versus language-specific properties of early word combinations (Bowerman, 1975b, 1978c). It was her clear thinking and respect for child language data that made her work stand out. This early work also contained seeds of concerns that took on greater focus in later years, such as the relationship of linguistic development and cognitive development (Bowerman, 1978c; Bowerman & Levinson, 2001).

In the mid-1970s, Melissa began consulting data from her own two children, Christy and Eva, for deep and thorough explorations of real-child-language evidence concerning important theoretical issues. The first concern focused on the acquisition of word meaning. Through a careful analysis of her own children's extensions of words over time, Bowerman was able to draw important inferences concerning the intensions of those words. She posited her prototype theory for the acquisition of word meaning (Bowerman, 1978a). Under this theory, she argued, children establish an early prototype for a word and from that word-prototype link they extend the word to new instances on the basis of similarity in one or more ways with the prototypical referent. The fact that those new referents did not necessarily share all semantic features or characteristics with the prototype or the same features with one another led her to argue that children extended words "complexively," on the basis of one or more features of the prototype. At the same time, she argued, the shared features were often perceptual, as had been argued in Clark's (1973) work, but they were also sometimes functional, as Nelson (1973) had proposed. This work immediately put Bowerman on the map as a researcher whose explorations into semantic matters would likely provide considerable insights and continuing challenges to the child language research community.

Bowerman also noticed a wealth of other types of fascinating phenomena in her children's speech, and these became the subject of further inquiry. Her children's production of causative verb errors ("Mommy, can you stay this open?" for "can you CAUSE this to STAY open"; Bowerman, 1978c, p. 384) led her to examine not only children's acquisition of causative verbs (Bowerman, 1974) but also competing theoretical claims of the status of causative verbs in adult English (Bowerman, 1982a, Bowerman & Croft, 2007). Her attention to children's errors with regard to the expression of Figures and Grounds (e.g., "Christy hit the jump rope on my lip," "I touched her hand to his legs"; Bowerman, 1978b) led to her exploration of the acquisition of the expression of such semantic elements, drawing extensively on Talmy's (1985) analyses. And the fact that her children's expression of theta-roles in verb-argument structures did not follow patterns predicted by nativist approaches led her to challenge the position that children are endowed with innate linking rules related to such expression (Bowerman, 1990).

One major focus of all of this work was on the timing of children's errors: Many types of errors emerged long after children were producing correct forms for the structures in question. This led Bowerman to posit (e.g., Bowerman, 1977, 1978d, 1979b, 1979c, 1979d, 1981a, 1982b, 1982c) that children's linguistic systems undergo reorganizational processes during development, and that these late errors provide evidence of clear advances in the child's knowledge of language. She has documented late errors and argued for such reorganization not only in the areas already mentioned (causative verbs, figure/ground expressions), but also, for example, in children's knowledge of semantically related verbs (e.g., the use of *put* and *take* for *make*, which gives evidence that the child has brought together these verbs for change of state and change of location; 1982c, 1983a), in the realms of space and time (1982c, 1983a), in the use of nouns as verbs ("I was just about to *scissor* it"; Bowerman, 1978e, p. 386), in the novel application of *un*-prefixation ("It won't unerase!"; Bowerman, 1978b; "He tippitoed to the graveyard and unburied her"; Bowerman 1983a, p. 455), in the organization of motion verbs (e.g., "I'm frowning out the door" for "I'm MOVING out the door in a frowning manner"; Bowerman, 1981b, p. 176), in the assignment of syntactic roles to noun arguments (Bowerman, 1981b), and in the expression of instruments and agents with *with* and *by* (Bowerman, 1983a).[1]

Bowerman has argued that such U-shaped curves in development provide evidence for "children's disposition to discover structure and regularity in their environment independently of any obvious or immediate instrumental gains" (1982c, p. 141). The late errors are clearly not in response to negative feedback, as that could only explain movement from incorrect to correct forms; and they clearly cannot be explained on the basis of communicative need, as the earlier forms are already correct and "presumably are maximally effective in communication" (1982c, p. 102). Instead, they suggest that children bring together forms that they previously had not seen as linked because "language constantly invites them to do so" (1982c, p. 140).

---

[1] I recall a discussion with Melissa way back in the 70s, while I was still a graduate student, in which she was reporting someone's evidence that children demonstrated early use of certain phonetic characteristics (e.g., the early use of sounds uncommon in early speech), and I recall her saying that she wouldn't care about this, as it did not reveal much about the deeper structural knowledge a child had.

Furthermore, such errors and their abatement pose challenges for theoretical issues concerning children's cutting back of errors when their speech becomes more adult-like (Bowerman, 1983b, 1985a, 1988b).

An important theoretical strand running through this research is the position that one of the tasks of the language-learning child is to discover how the language she is learning packages meaning (Bowerman, 1983a, 1985b, 1988a); much of Bowerman's work examines the extents to which language-universal factors, on the one hand, and language-specific factors, on the other, play roles in that process of discovery. Bowerman's gift has been to examine language-specific patterns in question with a fine-toothed comb in order to address this issue (Bowerman, 1980, 1993, 1994). A telling example comes from her (1979a, 1986) work on the acquisition of conditionals (*if...then* clauses), which emerge late in children's speech. She first explores in detail whether the late emergence is due to cognitive factors, or maybe even pragmatic factors. She rejects both possibilities on the basis of early attempts by children, using other structures, to express exactly the kinds of cognitive and pragmatic messages conveyed by conditionals. She then goes on to explore the types of conditionals children learn early and the types they learn late, and she discovers that there are some aspects of acquisition that appear "universal" and some language-specific: Children's use of conditionals for low-hypothetical future predictives ("If we go out there we haf' wear hats"; Bowerman, 1986) appears to have universal roots. In contrast, English-speaking children appropriately differentiate *if* future predictives from *when* future predictives, a distinction relevant for English but not for, say, German. The child thus shows early attention to how the language she or he is learning cuts up the semantic space for predictives.

The two interlinking paths that Melissa embarked on early in her career—exploring crosslinguistic evidence and the mysteries it can help to resolve and examining theoretical issues based on close consideration of the data—took on slightly new directions when she moved from the University of Kansas to the Max Planck Institute for Psycholinguistics, in Nijmegen. Melissa's work was influenced by both her own new acquisition of (and resulting fascination with) Dutch and by the innumerable top-ranking researchers with whom she was able to interact on a daily basis at the Institute, including the visiting researchers so welcome at the Max Planck. These included Soonja Choi, Lourdes de León, and Penny Brown, among others. She began to focus even more intensively on children's acquisition of linguistic means to express spatial relations, motion events, and cutting and breaking events.

Melissa Bowerman and Soonja Choi began a long-standing collaboration on young children's developing abilities in English, Dutch, and Korean for the expression of spatial relations (Bowerman, 1996a, 1996b; Bowerman & Choi, 2001; Bowerman, de León, & Choi, 1995; Choi & Bowerman, 1991). They discovered that from very early on, the linguistic patterns of children speaking English and children speaking Korean looked more like their adult counterparts than like one another. This work, like Bowerman's previous work, was seminal in prompting a new wave of research, both into crosslinguistic studies of children's acquisition of spatial relations and into the earliest, even prelinguistic, categorization of such relations (Bowerman, in press; Bowerman, Brown, Eisenbeiss, Narasimhan, &

Slobin, 2002; Bowerman & Choi, 2003; Casasola, Wilbourn, & Yang, 2006; Choi, 2006; Choi, McDonough, Bowerman, & Mandler, 1999; Majid, Bowerman, Kita, Haun, & Levinson, 2004; van Staden, Bowerman, & Verhelst, 2006).

A similar flurry of research has surrounded crosslinguistic patterns of acquisition in relation to cutting, breaking, and opening events (Bowerman, 2005; Majid, Bowerman, van Staden, & Boster, in press; Majid, Gullberg, van Staden, & Bowerman, in press; Majid, van Staden, Boster, & Bowerman, 2004). Studies of a variety of languages from distinct language families have shown, again, that there are certain universal characteristics (e.g., a clear distinction between events involving material destruction—i.e., cutting and breaking—and events involving separating, opening, and the like) and certain language-specific differences. The latter include, for example, where the boundaries are placed between cutting and breaking events and whether or not there are general verbs (like English *cut* and *break*) that encompass more specific verbs (*slice, smash*), or only the more specific verbs.

Throughout all of this work, Melissa Bowerman has demonstrated over and over again what a happy marriage between theory and empirical evidence looks like. Her work stands as a model for us all of the nature of true scholarship and science. As one researcher puts it, one can always turn to Melissa when in need of "a well-balanced and knowledgeable idea of what people from competing perspectives are proposing as 'solutions' to issues in the field" (Berman, this volume). The field of child language owes Melissa Bowerman a great debt, and her work promises to continue to be at the forefront of the theoretical edge in the field (e.g., Bowerman & Brown, 2007). The present volume is offered as a tribute to and in gratitude for the wealth of scholarship that Melissa Bowerman has bestowed upon us all.

The chapters presented in this volume reflect a composite picture of some of the wide areas of endeavor in Bowerman's research. The organization of the volume is, rather suitably, a complexive one. We begin with work by two leaders in the area of the acquisition of word meaning, one of these a long-standing colleague of Melissa's, the other a former PhD student of Melissa's who has become a leader in her own right. The first chapter, by Dedre Gentner in collaboration with Lera Boroditsky, lays out in detail the current status of their position on the acquisition of nouns and verbs across languages. Gentner's own ground-breaking work in this area (Gentner, 1982; Gentner & Boroditsky, 2001) has engendered multiple research programs examining the factors contributing to the ease or difficulty of learning distinct classes of words, nouns versus verbs chief among these. Gentner and Boroditsky conduct an analysis of children's acquisition of nouns and verbs in Navajo, a language in which verbs figure prominently: Navajo is a polysynthetic language, in which verbs carry multiple affixes and noun arguments are optional. Using data collected by parents using a Navajo CDI-type checklist, Gentner and Boroditsky find that, despite the prominence of verbs in the language, young Navajo-speaking children still have more nouns than verbs in their speech, whether one judges on the basis of raw numbers of each or the percentage of the nouns and verbs from the checklist in the children's speech. These authors conclude that the Navajo data are further support for the complementary hypotheses, the *natural partitions* hypothesis and the *relational relativity* hypothesis.

In the second chapter, Esther Dromi, well-known for her careful analyses of the acquisition of word meaning, first provides a rich review of theories on this topic since the early 1970s. She looks at these theories and their evolution with 20-20 hindsight, which clarifies how the field has moved from the early categorical views of children's word meanings to more current dynamic systems and emergentist perspectives. Via a new look at her own data from her daughter Keren, she argues that a rich examination of children's early word use provides a complex picture of semantic development, a picture that reflects the best components of the theories that have evolved over the last 40 or so years. These include the claims (1) that early words might not carry categorical meanings from the outset; (2) that at early phases, words may be embedded in schematic representations of contexts; (3) that such words may undergo a lengthy process of decontextualization; (4) that timing is important (early words are slow to be learned, are context-bound, and rely on perceptual salience; later words are acquired more rapidly, are more referential, and are mapped more efficiently, wherein the child can use social and interactive cues); and (5) that conventional, symbolic, and categorical uses of words are emergent properties of the lexicon.

From the acquisition of word meaning, we move on to crosslinguistic patterns and the acquisition of lexical semantics. Two related chapters report on work conducted by close research colleagues of Melissa's. In chapter 3, Lourdes de León, who teamed up with Melissa in the 1990s to work on the Mayan language Tzotzil, addresses the acquisition of 'fall' and 'eat' verbs in Tzotzil. These are of interest because for each there is a wide range of specific verbs, and there is no general verb for either. As understanding falling and eating may entail prelinguistic concepts, the acquisition of the Tzotzil verbs can provide some further insight into the relative roles of cognitive and linguistic influences on early verb learning. Through an examination of two girls' speech, as well as that of caregivers, de León argues that already in the one-word period, children are sensitive to the semantic structure of their native language. At the same time, she argues for contributions from both cognition and semantics in development, because (cognitive) attention to gravity effects appears to be the best explanation for the precocious acquisition of the word *p'aj* 'fall from high' relative to other verbs for falling.

In chapter 4, Bhuvana Narasimhan and Penelope Brown, two colleagues of Melissa's working on the expression of space at the Max Planck Institute for Psycholinguistics in Nijmegen, take up a similar concern, that of children's early preference for general versus specific categories. Narasimhan and Brown examine children's expression of containment in two languages—one a Mayan language, Tzeltal, closely related to the Tzotzil studied by de León, the other Hindi. The "Semantic Specificity Hypothesis," they argue, would predict that children should (1) acquire semantically specific terms as early as semantically general terms; (2) use such expressions appropriately; and (3) underextend semantically general terms.

Through an examination of two children's speech, as well as that of caregivers, in each language, Narasimhan and Brown argue that the data for both languages are inconsistent with the hypothesis. In Hindi, children's acquisition of the most general form occurs early, following frequency of input, and is not restricted semantically; in Tzeltal, one of the more general forms is learned first, followed quickly by many of the very specific forms. However, the general forms are not always preferred, as another general form in Tzeltal is not acquired until later.

From crosslinguistic patterns and the acquisition of lexical semantic structure we turn to crosslinguistic patterns and the theoretical understanding of event structure and of motion events. In Bowerman's own work, theoretical models have figured crucially—either, on the one hand, as sources of insight into the structural challenges facing the child learning language, or, on the other, as theoretical models that can be critically tested through evidence from child language. In this section, three chapters written by close colleagues and collaborators of Melissa's provide new theoretical analyses and insights that could have important ramifications for similar such considerations of child language data in the future.

In chapter 5, William Croft, a long-standing expert on linguistic typology and on construction grammar approaches to linguistic analysis, addresses the nature of the causal-aspectual structure of events, drawing on a force-dynamic approach to the assignment of thematic roles in clauses. He proposes that a proper treatment of event structure and the assignment of argument roles within clauses relating to those events requires two major components—aspectual structure and force-dynamic structure. Within every event, he posits, each participant undergoes its own subevent, and these subevents are related causally to effect a force-dynamic chain within the larger event structure. Each subevent should be described with its own aspectual/construal scale, which, he proposes, involves time (t) and qualitative state (q) as its dimensions. With time and qualitative state acting as features, a full range of aspectual types can be captured; Croft argues that all predicates are flexible and have a range of aspectual potential, with most having at least two or three possible construals, some (e.g., *touch*) many more. When a third dimension, force dynamics, is added relating the t/q subevents for each participant in an event, the larger event structure is adequately captured as a causal chain of subevents causing other subevents.

In chapter 6, Soonja Choi, who, as noted above, has collaborated extensively with Bowerman on comparisons of the acquisition of Korean with the acquisition of English and Dutch, explores the expression of PATH and CAUSE in Verb-framed and Satellite-framed languages (Talmy, 1985). V-framed languages typically encode PATH of motion in the main verb, while S-framed languages encode PATH in "satellites" (particles, affixes); conversely, S-framed languages encode CAUSE in the main verb, while V-framed languages do not. Through elicited production of descriptions of motion events by speakers of four languages, English (S-framed), Spanish, Korean, and Japanese (all V-framed), she explores possible syntactic and cognitive ramifications of this typological difference. With regard to the expression of PATH in spontaneous motion contexts, she finds two critically distinct types of PATH: "endpoint" paths, in which the Ground is the semantic goal or source of motion, and "trajectory" paths, in which the Ground is the path itself. For the former, "endpoint" paths, speakers of all four languages used intransitive verbs to express motion. However, for "trajectory" paths, speakers of the V-framed languages used transitive constructs, while speakers of English, the S-framed language, used intransitive constructs. She argues that it is the syntax of V-framed languages that allows this distinction, and that it is not the choice of verb itself that controls the difference between transitive and intransitive constructs in V-framed languages, but the type of path itself.

With regard to CAUSE, Choi similarly finds differences: While all languages use transitive constructs when an explicit agent is present, they differ when an explicit agent is not present, when both spontaneous and caused motion are involved, or when there is indirect causation. In these cases, speakers of English favor transitive and passive constructs, and the expression of the causation. When motion is only implied (e.g., a woman is first in a room, and then out of a room, but no movement is shown), English speakers do not express motion or path, focusing instead on change of state; Japanese and Korean speakers tend to express paths; and Spanish speakers fall between these two extremes. Choi concludes that the lexicalization patterns of the language influence the treatment of different types of PATH and whether causes or trajectories are highlighted by speakers. At the same time, she argues, languages do not fall into a strict dichotomy, but, rather, form a continuum.

In chapter 7, Dan Slobin, one of the most tireless advocates for crosslinguistic studies of child language, continues the exploration into PATHS, with an eye to exploring how paths of motion relate to the expression of paths of vision across languages. He asks whether differences across S-framed and V-framed languages in their expression of physical paths carry over into their expression of visual paths. He first examines the expression of visual paths in four languages, English, Russian (both S-framed), Spanish, and Turkish (both V-framed). He finds that, while there are commonalities across these languages in certain means of expressing paths of vision, the S-framed languages, which allow more elaborate path descriptions in relation to physical paths, also allow more, and more elaborate, combinations of components expressed in relation to visual paths. He suggests that, just as the structure of the language directs "thinking for speaking" about physical paths, it by extension also influences conceptualizations regarding paths of vision.

Expanding this exploration to the development of the expression of visual paths in children's speech, Slobin considers children's (and caregivers') productive descriptions of paths of vision both in CHILDES transcripts and in transcripts of the *Frog Stories* (Mayer, 1969). He argues that there is evidence from early on of language-specific influence on children's expressions. Among the differences across the four groups is the use of boundary-crossing adverbials in Spanish, a distinction between path vs. placement functions of path markers in Russian and Turkish, and more elaborate paths in English. He thus concludes that these data support the claim that language "filters" and "packages" concepts from the start.

In the final section, we turn from the consideration of crosslinguistic patterns and the structure of events and motion to a focus on the more general question of what influences children's language development. In chapter 8, Eve Clark, another of the best-known researchers of child language, and the first person ever to collaborate with Bowerman (on a study concerning phonological development!) (Clark & Bowerman, 1986), examines the role of the input in children's developing systems. Clark argues that adults "shape the way children speak," and children make use of the information adults provide by conforming to the principles of

Conventionality and Contrast. Clark suggests that adults offer information to children in two fashions. First, adults offer appropriate terms for things, relations, and events, as well as information that elaborates on the relation between those conventional terms and others. (For example, they might comment on distinguishing properties of a new referent, or on common membership of this word/category with others in a larger, superordinate category, or on meaning relations between words.) The second way in which adults shape children's language is by providing feedback, in the form of reformulations, when children make errors. Adults do this, according to Clark, 50% to 70% of the time when children make errors, and they do so in all areas of the grammar—phonology, morphology, syntax, and the like. Such reformulations are provided usually as side sequences (66% of the time) or embedded corrections. Clark's evidence that these offers from adults are significant in language development comes from her examination of children's responses in immediately following turns: Children repeat what was said, they acknowledge the correction, or they reject it. This is not to say that the correction is taken up flawlessly, because, Clark points out, correcting errors may take time because children sometimes need to override well-entrenched patterns. Clark concludes that child-directed speech ultimately plays a crucial role in language acquisition by children.

A distinct perspective is taken in chapter 9, by Ping Li, a former PhD student of Melissa's, and one whose own reputation is rapidly gaining stature. Li examines the acquisition of meaning from a connectionist–emergentist perspective of language development. He argues that the child's discovery of meaning emerges as a natural outgrowth of the processing of statistical probabilities—the frequency of co-occurrence of form-to-form, form-to-meaning, and meaning-to-meaning mappings. Li discusses the development of language in three realms, that of tense/aspect, that of cryptotypes (or covert semantic categories embedded within a form like *un-* in combination with the roots to which it attaches), and that of lexical structure. Through an analysis of children's acquisition of tense and aspect in Chinese and a comparison with their acquisition of similar, yet not identical, structures in other languages, Li comes to the conclusion, like others in this volume and like Bowerman in so much of her work, that children are highly sensitive to the language-specific properties of the input, and they extract systematic patterns from it. Li also reports computational modeling of the acquisition of verbs that can take *un-* and of lexical–semantic structure in language. In the case of *un-*, hierarchical cluster analysis reveals that a computational model can develop clusters of verbs that do and do not take *un-* on the basis of statistical probabilities. Such probabilities defy description as involving "rules" for inclusion, as the cryptotype involves "interactive gangs" of minicryptotypes whose members vary on the number of features relevant to the group, on how strongly each feature is activated, and on how strongly the features overlap across members.

Li also reports on computational modeling of the development of lexical structures—word classes and word semantics—as emergent properties of the system. Using DevLex, an unsupervised learning model (i.e., one with no feedback regarding correct and incorrect forms), Li and colleagues exposed the system to real-world parental input culled from CHILDES. On the basis of transitional probabilities of co-occurrences between words in the input, and of associative strength between units (e.g., units gained associative strength if they were activated at the same time), the system was able to gradually develop word classes and semantic classes (such as animals, people, food, etc.). While the initial organization and category membership was diffuse and distributed, eventually, through continuous adaptation to the input structure, the later organization became more focused and more localized. Li concludes, "the semantic structure of the lexicon, whether it be overt or covert, can emerge from the interaction between the learner and the linguistic input in the form-meaning mapping process...."

Chapter 10 tackles a somewhat distinct theoretical question, one that draws on research involving children with Specific Language Impairment (SLI) to gain insights concerning language development in general. Mabel Rice, well-known for her work in both child language disorders and theoretical approaches to SLI, and one of the first PhD students coming out of Melissa's Kansas University days, takes a fresh look at language abilities in children with SLI. She turns the tables on the normal perspective on children with SLI (as children with language difficulties or deficits) and raises the challenge of trying to solve a conundrum: How is it that children with SLI can demonstrate deficits in learning some aspects of language, and yet show robust abilities in other areas of linguistic development? Rice reviews a wealth of proposals that have been made concerning the best explanation for the causal deficits in children with SLI. These include a possible breakdown in learning processes, including memory limitations or general cognitive limitations; possible domain-specific linguistic limitations; and possible genetic causes (which, she points out, could be consistent with either of the first two).

Rice argues that the hallmark problems that SLI children show in language development are (1) delay in the acquisition of vocabulary (virtually all SLI children are late talkers—but not all late talkers have SLI); (2) problems with grammatical tense marking; and (3) late onset of overregularization errors. Yet SLI children show robust abilities in the discovery of latent linguistic structure in a variety of other areas. They produce few morphological errors, they avoid overt errors in a wide range of constructs (including those in which they are weak), and they show no special/added difficulties if they are growing up as bilinguals and have to face more than one language. Rice argues that one of the fundamental lessons from work on SLI is that it has revealed that language acquisition involves multiple linguistic dimensions with differentiated timing mechanisms. Since acquisition is protracted in SLI children, this provides a window into what aspects of development may or may not necessarily be connected, in a way that we cannot see with nonaffected children, whose acquisition may give an erroneous impression of language as a unitary construct with co-linear dimensions of development. What SLI has revealed is that certain aspects of development, especially morphosyntactic development, can be out of synchrony with other aspects of linguistic development.

The final chapter, by Virginia Mueller Gathercole, examines the contributions of cognitive development and linguistic structure, including semantic and syntactic aspects of structure, to the development of scalar predicates. "Scalar predicates" here include a wide range of related structures that encode specification of the degree to which a property or quantity is present. Included are structures built on adjectives and on the quantifiers *much* and *many*— chief among these *A-er*, *A-est*, *very A, so A, too A, as A as, A enough; more (N), most (N), very much/many (N), so much/many (N), too much/many (N), as much/many (N), enough (N).* By analyzing data from two children's spontaneous utterances over time, I trace children's semantic and syntactic use of these structures. The data reveal some striking phenomena: First, children begin using these structures in very restricted, small-scale formal patterns (e.g., *many* and *how many* only in reference to age; *too A* only with *late* and *heavy* to mean "can't"; initial use of *much* always with Determiner modifiers— e.g., *too much*; and so forth). Second, early uses involve simpler cognitive concepts such as intensification, rather than more complex concepts such as scalarity. Third, the evolution of the full system proceeds small step by small step, at each turn the children expanding their usage of forms to encompass a wider set of forms. Fourth, syntactic development takes place over a long, protracted period, with the development of quantifier phrases ("as many N," "so much N," "such a big guy," "taller than he is fat," and the like) and stacked quantifier phrases ("much too big," "much bigger," "as much nicer," etc.) lasting well beyond the ages studied here (up to age 6). Fifth, the child's initial use of predicates that express relative position of a property along a scale, as seen from a lower level upwards on the scale ("as old as me," "big enough to V," etc.), is nonscalar. This leads children to use and interpret these scalar forms (as well as others, such as *until*) inappropriately. Finally, children's developing understanding of scalarity appears linked with their developing understanding of number, and they draw on this link in their expression of scalarity ("I'm 150 tired"). The data lead to the conclusion that the child's developing cognitive understanding acts hand in hand with the child's developing syntactic and semantic abilities and that together they "invite" the child towards a full development of the relevant structures.

As an introduction to each chapter, each author provides a short personal statement of how Melissa Bowerman has played a major role in his or her work and life. Interspersed among these, as well, are statements from a few other researchers for whom Melissa has played significant roles, either as their teacher (Jidong Chen, Ronald Schaefer, Angelika Wittek) or as colleague (Leonard Talmy, Ruth Berman, Martha Crago). These statements speak eloquently for themselves; together they provide at least a small glimpse of how rich and life-changing it can be to have someone as incomparable as Melissa Bowerman in one's academic (and personal) life.

So without any further ado, we will BREAK OFF here, CUT to the chase, and save SPACE for the chapters to come. The hope is that these new studies will help MOVE the field forward in ways that will lead to new and LATER EMERGING theories and PATHS of inquiry, in a MANNER that is suitably UN-assuming IN honor of the amazing woman who is the CAUSE of the production of this volume.

REFERENCES

Bowerman, M. (1971). Review [Lois Bloom, *Language development: Form and function in emerging grammars*]. *American Scientist, 61*, 369–370.

Bowerman, M. (1973a). *Early syntactic development: A cross-linguistic study with special reference to Finnish*. New York: Cambridge University Press.

Bowerman, M. (1973b). Structural relationships in children's utterances: syntactic or semantic? In T. E. Moore (Ed.), *Cognitive development and the acquisition of language* (pp. 197–213). New York: Academic Press..

Bowerman, M. (1974). Learning the structure of causative verbs: A study in the relationship of cognitive, semantic, and syntactic development. *Papers and Reports on Child Language Development, 8*, 142–178.

Bowerman, M. (1975a). Commentary and reply to Bloom, L., Lightbown, P., & Hood, L. Structure and variation in child language. *Monographs of the Society for Research in Child Development 40* (2, Serial No. 160), 80–90.

Bowerman, M. (1975b). Cross-linguistic similarities at two stages of syntactic development. *Foundations of Language Development* (Vol. 1. pp. 267–282). New York: Academic Press.

Bowerman, M. (1976a). Commentary on M. D. S. Braine, Children's first word combinations. *Monographs of the Society for Research in Child Development 41* (1) serial no. 164, 98–104.

Bowerman, M. (1976b). Semantic factors in the acquisition of rules for word use and sentence construction. In D. Morehead & A. Morehead (Eds.), *Directions in normal and deficient child language* (pp. 99–179). Baltimore: University Park Press.

Bowerman, M. (1977). The acquisition of rules governing "possible lexical items": Evidence from spontaneous speech errors. *Papers and Reports on Child Language Development, 13*, 148–156.

Bowerman, M. (1978a). The acquisition of word meaning: An investigation of some current conflicts. In N. Waterson & C. Snow (Eds.), *Development of communication: Social and pragmatic factors in language acquisition* (pp. 263–287). New York: Wiley.

Bowerman, M. (1978b, May 19–22). *Reorganizational processes in lexical and syntactic development.* Paper prepared for workshop-conference on "The State of the Art" in Language Acquisition: University of Pennsylvania.

Bowerman, M. (1978c). Semantic and syntactic development: A review of what, when, and how in language acquisition. In R. L. Schiefelbusch (Ed.), *Bases of language intervention* (Vol. 1, pp. 97–189) Baltimore: University Park Press.

Bowerman, M. (1978d). Systematizing semantic knowledge: Changes over time in the child's organization of word meaning. *Child Development, 49*, 977–987.

Bowerman, M. (1978e). Words and sentences: Uniformity, individual variation, and shifts over time in patterns of acquisition. In F. D. Minifie & L. L. Lloyd (Eds.), *Communicative and cognitive abilities: Early behavioural assessment* (pp. 349–396). Baltimore: University Park Press.

Bowerman, M. (1979a). The acquisition of complex sentences. In P. Fletcher & M. Garman (Eds.), *Language Acquisition* (pp. 285–305). Cambridge: Cambridge University Press.

Bowerman, M. (1979b, March 30–April 1). *Explorations in recombinant semantics: The child's acquisition of patterns for lexicalizing the notion of motion*. Paper prepared for Sloan Workshop on "Words and Concepts," Stanford University.

Bowerman, M. (1979c). Systematizing semantic knowledge: Changes over time in the child's organization of word meaning. *Child Development, 49*, 977–987.

Bowerman, M. (1979d). Words and sentences: Uniformity, variation, and shifts over time in patterns of acquisition. In F.D. Minifie & L.L. Lloyd (Eds.), *Communicative and cognitive abilities—Early behavioral assessment* (pp. 349–396). Baltimore: University Park Press.

Bowerman, M. (1980). The structure and origin of semantic categories in the language learning child. In M. Foster & S. Brandes (Eds.), *Symbol as sense* (pp. 277–299). New York; Academic Press.

Bowerman, M. (1981a). Beyond communicative adequacy: From piecemeal knowledge to an integrated system in the child's acquisition of language. *Papers and Reports in Child Language Development, 20*, 1–24.

Bowerman, M. (1981b). The child's expression of meaning: Expanding relationships among lexicon, syntax, and morphology. In H. Winitz (Ed.), *Native language and foreign language acquisition* (pp. 172–189). New York: The New York Academy of Sciences.

Bowerman, M. (1982a). Evaluating competing linguistic models with language acquisition data: Implications of developmental errors with causative verbs. *Quaderni di Semantica, 3*(1), 5–66.

Bowerman, M. (1982b). Reorganizational processes in lexical and syntactic development. In E. Wanner & L. R. Gleitman (Eds.), *Language acquisition: The state of the art* (pp. 319–346). New York: Academic Press.

Bowerman, M. (1982c). Starting to talk worse: Clues to language acquisition from children's late speech errors. In S. Strauss & R. Stavy (Eds.), *U-shaped behavioral growth* (pp. 101–146). New York: Academic Press.

Bowerman, M. (1983a). Hidden meanings: The role of covert conceptual structures in children's development of language. In D. R. Rogers & J. A. Sloboda (Eds.), *The acquisition of symbolic skills* (pp. 445–470). New York: Plenum.

Bowerman, M. (1983b). How do children avoid constructing an overly general grammar in the absence of feedback about what is not a sentence? *Papers and Reports on Child Language Development 22*, 23–35.

Bowerman, M. (1985a). Beyond communicative adequacy: From piecemeal knowledge to an integrated system in the child's acquisition of language. In K. E. Nelson (Ed.), *Children's language* (Vol. 5, pp. 369–398). Hillsdale, NJ: Erlbaum.

Bowerman, M. (1985b). What shapes children's grammars? In D. Slobin (Ed.), *The crosslinguistic study of language acquisition* (Vol. 2, pp. 1257–1319). Hillsdale, NJ: Erlbaum.

Bowerman, M. (1986). First steps in acquiring conditionals. In E. Traugott, C. A. Ferguson, J. Snitzer Reilly, & A. ter Meulen (Eds.), *On conditionals* (pp. 285–307). Cambridge, UK: Cambridge University Press.

Bowerman, M. (1988a). Inducing the latent structure of language. In F. S. Kessel (Ed.), *The development of language and language researchers: Essays in honor of Roger Brown* (pp 23–50). Hillsdale, NJ: Erlbaum.

Bowerman, M. (1988b). The "no negative evidence" problem: How do children avoid constructing an overly general grammar? In J. Hawkins (Ed.), *Explaining language universals* (pp. 73–101). Oxford: Basil Blackwell.

Bowerman, M. (1989). Learning a semantic system: What role do cognitive predispositions play? In M. L. Rice & R. L. Schiefelbusch (Eds.), *The teachability of language* (pp. 133–169). Baltimore: Paul H. Brookes.

Bowerman, M. (1990). Mapping thematic roles onto syntactic functions: Are children helped by innate linking rules? *Linguistics, 28*, 1253–1289.

Bowerman, M. (1993). Typological perspectives on language acquisition: Do crosslinguistic patterns predict development? In E. V. Clark (Ed.), *Proceedings of the Twenty-fifth Annual Child Language Research Forum* (pp. 7–15). Stanford, CA: Center for the Study of Language and Information.

Bowerman, M. (1994). From universal to language-specific in early grammatical development. *Philosophical Transactions of the Royal Society of London B, 346*, 34–45.

Bowerman, M. (1996a). Learning how to structure space for language—A crosslinguistic perspective. In P. Bloom, M. Peterson, L. Nadel, & M. Garrett (Eds.), *Language and space* (pp. 385–436). Cambridge, MA: MIT Press.

Bowerman, M. (1996b). The origins of children's spatial semantic categories: Cognitive vs. linguistic determinants. In J. J. Gumperz & S. C. Levinson (Eds.), *Rethinking linguistic relativity* (pp. 145–176). Cambridge, UK: Cambridge University Press,

Bowerman, M. (2005). Why can't you "open" a nut or "break" a cooked noodle? Learning covert object categories in action word meanings. In L. Gershkoff-Stowe & D. Rakison (Eds.), *Building object categories in developmental time* (pp. 209–239). Mahwah, NJ: Erlbaum.

Bowerman, M. (2007). Containment, support and beyond: Constructing topological spatial categories in first language acquisition. In M. Aurnague, M. Hickmann, & L. Vieu (Eds.), *The categorization of spatial entities in language and cognition* (pp. 177–203). Amsterdam: John Benjamins.

Bowerman, M., & Brown, P. (Eds.). (2007). *Crosslinguistic perspectives on argument structure: Implications for learnability.* Mahwah, NJ: Erlbaum.

Bowerman, M., Brown, P., Eisenbeiss, S., Narasimhan, B., & Slobin, D.I. 2002. Putting things in places: Developmental consequences of linguistic typology. Online *Proceedings of the Child Language Research Forum 2002.* http://cslipublications.stanford.edu/CLRF/2002/CLRF-2002-title.html.

Bowerman, M., & Choi, S. (2001). Shaping meanings for language: Universal and language-specific in the acquisition of spatial semantic categories. In M. Bowerman & S. C. Levinson (Eds.), *Language acquisition and conceptual development* (pp. 475–511). Cambridge, UK: Cambridge University Press.

Bowerman, M., & Choi, S. (2003). Space under construction: Language-specific spatial categorization in first language acquisition. In D. Gentner & S. Goldin-Meadow (Eds.), *Language in mind* (pp. 387–427). Cambridge: MIT Press.

Bowerman, M., & Croft, W. (2007). The acquisition of the English causative alternation. In M. Bowerman & P. Brown (Eds.), *Crosslinguistic perspectives on argument structure: Implications for learnability.* Mahwah, NJ: Erlbaum.

Bowerman, M., de León, L., & Choi, S. (1995). Verbs, particles, and spatial semantics: Learning to talk about spatial actions in typologically different languages. In E. V. Clark (Ed.), *Proceedings of the Twenty-seventh Annual Child Language Research Forum* (pp. 101–110). Stanford, CA: Center for the Study of Language and Information.

Bowerman, M., & Levinson, S.L. (Eds.). (2001). *Language acquisition and conceptual development.* Cambridge: Cambridge University Press.

Casasola, M., Wilbourn, M. P., & Yang, S. (2006). Can English-learning toddlers acquire and generalize a novel spatial word? *First Language, 26*(2), 187–205.

Choi, S. (2006). Influence of language-specific input on spatial cognition: Categories of containment. *First Language, 26*(2), 207–232.

Choi, S., & Bowerman, M. (1991). Learning to express motion events in English and Korean: The influence of language-specific lexicalization patterns. *Cognition, 41*, 83–121.

Choi, S, McDonough, L., Bowerman, M., & Mandler, J. (1999). Early sensitivity to language-specific spatial categories in English and Korean. *Cognitive Development, 14*, 241–268.

Clark, E. V. (1973). What's in a word? On the child's acquisition of semantics in his first language. In T. E. Moore (Ed.), *Cognitive development and the acquisition of language* (pp. 65–110). New York: Academic Press.

Clark, E. V., & Bowerman, M. (1986). On the acquisition of final voiced stops. In J. A. Fishman (Ed.), *Festschrift for Charles A. Ferguson* (pp. 51–68). Amsterdam/Berlin: Mouton.

Gentner, D. (1982).. Why nouns are learned before verbs: Linguistic relativity versus natural partitioning. In S. Kuczaj (Ed.), *Language development: Language, cognition, and culture* (pp. 301–334). Hillsdale, NJ: Erlbaum.

Gentner, D., & Boroditsky, L. (2001). Individuation, relativity and early word learning. In M. Bowerman & S. Levinson (Eds.), *Language acquisition and conceptual development* (pp. 215–256). New York: Cambridge University Press.

Majid, A., Bowerman, M., Kita, S., Haun, D., & Levinson, S. C. (2004). Can language restructure cognition: The case of space. *Trends in Cognitive Science, 8*, 108–114.

Majid, A., Bowerman, M., van Staden, M., & Boster, J. (in press). The semantic categories of cutting and breaking events: A crosslinguistic perspective. [Special issue] *Cognitive Linguistics.*

Majid, A., Gullberg, M., van Staden, M., & Bowerman, M. (in press). How similar are semantic categories in closely related languages? A comparison of "cutting and breaking" in four Germanic languages. *Cognitive Linguistics.*

Majid, A., van Staden, M., Boster, J. S., & Bowerman, M. (2004). Event categorization: A cross-linguistic perspective. *Proceedings of the 26th Annual Meeting of the Cognitive Science Society* (pp. 885–890).

Mayer, M. (1969). *Frog, where are you?* New York: Dial Press.

Nelson, K. 1973. Structure and strategy in learning to talk. *Monograph of the Society for Research in Child Development*, 38 (1–2 serial no. 149).

Talmy, L. 1985. Lexicalization patterns. In T. Shopen (Ed.), *Language typology and syntactic description: Vol. 3. Grammatical categories and the lexicon* (pp. 59–149). Cambridge, UK: Cambridge University Press.

van Staden, M., Bowerman, M., & Verhelst, M. 2006. Some properties of spatial description in Dutch. In S. C. Levinson & D. Wilkins (Eds.), *Grammars of space* (pp. 477–513). Cambridge, UK: Cambridge University Press.

Acknowledgments

I wish to express my deepest gratitude to all of those reviewers who provided comments on earlier drafts of the chapters presented here: Ayhan Aksu, Martyn Barrett, Gina Conti-Ramsden, Kenneth Drozd, Susan Gelman, Erika Hoff, Soohee Kim, Stan Kuczaj, Bill Merriman, Julian Pine, Clifton Pye, Caroline Rowland, Ron Schaefer, Yasuhiro Shirai, Nick Sobin, Anna Theakston, Marilyn Vihman, Dick Weist, and Feryal Yavas. Thanks also to Cathleeen Petree and Mimi Williams of Erlbaum/Taylor & Francis for their assistance throughout the duration of this project.

Contributors

Ruth A. Berman
Professor Emeritus
Linguistics Department
Tel Aviv University
Ramat Aviv, Israel

Lera Boroditsky
Assistant Professor
Department of Psychology
Stanford University
Palo Alto, California, U.S.A.

Penelope Brown
Scientific Staff Member
Max Planck Institute for Psycholinguistics
Nijmegen, the Netherlands

Jidong Chen
Department of Linguistics
California State University, Fresno
Fresno, California, U.S.A.

Soonja Choi
Professor of Linguistics
Department of Linguistics and Asian/Middle Eastern Languages
San Diego State University
San Diego, California, U.S.A.

Eve V. Clark
Richard W. Lyman Professor and Professor of Linguistics
Department of Linguistics
Stanford University
Stanford, California, U.S.A.

Martha Crago
Vice-rectrice
International et Relations Institutionelles
Université de Montréal
Succursale Centre-ville
Montréal, Québec, Canada

William Croft
Professor of Linguistics
Department of Linguistics
University of New Mexico
Albuquerque, New Mexico, U.S.A.

Lourdes de León
Researcher and Professor of Linguistics
Center for Research and Graduate Studies in Social Anthropology (CIESAS)
Maestría en Lingüística Indoamericana
Juárez, México

Esther Dromi
Associate Professor
Human Development and Education
Tel Aviv University
Tel Aviv, Israel

Virginia C. Mueller Gathercole
Professor, School of Psychology
and
Co-Director, ESRC Centre for Research on Bilingualism in Theory and Practice
Bangor University
Bangor, Gwynedd, Wales, U.K.

Dedre Gentner
Director, Cognitive Science Program
Professor, Department of Psychology
Professor, School of Education and Social Policy
Northwestern University
Evanston, Illinois, U.S.

Ping Li
Professor of Psychology
Department of Psychology
The Pennsylvania State University
University Park, Pennsylvania, U.S.A.

Bhuvana Narasimhan
Assistant Professor
Department of Linguistics
University of Colorado
Boulder, Colorado, U.S.A.

Mabel Rice
Fred and Virginia Merrill Distinguished Professor of Advanced Studies
and
Director, Center for Biobehavioral Neurosciences of Communication Disorders
and
Director, Child Language Doctoral Program
University of Kansas
Lawrence, Kansas, U.S.A.

Ronald P. Schaefer
William and Margaret Going Professor
Head, Center for International Programs
and
Associate Dean SIUE Graduate School
Department of English Language and Literature
Southern Illinois University
Edwardsville, Illinois, U.S.A.

Dan I. Slobin
Professor Emeritus of Psychology and Linguistics
Research Psychologist
Institute of Human Development and Institute of Brain and Cognitive Sciences
University of California
Berkeley, California, U.S.A.

Leonard Talmy
Professor Emeritus
Department of Linguistics
Center for Cognitive Science
State University of New York
Buffalo, New York, U.S.A.

Angelika Wittek
Head of Student Exchange Office
ETH Zürich
Zürich, Switzerland

Part I

Learning Words

Personal Tribute

DEDRE GENTNER

When I think back to my first meetings with Melissa, two events fuse together into one brilliantly evocative memory. One was Melissa's talk "Learning the Structure of Causative Verbs" at the 1974 Stanford Child Language Research Forum. This talk was intensely exciting to me. I was working on verb semantics also, and this work was so rich that I had dozens of questions and speculations, all of which I wanted to try out on Melissa that very night. Not long after, Melissa visited the University of Washington (where I was an assistant professor), and Phil Dale, my generous senior colleague, invited me to his house to meet her. I appeared at his door bearing a huge stack of papers and books. (I was obviously none too swift at catching on to the appropriate behavior for assistant professors, but luckily Phil was an unusually kind and supportive senior colleague.) Melissa, not one to hold back, dived right in, and soon we had covered Phil's living room floor with notes and diagrams, while Phil benignly looked on. It was then that we took up the great question of "Factorialization: Creeping or Sweeping?"—our code name for whether semantic reorganization occurs in tiny local increments or instead in one moment of grand insight. Needless to say, this question needed a lot of refining, and over the years we kept working away at it.

We continued to meet in various ways—one vivid memory is of my practicing Melissa's talk as we hurtled through the dark toward Stanford, where she was supposed to give a talk that she feared she would be too hoarse to deliver. Although we repeatedly squandered her precious remaining voice on digressions and moments of hilarity, in the end she somehow managed to give the talk herself, to great effect. In 1984, after Melissa had joined the Max Planck Institute, I visited her for a longer stay with the goal of planning joint research. We talked about dozens of possibilities and finally settled on comparing the systems of spatial prepositions in Dutch and English, something Melissa had already begun to work on.

Over the next few years we designed and ran an elicitation study with 50 Dutch children and 50 American children, ranging from 2 to 5 years of age. We focused on the acquisition of terms for support (lexicalized as *on* in English, and as three narrower categories—*op, aan, om,* in Dutch). Our results were very strong and clear, although not quite what either of us had predicted. These puzzling results fortuitously provided us with the need to meet each year to analyze and reanalyze the data and work on how to write about it, and to polish our small but serviceable repertoire of duets for voice and flute. (Now that we've actually written a version, I can only hope we quickly develop another long-term project!) Our meetings were often at the Max Planck Institute in Nijmegen, where Melissa was always the center of a dozen fascinating research interactions. Other times we met in various spots around the globe (the oddest of which perhaps was a former utopian settlement called New Harmony). Here the main distraction from finishing the paper was the fascinating discussions we had on everything from how children connect language to the world (the topic of this chapter) to mental models of contagion to a theory of humor—never forgetting the great question of semantic reorganization during language learning, which had now metamorphosed from "creeping or sweeping" into a set of more specific processing questions.

Of the many things I am grateful for in my career, my friendship and colleagueship with Melissa rank in the very top set. It's a great gift to have a friend who is not only a deep, incisive thinker with comprehensive knowledge of her field, but who also possesses a wonderfully original turn of mind and a lively intellectual curiosity about everything under the sun.

Melissa's ground-breaking work on crosslinguistic semantic differences and their implications for language learning have had a profound impact on theories of cognitive and linguistic development. As her friend I've been lucky enough to experience her insights first-hand, and in the most delightful way. I'm honored to be part of this Festschrift volume.

1

Early Acquisition of Nouns and Verbs

Evidence from Navajo

DEDRE GENTNER
Northwestern University

LERA BORODITSKY
Stanford University

Which words do children learn earliest, and why? These questions bear on the developmental origin of language and its connection to thought. The striking dominance of nouns in early English vocabularies has led researchers to ask whether there is something special about the link between nouns and concrete objects (e.g., Gleitman, Cassidy, Papafragou, Nappa, & Trueswell, 2005; Kako, 2004; Macnamara, 1972). Gentner (1982) proposed a conceptual explanation for this early noun dominance: The mapping between words and experience is easier for nouns because of the greater perceptual learnability of their referents in children's early experience.

Gentner proposed two interrelated hypotheses concerning learnability: the *natural partitions hypothesis* and the *relational relativity hypothesis*. The *natural partitions hypothesis* states that concrete objects and entities are easier to individuate in the world (and therefore easier to label) than are the relational constellations that form the referents of verbs or prepositions (Gentner, 1981, 1982; Gentner & Boroditsky, 2001). This is in part a specific case of a general pattern referred to as the *relational shift* in cognitive development (Gentner, 1988; Halford, 1992). Relations require the presence of the entities they link; thus it appears that entities are psychologically represented before the relations between them. For example, young children given a similarity task often respond according to object similarity, even when they are given repeated feedback that the correct response should be based on relational similarity. In contrast, older children can readily focus on relational similarity (Gentner & Rattermann, 1991; Rattermann & Gentner, 1998). Further, there is evidence that in adult encoding of scenes, object attributes are encoded before the relations between them (Sloutsky & Yarlas, in preparation). The early object advantage in part reflects this priority of entities over the relations between them. But another contributor to the object advantage is relational relativity.

The *relational relativity hypothesis* states that verb meanings are more variably composed across languages than are noun meanings—that is, relational terms such as verbs and prepositions vary crosslinguistically in their meanings to a greater degree than do concrete nouns. Because objects are readily individuated in the world, the denotations of concrete nouns can be derived by linking a word with an existing concept. But the meanings of verbs and prepositions (even in concrete perceptual arenas) are not "out there" in the same sense. This means that children cannot learn verbs from the word-to-world mapping alone; they must discover how their particular language chooses to combine the elements of experience into verb meanings.

A related approach has been taken by Markman (1989) and Waxman (1990), who have argued for early constraints or linkages relating nouns to objects and categories. For example, Markman's whole-object constraint refers to a child's tendency to assume that a novel word applied to an object refers to the whole object, rather than some part or characteristic of the object. This is clearly related to the natural partitions hypothesis, except that under that hypothesis, not all objects are equally likely to be taken as wholes. As discussed later, some entities are more readily individuated than others. Another related proposal is Markman's taxonomic constraint, which refers to a child's willingness to extend a novel label for an object to other objects of the same kind (and not, for example, to those that are thematically linked). Likewise, Waxman (1990) proposes an early noun-category linkage that forms the basis for further more differentiated language learning. Like the natural partitions hypothesis, these early linkages or constraints would predict an initial advantage for nouns that name concrete objects and entities. However there are some differences between these positions. The taxonomic constraint and the noun-object linkage both propose an innate or very early linkage between words and *categories.* The natural partitions hypothesis concerns the relation between a word and a referent; there is no theoretical commitment to the early existence of categories. We suggest that early categories arise out of the process of word extension, rather than determining the set of extensions.

The position of noun dominance in children's early word learning has amassed considerable empirical support. In English, nouns predominate in early production (Gentner, 1982; Huttenlocher, 1974; Nelson, 1973) and in comprehension (Goldin-Meadow, Seligman, & Gelman, 1976). The use of a novel word directs children's attention toward object meanings (Markman, 1989; Markman & Hutchinson, 1984; Waxman, 1990) even as early as 13 months of age (Waxman & Markow, 1995). Further, Gentner (1982) produced evidence that the noun advantage holds across several languages, and here too there is supporting evidence (Au, Dapretto, & Song, 1994; Bates, Bretherton & Snyder, 1988; Bornstein et al., 2004; Caselli et al., 1995; Dromi, 1987; Kim, McGregor & Thompson, 2000; Ogura, Dale, Yamashita, Murase, & Mahieu, 2006).

Yet despite this support, the universality of a noun bias in early vocabularies has received a good share of controversy. On theoretical grounds, Nelson (1973) and Gopnik and Meltzoff (1993) have argued that children's well-attested interest in dynamic changes, motion, and causality should lead them to name the kinds of concepts that are usually conveyed by verbs. Furthermore, some researchers have argued that the noun advantage in English results from features of the linguistic input that make nouns salient to children, rather than from semantic-conceptual regularities (Gopnik & Choi, 1995; Tardif, 1996).

Gentner (1982) had considered this possibility and noted that there are at least four nonsemantic features of English that could account for the noun advantage in early vocabulary. These include word frequency, word order, morphological transparency, and patterns of language teaching. She argued that the frequency possibility—that nouns are learned before verbs because they are more frequent in English input—is unlikely, because nouns represent only 6% of the most frequent words used in the English language, as compared to verbs at 20%. More convincingly, an advantage for nouns over verbs has been found for learning new words in studies that controlled frequency and position in sentence (Childers & Tomasello, 2002; Schwartz & Leonard, 1980) as well as phonology (Camarata & Leonard, 1986). Gentner also considered morphological transparency—that is, how easily a root can be perceived within the surrounding word. In English (as in many languages) verbs can take a greater variety of affixes and inflections than nouns; hence the sound–meaning relation may be more difficult to perceive for verbs, resulting in a disadvantage in acquisition. To test whether the early noun advantage results from greater morphological transparency, she considered Mandarin Chinese, in which verbs and nouns have equivalent morphological transparency (Mandarin having virtually no inflections). Data collected by Erbaugh show a strong advantage for nouns in early Mandarin (Erbaugh, 1992); this suggested that differential morphological transparency cannot be the whole explanation for the noun advantage. Indeed, as discussed below, Imai, Haryu, Okada, Li, & Shigematsu (2006) suggest that Mandarin's lack of morphological difference between nouns and verbs may actually make verbs harder to learn. The third factor considered by Gentner was patterns of teaching—the possibility that American parents lead their children to focus on object names by our practice of labeling objects for children. However, even in Kaluli, in which cultural practice does not emphasize the teaching of object names (Schieffelin, 1985), children still showed twice as many nominals as predicates in their early vocabularies.

The fourth factor considered was word order. As Slobin (1973) has pointed out, words in utterance-final position are highly salient to children and especially likely to be learned. Thus the early noun advantage in English might be a result of its SVO word order. Gentner attempted to rule out this possibility by considering languages such as Japanese, Turkish, Kaluli, and German, in which verbs tend to appear in final positions. Since the early noun advantage persisted even in these languages, the conclusion was that word order cannot be the sole cause of the early noun dominance in English. Thus, Gentner concluded that although word order and other input factors have important effects on children's learning, they do not by themselves account for early noun dominance. Semantic and conceptual factors must be part of the explanation.

These conclusions, however, must be regarded as provisional. The crosslinguistic data were provided by different researchers, most of whose projects were not specifically directed at early vocabulary acquisition. Further, these data were collected prior to the introduction of the MacArthur checklist. The methods varied considerably across studies, and included taped sessions, ongoing journals, and retrospective reports.

Fortunately, the paucity of crucial data in this arena has not gone unaddressed. The past decade has seen direct investigations of patterns of vocabulary growth in languages of varied typology (e.g., Au et al., 1994; Choi & Gopnik, 1995; Gopnik & Choi, 1995; Pae, 1993; Tardif, 1996). Researchers have sought out "verb friendly" languages such as Mandarin and Korean—languages whose input features should act to promote verb learning. Gentner and Boroditsky (2001) reviewed this work and concluded that the best available data bear out the hypothesis: Nouns predominate in early vocabularies in Chinese and Korean as well as in Indo-European languages (see also Bornstein et al., 2004). But even if this conclusion holds up, it still rests on a relatively small sample of the world's languages. To determine whether early noun dominance is a universal pattern, we need a broader sample of languages. In this chapter we investigate early word learning in Navajo, a language that is typologically different from those studied to date. We begin with a brief reprise of the theoretical claims, whose inception owed much to the work of Melissa Bowerman.

THEORY

Gentner's (1981, 1982, 2006) hypothesis concerns the mapping from language to the world. It has two parts: natural partitions and relational relativity. The first has been widely noted, but the second has often been overlooked; yet it is, to our thinking, the more interesting of the two claims. The natural partitions hypothesis is that

> ...there are in the experiential flow certain highly cohesive collections of percepts that are universally conceptualized as objects, and that these tend to be lexicalized as nouns across languages. Children learning language have already isolated these cohesive packages—the concrete objects and individuals—from their surroundings. Because the language they are learning will have selected the same set of concrete objects as its nominal referents, children need only match preconceived objects with co-occurring words. (Gentner, 1982, p. 324)

The relational relativity hypothesis is the other essential element of this position:

> In a given perceptual scene, different languages tend to agree in the way in which they conflate perceptual information into concrete objects, which are then lexicalized as nouns. There is more variation in the way in which languages conflate relational components into the meanings of verbs and other predicates.... Loosely speaking, noun meanings are given to us by the world; verb meanings are more free to vary across languages. (Gentner, 1981, p. 169)

To motivate the relational relativity hypothesis, consider that the child's task during word learning is to discover the mapping between words in the stream of speech and their referents in the stream of experience. The idea that this might be especially difficult for relational terms was inspired in large part by Melissa Bowerman's (1974, 1976, 1982) seminal research on children's learning of verbs and other relational terms. She found that children make semantic errors with verbs and other relational terms—even quite late in language learning, and often after a period of correct but rather conservative usage. Some of these errors involve creating causative usages, such as "But I can't eat her!" (meaning "I can't make her eat") and "Don't dead him" (as mother picks up a spider). Others seem to draw on a space–time analogy that the child has generalized beyond its adult borders, as in "Can I have some candy behind dinner?" Such errors drive home the challenges children face in fully mastering the semantic systems governing verbs in their language.

Another motivation for this idea was the work of Talmy (1975), which showed that the meanings of verbs and other relational terms differ markedly across languages (see also Bowerman, 1985; Clark, 1993; Maratsos & Chalkley, 1980; Slobin, 1996). Talmy showed that languages differ in which semantic elements are incorporated into motion verbs: the path of the moving figure (as in Spanish), the manner of its motion (as in English), or the shape of the moving figure (as in Atsugewi). Further research has shown many more examples of crosslinguistic variability in the semantics of relational terms. For example, differences from English have been found in the spatial semantics of Mayan languages such as Tzeltal (e.g., Bohnemeyer, 1997; Brown, 1994, 1998; de Leon, 2001; Levinson, 1996) and Cora (Casad & Langacker, 1985) and in verbs of support and containment in Korean (Bowerman & Choi, 2003; Choi & Bowerman, 1991).

Talmy did not himself claim that verbs are more variable in their semantics than nouns. But his findings for verbs offered a path toward understanding why children learn nouns before verbs. If verb meanings are linguistically shaped, then learning how verbs refer is embedded in language learning. In contrast, if at least some noun meanings are "given by the world," then these nouns can be learned before the infant has penetrated the semantics of her language. This means that to bind a relational term to its referent the child must not only pick out the word but must also discover which particular set of the available conceptual elements is included in verb meaning in his or her language. In contrast, for entities that can be individuated prelinguistically, the mapping of word to world reduces to the task of matching the linguistic label to a preexisting concept.

The chief prediction of the NP/RR hypothesis is that there will be a predominance of names for objects and individuals over names for relations in very early vocabularies. A second prediction follows from the conjecture that "Object-reference mappings may provide natural entry points into language—an initial set of fixed hooks with which children can bootstrap themselves into a position to learn the less transparent aspects of language" (Gentner, 1982, p. 329). This suggests that as vocabulary size increases, there should be an increase in the proportion of relational terms.

A third prediction applies *within* the noun class, rather than between form classes. If conceptual individuability is what drives the noun advantage, there should be differential acquisition *within* the noun class, as well as between nouns and verbs. Names for entities that are easily individuated should be acquired before names for entities that are not. How might we decide which these should be? Gentner and Boroditsky (2001) suggested three sources of insight into individuability: (1) Gestalt principles of good objecthood; (2) findings from infancy as to which kinds of objects are individuated early; and (3) crosslinguistic regularities as to which kinds of entities tend to be treated as individuals for grammatical purposes. Gestalt perceptual principles include *common fate*—a propensity for the parts to move together—and *coherence*—the perceived organization of parts into a whole. Animate beings are likely to be high in both of these. Research on prelinguistic infants suggests that they expect continued "objecthood" when they perceive a stable perceptual structure moving against a background (common fate), and later come to use perceptual well-formedness or coherence as a predictor of continued stability (Baillargeon, 1987; Spelke, 1990). Taken together, these suggest that animate beings might be especially easy to individuate. The third line of evidence as to what is naturally individuated, though indirect, is intriguingly consistent with the above patterns. Linguistic analyses of grammatical patterns across languages suggest a continuum of individuation in which animate beings (especially humans) are the most likely entities to be grammatically individuated (i.e., countable and pluralizable) across languages, with concrete objects and substances (in that order) less likely to be individuated (Croft, 1990; Lucy, 1992; see Imai & Gentner, 1997).

This line of reasoning implies that within the noun class, the proportion of terms for animates should be especially large early on. Of course, this prediction is not unique to the NP/RR account. Names for people and other living beings might be learned early in part because of their social–emotive salience (e.g., Nelson, 1973). A predominance of names for animate beings—including names for individuals—would therefore be consistent with the NP/RR account, but not uniquely so.

We can distill the above predictions as follows: (1) Names for objects and entities should predominate over verbs in early vocabulary; (2) as vocabulary increases, the proportion of verbs should increase; (3) among nominals, names for animate entities, including proper names, should be strongly represented in early vocabulary.

NAVAJO

In this chapter we consider the acquisition of Navajo. The Navajo language is of interest because it represents a language type about which little is known with respect to vocabulary acquisition. Navajo is a member of the Athapaskan language group, along with Apache, Chipewyan, Tlingit, and others. Athapaskan is a widespread family, extending from northwestern Canada and Alaska south to northern Mexico. Unlike many Amerindian languages, Navajo is still a healthy language being acquired naturally by children. Further, Navajo has several properties that may favor verbs in early acquisition, as discussed below.

In Navajo, as in other Athapaskan languages, verbs are heavily inflected. Each verb has 14 to 16 prefix positions, each reserved for a class of morphemes, though positions need not necessarily be filled. The full description of these prefix positions is beyond the scope of this chapter (see Young & Morgan, 1987, for details). Verb prefixes represent subject and object (direct and indirect), subaspect and mode (functionally similar to tense in English), and a variety of adverbial and thematic concepts. A full range of sentential variation can be expressed by deleting, adding, or substituting prefixes as exemplified below. Verbs can also be suffixed by clause subordinators, nominalizers, framing elements, or any of a small number of adverbial enclitics. Examples are:

(1) a. bitsuarharshfararh
b. Third person object + 'away from, separating from P' + 'one after another' + first person singular subject + transitive, caused + 'gather, collect object'
c. 'I pick them out of it one after another' (e.g., burrs from a fleece). (Lit: I collect them away from it one after another)

(2) a. arzaashtuap
b. 'own' + 'mouth' + first person singular subject + transitive, caused + perfective, 'handle solid roundish object'
c. 'I put it (a solid roundish object, e.g., a piece of candy) into my mouth.'

(3) a. bizaashjoof
b. Third person possessor + 'mouth' + first person singular subject + transitive, caused + imperfective, 'handle noncompact matter'
c. 'I am putting it (noncompact matter, e.g., hay) into its (his, her) mouth.'

(4) a. bizaashkaah
b. Third person possessor + 'mouth' + first person singular subject + ? + imperfective, 'handle something in an open container'
c. 'I am pouring it (something in an open container, e.g., a glass of water) into its (his, her) mouth.'

(5) a. bighadiunishtuaah
b. Third person object + 'away from P (coercively)' + 'related to oral noise' + third person indefinite object + imperfective + first person singular subject + transitive, caused + 'handle solid roundish object'
c. 'I am trying to persuade her.' (Lit: I am getting something away from her in a way that involves oral noise.)

(6) a. ahidaaftuer
b. 'each other' + distributive plural + ? + active voice? + 'be, become'
c. 'They resemble each other.'

(7) a. chuirnirnarardiunirfdlarard
b. 'horizontally outward' + reversionary, 'back' + 'again' + 'fire or light' + perfective + third person subject + caused + perfective, 'rip, tear, crack, break'
c. 'The sun came back out again.' (Lit: It caused light to break back out again horizontally.)

Navajo verb morphology is more productive than its noun morphology. For example, Young and Morgan's (1992) *Analytical Lexicon of Navajo* contains approximately 6,245 nouns, as compared with some 9,000 verb bases (analogous to English infinitives). Moreover, a large proportion of nouns appear to be formed from verbs. The lexicon contains only 265 stem nouns, "many of which also function as verb stems," from which about 2,245 nouns are derived through compounding and inflection (Young & Morgan, p. 961). In contrast, there are about 4,000 entries for "verbal nouns," including nominalized verbs and compounds of nominal and verbal stems (pp. 964–965). Navajo thus contrasts strongly with many of the languages in which vocabulary acquisition has been studied (e.g., English, Italian, Korean and Mandarin) in its morphological complexity overall, and especially in the verb.

How does the structure of Navajo affect input to children? First, since Navajo verbs incorporate obligatory pronominal prefixes, verbs can stand alone as sentences. This fact that verbs can stand alone as acceptable utterances (as in Italian, Korean, and Mandarin) might make verbs more accessible in the input (Au et al., 1994; Caselli et al., 1995; Choi & Gopnik, 1995). Another input factor that may favor verbs in Navajo acquisition is word order. In subject-verb-object (SVO) languages like English, nouns frequently occur in the salient sentence-final position (Slobin, 1973). Navajo is an SOV language (or perhaps more properly, a topic/object/verb language) (Young & Morgan, 1992). Thus verbs ordinarily occur in the salient sentence-final position.

Another factor that could affect acquisition is the relative morphological transparency of nouns versus verbs—the degree to which children can perceive the same stem across different uses (Gentner, 1982). On this count the Navajo language is mixed. As in most languages, verbs take a greater variety of affixes than nouns.[1] As mentioned above, verbs can take up to 14 to 16 prefix positions, and use of 11 prefixes is fairly typical. Navajo nouns have fewer markings. They can be inflected for possession and plural,[2] and stem nouns[3] may also take other suffixes, including particularizers and a small number of adjectival enclitics, perhaps coming to four or five affixes. But although verbs have greater morphological complexity than nouns, they may have the advantage over nouns on another aspect of morphological transparency. Most affixes to verbs come before the verb, so that

---

[1] In Navajo (as in other highly morphologized polysynthetic languages), distinctions in complexity between verbal and nominal inflection systems are sometimes obscured by the difficulty of drawing a clear distinction between morphology and syntax. However, the conclusion appears safe that verbs take more markings than nouns.

[2] Possession is obligatory for some nouns, including kin terms, anatomical terms, and habitats. Only kinship terms and names of age-sex groups form simple plurals, but many nouns form distributive plurals.

[3] Verbal nouns can (and sometimes must) have verbal inflection patterns; e.g.,

teacher = *baruorftauir* (for-her-she-learns-[nominalizer]).
my teacher = *shibaruorftauir* (my + baruorftauir)
OR *irirnirshtauir* (for-her-I-learn-[nominalizer])

This would of course add to the overall complexity of noun marking patterns. However, the constituents of most verbal nouns are likely to be slightly more conventionalized or "frozen" than those of the verb proper.

the root of a Navajo verb almost always occupies the salient word-final position. Nouns are more prone to take affixes at the end, thus making the root more difficult to perceive within the surrounding word (Watson, 1976). On balance, we would consider Navajo somewhat more verb-friendly than noun-friendly.

The semantic properties of Navajo verbs are also worth noting. Navajo verbs with their rich morphology seem more semantically complex—particularly in incorporating features of the object noun—than, say, English verbs, and this might make them harder to learn. On the other hand, as Brown (1998) has suggested, "heavy" verbs that are semantically rich may be easier to acquire than leaner verbs, because they require less abstraction from context (see also Gentner & Boroditsky, 2001; Tardif, 2005). To investigate the effects of this combination of input factors on language acquisition, we conducted a study of early child vocabulary in Navajo. Navajo provides a new entry to the annals of nouns and verbs in early vocabulary.

Our method of approach was to create a Navajo checklist modeled after the MacArthur Communicative Development Inventory for Infants (MCDI). The MCDI and its variants have proven to be an invaluable tool for the assessment of early vocabulary learning and for crosslinguistic comparison. A variety of methods has been used to assess early word learning, but the two methods most commonly used are transcriptions of taped sessions and retrospective reports of the child's vocabulary, generally using a checklist. Other forms of retrospective report, such as asking parents to recall and list their children's words, are sometimes used, but the checklist method has the advantage of being a recognition task; recognition provides a more sensitive memory assessment than does recall. The checklist method also has several important advantages over the transcript method (as amplified in the "Discussion"). For these reasons, the checklist method seemed best for our purposes.

Checklist construction is guided by the psychology of parental report. The basic premise is that recognition (while not perfect) is in general far more sensitive than recall. Therefore, the first goal of checklist construction is to ensure that *all* the words a child may say are on the list. Having extra words on the list, to which parents mostly say no, is not a problem (unless of course the number is so large that the task becomes too onerous to the parent). Indeed, it is important that there be some words to which a given parent says no, to ensure that she or he is not simply saying yes to everything. But if words are missing, the cost is greater. For missing words, the burden is on the parent to realize this and to somehow dredge the word out of her mind. Any such missing words are effectively being tested in a relatively insensitive recall task instead of a sensitive recognition task. In sum, the penalty is high for an error of exclusion and low for an error of inclusion. Because of these considerations, in checklist research, it is common to report the "percent opportunity filled" measure introduced by Caselli et al. (1995)—the percentage of a given class checked off for a given child. A very high percentage is cause for concern that the child's vocabulary may have exceeded the checklist's capacity.

With this logic in mind, and because our hypothesis was that verb acquisition would lag behind noun acquisition, a key goal was to ensure that all possible verbs a child would say were included on the list. We began with the English version of the MacArthur Communicative Development Inventory for Infants. We increased the proportion of verbs on the list by adding 73 verbs that were used in a Korean checklist by Au et al. (1994) as well as 13 additional verbs adapted from Gopnik and Choi (1995). Of course, when the large list was translated into Navajo (in stage 1 of the checklist construction, described below), some of these verbs were rejected as unnatural; but others did have equivalent or related Navajo forms, and still others reminded the translators of other Navajo verbs.

The Checklist

To prepare a checklist appropriate for Navajo, we consulted with Navajo language researchers and educators (Werner, Morgan, & Nichols), with several first-language speakers of Navajo, and with expert translators (Shorty, Yazzi, King, & Begaye). Several stages of adaptation were necessary. We began with the English version of the MacArthur Communicative Development Inventory for Infants. We then increased the number of verbs in a rather indiscriminate way (knowing that refinements would occur later) with 86 Korean verbs taken from Au et al. (1994) and from Gopnik and Choi (1995).

The checklist was translated in three stages. In stage 1, the initial translation was done by Anthony Yazzi, a native Navajo speaker residing in the Chicago area, and Bill Nichols, a graduate student of Navajo. Anthony Yazzi added further words, including child forms of many words and other words that are specific to Navajo culture (e.g., *coyote*). Stage 2 was carried out on the reservation by Nichols and Begaye. They elicited from several speakers, including parents not included in the study, the forms typically used by children, as well as other words likely to be known by children. We adopted a liberal criterion for verb forms and included all forms of a given verb that speakers considered likely to be present in children's vocabularies. This was done both for methodological reasons (to ensure that any bias was in favor of verbs)[4] and on the theoretical grounds that children may learn different verb forms as separate words (Tomasello, 2000). In stage 3, the revised checklist was again vetted by several native speakers, notably by William Morgan, a Navajo researcher educator and coauthor of the *Analytical Lexicon of Navajo* (Young & Morgan, 1992).[5]

The final checklist contained 479 words frequently found in children's vocabularies: 239 nouns and 163 verbs. The checklist was divided in the fashion of the MacArthur inventory into 19 sections, such as Animal words, Vehicle words, and

---

[4] Of course, this runs the risk of overestimating the child's verb knowledge, because two forms of the same verb could be counted as two different verbs.

[5] As would be predicted from the relational relativity hypothesis, nouns were fairly easy to translate into Navajo, but verbs were more difficult, and sometimes required an idiomatic or metaphoric expression. To deal with these complexities, for each English verb we constructed a naturalistic sentence in which it might occur in English speech to children. Then, the Navajo informants constructed equivalent Navajo sentence(s), and the Navajo verb that best carried the sense of the English verb was chosen and rendered in a form that would be natural in speech with very young children. Similar procedures were followed for adjectives. Many English adjectives are realized as nominalized descriptive verbs in Navajo. As in Korean, this acts to increase the size of the verb class in Navajo.

Action words (see Table 1.1). Note that the total number of verbs (163) is greater than the number of Action words in the table (135) because not all verbs are action verbs. The final step was to have the checklist and instructions tape-recorded by Ed Shorty, a local radio broadcaster. This was done so that literacy would not be necessary for participation—an important step, because relatively few people are literate in Navajo. Caretakers were provided with the taped version along with the paper version of the checklist. A sample of roughly one-fifth of the checklist is given in appendix A, along with English translations and our categorization as to noun, verb, or other. The entire checklist can be obtained by request.

Site and Subject Selection

The Navajo reservation straddles the state lines of Utah, New Mexico, and Arizona, and has 150,000 to 250,000 residents. The number of Navajo monolinguals is rapidly declining, and many young people communicate primarily in English. To find infants with monolingual caretakers, the experimenters contacted workers at Navajo Women Infant Children (WIC) clinics in two rural chapters (local governmental districts). For the same reason, we sought families in relatively remote locations. WIC clinicians referred us to four of the families on the basis of their known proficiency in Navajo and likelihood of monolingual experience. A fifth subject was referred to us by an interview candidate.

Experiment 1a

Method

Experimenters. Two experimenters conducted research on the Navajo reservation with Northwestern's Ethnographic Field School under the direction of Dr. Oswald Werner. Both experimenters (Bill Nichols and Nathan Bush) were graduate students in anthropology studying with Dr. Werner. The senior experimenter, Bill Nichols, was the Deputy Director of the Field School, with three seasons' experience conducting cultural research on the Navajo reservation.

Participants. Five Navajo caretakers—mothers and grandmothers of infants aged 18 to 26 months—participated in this study. The infants were two boys and three girls who lived in remote locations on the Western part of the reservation and were being raised primarily monolingual in Navajo.

Materials and Procedure. For three of the children the interviews were conducted at the children's homes. For the other two, the interviews were conducted in a WIC clinic. Caretakers were told that the experimenters were interested in the early vocabularies of babies being raised in Navajo. The caretakers were given the Navajo checklist and the study was explained. The tape of the words was played for them as they went through the checklist. They were encouraged to pause, ask questions, or review the tape at their discretion. For each word on the checklist, caretakers were asked to indicate (1) whether the child understands the word, and

TABLE 1.1 Navajo Children's Productive Vocabulary: Numbers of Words Acquired per Checklist Category

Category (number of possible responses)	Child Gender/Age in months				
	1 M/23	2 F/18	3 F/25	4 F/19	5 M/26
Animal sounds (9)	3	4	4	6	6
Animals (36)	4	6	13	12	13
Vehicles (9)	0	0	0	1	1
Toys (8)	1	0	1	1	1
Food (31)	4	0	5	12	9
Clothing (19)	0	0	1	6	5
Body parts (20)	0	0	1	12	11
Rooms & furniture (25)	0	0	1	3	7
Household items (34)	0	0	0	6	1
Things in nature (27)	1	1	1	6	3
People (20)	2	0	4	8	14
Games & routines (24)	7	6	7	13	18
Action words (135)	2	2	1	22	34
Temporal words (8)	0	0	0	0	0
Descriptive words (37)	0	1	2	7	11
Possessives (11)	0	7	2	5	9
Question words (6)	0	0	0	3	4
Prepositions (11)	0	2	2	2	2
Quantifiers (8)	1	2	2	2	2
Words added by caretakers	8	2	7	7	54
Total productive vocabulary	33	31	47	134	205

Note Numbers in the table are the number of words reported in each category. Numbers in parentheses next to the category descriptions represent the total number of possible responses in that category. Words added by caretakers are listed separately at the bottom of the table.

(2) whether he or she also spontaneously says the word. They were also asked to tell the experimenter if any checklist item reminded them of some item not on the checklist that they had forgotten to mention. For three of the children, the caretakers were also asked to recall as many as possible of the words they had heard their child say, whether in Navajo or in another language, before they filled out the checklist.[6]

[6] Due to experimenter error, this was not done for two children (child #2 and child #3). This meant that proper names were not collected for these two children, probably resulting in an undercounting of their animate nouns. (The number of proper nouns for people ranged from 2 to 12 among the other three children.)

Results The infants' productive vocabulary in Navajo ranged from 31 to 205 words. Table 1.1 shows a breakdown of the infants' words in each of the CDI categories, as well as the number of words added by parents. As Figure 1.1a shows, all five infants produced more nouns than verbs, $t(4)=3.52$, $p < .05$. (All tests are two-tailed.) The mean noun–verb ratio was 3.26:1 overall. This finding is consistent with the central prediction of the natural partitions/relational relativity hypothesis that nouns for objects and entities should be acquired earlier than verbs and other relational terms. This was true in our data, even though we adopted a very liberal criterion for scoring vocabulary items as verbs. Many descriptive terms and adjectival expressions (e.g., 'it is red') were included as verbs in our counts.

The second prediction of the NP/RR hypothesis is that as vocabulary size increases, so should the proportion of relational terms. Consistent with this prediction, the results show that the greater the child's total Navajo productive vocabulary, the greater was the proportion of verbs, $r = .981$, $p = .003$, $N = 5$.

Figure 1.1b shows the children's total Navajo vocabularies—both words produced and words comprehended but not produced. Here too the pattern of results supports the prediction. Nouns predominate in the smallest vocabularies; only the one child who attained a productive vocabulary of over 200 Navajo words shows a proportion of verbs comprehended and produced that is equal to or greater than that for nouns.

A third prediction of the NP/RR hypothesis is that names for animate entities (including proper names) will be especially prominent early in acquisition. Figure 1.2 shows the proportion of animate nouns among nouns in children's vocabularies. As predicted, names for animate entities comprised a substantial proportion (a mean of 66.3% overall) of the early noun vocabularies. Considering the initial dominance of animate nouns in early vocabularies, it would also be expected that the proportion of animate nouns should decrease with increasing vocabulary. Figure 1.2 shows a nonsignificant trend in this direction.

Percent Opportunity Filled A possible concern is that the noun advantage was an artifact of our having too few verbs (relative to the nouns) on our checklist. We believe such a ceiling effect is unlikely, because even the child with the largest vocabulary was reported to produce less than a third of the verbs on the checklist. However, to be certain, we applied the "percent opportunity filled" measure to the children's productive vocabularies. If the noun advantage results from the artifact of having included too few verbs on the checklist, then the percent opportunity filled will be higher for verbs than for nouns. Reassuringly, the results showed a trend in the opposite direction. The mean percent opportunity filled for nouns (14.8%) was actually higher than that for verbs (10.8%), marginally significant, $t(4) = 2.27$, $p = .09$.) Thus the observed noun advantage did not result from an insufficient number of verbs on the checklist.

Added English Words As noted above, for three of the five children, additional Navajo words were reported by caretakers. Many of these words were names of relatives and other items commonly added to checklists. However, there were also some added English words (not included in the data reported above). The English

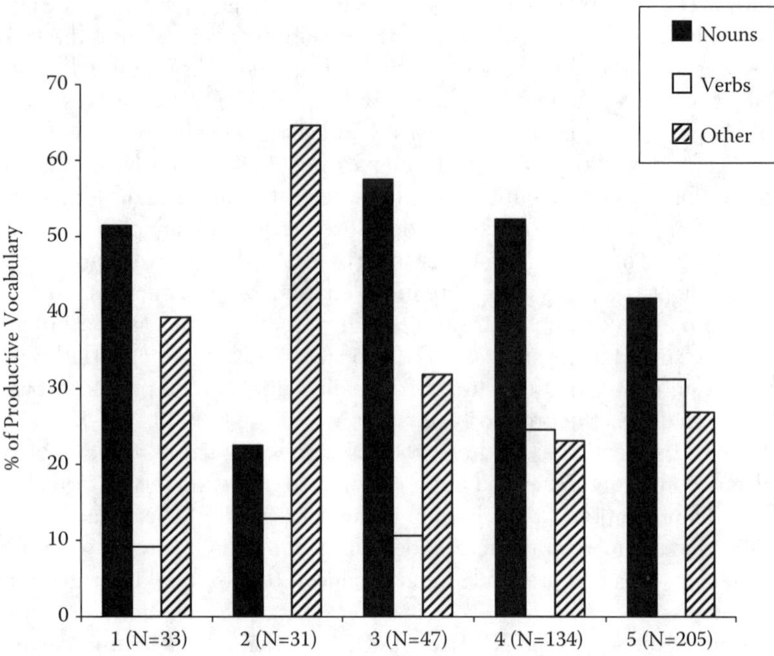

Figure 1.1a Proportions of nouns and verbs in Navajo productive vocabulary.

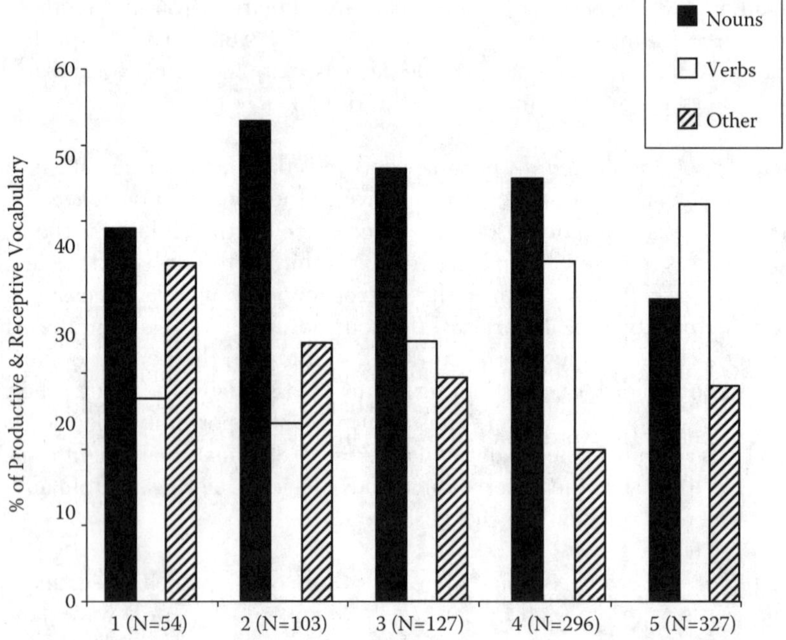

Figure 1.1b Proportions of nouns and verbs in Navajo productive and receptive vocabulary.

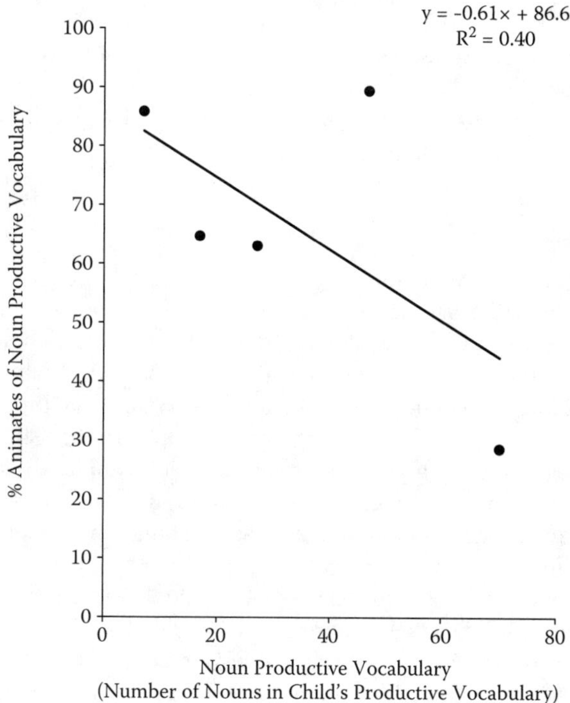

Figure 1.2 Proportion of animate nouns plotted against vocabulary size.

(and Navajo) productive vocabulary sizes were 8 (33) for child 1; 50 (134) for child 4; and 125 (205) for child 5. This led to a concern: Were these English words evidence that the children were not truly monolingual, or were these words simply English loan words into Navajo that the children had learned in the course of normal Navajo discourse?

Like other Amerindian languages, Navajo has borrowed many items from English (Young & Morgan, 1992). In child language, these include *ouch*, *OK*, *ice cream*, *TV*, *duck duck goose*, and *Hey, man*. The bulk of the children's English words (63%) were nouns. This is consistent with the possibility that the English words are loan words; crosslinguistically, nouns are the grammatical class most likely to be borrowed in language contact (Haugen, 1950; see also Gentner, 1981). To assess whether the words that showed up in children's vocabularies were in fact loan words, we conducted a follow-up study.

Experiment 1b

We constructed a questionnaire containing all the English words reported by caretakers. To operationalize the idea of linguistic borrowing, we asked an expert Navajo rater to assess the likelihood that a Navajo speaker would use the

English word in the course of a Navajo conversation (a scale of 1 = very likely to 7 = very unlikely was used). Ratings were obtained in an interview with an expert informant, Larry King, a Navajo language tutor who lives in Shiprock. Over 70% of the English words added by caretakers were rated as very likely to be borrowings (rated as 1 or 2). It is very likely, then, that the children learned these words in the course of normal Navajo acquisition.

Discussion

We began with three predictions: (1) Nouns should predominate in early vocabulary; (2) the proportion of verbs should be low initially and should increase with vocabulary size; and (3) among nouns, terms for animates should be acquired especially early. We found evidence for all three of these. Nouns outnumbered verbs in early Navajo vocabulary by a factor of over 3 to 1. The proportion of verbs began low and increased with vocabulary size. Finally, although strong conclusions regarding developmental change must await a larger sample, the results showed the predicted pattern that among nouns, terms for animate beings predominated in early vocabulary and tended to decrease as vocabulary increased.

These findings are consistent with the hypotheses of natural partitions and relational relativity, according to which object names are learned earlier than relational terms because objects are more easily individuated than are the referents of relational terms. According to this hypothesis, relational terms have two strikes against them: First, relations in general are typically noticed and encoded after the objects they apply to; and, second, because relational terms differ crosslinguistically (relational relativity), learning their meanings requires some experience with the semantic patterns of the language.

Comparison with Other Findings The question of noun dominance in early vocabulary acquisition has been intensely debated over the last decade. This controversy has had the valuable effect of inspiring the investigation of languages that differ from English in their typological properties, particularly those that seem likely to make the language "verb-friendly" for infants learning their first words. There is general agreement that input factors should have some influence, from Gentner's (1982) paper through the present. The question is whether semantic factors in the early word-to-world mapping also play a substantial role, or whether the findings can be explained most economically in terms of input factors that favor verbs or nouns.

Unfortunately, these studies have led to differing conclusions among different researchers (and in some cases even the *same* researchers) studying the same language. We believe these difficulties stem largely from differences in methodology that have led to non-commensurable results. In hopes of achieving greater convergence, we briefly review two prominent cases of verb-friendly languages: Korean and Mandarin.

Korean Korean is a clear candidate for a verb-friendly language and has recently been examined extensively. It has SOV word order and is a pro-drop language, so verbs often appear alone or in the salient utterance-final position. Choi and Gopnik (1995) examined a sample of Korean adult speech to children and found almost twice as many verbs as nouns (19.8 verbs vs. 11.9 nouns per 100 utterances). Thus if input factors dominate, Korean children should learn verbs earlier than nouns. Choi and Gopnik examined children's early vocabularies by analyzing spontaneous speech samples and by asking Korean parents to report on their children's vocabularies, using a modified version of Gopnik's relational inventory questionnaire and encouraging parents to list other words their children said. They found that the proportions of nouns (excluding proper nouns) and verbs in the first 50 words were 44% and 31%, respectively. This proportion for nouns is substantially lower than the 60 to 70% range typically found in English, suggesting that input factors determine infants' first words.

However, other studies of Korean have reached different conclusions. Au et al. (1994) first confirmed Choi and Gopnik's finding that Korean input to children is verb-favored. Verbs were four times more likely than nouns to appear in the salient final position in Korean language to children (46% vs. 10%). In English, the reverse was found: Verbs occupied 9% of the utterance-final positions, and nouns 30%. But despite this verb advantage in input, when Au and her colleagues examined early vocabularies of Korean children (using an adapted MacArthur CDI parental checklist) they found a noun to verb advantage of roughly 4 to 1. Strikingly, Korean children produced four times as many nouns as verbs despite an equally strong input advantage in the reverse direction. Pae (1993) corroborated this finding of noun dominance in her comprehensive study of early Korean acquisition. She used a MacArthur checklist adapted for Korean to assess the vocabularies of 90 children living in Seoul between the ages of 12 and 23 months. She found a strong noun advantage throughout, comparable to that for English. Most children (87 of the 90) used a noun as their first word, and none had a verb as first word. Nouns increased rapidly; at 51 to 100 words, the productive vocabularies contained 50 to 60% nouns and about 5% verbs. Overall, Pae found a large advantage for nouns over verbs in Korean early vocabularies, roughly equivalent to that found in a comparable English sample. Finally, Bornstein, Cote et al. (2004), in a large crosslinguistic study of early vocabularies, also found that nouns outnumbered verbs in early Korean. What gives rise to these divergent results? Studies of Mandarin, another "verb-friendly" language, may shed light on this issue.

Mandarin In Mandarin, verbs and nouns have equivalent morphological transparency in that neither nouns nor verbs are inflected. Mandarin is also a pro-drop language: The subject of a sentence can often be omitted. Word order is SVO, just as in English, but subject-dropping creates verb-initial (VO) and verb-only sentences, both of which give the verb a more salient position than the middle position it occupies in the English SVO sentence (Slobin, 1973). Tardif (1996) hypothesized that these input factors would promote the acquisition of verbs. She estimated the vocabularies of 10 Mandarin-speaking infants using one-hour taped transcriptions of their spontaneous interactions with caregivers. She reported a mean of 19 nouns (13.8 with proper names excluded) and 19.1 main verbs. Tardif concluded that the early noun advantage is not universal, and that the relative rate of acquisition of nouns and verbs depends on linguistic factors.

Fortunately, the work did not end there. In an important study, Tardif, Gelman, and Xu (1999) revisited early Mandarin acquisition and compared spontaneous speech samples taken in different contexts with the results of a checklist task. They established two important findings: (1) Spontaneous speech samples are highly vulnerable to contextual variability, and (2) spontaneous speech samples are likely to severely underestimate children's vocabularies. Their results further suggested that this underestimation is likely to be particularly severe for nouns. Tardif and her colleagues tape-recorded 20-month-old English and Mandarin children in naturalistic interactions with caregivers in three controlled contexts: noun-favorable (reading a picture book together), verb-favorable (playing with a mechanical toy that offered several different activities), and neutral (playing with various toys). The observational (transcript) data showed striking variability across contexts. The noun-to-verb ratios for Mandarin children were 2.2, .62, and .51 for noun-friendly, neutral, and verb-friendly contexts, respectively. The English children's transcript results showed comparably high variability, with N/V ratios of 3.3, 1.0, and .7 for noun-friendly, neutral, and verb-friendly contexts. These finding demonstrate the problems with using small samples of transcribed speech to assess total vocabulary. A researcher who relied on transcript data could conclude that Mandarin children have twice as many nouns as verbs, or half as many, depending on which context happened to occur. Indeed, depending on the context, one could even conclude that English, a notoriously noun-friendly language, shows a verb advantage in early vocabularies.

Tardif et al. then compared these transcript results with the results of checklists applied to the same Mandarin and English children. They found that the transcript results were far less comprehensive than the checklist results. Pooling all words from the three different contexts, the average number of types revealed for each child was 56.7 for Mandarin and 60.2 for English. The checklist results for these same children revealed 316 types for Mandarin and 160 types for English. The Mandarin checklist vocabulary is four times greater than Tardif's (1996) report of 73.7 words based on transcript data from slightly *older* children (22 months). It appears that the transcript results seriously underestimate the children's vocabularies. In addition to revealing a larger vocabulary than the observational data, the checklist results revealed a clear noun advantage: Mandarin children showed 2.4 times as many nouns as verbs.

The Mandarin vocabularies showed a clear noun bias, consistent with the natural partitions hypothesis. However, we also note that the noun advantage was considerably less pronounced in Mandarin than in English, consistent with the claim that Mandarin is a verb-friendly language (Choi & Gopnik, 1989; Gentner, 1982; Tardif, 1996).

This research makes it clear that transcripts of observational data cannot be equated with the child's productive vocabulary. Transcripts are likely to greatly underestimate the total vocabulary size; they also are likely to provide misleading results as to noun–verb composition. In part this results from patterns of usage: People tend to use a large variety of nominal types, each fairly infrequently, and a small number of relational types, each fairly frequently (Gentner, 1981). This means that verbs will tend to show up in a large range of contexts, but nominals will tend to be restricted to particular contexts. (For example, you may have not said the word *tiger* for weeks.) Because nouns are used in a more referentially specific manner than are verbs, transcripts are likely to underestimate nouns relative to verbs (Gentner & Boroditsky, 2001; Bates, Bretherton, & Snyder, 1988). Consistent with this suggestion, Gopnik and Meltzoff (1984) found that across several observational sessions with a group of 1- to 2-year-olds, 75% of the relational terms and only 25% of the nominals occurred in more than one session. Thus, more nouns than verbs are likely to be missing from any given transcript.

What about very early acquisition? In both Mandarin and English, mothers reported that their children's first object word had preceded their first action word (Gelman & Tardif, 1998). This accords with the first vocabularies of two Mandarin-speaking children with under 50 words, reported by Gentner (1982) using parental data collected by Mary Erbaugh (1992) in Taiwan (both parental vocabulary lists, and transcriptions of natural interaction sessions). For both children, nominals (including proper nouns) were the dominant class (.65 and .59 mean proportions). For example, at age 1.6, the child Xiao-Jing had 37 words, of which 22 were nouns, seven were relational terms (e.g., 'go,' 'come,' 'pick-up'), and two were modifiers. These results bear out the claim that even in verb-friendly languages, there are semantic-conceptual factors that favor object names as the first word-to-world mappings.

One might ask whether the use of a checklist results in overestimating vocabulary—perhaps the proud parents exaggerate, and mistakenly attribute extra words to their child's vocabulary. Although this surely must occur, Tardif et al.'s (1999) results actually showed that the opposite can occur as well. Parents omitted a small number of words that the children had in fact produced in the observational settings. That is, some words appeared in the transcript but not in the checklist. However, the degree of underestimation on the checklist was on the order of a few percent—far less severe than the 60 to 80% underestimate given by the transcript method relative to the checklist.

Another question is whether checklists overrepresent the proportion of nouns. Pine, Lieven, and Rowland (1996) suggested that there may be a noun bias in maternal reporting on checklists, based on findings that recognition is better for nouns than for verbs (e.g., Asmuth & Gentner, 2005; Gentner, 1981; Kersten & Earles, 2004).

However, they also pointed out several factors that favor checklists over observational transcripts for estimating the relative proportions of different vocabulary classes: Observational measures are generally less comprehensive and therefore less reliable than checklist reports; transcript data are highly sensitive to the context in which they are recorded; and transcript data are frequency-sensitive—words that a child knows, but rarely uses, are likely to be missed in a taped session, whereas they may appear on a checklist.

These concerns are more important than has generally been realized, because the method chosen for assessing child vocabulary has a strong effect on the outcome. For example, studies that have used checklist data have found that nouns predominate in early vocabulary (e.g., Au et al., 1994; Caselli et al., 1995; Pae, 1993; Tardif et al, 1999), while studies using taped observational sessions or interview tasks have typically found no noun advantage (Choi & Gopnik, 1995; Tardif, 1996; but see Pae, 1993). One obvious implication is that meaningful comparisons of word acquisition across languages can only be achieved if the studies use the same methods. Taking Tardif et al.'s (1999) findings into account, we suggest that although observational transcripts are valuable for many purposes, they are not suitable for assessing total vocabulary or for assessing the relative proportions of different word classes.

The checklist method is less susceptible to problems of contextual variability and is also more likely to produce a more complete assessment of a child's total vocabulary. However, the checklist method is also not perfect. Its limitations include: (1) It can discourage proper nouns, unless parents are encouraged to provide them; (2) its success depends on having an inclusive, language-appropriate list; (3) it asks first for nouns, possibly leading to fatigue factors in reporting verbs (this could be remedied); (4) it may underestimate phrases used as wholes; (5) for heavily morphologized languages it may be difficult to decide how to count words; and (6) the context of use is not provided. Despite these flaws, in our view the CDI remains the single best method for estimating overall vocabulary when detailed longitudinal data are not available (see also Pine et al. (1996) for a comparison of transcript and checklist methods).

Another source of discrepancy between different studies lies in the criteria used to score verbs and nouns. Some studies have excluded proper names from the noun count. Such exclusion is reasonable for evaluating hypotheses that posit a noun-category linkage, but not for evaluating the natural partitions hypothesis, which encompasses names for individuals as well as classes. Indeed, to test the corollary prediction of the natural partitions hypothesis—that names for animate beings will be particularly early—*requires* that proper names be counted. Another source of variation is the criteria for relational terms; for example, whether adjectival meanings should be included if they are expressed as verbs. The checklist method will gain in utility as clear criteria are developed for classifying early words.

Learning New Verbs Another way to approach the acquisition issue is to look at children's relative ability to *learn* new nouns and verbs. When new words are taught to young English-speaking children, they acquire nouns more rapidly than verbs (Childers & Tomasello, 2006; Schwartz & Leonard, 1980). Does this noun advantage hold up crosslinguistically? Imai, Haryu, and Okada (2005; Imai et al., 2006) have found a noun advantage in word-learning among preschool children across Mandarin, English, and Japanese. They showed children a video scene of a person carrying out a novel action with a novel object, and labeled it with either a novel noun or a novel verb. Then the children were asked to generalize the new word to a new scene, which either showed the same object in a new action (correct for the noun, but not for the verb) or the same action with a new object (the reverse pattern). The results showed a noun advantage across all languages. All three groups—Mandarin, Japanese, and English—generalized novel nouns correctly by 3 years, but did not generalize novel verbs correctly until 5 years of age. These results are consistent with there being a general noun advantage in early learning.

Interestingly, Mandarin children given the same task lagged behind the other two groups in their verb learning; even at 5 years of age, they tended to map the verb to the object rather than the action. They did not correctly generalize the verbs until 8 years of age (Imai et al., 2006). Imai and her colleagues were able to develop a version of the task such that 5-year-old Mandarin children could extend the verbs correctly, but the greater difficulty Mandarin children experience with the standard task calls for a rethinking of what makes for a verb-friendly language. Gentner's (1982) original suggestion of Mandarin as a verb-friendly language was based on the fact that it has an equal degree of added morphology on nouns and verbs (i.e., none). But Imai et al. speculate that the lack of *any* morphology on nouns and verbs in Mandarin may in fact make it more difficult for children to separate the syntactic classes of nouns and verbs (see also Kim et al., 2000). Tardif (1996) focused on another factor that might make Mandarin verb-friendly: namely, argument-dropping (the ability to omit nouns in a sentence). This permits verb-final and even verb-only sentences, which might help children attend to verbs. But here too, one must ask whether argument-dropping is always helpful. In the absence of morphological marking, a Mandarin child hearing a single word cannot know whether it is a noun or a verb. This could impede verb learning, particularly if (as seems likely) children sometimes take verbs to refer to objects. Clearly, Mandarin poses some tricky issues for child language researchers.

Conceptual and Linguistic Factors: A Rapprochement? We have argued for the importance of semantic-conceptual factors in early word acquisition, but linguistic input factors are also important. Discovering word meanings requires both isolating the word within the speech stream and individuating the referent within the experiential stream (and connecting them). The relative difficulty of isolating the *word* in the stream of speech is influenced by linguistic factors such as word order and stress. The relative difficulty of individuating the *referent* in the stream of experience is influenced by perceptual and conceptual factors that inherently favor concrete nouns over verbs and other relational terms. Thus both input factors and conceptual factors will influence the child's acquisition rate.

Studies of verb-friendly languages show the influence of both conceptual and input factors. We earlier discussed the findings of Tardif, Gelman, and Xu (1999), which suggest that young Mandarin children have more nouns than verbs, consistent with the natural partitions hypothesis, but also show a greater proportion of verbs than English-speaking children, consistent with the idea that input factors can accelerate verb acquisition. In her recent work, Tardif (2005) has found a similar pattern: Children learning Mandarin show clear noun dominance in their first 20 words, consistent with the natural partitions hypothesis; but their subsequent verb acquisition seems to proceed much more rapidly than in a comparable group of children learning English. Ogura et al. (2006) studied parental interactions in Japanese and English in interactive parent–child sessions. They found that children of both languages showed noun dominance early in acquisition. This was particularly interesting in light of the fact that verbs were considerably more prominent in the Japanese input than in the English input. Further, the proportion of verbs increased over language development for both language groups. So far, the results simply follow the natural partitions hypothesis. However, consistent with the presence of input effects, the proportion of verbs increased more rapidly in Japanese children than in English children. Likewise, Kim et al. (2000) reported that both Korean and English children learned more nouns than verbs in their first 50 words; but the Korean children learned significantly more verbs than English children. In a comprehensive review of recent research, Ogura et al. concluded that early noun dominance holds for Mandarin, Korean, and Japanese, just as for English, but also that children learning the former three languages show more rapid verb acquisition than children learning English. The ease of establishing the word-to-world mapping depends both on how easy it is to individuate the word's referent in the experiential stream (the realm of the natural partitions hypothesis) and on how easy it is to pick out the word in the stream of speech.

Convergent evidence that both conceptual and linguistic factors are at play comes from the human simulation paradigm of Gleitman and her colleagues, which provides a different method of assessing the relative difficulty of picking out referents in the world. Gillette, Gleitman, Gleitman, and Lederer (1999) showed adult subjects silent videos of mothers talking to young children; beeps marked the instance of a particular noun or verb, and the subject was asked to guess the word uttered at the beeps. After six different instances of a given word, subjects guessed correctly 45% of the time for nouns, but only 15% of the time for verbs. Their accuracy at guessing verbs almost doubled (to 29%) if they were told which nouns were used in the sentence. Further, when Gillette et al. added nonsense syntactic frames (e.g., "Gorp the fendex.") as well as the nouns used, the percentage of correct verb guesses rose to 90%—evidence of the role of syntactic frames in deriving verb meanings (Fisher, 1996; Gleitman & Gleitman, 1992). Even for adult English speakers, who already know the verbs of the language, picking out the referents of highly familiar verbs cannot be reliably achieved without help from known bindings between nouns and objects. This pattern is consistent with findings from the analogy literature that, in general, people need to know the objects in a scene before they can grasp the relations between them. Thus the early learning of concrete nouns may provide the scaffolding children need to learn verb meanings (Gentner, 1982, 2006).

CONCLUSIONS

The insight that words refer to specific aspects of the external world is one of the great discoveries of early childhood. The intuition underlying the natural partitions hypothesis is that concrete and proper nouns are the ideal starting point for making this connection, because they can act as simple referential pointers to things that the child has already individuated (or can readily discern). In contrast, as Bowerman's work has so convincingly demonstrated, it is highly unlikely that children can prelinguistically individuate the referents of verbs. Verb conceptual components don't fall into inevitable clumps ready to be named, as evidenced by the fact that different languages carve them up very differently.

These results extend the natural partitions findings to Navajo. We found that object terms predominated in early Navajo vocabulary, and that terms for animate beings were especially prominent in the early Navajo noun vocabularies. There was also evidence that the proportion of relational terms increased with vocabulary size. These findings are interesting in that some aspects of the Navajo language might be expected to make verbs more salient in the input to children. More generally, Navajo represents an Athapaskan language, a very different language type from those studied so far. Thus, these results provide evidence for the generality of the natural partitions hypothesis.

The natural partitions hypothesis, in its strongest form, predicts that noun dominance is universal in early language acquisition; and more generally, that the individuability of the referent is a major factor in early word learning. Our results for Navajo, and our review of findings from the current literature, are consistent with these claims.

The natural partitions hypothesis predicts that nouns will form the child's first referential mappings from language to the world. The mapping between nouns and concrete entities can be achieved even at the very outset of language understanding. These first connections provide an easy first case of a reference relation and perhaps give the child the idea that other more opaque words must also have referents. And once learned, nouns provide semantic and syntactic frames to aid in mapping the verb to its meaning. In this way, the early acquisition of simple nouns may pave the way for learning verbs and other relational terms.

ACKNOWLEDGMENTS

We thank William Nichols, who helped design and conduct the studies as part of his graduate training in anthropology at Northwestern. We especially thank Dr. Oswald Werner for his advice on Navajo language and culture and for his assistance in reaching the Navajo community. Without their help the study could not have been done. We also thank William Morgan, Ed Shorty, Larry King, Kenneth Begaye, and Anthony Yazzi for their invaluable help in constructing and presenting the Navajo checklist, and Nathan Bush for his help as an experimenter. This chapter was partially prepared while Dedre Gentner was a fellow at the Center for Advanced Study in the Behavioral Sciences. We gratefully acknowledge the financial support of the William T. Grant Foundation, Award #95167795.

APPENDIX 1.A Examples of Checklist Items, Showing MCDI Category and Our Classification as to Noun, Verb, or Other

Navajo word	English gloss	Word type	Noun/ verb/ other	Animate
k'iVniVtiViVh	You break it [stick-shaped object].	MCDI: action words	verb	
k'iV'eVltvo'	It [slender stiff object, or mechanism] broke.	MCDI: action words	verb	
sits'il	It shattered/bloated.	MCDI: action words	verb	
niV'aah	You bring/carry it [round, compact object].	MCDI: action words	verb	
nich'iish	You brush [e.g., teeth].	MCDI: action words	verb	
nishoVoVh	You brush [e.g., dirt off your dress].	MCDI: action words	verb	
yishtiViVf	I carry it along [e.g., rifle/spear/pole].	MCDI: action words	verb	
naVniVfjid	I carried it on my back.	MCDI: action words	verb	
daVdi' nishtvivih	I am closing it [stick-shaped object, e.g., door].	MCDI: action words	verb	
daV' niV'aah	You close it [compact object e.g., a box].	MCDI: action words	verb	
da'deelkaal	It is closed.	MCDI: action words	verb	
yisbvas	I am driving/rolling it along.	MCDI: action words	verb	
da'iViVniVilbvavas	We [severally] drive.	MCDI: action words	verb	
hoV'vaVvaVfdaVaVz	It splashed over the rim.	MCDI: action words	verb	
vavadiVziViVd	You spread it out [e.g., sand, coals].	MCDI: action words	verb	
niVdii'aah	You get it [roundish, compact object].	MCDI: action words	verb	
yoVoV'ahiVfhan	You throw it away.	MCDI: action words	verb	
shiVf hozh	You tickle me.	MCDI: action words	verb	
wvivivavo	meow	MCDI: animal sounds	other	
pbpbpbpbpbp	vroom	MCDI: animal sounds	other	
wuVh wuVh	woof woof	MCDI: animal sounds	other	
tsiVdii	bird	MCDI: animals	noun	yes
ch'osh	bug	MCDI: animals	noun	yes
gah	bunny	MCDI: animals	noun	yes

APPENDIX 1.A (continued) Examples of Checklist Items, Showing MCDI Category and Our Classification as to Noun, Verb, or Other

Navajo word	English gloss	Word type	Noun/ verb/ other	Animate
k'aaloVgi	butterfly	MCDI: animals	noun	yes
moVsiV	cat	MCDI: animals	noun	yes
gaVagii	crow	MCDI: animals	noun	yes
dlvoVvoV'	prairie dog	MCDI: animals	noun	yes
Shigaan	my arm	MCDI: body parts	noun	
shits'eVeV	my belly button	MCDI: body parts	noun	
tf'eestsooz	diaper	MCDI: clothing	noun	
biil	traditional dress	MCDI: clothing	noun	
ch'ah	hat	MCDI: clothing	noun	
yiVftseViV	It is dried up.	MCDI: descriptive words	verb	
bii aVdin	It's empty/There is nothing inside.	MCDI: descriptive words	verb	
tsxviVviVf	fast	MCDI: descriptive words	other	
biVighah	That's fine (It works/fits).	MCDI: descriptive words	verb	
toV	water	MCDI: food	noun	
toVdilchxoVshiV	soda	MCDI: food	noun	
naadvaVvaV'	corn	MCDI: food	noun	
ayaV	ouch	MCDI: games and routines	other	
waV	uh oh	MCDI: games and routines	other	
aVammmm	yum yum	MCDI: games and routines	other	
t'aVaVshvovodiV	please.	MCDI: games and routines	other	
bee nahalzhohiV	broom/brush	MCDI: household items	noun	
bvavaha'iVizhahiV	cup (with handle)	MCDI: household items	noun	
feits'aat'vaVhiV	dish/plate	MCDI: household items	noun	
bilataVaV'iV	fork	MCDI: household items	noun	
toVzis bii adlaVniV	glass	MCDI: household items	noun	

(continued)

APPENDIX 1.A (continued) Examples of Checklist Items, Showing MCDI Category and Our Classification as to Noun, Verb, or Other

Navajo word	English gloss	Word type	Noun/verb/other	Animate
naak'ei siniliV	eyeglasses	MCDI: household items	noun	
bee atsidiV	hammer	MCDI: household items	noun	
bee aVndiVtviVviVhviVviV	keys	MCDI: household items	noun	
t'ahkvo'	iil lamp	MCDI: household items	noun	
beVeVsh	fnife	MCDI: household items	noun	
adee'	ladle	MCDI: household items	noun	
ts'aa'	basket	MCDI: household items	noun	
yiVftseViV	It is dried up.	MCDI: modifiers	verb	
bii aVdin	It's empty./There is nothing inside.	MCDI: modifiers	verb	
tsxviVviVf	fast	MCDI: modifiers	other	
biVighah	That's fine (It works/fits).	MCDI: modifiers	verb	
shiVnaaiV	my older brother	MCDI: people	noun	yes
shizheV'eV	my father	MCDI: people	noun	yes
at'eed	girl	MCDI: people	noun	yes
shimaVsaVniV,	my maternal grandmother	MCDI: people	noun	yes
shinaVliV	my paternal grandparent	MCDI: people	noun	yes
shicheii	my maternal grandfather	MCDI: people	noun	yes
shimaV	my mother	MCDI: people	noun	yes
baV'oVfta'iV	teacher	MCDI: people	noun	yes
ooljeVeV'	moon	MCDI: places/things in nature	noun	
joVhonaa'eViV	sun	MCDI: places/things in nature	noun	
chaha'oh	shade/ramada	MCDI: places/things in nature	noun	
chizh	firewood	MCDI: places/things in nature	noun	
hooghaniVmaVziV	hogan	MCDI: places/things in nature	noun	

APPENDIX 1.A (continued) Examples of Checklist Items, Showing MCDI Category and Our Classification as to Noun, Verb, or Other

Navajo word	English gloss	Word type	Noun/ verb/ other	Animate
ni	[used for emphasis, singular] you/your/yours	MCDI: possessives	other	
daanihiV	[used for emphasis, plural] (severally)	MCDI: possessives	other	
nVlaVaVhdi	at a remote and invisible location	MCDI: prepositions	other	
naVt'vaVvaV'	back (in the direction from whence one came)	MCDI: prepositions	other	
yaago	downward	MCDI: prepositions	other	
woVne'	in/inside [e.g., a hogan]	MCDI: prepositions	other	
bik'i	on it [e.g., put the saddle "on" the horse]	MCDI: prepositions	other	
bikaVaV	on it [e.g., the snow], against a horizontal plane	MCDI: prepositions	other	
deigo	upwards	MCDI: prepositions	other	
nViVleVidi	over there/yonder/at a remote but visible location	MCDI: prepositions	other	
naVaVnaV	again	MCDI: quantifiers	other	
bilaVahgo	being beyond it in quality or quantity	MCDI: quantifiers	other	
dooda	no	MCDI: quantifiers	other	
hait'eVego	how (in what manner)	MCDI: question words	other	
haV'aVt'iViV	what	MCDI: question words	other	
hahgo	when (at what future time)	MCDI: question words	other	
ch'iiyaVaVn	kitchen	MCDI: rooms and furniture	noun	
bii' naV'aVkaVhiV	oven	MCDI: rooms and furniture	noun	
biij'eVheVdaVhiV	outhouse (place you go out to)	MCDI: rooms and furniture	noun	
bii' azk'aVziV	refrigerator	MCDI: rooms and furniture	noun	

(continued)

APPENDIX 1.A (continued) Examples of Checklist Items, Showing MCDI Category and Our Classification as to Noun, Verb, or Other

Navajo word	English gloss	Word type	Noun/ verb/ other	Animate
niVfch'ih naalkidiV	tv	MCDI: rooms and furniture	noun	
abiVniV	morning	MCDI: temporal words	other	
tf'veVveV'	night	MCDI: temporal words	other	
k'ad	now	MCDI: temporal words	other	
diViVjviV	today	MCDI: temporal words	other	
yiskvaVvago	tomorrow	MCDI: temporal words	other	
diViVtf'veVveV'	tonight	MCDI: temporal words	other	
joof	ball	MCDI: toys	noun	
naaltsoos woVlta'iV	book	MCDI: toys	noun	
aweVeVshchiViVn	doll	MCDI: toys	noun	
aVazdaa	you're lying	added—Navajo	verb	
ch'il	weed/shrub	added—Navajo	noun	
aVniVleVeVh	you make it	added—Navajo	verb	
Zha Zha	Zandria (cousin)	added—Navajo	noun	yes
duck duck goose	duck duck goose	added— English	other	
excuse me	excuse me	added—English	other	
hurt	hurt	added—English	other	
outside	outside	added—English	other	
see you	see you	added—English	other	
pretty	pretty	added—English	other	
bye	bye	added—English	other	
airplane	airplane	added—English	noun	
banana	banana	added—English	noun	
blanket	blanket	added—English	noun	
chili	chili	added—English	noun	
corn	corn	added—English	noun	
dad	dad	added—English	noun	yes
diesel	diesel	added—English	noun	
orange	orange	added— English	noun	

APPENDIX 1.A (continued) Examples of Checklist Items, Showing MCDI Category and Our Classification as to Noun, Verb, or Other

Navajo word	English gloss	Word type	Noun/ verb/ other	Animate
pamper	pamper	added—English	noun	
look at	look at	added—English	verb	
love	love	added—English	verb	
move over	move over	added—English	verb	
open	open	added—English	verb	
play	play	added—English	verb	

REFERENCES

Au, T. K., Dapretto, M., & Song Y. K. (1994). Input vs. constraints: Early word acquisition in Korean and English. *Journal of Memory and Language, 33*, 567–582.

Baillargeon, R. (1987). Object permanence in 3.5- and 4.5-month-old infants. *Developmental Psychology, 23*, 655–664.

Bates, E., Bretherton, I., & Snyder, L. (1988). *From first words to grammar: Individual differences and dissociable mechanisms.* Cambridge, UK: Cambridge University Press.

Bohnemeyer, J. (1997). Yucatec Mayan lexicalization patterns in time and space. In M. Biemans & J. v.d. Weijer (Eds.), *Proceedings of the CLS opening academic year 1997–1998* (pp. 73–106). Tilburg, Netherlands: Center for Language Studies.

Bornstein, M. H., & Cote, L. R., with Maital, S., Painter, K., Park, S.-Y., Pascual, L. et al. (2004). Crosslinguistic analysis of vocabulary in young children: Spanish, Dutch, French, Hebrew, Italian, Korean, and American English. *Child Development, 75*(4), 1115–1139.

Bowerman, M. (1974). Learning the structure of causative verbs: A study in the relationship of cognitive, semantic, and syntactic development. *Papers and Reports on Child Language Development 8*, 142–178.

Bowerman, M. (1976). Semantic factors in the acquisition of rules for word use and sentence construction. In D. M. Morehead & A. E. Morehead (Eds.), *Normal and deficient child language* (pp. 99–179). Baltimore, MD: University Park Press,.

Bowerman, M. (1982). Reorganizational processes in lexical and syntactic development. In E. Wanner & L. R. Gleitman (Eds.), *Language acquisition: The state of the art* (pp. 319–346). New York: Cambridge University Press.

Bowerman, M. (1985). What shapes children's grammars? In D. I. Slobin (Ed.), *The crosslinguistic study of language acquisition: Vol. 2. Theoretical issues.* Mahwah, NJ: Erlbaum.

Bowerman, M., & Choi, S. (2003). Space under construction: Language-specific spatial categorization in first language acquisition. In D. Gentner & S. Goldin-Meadow (Eds.), *Language in mind: Advances in the study of language and cognition* (pp. 387–428). Cambridge, MA: MIT Press.

Brown, P. (1994). The ins and ons of Tzeltal locative expressions: The semantics of static descriptions of location. *Linguistics, 32*, 743–790.

Brown, P. (1998). Children's first verbs in Tzeltal: Evidence for an early verb category. *Linguistics, 36*(4), 713–753.

Camarata, S., & Leonard, L. B. (1986). Young children pronounce object words more accurately than action words. *Journal of Child Language, 13,* 51–65.

Casad, E. H., & Langacker, R. W. (1985). "Inside" and "outside" in Cora grammar, *International Journal of American Linguistics, 51,* 247–281.

Caselli, M. C., Bates, E., Casadio, P., Fenson, J., Fenson, L., Sanderl, L. et al. (1995). A crosslinguistic study of early lexical development. *Cognitive Development, 10,* 159–199.

Childers, J. B., & Tomasello, M. (2002). Two-year-olds learn novel nouns, verbs, and conventional actions from massed or distributed exposures. *Developmental Psychology, 38*(6), 967–978.

Childers, J. B., & Tomasello, M. (2006). Are nouns easier to learn than verbs? Three experimental studies. In K. Hirsh-Pasek & R. Golinkoff (Eds.), *Action meets word: How children learn verbs.* Oxford: Oxford University Press.

Choi, S., & Bowerman, M. (1991). Learning to express motion events in English and Korean: The influence of language-specific lexicalization patterns. *Cognition, 41,* 83–121.

Choi, S., & Gopnik, A. (1995). Early acquisition of verbs in Korean: A crosslinguistic study. *Journal of Child Language, 22*(3), 497–529.

Clark, E. V. (1993). *The lexicon in acquisition.* Cambridge, UK: Cambridge University Press.

Croft, W. A. (1990). *Typology and universals.* Cambridge, UK: Cambridge University Press.

de Leon, L. (2001). Finding the richest path: Language and cognition in the acquisition of verticality in Tzotzil (Mayan). In M. Bowerman & S. C. Levinson (Eds.), *Language acquisition and conceptual development* (pp. 544–565). Cambridge, UK: Cambridge University Press.

Dromi, E. (1987). *Early lexical development.* Cambridge, UK: Cambridge University Press.

Erbaugh, M. S. (1992). The acquisition of Mandarin. In D. I. Slobin (Ed.), *The crosslinguistic study of language acquisition* (Vol. 3, pp. 373–455). Hillsdale, NJ: Erlbaum.

Fisher, C. (1996). Structural limits on verb mapping: The role of analogy in children's interpretations of sentences. *Cognitive Psychology, 31,* 41–81.

Gelman, S. A., & Tardif, T. (1998). Acquisition of nouns and verbs in Mandarin and English. In E. Clark (Ed.), *Proceedings of the 29th Annual Stanford Child Language Research Forum.* Stanford: Center for the Study of Language and Information.

Gentner, D. (1981). Some interesting differences between verbs and nouns. *Cognition and Brain Theory, 4*(2), 161–178.

Gentner, D. (1982). Why nouns are learned before verbs: Linguistic relativity versus natural partitioning. In S. Kuczaj (Ed.), *Language development: Language, cognition, and culture* (pp. 301–334). Hillsdale, NJ: Erlbaum.

Gentner, D. (2006). Why verbs are hard to learn. In K. Hirsh-Pasek & R. Golinkoff (Eds.), *Action meets word: How children learn verbs* (pp. 544–564). Oxford, U.K.: Oxford University Press.

Gentner, D., & Boroditsky, L. (2001). Individuation, relativity and early word learning. In M. Bowerman & S. Levinson (Eds.), *Language acquisition and conceptual development.* New York: Cambridge University Press.

Gentner, D., & Rattermann, M. J. (1991). Language and the career of similarity. In S. A. Gelman & J. P. Byrnes (Eds.), *Perspectives on thought and language: Interrelations in development* (pp. 225–277). London: Cambridge University Press.

Gillette, J., Gleitman, H., Gleitman, L., & Lederer, A. (1999). Human simulations of vocabulary learning. *Cognition, 73*(2), 135–176.

Gleitman, L. R., & Gleitman, H. (1992). A picture is worth a thousand words, but that's the problem: The role of syntax in vocabulary acquisition. *Current Directions in Psychological Science, 1,* 31–35.

Gleitman, L. R., Cassidy, K., Papafragou, A., Nappa, R., & Trueswell, J. T. (2005). Hard words. *Journal of Language Learning and Development, 1,* 23–64

Goldin-Meadow, S., Seligman, M., & Gelman, R. (1976). Language in the two-year-old. *Cognition, 4,* 189–202.

Gopnik, A., & Choi, S. (1995). Names, relational words, and cognitive development in English and Korean speakers: Nouns are not always learned before verbs. In M. Tomasello & W. E. Merriman (Eds.), *Beyond names for things: Young children's acquisition of verbs* (pp. 63–80). Hillsdale, NJ: Erlbaum.

Gopnik, A., & Meltzoff, A. N. (1984). Semantic and cognitive development in 15-to-21-month-old children. *Journal of Child Language, 11,* 495–513.

Gopnik, A., & Meltzoff, A. (1993). Words and thoughts in infancy: The specificity hypothesis and the development of categorization and naming. In C. Rovee-Collier & L.P. Lipsitt (Eds.), *Advances in infancy research* (pp. 217–249). Norwood, NJ: Ablex.

Halford, G.S. (1992). Analogical reasoning and conceptual complexity in cognitive development. *Human Development,* 35(4), 193–218.

Haugen, E. (1950). The analysis of linguistic borrowing. *Language, 26,* 210–231.

Huttenlocher, J. (1974). The origins of language comprehension. In R. L. Solso (Ed.), *Theories in cognitive psychology: The Loyola Symposium.* Potomac, MD: Erlbaum.

Imai, M., & Gentner, D. (1997). A crosslinguistic study of early word meaning: Universal ontology and linguistic influence. *Cognition, 62,* 169–200.

Imai, M., Haryu, E., & Okada, H. (2005). Mapping novel nouns and verbs onto dynamic action events: Are verb meanings easier to learn than noun meanings for Japanese children? *Child Development, 76,* 340–355.

Imai, M, Haryu, E, Okada, H., Li, L. & Shigematsu, J. (2006). Revisiting the noun-verb debate: A crosslinguistic comparison of novel noun and verb learning in English, Japanese- and Chinese-speaking children. In K. Hirsh-Pasek & R. Golinkoff (Eds.), *Action meets word: How children learn verbs* (pp. 450–476). Oxford: Oxford University Press.

Kako, E. T. (2004). Information sources for noun learning. *Cognitive Science, 29,* 223–260.

Kersten, A.W., & Earles, J.L. (2004). Semantic context influences memory for verbs more than memory for nouns. *Memory & Cognition* 32(2), 198–211.

Kim, M., McGregor, K. K. & Thompson, C. (2000). Early lexical development in English and Korean-speaking children: Language-general and language-specific patterns. *Journal of Child Language* 27, 225–254.

Levinson, S. C. (1996). Frames of reference and Molyneux's question: Crosslinguistic evidence. In P. Bloom, M. A. Peterson, L. Nadel, & M. F. Garrett (Eds.), *Language and space* (pp. 109–169). Cambridge, MA: MIT Press.

Lucy, J. A. (1992). *Language diversity and thought: A reformation of the linguistic relativity hypothesis.* Cambridge, MA: Cambridge University Press.

Macnamara, J. (1972). Cognitive basis of language learning in infants. *Psychological Review, 79,* 1–13.

Maratsos, M. P., & Chalkley, M. A. (1980). The internal language of children's syntax: The ontogenesis and representation of syntactic categories. In K. Nelson (Ed.), *Children's language* (Vol. 2, pp.). New York: Gardner Press.

Markman, E. M. (1989). *Categorization and naming in children: Problems of induction.* Cambridge, MA: MIT Press.

Markman, E. M., & Hutchinson, J. E. (1984). Children's sensitivity to constraints on word meaning: Taxonomic versus thematic relations. *Cognitive Psychology, 16,* 1–27.

Nelson, K. (1973). Structure and strategy in learning to talk. *Monographs of the Society for Research in Child Development, 38* (Serial Nos. 1–2), 1–136.

Ogura, T., Dale, P., Yamashita, Y., Murase, T., & Mahieu, A. (2006). The use of nouns and verbs by Japanese children and their caregivers in book-reading and toy-playing contexts. *Journal of Child Language, 33,* 1–29.

Pae, S. (1993). *Early vocabulary in Korean: Are nouns easier to learn than verbs?* Unpublished doctoral dissertation, University of Kansas, Lawrence.

Pine, J. M., Lieven, E. V. M., & Rowland, C. (1996). Observational and checklist measures of vocabulary composition: what do they mean? *Journal of Child Language, 23,* 573–589.

Rattermann, M. J., & Gentner, D. (1998). The effect of language on similarity: The use of relational labels improves young children's performance in a mapping task. In K. Holyoak, D. Gentner, & B. Kokinov (Eds.), *Advances in analogy research: Integration of theory & data from the cognitive, computational, and neural sciences* (pp. 274–282). Sophia: New Bulgarian University.

Schieffelin, B. B. (1985). The acquisition of Kaluli. In D. I. Slobin (Ed.), *The crosslinguistic study of language acquisition* (Vol. 1). Mahwah, NJ: Erlbaum.

Schwartz, R. G., & Leonard, L. B. (1980). Words, objects, and actions in early lexical acquisition. *Papers and Reports in Child Language Development, 19,* 29–36.

Slobin, D. I. (1973). Cognitive prerequisites for the development of grammar. In C. Ferguson & D.I. Slobin (Eds.), *Studies of child language and development.* New York: Holt, Rinehart & Winston.

Slobin, D. I. (1996). Two ways to travel: Verbs of motion in English and Spanish. In M. Shibatani & S. A. Thompson (Eds.) *Essays in syntax and semantics* (pp. 195–220). Oxford: Oxford University Press.

Sloutsky, V. M., & Yarlas, A. S. (submitted). Processing of information structure: Mental representations of elements and relations.

Spelke, E. S. (1990). Principles of object perception. *Cognitive Science, 14,* 29–56.

Talmy, L. (1975). Semantics and syntax of motion. In J. Kimball (Ed.), *Syntax and semantics* (Vol. 4, pp. 181–238). New York: Academic Press.

Tardif, T. (1996). Nouns are not always learned before verbs: Evidence from Mandarin speakers' early vocabularies. *Developmental Psychology, 32*(3), 492–504.

Tardif, T., (2005, April). *But are they really verbs?* Paper presented at the meeting of the Society for Child Development, Atlanta, Georgia.

Tardif, T., Gelman, S. A., & Xu, F. (1999). Putting the noun bias in context: A comparison of English and Mandarin. *Child Development, 70*(3), 620–635.

Tomasello, M. (2000). Do young children have adult syntactic competence? *Cognition, 74*(3), 209–253.

Watson, C. S. (1976). Factors in the discrimination of word-length auditory patterns. In S. K. Hirsh, D. H. Eldredge, I. J. Hirsh, & S. R. Silverman (Eds.), *Hearing and Davis: Essays honoring Hallowell Davis* (pp. 175–189). St. Louis, MO: Washington University Press.

Waxman, S. R. (1990). Linguistic biases and the establishment of conceptual hierarchies: Evidence from preschool children. *Cognitive Development,* 5,123–150.

Waxman, S. R., & Markow, D. B. (1995). Words as invitations to form categories: Evidence from 12- to 13-month-old infants. *Cognitive Psychology, 29,* 257–302.

Young, R. W., & Morgan, W. Sr. (1987). *The Navajo language: A grammar and colloquial dictionary.* Albuquerque, NM: University of New Mexico Press.

Young, R. W., & Morgan, W., Sr., with Midgette, S. (1992). *Analytical lexicon of Navajo.* Albuquerque, NM: University of New Mexico Press.

Personal Tribute

ESTHER DROMI

I first met Melissa Bowerman in the Fall of 1977, shortly after I had arrived as a doctoral student in Lawrence, Kansas. In those days when e-mail communication or Internet searches were nonexistent, Melissa Bowerman was already an internationally recognized researcher who was well known for her seminal work on early syntactic development in Finnish (Bowerman, 1973). I applied to the graduate program at the University of Kansas because I was eager to study under her supervision and wanted to investigate the development of Hebrew as a first language.

During my first semester at the University of Kansas, I participated in Bowerman's graduate seminar on child language. During that time, Melissa was deeply interested in late-emerging errors. She was busy documenting and analyzing ungrammatical spontaneous productions of her two daughters, Christy and Eva (as well as a few other children). Her observation that children's use of causative verbs in English change over time convinced her that as the linguistic knowledge becomes more complete, the underlying hidden semantic representations undergo important changes (Bowerman, 1974, 1985, 1988). I still remember that from one week to the next, I poured over the fascinating readings (using an English–Hebrew dictionary for every other word) and counted the days until the following seminar meeting. I was astonished by Melissa's rich knowledge—and no less by her sweet and hospitable personality. I could hardly believe that a professor who was so notable could also be so attentive to the novel ideas of every participant in the seminar. Melissa's bottomless interest in every proposal that was made by first year students was extraordinary and highly supportive for all of us.

In her 1988 chapter, Bowerman devoted a whole section to describing her strong commitment to data collection. She reported that from Roger Brown, her esteemed PhD advisor at Harvard, she acquired the strong urge to become intimately familiar with spontaneous child language data. "Roger's faith in the power of careful observation to start off a fruitful chain of questioning and analysis was immensely inspiring" (1988, p. 36). Melissa also admitted that a strong commitment to data collection is costly and sometimes frustrating. At the same time, Bowerman did not hide her view that hypotheses that are derived from a systematic examination of a comprehensive body of data may lead to generalizations that are much more far-reaching than the results of a well-designed experimental study. This is not to say that theory and experimentation are unimportant (e.g., Bowerman, 1977, 1978, 1980, 1985).

I was extremely lucky when Melissa agreed to act as the chairperson of my doctoral dissertation, which was a diary study of my own daughter Keren. My goal in this project was to investigate how meanings of words are constructed at the outset of speech. I was hoping that a highly disciplined diary study, involving rich and nonselective data, would contribute to the theorizing on word meaning acquisition. I also wished to increase the attention of child language researchers to the value of crosslinguistic evidence from Hebrew, my mother tongue.

At the time of writing this chapter, Keren (who was 10 months old at the beginning of data collection) is already a mother, and the field of word meaning acquisition is exceedingly active and proliferating with new ideas and innovative experimental techniques. In retrospect, I think that my diary study resulted in a wealth of findings, as well as important theoretical generalizations, that are still relevant and timely today. Many years of active research in this field have proved that sophisticated multifaceted models of word meaning acquisition are needed to explain how young children learn what words mean. Bowerman's contention that intimate familiarity with data can result in far-reaching hypotheses has indeed proven to be true. I am so fortunate that Melissa was inspired by her own academic mentor and went on, as my advisor, to instill in me the deepest commitment to the demanding but also fulfilling journey of scientific endeavor. The training with Melissa during my graduate work in Kansas contributed invaluably to my academic career, a fact for which I am deeply grateful.

2

Old Data—New Eyes
Theories of Word Meaning Acquisition

ESTHER DROMI
Tel Aviv University

INTRODUCTION

This chapter reexamines the intriguing question of how 10- to 18-month-old infants get to know what words mean. The chapter begins with a condensed historical overview of theoretical models of word meaning acquisition, which are grouped according to major theoretical trends. The second section briefly describes the Hebrew corpus that I collected almost thirty years ago and presents the system I used for data analysis. In the third and fourth sections, I summarize the main results on meaning acquisition and reiterate theoretical claims that I have been making based on my familiarity with Keren's naturalistic data. In the last section, I discuss the old findings with new eyes, reflecting on the generalizations of my original findings with reference to current theoretical models of word meaning acquisition. I show that present day accounts in fact make predictions that very well accord with observations that were first reported in my doctoral dissertation. My intention is to demonstrate the value of investing that extraordinary effort into collecting a complete data set and of analyzing it at various levels of specificity. I also attempt to show that a rich child language database can be used over many years for testing competing theoretical accounts.

A CONDENSED HISTORY OF THEORETICAL ACCOUNTS OF WORD MEANING ACQUISITION

The earliest models of word meaning acquisition were published in the 1970s by Clark (1973), Nelson (1973), and Bowerman (1977). Each model was unique at the time of its publication, and yet all three models shared the common underlying assumption that word meaning representations of the first words are categorically represented in the child's mind. Clark claimed that at the beginning of word use, children attach only a few general and perceptually salient semantic features to the meaning representation of new words; therefore, the child uses the word more flexibly than does the adult (e.g., applying *doggy* to all four-legged animals). Gradually, children accumulate more specific semantic features, and thus narrow down the extension of new words. Nelson (1973) objected to the idea that the form of referents dictated the initiation of category formation. She claimed that the child initially perceives objects as functional wholes and assigns objects to a particular category on the basis of what they can do and what one can do with them. A basic assumption of both Clark and Nelson was that children use words to name a set of exemplars sharing perceptual or functional attributes. Bowerman (1978, 1980) was the first researcher who questioned this premise. She reported that some words that Christy and Eva used were extended to exemplars that apparently did not share any attributes with each other (e.g., "kick" to sudden contact of a limb with any object, to hands or legs moving, and to propelled objects of several shapes). Bowerman hypothesized that initially children map a new word onto a prototype (i.e., the best exemplar), which usually comprises the referent to which adults have most frequently applied this word. After an initial period in which the child's use of the word is restricted to one exemplar (or a set of closely similar exemplars), it is extended to other referents that are included in the same category. These referents, however, need not share all attributes with the original "best exemplar." As later extension relates to the child's mental ability to decompose and recompose abstract features in new ways, words might be deliberately used to label extremely dissimilar exemplars, across adult grammatical categories, and to novel instances that barely resemble any other member of the class on a single or a number of shared recognizable features.

Bowerman's prototype model was revolutionary in two important ways: She was the first to propose that early misuses of words reflect broad definitions of meaning, and early words may take several routes to word meaning. Her model predicted that the development of meaning, at least in some cases, follows a developmental path from specific to general and not vice versa. Second, Bowerman was also the first researcher to highlight the role of parental input in learning the meanings of early words. In her opinion, initial uses of new words were closely tied to the ways adults use the same words. Bowerman, who saw children as highly competent learners, hypothesized that children analyze word meanings by way of detailed comparisons that they are able to make among repeated instances in which they hear words. In that sense, she called attention to the fact that various linguistic and nonlinguistic cues in concert direct children to the initial definition of word meaning.

Three models of word meaning acquisition were published during the beginning and mid-1980s. In retrospect, I would argue that these models were transitional in the sense that they expressed dissatisfaction with the categorical view of early representation of meaning, and yet could not relinquish this notion altogether. Schlesinger's (1982) word referent pairing model refuted the argument that early words are tied to categories from their outset. He proposed that a first step in learning the meaning of a new word involves its association or pairing with only one referent. In a gradual process of pairing words with additional exemplars, the child eventually generates an underlying representation of a concept (i.e., a protoverbal element in Schlesinger's terminology). According to this proposal, the generation of categorical representations is the outcome of growing language experience and is achieved by the application of general learning processes such as (1) discrimination learning and (2) positive cue extraction.

A lively description of the process of word meaning acquisition appears in Schlesinger's (1982) book:

> A bushy tail may have become a cue for a "fox," but when it later turns out that animals called by other names have bushy tails, discrimination learning may set in. That is, the child will note properties of the different kinds of bushy tails—those that are cues for "fox" and those that are not. (p. 127)

Schlesinger's model not only predicted that meaning will develop from specific exemplars to general abstractions, but it also outlined a crucial role for the initial mapping of words and their hypothesized referents. Schlesinger perceived the child as an active constructor of internal representations of meanings, and he asserted that contextual, perceptually salient nonlinguistic information directs the child to fast mapping. Although Schlesinger himself never used this term, it is clear that in his model the initial correct pairing of a new word with its intended referent is a crucial step without which conventional meaning will not be established. According to Schlesinger, covert but active processes, by which children compare their assumptions about a word's meaning to linguistic evidence they gather from the linguistic input, bring children to appreciate the categorical nature of word meanings.

The role of nonlinguistic parameters encompassed a central theme in two other word meaning models of the eighties. Nelson's (1985) event representation or script theory, and Barrett's (1986, 1995) multiroute model shared the underlying idea that early words might not carry categorical meanings from their outset. Nelson (1985) and Nelson and Lucariello (1985) suggested that during the early phase of word learning, children attach new words to unpartitioned event representations. Instead of using words to signify object concepts, children label sets of relations in which these objects may take a role. According to this view, during late infancy children build up holistic mental representations of the frequently occurring events in their lives. But they only gradually analyze these event representations into their constituent components of people, objects, actions, and relations. Nelson argued that early words are preconceptual and hence should not be regarded as true words. She suggested calling such words prelexical expressions or wordlike productions. According to this account, only after the child is able to partition an event representation into its main nonlinguistic components can words become true referential expressions. In other words, true lexical items enter the child's vocabulary toward the second half of the second year of life and are manifested linguistically by (1) the dropout of some early words, (2) the emergence of clear object denotation, and (3) the beginning of word combinations.

The idea that categorical use of words evolves from a preliminary "workout" period is incorporated in Barrett's model too. Whereas Nelson argued that all early expressions are noncategorical, Barrett proposed to differentiate between two subgroups of early words: (1) context-bound or social pragmatic words and (2) referential words. He argued that these two classes of words coexist in early lexicons and follow distinct routes to conventional meaning. Context-bound words are initially mapped onto holistic unanalyzed representations, whereas referential words are initially mapped onto mental representations of categories that are organized around prototypes (Barrett, 1986, 1995).

The multiroute model postulates five hypothetical levels in the process of meaning acquisition. Words differ with regard to their entry level, and not all words will demonstrate a transition through all of the five levels in their developmental projection. Level A characteristically entails either an initial mapping of a new word onto an event representation or its attachment to the representation of the prototype of a category. At level B, the child modifies the event representation. Changes may include the addition of several actors or possible objects that participate in the represented event. At level C, the child disembeds and subsequently uses a single constituent in the event representation as the prototypical referent for the word. At level D, words that initially presented context-bound behaviors, and words that exhibited referential use from their outset, expand their referential scope. This expansion relates to the identification of the principal features that characterize the prototype of the category. At level D, the child is aware of the underlying category that is attached to the word, and hence might now overextend a word for a referent that is similar to the prototype. Level E entails the refinement of the underlying semantic representation of words, which includes organization of words into semantic fields, recession of overextension, and contraction of referential scope.

The multiroute model explained well the diverse findings on initial mapping of various kinds of early words. Its originality lies in the creative idea that time and experience play an important role in meaning development and that therefore a lengthy process of decontextualization is often observed for some early words. Barrett's (1995) model also contributed to our understanding that various functional interrelations operate in the gradual refinement of the meaning relations among different words in the child's lexicon. This model explained better than previous models why some words show consistent patterns of word extension from their outset, although others generalize or refine their referential scope over time.

A third wave of theories began with the revolutionary suggestion of Markman (1989) that in acquiring the meanings of words children utilize a set of a priori built-in constraints that direct their initial mappings of words onto their referents. Markman's innovative idea strongly influenced the theoretical proposals as well as the research methods for investigating word meaning acquisition. Markman and other constraint theorists (e.g., Carey, 1993; Clark, 1983, 1988, 1993; Markman, 1989, 1991, 1993; Markman & Hutchinson, 1984; Markman & Wachtel, 1988; Merriman & Bowman, 1989; Merriman, Marazia, & Jarvis, 1995; Soja, Carey, & Spelke, 1991) claimed that the existence of linguistic constraints explain the accelerated speed and great accuracy by which children accumulate new words. Constraint theorists have tried to explicate how young children may solve the logical problem of generating possible hypotheses about the meaning of a new word. Quine (1960, cited in Markman, 1993; Carey, 1993; Naigles, Gleitman, & Gleitman, 1993 and in many other publications) long ago posed this question about the problem of correct mapping: How is it that when a person hears a new word he or she immediately knows to which aspect of the complex observational situation this word refers? Carey, for instance, demonstrated the problem of correct mapping with the following example:

> Suppose a child hears "that's a cup" when the speaker is indicating a brown plastic cup half filled with coffee. Suppose also that the child does not know any word which refers to any aspect of this situation. "Cup" could refer to cups, tableware, brown, plastic, coffee, being half full, the front side of the cup and the table, the handle, any undetached part of a cup, a temporal stage of the cup (that is the particular cup at some particular time), the number one, the cup shape, and so on for an infinitude of possibilities. (1993, p. 88)

Markman (e.g., 1989, 1991, 1993) articulated three constraints—*whole object*, *taxonomic*, and *mutual exclusivity*—to explain how the inductions of word meanings are so often correct from the outset, how quickly young children learn the meanings of new words, and what mechanisms might motivate young children to learn terms other than object words (e.g., labels for properties, parts of objects, categories of objects). Markman postulated that when children are exposed to a new word in the presence of a novel object, they assume that: (1) the new word labels the *whole object*, rather than its parts, substance, or other properties; and (2) the new word labels a class of objects of similar kind (*taxonomy*) rather than objects that are thematically related (e.g., a pencil and paper, a doggie and a bone). In addition, when children hear a new word applied to an object for which they already have a name, they assume that the new word cannot be a second name for the same object (*mutual exclusivity*); hence, the child links the new word to some property of that object or one of its salient parts (see also Carey, 1993).

Clark (1983a, 1983b, 1988, 1990), who joined the constraints theorists, offered two additional constraints: *contrast* and *conventionality*. According to Clark, from a very young age, and even before children start to produce their first words, they already appreciate the usefulness of these two important linguistic constraints. First, any word in the lexicon *contrasts* in meaning with any other word, and second, every word in the language has a *conventional* meaning that is shared by all speakers in the same language community. Clark summarized empirical evidence to support her claim that conventionality and contrast preempt the use of synonymous words, and that children utilize new words and innovative lexical forms to fill in lexical gaps (Clark, 1993).

Along with the flourishing experimental work that evolved from specific hypotheses on the instrumental role of linguistic constraints in early word meaning acquisition, researchers also raised serious objections to the idea of linguistic constraints (Gathercole, 1987, 1989; Nelson, 1988). Nelson, for example, questioned the proposal that lexical constraints are innate and are present from the beginning of the one-word stage. She invoked descriptions of early complexive uses of words (e.g., Bowerman, 1978) and highlighted the fact of contextual use of first words by young children. She also questioned the scope of the constraints account, arguing that it might be relevant to object words only (Bloom, 1994). Finally, she also objected to the all-or-nothing implication of constraints. An assumption of innate and universal constraints, Nelson argued, would not allow for individual differences. Gathercole (1987, 1989) presented a strong set of arguments against Clark's position that lexical meanings always contrast. She cited a rich set of examples for noncontrastive use of words by young children and by adults. Gathercole argued that it is important to consider pragmatic principles in studying early language, and to test mothers' input practices in order to better understand how children construct their lexical knowledge.

In 1994, Golinkoff, Mervis, and Hirsh-Pasek initially introduced the idea that meaning acquisition is guided by a set of lexical principles (rather than built-in constraints) that consist of intelligent strategies that young children entertain in order to increase the likelihood of forming certain word-meaning hypotheses. Lexical principles direct children toward some conclusions and not others; however, they are not deterministic and their relative significance changes over time. According to this proposal it is important to distinguish between those lexical principles that are operating early, and those that operate later on. Early operating principles (i.e., the "first tier") include the simple strategies of reference, extendibility, and object scope. These principles are prerequisites for the beginning of vocabulary learning. Later operating principles (i.e., the "second tier") include the more advanced strategies of categorical scope, novel name—nameless category (N3C), and conventionality, which the child constructs on the basis of accumulated experience with language. The contribution of this model to theories of word meaning acquisition lay in its attempt to combine previous proposals in order to seek a unified structure that would explain word meaning acquisition from its beginning and throughout the second year of life. This model also introduced for the first time the idea that co-occurring principles direct word learning and these principles may not be the same at different developmental levels.

I see a fourth wave of theorizing on word–meaning acquisition with the bulk of discussions and experimental research on the role of social contexts in the course of early lexical learning (Tomasello, 1992; Tomasello & Akthar, 1995; Tomasello & Farrar, 1986). In a sequence of several experimental studies, Tomasello and colleagues tested the hypothesis that young infants (as young as 19 months) are sensitive to social cues that adults provide to facilitate the mapping of new words with unnamed novel objects or novel actions (e.g., Tomasello & Barton, 1994; Tomasello

& Farrar, 1986). They showed that during the beginning of the second year of life, toddlers are able to match a nonsense word (e.g., *toma*) with a referent on the basis of the adult's intended use of a label by this word. This finding, they argued, clearly demonstrates that from a very young age infants pick up subtle social cues from the adults who direct their attention to relevant aspects of the situation being discussed. As partners in the social-pragmatic game, adults provide implicit and explicit modeling examples. Parents are attuned to their child's focus of attention and most often talk about those aspects of the situation that are in the child's current focus of attention (Harris, 1992; Masur, 1982; Ringwald-Frimerman, 2003). When adult–child interactions are fruitful and the implicit conditions for a communicative flow are fulfilled, word meaning acquisition becomes a kind of apprenticeship in which the social environment feeds word learning at an acceptable rate (Baldwin & Tomasello, 1998; Hollich et al., 2000; Ringwald-Frimerman, 2003).

When do children begin to effectively exploit social knowledge in determining what a new word might mean? An answer to this question is found in the revised model of Hollich, Golinkoff, and Hirsh-Pasek, a model known as the emergentist coalition model (Golinkoff & Hirsh-Pasek, 2006; Hollich et al., 2000). The emergentist coalition model holds that children have access to a number of co-occurring cues for word learning (including perceptual, social, and linguistic), which they utilize at different times along the extended process of word meaning acquisition (Golinkoff & Hirsh-Pasek, 2006; Pruden, Hirsh-Pasek, Golinkoff, & Hennon, 2006). At the outset of speech children associate new words with the most salient object that they perceive in the immediate environment (see also Smith, 1999). Later on, infants begin to appreciate the importance of the social cues that adults provide in order to signal the intended meaning of a new word to the child.

The idea that sophisticated understanding of inherent communicative intentions that are unique to humans evolve from cognitively simpler mechanisms is closely tied to the theoretical framework of dynamic systems theory and connectionism (Bates & Elman, 2000; Bidell & Fischer, 2000; Elman et al., 1996; Granott & Parziale, 2002; MacWhinney, 1999; Smith, 1995, 1999; Spencer et al., 2006; Thelen & Bates, 2003; Thelen & Smith, 1994; VanGeert, 1994). In a paper that compares dynamic systems theory and connectionism, Thelen and Bates (2003) laid out four principles that characterize language learning:

> 1) that it is function, rather than rule-driven; 2) that language acquisition is highly bidirectional and multi-layered; 3) that language is learned from the input in a statistical or probabilistic way; 4) that language learning is nonlinear, whereby gradual changes can lead to emergent properties. (p. 381)

Later on in the same paper, Thelen and Bates added a fifth characteristic dealing with the notion of changes in the underlying representation: (5) that "sometimes-surprising reorganizations can result from these nonlinearities" (Thelen & Bates, 2003, p. 381). In accordance with this set of tenets, Bates proposed that language development constitutes an example of a highly specified human capacity that can be explained on the basis of simple connectionist principles of evolution and interaction, the plasticity of the human brain, and experiential sudden catastrophic reorganizations or transformations that can take place in underlying representations (Bates & Elman, 2002; Elman et al., 1996; MacWhinney, 1999; Smith, 1999; Thelen & Bates, 2003).

Smith (1999) examined the position that high-level word-learning strategies are derived from basic mechanisms of greater generality. She showed how primary associative and attention mechanisms that infants already possess during the second half of the first year of life are used for labeling objects of similar shapes. According to this view, the growing experience with words during the beginning of speech has an important role of adding to and strengthening the association between objects and linguistic labels. The results of a recent experimental study on mapping of words by 10-month-old babies, in which the preferential looking paradigm was used (Pruden et al., 2006), provides additional support to the claim that at an early age infants pair words with perceptually salient objects. On the basis of their results, Pruden et al. argue that prior to their first birthday infants lean on perceptual rather than on social cues in associating words and their referents. Later on, at the age of 12 months, infants become sensitive to social cues, but cannot yet recruit them in all circumstances for word learning. Only after gaining a wealth of experience in learning new words (when they are about 18 to 24 months of age) do children begin to utilize social pragmatic cues for rapid and efficient word learning (Pruden et al., 2006).

During the last three decades our understanding of the multiple factors that are involved in word meaning acquisition has significantly increased. Bowerman's strong conviction that language development involves hidden underlying reorganizations has gained considerable empirical support.

THE OLD DIARY STUDY

The database for my investigation comprised the complete record of all the words that my daughter acquired and repeatedly used from the emergence of her first comprehensible word ("bow wow" for a dog) and until she started to productively combine words. The one-word stage lasted in Keren's case about 8 months, between the ages of 10(12) and 17(23) months. During this time she accumulated a productive lexicon of 337 different Hebrew words. I employed a carefully controlled case study to collect as much information as possible on the use of each of these words in different contexts over time. I utilized three independent means for data collection: (1) a handwritten diary that included descriptions of all her productions together with the linguistic and nonlinguistic contexts for their use; (2) nine periodic audio recordings ranging in length from 55 to 180 minutes each, which provided a representative picture of her typical discourse and regular use of words in the course of natural interactions with parents; and (3) four 30-minute video-recorded sessions that presented verbal and visual aspects of early interactions in semistructured play situations at home (Dromi, 1987, chapter 7). I designed the combination of these data collection procedures to compensate for the drawbacks inherent in each procedure alone. It also provided the means for conducting various measures of reliability and validity on the data, which were found to be reasonably high (Dromi, 1987, pp. 84–89). These measures clearly indicated that although I, the mother-researcher, collected data constantly and for a relatively long period of time, the record was accurate and representative of the actual course of the child's lexical development, reflecting both the emergence of new words and changes in the use of old words throughout time.

In the course of data analysis, weekly scores were given to each word in Keren's vocabulary on various form and meaning dimensions. Preplanned codes were operationally defined and also tested for interjudge reliability (see description and illustration of the coding systems for reference and extension in Dromi, 1987, chapter 8). The scores given to all words reflected quantitative changes in the number of words, qualitative measures of grammatical categories of all words, and each word's extension relative to the meaning of that word in adult speech. As will be shown below, the procedure of repeated scoring for each word provided crucial information for the identification of underlying conceptual and linguistic processes in word meaning acquisition.

In order to capture changes over time in word meanings, I adopted a distinction originally proposed by Frege (1892/1974) to distinguish between reference and sense in the representation of meaning. Anglin (1977, 1983) integrated Frege's distinction into the study of early language development and also provided an explanation of why the meanings of children's words ought to be represented at two distinct levels: The level of extension and the level of intension. "The extension of a term of reference includes all the objects which an individual is willing to denote with that term of reference, whereas the intension of a term of reference is the set of properties which an individual believes to be true of the instances of the category denoted by that term" (Anglin, 1977, p. 27).

According to this definition, the extension of the word *animal*, for example, would be: cow, dog, cat, elephant, crocodile, penguin, mink, etc. Its intension would be: It lives, it digests, it reproduces itself, it is capable of spontaneous motion, and so on (Anglin, 1983). Conceptual word meaning representations include both the extension and the intension aspects of a category of objects or events that are denoted by a word. It is logical to assume, then, that the extension and the intension of a word are intrinsically tied and are concurrently constructed in the mental lexicon. Although it is difficult to differentiate extension from intension on the basis of behavioral data, it is feasible to utilize the logical distinction between these two phenomena when analyzing repeated spontaneous productions of children at the one-word stage.

I assessed Keren's early word extensions in order to (1) document changes over time in the ways she used a particular word throughout the one-word stage and (2) compare Keren's extensions with the extensions of the same words by adults. These offered a powerful means of testing the extent to which Keren's uses of words reflected adults' conventional meanings. The relations between the child's and the adult's extension of the same word might take one of the following five logical forms: identity, partial overlap, mismatch, underextension, or overextension (Anglin, 1977, 1983; Clark, 1983; Reich, 1976).

Repeated uses of each of Keren's new and old words in any given week of study helped in determining the assignment of each word to one of mutually exclusive extension categories. Words that she used restrictively during a given week, for a single referent only or for a very limited subset of instances from the corresponding adult category, received an assignment to the category of underextension. Words demonstrating flexible use for a number of different referents that belonged to a corresponding adult category were assigned to the category of regular extension. I classified as overextension Keren's overly broad use of a word for a class of referents, some of which fell outside of the corresponding adult category for the same word (e.g., using the word *car* for all kinds of vehicles).

Keren repeatedly used a certain number of words in contexts that differed from those adults would use. Although these words were uttered consistently and recorded in high frequency, it was never clear to me which aspect of the situation they encoded. She used some words ambiguously for actions and related objects (e.g., the word *sus* 'horse' for bouncing movements, riding, and horses); others sounded as if they were used associatively rather than referentially (e.g., the word *dod* 'uncle' used for strangers and for whenever the child heard noises coming from outside). Still other words exhibited a pattern of shifting referential behaviors, so that it remained unclear as to whether they were terms for specific objects, actions, or relations or were employed as cover terms for whole unanalyzed situations (e.g., *niyar* 'paper' used for pieces of paper, pencils, drawing, a painting, newspapers, appliqué on a pillow case, chalk marks on the sidewalk). I assigned such words to the category of unclassified extension (see more examples in Dromi, 1987, 1993, 1999).

SUMMARY OF THE RESULTS ON CHANGES OVER TIME IN WORD MEANINGS

The four extension categories were unequally represented in Keren's corpus of single words. Of all the words that were learned throughout the stage, 66% exhibited categorical, or regular, extension at one time or another, and the other 33% showed overly restricted, overly broad, or unclassified behaviors. It was interesting to note that overextensions, which throughout the seventies were so extensively discussed in the word meaning literature, were recorded for only one third of Keren's vocabulary of single words. This behavior appeared as rarely as underextension or unclassified extension; it emerged relatively late and was recorded much more often toward the end of the study and shortly before word combinations emerged.

The question of when in its history a word showed certain extension behavior was among the most important questions to be explored. I found that almost all underextensions were recorded during the initial uses of a new word and that this behavior persisted for a relatively short period of time (M = 2 weeks, range = 1–10 weeks). In contrast, overextensions were almost always recorded after a few weeks of correct or restricted use of the same word. This behavior was transient for some words and longer lasting for others. Half of the words that showed regular extension were recorded as such from the first week of their use, whereas the other half showed underextension or unclassified behaviors prior to the recording of categorical adult meaning. Unclassified behaviors, which comprised the most idiosyncratic and least conventional uses of words, were mainly recorded during initial weeks of production. Words that showed this behavior exhibited it over a long period of time (M = 7 weeks, range = 1–24 weeks). It is interesting to note that Keren was consistent in using such words in her own way despite my regular attempts to provide examples of how to use conventional words in cases of Keren's irregular or unclear extension.

A strong relationship emerged between the timing of a new word's acquisition and the pattern of extension it exhibited during the first week of its use and over time. During the first four months of study, all four extension types were recorded, but it was impossible to predict which words would initially show underextension and which would be used categorically from the outset. I found it extremely challenging to try and explain why some words from their outset conveyed conventional meanings, yet others demonstrated unclassified behaviors. A striking finding for this first phase was the complete lack of initial overextensions. No word in Keren's vocabulary of the first four months was overextended during its first week of use. Initial unclassified behaviors, on the other hand, were recorded frequently, and during some weeks even predominated.

This unpredictable pattern of extension altered suddenly during the fifth month of study. This change appeared shortly before I documented a lexical spurt that was manifested in an abrupt change in the rate of learning new words during the 25th, 26th, and 27th weeks of data collection. In that particular short interval of time, Keren accumulated 150 new words, which constituted one third of her productive single-word vocabulary. Starting at the lexical spurt interval and onward, 30 to 40% of Keren's new words showed underextension during the first week of use, and over 50% of the new words showed regular extension from their outset. The tendency of new and old words to exhibit conventional categorical meanings was ever-growing toward the last few weeks of the stage. Overextensions of new words during their first week of use were recorded only during the second half of the research. Unclassified extension behaviors in new words declined considerably at this phase, until they completely disappeared five weeks before the beginning of multiword productions.

Figure 2.1 depicts the relative distribution of all Keren's words in the four extension categories during each week of study. The interrelationship between the four curves in this figure confirms that overextension and underextension behaviors remained relatively low and stable throughout the period of study, whereas unclassified extension was correlated negatively with regular extension. It is obvious that, with time, more and more words entered the category of regular extension, as fewer and fewer words showed unclassified behaviors. The gradual and systematic increase in the number of regularly extended words strongly suggested to me that, with time, Keren's lexical system became more and more conventional, with very few words showing overly restricted or overly broad extensions.

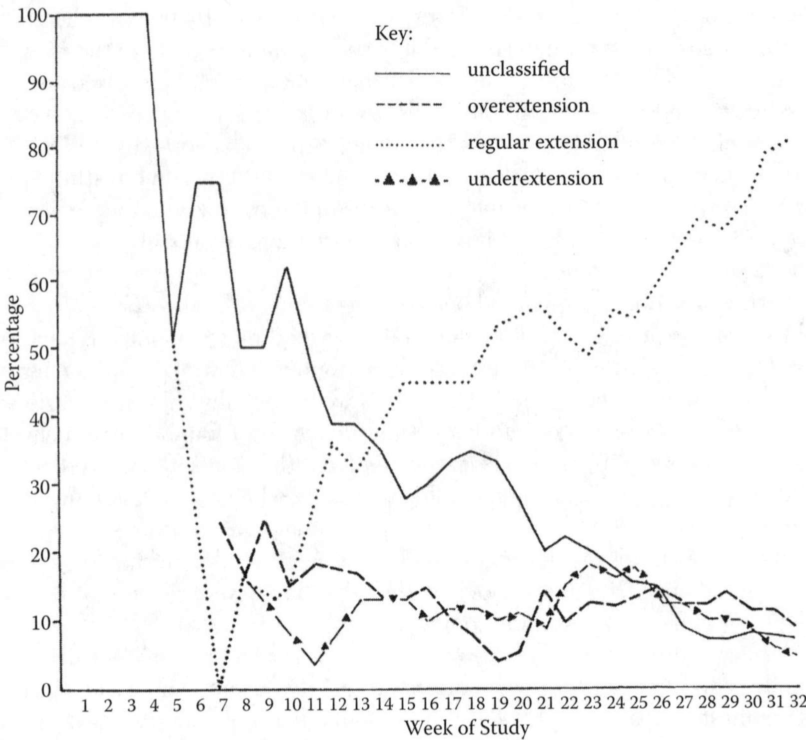

Figure 2.1 The relative distribution of extension classes for all the words that Keren used throughout the one word stage.

THEORETICAL IMPLICATIONS OF THE CASE STUDY RESULTS

My findings led to the conclusion that Keren's lexical abilities differed qualitatively at the beginning and at the end of the one-word stage. I argued that underlying cognitive and linguistic developments that take place throughout that developmental period are linked to the variance in the prevalence of the different extension categories as well as the course observed in the natural history of meaning in each single word. Examination of changes in the extension of a single word over time produced an extension profile for that word. In Keren's corpus of 337 different words in Hebrew, I identified as many as 58 different profiles of extension (Dromi, 1987, p. 145). On the basis of this great variability, I concluded that different words take various routes as their meanings develop. I attributed the link that most words demonstrated—between the timing of acquisition and the extension profile—to an interaction between the child's cognitive and linguistic abilities and the nature of input conditions. I proposed that during the first few months of study, the extension of a new word was highly conditioned by the modeling of that particular word to the child. I showed that words that were modeled in opaque nonlinguistic contexts were initially used by Keren in an ambiguous and nonreferential way. On the other hand, words that were modeled in contexts that allowed clear orientation to the referent that was named by the word were used correctly by Keren even during the earliest phase of the study.

In my dissertation (Dromi, 1982), I claimed that early nonreferential uses of words provided strong empirical support for Mandler's supposition that schematic and categorical representations can coexist in human cognition. Mandler (1979, 1983), who studied memory representations in adults, explained the distinction between categorical and schematic cognitive representations. She claimed that a scheme is a structure that is organized around contiguities of space and time, unlike categories, which are based on similarity relationships among the members of a class. I suggested that during the early phases of the one-word stage, children may fail to correctly map a word onto a single component of a situation (i.e., an agent, an object, or an action). In such cases, the word is automatically embedded in the schematic representation of the context in which it was modeled to the child. Inasmuch as the child is not yet aware of the conceptual nature of word meanings, she uses this word in a nonreferential manner.

In several publications (Dromi, 1987, 1993, 1999), I have argued that the first few months of word learning are in fact *a preparatory phase* during which the child learns each new word as a special case at a slow rate. Idiosyncratic patterns of word extension are noticed during this phase, because children are not equipped yet with the mature notion that words must be associated with underlying concepts. The initial extension of a new word in this period is highly dependent on the characteristics of input and the conditions of adult modeling, thus impeding predictions about what the extension of a new word would be during that time.

Following the lexical spurt, Keren's words were less malleable with respect to input conditions and tended to indicate conventional meanings from their very first applications. She used many words first to denote a single referent, possibly the prototype of the underlying category, and she immediately extended others to a number of referents belonging to the same category in adult speech. I explained the relationship between the lexical spurt and the change in extension behaviors of words as the result of a new skill that Keren attained in the ability to initially map new words onto their referents. *The second phase* of the stage was characterized by much more efficient word learning that was marked by consistent, categorical, and conventional use of new words. During the second phase, the child maps words correctly, immediately attaches words to underlying concepts, and shows context-free uses of new words from their outset. I hypothesized that Keren's utilization of linguistic cues was much greater in the second phase of the stage than in the first phase. Such cues free the child from reliance on observational data and enhance more efficient learning of new meanings (Dromi, 1999).

To sum up, I claimed that, following the lexical spurt, the child's linguistic behaviors are much more directed by internal cognitive organization of experiences as well as by linguistic cues than by the immediate nonlinguistic contexts in which new words are modeled. Therefore, during that phase words are symbolic, conventional, and context-free entities.

REFLECTIONS: OLD DATA—NEW EYES

On the basis of rich empirical data on only one child, my own daughter Keren, I concluded that throughout the one-word stage children's linguistic system undergoes a major structural change as it becomes more highly differentiated, symbolic, and conventional. I argued that the acquisition of the major principles for conventional use of words is neither instantaneous nor general across the board. My claim was that the child gradually learns to appreciate the fact that words convey consistent categorical meanings; that they are attached to either object concepts or to actions and relations; that words must be conventional both in terms of their form and their underlying meaning; and that words can stand for specific referents, classes of referents, and relations even in their absence in the immediate physical context.

When I wrote my dissertation in the early 1980s, categorical theories of word meaning acquisition predominated. At that time, my claim that not all words are learned as labels for already existing categories raised questions. It was not so clear if Keren demonstrated an idiosyncratic pattern of word learning because she was a precocious learner of language, and whether my findings and theoretical claims could be at all generalized to other children learning other languages (e.g., Dromi, 1990; Nelson, 1990).

In close proximity to my dissertation, Barrett (1986) published the English language data that he collected from his son Adam. Barrett (1986, 1995) reported that not all early words showed categorical extension from their outset; Adam produced some words initially in only very specific contexts. Barrett's most famous example of context-bound word use was the word *duck*, which Adam initially uttered only while taking a bath and hitting a specific toy duck off the edge of the bathtub. As Adam's lexical development proceeded, the context-bound word *duck* that was initially produced in just one situation was uttered in a much wider range of contexts until it became completely context-free. On the basis of this example and a few others, Barrett concluded that "the reference of the word after decontextualization seems to derive from one of the core aspects of the event which previously elicited context bound use of the word" (1995, p. 371).

Harris et al. (1988) documented the contexts in which the first 10 words were used by four English-speaking participants. They found that more than 50% of the 40 words studied were initially used in a context-bound manner. Barrett, Harris, and Chasin (1991) and Harris (1992) reported that by age 2, all but three of the initially recorded context-bound words showed referential meaning. A pivotal finding in this research program addressed the relationship between the characteristics of mothers' modeling practices and the extension of the same words by their children. The analysis of longitudinal speech samples indicated that children's initial productions resembled the most frequent contexts in which the mothers modeled the same words. Mothers' modeling behaviors correlated significantly with the child's initial extension of the word. However, the relationship between mothers' input practices and children's subsequent uses of the same words was dramatically weaker. Later acquired words and later uses of the same words were not tied to the nonlinguistic characteristics of the input. This finding is supportive of the argument that as children grow older their reliance on selective perceptual aspects of the modeling contexts decreases.

Theoretical explanations for nonreferential use of early words were provided during the eighties by a number of researchers who postulated, often independently of one another, that nonreferential words lack categorical properties and are initially connected to undifferentiated representations of unanalyzed situations, separate scenes, or single events. These researchers, including myself, argued that context-related productions might be triggered by the identification of a single component of an event, as well as by the activation of an overall scripted representation (e.g., Barrett, 1986; Dromi, 1982, 1987, 1993; Gillis, 1986; Nelson, 1985; Nelson & Lucariello, 1985; Schank & Abelson, 1977; Tomasello, 1992).

Clark's (1983, 1988, 1993) principles of contrast and conventionality, which she proposed in the late eighties, also deserve mention here. It is very clear that these two constraints explain why, following the lexical spurt, children refuse to produce words for which they have not been able to attach categorical meanings. The phenomenon of the replacement of old idiosyncratic words with conventional words is remarkable. It shows that the child does not give up old forms for new ones so easily. Keren initially juxtaposed old forms that were initially attached to script representations with new categorical words, as if she were trying to translate the meanings of the conventional words by relying on old meanings that she had. Consider the following two examples:

(1) At age 17(5): In the living room; K brings a red balloon to M. She hands it to M and says: *alon* [*balon*] ('a) balloon'/ *hupa* '?'/ *hupa* was K's earlier word for round objects and any abrupt contact of body parts, mainly legs, with the floor;

(2) At age 15(16): In K's room; K is sitting on the floor and playing with plastic toy animals. She takes a horse out of the box and says: *dio* 'giddi-up'. M asks K: *ma ze?* 'What is this?' K answers: *sus* '(a) horse'/ *dio* 'giddiup.' (Dromi, 1987, p. 51)

Timing of acquisition is a major factor in word meaning acquisition. In Barrett's (1986, 1995) multiroute model, time is reflected by the sequence of steps that a word may take en route to conventional meaning. Barrett argued that context-bound words emerge early and show a longer, more complex developmental path than do words that are learned later and show referential behaviors from their outset. In Hollich et al.'s emergentist coalition model (2000), timing is also a most visible and important factor for predicting how words will be learned. Early words are mapped onto referents on the basis of perceptual salience cues, and later acquired words are mapped more efficiently as the child can utilize social and interactive cues to direct attention to the referent that is labeled by the adult (Golinkoff & Hirsh-Pasek, 2006; Hirsh-Pasek & Golinkoff, 1996; Hollich et al., 2000).

My careful analysis of Keren's rich data led me to the conclusion that input and experience play a crucial role in the construction of linguistic knowledge. The role of input and experience was first highlighted in Schlesinger's (1982) word-referent pairing model. Two major arguments initially made by Schlesinger reappear in the work of present-day child language researchers who operate within the social pragmatic theoretical framework (Baldwin, 1995; Baldwin & Tomassello, 1998; Tomassello & Akhtar, 1995; Tomassello & Farrar, 1986). The first argument is that children initially match words with single referents on the basis of a simple one-to-one mapping strategy. The second is that early words do not comprise labels for predefined concepts, but rather they facilitate the gradual construction of underlying concepts (Smith, 1999).

Those committed to the application of dynamic systems theory to language development in general, and to word meaning acquisition in particular, view the formulation of cognitive categories that underlie words as a gradual process that subscribes to species-general mechanisms of change (Elman et al., 1996; Hollich et al., 2000; Plunkett, 1997; Smith, 1995; Thelen & Bates, 2003; Thelen & Smith, 1994). According to this account, environmental factors play a central role in the generation of internal structuring that is also based on the child's growing processing abilities. These abilities include the child's capacity to attend to nonverbal cues, to match words with nonlinguistic referents, and to form categories on the basis of accumulating positive and negative cues (Schlesinger, 1982). Covert but active processes, by which the child compares assumptions about a word's meaning to linguistic evidence that she gathers from the linguistic input, bring her to appreciate the categorical nature of words. Thelen and Bates (2003) emphasized the important role of the child's gradual restructuring of external information that turns into an internalized rule system or a new generalized ability (see also Spencer et al., 2006).

My finding that at least some early words are in fact verbal behaviors that lack the linguistic status of referential words and are produced within repeated routinized contexts of everyday experiences supports the view that from simple procedures much more sophisticated abilities emerge (Bidell & Fischer, 2000; Granott & Parziale, 2002; Van Geert, 1994). In this chapter, I have shown that by a continuous process of decontextualization, early vocalizations gradually become more symbolic. They are detached from the restricted schemes in which they were initially embedded, and begin to represent sets of referents or relations. As symbolic tools, words are separate from their intended referents not only in time and space, but also by the very fact that they become conventional and begin to convey socially agreed upon meanings (Bates, 1979; Hollich et al., 2000; Piaget, 1962).

I have argued that the diversity of lexical extensions that I documented in Keren's lexical behaviors prior to the lexical spurt indicate that self-organization is the end result of a developmental process and that, given a diversity of possibilities, the human mind selects the best solution to a problem (Elman et al., 1996; Spencer et al., 2006; Thelen & Bates, 2003). The long process of word meaning acquisition that results in reorganization and appreciation of principles such as conventionality on the one hand and categorical meaning on the other can be characterized as emergent knowledge. The initial phase of the one-word stage is mandatory for the future generation of categorical thinking and specific word-learning mechanisms. The dynamic system theory explains very well why initially words are accumulated so slowly, behave so differently from adults' words, and rely so heavily on the characteristics of input and environmental factors (Smith, 1999). Hollich et al. (2000) suggested that present-day models of word-meaning acquisition should entertain at least three assumptions:

> a) that children are exposed to multiple inputs; b) that the weights of these inputs change over time through guided distributional learning; and c) that the result of this process is emergent principles of word learning that move from immature to mature and from domain-general to domain-specific principles. (2000, p. 29)

Keren's old diary data can be used as naturalistic empirical evidence that this is indeed the case.

An illuminating example from Keren's diary demonstrates how a conventional word in adult speech can initially be used by the child in a highly associative way and without any recognized referential meaning:

> Age 13(8): In K's room; F and M are talking about going out tonight. K seems not to be paying attention. She is running around with her ball. M draws a schematic map of town on a piece of paper and says to F: *ani efgosh otxa po al yad hasha'on shel yaffo/* 'I shall meet you right here near Jaffa Clock.' (Jaffa Clock is a central location in Jaffa). K comes closer to parents. She points to the piece of paper and says: ~ "tick tock" (her word for watches, clocks, and other jewelry and also a word for bringing little objects to the ear). (Dromi, 1993, p.48)

It seems to me that the word 'clock' was elicited in that particular instance as a result of a simple sound–word association only because Keren recognized a familiar string of sounds *sha'on* 'clock,' which is also the name of the central square in Jaffa. I am certain that at this early phase Keren did not yet know what the word 'clock' or 'watch' in Hebrew meant and she used the word in a nonreferential manner. A few months later, Keren learned the full meaning of this word.

How much can be learned from a systematic analysis of only one child's diary? Was this study facilitative of theoretical generalizations that later on proved fruitful? It took me over two decades to realize that my disciplined case study research, which I formally completed in 1982, will keep me intellectually busy throughout my entire academic career. Now, when I look back at the naïve theories of the early seventies, I am amused by their simplicity. Many years of active empirical research in this field have proved that sophisticated multifaceted models of word meaning acquisition are needed in order to explain how young children learn what words mean.

ACKNOWLEDGMENTS

I would like to express my deep gratitude to Ginny Gathercole for inviting me to contribute a chapter for this volume. I also want to thank two anonymous reviewers for very helpful comments on an earlier draft. Finally, I wish to thank Dee B. Ankonina for her editorial assistance.

REFERENCES

Anglin, J. M. (1977). *Word, object and conceptual development.* New York: Norton.

Anglin, J. M. (1983). Extensional aspects of the preschool child's word concepts. In T. Seiler & W. Wannenmacher (Eds.), *Concept development and the development of word meaning* (pp. 247–266). New York: Springer-Verlag.

Baldwin, D. A. (1995). Understanding the link between joint attention and language. In C. Moore & P. J. Dunham (Eds.), *Joint attention: Its origins and role in development.* Hillsdale, NJ: Erlbaum.

Baldwin, D. A., & Tomassello, M.(1998). Word learning: A window on early pragmatic understanding. In E. V. Clark (Ed.), *Proceedings of the Stanford Child Language Research Forum.* Stanford, CA: Center for the Study of Language and Information.

Barrett, M. D. (1986). Early semantic representations and early word usage. In S. Kuczay & M. D. Barrett (Eds.), *The development of word meaning.* New York: Springer.

Barrett, M. D. (1995). Early lexical development. In P. Fletcher & B. MacWhinney (Eds.), *The handbook of child language* (pp. 362–392). Oxford: Blackwell.

Barrett, M. D., Harris, M., & Chasin, J. (1991). Early lexical development and maternal speech: A comparison of children's initial and subsequent uses of words. *Journal of Child Language, 18*, 21–40.

Bates, E., (1979). *The emergence of symbols: Cognition and communication in infancy.* New York: Academic Press.

Bates, E., & Elman, J. (2002). Connectionism and the study of change. In M. Johnson (Ed.), *Brain development and cognition: A reader.* (2nd ed., rev.). Oxford: Blackwell. (Original work published 1993).

Berman, R. (1985). Acquisition of Hebrew. In D. Slobin (Ed.), *The crosslinguistic study of language acquisition.* Hillsdale, NJ: Erlbaum.

Bidell, T. R., & Fischer, K. W. (2000). The role of cognitive structure in the development of behavioral control: A dynamic skills approach. In W. J. Perrig & A. Grob (Eds.), *Control of human behavior, mental processes, and consciousness: Essays in honor of the 60th birthday of August Flammer* (pp. 183–201). Mahwah, NJ: Erlbaum.

Bloom, P. (1994). Possible names: The role of syntax-semantics mapping in the acquisition of nominals. *Lingua*, 92, 297–329.

Bowerman, M. (1973). *Early syntactic development: A crosslinguistic study with special reference to Finnish.* Cambridge, UK: Cambridge University Press.

Bowerman, M. (1974). Learning the structure of causative verbs: A study in the relationship of cognitive, semantic, and syntactic development. *Papers and Reports on Child Language Development, 8*, 142–179.

Bowerman, M. (1977). The acquisition of rules governing "possible lexical items": Evidence from spontaneous speech errors. *Papers and Reports on Child Language Development, 13*, 148–156.

Bowerman, M. (1978). The acquisition of word meaning: An investigation into some current conflicts. In N. Waterson & C. Snow (Eds.), *The development of communication.* New York: John Wiley.

Bowerman, M. (1980). The structure and origin of semantic categories in the language learning child. In M. Foster & S. Brandes (Eds.), *Symbol as sense.* New York; Academic Press.

Bowerman, M. (1985). What shapes children's grammar? In D. Slobin (Ed.), *The cross-linguistic study of language acquisition*. Hillsdale, NJ: Erlbaum.

Bowerman, M. (1988). Inducing the latent structure of language. In F. Kessel (Ed.), *The development of language and language researchers: Essays in Honor of Roger Brown*. Hillsdale, NJ: Erlbaum.

Carey, S. (1993). Ontology and meaning—Two contrasting views. In E. Dromi (Ed.), *Language and cognition: A developmental perspective* (pp. 88–103). Norwood, NJ: Ablex.

Clark, E. V. (1973). What's in a word? On the child's acquisition of semantics in his first language. In T. E. Moore (Ed.), *Cognitive development and the acquisition of language*. New York; Academic Press.

Clark, E. V. (1983a). Convention and contrast in acquiring the lexicon. In B. Seiler & W. Wannenmacher (Eds.), *Concept development and the development of word meaning* (pp. 67–89). Berlin, Germany: Springer-Verlag.

Clark, E. V. (1983b). Meanings and concepts. In P. H. Mussen (Ed.), *Handbook of child psychology: Vol. 3. Cognitive development* (pp. 787–840). New York: Wiley.

Clark, E. V. (1988). On the logic of contrast. *Journal of Child Language, 15*, 317–337.

Clark, E. V. (1993). *The lexicon in acquisition*. Cambridge, UK: Cambridge University Press.

Dromi, E. (1982). *In pursuit of meaningful words: A case study analysis of early lexical development*. Unpublished doctoral dissertation, University of Kansas.

Dromi, E. (1987). *Early lexical development*. London: Cambridge University Press.

Dromi, E. (1990). Word meaning acquisition in the one word stage: A reply to Nelson's review of *Early lexical development. First Language, 10*, 75–82.

Dromi, E. (1993). The mysteries of early lexical development. In E. Dromi (Ed.), *Language and cognition: A developmental perspective* (pp. 32–60). Norwood, NJ: Ablex.

Dromi, E. (1999). Early lexical development. In M. Barrett (Ed.), *The development of language*. London: UCL Press.

Elman, J. L., Bates, E. A., Johnson, M., Karmiloff-Smith, A., Parisi, D., & Plunkett, K. (1996). *Rethinking innateness: A connectionist perspective on development*. Cambridge, MA: MIT Press.

Frege, G. (1974). On sense and reference. In F. Zabeeh, E. D. Klemke, & A. Jacobson (Eds.), *Readings in semantics*. Urbana: University of Illinois Press. (Original work published 1892.)

Gathercole, V. C. (1987). The contrastive hypothesis for the acquisition of word meaning: A reconsideration of the theory. *Journal of Child Language, 14*, 493–531.

Gathercole, V. C. (1989). Contrast: A semantic constraint? *Journal of Child Language, 16*, 685–702.

Gelman, S. A., & Markman, E. M. (1986). Understanding natural kind terms: A developmental comparison. *Papers and Reports on Child Language Development, 25*, 41–48.

Gillis, S. (1986). The child's "Nominal Insight" is actually a process: The plateau-stage and vocabulary spurt in early lexical development. *Antwerp Papers in Linguistics, 45*.

Golinkoff, R. M., & Hirsh-Pasek, K. (2006). Baby wordsmith: From associationist to social sophisticate. *Current Directions in Psychological Science, 15*, 30–33.

Golinkoff, R. M., Mervis, C. B., & Hirsh-Pasek, K. (1994). Early object labels: The case for a developmental lexical principles framework. *Journal of Child Language, 21*, 125–155.

Granott, N., & Parziale, J. (2002). Microdevelopment: A process-oriented perspective for studying development and learning. In N.Granott & J. Parziale (Eds.), *Microdevelopment: Transition processes in development and learning*. Cambridge, UK: Cambridge University Press.

Harris, M. (1992). *Language experience and early language development: From input to uptake*. Hillsdale, NJ: Erlbaum.

Harris, M., Barrett, M. D., Jones, D., & Brookes, S. (1988). Linguistic input and early word meaning. *Journal of Child Language, 15*, 77–94.

Hirsh-Pasek, K., & Golinkof, R. M. (1996). *The origins of grammar: Evidence from early language comprehension*. Cambridge, MA: MIT Press.

Hollich, G. J., Hirsh-Pasek, K., & Golinkoff, R. M., Brand, R. J., Brown, E., Chung, H. L. et al. (2000). Breaking the language barrier: An emergentist coalition model for the origins of word learning. *Monographs of the Society for Research in Child Development, 65*(3, Serial No. 262).

MacWhinney, B. (1999). The emergent of language from embodiment. In B. MacWhinney (Ed.), *The emergence of language*. Hillsdale, NJ: Erlbaum.

Mandler, J. M. (1979). Categorical and schematic organization in memory. In C. R. Puff (Ed.), *Memory organization and structure*. New York: Academic Press.

Mandler, J. M. (1983). Representation. In J. H. Flavell & E. M. Markman (Eds.), *Cognitive development* (Vol. 1, pp. 255–287). New York: Wiley.

Markman, E. M. (1989). *Categorization and naming in children: Problems of induction*. Cambridge, MA: MIT Press.

Markman, E. M. (1991). The whole object, taxonomic, and mutual exclusivity assumptions as initial constraints on word meanings. In J. P. Byrnes & S. A. Gelman (Eds.), *Perspectives on language and thought: Interrelations in development* (pp. 72–106). Cambridge, UK: Cambridge University Press.

Markman, E. M. (1993). Ways in which children constrain word meanings. In E. Dromi (Ed.), *Language and cognition: A developmental perspective* (pp. 61–87). Norwood, NJ: Ablex.

Markman, E. M., & Hutchinson, J. E. (1984). Children's sensitivity to constraints in word meaning: Taxonomic vs thematic relations. *Cognitive Psychology, 16*, 1–27.

Markman, E. M., & Wachtel, G. F. (1988). Children's use of mutual exclusivity to constrain the meanings of words. *Cognitive Psychology, 20*, 121–157.

Masur, E. F. (1982). Mother's responses to infants' object-related gestures: Influences on lexical development. *Journal of Child Language, 9*, 23–30.

Merriman, W. E., & Bowman, L. L. (1989). The mutual exclusivity bias in children's word learning. *Monographs of the Society for Research in Child Development* (serial no. 220).

Merriman, W. E., Marazita, J., & Jarvis, L. (1995). Children's disposition to map new words. In M. Tomasello & W. E. Merriman (Eds.), *Beyond names for things*. Hillsdale, NJ: Erlbaum.

Mervis, C. B. (1987). Child-basic object categories and early lexical development. In U. Neisser (Ed.), *Concepts and conceptual development: Ecological and intellectual factors in categorization* (pp. 201–233). New York: Cambridge University Press.

Naigles, L. G., Gleitman, H., & Gleitman, L. R. (1993). Children acquire word meaning components from syntactic evidence. In E. Dromi (Ed.), *Language and cognition: A developmental perspective* (pp. 104–140). Norwood, NJ: Ablex.

Nelson, K. (1973). Structure and strategy in learning to talk. *Monograph of the Society for Research in Child Development, 38*(1–2 serial no. 149).

Nelson, K. (1985). *Making sense: The acquisition of shared meaning*. New York: Academic Press.

Nelson, K. (1988). Constraints on word learning? *Cognitive Development, 3*, 221–246.

Nelson, K. (1990). Development of meaning and meaning of development in the single word period: A review of E. Dromi. Early lexical development. *First Language, 10*, 61–73.

Nelson, K., & Lucariello, J. (1985). The development of meaning in first words. In M. D. Barrett (Ed.), *Children's single-word speech* (pp. 59–87). New York: John Wiley.

Piaget, J. (1962). *Play, dreams and imitation in childhood.* New York: Norton.

Plunkett, K. (1997). Theories of early language acquisition. *Trends in Cognitive Sciences, 1*(4), 146–153.

Pruden, S. M., Hirsh-Pasek, K., Golinkoff, R. M., & Hennon, E. A (2006). The birth of words: Ten month olds learn words through perceptual salience. *Child Development, 77,* 266–280.

Quine, W. V. 0. (1960). *Word and object.* Cambridge, MA: MIT Press.

Reich, P.A. (1976). The early acquisition of word meaning. *Journal of Child Language, 3,* 117–123.

Ringwald-Frimerman, (2003). From communication to language in two linguistic environments: Speaking and signing. Unpublished doctoral dissertation, Tel Aviv University.

Schank, R. C., & Abelson, R. P. (1977). *Scripts, plans, goals and understanding: An inquiry into human knowledge structure.* Hillsdale, NJ: Erlbaum.

Schlesinger, I. M. (1977). The role of cognitive development and linguistic input in language acquisition. *Journal of Child Language, 4,* 153–169.

Schlesinger, I. M. (1982). *Steps to language.* Hillsdale, NJ: Erlbaum.

Slobin, D. I. (1985). Introduction: Why study acquisition crosslinguistically? In D. I. Slobin (Ed.), *The crosslinguistic study of language acquisition* (Vol. 1, pp. 3–23). Hillsdale, NJ: Erlbaum.

Smith, L. B. (1995). Self-organizing processes in learning to learn words: Development is not induction. In C. A. Nelson (Ed.), *The Minnesota symposia on child psychology* (Vol. 28). Mahwah, NJ: Erlbaum.

Smith, L. B. (1999). Children's noun learning: How general learning processes make specialized learning mechanisms. In B. MacWhinney (Ed.), *The emergence of language.* Mahwah, NJ: Erlbaum.

Soja, N. N., Carey, S., & Spelke, E. S. (1991). Ontological categories guide young children's inductions of word meaning: Object terms and substance terms. *Cognition, 38,* 179–211.

Spencer, J. P., Corbetta, D., Buchanan, P., Clearfield, M., Ulrich, B., & Schoner, G. (2006). Moving towards a grand theory of development: In memory of Esther Thelen. *Child Development, 77,* 1521–1538.

Thelen, E., & Bates, E.A. (2003). Connectionism and dynamic systems: Are they really different? *Developmental Science, 6,* 378–391.

Thelen, E., & Smith, L. B. (1994). *A dynamic systems approach to the development of cognition and action.* Cambridge, MA: MIT Press.

Tomasello, M. (1992). *First verbs: A case study of early grammatical development.* Cambridge, UK: Cambridge University Press.

Tomasello, M., & Akhtar, N. (1995). Two-years-olds use pragmatic cues to differentiate reference to object and actions. *Cognitive Development, 10,* 201–224.

Tomasello, M., & Barton, M. (1994). Learning words in nonostensive context. *Developmental Psychology, 30,* 639–650.

Tomasello, M., & Farrar, J. (1986). Joint attention and early language. *Child Development, 57,* 1454–1463.

Van Geert, P. (1994). *Dynamic systems of development: Change between complexity and chaos.* New York: Prentice-Hall.

Part *II*

Crosslinquistic Patterning and Acquisition of Lexical Semantics

Personal Tribute

RUTH A. BERMAN

My first meeting with Melissa Bowerman was at the Stanford Child Language Research Forum in 1978, when I was just entering the child language research community, on my first sabbatical at Berkeley. Her readiness to sit down and chat at length, the serious and careful attention she accorded someone unknown to her, and her thoughtful responses to my queries—these are traits that I now know to be typical of Melissa, though not necessarily of academia at large. Her groundbreaking (1974) paper on the acquisition of causative verbs by Christy and Eva, her daughters, whom I have since come to know and love, generated a spate of research in this domain in English as well as other languages—typical of Melissa's impact on the field. It also sparked all my subsequent work on children's development of derivational morphology and word-formation—which started out with analysis of how causatives are expressed morphologically in Hebrew, and how this affects their acquisition, and a comparison with the very different structural and developmental patterns that Melissa had revealed for English.

The subtitle of her 1974 paper, "A study in the relationship of cognitive, semantic, and syntactic development," reflects a theme that has motivated much of Melissa's work since her graduate studies under Roger Brown at Harvard. In fact, that early study of Melissa's bore the marks of major features of all her work: a deep concern for issues of semantics, combined with careful attention to the structural details of how semantic categories are expressed linguistically, and a meticulous consideration for the divide and overlap between semantics and cognition. Over the years, she has always taken pains to learn and understand different approaches and theoretical perspectives, afterwards proceeding to pursue her own path in a non-combative, non-contentious fashion. I often find myself reading something by Bowerman when I feel in need of a well-balanced and knowledgeable idea of what people from competing perspectives are proposing as "solutions" to issues in the field. And I trust that my own work has been guided by another feature of Melissa's research: a deep respect for authentic child language data and the conviction that they are indispensable for addressing any issue in the field.

Melissa and I have crossed paths at different times and places since that first meeting at Stanford. I recall with pleasure her participation in the 1979 Tel Aviv University workshop on U-shaped learning and her visit in 1997 to our home at Beth Herut (where she was hoping to get in some good bird-watching as well), an excursion with Dan Slobin to the Dokumenta at Kassel, and chats over cups of soup in the MPI cafeteria. Perhaps most vivid of all is getting together in her and Wijbrandt's house in Nijmegen, a home away from home for me on the many occasions I have spent there. The environment is always one of warm and comforting talk and meals, while Melissa also, to cite from her biography in Frank Kessel's collection in honor of Roger Brown, "tends a houseful of children and pets and tries to find time to play chamber music." A woman of many parts indeed.

Dear Melissa, what I wish for you as you enter your retirement years is that you enjoy this stage in your life as much as I do mine. But I hope, in the interests of your students, your colleagues, and the entire child language community, that you continue to pursue your work, which I trust will remain a source of interest and insights for us oldtimers as well as for newcomers to the field.

Personal Tribute

ANGELIKA WITTEK

These lines give me the chance to put down in words my reflections toward Melissa Bowerman's

~~skeptical but fair~~,

~~constantly questioning but supportive~~,

~~distinctively stimulating~~,

~~thought-provoking but modest~~,

~~insisting but patient~~,

~~strikingly thorough and reflective~~,

~~undoubtedly attentive~~,

~~unprejudiced~~,

~~absolutely accurate but creative~~,

simply indescribable

way of handling scientific thoughts and their originators. Admittedly, none of these attributes really captures what made my time as a PhD student of Melissa's so precious and unique. In the face of such inadequacy of words, a simple S-V-O construction—without modifiers—directed to Melissa might be more appropriate: I thank you.

Personal Tribute

LOURDES DE LEÓN

I want to thank Melissa Bowerman for her contagious passion for children's words and worlds across languages. I thank her for walking me through some of her daughters' diaries. In her own special way, she presented the children's words as a language and a culture of their own; these could be discerned by the researcher from the contexts of use, from the moments in which they were used, and from the meanings each word had in the adult language.

Melissa came to the Mayan Tzotzil-speaking village of Nabenchauk, Zinacantán, to do fieldwork with me in 1992. I was struck by how she moved around naturally, as if she had been there all her life. As a daughter of an anthropologist and an anthropologist of children herself, she felt at home right away. She became fascinated by the intricacies of Tzotzil semantics and found creative and fun ways to elicit verbs or body part terms, e.g., for 'the leg of a machete,' or for 'the hand of a juice press,' or for the 'nose of a knife,' or for the 'teeth of a stapler.'

The root *xoj* 'to insert ringlike object into longish object,' was her favorite. When I gave her an example produced by a child her eyes sparkled. I will never forget when she tried to pronounce words with a glottal stop; her whole face lit up, and the sound exploded out with a laugh.

Melissa's mind has the best qualities of a child's mind: refreshing, creative, and sensitive. I thank her for sharing with me her unique way of looking at children's language.

3

Mayan Semantics in Early Lexical Development
The Case of the Tzotzil Verbs for 'Eating' and 'Falling Down'

LOURDES DE LEÓN

Center for Advanced Studies in Social Anthropology (CIESAS-México)

INTRODUCTION

Many recent studies of early lexical acquisition have addressed the induction problem. How do children associate new words with appropriate referents out of the many possibilities available? Quine's (1964) question of referential indeterminacy is particularly intriguing in the context of Mayan languages. How do children learning Tzotzil know that a verb like *lo'* 'eat soft food,' or *ve'* 'eat.corn or grain-based food' refers to the action of eating food with such characteristics and does not refer to the food itself (a banana or a tortilla)? Or how do adults know that when young children use these verbs as bare roots they refer to an action and not to an object?

Children may make use of a variety of information to reduce the multiple possibilities of reference. What kind of clues do Mayan children receive to break into the semantic structure of their native language? What are the cognitive constraints guiding them, and how do they interact with the very specific semantics of a Mayan language like Tzotzil?

In the last decade, increasing research in the acquisition of non-European languages has brought typological diversity to bear on these questions, to test and expand the field of studies about early lexical development. Studies on Korean (Choi & Gopnik, 1995), Mandarin Chinese (Tardif, 2006, 1996; Tardif, Gelman,

& Xu, 1999), Tzotzil (de León, 1999a), and Tzeltal (Brown, 1998) have shown that children can learn verbs as early as or earlier than nouns. Studies in the area of spatial semantics have shown that the semantics of the native language guides children very early into learning spatial categories encoded in verbs (Bowerman, 1989, 1996, 2005; Bowerman & Choi, 2001, 2003; Bowerman & Levinson, 2001; Choi & Bowerman, 1991; de León, 2001a). Other studies with children learning Japanese and Korean have explored how language might influence speakers' construals of entities distinguished by shape or substance (Gathercole & Min, 1997; Imai & Gentner, 1997).

The present chapter looks at the development of verbs in two semantic areas characteristic of Mayan languages: 'eating' and 'falling,' for which verbs are learned before children reach the 50-word mark.[1] I argue here that Tzotzil semantic structure leads children from the beginning into learning to refer to specific *types* of actions that covertly categorize objects by features such as dimensionality, orientation, texture, consistency, and material in the semantic areas where the language offers these options (e.g., 'falling,' 'eating,' 'holding,' 'breaking,' 'change of posture' actions).[2] Elsewhere I have shown the effect of Tzotzil semantic structure on the acquisition of spatial terms denoting containment, support, contact, gravity (Bowerman, de León, & Choi, 1995; de León, 2001a, 2001c), and body posture (de León, 2005). In a language where children have an early preference for verbs, early semantic development is of interest in terms of how action reference may interact with the organization of object categorization (see Bowerman, 2005 for English; Brown, 2007). This point may open up new avenues into understanding the subtleties of lexical development and semantic typology.

TZOTZIL AND COGNITIVE CONSTRAINTS ON EARLY LEXICAL DEVELOPMENT

Psycholinguistic theories of lexical development have postulated constraints or presuppositions for word learning in regards to object reference, action reference, and spatial vocabulary (E. Clark, 1993). These theories have basically posited a relation between conceptual and linguistic development. In her seminal work, Gentner (1982; Gentner & Boroditsky, 2001; see Gentner & Boroditsky, this volume) has held that object reference is learnt earlier due to "cognitive simplicity." Markman has posed the "whole object constraint," which predicts that new words refer to whole objects and not to parts, substances, color, or other properties (Markman, 1989). In connection with verb learning, some theories have posited that children go from general to specific meanings. Light verbs such as 'make,' 'go,' 'give,' and

[1] In de León (2005) I examine how the verbs referring to posture are acquired by the two girls of the study.

[2] Brown (2001) has argued that semantic specificity in Tzeltal plays an important role not only in acquiring specific verbs, but also general verbs such as 'going up' and 'going down.' See Brown (2007) for 'cut' and 'break' verbs in Mayan Tzeltal (closely related to Tzotzil).

'put' would enter before specific ones, in part for ontological reasons (Clark, 1993, p. 55).

Many have challenged these positions (Brown, 1998; Choi & Gopnik, 1995; de León 1999a, 1999b, 2001b; Gathercole & Min, 1997; Gathercole, Thomas, & Evans, 2000; Narasimhan & Brown, this volume; Nelson, 1981; Tardif, 1996, 2006; Tardif, Gelman, & Xu, 1999). Elsewhere I have argued that the predictions above are, in general terms, disconfirmed by Tzotzil acquisition data. In regards to the nouns-first hypothesis, Tzotzil children learn action reference earlier than or as early as object reference. This finding is consistent with patterns of verb frequency and saliency in the input. In connection with light verbs coming first, Tzotzil learners have 'go,' 'want,' and 'give,' but they also learn semantically rich Tzotzil verbs like *ti'* 'eat fleshy food,' *kuch* 'carry on back,' or *xoj* 'insert long object into ring-shaped object' right from the beginning. I have not recorded the use of light verbs instead of specific ones; rather, I have discovered that specific verbs develop within the borders of specific categories. With regard to spatial language, specific terms denoting shape, location, and position are used in locative expressions, and I have found no tendency toward generalization (de León, 2001a, 2001c). In the present chapter, I explore the development of categories of eating, and delve more deeply into verbs denoting falling actions, reported in de León (2001a).

Tzotzil Adult Language

Let us look first at the adult language. At the heart of the Tzotzil language is a set of roots with consonant-vowel-consonant (CVC) form. These roots are the basis for the derivation of different grammatical classes such as nouns, adjectives, numerals, and verbs. Among these roots, approximately 850 are verbal (Haviland, 1994a, p. 699). Nominal roots are semantically similar to nouns in other languages. However, verbal roots have their own particularities that make them unique to this language, or perhaps to Mayan languages. The semantic specificity of verbal roots in Tzotzil and Tzeltal has been the major motivation of several studies of "native categorization" conducted in the 1960s. One classic work was that of Berlin on classifiers and 'eating' verbs in Tzeltal (Berlin, 1967).[3]

The semantic features that contribute to verb semantics have to do with spatial notions that intersect with other dimensions such as texture, size, and collectivity. Haviland has distinguished the following semantic domains (1994a, p. 726):

(i) *Shape*: one, two, or three dimensions (flat, elongated, round, spherical).
(ii) *Position or posture*: distinguished for the Gestalt of a Figure with a specific anatomy in relation to a Ground (sitting, standing, lying, kneeling, reclining, etc.).
(iii) *Colocation*: involves the juxtaposition of multiple Figures that are hanging (e.g., banana bunch).

[3] Berlin (1967) examines, in fact, Tzeltal and Navajo categories of eating. Both languages show very suggestive parallelisms, which indicate patterns of semantic structuring for 'eating' categories shared by languages.

(iv) *Collections*: groups or heaps of objects arranged in a specific way where something is on top of something else.
(v) *Texture*: surface, substance, consistency, material.
(vi) *Perceptual properties* of objects: dimension and visual particularities.[4]

Table 3.1 presents examples of some sets of roots in Zinacantec adult Tzotzil. Columns indicate root classes distinguished on the basis of transitivity and position—a distinction which is based on morphological profiles characteristic of each root class (Haviland, 1994a, 1994b). Rows indicate semantic dimensions organizing each subset of verbs. The boxed areas indicate the roots that I examine in this chapter. They belong to the intransitive class (i.e., 'falling' verbs) and transitive class (i.e., 'eating' verbs).

Table 3.2 presents the dimensions or components of the semantic space of the set of falling verbs. We first notice that all the verbs belonging to this category share the dimension 'gravity effect.' The most general and least specified verb of the set would be *p'aj* 'fall from high,' which denotes free fall of any kind of object, be it animate or inanimate. Other verbs are distinguished on the basis of visual features such as dimensionality of the Figure—whether it is one-dimensional (e.g., post, tree), two-dimensional (e.g., bicycle, board), or three-dimensional (e.g., person, pot). The feature of "angle of Figure with respect to Ground" is encoded in the verbs *lom* and *jin*. It applies, for *lom*, to a 90° angle and, in general, to one-dimensional objects such as posts and trees, and, for *jin*, to two-dimensional objects such as bicycles and fences. *Lom* is also used metaphorically to refer to a drunk man falling down, without control. The feature of "orientation of Figure during the fall" applies to three-dimensional objects that have a main axis of the kind front/back/side, and it thus discriminates between falling forwards, backwards, or sideways. Another feature encoded in this set is the contact of Figure and Ground, where the Ground is normally the horizontal plane and the Figure is specified by its resulting body posture, i.e., falling motion backwards (*jach'*). Resulting change of posture is encoded in the verbs *javk'uj* 'falling with legs upwards' and *valk'uj* 'falling with head downwards.' Table 3.3 presents the set of Tzotzil 'eating' verbs.[5]

In Tzotzil there is no general term for 'eating.' The main distinction between the verbs is drawn on the basis of *texture* or *consistency* of the edible object (Figure) as experienced by the mouth of the agent (Ground). The main dimensions of the subset of eating verbs are "corn or grain-based" (*ve'*), "fleshy" (*ti'*), "soft" (*lo'*), and "crunchy" (*k'ux*).

The verb *ve'* could be thought of as the most general verb, but it cannot be used in place of the other verbs of the set. It denotes eating corn or grain-based food, and also the event of the meal itself (which always involves tortillas). Apart from

[4] Brown (1994) has reported similar semantic categories in Tzeltal and has associated some of them with locative functions.

[5] *-uch* 'drink,' *tz'un* 'suck' (e.g., sugar cane from corn stalk pulp) and *chuchu'* 'nurse' refer to liquid ingestion and are not included in the domain of 'eating,' which involves solid foods. Children learn the verb *chuchu'* 'nurse' among their first 10 words.

TABLE 3.1 Some Examples of Sets of Tzotzil Verb Roots

	Intransitive	Transitive	Transitive Positional	Positional
Position				*va'* 'stand vertically' *kot* 'standing on four legs' *chot* 'sit' *kej* 'kneel down' *jav* 'lie face up' *vuch* 'stand, face up' *nuj* 'face down'
Insertion		*ch'op* 'insert fingers' *mul* 'insert briefly' *jul* 'inject'	*tik'* 'insert in container' *xoj* 'insert, (ring or tubular shaped object)' *p'aj* 'insert with force'	
Separation	*k'as* 'break, 3D' *vok'* 'break'	*jav* 'cut in half' *tuch'* 'cut ID' *jet* 'cut, separate' *k'ut* 'break by twisting'	*jat* 'tear' *jis* 'cut in strips' *t'ol* 'slice horizontally' *xut* 'break in small pieces'	
Gravity effect	*p'aj'* 'fall from high' (e.g., off a cliff, off a table, etc.) *jach'* 'slip and fall' (e.g., person on mud, ice, etc.) *lom* 'fall down in a 90° angle' (e.g., tree, post) *jin* 'fall and turn over' (e.g., chair, table, car, heap of rocks)			*javk'uj* 'with legs upwards' (as a result of falling) *valk'uj* '(fall) upside down'
Eat		*ve'* 'eat (with tortilla)' *ti'* 'bite, eat fleshy food' *lo'* 'eat soft food' *k'ux* 'eat crunchy food' (e.g. corn, popcorn) *tz'un* 'suck' (i.e. sugar cane of corn stalk pulp)		
Hold		*kuch* 'carry on back' *pet* 'carry in arms'		

TABLE 3.2 Semantic Dimensions of the Set of 'Falling' Verbs

Verb	Gloss	Grav. effect	Dim. of Fig.			Angle of Fig./G.	Orient. of Fig. during fall			Fig./G. contact	Resulting body posture
			1	2	3		F	B	S		
p'aj	'fall from high'	+	-	-	-	-	-	-	-	-	-
jach'	'slip and fall'	+	-	-	+	-		+		+	-
lom	'fall in a 90° angle'	+	+	-	-	+	-	-	-	-	-
jin	'fall and turn over'	+	-	+	-	+	-	-	+	-	-
javk'uj	'(fall) "backwards with legs upwards'	+	-	-	+	-	-	+	-	-	+
valk'uj	'(fall) forwards on head'	+	-	-	+	-	+	-	-	-	+

Key **B:** Backwards, **Dim.**: Dimensionality, **Fig.**: Figure, **F:** Frontwards, **Grav.**: Gravity, **G:** Ground, **Orient**: Orientation, **S**: Sideways.

TABLE 3.3 Tzotzil 'Eating' Verbs

ve'	'eat corn or grain-based food' (extension to eat a meal)
ti'	'eat fleshy food' (i.e., meat, chili, bean, mushroom), 'bite,' 'sting'
lo'	'eat soft food' (i.e., fruit, dough, cheese, candy, gum)
k'ux	'eat crunchy food' (i.e., popcorn, corn on the cob, chips)

eating tortillas it can also be used to refer to actions of eating bread, cookies, or dough-based edibles (e.g., cake).

This initial description does not capture the full use of these verbs, however. Some of the verbs are extended beyond these uses. For example, the set of arguments that the verb *ti'* can take includes not only meat, but beans, mushrooms, and chillies. Berlin argues, for the closely related language Tzeltal, that the criterion guiding the *ti'* category is "fleshy" edible (1967).[6] However, *ti'* also means 'bite' and 'sting' and, by extension, a 'biting' feeling of pain caused by an external agent (e.g., tightness of clothes). *Lo'* 'eat soft food' is prototypically associated with fruit, but it is nowadays extended to candy and chewing gum. *Ve'* 'eat corn or grain-based food, or eat a meal (with tortilla)' can, as noted above, take tortilla, bread, cookies, and tamales as arguments, but also applies to the social event of a meal.

[6] Berlin argues that the feature "fleshy" for the closely related Tzeltal verb *ti'*, explains the inclusion of eating mushrooms and beans in this category. He argues also that, alternatively, the inclusion of mushrooms and chillies can also be explained by the categorization of these two edibles as "animals," under the numeral classifier *kojt*, which applies to animals and four-legged objects (1967, p. 5).

Predictions for Acquisition

What might one predict for the acquisition of these verbs? For the verbs of 'falling,' a cognitive approach might predict that effect of gravity may play a central role. This prediction is based on the claim that there are cognitive biases at work in the acquisition of spatial language and that children may map words to preexisting spatial notions. In this case, Tzotzil learners would be guided by a prelinguistically acquired notion of gravity effect (Bloom, 1973; H. H. Clark, 1973; Mandler, 1996; McCune-Nicholich, 1981, 2006; Nelson, 1974; see Choi & Bowerman 1991, for discussion). Consistent with the idea that early spatial words are mapped to pre-established spatial concepts, researchers have found that generalization often takes place very rapidly (McCune-Nicholich, 1981; see Bowerman & Choi, 2001, p. 479, for discussion). In the case of the 'falling' verbs examined here, the spatial notion of gravity may arguably lead children to overextend the members of this verb category to any falling event at the early stages of acquisition. If children go from general to specific notions, the specific perceptual discriminations would arguably come later for this set of verbs.

In the case of 'eating' verbs, the learning task may not be simple, since there is no superordinate verb for the set of 'eating' verbs, and the members of the set do not show any clear-cut taxonomic relations.[7] If there is an underlying covert category it would be texture or consistency.

For both 'falling' and 'eating' verbs, Tzotzil children have to pay attention to several classificatory criteria. In the case of 'falling' verbs, the criteria have to do with perceptual properties: vertical motion, main axis, dimensionality, directionality of motion, body posture. For 'eating' verbs, texture or consistency of the Figure is a central feature; but the broader extensions of the verbs may make this less than obvious for a child.

These verbs are among the first 50 words that Tzotzil-speaking children produce, so their acquisition can help clarify some important theoretical issues. Among these is the question of the relative roles of cognitive, perceptual, semantic, and language-specific factors in the acquisition of verb meaning.

DATA AND METHODOLOGY

Subjects

The study was conducted in the hamlet of Nabenchauk, Zinacantán, in the state of Chiapas, Mexico, where Tzotzil Mayan is learned by children in a predominantly monolingual environment. The community has around 3,000 inhabitants who carry out mainly agricultural work. Longitudinal data were collected as part of a linguistic and anthropological study of Tzotzil language acquisition and

---

[7] Brown (2007) points out that the set of of verbs referring to 'cutting and breaking' actions in Tzeltal does not have an overarching verb either: "cutting and breaking actions are finely differentiated according to the spatial and textural properties of the theme object, with no superordinate term meaning either 'cut in general' or 'break in general'" (p. 1). This is very similar for Tzotzil 'eating' verbs, and 'cutting' and 'breaking' verbs, for that matter.

socialization. Data come from two girls, Cande and Tinik. The data for Cande cover from 1;6 to 2;0, and the data for Tinik cover the period from 1;7 to 2;0. Spontaneous utterances were audio- and videotaped by the researcher in biweekly visits of four hours each day for Tinik. Data for Cande were obtained in monthly visits and during in-home stays during the summer. Transcription was carried out by the researcher with the help of the caregiver. Table 3.4 gives information about ages, MLU, hours, and number of analyzed utterances.

TABLE 3.4 Subjects, Ages, MLU, Material, and Number of Utterances

	Age	MLU	Analyzed audio/video	# of analyzed utterances
Cande	1;6	1	5 hours	80
	1;7	1	6 hours	70
	1;8	1	6 hours	80
	1;9	1	6 hours	80
Tinik	1;7.5	1	12 hours	125
	1;8	1	6 hours	70
	1;9	1	6 hours	70
	1;10	1	6 hours	70
	1;11	1.5	6 hours	75
	2	1.8	6 hours	70

Data Codification

As in previous studies (Choi & Gopnik, 1995; de León, 1999a, 1999b; see also Gentner, 1982), I have followed semantic and morphological criteria to codify children's grammatical categories. At a semantic level, words were identified as verbs if they were used in reference to actions or activities. At a morphological level, the components of forms were identified in terms of their similarity to adult forms. Since these children are in transition between one-word utterances and early combinations, I will be using the terms *verbal root*, *verb*, or *action name* interchangeably, if the roots approximated the adult forms, and if they were used in reference to actions.

The criteria used to determine the acquisition of a verb were that (1) it was produced spontaneously, (2) it was not a repetition of a previous utterance, and (3) it was produced at least three times in different contexts per monthly session.

EARLY VERBAL ROOTS IN CANDE'S AND TINIK'S SPEECH

The first children's productions were bare CVC roots with no affixes (de León, 1999a). This is surprising since the roots are bound forms and adults never use the roots in isolation. In de León (1999a) I argued that a combination of factors—frequency, prosody, saliency, and semantic weight—in the adult input contribute to the isolation of the root.

Tables 3.5 and 3.6 show the "action names" produced by the girls of the study. Boxed areas include the verbs that I will be examining in this chapter.

The whole set of early verbal roots shows, in general, consistency with the conceptual areas covered in early vocabularies documented for other languages (McCune-Nicholich, 2006; Tardif, 2006; Tomasello, 1992):

(1) a. Disappearance
b. Motion
c. Spatial notions of support, contact, containment, gravity effect, and separation (see de León, 2001a)

But they also reflect Tzotzil semantic preoccupations, such as those in (2), which subdivide major conceptual areas in complex ways.

(2) a. Corporal posture and shape
b. Specification of support, contact, and containment actions
c. Specification of eating actions
d. Specification of verbs of 'breaking' and 'division'
e. Specification of holding actions

Earlier studies on the acquisition process in Tzotzil learners have revealed that, on the one hand, the children learn general verbs consistent with adult usage: Motion verbs appear early, starting with the verbs *bat* 'go' and *och* 'enter' (see de León, 1999b). The general verbs *k'an* 'want' and *ak'* 'give' are also very frequent in the input and in the children's productions. At the same time, verbs denoting containment, support, contact, gravity, separation, body posture, eating, and holding are also present right from the start. The semantic categories develop in a Tzotzil fashion, with no extensions beyond each category, and with no "light" verb usage prior to the use of rich verbs (Clark, 1993; Ninio 1999a, 1999b). Within the specific Tzotzil categories themselves, the studies have revealed that children do not overgeneralize one verb to denote a general category and later learn the specific meanings. Meaning contrasts within a given category are present from the beginning, with some errors revealing children's analytical productivity. In the present study, I examine, among other things, whether the acquisition of the two sets of verbs of interest follow the same conservative tendency.

Acquisition of 'Falling' Verbs

In de León (1997, 2001a) I argued that the expression of vertical motion appears very early in Tzotzil acquisition, starting with the verb *p'aj* 'fall from high.' The category of falling verbs develops early, and the child gradually builds up contrasts based on manner of fall, angle of orientation of the Figure, contact of the base of the Figure and the Ground, and body posture resulting from the fall, consistent with the adult forms.

TABLE 3.5 First Verbal Roots Produced by Cande at the One-Word and Early Combination Period

Verbal root	Gloss	Verbal root	Gloss
DISAPPEARANCE			
ch'ay	'lose'	*laj*	'finish'
poj	'steal'		
DESIRE			
k'an	'want'		
MOTION			
bat	'go'	*sut*	'return'
la'	'come' (supl.)	*mam (=xanav)*	'walk'
Fall			
p'aj	'fall from high'	*jin*	'fall and turn over'
jach'	'slip over'	*javk'uj*	'with legs upwards' (as a result of falling)
SUPPORT			
Posture			
pepex->chot	'sit down'		
kot	'stand on four legs'		
Support from high			
kaj	'place on a high surface'	*kuch*	'carry on back'
pet	'hold on arms'		
CONTACT			
lap	'put on clothes'	*baj*	'close'
pak	'fold"		
CONTENT			
xoj	'insert ring'	*kokon*	'pour into container'
tzaj	'submerge in liquid'	*tik'*	'put in container'
SEPARATION			
jam	'open'		
Break			
jat	'tear'	*cho'*	'peal'
jav	'cut in halves'	*jos*	'scrape'
ACTIVITY			
Eat			
ti'	'eat fleshy food, bite'	*ve'*	'eat corn or grain-based food'
lo	'eat soft food'	*k'ux*	'eat crunchy food'
Other Activities			
k'el	'see'	*nit'*	'pull'
tza'tza' (CDS)	'defecate'	*maj*	'hit'
chuchu'	'nurse'	*xi'*	'fear'
sa'	'find'	*tzi'*	'fart'
tam	'grab'	*net'*	'press'
k'ux	'hurt'	*tij*	'play music'
CHANGE OF STATE			
toj	'cool'	*ta'aj*	'cooked'

TABLE 3.6 First Verbal Roots Produced by Tinik at the One-Word and Early Combination Period

Verbal root	Gloss	Verbal root	Gloss
DISAPPEARANCE			
nak'	'hide'	*poj*	'steal'
ch'ay	'lose'	*laj*	'finish'
DESIRE			
k'an	'want'		
MOTION			
och	'enter'	*sut*	'return'
bat	'go'		
Fall			
p'aj	'fall from high'	*lom*	'fall in a 90° angle'
jach'	'slip over'	*javk'uj*	'with legs upwards' (as a result of falling)
		valk'uj	'on head' (as a result of falling)
SUPPORT			
Posture			
pepex ->chot	'sit'	*nuj*	'face down'
kej	'kneel down'	*va'al*	'stand up'
kot	'stand on four legs'		
Located on high surface			
kaj	'located on high surface'	*jok'*	hanging'
luchul	'perched'		
Carry			
kuch	'carry on back'	*pet*	'carry on arms'
CONTACT			
mak	'close'	*lutz*	'cover'
CONTAINMENT			
tik'	'put in container'	*xoj*	'insert ring'
SEPARATION			
lok'	'take off'	*jam*	'open'
Break			
jat	'tear'		
ACTIVITY			
Eat			
ve'	'eat corn or grain-based food'	*ti`*	'eat fleshy food, bite'
		lo'	'eat soft food'
Other Activities			
jax	'wash hands (formal)'	*nit'*	'pull'
xuj	'push'	*maj*	'hit'
jip	'throw'	*k'abin*	'pee'
vay	'sleep'	*vi*	'look!'
kej	'put away'		

Tables 3.7 and 3.8 show the evolution month by month of this class of verbs in the speech of Cande and Tinik within the one-word and early combination period.

These tables show that both children start with the verb *p'aj* 'fall from high.' The children use this for trajectory on a vertical axis, which is consistent with adult usage and with possible cognitive predictions about children's early attention to the effects of gravity (Mandler, 1996; McCune-Nicolich, 1981). Importantly, the children never use this verb to refer to other kinds of falls, where the axis or the manner of falling is codified in the semantics of the verb.

Examples of Cande's use of *p'aj* are shown in (3) and of Tinik's use in (4).

(3) Cande:

p'aj (Aunt Lucia is holding a piece of tortilla while sitting by Cande's side. The girl notices that it falls from her aunt's hand to the ground) (she pronounces it as /baj/) (1;6)

p'aj (she looks at a potato bug walking along the line of a table board and describes it as falling down from high) (1;7)

p'aj (she sees the researcher's daughter walking on the roof and warns she is going to fall down) (1;8)

(4) Tinik:

p'aj (her doll falls from her hand to the ground) (1;7)

p'aj (a coin falls from her mother's hand to the ground) (2;0: 3) (2;0.21)

p'aj (a peach falls off a tree) (2;1;2)

TABLE 3.7 Early 'Falling' Verbs in Cande

Gravity	1;6	1;7	1;8	1;9
'fall from high'	*p'aj*			
'fall on side'		*jin*		
'fall (90° angle)' e.g., tree, lamp post	-	-	-	-
'slip over'			*jach'*	
'(fall) backwards with legs upwards'				*javk'uj*

TABLE 3.8 Early 'Falling' Verbs in Tinik

Gravity	1;7	1;8	1;9	1;10	1;11	2;0
'fall from high'	*p'aj*					
'fall' (90° angle)					*lom*	
'slip over'						*jach'*
'(fall) on head'					*valk'uj*	
'(fall) backwards with legs upwards'					*javk'uj*	

In Cande's speech, the next verb to enter is *jin* 'fall on side,' as in (5), at age 1;7; then *jach'* 'slip over,' as in (6), at 1;8; followed by *javk'uj* 'fall with legs upwards,' as in (7), at 1;9.

(5) *jin* (she tells her mother that her father's bike turned over) (1;6)
jin (she notices a chair that falls on its side) (she uses it for chairs and tables) (1;7)
jin (she comments that a small toy car turns over while she plays with it) (1;7)

(6) *jach'* (she walks and slips over) (1;8)
jach' (LL is holding her in her arms and loses balance, so she says *jach'*) (1;8)
jach' (she is sitting down and falls forward) (error) (1;9)

(7) *javk'uj* (describes her cousin Ran who fell backwards off his chair) (1;9)
javk'uj (describes a doll that fell backwards) (1;10)

In Tinik's speech, *p'aj* is followed by *lom* 'fall from vertical position in 90° rotation,' *valk'uj* 'fall forwards with head down,' and *javk'uj* 'fall backwards with legs upwards,' as in (8) through (10), at 1;11; and finally, by *jach'* 'slip over,' as in (11), at 2;0.

(8) *lom* (she stands up a toy tree, and it falls on its side) (1;11)
lom jun (= *lom li june*) 'one fell' (referring to a plastic rooster that falls on its side) (1;11.26)
lom-es (fall + causative) (she blames another girl for causing a toy horse to fall on its side) (2;1.2)
lom (a toy fence falls on its side) (2;2)

(9) *valk'uj* (describes another girl who fell head down) (1;11)
valk'uj (describes a girl in a picture who is head down) (1;11)

(10) *javk'uj* (she describes another girl that fell down backwards) (1;11)
javk'uj (describes researcher doing this particular motion) (1;11)

(11) *jach'* 'slip over' (walks and loses balance) (repeated on several occasions) (2;0)
jach' (walks and feels she is losing her balance and may slip over) (2;2)
i jach' (falls forward with hands on ground, but her feet do not lose contact with the ground. I ask her father, and he says 'It is not correct to say that.') (2;2)

Interestingly, we see the two girls producing similar errors in their early use of the verb *jach'* 'slip over.' They both pay attention to the feature "lose base" (of Figure and Ground contact), but they do not distinguish directionality of fall—adults codify the feature "direction backwards" as part of the semantics of the verb. The error shows the girls have both noted the Figure/Ground contact feature, but not the "orientation of fall" feature. The extension of *jach'* 'slip over' to actions that denote to 'fall forward' reveals that the children have learnt the dimension of the Figure/Ground angle, as well as the Figure/Ground contact in the semantics of the category. Orientation of fall does not seem to be added to the semantics of the verb until later. I should comment here that for both girls, the error made with *jach'* 'slip over' occurred with them as subjects of the action. Loss of base is perhaps a more salient experiential and subjective factor than orientation of fall, and this may affect early understanding of the semantics of the verb.

In summary, these data show that both girls use *p'aj* 'fall from high' as the first verb of the 'falling' category. This verb is, in fact, among the earliest verbs acquired by both children: Cande had it among her first five words (de León, 1999a), Tinik among her first 10 words. I have argued (de León, 1997, 2001a) that *p'aj*'s association with gravity effect has, most probably, a perceptual-cognitive motivation. However, the children soon use words encoding further specification related to dimensionality, angle of fall, orientation of fall, and Figure/Ground contact. Orientation of fall is acquired last. The category of 'falling' is learnt within its boundaries. It involves the abstraction of perceptual features, the categorization of permanent properties (dimensionality), and perception of transitory states (angle of Figure and Ground, orientation of falling motion, resulting body posture). The task of learning these verbs is clearly not "cognitively simple," since it involves reference to abstract dimensions of a perceptual nature that interact at several levels. The two children of the study manage to learn such reference by two years of age.

Acquisition of 'Eating' Verbs

The data for 'eating' verbs will be presented separately for the two children.

Cande's Eating Verbs Cande has a dense corpus of eating verbs. Recall that in her case, I lived with the family for periods of time at different parts of the year, sharing everyday life.

Table 3.9 shows the development of verbs for eating in Cande's speech. Cande starts with the root *ti'* 'eat fleshy food, bite,' followed by *lo'* 'eat soft food,' and then by *ve'* 'eat corn (eat meal),' and *k'ux* 'eat crunchy food.'

The semantic development within each verb is of interest. Table 3.10 shows Cande's uses of the verb *ti'* 'eat fleshy food, bite.'

TABLE 3.9 Development of 'Eating' Verbs in Cande

Eat	1;6	1;7	1;8	1;9	1;10	1;11	2;0
'eat fleshy food, bite'	*ti'*						
'eat soft food'		*lo'*					
'eat corn or grain-based food (eat meal)'			*ve'*				
'eat crunchy food'			*k'ux*				

TABLE 3.10 Development of Cande's Use of the Verb ***ti'*** 'eat fleshy food,' 'bite,' 'sting'

	1;6	1;7	1;8	1;9	1;10	1;11	2;0
ti' 'eat fleshy food,' 'bite'	hurt, sting	teeth or bite?	bite? (said of a dog)	eat chicken			
			sting (said of an insect)	sting (said of a needle)			
					eat fleshy food (said of raw and cooked meat)		
					eat fleshy food, eat chili		eat fleshy food
titi' (BT) 'meat' ('bite bite')	sausage	raw meat/ chicken	raw meat/ chicken	raw chicken	chicken feathers, hanging meat	chorizo, bean	
					dead chicken with feathers		

Cande first used *ti'* at 1;6 referring to 'hurt,' to express pain caused by tight pants. At 1;7 Cande used it while making a biting gesture with her teeth, which made it unclear whether she referred to her own teeth or to the intention to bite. At 1;8 her uses meant 'sting,' or 'bite.' This may be related to the fact that children are warned not to get close to insects or to dogs with the utterance *ta sti'ot* 'it is going to bite/sting you.' Later Cande used *ti'* with food arguments such as *'ich* 'chili,' *chorizo* 'sausage,' and *chenek'* 'beans.' For 'chicken,' 'pork,' and 'meat,' the normal prototypes for *ti'*, she only uses *ti'* or *titi'* with no expressed argument. This last form *titi'* means literally 'bite bite' and refers prototypically to kinds of meat (e.g., beef, pork, or chicken). Adults can use it as a noun *mi ch-a-k'an titi'* (int. ICP-2E-want eat.fleshy.eat.fleshy)[8] 'do you want meat?' but they also use it as a verb *mi ch-a-titi'* (INT ICP-2E-eat.fleshy.eat.fleshy) 'do you want to eat.fleshy?'

[8] In these and the following examples, the following codes will be used: CL = clitic, DEM = demonstrative, E = ergative, POS = possessive, A = absolutive, IMP = imperative, INT = interrogative, ICP = incompletive, NUM = numeral, NEG = negation, PT = particle, SUBJ = subject.

TABLE 3.11 Development of the Denotation of ***lo'*** 'eat soft food' in Cande

	1;7	1;8	1;9	1;10	1;11	2;0
lo' 'eat.soft. food' (e.g., fruit, vegetables, sweets)	eat berries eat banana	eat berries banana peach	eat soft food	eat soft food	eat soft food	eat soft food
			eat lollypop	eat candies	eat candies	
			eat dough	eat dough	eat dough	eat dough
				(eat) carrot	eat vegetable	eat vegetable
lolo' 'fruit'				banana		banana
lo'bol 'banana'						fruit

Normally, adults point at a live chicken when talking to young children, and say, *mi ch-a-ti'* (INT ICP-2E-eat.fleshy), 'do you want to eat.fleshy?' At 1;7 Cande uses the reduplicated form *titi'* to refer to raw chicken/meat; at 1;10 she extends it to a dead chicken still with feathers, and to feathers stuck on the ground.

Cande's progression in the verb meaning shows that she is learning to refer to actions of eating 'fleshy food' by first using it for 'biting' (the instrument), where she is the experiencer of the action ('biting or stinging feeling,' e.g., clothes or insects). She then moves into kinds of 'bitable' objects.

Table 3.11 shows Cande's use of the verb *lo'* 'eat soft food.' Cande starts by using the verb form *lo'* three months before the reduplicated noun form, *lolo'* 'fruit.' She initially starts, at 1;7, by using the verb to refer to both eating berries and eating bananas. At age 1;8 she also uses this verb to refer to 'eat fruit (peach),' pointing at peaches in a tree. At 1;9 her use of the verb is very similar to the adult norm: She has extended the use of the verb to mean 'eat fruit,' for all kinds of fruit, and she has also started extending the use to 'eat lolly' and 'eat dough' (soft stuff). By age 1;10 she has extended its denotation to 'eat candies,' and she has also tentatively introduced carrots as members of the category. (She found some carrots inside a basket and was unsure of what they were and pointed at them saying *lo'*? 'eat soft food?'). By age 1;11 she extended the denotation of *lo'* to 'eat vegetables,' to refer to cooked leafy vegetables, chayote, and potatoes. It was not until 1;10 that she started to use the reduplicated noun form *lolo'* 'fruit' to refer to a banana. And it was not until 2;0 that she used the adult form *lo'bol* 'banana' to refer to 'fruit.' Thus, she built up her category for *lo'* through reference to the 'action on soft edible things' long before she had the term for the object referents.

Let us now move to the development of Cande's use of the verbs *k'ux* 'eat. crunchy food' and *ve'* 'eat.corn or grain-based food.' Table 3.12 shows Cande's use of *k'ux*. She starts at 1;10 by referring to eating crunchy foods in relation to popcorn and potato chips. By 2;0 she uses *k'ux* for eating sugar cane and corn on

TABLE 3.12 Development of the Denotation of *k'ux* 'eat crunchy food' in Cande

	1;10	1;11	2;0	2;1
k'ux 'eat crunchy food'	eat popcorn	eat popcorn	eat popcorn	eat popcorn
	eat potato chips		eat potato chips	eat potato chips
			eat sugar cane	eat sugar cane
			eat corn on the cob	eat corn on the cob
				eat pork rind

TABLE 3.13 Development of the Denotation of *ve'* 'eat.corn or grain-based Food (eat a meal)' in Cande

	1;6	1;7	1;8	1;9	1;10	1;11	2;0	2;1
ve' 'eat.corn' 'eat a meal'					meal	>	>	
							eat cookie	eat cookie, bread
							meal	
vaj 'tortilla'	meal		tortilla					

the cob as well. By 2;1 she adds pork rind as another not very common but highly valued crunchy food.

Table 3.13 shows Cande's use of *ve'*. At age 1;6 Cande uses *vaj* 'tortilla' in association with 'eat a meal' in a way that suggests a parallelism between *titi' / ti'* and *lolo' / lo'*, where there is a semantically related noun/verb pair—in this case, *vaj* 'tortilla'/*ve'* 'eat with tortilla (meal).'[9]

Tinik's 'Eating' Verbs Tinik has a smaller inventory of 'eating' verbs than Cande. Three verb roots, *ti'*, *lo'*, and *ve'*, appear at the age of 1;7, as shown in Table 3.14. Table 3.15 shows the gradual development of the denotation of 'eating' verbs.

Tinik's early uses of these three forms are appropriate. At 1;9 and 1;10, she makes interesting errors using the verbs *ti'* and *lo'* to refer to the action of 'eating a cookie.' Cookies are introduced foods and are normally referred to by the verb *ve'* 'eat.corn.' This is the only error made with these verbs, so it is not clear if there is some sort of underspecification or an extension based on the kind of eating action being performed and the instrument (tongue, teeth) used when eating cookies.

9 Interestingly enough in Chol, another Mayan language, the general verb *k'ux* 'eat' is now incorporating the argument *k'uxwaj* 'eat.tortilla' to refer to the action of having a meal with tortilla (*waj*). The grammaticalization process looks similar to what Cande does.

TABLE 3.14 Tinik's 'eating' Verbs

Eat	1;7	1;8	1;9	1;10	1;11	2;0
'eat.meat, bite'	*ti'*	>	>	>	>	>
'eat soft food'	*lo'*	>	>	>	>	>
'eat corn or grain-based food'	*ve'*	>	>	>	>	>
'eat grain'	–	–	–	–	–	–

TABLE 3.15 Development of 'eating' Verbs in Tinik

	1;7	1;8	1;9	1;10	1;11	2;0
ti' 'eat.meat'	points at a live chicken	points at a live chicken		?		
				eat.meat °eat cookie		eat.meat
					raw chicken	
						bite
lo' 'eat.soft food'						
'eat vegetable,' 'eat soft food,' 'eat candy' (chewing gum, lolly)	eat.soft food (plum)		eat.soft. food eat cookie (dog)	eat.soft. food		eat.soft. food eat candy
ve' 'eat.corn' (meal)	(want) meal					meal
						jve'eltik 'we eat a meal'
k'ux 'eat.crunchy food'	–	–	–	–	–	–

To summarize, the acquisition of eating verbs by the two children indicates that they do not generalize one verb to denote all kinds of eating, but draw distinctions from the beginning. Errors occur within the boundaries of the category.

Input The very specific semantics of the Tzotzil verbs examined here raises the obvious question of how Tzotzil semantics for 'eating' and 'falling' actions are presented to the child in the input. In a semantic space of falling verbs where gravity plays a role, how do input factors interact, if they do, with the perceptual-cognitive factors? In order to assess the role of the input, I examined a sample of two caregivers' speech addressed to Cande. The two samples consist of 300 utterances overall: 100 utterances from the mother and 200 from the aunt, representing 55

TABLE 3.16 Percentage of Tokens of Verbs Shared by Both Caregivers

	Mother	Aunt
Number of utterances	100	200
Number of verb types	55	50
Number of verb tokens	140	250
	% of tokens	% of tokens
EXISTENCE		
oy 'existence'	1%	4%
DISAPPEARANCE		
laj 'finish'	3%	2%
DESIRE		
k'an 'want'	2%	1%
MOTION		
tal 'come'	2%	8%
ba 'go' *(aux)*	3%	4%
bat 'go'	5%	15%
yul 'arrive'	1%	1%
ay 'return'	4%	2%
och 'enter'	1%	1%
TRANSFERENCE		
ak' 'give'	3%	3.6%
ich 'take'	3%	1%
pik 'grab'	1%	2%
PERCEPTION		
k'el 'look'	6%	6%
il 'see'	1%	4%
SPEECH		
ut 'say'	7%	14%
al 'say'	1%	3%
k'op 'speak'	1%	1%
SEPARATION		
jos 'peel'	1%	1%
ACTIVITIES		
pas 'make'	4%	1%
lo' 'eat soft food'	8%	3%
ch'u 'nurse'	1%	1%
nit' 'pull'	2%	1%
mala 'wait'	2%	1%

verb types (140 tokens) for the mother and 50 verb types (250 tokens) for the aunt. The verbs used by the two caregivers are shown in Table 3.16, organized by semantic category.

The highest rate of verb tokens and types is concentrated in the areas of motion, speech, perception, and transference. However, if we look at activity verbs, many

TABLE 3.17 Eating and Falling Verbs Not Shared by the Two Caregivers

	mother	aunt
ti' 'eat.fleshy food'	2%	
ve' 'eat.corn'		3%
k'ux 'eat crunchy food'		2%
p'aj 'fall'	1%	
lom 'fall on side'	1%	
javk'uj 'fall with legs upward'		2%

of which are semantically specific (with the exception of *pas* 'make'), *lo'* 'eat soft food' is the one with the highest percentage occurrence. In fact, of the whole set of verbs produced by Cande's mother *lo'* is the one with the highest frequency (8%). As for her aunt, *lo'* has a lower rate than other general verbs of the broad categories, but it is the highest among specific verbs and is used at the same rate as *ve'* 'eat corn or grain-based food' (see Table 3.17).

Ti' and *k'ux* are also present, but not shared by both caregivers in the input data (see Table 3.17). These data suggest that the input is indeed providing labels for categories that are organized by texture, shape, and so on, and does not rely solely on basic level labels.

Table 3.17 shows the verbs in the input not shared by the two caregivers. With regards to falling verbs, the input shows that they were only used by one caregiver, at a lower frequency than the eating verbs. I should say, however, that I have encountered a higher frequency of falling verbs in other contexts, where the young child is starting to walk and is constantly warned not to fall down. In these cases the adults warn the child not to 'slip over' (*jach'*).

I have argued that the verb *p'aj* 'fall from high' is among the first five to ten words used by the children of the study. This early acquisition is most probably due to the influence of a perceptual-cognitive factor related to attention to gravity effect. The gradual construction of the Tzotzil category is apparently driven by the interaction between perceptual-cognitive forces and Tzotzil semantics.

DISCUSSION

In this chapter I have explored how two Tzotzil learners develop two semantic categories typical of Mayan languages: the set of intransitive verbs for 'falling' and transitive verbs for 'eating.' I have shown that children build up each category in a conservative manner. They do not overgeneralize one verb to denote all kinds of falling or eating actions, but learn verb by verb, making errors that reveal sensitivity to the limits of each category. In my work on spatial development in Tzotzil (de León, 2001a; 2001b), I have weighed out the relation between cognitive predispositions and semantic structure. I have found an interrelation between the two factors, showing that spatial notions such as gravity, contact, and support interact with Tzotzil-specific semantic structure. I have also shown that Tzotzil provides its own spatial concepts not derived from more general cognitive ones—e.g., the verb *xoj* 'put in ring-like object' (i.e., finger in ring, arms in sleeves, etc.). In this chapter, I have further explored the growth of the category of 'falling' verbs and 'eating' verbs. For the former, I have found that the cognitive factor of "effect of gravity" plays a role in starting out the category. In fact, if we look at our input sample, although several falling verbs are present in the speech of both caregivers, they are much less frequent than the set of 'eating' verbs. Tzotzil learners, however, start with the verb *p'aj* 'fall from high' and then gradually build up contrasts based on angle of Figure, and loss of base from Ground. *P'aj,* however, is never generalized by the children of the study to express other kinds of falling actions. Furthermore, they carve out the 'falling' actions category within the borders set by Tzotzil, paying attention to perceptual features such as angle and stability.

Eating verbs are frequent in the input, and are acquired early. If we look at the early vocabularies in other languages, food terms are among the earliest ones to appear (Clark, 1993; Tardif, 2006). However, whereas English-speaking children or even Mandarin-speaking children have about 10 food terms (nouns), Tzotzil children have three to four eating verbs that cover several kinds of foods. The Mayan children of the study learn to categorize "edibles" on the basis of the association between action and the texture and consistency of the object argument before they label objects at a basic level. In fact, Tzotzil categories for eating override "natural" taxonomies. There is no superordinate verb for the set. The underlying semantic contrasts run along dimensions such as "soft," "fleshy," "hard," or "grain-based." This shows that language can provide classificatory criteria that do not depend directly on ontological or cognitive restrictions for learning action words. One restriction which is clearly not operating is a "whole-object constraint" (Markman, 1989). The Tzotzil children of the study refer to edible objects through verbs and not through nouns. The set of verbs denotes covert object categories mainly organized by consistency and texture.

The sets of falling verbs illustrate perceptual-cognitive forces at a primary level (the effect of gravity), but with Tzotzil organization. 'Eating' verbs illustrate the possibility of learning action categories that do not depend directly on ontology or cognition in an obvious way, but which build on Tzotzil linguistic taxonomies.

In connection with the acquisition of action words, Clark has remarked that children may have "action" as an ontological type distinct from that of objects, but that they would start with general notions of action denoted by verbs such as 'to do,' 'to get,' 'to go,' 'to put' (1993, p. 55, see also Ninio, 1999a, 1999b). She argues that actions are complex given the multiplicity of different actions that can be referred to by the same verb and, for this reason, children learn them in a slower fashion than nouns (see also Gentner & Boroditsky, 2001).

> ...The same holds for acts of eating: One eats apples, blackberries, celery sticks, salmon, crab, steak, cucumber salad, and candy-floss—all with different actions some with and some without utensils, yet all receive the same label in English: The verb *to eat.* This diversity could make action categories harder to identify as categories initially, so children might take longer both to

> form categories and to attach labels to them (Clark, 1978b, Gentner, 1982, and Maratsos, 1990 cited in Clark, 1993, p. 55).[10]

Tzotzil provides the perfect example of a language that does discriminate among 'eating actions.' It does it also with holding, breaking, falling, and inserting actions, which are all very specific. In this connection, the role of semantically specific verbs and their effect in early lexical acquisition in some languages has been addressed for Tzeltal Mayan (Brown, 1998; Narasimhan & Brown, this volume) and for Chinese (Tardif, 2005). Brown (1998) has argued that "verb-semantic specificity" in Tzeltal (a close neighbour of Tzotzil) leads children to prefer verbs over nouns in their early lexical development. In a recent paper, Tardif (2005) examines the semantic richness of Mandarin Chinese verbs, contrasting the example of the English verbs *to carry* and *to push*, which encompass many actions of carrying or pushing objects, to the varied collection of verbs for carrying and pushing in Chinese, where they are used frequently at a "basic level." She finds an inverse situation with nouns: Nouns in English are more specific than nouns in Mandarin. What her findings indicate is that the distribution of the semantic or "referential" load in a language may have an effect on children's early lexical preferences for verbs or nouns. Her data showing early acquisition of Chinese verb semantics confirm this view. As with Tzeltal and Chinese, verb semantic specificity in verb semantics seems to play a role in Tzotzil children's early preference for verbs (de León, 1999a, 1999b). Along these lines, Bowerman has recently argued that

> [in English] information about objects is in fact heavily concentrated in nouns. In many other languages the task of imparting object information is far more extensively shared by other parts of speech, in verbs, prepositions, particles, and verb affixes. (2005, p. 211)

Bowerman also draws our attention to the fact that verbs such as *break* and *open*, learned early in English, implicitly denote covert object categories, similar to what I have described for Tzotzil. Tzotzil eating verbs clearly show how semantic specificity in action words can lead children to organize covert "object" categories without resorting to basic level labels for edible objects.

The case of Tzotzil 'falling' verbs raises the same theoretical issues related to semantic "density" and lexical learning. However, these verbs pose a different learning task. The semantics inherent in each of these intransitive verbs encodes perceptual features related to *intrinsic* properties of the implied object argument; for example, having a main axis (*jin*); longish, and standing vertically (*lom*); or animate, standing on a base (*jach'*). But they also refer to *transitory* states, such as falling from high, falling on one side, slipping, or tumbling down. These transitory actions are not inherent properties of the argument of the verb, but are associated with sudden changes of states resulting from accidental events. What

---

[10] Bowerman (2006, p. 224) points out that the English verb *eat* emerges between 17 and 18 months and is rapidly extended to a wide range of solid foods. Likewise *drink* emerges between 18 and 20 months and is extended in a short period of time to liquid drinkables in the speech of two children studied longitudinally.

seems relevant here is that the abstract perceptual features and the *transitory* states seem to play a role in early categorization. This concurs with McCune-Nicholich's (2006) position that experiential factors, such as sudden changes of states experienced by an agent, may guide children in their early lexical development.

Overall we see an interaction between some perceptual-cognitive factors and Tzotzil-specific semantic structure of each verb. For 'falling' verbs visual perception and cognition may trigger early production of descriptions of gravity effects, but Tzotzil semantics then organizes the category. For 'eating' verbs the mouth's perception of texture, consistency, or corn-based flavour seems to be the driving force. Thus, Tzotzil exemplifies a fascinating complexity, whereby several explanations and driving forces must be posited to interact, and no one answer can solve the acquisitional puzzle.[11] This leads to the conclusion that early lexical learning is guided by the *particular* intersection of linguistic and cognitive factors in the native language. The different weights these factors have in the learning task is particular to the language being learned.

ACKNOWLEDGMENT

I gratefully acknowledge Ginny Gathercole's thoughtful comments on a previous version of the chapter. Any errors or misconceptions are my own responsibility. The names of the children were changed for reasons of confidentiality.

REFERENCES

Berlin, B. (1967). Categories of eating in Tzeltal and Navajo. *International Journal of American Linguistics, 33*(1), 1–6.

Berlin, B. (1968). *Tzeltal numeral classifiers: A study in ethnographic semantics.* The Hague and Paris: Mouton.

Bloom L. 1973. *One word at a time: The use of single word utterances before syntax*. The Hague: Mouton.

Bowerman, M. (1989). Learning a semantic system: What role do cognitive predispositions play? In M. L. Rice & R. L. Schiefelbusch (Eds.), *The teachability of language* (pp. 133–169). Baltimore, MD: Paul H. Brookes.

Bowerman, M. (1996). Learning how to structure space for language—A crosslinguistic perspective In P. Bloom, M. Peterson, L. Nadel, & M. Garret (Eds.), *Language and space* (pp. 385–436) Cambridge, MA: MIT Press.

Bowerman, M. (2005). Why can't you "open" a nut or "break" a cooked noodle? Learning covert object categories in action word meanings. In L. Gershkoff-Stowe & D. Rakison (Eds.), *Building object categories in developmental time* (pp. 209–243). Mahwah, NJ: Erlbaum.

[11]The following quote by Küntay and Slobin (1997, p. 284) nicely reflects the problem: "...[E]ach language presents the learner with a particular set of multiply-intersecting problem spaces. Part of acquiring a language lies in determining the relevant cues to each of those spaces" (see Brown, 1998 for the same argument).

Bowerman, M., & Choi, S. (2001). Shaping meanings for language: Universal and language specific in the acquisition of spatial categories. In M. Bowerman & S. Levinson (Eds.), *Language acquisition and conceptual development* (pp. 475–511). Cambridge, UK: Cambridge University Press.

Bowerman, M., & Choi, S. (2001). Shaping meanings for language: Universal and language-specific in the acquisition of spatial semantic categories. In M. Bowerman & S. Levinson (Eds.), *Conceptual and linguistic development* (pp. 475–513). Cambridge, UK: Cambridge University Press.

Bowerman, M., & Choi, S. (2003). Space under construction: Language-specific spatial categorization in first language acquisition. In D. Gentner & S. Goldin-Meadow (Eds.), *Language in mind: Advances in the study of language and thought* (pp. 387–428). Cambridge, MA: MIT Press.

Bowerman, M., de León, L. & Choi, S. (1995). Verbs, particles, and spatial semantics: Learning to talk about spatial actions in typologically different languages. In *The Proceedings of the 27th Annual Child Language Research Forum* (pp. 101–110). Stanford, CA: Stanford Linguistics Association and Center for the Study of Language and Information.

Bowerman M., & Levinson. S. (Eds.). (2001). *Conceptual and linguistic development.* Cambridge, UK: Cambridge University Press.

Brown, P. (1994). The ins and ons of Tzeltal locative expressions: The semantics of static descriptions of location. *Linguistics, 32*, 743–790.

Brown, P. (1997). Isolating the CVC root in Tzeltal Mayan: A study of children's first verbs. In *The Proceedings of the 28th Child Language Research Forum* (pp. 41–52). Stanford, CA: Center for the Study of Language and Information.

Brown, P. (1998). Children's first verbs in Tzetal: Evidence for an early verb category. *Linguistics, 36*(4), 715–753.

Brown, P. (2001). Learning to talk about motion UP and DOWN: Is there a language specific-bias for verb learning? In M. Bowerman & S. Levinson (Eds.), *Conceptual and linguistic development* (pp. 512–543) Cambridge, UK: Cambridge University Press.

Brown, P. (2007). "She had just cut/broken off her head": Cutting and breaking verbs in Tzeltal. [Special issue] *Cognitive Linguistics, 18*(2).

Choi, S. (2000). Caregiver input in English and Korean: Use of nouns and verbs in book-reading and toy-play contexts. *Journal of Child Language, 27*(1), 69–96.

Choi, S., & Bowerman, M. (1991). Learning to express motion events in English and Korean: The influence of language-specific lexicalization patterns. *Cognition, 4*, 83–121.

Choi, S., & Gopnik, A. (1995). Early acquisition of verbs in Korean: A cross-linguistic study. *Journal of Child Language, 22*, 497–529.

Clark, E. V. (1993). *The lexicon in acquisition.* Cambridge, UK: Cambridge University Press.

Clark, H. H. (1973). Space, time, semantics, and the child. In T. E. Moore (Ed.), *Cognitive development and the acquisition of language* (pp. 27–73). New York: Academic Press.

de León, L. (1994). Exploration in the acquisition of geocentric location by Tzotzil children. *Linguistics, 32*(4–5), 857–885.

de León, L. (1997). The acquisition of vertical path in Tzotzil (Mayan): Cognitive vs. linguistic determinants. In *Proceedings of the 28th child language research forum* (pp. 183–197). Stanford, CA: Stanford Linguistics Association and Center for the Study of Language and Information.

de León, L. (1999a). Verb roots and caregiver speech in Tzotzil Mayan acquisition. In L. Michaelis & B. Fox (Eds.), *Language, cognition, and function* (pp. 99–119). Stanford University, CA: Stanford Center for Language and Information.

de León, L. (1999b). Verbs in early Tzotzil syntax. [Special issue] *International Journal of Bilingualism, 3* (2–3), 219–240.

de León, L. (2001a). Finding the richest path: the acquisition of verticality by Tzotzil children. In M. Bowerman & S. Levinson (Eds.), *Conceptual and linguistic development* (pp. 544–564). Cambridge, UK: Cambridge University Press.

de León, L. (2001b). Why Tzotzil children prefer verbs over nouns: The role of linguistic, cognitive, and cultural factors. In M. Almgren, A. Barreña, M. J. Ezeizabarrena, I. Idiazabal, & B. McWhinney (Eds.), *Research on language acquisition. Selected papers of the Proceedings of the 8th International Congress for the Study of Child Language.* San Sebastián, País Vasco: Cascadilla Press. CD ROM.

de León, L. (2001c). ¿Cómo construir un niño zinacanteco?: Conceptos espaciales y lengua materna en la adquisición del tzotzil. In C. Rojas Nieto & L. de León (Eds.), *Estudios de adquisición del lenguaje: Español, lenguas mayas, euskera* (pp. 99–124). México: CIESAS-UNAM.

de León, L. (2005). *La llegada del alma: Lenguaje, infancia y socialización entre los mayas de Zinacantán.* México: CIESAS-INAH-CONACULTA.

Gathercole, V. C. M., & Min, H. (1997). Word meaning biases or language-specific effects? Evidence from English, Spanish, and Korean. *First Language, 17,* 31–56.

Gathercole, V. C. M., Thomas, E. M., & Evans, D. (2000). What's in a noun? Welsh-, English-, and Spanish-speaking children see it differently. *First Language, 20,* 55–90.

Gentner, D. (1982). Why nouns are learnt before verbs: Linguistic relativity versus natural partitioning. In S. A. Kuczaj (Ed.), *Language development* (Vol. 2, pp. 301–334). Hillsdale, NJ: Erlbaum.

Gentner, D., & Boroditsky, L. (2001). Individuation, relativity, and early word learning. In M. Bowerman & S. Levinson (Eds.), *Language acquisition and conceptual development* (pp. 199–256). Cambridge, UK: Cambridge University Press.

Gopnik A., & Choi, S. (1995). Names, relational words, and cognitive development in English and Korean speakers: Nouns are not always learned before verbs. In M. Tomasello & W. Merriman (Eds.), *Beyond names for things: Young children's acquisition of verbs.* (pp. 63–80). Hillsdale, NJ: Erlbaum.

Haviland, J. B. (1992). Seated and settled: Tzotzil verbs of the body. *Zeitschrift fur Phonetik, Sprachwissenschaft und Kommunikationsforschung, 45*(6), 534–561. Berlin: Akademie Verlag.

Haviland, J. B. (1994a). "Ta xetel xulem" [The buzzards were circling]: Categories of verbal roots in (Zinacantec) Tzotzil. *Linguistics, 32,* 791–743.

Haviland, J. B. (1994b). Verbs and shapes in (Zinacantec) Tzotzil: The case of "insert." Universidad de Guadalajara, [Special issue] *Función, 15–16,* 83–117.

Imai, M., & Gentner, D. (1997). A cross-linguistic study of early word meaning: Universal ontology and linguistic influence. *Cognition, 62,* 169–200.

Mandler, J. (1996). Preverbal representation and language. In P. Bloom, M. Peterson, L. Nadel, & M. Garrett (Eds.), *Language and space* (pp. 365–384). Cambridge, UK: Cambridge University Press.

Maratsos, M. (1990). Are actions to verbs as objects are to nouns? On the differential semantic bases of form, class, category. *Linguistics, 28,* 1351–1379.

Markman, E. (1989). *Categorization and naming in children: Problems of induction.* Cambridge, MA: MIT Press.

McCune-Nicolich, L. (1981). The cognitive bases of relational words in the single-word period. *Journal of Child Language, 8,* 15–34.

McCune-Nicolich, L. (2006). Dynamic event words: From common cognition to varied linguistic expression. *First Language, 26,* 233–255.

Nelson, K. (1974). Concept, word, and sentence: Interrelations in acquisition and development. *Pychological Review, 81,* 267–285.

Nelson, K. (1981). Individual differences in language development: Implications for development and language. *Developmental Psychology, 17,* 170–187.
Ninio, A. (1999a). Pathbreaking verbs in syntactic development and the question of prototypical transitivity. *Journal of Child Language, 26,* 619–653.
Ninio, A. (1999b). Model learning in syntactic development: Intransitive verbs [Special issue] *International Journal of Bilingualism, 3,* 111–131.
Quine, W. (1964). *Word and object.* Cambridge, MA: MIT Press.
Tardif, T. (1996). Nouns are not always learned before verbs: Evidence from Mandarin speakers' early vocabularies. *Developmental Psychology, 32,* 492–504.
Tardif, T. (2006). But are they really verbs? In K. Hirsh-Pasek & R. M. Golinkoff (Eds.), *Action meets word: How children learn verbs* (pp. 477–498). Oxford: Oxford University Press.
Tardif, T., Gelman, S. A., & Xu, F. (1999). Putting the "noun bias" in context: A comparison of English and Mandarin. *Child Development, 70,* 620–635.
Tomasello, M. (1992). *First verbs.* Cambridge, UK: Cambridge University Press.

Personal Tribute

PENELOPE BROWN and BHUVANA NARASIMHAN

I (PB) first met Melissa on my arrival at the Max Planck Institute (MPI) in September 1991, along with a new project group on Space headed by Stephen Levinson. Trained as a linguistic anthropologist, I was at that time immersed in Tzeltal adult spatial language and had never dreamed that I would get interested in child language. Melissa herself, by then a long-term member of the MPI, was also immersed in spatial language—the semantic distinctions lexicalized in words like *in* and *on*, *af*, *op*, and *aan*, tight and loose fitting insertion and extraction, and the like—and the difficulties these pose for first language learners. She was promptly adopted as an honorary member of the new Project Group, and her enthusiasm, clear thinking, and sense of humor have kept us all on our toes.

I (BN) met Melissa during a conference on spatial language in Arizona in 1996, when I was first getting interested in word meaning as a graduate student. I arrived at the MPI in 1999, and during my years here Melissa has become a role model in many ways. These are the qualities with which she dazzles us: the art of arguing gently but firmly, seeing the big picture and simultaneously the smallest details, appreciating the absurd in any situation, and writing the most lucid prose. But it is the small things that I appreciate the most: a kind word to a nervous student, a timely joke to revive a flagging conversation, a book or newspaper clipping in the mailbox about something funny or interesting, advice about how one might smuggle small rodents in strange airports, a single observation that can save hours of labor ("Have you looked at Rispoli 1991?").

We are both glad and grateful for the richness of our collegial contact with Melissa, for her insights and her editorial patience, for innumerable lunchtime discussions about everything in the universe. Most of all we are grateful for the continuing inspiration that Melissa provides to us in multiple ways: in asking the interesting questions, insisting on precise and testable approaches to answering them and on clarity of expression in reporting what we've discovered, and always remembering *the* pertinent example of child language usage that most poignantly addresses any point ever raised by any speaker.

4

Getting the INSIDE Story
Learning to Express Containment in Tzeltal and Hindi[1]

BHUVANA NARASIMHAN
University of Colorado, Boulder

PENELOPE BROWN
Max Planck Institute for Psycholinguistics, Nijmegen

INTRODUCTION

This chapter compares young children's uses of semantically specific and general relational containment terms (e.g., *in, enter, insert*) in two unrelated languages, Hindi and Tzeltal, with the aim of assessing the role of a semantic specificity preference in children's vocabulary acquisition.

How children learn the meanings of words is a core puzzle in the study of language acquisition. There are commonalities in the general types of semantic notions that tend to get lexicalized across languages and those that are acquired early—for example, concepts of motion, possession, attribution, and the existence, location, and disappearance of objects (Bowerman, 1973; R. Brown, 1973; E.V. Clark, 1973; Johnston & Slobin, 1979; Slobin, 1973, 1985). There is also, however,

[1] This chapter began as a talk at a workshop in honor of Melissa Bowerman held at the Max Planck Institute, Nijmegen, on April 3, 2002. The chapter is an offshoot of a crosslinguistic study on motion verbs presented at the Stanford Child Language Research Forum in April 2002 (Bowerman et al., 2002), part of which we also presented at the Netherlands Eerste Taal (NET) Conference in Nijmegen in March 2002; a revised version will appear in Slobin et al., in press. We are grateful for the help in understanding our data provided by our collaborators, and for the feedback from many others at these forums.

wide variation in how languages cut up the world into semantic categories, variation which is perhaps most systematically documented for the spatial domain (e.g., Ameka & Levinson, 2007; Levinson & Meira, 2003; Levinson & Wilkins, 2006; Majid, Enfield & van Staden, 2006). Children beginning to speak have to integrate the ways in which speakers around them use words in particular contexts with the prelinguistic categories they have already formed, in order to prune or expand these categories. They may have to create new categories, so that they can use words in the situations that call for them and not in others. They do this at an astonishing rate and from a very young age.[2] The categories that they form also look language-specific from a very young age, as demonstrated by the work of Bowerman and her colleagues since the early to mid-1990s (Bowerman, 1996; Bowerman & Choi, 2001, 2004; Brown, 2001, 2008; Choi & Bowerman, 1991; de León, 2001). How children do this is still something of a mystery.

In the abundant literature on this subject, the issue of how children acquire the meanings of relational terms—verbs, adpositions, particles—has been the focus of much attention, especially in the domain of space (Choi & Bowerman, 1991; Clark, 1973; Coventry, Prat-Sala & Richards, 2001; Gentner, 1978, 1982; Huttenlocher, Smiley, & Charney, 1983; Johnston, 1984; Johnston & Slobin, 1979; Landau & Stecker, 1990; McCune-Nicolich, 1981; Piaget & Inhelder, 1956, among many others). Some researchers have suggested that, due to the transitory nature of events, labels for events are harder to acquire than are labels for concrete objects (Gentner & Boroditsky, 2001; chapter 1, this volume; Imai, Haryu, & Okada, 2002; Mintz & Gleitman, 2002). The linguistic framing of events has been proposed as an important factor in helping children extract event categories from the perceptual flux in which events are embedded (Fisher, Hall, Rakowitz, & Gleitman, 1994; Gleitman, 1990), and Genter and Boroditsky (2001) have argued that there is more crosslinguistic variation in how languages construe events than in the labeling of objects.[3]

Yet, as Gentner and Boroditsky point out, not all the events which are labeled in language are alike; they vary in perceptual and cognitive complexity. One dimension of difference in words used to label events has to do with how much information about the event is packaged into the word. Some event labels are "general" or "light" covering a wide range of situations—as, for example, the English verbs *do, make, get, give*. Others are much more specific to particular situations. For example, the Mayan language Tzeltal divides the domain of eating into many different kinds of eating, with distinct verbs for 'eat tortilla-like things,' 'eat meat-like things,' 'eat soft things,' 'eat crunchy things,' 'eat sugarcane,' and others. Semantically specific verbs of this sort, unlike more general verbs (like 'give,' 'get,' etc.), subcategorize for specific properties of objects; such verbs encode "covert object categories" (Bowerman 2005, 2008).

[2] See Carey (1978), who estimated that children must learn on the order of five words a day from age 1;6 to age 6.

[3] Some researchers have argued that there is much more crosslinguistic diversity in noun semantics than psychologists have believed (Brown, 2001; Gathercole, Thomas, & Evans, 2000; Lucy, 1992).

This leads to the following question: Do children find relational expressions of a particular level of specificity easier to learn? A number of researchers have observed that children learning Indo-European languages initially rely on semantically very general verbs; in their first year of speaking they make heavy use of verbs like 'do,' 'make,' 'want,' 'go,' 'give,' 'get' (Clark, 1993; Goldberg, 1996; Ninio, 1999a, 1999b), suggesting that these light verbs are easy to learn. This contrasts with the equally plausible but incompatible possibility that labels for events that stand for particular schemas denoting specific (classes of) objects (e.g., *bake*, which applies to certain classes of objects such as cakes, bread, etc.) are easier to learn than those for events that are more abstract (e.g., *make*, which is relatively semantically general, ranging over many different types of objects and event types). There is some evidence that event labels denoting actions or states specific to particular (classes of) objects can be acquired at the same time as event labels that are more abstract (e.g., Brown 1998, 2001, for Tzeltal; de León, this volume for the related language Tzotzil). Gentner and Boroditsky (2001) relate early use of semantically specific verbs in languages like Tzeltal to the fact that such verbs refer to coherent event schemata that are more highly individuated and hence, in general, perceptually salient for children. Further, labels that conflate more elements of the event (e.g., verbs such as *enter*, which conflates motion and containment), might also be preferred by children over labels that are more general and apply to a wider range of contexts (e.g., particles such as *in*, used in both static and dynamic contexts) (cf. Gentner & Boroditsky, 2001).

One confounding factor in exploring the role of semantic specificity in the acquisition of relational terms has to do with input frequency (cf. Theakston, Lieven, Pine, & Rowland, 2004). Since semantically specific terms tend to be less frequent than general expressions, an absence of such expressions in children's early production might well arise from their sparsity in the input. But children's use of relational expressions in particular contexts may provide some evidence of a semantic specificity preference. For instance, children may not initially generalize their uses of semantically general expressions in a productive way even if they occur frequently and are extended to a wide range of contexts in the input. Rather, they might use semantically general expressions often but "in an overly conflationary manner, retaining the objects as well as the relational elements" (Gentner & Boroditsky, 2001, p. 245). Further, semantically specific terms might be acquired early even if relatively infrequent in the input, since they apply to a smaller range of situations by virtue of conflating more semantic elements in their meaning. Hence they do not place demands on children to generalize very widely across diverse contexts of use at a stage when the child may not have had sufficient exposure to the input to determine the appropriate basis for generalization.

The role of semantic specificity in child vocabulary acquisition has not been systematically explored across languages in a single semantic domain, nor for relational terms other than verbs (e.g., for case, adpositions, spatial nominals). Crosslinguistic data can be examined to see whether semantically specific relational expressions that occur with comparatively low frequency in the input are nevertheless acquired as early as semantically general expressions, and whether children initially show a tendency to severely restrict their uses of semantically general terms. This chapter performs this comparison for the domain of containment relations. In Figure 4.1 we schematize the contrast between the types of lexicalization we are addressing, for the domain of containment relations. The circles represent the situations in which a particular linguistic expression applies. Containment terms with relatively specific meanings cover a small range of situations and are represented by the smaller circles (e.g., Tzeltal semantically specific insertion verbs, such as *tik'* 'insert [into something that has opening into an 'inside,' i.e., a 3D container of some sort]' or *lut* 'lodge tightly between objects [e.g., parallel objects (lips) or a forked object (tree branches)]'). Terms with relatively general containment senses cover a wide range of situations and are represented by larger circles (e.g., 'enter'). The most general terms, compatible with both static and dynamic containment contexts (e.g., 'in') are shown in the largest circle.

The "semantic specificity hypothesis" proposes that children's early relational meanings are "overly conflationary," retaining properties of the objects involved in the events to which relational labels are applied. It also suggests that children may be overly context-bound by virtue of inappropriately conflating more *relational* elements (e.g., containment and motion) in the use of semantically general expressions (such as locative case-markers that apply to both static and dynamic contexts). If children have a preference for semantically specific expressions, those that are used for a narrow range of contexts, we would expect them to (1) acquire semantically specific terms at least as early as semantically general terms; (2) use such expressions appropriately even if they occur with relatively low frequency in

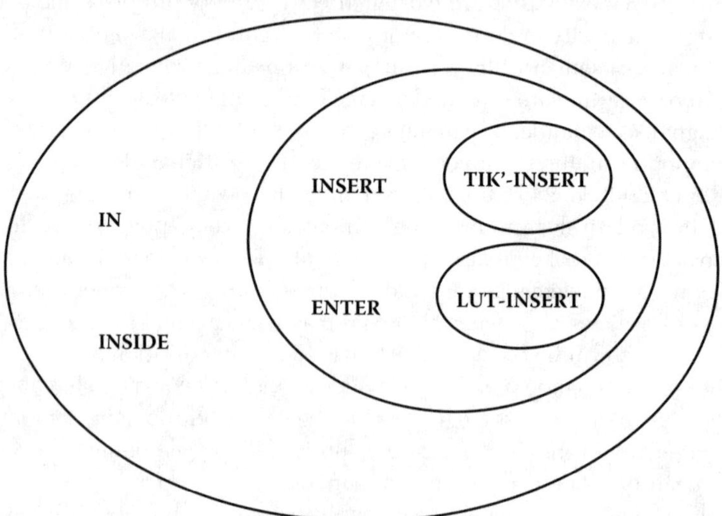

Figure 4.1 General and specific containment terms.

the input; and (3) initially underextend semantically general forms even if they are used frequently and in a diverse range of contexts by caregivers.

In the present study we focus on children's and caregivers' uses of a set of terms of different syntactic categories, all of which encode the semantic notion of containment or motion into containment. We have several reasons for thinking that this approach can help us to evaluate the "semantic specificity hypothesis." First, containment is an important notional concept, one especially salient to children (Piaget & Inhelder, 1956; Slobin, 1985)—young children put things into containers when possible, and presume that 'put-in' is the meaning of nonsense verbs in container contexts (Clark, 1993; Jensen de López, 2002). Across languages, a prototypical notion of containment is frequently lexicalized; Wierzbicka (1996) claims INSIDE as a semantic universal, although the linguistic categorization of the domain can vary across languages (Brown, 1994; Bowerman, de León & Choi, 1995; Haviland, 1994). Second, by comparing forms within the same semantic domain, one avoids the risk of confounding variables. For example, a semantically specific form in a particular domain (e.g., 'eat-tortilla') might be preferred over a "light" form in another domain (e.g., 'make') because the particular semantics of that domain (e.g., eating) proves inherently attractive to the child rather than because the specificity of the verb is favored by the child. Third, by comparing terms belonging to different form classes (e.g., case markers and spatial nominals in Hindi, verbs, directionals and spatial nominals in Tzeltal), we can examine the issue of semantic specificity across form class distinctions. Fourth, we have comparable situations involving containment in both the Hindi and Tzeltal data sets of child–caregiver interactions, collected longitudinally to allow for the study of developmental change. And fifth, by comparing children's uses of containment terms with those of their caregivers, we can establish the extent to which frequency and diversity of contexts of use in the input influence children's uses as well.

Hindi and Tzeltal, two languages spoken on opposite sides of the world, contrast nicely in their lexical resources for talking about things being IN and entering INTO containment.[4] In the next section we spell out these lexical resources and set out the hypotheses we will entertain concerning the role of semantic specificity in children's approach to learning these words. Then we describe our data-collection and methodological procedures. In the next two sections, we inspect Hindi and Tzeltal-speaking caregivers' input, as well as children's early language production at two time points—at the two-word stage and a few months later—to show what forms the children use and which forms they prefer when talking about containment. Finally, we draw some conclusions about the role of semantic specificity in influencing children's early word productions.

[4] Hindi is spoken by about 360 million speakers, primarily in the Indian subcontinent. The data reported in this study come from Narasimhan's longitudinal corpus of four children collected in New Delhi. Tzeltal is spoken by approximately 250,000 Mayan indigenous people in Chiapas, Mexico. The Tzeltal data come from Brown's longitudinal corpus of five children, in the community of Tenejapa.

LEXICALIZATION OF THE CONTAINMENT DOMAIN IN HINDI AND TZELTAL

We define containment broadly to mean inclusion of (part of) one entity within the boundaries of a second entity which might be three-dimensional (e.g., *walk into the room*), two-dimensional (e.g., *the dot is in the circle*), or one-dimensional (e.g., *the point is in the line).* Motion into containment then involves boundary crossing to a place or region conceptualized as enclosed, containerlike in some way. A basic containment notion (IN, INSIDE) is taken to be a primitive in linguistic and psycholinguistic theories (e.g., Jackendoff, 1983; Miller & Johnson-Laird, 1976; Wierzbicka, 1996).[5] Such a notion of containment can be expressed in words from a variety of syntactic categories, including verbs (*enter, insert*), adpositions (*in, into*), particles (*in*), and spatial nominals (*inside*), among others (cf. Jackendoff, 1990).

What words in everyday speech to children are used in talking about relations of containment? Hindi and Tzeltal are both "verb-framed" languages (Talmy, 1985, 1991), both having basic-level verbs meaning 'enter' and other path-encoding motion verbs. Yet the resources for talking about containment situations go well beyond verbs; we shall look at the relevant forms across all word classes to get a sense of which forms, in which word classes, are preferred in children's early uses in these two languages. We restrict ourselves to forms frequent in speech of young children.

Containment Expressions in Hindi

In Hindi,[6] containment is expressed with the verbs *ghus* 'enter' and *ghus-aa* 'enter-CAUSE,' as well as with nonverbal spatial relators such as the locative case-marker *mE* 'in(to)' and the spatial nominal *andar* 'inside.' The verbs *ghus* and *ghusaa* select Ground expressions which occur as noun phrases that are case-marked with the locative case marker *mE* 'in(to)' or as possessed spatial nominals such as *X ke andar* 'X=GEN inside'; that is, 'X's inside.' The spatial nominal can also occur in isolation (e.g., *andar jaa* 'inside go'). The locative case-marker and spatial nominal may also occur with verbs that do not encode the notion of containment in themselves, to describe caused motion (e.g., *Daal* 'put/drop') or spontaneous motion (e.g., *jaa* 'go') into containment. The basic kinds of schemata for predicating containment in Hindi are given in (1):

[5] But see Haviland (1994) for an argument against the universality of such a primitive, based on data from Tzotzil, a Mayan language closely related to Tzeltal.

[6] Hindi transcribing conventions include: E (nasalized close mid front vowel /e/), D (retroflex plosive), and = (which, following the Leipzig glossing rules, indicates a clitic boundary between a root and a case postposition).

(1) Schemata for location/motion predications in Hindi[7]

a. Transitive motion:

Agent	**Figure**[8]	**Ground + Loc.Case/ Spatial Nominal**	**Verb**
NP	NP	NP = Loc	VERB
us = ne	*kitaab-ϕ*	*thaele =* ***mE***	***ghus-aa-****yii*
he = Erg	book-Nom	bag = Loc	enter-Caus-Sg.Fem.Prf

'He inserted/crammed the book in the bag.'

NP	NP	NP = Gen Spatial Nominal	VERB
us = ne	*kitaab-ϕ*	*Dibbe = ke* ***andar***	*rakh-ii*
he = Erg	book-Nom	box = Gen inside	put-Sg.Fem.Prf

'He put the books inside the box.'

b. Intransitive (motion):

Figure	**Ground + Loc.Case /Spatial Nominal**	**Verb**
NP	NP = Loc	VERB
wo	*kamre =* ***mE***	***ghus****-aa*
he-Nom	room = Loc	enter-Sg.Msc.Prf.

'He entered the room.'

c. Intransitive (location):

Figure	**Ground + Loc.Case /Spatial Nominal**	**Verb**
NP	NP = Gen Spatial Nominal	VERB
wo	*Dibbe = ke* ***andar***	*hae*
it-Nom	box = Gen inside	be.3Sg.Pres

'It is in the box.'

Some examples from the child language database instantiating the schemas above are provided in (2) to (4):

(2) *wo... usii = ke* ***andar ghus*** *jaa-tii hae*
it-Nom...that.only = Gen inside enter go-Fem.Imprf be-3Sg.Pres
'it [car]...enters inside only that.' (Child, 27 months)

(3) *gaaD|ii = ke* ***andar*** *rakh do is = ko*
car = Gen inside put give.Imp this = Acc
'Put this inside the car.' (Mother, when child is 20–21 months)

(4) *gol-ϕ is =* ***mE*** *lag-aa-o*
round-Nom this = Loc attach-Caus-Imp
'Put the round (thing) in this.' (Mother, when child is 20–21 months)

These containment terms can be grouped in cross-cutting ways on the basis of semantic specificity. One distinction is based on what semantic elements are conflated in their meanings (Talmy, 1985). Whereas verbs that conflate caused or

---

[7] Hindi gloss conventions: *Erg*: Ergative; *Nom*: Nominative; *Acc*: Accusative; *Dat*: Dative; *Gen*: Genitive; *Loc*: Locative; *Ins*: Instrumental; *NF*: Nonfinite verb; *Pst*: Past tense; *Pres*: Present tense; *Fut*: Future tense; *Sg*: Singular; *Msc*: Masculine; *Fem*: Feminine; *Imprf*: Imperfective; *Part*: Participle; *Prf*: Perfect; *Ind.caus*: Indirect causative.

[8] We use the terms *Figure* and *Ground* in Talmy's (1985) sense: Figure is the object being located; Ground is the object or place in relation to which it is located.

spontaneous motion with containment (*ghus* 'enter,' *ghusaa* 'enter-CAUSE') are restricted to expressing containment in dynamic contexts (motion into containment), the nonverbal spatial relators (case-marker *mE* 'in(to)' and spatial nominal *andar* 'inside') are more general and can be used to express containment in both static and dynamic contexts. Cross-cutting the conflated-unconflated distinction is the dimension of selectional restrictivity. The case-marker *mE* can be used for two-dimensional Ground objects (e.g., surface of wall, ceiling, in examples 5, 6) as well as three-dimensional Ground objects (e.g., cup, in example 7), whereas the spatial nominal *andar* is typically used with three-dimensional Ground objects (e.g. bowl, apple, in examples 8, 9). In addition, the spatial nominal *andar* tends to be used for whole inclusion, whereas *mE* tolerates partial inclusion as well.[9]

(5) *tasviir-ϕ* *diiwaar* = ***mE*** *Tang-ii* *hu-ii* *hae*
Picture-Nom wall = Loc hang-Sg.Fem.Prf be-Sg.Fem.Prf be.3Sg.Pres
'The picture is suspended ON the wall.' [lit.: IN]

(6) *kiiD|aa-ϕ* *chat* = ***mE*** *lag-aa* *hu-aa* *hae*
Insect-Nom ceiling = Loc attach-Sg.Msc.Prf be-Sg.Msc.Prf be.3Sg.Pres
'The insect is attached ON the ceiling.' [lit.: IN]

(7) *seb-ϕ* *kap* = ***mE*** *rakh-aa* *hu-aa* *hae*
Apple-Nom cup = Loc place-Sg.Msc.Prf be-Sg.Msc.Prf be.3Sg.Pres
'The apple has been placed IN the cup.'

(8) *seb-ϕ* *kaTorii* = *ke* ***andar*** *hae*
Apple-Nom saucer = Gen inside be.3Sg.Pres
'The apple is INSIDE the bowl.'

(9) *tiir-ϕ* *seb* = *ke* ***andar*** *hae*
arrow-Nom apple = Gen inside be.3Sg.Pres
'The arrow is INSIDE the apple.'

Comparing across form classes, we see that the verbs *ghus/ghus-aa* 'enter/enter-CAUSE' are more semantically specific than the spatial nominal (*andar*) and case-marker (*mE*), not only in terms of conflation of semantic elements but also with respect to the types of objects they select for (typically 3D Ground objects, with 2D objects being dispreferred).

Containment Expressions in Tzeltal

Unlike Hindi, Tzeltal has no case marking on nouns and no spatial adpositions (there is only one semantically general preposition in the language). Containment relations are most naturally expressed in verbs. In addition to the intransitive *och* 'enter,' and its transitivized form *otz-es* 'enter-CAUSE,' there is a wide range of semantically specific "insertion" verbs used in everyday discourse, including *ch'ik*

[9] The Hindi examples are taken from an elicited production task with adults, using the "BowPed" picture book series designed to elicit IN-ON terms in various languages (Bowerman & Pederson, 1992).

'insert between two other things [e.g., person between two others, or money tucked in between skirt and belt]),' *tik'* 'insert [into something that has an opening into an "inside," i.e., a 3D container of some sort],' *lut* 'lodge tightly between objects [e.g., parallel objects (lips) or forked object (tree branch)]' (see examples 14–16 below). These verbs form a contrasting set of terms for referring to particular types of insertion events differentiated with respect to the geometric properties of Figure, Ground, and their spatial relationship.[10] A second possibility in Tzeltal is to use a noninsertion verb along with the directional *ochel* 'entering,' indicating that the action of the verb takes place in an 'entering' direction (examples 13, 17). Finally, there is one nonverbal spatial relator for containment relations, the spatial nominal *y-util* 'its-inside' (example 17).[11]

The basic intransitive and transitive schemata for location and motion predications of a Figure in relation to a Ground in Tzeltal are given in (10).[12]

(10) Schemata for location/motion predications in Tzeltal

a. Intransitive:

Verb				**(Directional)**	**Prep**	**Ground (Figure)**
ya	*x-*	***och-***	*0*	*al*	*ta*	*koral*
ICP	ASP-	enter-	3A	DIRcome	PREP	corral

'He's coming into the corral.'

[10] There are more than 50 Tzeltal roots whose semantic content includes reference to containment in some sense. This is not a clearly bounded set because many Tzeltal verbs are sensitive to spatial properties of the Figure/Ground relation achieved by the verb (Brown, 1994). Insertion scenes merge into those of attachment, holding (in hand or arm), carrying, and positioning of objects. No syntactic properties (to our knowledge) demarcate these (to a speaker of English) distinct notional sets. It is also a peculiarity of many of these specific verbs that they do not categorize insertion events per se but rather the configuration of Figure/Ground objects where one is inserted in the other; depending on the syntax they can flip which is Figure and which is Ground. For example, *xoj* 'insert-solid-object-into-containment relation' can be used to talk about inserting a ring onto a pole or inserting the pole into the ring (see Brown, 1994 for details). What these verbs mean is more like 'achieve a certain Figure/Ground relationship such that one item is INSIDE another one.' This Figure/Ground reversibility is even true for the canonical "enter" verb *och*. It is not true, however, for the three semantically specific verbs found in the early Tzeltal data discussed here.

[11] *Y-util* 'its-inside' is also in a contrast set with about 20 other "relational nouns" used to specify spatial relationships between objects. These include *y-olil* 'its middle,' *s-ba* 'its topside,' *y-anil* 'its underneath,' *y-ajk'ol* 'its-uphill (uphillwards or above it),' *y-alan* 'its-downhill (downhillwards or below it),' and a number of more concrete bodypart terms ('its-head,' 'its-back,' 'its-belly,' etc.). See Levinson (1994), Brown (2006) for details.

[12] The grammatical abbreviations for Tzeltal are as follows: 1, 2, 3E = lst, 2nd, 3rd person ergative; 1,2,3 A = lst, 2nd, 3rd person absolutive, 1plincl = lst plural inclusive, 1plexcl = lst plural exclusive; ASP = neutral aspect, ICP = incompletive, CMP = completive, ACS = achieved change of state; ART = definite article, CAUS = causative suffix, CL = sentence-final clitic, DEIC = deictic particle, DIR = directional, IMP = imperative, NEG = negative, PT = particle, PREP = preposition, VOC = vocative, ! = proposition assertion ('it is the case that…').

b. Transitive:

Verb					**(Directional)**	**Prep**	**Ground**	**(Figure)**	**(Agent)**
ya	*k-*	***otz-***	***es-***	*O*	*tal*	*ta*	*s-koral*	*te*	*wakax-e*
ICP	3E-	enter-	CAUS-	3A	DIRcome	PREP	3E-corral	ART	bull-CL

'I make the bull enter (in)to its corral.'

Some examples from the Tzeltal child database follow:

(11) Intransitive 'enter'

eso ***och****-O* *ix* *ta* *sit.*
thus enter-3A ACS PREP eye
'Thus it has entered (someone's) eye.' [soap liquid]

(12) Transitive 'enter'

ma *me* *'w-****otz-es****-O* *ajch'al tey* *ta* *ja'* *i* *antun*
NEG PT 2E-enter-CAUS-3A mud DEIC PREP water DEIC VOC
'Don't make mud enter there into the water, Antun.' [i.e., 'Don't put mud into the water.']

(13) Verb + directional 'entering'

ma *x-a'w-****ak'****-O* ***ochel*** *ta* *kajpe*
NEG ASP-2E-put-3A entering PREP coffee
'Don't put it entering (in)to the coffee.' [toy car, into coffee beans spread out to dry]

(14) Transitive specific verb: *tik'* 'insert into container with definable entry place' [grandmother tells child to insert puzzle piece in board]

li' *x-a'-****tik'****-O* *i* *xawin* *i*
here ASP-2E-insert-3A DEIC cat DEIC
'Here you should insert this cat [puzzle piece].'

(15) Transitive specific verb: *lut* 'insert tightly between two supports' [e.g., into mouth]

ma *x-a'-****lut****-O* *mene,* *ay-O* *y-ajch'alel*
NEG ASP-2E-insert.between-3A that.one EXIST-3A 3E-mud
'Don't insert that one between things [i.e., your lips], it has mud (on it).'

(16) Transitive specific verb: *ch'ik* 'insert between'

ch'ik*-O* *ix* *a*
insert.between-3A ACS DEIC
'(You) inserted it there.' [gum into mouth]

(17) Containment expressed in a directional adverb and spatial nominal *y-ut(il)*

ik'-a *laj* ***ochel*** *li'* *ta* ***y-ut(il)*** *na'* *ini*
take-IMP QUOT DIRenter here PREP 3E-inside house here
'Take this one entering here to the inside of the house [i.e., take it into the house].'

(18) Stative containment with a positional adjective derived from a positional verb root
[MAN (age 8) tells Frog story]

xojol*-O* *s-jol* *ta* *ala* *tepil-e*
inserted-3A 3E-head PREP DIM shoe-CL
'His head is inserted in the little shoe.'

As in Hindi, containment terms in Tzeltal are classifiable in cross-cutting ways based on conflation patterns and selectional restrictions. The verbs *och* 'enter' and *otz-es* 'enter-CAUSE' express containment in dynamic contexts (motion into containment); the directional adverb *ochel* 'entering' and the spatial nominal *y-util* 'its-inside' are more general and can be used to express containment in both static and dynamic contexts. Within the class of verbs, this conflation pattern distinction is cross-cut by the dimension of selectional restrictivity. *Och* 'enter' and *otz-es* 'enter-CAUSE' are relatively semantically general with respect to the kinds of objects which constitute the denotata of their arguments. Many other insertion verbs encode specific properties of the Figure or Ground objects they can be predicated of—for example, *ch'ik* 'insert-between-things' (e.g., firewood into fire), *lap* 'insert long-thin-sharp-thing through flexible Ground' (e.g., safety-pin in cloth, needle through mat), or *tik'* 'insert into container with opening' (e.g., rabbit into hutch; see examples 14–16 above). In contrast to Hindi, although Tzeltal has a general-specific contrast within the class of caused motion-into-containment verbs, there is no similar distinction within the class of nonverbal spatial relations expressing containment (i.e., with the relational noun *y-util* 'its inside'). There is no form in Tzeltal with a meaning of IN as general as that for Hindi *mE*.

Summarizing, Hindi and Tzeltal have unconflated words encoding containment alone (*andar, mE* in Hindi; *y-util* in Tzeltal), as well as verbs encoding motion into containment (*ghus/ghus-aa* 'enter/enter-CAUSE' in Hindi, *och/otzes* 'enter/enter-CAUSE' and many more specific insertion verbs *tik', lut*, etc. in Tzeltal). Further, there is a cross-cutting dimension having to do with the (selectional) restrictions imposed by the relational term on the type of object or subtype of containment relation. The spatial nominal *andar* in Hindi prefers Ground objects that are three-dimensional, and implies (but does not entail) complete inclusion, whereas the case-marker *mE* can be used for two-dimensional Ground objects as well. In Tzeltal, there is one spatial nominal for containment, *y-util* 'its-inside,' used with Ground nominals referring to three-dimensional objects that have an 'inside,' as well as one used for two-dimensional relations, *y-ol(il)* 'between' 'in middle of.' But in the verbal domain there is both a general verb encoding motion into containment (*och/otz-es*) and a range of specific verbs of motion into containment which encode properties of the Figure and Ground as well (*tik', lut*, etc.).[13]

THE STUDY

The previous two sections demonstrate a contrast between the two languages in the encoding of (motion into) containment. The specific-general distinction is

[13] In characterizing the semantics of these forms, we are ignoring for the purposes of our analysis more subtle semantic restrictions associated with these forms. For instance, while *ghus-aa* 'enter-CAUSE' in Hindi can be used in the sense of *insert*, it can also be used in contexts where English verbs for tight-containment such as *stuff, cram* are typically used. Further, we have omitted, for the purposes of this analysis, relatively low-frequency verbs such as *ghuseD|* 'shove in, cram' and *ThUUs* 'force down, cram in.'

exemplified in nonverbal relational terms in Hindi (spatial noun, case-marker), whereas in Tzeltal this distinction appears within the verbal domain. Hindi does conflate motion and containment in the verb; however, it lacks the rich set of distinctions in containment verbs found in the Tzeltal verb lexicon. But these typological contrasts in adult language reveal what distinctions *can* be made, not what distinctions *are* made in the input to children. In order to examine "typology in use," we examine the patterns of use of containment expressions in the input to children acquiring Hindi and Tzeltal. We follow with an examination of the use of containment terms in the speech of two children in Hindi and two children in Tzeltal.

Method

Both the adult and child data come from samples of spontaneous language production of two Hindi children ("ISH" and "MAN") and two Tzeltal children ("LUS" and "XAN"), described below. From these samples, we examine both the adult usage of containment terms in the input and children's first uses of containment forms in early acquisition.

Adult Usage in the Input We begin by tabulating the frequency of different containment expressions in caregivers' input speech to children in each of the two languages. Since children cannot know a priori which containment term is semantically general or specific, they must rely on the range of contexts in which these expressions are used in the input. We therefore also establish a profile of contextual diversity of use for each containment term in caregivers' speech to children. This profile might not necessarily correspond to adult intuitions regarding the semantic specificity of containment expressions as outlined above. For instance, even though Hindi *mE* 'in(to)' can be used in both static and dynamic contexts, and with two- and three-dimensional Ground objects in adult language, it might be that caregivers overwhelming use *mE* in dynamic (motion) contexts with three-dimensional Ground objects in talking to their children. In such a case, the diversity of uses of *mE* would not be distinguishable from that of the verbs *ghus* 'enter,' *ghus-aa* 'enter-CAUSE.' The predictions of the semantic specificity hypothesis have to be evaluated in relation to the extensional patterns of the different containment expressions in caregivers' input to children.

Children's Acquisition Having established a profile of the distributional patterns in the input, we can investigate (1) whether children use semantically specific forms as early as they use semantically general forms, even if the former occur infrequently in the input; (2) whether they use such forms appropriately; and (3) whether children initially restrict semantically general forms to a limited set of situations. For instance, even though *mE* in Hindi or *och, otzes* in Tzeltal might be used in a variety of contexts in the input, children might start out using them in highly specific ways, perhaps limited to specific types of objects encountered frequently in association with use of these forms.

In evaluating productivity in children's extensional patterns of use we examine the range of extralinguistic contexts to which containment expressions are applied. For instance, although children's linguistic productivity with a particular expression (e.g., uses of *mE* with a range of different Ground and Figure nominals, and/or co-occurring with a variety of different verbs) would indicate that children are applying the expression to a range of different objects and types of events, the lack of linguistic diversity does not necessarily imply a lack of extensional diversity. For instance, children might restrict their uses of *mE* to just a pronoun (e.g., *is=mE* 'this in'), but the pronoun could be applied to a whole range of different referents (e.g., a basket, a tub, a room, a bag, a picture book, etc.) and different types of events (causative or spontaneous motion, static location). In contrast to the methodology applied in much prior research, we rely not only on the *linguistic* contexts of use but also on the diversity of *situational* contexts of use. These together provide a more accurate measure of patterns of semantic extension of a particular containment expression than linguistic contexts of use alone.

Data Collection and Coding For each language, we examined selected samples of the spontaneous language production of two children, drawn from larger longitudinal databases of videotaped natural interaction of family members and the children (at ages 1;8 to 2;8). The children were audio- and videotaped in naturally occurring and seminaturalistic contexts in their homes, interacting with their caregivers and siblings (and sometimes with the researchers), playing with toys, reading books, or just being together with caregivers (and often other children) either indoors or outdoors. Data were drawn from two time points: roughly the early two-word stage (t1), and three to six months later (t2). The criterion of beginning at the two-word stage led to data being sampled from children whose ages differed by several months from each other. Details of the child samples are shown in Table 4.1.

Representative samples of the input in the two languages were taken from sessions taped prior to the children's t1 samples (referred to as "t0"), for the purpose of comparison with children's speech at t1. To examine any changes in the input patterns over time, we also examined caregivers' input at children's t1 samples. Note that, in both Hindi and Tzeltal societies, input speech is not necessarily primarily from the mother, so we have included the speech of siblings and other caregivers in the input samples. Details of the input samples are also given in Table 4.1.

From both the child and adult samples we extracted all utterances with relational forms encoding containment, including static uses of these terms (locational), temporal uses, and uses in contexts of caused and spontaneous boundary-crossing motion into a container, broadly construed. Utterances addressed directly to the children as well as to other interlocutors present in the context were included. Immediate self-repetitions and exact imitations of prior utterances were excluded.

TABLE 4.1 Child and Input Samples at Two Time Points*

Speaker, sample	No. of sessions	Approximate duration	Age of focal child
Hindi child data			
ISH t1	5 sessions	3.75 hours	1;8–1;9
ISH t2	3 sessions	2.25 hours	2;3
MAN t1	4 sessions	3 hours	2;2–2;4
MAN t2	3 sessions	2.25 hours	2;7–2;8
Hindi input			
Mother, ISH t0	4 sessions	3 hours	1;4–1;5
Brother, ISH t0	4 sessions	3 hours	1;4–1;5
Mother, ISH t1	4 sessions	3 hours	1;7– 1;9
Brother, ISH t1	4 sessions	3 hours	1;8–1;9
Mother, MAN t0	4 sessions	3 hours	2;1–2;2
Mother, MAN t1	2 sessions	1.5 hours	2;2–2;3
Tzeltal child data			
LUS t1	6 sessions	8 hours	1;11–2;0
LUS t2	2 sessions	3 hours	2;5
XAN t1	4 sessions	6 hours	2;2
XAN t2	3 sessions	4.5 hours	2;7–2;8
Tzeltal input			
Cousins, mother, aunts, LUS t0	3 sessions	5.5 hours	1;6
Cousins, grandmother, aunts, LUS t1	6 sessions	8 hours	1;11–2;0
Sibling, cousins, mother, father, aunts, grandmother, XAN t0	5 sessions	6 hours	1;10–2;0
Sibling, cousins, mother, father, aunt, XAN t1	4 sessions	6 hours	2;2

*t0 = first time point at which input to the child was sampled (prior to t1)
t1 = first time point at which child's utterances were sampled (beginning of two-word stage), and second time point at which input to the child was sampled
t2 = second time point at which child's utterances were sampled

Hindi Data

Hindi Input The input in the case of the child ISH comes from the mother and the child's 3-year-old brother (pooled in the table below). In the case of MAN, the input is provided by the child's mother. The number of uses of the different forms at two different time points, t0 and t1, for the input to the two children is shown in Table 4.2.

In terms of sheer frequency of use, the term *mE* predominates in the input to both children and at both time points. The term *andar* is used far less frequently, although its relative proportion of use increases over time. The terms *ghus* and *ghusaa* were not used in the input at all in the sessions sampled for this study.

In Table 4.3 we illustrate the range of the types of contexts of use for the different containment terms in the input to MAN and ISH at t0. The patterns of input to MAN quite clearly show greater semantic generality for *mE* (measured as contextual diversity of use) relative to *andar* at both time points. The term *andar* is used for three-dimensional Ground objects such as the house or a room. It is also used

TABLE 4.2 Frequency of Containment Terms in the Hindi Input

	ISH		MAN	
	t0	t1	t0	t1
mE 'in'	45 (93.8%)	69 (64.5%)	81 (95.3%)	46 (79.3%)
andar 'inside'	3 (6.25%)	38 (35.5%)	4 (4.7%)	12 (20.7%)
ghus/*ghus-aa* 'enter/enter-CAUSE'	0	0	0	0
Total no. of containment terms	48	107	85	58

in both static and caused or spontaneous motion contexts. The term *mE* is used not only for three-dimensional Ground objects such as a cup, a shelf, and a bottle, but also two-dimensional objects (such as a chart with pictures on it) and distributed objects (such as an array of toy animals). In addition to static and caused/spontaneous motion contexts, *mE* is used for nonspatial contexts as well—for example, to indicate a later point in time (*baad=mE* 'after in') or to refer to events such as festive occasions (e.g., 'IN the wedding'). In the case of input to the child ISH, we find that both *mE* and *andar* are used in a range of contexts in both the brother's and the mother's speech. But, as in the case of input to MAN, we find that *mE* is used in a wider variety of contexts than *andar* and with a wider range of Figure and Ground objects. The number of nonspatial uses is relatively limited compared to what was found for input to MAN.

In summary, we find that the verbs *ghus* 'enter' and *ghus-aa* 'enter-CAUSE' are not attested at all in the input samples selected for this study. At both time points, t0 and t1, the form *mE* is both more frequent and used in a wider range of static and dynamic contexts, and with a greater variety of Figure and Ground objects, than the form *andar.* If distributional patterns in the input play a predominant role in influencing children's use of these forms, we would expect a similar pattern of usage in the children's speech as well. If, on the other hand, children home in on terms that are used in a narrower range of contexts than terms that are more general, we would expect early use of *andar* despite its low frequency (relative to *mE*) in the input. Further, under the specificity hypothesis, children would be predicted to use the term *mE* in a narrower range of contexts than the adults and older children providing the input do, especially in the early stage of development, at t1.

Hindi Child Data Despite using relatively broad criteria for inclusion in our samples (excluding only immediate self-repetitions and exact imitations), at time point 1 when the children are just beginning to combine two words together we find relatively few expressions involving containment in the Hindi children's speech. The number of expressions the children use to explicitly encode containment remains low at time point 2. The data for both children are given in Table 4.4.

TABLE 4.3 Selected Types of Contexts of Use: Containment Expressions in the Hindi Input to MAN and ISH at t0

Broad context of use	Linguistic form for IN	Specific context of use	
		MAN samples	**ISH samples**
Stative	*andar*	child (staying) inside the house toys in room/cupboard	cat seated inside a location in picture book
Spontaneous motion		child inside house	child inside house
Nonspatial		—	child squishes plasticine animal within one instant
Caused motion	*mE*	bottle in water toy horse in hand oil in hair aubergine in hand book in the hand tea in toy cup toy block in a location ingredients in the vegetables (remove) oil from inside bottle (remove) toy cow from 'in' group of other animals	clarified butter and salt 'in' bread pencil in hand tea from container into cup cushion 'in' toy sofa toy cow in between two plastic blocks on rod doll in hospital
Stative		ducks (live) in water toffee in shelf food sticking in the throat ache in tooth toy lion in array of toy animals little boy (living) in the neighbourhood lullabies (sung) in village child (folding palms) in temple pictures 'in' a chart (making) bread in toy utensil hair 'in' toy horse mosquitos in the house electricity in light switch	narrating incident that happened 'in' school brother's actions taped in camera pictures of blocks 'in' box lid banana 'in' a tree picture of hippo in hand picture of snake 'in' box lid story in picture book cord of toy phone around ('in') neck picture of rhino in array of cards ache in head

TABLE 4.3 (continued) Selected Types of Contexts of Use: Containment Expressions in the Hindi Input to MAN and ISH at t0

Broad context of use	Linguistic form for IN	Specific context of use	
		MAN	**ISH**
Non-spatial	*mE* (cont'd)	language in which child is reciting lullaby eating toffees at ('in') a later point catching butterfly at ('in') a later point using the phone at ('in') a later point wearing slippers at ('in') a later point child getting off bed in a little while festivity in which fireworks are lit what is eaten at a meal	children getting into fights pictures 'in' child's knowledge [child recognizes pictures]
Spontaneous motion		toy monkey in water child in the temple doll in a box electric current from within light switch tape recorder from within which songs are heard	crocodile in water child in mother's lap plastic block in slot

TABLE 4.4 Frequency of Containment Expressions in Child Hindi

	ISH		MAN	
	t1	**t2**	**t1**	**t2**
mE 'in'	24 (96%)	11 (47.8%)	30 (91%)	45 (98%)
andar 'inside'	1 (4%)	10 (43.5%)	3 (9%)	1 (2%)
ghus 'enter'	0	2 (8.7%)	0	0
ghusaa 'enter-Cause'	0	0	0	0
Total:	25	23	33	46

Despite the few cases, the patterns are quite clear: Use of the different containment expressions by the children shows a similar pattern to that in the input. The frequency of use of *mE* is higher than that of *andar* for both ISH and MAN at time point 1 and at time point 2. The use of *andar* is relatively early in the case of MAN and ISH even in this limited sample, if we apply the criterion of early use once, spontaneously. But there is no evidence that the more specific term *andar* is used more frequently by children than by adults at t1, such that, early on, they produce a more balanced distribution of *mE* and *andar* than is found in the input. At a later point in time (t2), ISH begins to produce more uses of *andar*, but a

TABLE 4.5 Selected Types of Contexts of Use: Containment Expressions Used by Two Hindi Children, MAN and ISH, at t1

Broad context of use	Linguistic form for IN	Specific context of use	
		MAN	**ISH**
Stative	*andar*	object inside plasticine bag	
Spontaneous motion		child inside house	toy-train in block-like object
Caused motion	*mE*	ball in lap belt inside basket lipstick in eyes	puzzle piece in slot
Stative		ball in market pictures in book snakes (live) in water plasticine toy in lap of 2nd toy king (in picture book) on chair fish (in picture book) in water	child (in picture book) in lap rat (lives) in nest fish (lives) in water flowers on a bush lentil soup in toy pan vegetables in toy pan
Spontaneous motion		container in spread out skirt child in lap child in room doll on couch clip from in hair	child in lap puzzle piece in slot train in water reptile in nest

similar increase in the uses of *andar* is also observable in the input at the second time point (t1). That is, any hypothetical preference for semantically specific forms does not induce the children to overuse specific forms relative to the patterns found in the input. The verb *ghus* 'enter' is also vanishingly rare, and *ghus-aa* 'enter-CAUSE' is entirely absent in the children's data.

Turning now to the contexts of use, we can investigate whether children tend to be initially more restrictive in the range of contexts in which they use semantically general containment expressions relative to adults. Tables 4.5 and 4.6 show the contexts of use for containment expressions produced by ISH and MAN at t1 and t2. There is no evidence that the use of *mE* is restricted to a limited set of contexts at t1 in the data of either ISH or MAN. Rather, the range of contexts of their initial uses of *mE* is comparable in diversity from the beginning to that found in adult input at t0 (from a time point several months earlier; see Table 4.1), as well as to their own production at a later time point, t2. Both children use *mE* in contexts of caused and spontaneous motion to a goal as well as for describing static locations. They also use *mE* for a range of Figure objects (ball, belt, toy lipstick, puzzle piece, plasticine figure) and Ground objects (lap, basket, eyes, storybook, water). Interestingly, despite the frequent uses of *mE* for nonspatial uses in the input to MAN, we find no such uses in MAN's own spontaneous production.

TABLE 4.6 Selected Types of Contexts of Use: Containment Expressions Used by Two Hindi Children, MAN and ISH, at t2

Broad context of use	Linguistic form for IN	Specific context of use	
		MAN	**ISH**
Caused motion	*andar*	toys in location (room/cupboard/house)	
Stative			object inside room mud inside room nothing inside box of toy stamps
Spontaneous motion			object in region behind/ under chair object under child who is seated toy inside train
Spontaneous motion	*ghus/andar*		child in space between the back of a chair and the wall toy car in region under (washing) machine
Caused motion	*mE*	powder 'in' face curlers 'in' fingers curlers in hair toy animals 'in' book surface salt in hand pencil in hand tea in toy containers liquid (from) in cup lid 'in' bottle	—
Stative		character (in book) in water one bear in lap of big bear character (in picture book) in boat character (in picture book) 'in' the stairs child in bus bear (in picture book) on chair lion (lives) in jungle ducks (live) in water boy (in picture book) on scooter toys in room story in picture book toy animals 'in' book surface	brother's fight in school child in swing father in a plane elephant in picture book
Spontaneous motion		cat in car water (in picture book) in flower	fish-shaped puzzle piece in water candle falling 'in' the outside child (going) in(to) class cockroach in nest insect in tea

Conclusions from the Hindi Data The Hindi data suggest that the strong form of the specificity hypothesis is not tenable. The most general, and the most frequent, containment form, the case-marker *mE*, emerges clearly as the preferred choice for encoding containment in early child Hindi, and is used early (at t1) and frequently. The spatial nominal *andar* 'inside' does make an appearance at time point 1 but is used rarely at that point in the data examined. The verb *ghus* 'enter' appears to be dispreferred, at least by our criteria, since it is used only twice at time point 2 by ISH, and in one of these instances, the verb was used after it was used by the child's older sibling in the same recording session. The semantic specificity hypothesis would also predict that children undergeneralize more general forms initially—for example, more at t1 than t2, using them only in highly context-bound ways. Undergeneralization of a particular form relative to adult usage is not always easy to demonstrate, since the child's nonuse of a particular form in a context where it might be used is not conclusive. However, the data show that from the beginning, at t1, the children use *mE* quite productively—that is, not restricted to a few contexts where it is repeatedly used. Nor does *mE* occur only with a limited number of Ground-object denoting nominals. It is used in static contexts (e.g., flowers arrayed all over a bush, vegetables in a toy pan) and dynamic contexts (e.g., for caused motion as in putting a puzzle piece in a puzzle board; spontaneous motion as in sitting in mother's lap), and with nominals denoting a variety of Ground objects (e.g., water, page in a book, mother's lap, slot in puzzle board). This finding echoes observations in Bowerman and Choi (2001) suggesting that children have early abilities to generalize the meaning of relatively abstract relational expressions that apply across a wide range of situations (e.g., in the use of English particles such as *in*, *up*).

The only evidence for a restriction in the Hindi children's usage patterns is seen in the absence of nonspatial reference with the use of *mE* in the spontaneous production of MAN, despite a number of such uses in the input at both t0 and t1. Since spatial referents are physical objects that can be seen and observed, whether they are two- or three-dimensional, whether they are small manipulable objects or large places like rooms and houses, it is likely that the child is better able to map labels onto them than onto less imageable notions of situations or points in time.

It is possible that the distribution of the various containment forms in the child's speech is just a reflection of the types of situations that were sampled. Perhaps the rare occurrence of *ghus*, and only at t1, and the relatively infrequent uses of *andar* (especially at t1) simply reflect the fact that the relevant opportunities for their use did not arise in the recording session (cf. Gentner & Boroditsky, 2001, p. 237). Further research is required to examine such a possibility. However, *mE*, rather than *andar* or *ghus*, was used by the children in contexts where *andar* was a possible lexical choice (e.g., static location of vegetables in a toy pan, putting puzzle pieces in puzzle slots, animal running into nest), as for example in (19):

(19) *bil=mE* *bhaag* *jaa-egaa.*
nest=Loc run go-3Sg.Msc.Fut.
'will run in the nest'

This example from the child ISH (produced when she sees a cockroach on the ground) provides some supporting evidence that children acquiring Hindi have no strong preference for the forms with more restricted semantics.

Tzeltal Data

Tzeltal Input Samples of input speech were extracted from the data for the two Tzeltal children some months before t1 (t0 in Table 4.3).[14] As in Hindi, the input data from Tzeltal exhibits a number of containment forms used in a variety of constructions in both static and dynamic contexts, and with different types of Ground and Figure object nominals. This is illustrated in the examples of input from adults and from older children aged 4 to 8 years (examples 20 to 31, drawn not only from t0 but also from t1 and t2 for both children). The elements with containment semantics are in boldface type.

och—Intransitive

(20) [MET is child's grandmother, the caregiver]
MET: *yak. jich ya x-**och**-O koel ini.* [pointing]
yes thus ICP ASP-enter-3A DIR this
'Yes, thus it enters descending here.' [road-building machine]

otz-es—Transitive

(21) CAL is a cousin of the two focal children, aged 5; CAN is another cousin]
CAL: *ma x-a'w-**otz-es**-be-O ix a men antun me'tik*
NEG ASP-2E-enter-CAUS-BEN-3A ACS there that Antun Mrs.
'Don't make it [puzzle piece] enter there any more for that Antun, Mrs.'

Specific Insert-Verbs—Transitive

(22) *tik'* 'insert into container with definable entry place'
CON: *ja' x-a'-**tik'**-O me yax antz*
! ASP-2E-insert-3A that green woman
'You should *tik'*-insert the green one, woman.' [CON tells LUS how to stack rings onto stick]

(23) *lut* 'insert between two supports' [e.g., into mouth]
MET: *ja'laj la s-**lut**-O bel tz'i' te paleta-e*
! QUOT CMP 3E-insert-3A DIR dog ART lollypop-CL
'She says the dog carried the lollipop away.' [lit: 'she says the dog held-in-mouth-between-parallel supports awaywards the lollipop']

(24) *ch'ik* 'insert parallel [i.e., long-thin-thing into others]'
MET: *majtek la '-**ch'ik**-be-n y-ej i bojch, antz*
not.at.all CMP 2E-insert-BEN-1A 3E-mouth DEIC gourdbowl, woman
'You didn't insert the edge of this gourd bowl (in your mouth), woman.'

---

[14] Tzeltal input data included speech of siblings and cousins (age 4 or older) present in the interactions, excluding only LUS, one of the children under study who was often also present in the sessions for her cousin XAN.

(25) *lap* 'insert-thin-sharp thing'
MLU: *ixtal men kuchilu ma me* ***'-lap**-be-0* *ta* *'-sil*
here that knife NEG if 2E-insert-BEN-3A PREP 2E-eye
'Here that knife, don't insert (it) [sharp thin thing] in your eye.'

(26) *xij* 'insert long thin thing parallel to others'
MAX: ***xij**-a* *k'ajk'. ya x-tak'aj-O tal waj j-we'-tik*
insert-IMP fire. ICP ASP-dry-3A DIR tortilla 1E-eat.tortillas-1plincl.
'Insert [stick] [into] fire. The tortillas will toast for us to eat.'

Direction of Motion 'Inwards': *ochel*

(27) CGR: *ma me '-t'uxan-be-ik* ***ochel*** *tz' in*
NEG if 2E-make.fall-BEN-pl DIRenter PT
'Don't make him fall inwards then.' [toy man, looking into corral at chickens]

Spatial Nominal—*y-util* 'its inside'

(28) XUN (age 11)
***och**-an ta **y-ut** na-e*
enter-IMP PREP 3E-inside house-CL
'Enter to the inside of the house.'

Nominalized Containment

(29) XUN (age 11)
XUN: *ay ya s-na'-ix s-**tik'**-el*
EXIST ICP 3E-know-ACS 3E-insert-NOM
'She already knows how to *tik'*-insert them.' (rings onto stick)

(30) CAN (age 4):
*ma (j)-na'-ix y-**otz**-es-el a ini*
NEG (1E)-know-ACS 3E-enter-CAUS-NOM DEIC this
'(I) don't yet know how to put this one in.' [lit: its enter-CAUSE-ing]

Static (Adjectival) Context

(31) CON: ***pach**-al-0*
be.sitting.bowl.shaped.object-DIS-3A
'It (a bowl-shaped object with corngruel in it) is sitting.'

The frequencies of use of the different containment terms in the Tzeltal input at t0 and t1 are summarized in Table 4.7. Children acquiring Tzeltal hear both general verbs for "entering" events such as *och* and *otzes*, much more specific insertion verbs such as *lut*, *ch'ik*, and *tik'* (and a number of others), and the spatial nominal *y-util*. Among the specific insertion verbs there are 17 different roots, including *ch'ol* 'pour-liquid-into-container,' *kap* 'insert-object-into-group,' *baj* 'hammer-in,' *matz'aj* 'get-stuck-in,' *tz'ot* 'twist-into-tight-fit,' *joy* 'put into encircling relation,'

TABLE 4.7 Frequency of Containment Terms in the Tzeltal Input [Roots Are in Boldface]

Input stem	LUS		LUS Total	XAN		XAN Total
	t0	t1		t0	t1	
Spontaneous motion						
och 'enter'	30 (41%)	10 (14%)	40	41 (42%)	37 (54%)	78
matz'*-aj* 'get.stuck in.mud'	0	0	0	6 (6%)	0	6
Caused motion—general verb						
otz*-es* 'enter-CAUSE'	1	5 (7%)	6	27(28%)	0	27
Directional—general						
och*-el* 'inwards, entering'	3	2	5	4	2	6
Caused motion—specific insertion verbs						
chop	0	0	0	0	1	1
chup	0	0	0	0	2	2
ch'ik	0	0	0	0	5 (7%)	5
ch'ol	1	1	2	3	0	3
kap	0	1	1	1	0	1
kojk*-on/****kojk****-ej*	3	0	3	0	0	0
latz	0	1	1	0	1	1
lut	0	1	1	0	2	2
pach	2	0	2	0	1	1
puk'	4	10 (14%)	14	0	7 (10%)	7
tik'	3	34 (47%)	37	2	0	2
t'um*(-an)*	1	0	1	0	0	0
tz'ap	1	0	1	0	1	1
xij	0	0	0	0	6 (8%)	6
xoj	1	0	1	0	0	0
Stative/Nonmotion IN words						
otz*-es-el* 'enter-CAUSE-NOM'	0	0		9 (9%)	2	11
jul*-el* 'pierce-NOM'	1	0	1	0	0	0
lut*-ul* 'inserted. between-ADJ'	4	0	4	0	0	0
pach*-ajtik* 'in.bowl-ADJ.PL'	1	0	1	0	0	0
pach*-al* 'in.bowl-ADJ'						
tik'*-lay-el*	0	0	0	0	1	1
'insert-DIST-NOM'	0	0	0	1	0	1
*s-****tik'****-el* '3E-insert-NOM'						
t'um*-ul* 'inserted.in.	0	1	1	0	0	0
water-ADJ'	2	1	3	0	0	0
xoj*-ol* 'inserted-ADJ'						
*y-****ut****/y-****ut****-il* 'its inside'	1	0	1	0	0	0
NOUN	13 (18%)	5 (7%)	18	3	0	3
*y-****ol****/y-****ol****-il* 'its middle/						
between' NOUN	1	0	1	0	0	0
Total IN words:	73	72	145	97	68	165

jul 'pierce-into,' *jut* 'pierce-into,' *lut* 'stick-in-between,' *pach* 'be-in bowl-shaped-container,' *puk* 'mix-into liquid,' *suk* 'put-in stopper,' *tik'* 'insert into container with opening,' *t'uman* 'immerse in liquid,' *xij* 'insert long thing lengthwise,' *xoj* 'put single object into/around another.' Children hear these verbs used both in their transitive forms and in their stative and nominalized forms.

The more general verb *och* 'enter' is also frequent, and for XAN is clearly the most frequent. However, *och* is not as prevalent as the form *mE* in Hindi. *Och* appears in a variety of syntactic forms (in intransitive form, in the directional *ochel*, causativized as *otz-es*, nominalized in *otz-es-el*). Like *mE* in Hindi, the Tzeltal children also hear *och* used in metaphorical (temporal) contexts, as in:

(32) XUN (age 11)

ya	*x-och-O*	*k'op*	*i*
ICP	ASP-enter-3A	fighting	DEIC

'This fighting will enter [i.e., begin].'

Turning to contexts of usage, we illustrate the types of contexts of use for the different contaiment terms in the input at t0 in Table 4.8.

Table 4.8 shows that *och* (along with its causativized form *otz-es*) is not only the most frequent containment term in the Tzeltal input, but it is also the most semantically general, as measured by the range of different contexts of use.[15] *Och* occurs in canonical containment situations of objects going into containers (ball into shoe, puzzle piece into board, frog into pot) and extends to tight containment (popbeads into each other, string into/onto toy animal). It also occurs in situations where the containment is two-dimensional (a split in a balloon) or involves movement into a region rather than a container (ball under chair, chicken into house, child into cart, child into place near the house where her brother is playing, person into house). *Och* also extends to temporal (or metaphorical) contexts (child entering school, work entering computer, child beginning (entering into) singing). A few static contexts are also represented with the nominalized form of *otzes* (*otzes-el*), and a number of noncontainment verbs co-occur with the directional *ochel* to indicate action toward containment (put into, immerse in liquid) or into a contained region (into house, between two things), or to express static events (looking inwards, smelling inwards).

In contrast with the Hindi data, however, the Tzeltal input also contains a range of other containment terms specialized to much more specific situations. A number of these occur in only one or two kinds of context in the data (*xij* for inserting sticks of firewood into the fire, *lut* for carrying or sticking something in the mouth, *pach* for wanting, carrying, or having corn gruel in a bowl, *puk'* for mixing corn gruel in a bowl). *Tik'* 'insert into container' is the only specific verb that extends to a variety of different kinds of contexts (puzzle piece into board, different objects into pocket or bag), including to the metaphorical insertion of anger into the child's

[15]We conjecture that child-directed speech from the older children (included as "input" in our study) may have contributed to the skewing toward semantically general expressions in the input.

TABLE 4.8 Selected Types of Contexts of Use: Containment Expressions in the Tzeltal Input to LUS and XAN at t0

Broad context of use	Linguistic form for IN	Specific context of use	
		LUS	XAN
Caused motion: general	*otz-es*	toys into toy truck	toy into bag hung around child's neck ring onto finger string onto toy car piece into puzzle doll's head back into doll's neck something into toy cart
	V + *ochel* + *y-ut(il)*	toy animals	toy animal, put away in house
Caused motion: specific	*ch'ol*	pouring water for toy animals	pouring water for toy animals pour water into toy cups
	tik'	Alux got his father angry (anger 'inserted') insert self	toys into blue sack toys into toy bag
	kap	—	insert self in between something (off camera)
	kojkon/kojkaj	pour water into container	—
	pach	telling child to hold it upright, don't spill [corngruel in bowl] carry [bowl of corngruel] upright	—
	puk'	mixing corngruel in water for child	—
Caused motion + direction	*t'uman* + *ochel*	dog inserted self in water	—
	xoj	frog's head into shoe	—
Spontaneous motion	*och*	Alux into school children into school permission to enter the school children entering house ball into shoe frog into pot, in book owl into tree, in book 'travellers' into toy car nothing in pot, in book toy animal into truck self into place where brother is playing toy into space between coffee bag and wall a load into truck	about child going to school tying string onto/into toy animal turkey into bucket pop beads into each other split in balloon child into house toys in back of toy truck toy car's tire into mud puzzle piece into board work into computer doll's head into neck something into cart

TABLE 4.8 (continued) Selected Types of Contexts of Use: Containment Expressions in the Tzeltal Input to LUS and XAN at t0

Broad context of use	Linguistic form for IN	Specific context of use	
		LUS	**XAN**
	och, y-ol	frog into water, in book	—
	och, y-ut	frog into water, in book	—
	matz'aj	—	toy car stuck in mud pretend announcement that car is stuck in mud
Nonmotion (nominalized or spatial noun)	*otz-es-el*	—	popbeads into each other piece into puzzle
	jul-el	child getting injection	—
	tik'-lay-el	—	toys into blue sack
	V+ *y-util*	dog smelling inside of pot, in book dog licks inside of pot, in book dog looking into pot, in book	toy car's inside place work inside computer
Stative/ locative	*och-el*	—	toy man looking in at the chickens
	lut-ul	boy on deer's antlers, in frog book	—
	pach-ajtik	bowl with contents upright	—
	xoj-ol	frog's head into shoe	—
	t'um-ul	frog in water in picture book	—
	y-ut	toy chicken thrown into the house dog in water, in book	—
	y-util	inside the little pot in book	—

father! While these terms (except for *tik'*) are used with far less frequency than *och* and *otzes*, they are used reliably in these very specific contexts.

The spatial nominal *y-ut(il)* is not used much in XAN's input data, and in LUS's data it is used mainly for one referent–inside the house. It also extends to inside a corral and inside a pot, and to the region inside water. A second spatial nominal *y-olil* 'its middle/between' is an occasional alternate for 'between' situations.

Tzeltal Child Data The data for the two Tzeltal children at time 1 and time 2 are summarized in Table 4.9. As in the case of Hindi, there are very few expressions involving containment (a total of 28 tokens in 14 hours of recording), and little diversity in the range of containment terms in the speech of the children acquiring Tzeltal at time point 1. All of these containment expressions are used in motion contexts, either spontaneous or caused. The verb used predominantly is the general verb *och* 'enter' (21/28 utterances). The other verbs used occasionally

TABLE 4.9 Frequency of Containment Terms in Child Tzeltal

	LUS		XAN	
	t1	t2	t1	t2
och 'enter'	8 (72.7%)	14 (73.7%)	13 (76.5%)	14 (58.3%)
otz-es 'make enter'	1 (9%)	0	0	2 (8.3%)
ch'ik 'insert [long thin thing parallel]'	0	3 (15.8%)	4 (23.5%)	4 (16.7%)
tik' 'insert [into container with opening]'	0	1 (5.2%)	0	2 (8.3%)
lut 'insert between'	2 (18.2%)	0	0	2 (8.3%)
y-ut(il) 'its inside'	0	1 (5.2%)	0	0
Total no. of containment terms	11	19	17	24

TABLE 4.10 Selected Types of Contexts of Use: Containment Expressions Used by Two Tzeltal Children, XAN and LUS, at t1

Broad context of use	Linguistic form for IN	Specific context of use	
		LUS	XAN
Caused motion	*otz-es*	puzzle piece	
Caused motion specific	*ch'ik*	—	firewood into fire
	lut	dog taking child's lollipop away in its mouth	—
Spontaneous motion	*och*	chicken into house puzzle piece into puzzle board chicken into yard	tortilla into container firewood into fire water into container into cart girl into toy cart bug into hole fly into crack fly under stool

include *otz-es* 'enter-CAUSE' (used once by LUS), as well as two semantically specific insertion verbs: *ch'ik* 'insert between' (by XAN) and *lut* 'insert tightly between' (by LUS). The spatial nominal *y-util* is not used at time 1 by either child, in either static or dynamic contexts.

The data for t2, about five months later, show that by now, the children are producing a somewhat higher number of containment expressions (n = 43 tokens in 7.5 hours of recording). The use of *och* 'enter' remains high (28/43 uses), and the number of uses of the caused motion verbs increases. These include the general 'insert' verb *otz-es* 'enter-CAUSE' and three specific verbs: *ch'ik* 'insert between parallel long thin things,' *lut* 'insert tightly between,' and *tik'* 'insert into container.' The spatial nominal *y-util* makes an appearance in LUS's data, but only in a single

TABLE 4.11 Selected Types of Contexts of Use: Containment Expressions Used by Two Tzeltal Children, XAN and LUS, at t2

Broad context of use	Linguistic form for IN	Specific context of use	
		LUS	XAN
Caused motion—general	*otz-es*		hand into puppet corncob into pail of corn kernels
Caused motion— specific	*ch'ik*		gum into mouth bowl edge into mouth [of baby] making toy duck insert her finger into its mouth
	tik'	mud into container	toy into cup
Spontaneous motion	*och*	flower into bucket handle onto toy pail balloon into bag something into car something over there ring onto ring toy something entered over there hand into puppet	make something enter her hand into puppet cows into box toy man into car toy into container ribbon in cup into her drink
Stative	*y-ut*	mother inside the house	

instance, in a static context. At both time points, the containment terms are used by the children in ways that are contextually appropriate (Tables 4.10 and 4.11).

Conclusions from the Tzeltal Data We have seen that the children's preferred form for talking about containment in Tzeltal is neither the unconflated general form *y-util* 'its-inside' nor the very specific verbs *ch'ik*, *lut*, *tik'*. Rather it is the general verb of spontaneous motion into containment, *och* 'enter,' which appears early and is used frequently at both t1 and t2. This is followed by the specific 'insert' verbs *ch'ik*, *lut*, and *tik'*, while the spatial nominal *y-util* emerges late.

Perhaps it is the case that Tzeltal children show a preference for specificity in a different way—perhaps they undergeneralize *och* 'enter' initially, and use it only in highly context-bound ways. However, as shown in Table 4.10, the use of *och* is already quite productive at t1, occurring with nominals denoting a variety of Ground objects (e.g., container, cart, crack, stool, hole, house, yard, puzzleboard) and Figure objects (e.g., tortilla, water, bug, fly, girl, puzzle piece, chicken). Nor do we find the opposite pattern, with children *over*generalizing the very specific verbs. Verbs such as *tik'* and *lut* are used appropriately, suggesting that children are respecting the selectional restrictions of these very specific verbs. A similar finding is reported by Choi and Bowerman (1991) for Korean children's early uses of semantically specific verbs (e.g., put into loose- vs. tight-fitting containment).

The preference in Tzeltal for *och* over specific verbs like *tik'*, *ch'ik*, etc., seems to confirm the conclusion drawn from the Hindi data that the strong form of the specificity hypothesis is not supported. Taken in conjunction with the Hindi data, this might suggest strong support in favour of a position that children prefer more frequent and/or semantically general forms over more specific ones. However, the Tzeltal children's earlier and more frequent use of the very specific verbs (*ch'ik*, *lut*, *tik'*) relative to the more general spatial nominal *y-util* suggests that children do not always prefer general, frequent forms either. While the frequency of the specific verb *tik'* in the input appears to be high (34 times in LUS's t1 data), in fact this is true for only one of the children and is due to the particular activity of playing with a puzzle board. But the frequency with which *y-util*, a general term, is used in the input is as high as or higher than the frequency of each of the specific verbs for both children. Based on input frequency alone, we might expect that the specific verbs and the spatial nominal should be used with roughly comparable frequencies by the children. However, we found that the specific forms were used more frequently than *y-util*, which was the least frequently used form for both children. The minimal use of *y-util* (and possibly, of Hindi *andar*) might be related to the fact that, like English *inside*, *y-util* is an optional, extra-specific manner of expressing location at the inside of a space construed as a container. This optional specificity contrasts with the obligatory specificity in the Tzeltal transitive verbs: In the latter case, if the situation is one captured by a specific verb, the specific verb will almost always be used.

Further, a number of the semantically specific verbs that share the semantic space of containment with *och* and *otzes* are also very early in the child data. One might want to argue that the specific verbs are used so infrequently in the children's data that we can dismiss them, that they are perhaps just frozen expressions. Given the nature of our data (naturally occurring production) we cannot entirely rule this out. However, each of these verbs is also infrequent in the input speech, and for a good reason: Their specificity means that they apply in a very narrow range of situations, and unless those situations arise in the sessions being filmed, the verbs will not appear. In another sense these verb *types* are not so infrequent: In the input data a total of 16 semantically specific transitive verb roots are used (as well as one intransitive: *matz'aj* 'to be stuck in mud'); they appear also in stative and nominalized forms. In both the children's speech and in the input speech, these verbs crop up whenever the relevant well-defined kind of situation occurs. The fact that these not very frequent verbs are acquired early suggests that there is in fact something salient about a verb used in only one or two different contexts, if those contexts happen to be ones important to a child.

GENERAL DISCUSSION

Our study shows that children talking about containment use relatively abstract relational forms early, irrespective of their syntactic category (case markers, verbs, or spatial nouns or adjectives), and they produce them frequently and in varied contexts of use. The general case-marker *mE* is used more than all other forms in Hindi, while in Tzeltal, the general verb *och* 'enter' is used more than the specific verb forms, even when the latter are pooled together. A semantic specificity preference does not play a strong role in children's acquisition of containment expressions in Hindi and Tzeltal. Children do not associate semantically general expressions with concrete, narrowly specified event schemas for a protracted period of their development. Any preference for sticking to very narrow, object-specific schemata in the use of a relational word, if it exists at all, must occur quite early and be relatively short-lived. Children appear capable of creating quite general relational categories at an early age: *mE* is used appropriately and productively in Hindi child language as early as 20 to 21 months. The only restriction we observed is in a lack of extensions of *mE* to the temporal domain.

Whereas children can generalize rapidly, our crosslinguistic comparison also shows that they are not driven by a global preference to construct a semantically general category of containment. In this respect, our findings echo the observations in Choi and Bowerman (1991) showing early, language-specific categorization of motion events in children acquiring English and Korean. Hindi children appropriately use very general terms such as *mE* which abstracts away from the distinction between stative and (caused) motion events, while Tzeltal children accurately restrict use of the general verbs *och* and *otzes* to spontaneous and caused motion contexts, respectively. Children are also appropriate in their use of the Tzeltal "insert" verbs which distinguish between very specific varieties of containment. The types of overgeneralization errors that one might expect if children were motivated by a tendency to create a general category of containment are not attested in these data. (See Narasimhan, 2005 for similar arguments regarding the semantic category of "Agent.")

It might be argued that early use of semantically specific verbs in Tzeltal constitutes evidence for a semantic specificity preference. For instance, despite the paucity of specific "insertion" verbs in the data, Tzeltal children are using several distinct IN verbs (*och*, *otzes*, *lut*, *ch'ik*) at an early age, which is compatible with the findings for Tzeltal verbs in other semantic domains. Semantically specific verbs are an important part of the vocabulary of Tzeltal children from their first productions at age 1;6 (Brown, 1998; see also Narasimhan & Gullberg, 2006). De León (1999a, 1999b, 2001, this volume) reports similar findings for children learning the closely related language Tzotzil, and Tardif (2006) reports the same for Chinese. A psychological explanation for the early acquisition of semantically specific verbs in languages like Tzeltal, Tzotzil, and Chinese was proposed by Gentner and Boroditsky (2001), who relate the early use of semantically specific verbs in these languages to the fact that such verbs refer to coherent event schemata that are more highly individuated and hence relatively perceptually salient for children. Further, as pointed out in Brown (1998), Tzeltal children's early use of specific verbs might be attributed to the highly differentiated patterns of lexicalization in Tzeltal (Brown, 1994, 2001) rather than to any semantic specificity preference. Faced with a rich set of forms encoding fine distinctions in one semantic domain after another, children acquiring Tzeltal may learn early to be conservative in generalizing the meanings of new forms.

Rapid, error-free generalization of language-specific semantic categories, as shown in our study, is something of a paradox. As many researchers have pointed out, the elements of a situation that are encoded by a relational expression are not easily inferred, suggesting that there might be a protracted period of learning characterized by restricted patterns of generalization and/or early errors. To resolve this paradox, Bowerman and Choi (2001, p. 497) suggest that "children construct spatial semantic categories over time on the basis of the way they hear words used in the input" but they also draw on "perceptual sensitivities and conceptual biases they bring with them to the task." In the process of acquiring the meanings of words, children "do not waste time on crazy possibilities and have some sense of what properties of situations are likely to matter" (Bowerman & Choi, 2001, p. 503). At the same time, characteristics of the language influence children's construction of semantic categories as well, including the *frequency* with which given words are used in the input, the *consistency* of the range of referents for which the words are used, the *number* of words used to label a particular semantic domain, and the *degree of overlap* in the referents for which different words are used (Bowerman & Choi, 2001, p. 498). Such a multifactorial account may not only explain the early and rapid acquisition of terms in the domain of containment in children learning different languages, but also children's sensitivity to the different factors that influence semantic category construction in their language (see Narasimhan & Gullberg, 2006). Further research is required to identify the relative contribution of the different factors that influence vocabulary acquisition in children learning different languages.

REFERENCES

Ameka, F., & Levinson, S.C., Eds. (2007). Towards a typology of locative predication. [Special issue] *Linguistics, 45*(5/6).

Bowerman, M. (1973). *Early syntactic development: A crosslinguistic study with special reference to Finnish.* Cambridge: Cambridge University Press.

Bowerman, M. (1996). Learning how to structure space for language: A crosslinguistic perspective. In P. Bloom, M. A. Peterson, L. Nadel, & M. F. Garrett (Eds.), *Space and language* (pp. 385–436). Cambridge, MA: MIT Press.

Bowerman, M. (2005). Why can't you "open" a nut or "break" a cooked noodle? Learning covert object categories in action word meanings. In L. Gershkoff-Stowe & D. H. Rakison (Eds.), *Building object categories in developmental time* (pp. 209–243). Hillsdale, NJ: Erlbaum.

Bowerman, M. (2007). Containment, support and beyond: Constructing topological spatial categories in first language acquisition. In M. Aurnague, M. Hickmann, & L. Vieu (Eds.), *The categorization of spatial entities in language and cognition: Developmental consequences of linguistic typology* (pp. 117–203). Amsterdam: John Benjamins.

Bowerman, M., Brown, P., Eisenbeiss, S., Narasimhan, B., & Slobin, D.I. (2002). Putting things in places: Developmental consequences of linquistic typology. In E. Clark (Ed.), *Proceedings of the Stanford Child Language Research Forum*, April 2002. Retrieved from: http://cslipublications.stanford.edu/hand/miscpubsonline.html

Bowerman, M., & Choi, S. (2001). Shaping meanings for language: Universal and language-specific in the acquisition of spatial semantic categories. In M. Bowerman & S. C. Levinson (Eds.), *Language acquisition and conceptual development* (pp. 475–511). Cambridge, UK: Cambridge University Press.

Bowerman, M., & Choi, S. (2004). Space under construction: Language-specific spatial categorization in first language acquisition. In D. Gentner & S. Goldin-Meadow (Eds.), *Language in mind: Advances in the study of language and cognition* (pp. 387–428). Cambridge, MA: MIT Press.

Bowerman, M., de León, L., & Choi, S. (1995). Verbs, particles, and spatial semantics: Learning to talk about spatial actions in typologically different languages. In E. V. Clark (Ed.), *The Proceedings of the 27th Annual Child Language Research Forum* (pp. 101–110). Stanford, CA: Stanford University Center for Language and Information.

Bowerman, M., & Pederson, E. (1992). Topological relations picture series. *Space stimuli kit 1.2.* Max Planck Institute for Psycholinguistics, Nijmegen.

Brown, P. (1994). The INs and ONs of Tzeltal static locative expressions: The semantics of static descriptions of location. In J. Haviland & S. C. Levinson (Eds.), *Spatial conceptualization in Mayan languages* [Special issue] *Linguistics, 32*, 743–790.

Brown, P. (1998). Children's first verbs in Tzeltal: Evidence for an early verb category. In E. Lieven (Ed.) [Special issue] *Linguistics, 36*(4),713–753.

Brown, P. (2001). Learning to talk about motion UP and DOWN in Tzeltal: Is there a language-specific bias for verb learning? In M. Bowerman & S. C. Levinson (Eds.), *Language acquisition and conceptual development* (pp. 512–543). Cambridge, UK: Cambridge University Press.

Brown, P. (2006). A sketch grammar of Tzeltal space. In S. C. Levinson & D. P. Wilkins (Eds.), *The grammar of space* (pp. 230–272). Cambridge, UK: Cambridge University Press.

Brown, P. (2007). Culture-specific influences on semantic development: Acquiring the Tzeltal 'benefactive' construction. In B. B. Pfeiler (Ed.), *Learning indigenous languages: Child language acquisition in Mesoamerica* (pp. 119–154). Berlin: Mouton de Gruyter.

Brown, P. (2008). Verb specificity and argument realization in Tzeltal child language. In M. Bowerman & P. Brown (Eds.), *Crosslinguistic perspectives on argument structure: Implications for language acquisition* (pp. 167–189). Mahwah, NJ: Erlbaum.

Brown, R. (1973). *A first language: The early stages.* Cambridge, MA: Harvard University Press.

Carey, S. (1978). The child as word learner. In M. Halle, J. Bresnan, & G. A. Miller (Eds.), *Linguistic theory and psychological reality* (pp. 264–293). Cambridge MA: MIT Press.

Choi, S., & Bowerman, M. (1991). Learning to express motion events in English and Korean: The influence of language-specific lexicalization patterns. *Cognition,* 41, 83–121.

Clark, E. V. (1973). Nonlinguistic strategies and the acquisition of word meanings. *Cognition, 2,* 161–182.

Clark, E. V. (1993). *The lexicon in acquisition.* Cambridge, UK: Cambridge University Press.

Coventry, K. R., Prat-Sala, M., & Richards, L.V. (2001). The interplay between geometry and function in the comprehension of "over," "under," "above" and "below." *Journal of Memory and Language, 44,* 376–398.

de León, L, (1999a). Verb roots and caregiver speech in early Tzotzil acquisition. In B. A. Fox, D. Jurafsky, & L. A. Michaelis (Eds.), *Cognition and function in language* (pp. 99–119). Stanford, CA: Stanford University Center for Language and Information.

de León, L, (1999b). Verb roots in Tzotzil early syntactic development. *International Journal of Bilingualism, 3,* 219–240.

de León, L, (2001). Why Tzotzil (Mayan) children prefer verbs: The role of linguistic and cultural factors. In M. Almgren, A. Barreña, M-J. Ezeizabarrena, I. Idiazabal, & B. MacWhinney (Eds.), *Research in child language acquisition: Proceedings of the 8th Conference of the International Association for the Study of Child Language* (pp. 947–967). San Sebastián, Spain.

Fisher, C. D., Hall, G., Rakowitz, S., & Gleitman, L. R. (1994). When it is better to receive than to give: Syntactic and conceptual constraints on vocabulary growth. In L. R. Gleitman & B. Landau (Eds.), *The acquisition of the lexicon* (pp. 333–375). Cambridge, MA: MIT Press.

Gathercole, V. C. Mueller, Thomas, E. M., & Evans, D. (2000). What's in a noun? Welsh-, English-, and Spanish-speaking children see it differently. *First Language 20*, 55–90.

Gentner, D. (1978). On relational meaning: The acquisition of verb meaning. *Child Development, 49*, 988–998.

Gentner, D. (1982). Why nouns are learned before verbs: Linguistic relativity vs. natural partitioning. In S. A. Kuczaj II (Ed.), *Language development: Vol. 2. Language, thought, and culture* (pp. 301–334). Hillsdale, NJ: Erlbaum.

Gentner, D., & Boroditsky, L. (2001). Individuation, relativity, and early word learning. In M. Bowerman & S. C. Levinson (Eds.), *Language acquisition and conceptual development* (pp. 215–256). Cambridge, UK: Cambridge University Press.

Gleitman, L.R..(1990). The structural sources of verb meanings. *Language Acquisition, 1*, 3–55.

Goldberg, A. (1995). *Constructions: A construction grammar approach to argument structure*. Chicago: University of Chicago Press.

Haviland, John. (1994). Verbs and shapes in (Zinacantec) Tzotzil: The case of "insert." *Functión, 15–16*, 83–117.

Huttenlocher, J., Smiley, P., & Charney, R. (1983). Emergence of action categories in the child: Evidence from verb meanings. *Psychological Review, 90*, 72–93.

Imai, M., Haryu, E., & Okada, H. (2002). Is verb learning easier than noun learning for Japanese children? 3-year-old Japanese children's knowledge about object names and action names. In B. Skarabela, S. Fish, & A. H.-J. Do (Eds.), *Proceedings of the 26th Annual Boston University Conference on Language Development* (Vol. 1, pp. 324–335). Somerville, MA: Cascadilla Press.

Jackendoff, R. (1983). *Semantics and cognition*. Cambridge, MA: MIT Press.

Jackendoff, R. (1990). *Semantic structures*. Cambridge, MA: MIT Press.

Jensen de López. K. (2002). *Baskets and body-parts. A cross-cultural and crosslinguistic investigation of children's spatial cognition and language.* Unpublished doctoral dissertation, Institute of Psychology, University of Aarhus, Denmark.

Johnston, J. R. (1984). Acquisition of locative meanings: *Behind* and *in front of*. *Journal of Child Language, 11*, 407–422.

Johnson, J. R., & Slobin, D.I. (1979). The development of static locative expressions in English, Italian, Serbo-Croatian, and Turkish. *Journal of Child Language, 6*, 529–545.

Landau, B., & Stecker, D. S. (1990). Objects and places: Syntactic geometric representations in early lexical learning. *Cognitive Development, 5*, 287–312.

Levinson, S. C. (1994). Vision, shape and linguistic description: Tzeltal body-part terminology and object description. *Linguistics, 32*, 791–855.

Levinson, S. C., & Meira, S. (2003). "Natural concepts" in the spatial topological domain—Adpositional meanings in crosslinguistic perspective: An exercise in semantic typology. *Language, 79*, 485–516.

Levinson, S. C., & Wilkins, D. P. (Eds.). (2006). *Grammars of space*. Cambridge, UK: Cambridge University Press.

Lucy, J. (1992). *Grammatical categories and cognition: A case study of the linguistic relativity hypothesis*. Cambridge, UK: Cambridge University Press.

Majid, A., Enfield, N. J., & van Staden, M. (Eds.). (2006). Parts of the body: Crosslinguistic categorization [Special issue] *Language Sciences*, *28*(2–3), 137–360.

McCune-Nicolich, L. (1981). The cognitive bases of relational words in the single-word period. *Journal of Child Language, 8*,15–34.

Miller, G. A., & Johnson-Laird, P. N. (1976). *Language and perception*. Cambridge, UK: Cambridge University Press.

Mintz, T., & Gleitman, L. (2002). Adjectives really do modify nouns: The incremental and restricted nature of early adjective acquisition. *Cognition*, *84*(3), 267–293.

Narasimhan, B. (2005). Splitting the action of 'agent': Case-marking in early child Hindi. *Journal of Child Language*, *32*, 787–803.

Narasimhan, B., & Gulberg, M. (2006). Perspective shifts in event descriptions in Tamil child language. *Journal of Child Language, 33*, 99–124.

Ninio, A. (1999a). Pathbreaking verbs in syntactic development and the question of prototypical transitivity. *Journal of Child Language, 26*, 619–653.

Ninio, A. (1999b). Model learning in syntactic development: Intransitive verbs. In M. M. Vihman (Ed.) [Special issue] *International Journal of Bilingualism,*

Piaget, J., & Inhelder, B. (1956). *The child's conception of space*. London: Routledge & Kegan Paul.

Slobin, D. I. (1973). Cognitive prerequisites for the development of grammar. In C. A. Ferguson & D. I. Slobin (Eds.), *Studies of language development* (pp.175–108). New York: Holt, Rinehart, & Winston.

Slobin, D. I. (1985). Crosslinguistic evidence for the language-making capacity. In D. I Slobin (Ed.), *The crosslinguistic study of language acquisition* (Vol. 2, pp. 1157–1256). Hillsdale, NJ: Erlbaum.

Slobin, D. I., Bowerman, M, Brown, P., Eisenbeiss, S., & Narasimhan, B. (in press). Putting things in places: Developmental consequences of linguistic typology. In J. Bohnemeyer & E. Pederson (Eds.), *Event representations in language and cognition*. Cambridge, UK: Cambridge University Press.

Talmy, L. (1985). Lexicalization patterns: semantic structure in lexical forms. In T. Shopen (Ed.), *Language typology and syntactic description* (Vol. 3, pp. 57–149). Cambridge, UK: Cambridge University Press.

Talmy, L. (1991). Path to realization: A typology of event conflation. *Proceedings of the 17th Annual Meeting of the Berkeley Linguistics Society* (pp. 48–519.). Berkeley, CA: University of California.

Tardif, T. (2006). But are they really verbs? Chinese words for actions. In K. Hirsh-Pasek & R. Golinkoff (Eds.), *Action meets word: How children learn verbs* (pp. 477–498). Oxford: Oxford University Press.

Theakston, A. L., Lieven, E. V. M., Pine, J. M., Rowland, C. F. (2004). Semantic generality, input frequency and the acquisition of syntax. *Journal of Child Language*, *31*(1):62–99.

Wierzbicka, A. (1996). *Semantics: Primes and universals*. Oxford: Oxford University Press.

Part III

Crosslinguistic Patterning and Events, Paths, and Causes

Personal Tribute

LEONARD TALMY

It is a pleasure to add to the thanks that will be accruing in this volume for Melissa Bowerman. Melissa's work and mine have been interacting for decades now—over the same period that we have been friends.

In our earliest interactions, Melissa's work showed that the overgeneralizations in the motion sentences of children acquiring English often follow the characteristic typological pattern that I had found in English for representing an event of Motion. In this pattern, the verb expresses Manner or Cause, while the satellite that follows it expresses Path. And Melissa found her children saying things like "Don't hug me off my chair" and "I'll jump that down" (about to jump onto a mat floating atop the tub water and force it down to the bottom). Melissa's corroboration of this pattern in such basic cognitive processes as the unselfconscious semantic–syntactic creations of children provided my first reassurance that the typology I was working on might have some psychological validity.

All along, Melissa has been a leader in the art of perceiving fine distinctions in semantic domains, notably that of space, and of determining how languages package them in different ways. Her work on how languages variously group together fine-grained concepts in the collective semantic area of containment, support, attachment, and girding stands out in this regard. Her work in teasing such distinctions apart has helped my own in this area, and most recently has amplified my latest paper on the fundamental elements of spatial schemas across languages. In this vein, Melissa's unsinkable efforts to ferret out the ineffable distinctions between the two Dutch prepositions *op* and *aan* yielded a result that addressed my work on force dynamics. Thus, she found that, while both forms indicate spatial contact between a Figure and a Ground, *op* indicates a Figure supported comfortably in what is conceptualized as a natural rest state through its contact with a Ground, whereas *aan* indicates that the Figure is being actively maintained against gravity or other pulling force through its contact with the Ground. Accordingly, flesh is said to be *op* the bones of a live person, but *aan* the bones of a dead person.

Later, Melissa formulated the strongest challenge to the view that, in certain conceptual domains such as that of space, there is a universally available inventory of fundamental conceptual elements that combine in different arrangements to form the schemas found in different languages. She proposed, on the contrary, that languages show differences in their spatial schemas idiosyncratic enough that they could not be traced to any universal elements. Accordingly, children acquiring such languages could not have any innate or prelinguistic advantage in learning the morphemes with such idiosyncratic elements and must rather learn them the hard way, purely from observation of adult usage. Since I did and do hold with the existence of a universally available inventory of basic spatial schematic elements, Melissa and I differ on this issue. Perhaps it is impolite to disagree with the person one is in the midst of praising. But I include this disagreement here because the strength of her evidence and arguments for the nonuniversalist position have forced me to refine the tenets of the universalist position and to better define where universality might hold and where open-ended language differences might enter.

It has been a pleasure over the years to discuss with Melissa the wonders and mysteries of language—as well as of philosophy, life, and the concerns that enter a friendship.

Personal Tribute

JIDONG CHEN

Life is a string of events, and knowing Melissa Bowerman and working with her on the Event Representation project has been one of the most crucial events in my life. Melissa is a real mentor, a model scientist, and she has been a mother and friend to me. She has so many amazing qualities that I hold in great respect and awe. I am blessed to have been her student—I have learned so many invaluable lessons from her both in academics and in life. Through her, I have come to realize what I want to do, and can do, as a researcher, teacher, and human being.

She is so famous but so modest, caring, and encouraging. That was my first impression of Melissa even before I started my graduate studies under her supervision. I was struck by her candor and warmth in her e-mails. She has always been an unfailing source of support during my years of study at the Max Planck Institute for Psycholinguistics in Nijmegen.

She led me into the extremely interesting field of first language development and cognitive development from a cross-linguistic perspective. Spatial relations, cutting and breaking events, and placement events—she presented a fascinating world of linguistic diversity and early language-specific learning! She totally changed my view of linguistic research: Never be wed to theories, look at real data (especially crosslinguistic data), and let the data speak. Be prepared to do fastidious work on the data, be extremely careful in the interpretation of the data, and be open to alternative explanations for the data.

Melissa Bowerman is an amazing teacher: She always treats students as equals and engages a great amount of time and effort to help. She has infinite patience with questions, puzzles, doubts, and frustrations. So many times she walked me through the theories and the statistics again and again until I fully understood; so many times she looked at my data line by line together with me, seeking the patterns; and so many times she read my draft papers again and again, and each time she filled every page with detailed comments and suggestions. She is sharp and critical, yet she always delivers her criticism in a very kind—and convincing—way.

She listens to students' ideas, even when they are very immature and fragmentary, and she manages to provide immediate insights that untangle the mess of those ideas. She is a perfectionist: Truthfulness and precision in regard to the data are what I learned most from her. Whenever I felt stuck in my research, discussion with her always pointed me to a new horizon; whenever I was in despair, she provided strength and hope.

In addition to all her amazing qualities as a researcher and teacher, Melissa is a selfless, loving person. She cares not only about her students' academic growth, but also about them as people. When I had difficulties living in a foreign country (visa problems, culture shock, financial crises), she always lent a hand.

I see in Melissa all the admirable merits of a human being: intelligence, faith, integrity, diligence, perseverance, discipline, and selflessness. She is always young and full of curiosity and love. She is true to science, to others, and to herself. I, like many others, owe a debt of gratitude and great admiration to this incomparable scientist. Thank you, Melissa!

Personal Tribute

WILLIAM CROFT

Melissa is one of those very special people that one feels very lucky to have met. I first met her nearly 20 years ago when she gave a talk at the University of Michigan, and we immediately became good friends. A couple of years later, we were together at a workshop in Santa Barbara and talked together about many things over the course of the workshop. Since then we have crossed paths all over the world, including a drive up the California coast to a workshop, and bird watching outside Taipei after a conference. At a critical time in my career, Melissa invited me to spend several months at the Max Planck Institute for Psycholinguistics in Nijmegen, where she worked. I will always be grateful for her generosity, support, and friendship.

Melissa is a scholar who has quietly but firmly changed the way we think about language, language acquisition, and the relationship between language and thought. I do not need to talk about her intellectual achievements; they are well known, and are reflected in her influence on the authors and in the contributions to this volume. What has always impressed me is Melissa's calm but insistent questioning of even her strongest intellectual opponents in conferences and talks: The most devastating critiques are presented in the simplest and sincerest fashion, which is often far more effective than polemicism. Melissa has a spirit of objective inquiry in understanding matters both linguistic and personal, both of which often evoke strong emotions in all of us. She once told me she attributed this to her anthropological background, both in family and education.

But Melissa is also a warm person, willing to see the humor in any situation. For example, she often recalls a time when she came to Manchester to work with me on a paper. I had fallen victim to one of those British colds, which after striking, lingers for weeks in a debilitating cough that prevents you from sleeping. Melissa herself unfortunately was laid low by a scallop in the previous night's dinner. So we worked on our paper, Melissa lying down and unable to get up, and I in a chair, unable to lie down for fear of coughing my head off.

The fields of linguistics and psychology, and their intersection in language acquisition, owe Melissa a huge debt. Those of us who know her personally owe her an even bigger debt.

5

Aspectual and Causal Structure in Event Representations

WILLIAM CROFT

University of New Mexico, Albuquerque

ARGUMENT LINKING AND EVENT REPRESENTATION: A FIRST ATTEMPT

In this chapter I describe a three-dimensional model for representing the causal-aspectual structure of events. It is almost universally accepted that both the causal and aspectual structure of events is relevant to grammatical analysis. The aspectual structure of events, called lexical aspect or by some, Aktionsart—others restrict this term to aspectual derivational morphology—interacts with grammatical aspect. Some linguists also argue that the aspectual structure of events influences argument linking—that is, the assignment of participants of events to clausal NP roles (Subject, Object, Oblique). The causal structure of events, or more generally the force-dynamic structure of events (Talmy, 1988), also influences argument linking. Some linguists, including myself, have argued that causal structure is the primary determinant of argument linking (Croft, 1991, 1998a, 1998b). These arguments are briefly recounted here, in order to motivate the topic of this chapter.

Most discussion of the argument linking question defines the semantic participant roles in terms of a small set of thematic roles (case roles in the early literature), such as agent, instrument, and patient. It has long been recognized that there are serious problems in defining thematic roles sui generis. Among the problems usually offered are the disagreements in the literature on the number of thematic roles and their definition. The chief criticism of thematic roles is that they cannot be defined independently of the events in which they occur. For this reason, most current approaches to argument linking define thematic roles in terms of their position in event structure, at least in principle. Once that is done, however, thematic roles are almost always taken as the input to the linguistic theory of linking semantics to syntax in argument structure.

These are undoubtedly major problems with thematic roles, but thematic roles suffer from an even more serious problem from a grammatical point of view. Even in the clear-cut cases of the most widely accepted thematic roles, there is no simple mapping from the thematic roles to syntactic roles. This fact is illustrated with the thematic roles of agent, instrument, and patient and the syntactic roles of Subject, Object, and Oblique in 1–3:

(1) **agent**: a volitional being that brings about a change

a. Subject: *TOMMY drove the car.*
b. Oblique: *The food was eaten* BY RACCOONS.
c. Object (see below): *Hilary persuaded* WILLARD *to retire.*

(2) **instrument**: an object under the control of an agent that brings about a change

a. Oblique: *Ellen cut the salami* WITH A KNIFE.
b. Subject: THE KEY *opened the door.*
c. Object: *I used* A KNIFE *to cut the knot.*

(3) **patient**: an object that undergoes a change of some sort

a. Object: *The man cleaned* THE CAR.
b. Subject: THE BOOK *was banned by the authorities.*
c. Oblique: *She nibbled* AT THE CARROT.

All of the three thematic roles can occur in all of the three syntactic roles in English. Arguably, agents do not occur as Objects. The example in 1c is usually analyzed as a "causee" role in the periphrastic causative construction. This is because Willard is functioning not just as the agent of the event of retiring, but also as the causee of Hilary's persuasion. However, Willard's two-sided thematic role is just another manifestation of the problem of defining thematic roles.

As a consequence of the many-to-many mapping between thematic roles and syntactic roles, and the continued reliance on thematic roles, theories of argument linking have to resort to additional devices to get the linkings right. The thematic roles have to be given additional properties, such as a ranking in a thematic role hierarchy and the designation of privileged roles (e.g., macro-roles, proto-roles, designated arguments, "most prominent role," and so on; see Croft 1998a for further discussion). But these additional properties are not derived from event structure, and in some theories, they are not even semantically motivated.

The approach advocated in Croft (1991, 1998a, 1998b) exploits further properties of event structure which offer a simple theory of argument linking. The crucial difference between this approach and others is that participant roles are not defined in terms of absolute positions in event structure but by the relative position of participants in a single event. For example, in all of the transitive examples in 1–3, the Subject participant "acts on" the Object participant: Tommy acts on the car, Hilary acts on Willard, the key acts on the door (by unlocking it), I act on the knife, and the man acts on the car. This relative relationship of participants is described as transmission of force and more generally as a force-dynamic relationship by Talmy (1976, 1988), whose semantic analysis inspired this model of argument linking. In the intransitive examples, there is no Object argument, only a Subject argument, which therefore does not violate the principle that Subject acts on Object. This is true even of the passive construction in 3b: Even though the Subject is the patient, the agent is not the Object.

The sequence of participants acting on other participants sets up a causal chain of the participants in the event. It is this causal chain that forms the semantic structure that is relevant to argument linking. A four-participant causal chain is illustrated in example 4 (adapted from Croft 1991:177), with the representation proposed in Croft (1991):

(4) *Sue broke the coconut for Greg with a hammer.*

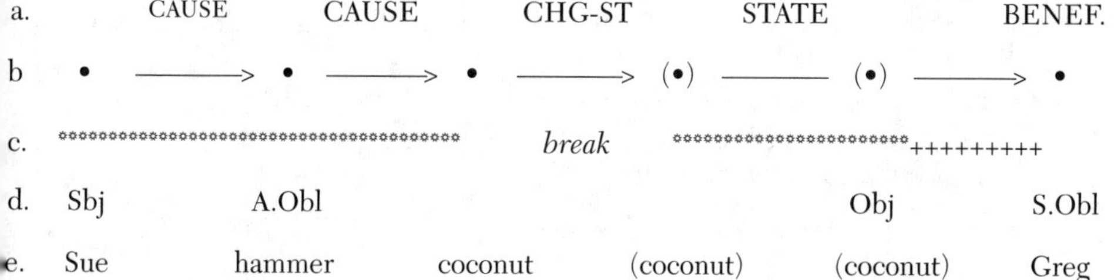

Line 4a gives the decomposition of the event into the segments of the causal chain. This decomposition of the event follows a long tradition. Line 4b gives the causal chain itself, for those segments involving two participants. The change-of-state and resulting state segments involve only one participant, which is indicated by parenthesized points in the chain. Line 4c introduces another critically important element of semantic structure, the part of the causal chain that is denoted or profiled (Langacker, 1987) by the verb (here, *break*). The semantic representation in (4) is a frame-semantic representation: A word such as *break* denotes or profiles a conceptual structure that itself assumes a larger conceptual structure as its background or frame (for arguments in favor of a frame semantic representation, see Fillmore, 1982, 1985; Croft & Cruse, 2004, chapter 2). Thus, the semantic representation has two parts: the frame structure as a whole, and the part that is profiled. In a frame-semantic model, both the profile and the frame are part of the meaning of a linguistic form.

The causal chain that forms the verb's semantic frame and the part of the causal chain that is profiled by the verb determine the linking to syntactic roles found in line 4d (the arguments in 4 are listed in line 4e). All argument linking is governed by a small number of universal linking rules. (1) The Subject and Object participants delimit the profiled part of the causal chain. (2) The subject is the initiator and the Object the endpoint of the causal chain. (This is the principle described in the discussion of examples 1–3 above.) Thus, *Sue* is Subject and *coconut* is Object.

(3) Oblique roles antecedent to the Object in the causal chain are linking to an Antecedent Oblique case marking (for example, *hammer* is governed by *with*), and Oblique roles subsequent to the Object are linked to a Subsequent Oblique case marking (for example, *Greg* is governed by *for*).

The third linking rule requires a division of case roles into antecedent and subsequent roles. This division is largely respected by the world's languages: Case markings (including prepositions and postpositions) are often polysemous, but they group together either antecedent roles only or subsequent roles only, with few exceptions (see Croft, 1991, chapter 5). In English, the antecedent markers include *with, by, of* and nonspatial (metaphorical) uses of *from* and *out of*. The subsequent markers include *to, for* and spatial path prepositions.

The linking rules apply straightforwardly when there is a clear asymmetrical causal (force-dynamic) relationship between participants, as with the traditional agent-instrument-patient thematic roles. In many cases, however, the relationship between participants is not clearly force-dynamic, or not clearly asymmetrical. In these cases, noncausal relations are generally construed as asymmetric relations in a consistent fashion, and argument linking then follows the linking rules given above.

One example will have to suffice here, the locative alternation:

(5) *Jane sprayed paint on the wall.*

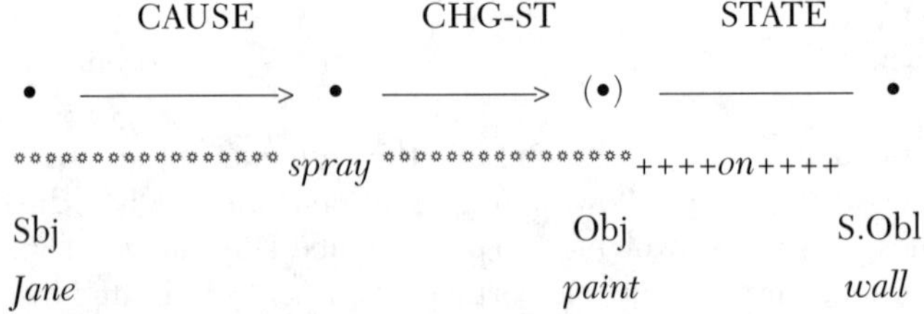

(6) *Jane sprayed the wall with paint.*

CAUSE CHG-ST STATE

• ——> • ——> (•) —— •

spray

Sbj A.Obl Obj

Jane *paint* *wall*

The paint functions as the Figure in the locative relationship with the wall, which functions as Ground (reference point). The Figure-Ground relationship is a locative one, not a causal one, but in this example, and in languages more generally, the Figure is conceptualized or construed as antecedent to the Ground, hence the arrangement in the causal chains in (5) and (6). The verb *spray*, however, profiles a different segment of the causal chain in the two examples (in other languages, overt derivational morphology distinguishes the two verb profiles). The profile determines the different assignment to Object, and consequently the use of the subsequent Path preposition *on* for *wall* in (5) and conversely the use of the antecedent preposition *with* for *paint* in (6). The possessed-possessor noncausal relation is also generally construed asymmetrically. Thus, the linking rules are universal—they hold across languages—but they are not global—they do not hold across all predicates, without further conventions of semantic construal of non-causal relations between participants in an event.

Further empirical evidence supporting the force-dynamic theory of argument linking is presented in Croft (1991, 1994, 1998a); see also Luraghi (2003). The force-dynamic theory is supported by much cross-linguistic evidence and by patterns of argument linking across a wide range of semantic classes of predicates. The central role of force-dynamic relations between participants in events for argument linking appears quite secure. In fact, the evidence presented in the cited works indicates that aspect plays almost no role in argument linking. However, there are serious problems with the semantic representation used in Croft (1991) and illustrated in (4).

The force-dynamic theory of argument linking separates causal and aspectual structure. But the representation in (4), (5), and (6) conflates causal and aspectual structure. Only two types of segments in the causal chain are distinguished in line 4b: A link headed with an arrow and a link designated by a line. The line indicates a noncausal relation, such as the resulting state in (4) or the spatial relations in (5) and (6). But the arrow indicates either a force-dynamic relation, such as that between the hammer and the coconut in (4), or a process, such as the change of state of the coconut in (4) or of the paint in (5) and (6). Thus, causal and aspectual subevents are conflated.

As a result of this conflation of aspect and causal structure in Croft (1991), some participants occur in more than one place in the so-called causal chain. This fact is represented by the parenthesized nodes representing the same participant in the chain. This representation appears somewhat ad hoc, but it may be justified (after all, other linguistic representation systems allow for multiple representations of the same entity). However, it causes serious problems for the linking rules. For example, if the coconut's role in the breaking event in (4) defines the endpoint of the profiled part of the causal chain, why does it extend all the way to the resulting state segment of the chain, instead of ending at the change-of-state segment or even the causal contact segment? It appears that the endpoint of the causal chain is at least partly stipulated (although it does fit the meaning of the verb *break*, which entails the resulting state).

A third problem with the representation in Croft (1991) is that the aspectual distinctions it makes are minimal. Only the state-process distinction is made. While this might suffice for argument linking, it cannot be an adequate representation of verbal aspect, which is an intricately complex linguistic semantic phenomenon.

A final problem with the representation is how causation is analyzed. In examples (4), (5), and (6), causation is analyzed as a transmission of force relation from one participant to the next in the causal chain; that is, causation is one participant acting on another participant. But the general philosophical analysis of causation is of one event causing another event. This is not simply a philosophical artifice. Participants have to do something in order to act on other participants: In many events, being acted upon means undergoing some event. Other linguists working on event structure have developed models of event representation that do distinguish aspect and causal structure, and treat causation as occurring between events. Two examples of representations that separate causal and aspectual operators are given in (7) and (8):

(7) *Jane dried the plate.*

[[Jane ACT] CAUSE [BECOME [plate <DRY>]]]
(Rappaport & Levin 1998, p. 107, with individuals supplied for variables)

(8) *Sally removed the book from the table.*

[**do´** (Sally, Ø)] CAUSE [BECOME NOT **be-on´** (table, book)]
(Van Valin & La Polla, 1997, p. 109)

The representations in (7) and (8) do not represent the force-dynamic causal chain, and extracting the causal chain from these representations is not a simple process (Van Valin & La Polla have a complex mechanism to derive argument linking that does not utilize force-dynamic relations between participants). However, the representation in Croft (1991) does not capture the fact that events cause other events, as well as conflating causal and aspectual structure. In sum, while the basic generalization in Croft (1991)—that force-dynamics and verb profile determine argument linking—appears to be empirically valid, the representation therein is inadequate to capture that generalization or other relevant properties of verbal semantics such as aspectual structure.

The remainder of this contribution presents a new analysis of verbal semantics that solves the representational problems presented above: It clearly separates aspectual and causal structure, it provides an unambiguous way to define a verbal profile, it provides a rich model of aspectual representation, and it represents both participants acting on other participants and events causing events. The starting point is an analysis of verbal or lexical aspect, which is presented in the following section. Once an adequate representation of verbal aspect is constructed, causal structure is integrated into the representation in the section on "Causal Structure and Aspectual Structure" below, producing a more complete representation of the major elements of verbal semantics that are relevant to grammar.

ASPECT: TOWARD A SEMANTIC REPRESENTATION

Lexical Aspectual Types (Construals)

The category of aspect is a notoriously vexing one (for a general survey up to 1990, see Binnick, 1991; for a survey of more recent literature, see Sasse, 2002). Comrie defines *aspect* as presenting "different ways of viewing the internal temporal constituency of a situation" (Comrie, 1976, p. 3). This broad definition is essentially correct, but when we turn to specific manifestations of aspect, things get more complicated.

Aspect is manifested both grammatically and lexically. Grammatically, many languages possess inflectional or periphrastic distinctions that modify "the internal temporal constituency of a situation," such as the distinction between Progressive and Simple Present in English, the distinction between Preterite (Aorist) and Imperfect in several Indo-European languages, and the distinction between Perfective and Imperfective in Russian. Grammatical aspect has been very difficult to define. One reason for this is that the semantic interpretation of the grammatical aspect categories often varies with the class of predicates (verbs and predicate adjectives and nominals) with which they are combined. This variation is generally attributed to differences in the lexical aspect (sometimes also called Aktionsart) of different classes of predicates. Lexical aspect is usually taken to be the inherent temporal structure of a situation: Some situations such as being an American are "naturally" enduring states, while others such as a window breaking are "naturally" punctual processes, and so on.

Most semantic analyses of lexical aspect take as their starting point a classification attributed ultimately to Aristotle but usually given in the form presented by Vendler (1967). Vendler distinguishes four types of lexical aspect, based on three semantic features: stative/dynamic (process), durative/punctual, and bounded/unbounded (or telic/atelic; aspect terminology is also notoriously ambiguous and overlapping):

(9) States: stative, durative, and unbounded (*be American, be polite, love*)
Activities: dynamic, durative, and unbounded (*sing, dance*)
Achievements: dynamic, punctual, and bounded (*shatter, reach [the summit]*)
Accomplishments: dynamic, durative, bounded (*cross [the street], read [the book]*)

States describe situations or events[1] that do not change over time (stative). The states that Vendler describes are also extended in time (durative) and do not have a "natural" endpoint (unbounded or atelic). Activities describe situations that involve change over time (dynamic/process), but in addition are unbounded and durative. Achievements also describe processes, but they describe a change of state that is instantaneous or at least conceptualized by the speaker as instantaneous—that is, occurring in just one point in time (punctual). The punctual change of state ends in a resulting state—for example, the shattered object or being at the summit.

[1] The terminology used in aspect analyses is hopelessly confused. A term such as *event*, for example, is used not just for the superordinate category (as in the common phrase *event structure*) but also for bounded processes in general and for achievements in particular. Of necessity I have chosen certain terms with one particular sense. Since *event* is used widely in the superordinate sense in the literature on "event structure" and argument linking, I have chosen that usage here, but also use the term *situation* suggested by Comrie (1976).

Accomplishments are processes that lead to a "natural" endpoint such as arriving at the other side of the street or the end of the book. They are durative, but in the process they "proceed toward a terminus" (Vendler, 1967, p. 101); later work describes this procession as an incremental progress (Dowty, 1991).

In fact, the relationship between verbs and lexical aspect is not one of simply assigning verbs into lexical aspect classes. Dahl (1985) puts it succinctly in his discussion of the relationship between grammatical aspect and lexical aspect:

> ...in addition to the fact that some aspectual notions are expressed by morphological means in some languages, it is also true for all languages that verbal lexemes differ in their 'aspectual potential'...As often happens, the theoretically nice distinction [between 'grammatical' and 'lexical' aspect] turns out to be rather difficult to apply in practice. To start with, we encounter the problem of separating out the 'inherent aspectual meaning' from contextual influences—after all, every occurrence of a verb is in a definite context, and there is no obvious way of determining what a 'neutral aspectual context' would be like. Also it turns out that there is an astonishing flexibility in how individual verbs may be used. (Dahl, 1985, pp. 26–27)

That is, a predicate does not inherently belong to a single aspectual type. Instead, it has the potential to be conceptualized or construed in multiple aspectual types (which we will also call construals). Moreover, one cannot assume that one of the aspectual types or construals is the "basic" one, although much discussion (including the discussion below) tends to assume this at least for convenience of exposition.

In addition to the flexibility of verbs that Dahl observes, it is clear that Vendler's classification of aspectual types requires revision. We briefly summarize the major problems with the Vendler classification here.

Stative predicates such as *know, see,* or *remember* (Vendler, 1967, p. 113–119) are construed as (transitory) states when they occur in the Simple Present:

(10) *I know how to do this.*

(11) *I see Mount Tamalpais.*

(12) *I remember her.*

But they can also be construed as achievements in the past tense:

(13) *I suddenly knew the answer.*

(14) *I reached the crest of the hill and saw Mount Tamalpais.*

(15) *I instantly remembered her.*

Vendler describes *see* and *know* as having two senses (Vendler, 1967, p. 113). However, the two "senses" depend on the grammatical context (tense-aspect constructions such as Simple Present or Past, further supported by adverbials such as *suddenly* or *instantly*). Instead, it is more accurate to say that *see* and *know*, and in fact English perception and cognition predicates in general, have an aspectual potential to be construed as either a state or an achievement in the appropriate semantic and grammatical context. Thus, state, achievement, and so on are not aspectual types of predicates but aspectual types or construals which different predicates have the potential to possess.

Another example of multiple aspectual potential is the category of disposition predicates such as *be polite* or *be friendly*. Dowty notes that *John is friendly* is a state, describing an inherent personality trait of John, whereas *John is being friendly* is an activity, describing a particular occasion of John behaving in a friendly manner (Dowty, 1979, p. 114). In our terms, disposition predicates allow alternative construals as a state and as an activity.

Smith (1991, pp. 55–58) argues that a fifth aspectual type or construal should be added to Vendler's original four types, which she calls "semelfactives"; this describes the temporal structure of examples such as:

(16) *Harriet coughed (once).*

Example (16) denotes a punctual event that does not lead to a different resulting state—after emitting the cough, Harriet "reverts" to her normal uncoughing state—(see also Carlson [1981, p. 39], who calls them "momentaneous"; and Talmy, [1985, p. 77], who describes them as the "full-cycle" class). Smith also notes that the same predicate *cough* can be used to describe an activity, when combined with a durative temporal adverbial or a progressive (Smith, 1991, p. 55):

(17) *Harriet coughed for five minutes.*

(18) *Harriet was coughing.*

In other words, *cough* has an aspectual potential to be construed as either a semelfactive or as an activity. Which construal is found depends on the tense-aspect construction *cough* occurs in (past tense, durative adverbial, progressive).

Another alternative construal reveals yet another aspectual type. The Progressive is unacceptable for most predicates usually construed as achievements because the Progressive applies to a durative situation:

(19) ?***The window is shattering.*

However, it is perfectly acceptable, under the right circumstances, to use the Progressive with some predicates typically considered to be achievements (Dowty, 1979, p. 137):

(20) *She's dying!*

(21) *He's falling asleep.*

(22) *They are reaching the summit.*

In these cases, the Progressive form describes a "run-up" process before the achievement of the change of state (and in fact, that change of state may not be achieved; see also Vendler 1967, p. 104).

Again, there are two alternative construals of the aspectual type of the situation, depending on the grammatical aspectual context. In this case, however, a new aspectual type must be recognized. Although *He's falling asleep* is durative and bounded, it is not an accomplishment. Accomplishments consist of an incremental, measurable change over time that leads to the resulting state, as indicated by the acceptability of a measure phrase:

(23) *I have read a quarter of the way through the newspaper.*

But the process leading up to falling asleep or dying is not an incremental, measurable process:

(24) **She has died/fallen asleep a quarter of the way.*

Croft (1998b, p. 74) named this aspectual construal a "run-up achievement": a nonincremental process leading up to a resulting state.

Further lexical aspectual distinctions have been proposed in the aspect literature. G. Carlson introduces a semantic distinction he describes as "object-level" vs. "stage-level" (Carlson, 1979, pp. 56–57); this distinction corresponds to what others have described as transitory vs. permanent or inherent. One effect of introducing this distinction is to divide states into transitory states, such as *be ill* or *be angry*, and inherent states such as *be American*. Whether a state is transitory or inherent is subject to construal in certain cases: For example, the predicate *be dry* is transitory when attributed to clothes, but inherent when attributed to a desert. Mittwoch identifies a third type of state, point states (Mittwoch, 1988, p. 234); examples include *be 5 o'clock, be on the point of Xing, be at the zenith* (e.g., the sun), *be exactly one hour since X, be on time.*

Dowty (1979, pp. 88–90) discusses a category which he calls "degree achievements," such as *cool, sink, age*. Dowty treats them as ambivalent—i.e., allowing alternative construals. But Hay, Kennedy, and Levin (1999, p. 132) argue persuasively against an ambivalence analysis, instead positing an analysis as an unbounded but directed change on a scale—i.e., a distinct aspectual type from (undirected) activities. In other words, Hay, Kennedy, and Levin argue for a distinct aspectual construal of an unbounded but incremental or measurable activity, so that activities are divided into directed or undirected bounded processes; see also L. Carlson (1981, p. 39), who describes directed activities as "dynamic"; Talmy (1985, p. 77), who describes them as "gradient verbs"; and Bertinetto and Squartini (1995), who describe them as "gradual completion verbs."

Finally, Talmy (1985, p. 77) distinguishes reversible (his "resettable") achievements (such as *open* or *close*), which can be reversed and therefore repeated, from irreversible ("nonresettable") achievements (such as most predicates of destruction or disintegration, such as *shatter, smash, die,* or *kill*), which cannot be reversed or repeated. Again, a predicate such as *break* may be reversible, as when it is applied to a repairable machine such as a washing machine, or irreversible, as when it is applied to a window or a stick.

If we gather together the different aspectual types/construals that have been proposed to characterize the aspectual potential of predicates, we have the following revisions and extensions to the Aristotle/Vendler classification:

(25) a. Three types of states: inherent, transitory, and point states, the last being a subtype of transitory states;
b. Two types of activities: directed activities and undirected activities;
c. Two types of achievements: reversible achievements and irreversible achievements;
d. Accomplishments;
e. Semelfactives;
f. Run-up achievements (not really achievements in Vendler's sense like [25c], but bounded, durative processes that do not involve incremental change)

This classification is not systematic. That is, it is not clear why there are the aspectual types that there are in the classification. Nor is it clear whether this classification is exhaustive, or whether there are further aspectual types that happen not to have been observed in the aspectual literature. In the following section, I present an analysis of lexical aspect that provides a coherent framework for the aspectual types given above. In this analysis, the possible aspectual types can in principle be extended from the classification given above, but the types already observed in the literature do represent more or less the full range of the most basic aspectual types.

An Analysis of Aspectual Types/Construals

The crucial analytical concept required to make sense of lexical aspect is temporal phase. Binnick (1991, pp. 194–207) argues that the notion of phase is essential for Aktionsart, which for him is derivational morphology for aspect:

> Since Streitberg there has been a great proliferation of schemes of *Aktionsarten* and of *Aktionsarten* themselves, too many to review here. Each scholar attempted to establish a logical taxonomy, a principled organization of the sundry *Aktionsarten* such that their various differences in meaning could be revealed and the set of all possible *Aktionsarten* be logically defined and organized. In the absence of a clearly defined concept of phase, these efforts were doomed to failure. (Binnick, 1991, p. 202)

A number of phasal analyses of lexical aspect have arisen recently. Space prevents me from offering a detailed discussion of these phasal analyses, and the following comments offer only a summary of their features and shortcomings, before presenting a more comprehensive phasal analysis. Binnick cites Woisetschlaeger (1982) as an early example of a phasal analysis. Woisetschlaeger uses a first-order predicate calculus semantic representation quantifying over subevents in time intervals—for example, specifying termination as the last subevent of the event (Woisetschlaeger, 1982, p. 22). However, Woisetschlaeger does not define qualitatively distinct subevents, apart from "pause" (event does not take place), and so does not capture the range of aspectual types described above.

A family of more fine-grained phasal analyses emphasizes the role of boundaries (Bickel, 1997; Breu, 1994; Johanson, 1996, 2000; Sasse, 1991). These analyses distinguish three possible phases of an event: an initial (inceptive) boundary transition; a "course" (Johanson) or middle; and a final boundary transition. Aspectual types are defined as to whether they include the initial or final boundaries or both. For example, in Bickel's notation, English *die* has two phases [ϕτ]: The run-up process (ϕ) and the final transition to death (τ; Bickel, 1997, p. 116). The simple past selects only τ and the progressive, only ϕ. In contrast, the Belhare verb *misen nima* '(get to) know'—like the English *know* illustrated in examples (11) and (14), has two phases [τϕ]: The inception (τ) and the resulting state (ϕ; compare Johanson's "initiotransformatives" (Johanson, 1996, p. 236). The simple present in (11) selects only ϕ and the past in (14) selects only τ. These analyses differentiate types of phases, but still not in a fine-grained enough fashion. In particular, the middle phase often does not distinguish state and process, let alone undirected vs. directed processes, and the final phase does not clearly distinguish completion (in the case of an accomplishment) vs. reversion to the original state (as with a semelfactive).

A somewhat different phasal analysis is offered by Klein (1994). Klein defines events in terms of the succession of possible states rather than the boundaries that hold between them. Klein distinguishes three aspectual types: 0-state, 1-state, and 2-state. A 0-state lexical content is always in that state—that is, there are no other states for the individual to which the lexical item is applied. An example would be the locative *be in* in the sentence *The Nile is in Africa*. A 0-state predicate corresponds to an inherent state in the description above. A 1-state lexical content denotes a particular state (or more precisely, phase, since the "state" may be stative or dynamic), but the state can be preceded by a "pretime" and followed by a "posttime" in which the state (phase) does not hold (Klein, 1994, p. 84). Finally, a two-state lexical content denotes at least two distinct states, a source state and a target state (Klein, 1994, p. 86). The target state corresponds to the resulting state in an achievement or accomplishment aspectual type. Klein argues that transitions from one state to another—boundaries—may be punctual or durative, and he does not semantically distinguish between the two possibilities (Klein, 1994, p. 88). Klein's analysis of aspectual types is embedded in a complex theory of time reference which we cannot do justice to here. Klein's analysis captures some elements of phases that the boundary-based analyses do not, but the reverse holds as well. Again, not enough semantic distinctions are made to capture all of the types described above.

Another type of phasal analysis is offered by Timberlake (1985). Timberlake assumes an interval temporal semantics like Woisetschlaeger, and focuses on boundaries. But he describes processes as a function from time intervals to situations and suggests that qualitative changes in state form a second dimension after that of time (Timberlake, 1985, pp. 50, 52–53). This is an important insight which is exploited here (this insight was developed here originally with Jerry Hobbs, independently of Timberlake and approximately at the same time).[2]

Our analysis of phase in lexical aspect, like Timberlake's, recognizes that aspectual phases involve not just one dimension, time, but two. Lexical aspect describes how events are construed as unfolding over time. But "unfolding" itself must be described. The unfolding of events is the sequence of qualitative states that characterize a particular event. The second dimension for representing lexical aspect is the qualitative states of the unfolding event.

Croft (in preparation) outlines a detailed two-dimensional phasal model of lexical aspect. In this model, events are represented in two dimensions, time (t) and qualitative states (q). Punctual event phases are points on t, and durative phases are extended on t. Stative phases are points on q (only one qualitative state holds over the relevant time period), while dynamic phases are extended on q (representing change from one qualitative state to another, possibly through intermediate states). With this basic set of distinctions, which can be represented geometrically, along with the concept of profile introduced already above, we can represent the range of aspectual types described.

A verb in a particular grammatical and semantic context denotes or PROFILES (Langacker, 1987) one (or possibly more) phase(s) of the ASPECTUAL CONTOUR of an event. (The phasal analyses described above generally describe the aspectual contour as a whole, from which a profile is selected, as in Bickel's model.) Example (26) compares the state and achievement aspectual construals of *see* from examples (11) and (14), repeated below. (The profiled phase in (26) is indicated with a solid line.)

(11) *I see Mount Tamalpais.*
(14) *I reached the crest of the hill and saw Mount Tamalpais.*
(26)

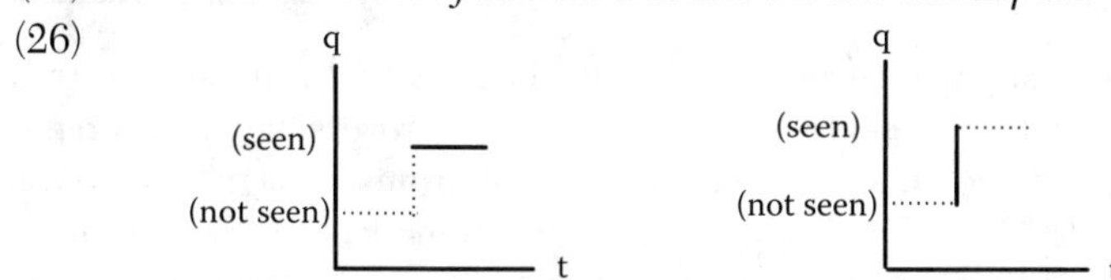

The t/q phase representations allow one to incorporate the aspectual construals and distinctions identified in the aspectual literature since Vendler's paper. These aspectual types can be grouped according to Vendler's original four-way classification.

[2] An early version of it was presented at the Summer Institute of the Linguistic Society of America at Stanford, California, in 1987 and at the Third Sommerschule der Deutschen Gesellschaft für Sprachwissenschaft, Hamburg, Germany in 1989.

Three kinds of states are illustrated in (27):

(27)

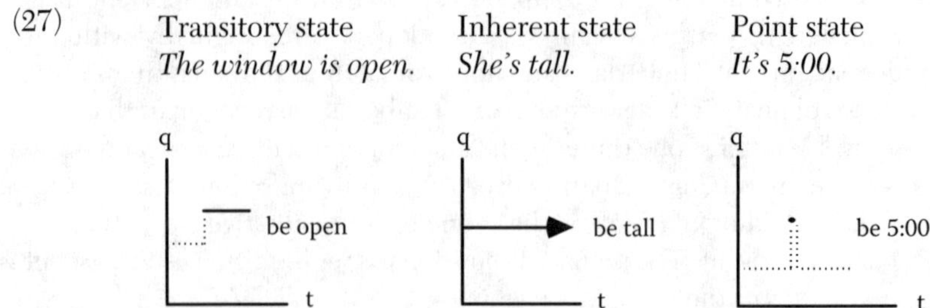

The first two types represent the distinction between transitory (stage-level) and inherent (object-level) states. Inherent states hold for the lifetime of the entity, which is represented by the arrow implying extension to the end of the t scale (t is relative to the lifetime of the entity). The third type represents point states. A variant of the inherent state type is an acquired inherent state, such as *dead* or *broken*. Unlike *be an American*, there is a period of time before which the dead or broken state holds, as with transitory states; but from that point onward it is an inherent state. Klein (1994, p. 85) distinguishes this type as a 1-state lexical content with a pretime and no posttime.

To these three kinds of states, there correspond three kinds of achievements:

(28)

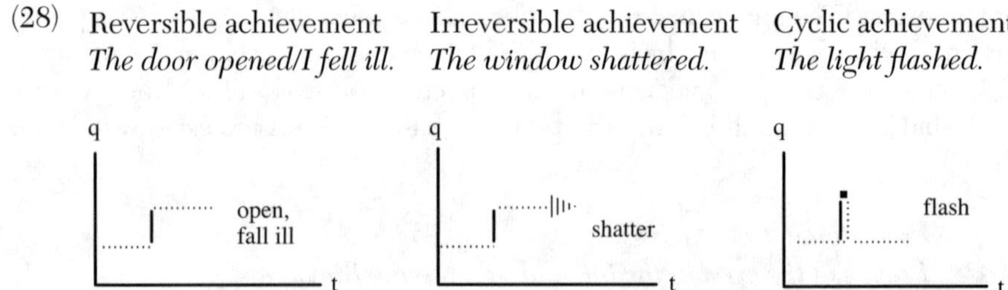

Reversible and irreversible achievements denote the punctual transition to transitory and inherent states, respectively. Reversible and irreversible achievements are both instances of directed achievements: a change from an original state q to a resulting state q'. Cyclic achievements are Smith's semelfactives: For example, the sound emission verb *cough* denotes a punctual transition to a punctual sound which then ceases. That is, the change from q to a point state q' implicates reversion to q after that point.

Following Hay et al. and their predecessors, two types of activities are distinguished:

(29)

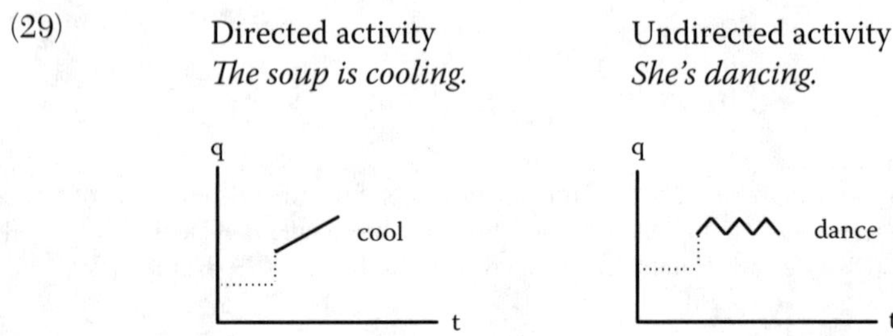

A directed activity is straightforwardly represented by a temporally extended incremental change on the q dimension. The incremental change can be thought of as a sequence of infinitesimal directed achievements. An undirected activity is represented by a cyclic change on the q dimension. This representation is not an arbitrary choice, in that undirected activities can be construed as iterated cyclical events: Dancing is repeated steps, talking is repeated sound emissions, and so on. Likewise, coughing (in the undirected activity construal) constitutes repeated individual coughing events.

Finally, there are two kinds of performances (bounded processes) corresponding to the two kinds of activities:

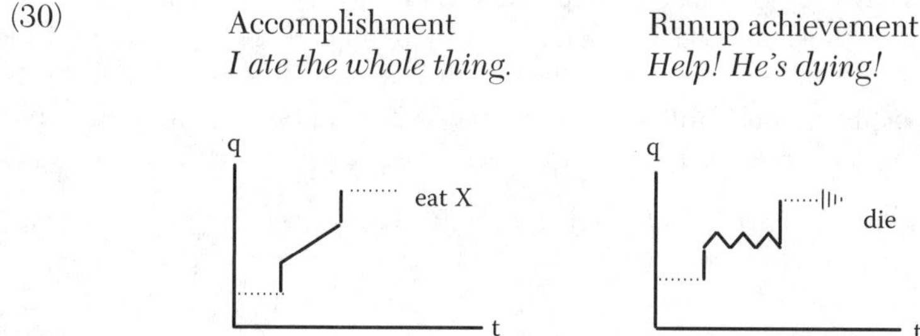

An accomplishment is a directed activity that is temporally bounded by its inception and completion phases (hence, three phases are here profiled). A run-up achievement is an undirected activity that is temporally bounded, since the process is not a measurable gradual change to the resulting state.

The t/q phasal representation provides a framework for systematically capturing the range of aspectual types that have been documented in the aspectual literature. There are three types of states, based on differences in duration on t (point, interval, entire scale). Reversible achievements, irreversible achievements, and cyclic achievements (semelfactives) represent punctual transitions to each of the three types of states. There are two types of durative processes, depending on whether or not incremental change is involved (the cyclic and incremental changes in q). Accomplishments and run-up achievements represent temporally bounded versions of the two types of activities, directed and undirected, respectively.

In principle, more complex profiles over more complex aspectual contours can be defined with the t/q phasal descriptive language. The types presented above, however, are the simplest aspectual types definable, profiling only one phase (the types of states, achievements, and activities) or a temporally bounded processual phase. (Achievements are processes in which the inceptive and completive transitions coincide.) In other words, simple predicates appear to have the aspectual potential to be construed in all and only these simple types. In this respect, the aspectual types reported in the aspectual literature do form a coherent class. In this respect also, the two-dimensional representation of aspect naturally captures this fact.

There is one exception to this generalization. The two-dimensional representation implies that a temporally bounded stative phase construal is just as simple as the temporally bounded processual construals, yet it has not been noted in the aspectual literature to my knowledge. This type is more complex than a temporally bounded processual phase. However, this is arguably the construal required by the so-called container adverbial *in X TimeUnit*. Sentences such as (31) and (32), where the container adverbial is applied to accomplishments and achievements that allow the run-up achievement construal, have the same profiles as the sentences in (30):

(31) *I ate the pizza in 10 minutes.*
(32) *He fell asleep in a few minutes.*

However, not all uses of the container adverbial with achievements require a run-up process. Instead, all the container adverbial denotes is that a state X time units long existed from some reference point, such as the present moment, to the achievement or inception (I am grateful to Paul Kay for pointing these examples out to me, though he used them to make a different point):

(33) *The TV show is starting in five minutes.* *The lights will go off in five minutes.*

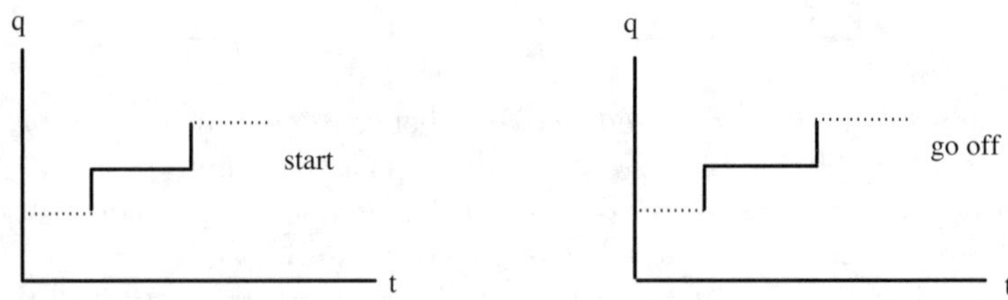

If we assume that the temporal profile of the sentence in (33) is determined by the container adverbial, just as they are in (31) and (32), then the profile of the aspectual contour is that of a temporally bounded state phase. This type then completes the inventory of possible minimal aspectual types or construals, according to the t/q phasal analysis, and further confirms the validity of this analysis of lexical aspect.

Space prevents us here from exploring the use of derivational and periphrastic constructions to describe more complex aspectual contours and profiles (see Croft, in preparation). Instead, we turn to the examination of the conceptual construal operations that define the aspectual potential of simple predicates.

Construal Operations and Aspectual Potential

A linguistic predicate (a verb or predicate adjective or nominal) does not necessarily fall under a single aspectual type. As Dahl puts it, with respect to aspect, predicates are remarkably flexible, and any given predicate will exhibit a range of aspectual potential. An example of a particularly flexible English predicate is *touch*. In the Simple Past tense, *touch* may be construed as a cyclic achievement, that is, an essentially instantaneous moment of contact:

(34) *Denise touched the painting.*

In the Past Progressive, *touch* may be construed as an undirected activity, not unlike other cyclic achievements, though this interpretation is easier to get with *keep* + Present Participle:

(35) *Denise was touching the painting/Denise kept touching the painting.*

More commonly, especially with inanimate Subjects, *touch* in the Progressive has a transitory state construal:

(36) *The chair is touching the painting.*

Touch may also be used to describe a (reversible) achievement, namely the transition to the transitory state profiled in (36):

(37) *She pushed the chair so far that it touched the painting.*

Finally, *touch* may also be used in the Simple Present:

(38) *The San Andreas Fault touches the east side of the campus.*

Goldsmith and Woisetschlaeger (1982) argue that in cases similar to examples (34) and (36), the Progressive/Simple Present contrast corresponds to a semantic distinction between "phenomenal" and "structural" properties of the situation. In our terms, this distinction would be characterized as "construed as transitory" and "construed as inherent," respectively. In this analysis, then, example (36) represents a construal of *touch* as a transitory state (but see below).

Touch represents a particularly versatile English predicate with respect to aspectual construal, but most predicates have at least two or three construals. For example, any process or transitory state predicate has a habitual construal in the Simple Present, which describes an inherent property of the grammatical Subject's behavior:

(39) *John hikes 10 miles every week.*
(40) *Sandy writes every morning between 7 and 8 a.m.*
(41) *Timmy is sick every winter.*

What sort of semantic processes allow for the alternative aspectual construals of predicates?

Linguists, particularly in the cognitive linguistic tradition, have identified a number of conceptualization processes or construal operations that are relevant to linguistic semantic analysis. A number of classifications of construal operations exists; the most comprehensive is that of Croft and Cruse (2004, chapter 3). Croft and Cruse classify construal operations under four major headings, all of which have a cognitive psychological basis: attention, comparison, perspective, and Gestalt. The construal operations responsible for alternative aspectual construals are instances of construal operations observed in other linguistic semantic domains.

One common construal operation of attention is selection (Langacker, 1987) or metonymy: A word may be used to describe two or more concepts associated in a semantic frame. For example, when one says *There's a purple finch in that tree*, one is normally asserting that the bird is in the space outlined by the branches of the tree, not that the bird is embedded in the trunk (Herskovits, 1985). That is, *that tree* is metonymically shifted to the associated concept of the space defined by the branches of the tree. In other words, the concept profile has shifted. Aspectual selection/metonymy is found with those predicates that allow either a directed achievement construal or a transitory (resulting) state construal, as can be seen from the t/q diagrams in (42):

(42) Transitory state — *I remember how to do this.* Directed achievement — *I remembered the answer.*

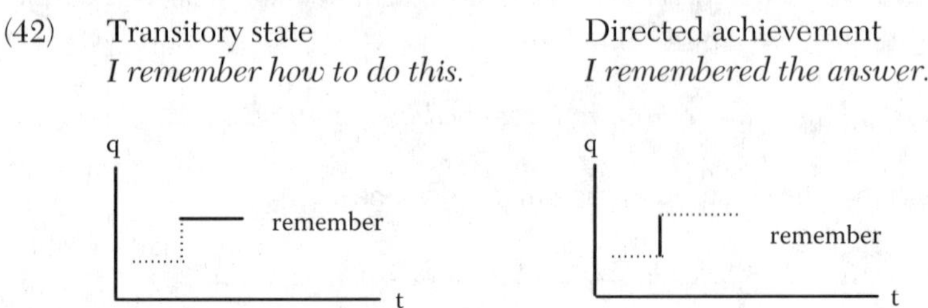

The two uses of *remember* share the same aspectual contour, but different phases are profiled in the different uses.

A construal operation of Gestalt that is found in aspect is described by Talmy (1985) as structural schematization: alternative ways to construe the structure of an object. An example is the alternative count and mass interpretations of *hair*: A *hair* profiles a single ("uniplex"—Talmy) object whereas *hair* profiles a plural ("multiplex") collection. The fact that English allows *hair* to have either construal is motivated by the fact that hairs frequently occur together in experience, and the association is strengthened by the fact that *hair* is usually used for strands from a common source (e.g., one person's head). The same phenomenon is found with the cyclic achievement and undirected activity construals of predicates such as *flash*, as Talmy himself observes (Talmy, 1985, p. 77):

(43) CYCLIC ACHIEVEMENT — *The light flashed.* UNDIRECTED ACTIVITY — *The light was flashing.*

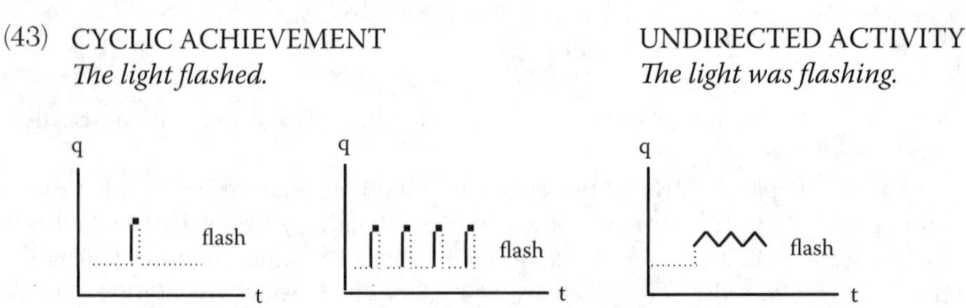

The alternative construals are of a single flash as a cyclic achievement, and iterated flashes as an undirected activity. Presumably the motivation for such verbs to have either construal is that light emission (and sound emission, bodily motions and contact) tend to occur either singly or in temporally contiguous groups.

Another construal operation of attention that is important for spatial conceptualization is the phenomenon of scalar adjustment (Croft & Cruse, 2004, pp. 51–53), also described as granularity. An example of spatial scalar adjustment is given in (44) and (45) (Croft & Cruse, 2004, p. 52, adapted from Talmy):

(44) *A squirrel ran across the road.*
(45) *The construction workers dug through the road.*

In the first example, the road is construed as a two-dimensional surface, as required by *across*; the actual third dimension of the thickness of the roadbed is ignored. This can be characterized as a coarse-grained spatial conceptualization: One so to speak turns down the magnification so that the much thinner third dimension shrinks to an infinitesimal thickness. The second example is a fine-grained conceptualization: One so to speak turns up the magnification so that the third dimension has extent and the road is now construed as a three-dimensional object.

Scalar adjustment accounts for several of the alternative aspectual construals described above. The geometric t/q representation allows for a direct representation of scalar adjustment. Scalar adjustment operates on both the t and q dimensions at once, further motivating the use of a two-dimensional representation of lexical aspect.

Dispositional predicates typically have two alternative construals: one as a transitory undirected activity describing a person's behavior on one occasion, and a second as an inherent state, that is, a personality trait of the person. The relationship between these two construals is given in (46):

(46) FINE-GRAINED | COARSE-GRAINED
Activity | Inherent state (incl. habitual)
He's being polite. | *He is polite.*

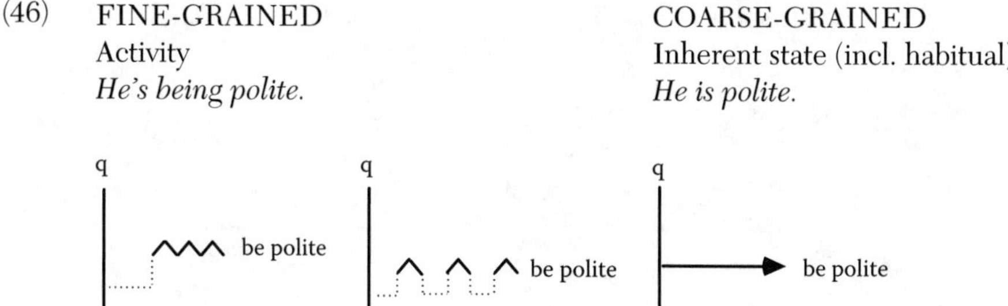

The left-hand diagram represents the single-occasion construal: a process which is therefore extended on the q dimension and with a relative short extension on the t dimension. The right-hand diagram represents the personality-trait construal: a state that is a point on the q dimension but is extended for the entirety of the t dimension. The middle diagram indicates the actual behavior of a polite person: On those occasions in which politeness is called for, the person behaves in a polite fashion. That is, the person engages in regular, repeated acts of politeness. If one turns down the magnification on this person's actions, then the events will no longer be extended on q. However, if the person really is polite, the point-like polite behavior events will extend through the person's lifetime—the scope of the coarse-grained, low-magnification construal on t. The pointline polite behavior events will be reconceptualized as a line extended through t—and this is the inherent state construal.

The same process can be described for the habitual construal of transitory processes and states:

(47) FINE-GRAINED
Activity
She is hiking through the woods.

COARSE-GRAINED
Inherent state (incl. habitual)
She hikes every weekend.

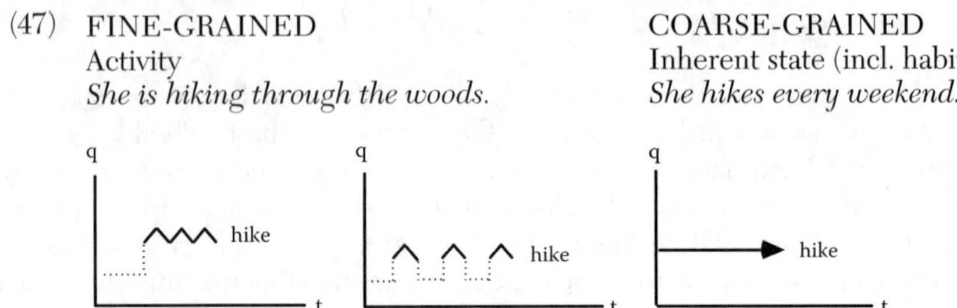

If a person regularly and repeatedly performs an action or enters into a state, then a coarse-grained, low-magnification construal will reduce the individual actions/states to points, but the repeated points over the person's lifetime will be reconceptualized as an extended line, that is, an inherent state.

A similar sort of scalar adjustment is found with those directed achievements that can be construed as accomplishments:

(48) FINE-GRAINED
Accomplishment
The bridge is collapsing.

COARSE-GRAINED
Directed achievement
The bridge collapsed at 9:15.

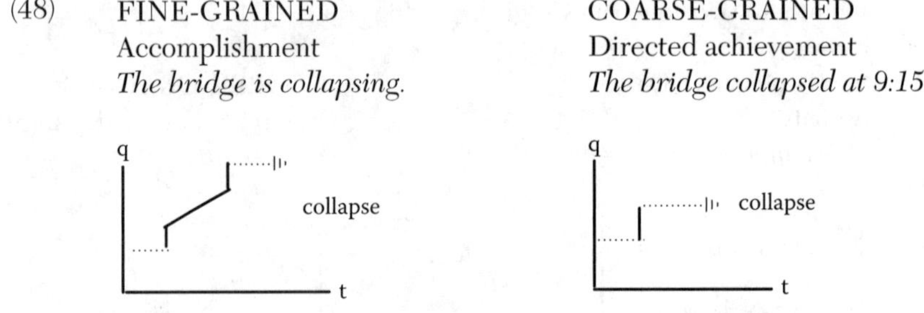

In the fine-grained scalar adjustment, the achievement is extended in t, but the increase in magnification also reveals the intermediate states on q that represent the incremental process from the intact bridge to the collapsed bridge. Likewise, for directed achievements that can be construed as run-up achievements, the fine-grained scalar adjustment both extends the event in time and reveals the intermediate states on q that represent the run-up process:

(49) FINE-GRAINED
Runup achievement
He's dying/He died in 3 hours.

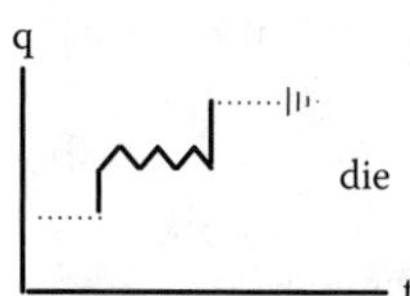

COARSE-GRAINED
Directed achievement
Jerry Garcia died on 8/9/95.

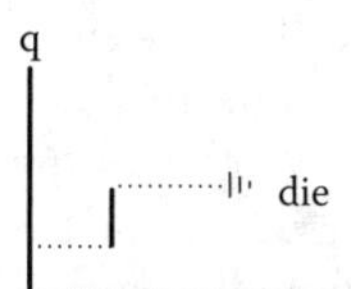

In the preceding examples, the fine-grained construal is expressed by the Progressive, because the fine-grained construal reveals a process extended in time. In the next example of alternative construals, the Progressive invokes a coarse-grained construal, since it reveals a process not present at a more fine-grained temporal scale:

(50) FINE-GRAINED
Inherent state
She resembles her mother.

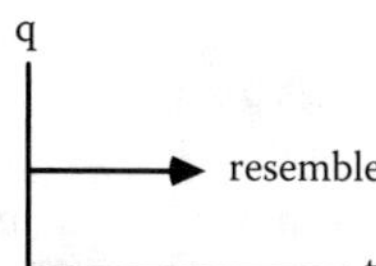

COARSE-GRAINED
Directed activity
She is resembling her mother more and more every year.

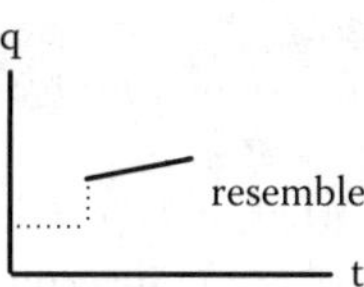

The fine-grained temporal construal describes a seemingly inherent state. A more coarse-grained temporal construal, extended over a significant part of the lifetime of the individual, reveals an incremental change of state, that is, a directed activity. The spatial analogy is that the earth appears to be flat at a close range, but its curvature is revealed at the much more distant (coarse-grained) range of the ocean's horizon.

The last example represents a slightly different scalar adjustment analysis:

(51) FINE-GRAINED
Transitory state (?)
Bill is lying on the bed.

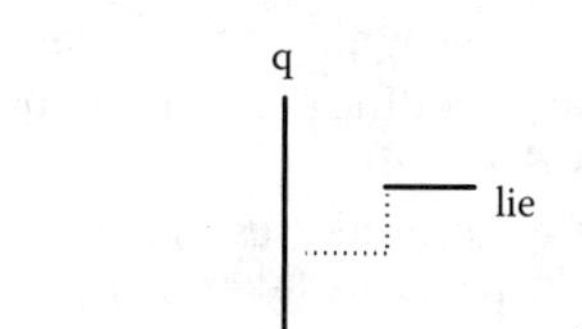

COARSE-GRAINED
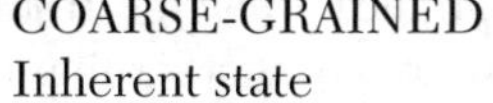
Inherent state
The forest lies to the east.

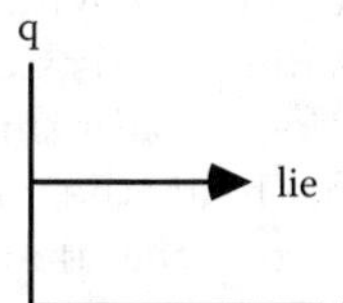

This is the contrast that Goldsmith and Woisetschlaeger describe as "phenomenal" versus "structural," and we analyzed as "construed as transitory" versus "construed as inherent." The scalar adjustment analysis holds for the t dimension. When discussing topographical, geological, or other relatively permanent features, the natural time scale is very coarse-grained, and if the relevant state persists over that time scale, then an inherent state construal is invoked. In contrast, a more fine grained time scale will invoke a transitory construal more easily.

Although the difference in scalar adjustment can lead to a difference in the nature of the state (transitory vs. inherent), there is no obvious difference in the q dimension, unlike the other examples of scalar adjustment described above. This is not necessarily contrary to the two-dimensional semantic analysis of lexical aspect presented here. After all, changes in granularity do not necessarily lead to changes in the extendedness of an event in either t or q. Nevertheless, there is an unusual feature of the semantic classes that allows the Progressive to construe an event as a transitory state in English. (This group is described as stative progressives by Dowty (1979, p. 173) and inactive actions by Croft (1991, p. 197).) These semantic classes include body posture verbs and some contact verbs (52–54), as well as certain mental and physiological process verbs (55–57):

(52) *Jim is standing at the top of the stairs.*
(53) *The box is lying on the bed.*
(54) *Johnny is touching my nose.*
(55) *I'm thinking.*
(56) *She's sleeping.*
(57) *The flowers are blooming.*

All of these situation types display an outward appearance of a transitory state, but seem to involve an internal or "invisible" process. Examples (52) and (54) involve the maintenance of a body posture, which requires some internal process (compare the neutral *Jim is at the top of the stairs*); in (53), this is reduced to the force of gravity and the support of the underlying object (the bed). Example (55) presumably reflects some outwardly invisible internal mental activity, while (56) and (57) reflect some internal physiological process. So it is possible that the fine-grained construal represented by the Progressive invokes some extendedness of the event on the q dimension, particularly for mental and physiological processes.

In this section, we have described how alternative aspectual construals of the same predicate emerge from conceptualization processes (construal operations) that are found in other linguistic semantic domains and that provide further evidence for the representation of lexical aspect presented here. The conceptualization processes can only be represented by an event structure of the sort argued for here. Selection/metonymy can only be understood by recognizing that a verbal aspectual meaning consists of a profiled phase of an overall aspectual contour, because selection involves shifting the profile (what is denoted) from one phase in the event frame to another. The various scalar adjustment processes make sense only by recognizing that the representation of lexical aspect involves two dimensions, time and qualitative states. Almost all of the scalar adjustment processes involve conceptually simultaneous adjustment of both the time scale and the qualitative state scale. A one-dimensional representation in terms of temporal phases, such as those mentioned on pages 149–150 cannot capture these two-dimensional construal operations. In the next section, we return to the question of integrating causal (force-dynamic) relations with verbal aspect.

CAUSAL STRUCTURE AND ASPECTUAL STRUCTURE

A proper representation of verbal semantics for grammatical analysis requires that force-dynamic relations be kept strictly separate from aspectual structure. The representation must unambiguously indicate what part of an event is profiled by a particular verb form. With respect to the representation in Croft (1991), a much richer representation of aspect is required. Finally, the representation must capture the fact that events cause other events, without losing the asymmetrical force-dynamic relationships that determine argument linking. The richer representation of verbal aspect is given above.

I propose that force-dynamic relations between participants be introduced as a third dimension, along with the time and qualitative state dimensions. There is a separate two-dimensional aspectual contour for each participant in the event. This aspectual contour represents what happens to that participant in the course of the event. The aspectual contours are then arranged in a linear causal chain in the third dimension, including the force-dynamic construals of noncausal relations between participants described above and in Croft (1991, 1998a).

The three-dimensional analysis can be illustrated with the transitive force-dynamic relation in (58):

(58) *Jack broke the window.*

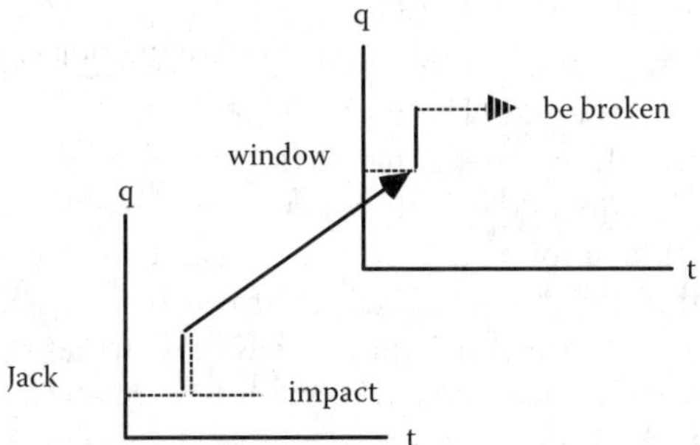

What happens to Jack is that he carries out an impact event, which is construed aspectually as a cyclic achievement. What happens to the window is that it undergoes a change of state, which is construed aspectually as an (irreversible) directed achievement. The transmission of force goes from Jack to the window, as indicated by the arrow linking the aspectual contours for Jack and the window at the point in time when the transmission of force occurs.

Each participant possesses its own t/q scale, while the causal chain introduces a third dimension to the representation. However, the three-dimensional representation in (58) is difficult to read on a two-dimensional page. For ease of reading, all participants are represented vertically on a single temporal scale, but each on its own qualitative scale:

(59)

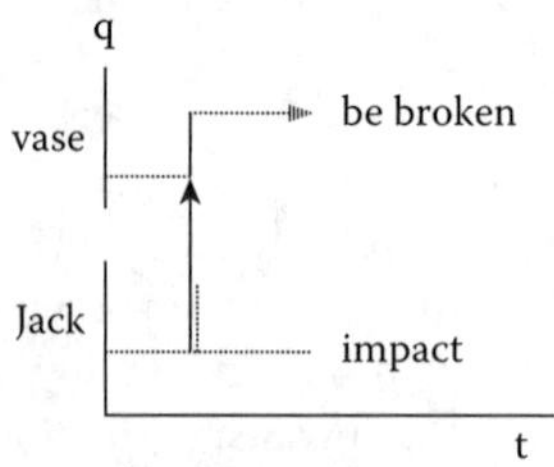

The alignment of the temporal scales clearly indicates the temporal alignment of each phase of each participant's aspectual contour. The break(s) in the q scales represent the separateness of the t/q dimensions for each participant. Hence, the horizontal dimension represents the unfolding of the event over time, and the vertical dimension the qualitative states/changes and, for visual clarity, the causal/noncausal interactions of participants in an event. As in the previous representations, the solid segments indicate the profiled part of the event representation, and the dotted-line segments represent the parts of the event in the event frame.

The three-dimensional representation of the event structure of predicates solves all of the representational problems enumerated on pages 143–144, without losing the value of the transmission-of-force model for argument linking. Aspectual structure is clearly separated from force-dynamic structure. Aspectual structure is represented in the t and q dimensions, and force-dynamic structure in the third dimension. The third dimension is also displayed in the vertical dimension as well, but the separation of the q scales for each participant allows one to treat each participant separately. The force-dynamic relationship between participants is now read vertically, following the participants named to the left of each q scale.

The crucial feature of the analysis of verbal semantics that allows us to separate each semantic dimension is to assign a subevent to each participant. These subevents can be thought of as what happens to each participant over the time course of the event. This feature of the analysis has two further benefits. First, the aspectual representation is rich enough to capture the alternative aspectual types or construals described above. Second, we can now represent causation as events causing other events, without losing the representation of transmission of force from one participant to another: Each participant's subevent causes the successive participant's subevent to occur.

In fact, the representation shows that events can be decomposed in two orthogonal ways. Events can be decomposed force-dynamically by breaking them down in terms of each participant's subevent. Events can also be decomposed temporally by breaking them down in terms of temporal phases.

We can illustrate further aspects of the new representation for examples given at the beginning of this chapter.

Example (1) is repeated below with its three-dimensional representation:

(1) *Sue broke the coconut for Greg with a hammer.*

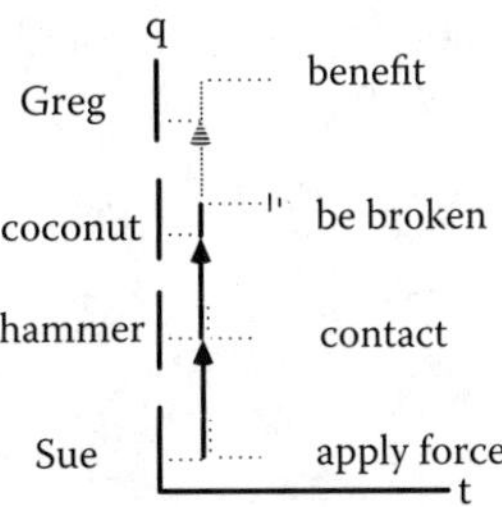

The overall aspectual construal of the event is punctual. Sue applies force to the hammer, presumably with a sudden motion. (Note that although Sue's application of force presumably takes time, the English verb, at least in the Simple Past tense, construes it as instantaneous.) The hammer makes contact with the coconut, also a punctual event. The coconut breaks, also punctual; the completed change of state entails that the resulting state is true. Finally the breaking of the coconut benefits Greg. In the representation for example (1), the profiled segment of the causal chain extends from Sue to the coconut. This is represented by the solid lines for the profiled phases for Sue, the hammer and the coconut, and the solid arrows for the causal relations linking the subevents for Sue, the hammer, and the coconut. There is no longer any ambiguity as to the position of the endpoint of the causal chain: It is simply the coconut's subevent, which includes the change of state and the necessarily entailed result state. The subsequent preposition *for* profiles the causal connection between the subevent of the coconut and the subevent involving Greg. The prepositional profile is represented by gray shading distinct from the dotted lines used for nonprofiled parts of the event frame.

Example (1) is an example of punctual causation: The profiled event is construed as a temporal point. Example (7) is an example of extended causation, and is represented below:

(7) *Jane dried the plate.*

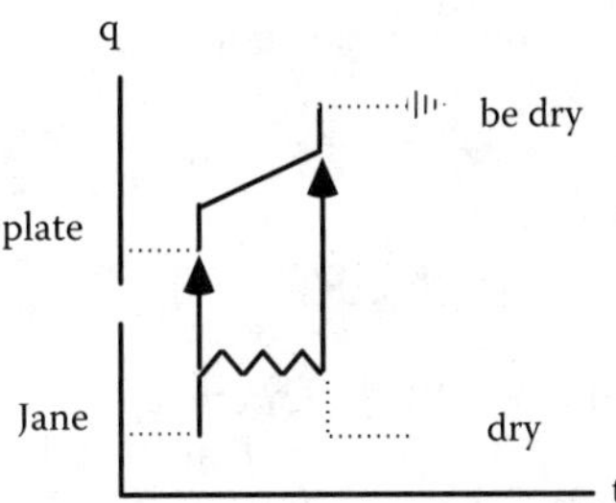

Jane engages in an undirected activity, the drying process (e.g., rubbing the plate with a dishcloth). The plate undergoes a directed change of state which is construed as bounded (i.e., an accomplishment) in the Past tense. Jane's activity causes the directed change of state of the plate over the profiled temporal interval. The force-dynamic relationship between Jane and the plate extends across the entire profiled temporal interval. This force-dynamic relationship is conventionally indicated only at the beginning and the end of the relevant temporal interval.

As a final example, we give the three-dimensional representation of example (8), also repeated below:

(8) *Sally removed the book from the table.*

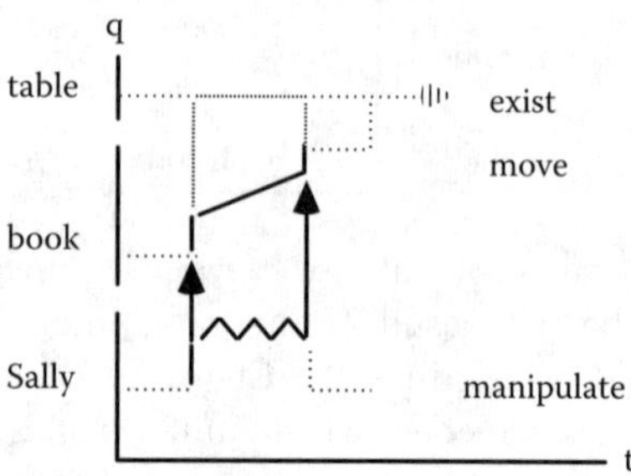

Sally engages in an undirected activity, the manipulation of the book. The book undergoes a directed change of state, the movement (change in location), which is construed as a bounded accomplishment in the Past tense. The bounded accomplishment construal means that Sally's starting to act causes the book to start to move, so the inception phases for both subevents are profiled. Sally's last instant of the action causes the book to be away from the table—so the book's completion phase is profiled, but Sally's cessation of action is not, since it doesn't cause the book to do anything. The relationship between the book and the table is noncausal, a spatial relationship (see "Aspect: Toward a Semantic Representation" above). As in the original force-dynamic representation, the noncausal relationship is represented by the absence of an arrowhead on the line joining the subevents for the book and the table. Again, since the event is durative, the noncausal spatial relation between the book and the table is represented by convention only at the beginning and the end of the interval. The table, which functions as the locative Ground object for describing the motion of the book, simply exists throughout the event.

With this powerful verbal semantic representation, we may continue to explore the role of verbal semantics and event structure in the grammar of human languages.

REFERENCES

Bertinetto, P. M., & Squartini, M. (1995). An attempt at defining the class of "gradual completion verbs." In P. M. Bertinetto, V. Bianchi, J. Higginbotham, & M. Squartini (Eds.), *Temporal reference, aspect and actionality: Vol. 1. Semantic and syntactic perspectives* (pp. 11–26). Turin: Rosenberg & Sellier.

Bickel, B. (1997). Aspectual scope and the difference between logical and semantic representation. *Lingua, 102*, 115–131.

Binnick, R. I. (1991). *Time and the verb*. Oxford: Oxford University Press.

Breu, W. (1994). Interactions between lexical, temporal and aspectual meaning. *Studies in Language, 18*, 23–44.

Carlson, G. N. (1979). Generics and atemporal *when*. *Linguistics & Philosophy, 3*, 49–98.
Carlson, L. (1981). Aspect and quantification. In P. Tedeschi & A. Zaenen (Eds.), *Syntax and semantics: Vol. 14.Tense and aspect* (pp. 31–64). New York: Academic Press.
Comrie, B. (1976). *Aspect*. Cambridge, UK: Cambridge University Press.
Croft, W. (1991). *Syntactic categories and grammatical relations: The cognitive organization of information*. Chicago: University of Chicago Press.
Croft, W. (1994). Voice: Beyond control and affectedness. In P. Hopper & B. Fox (Eds), *Voice: Form and function* (pp. 89–117). Amsterdam: John Benjamins.
Croft, W. (1998a). Event structure in argument linking. In M. Butt & W. Geuder (Eds.), *The projection of arguments: Lexical and compositional factors* (pp. 21–63). Stanford, CA: Center for the Study of Language and Information.
Croft, W. (1998b). The structure of events and the structure of language. In M. Tomasello (Ed.), *The new psychology of language: Cognitive and functional approaches to language structure* (pp. 67–92). Mahwah, NJ: Erlbaum.
Croft, W. (In preparation). *Verbs: Aspect and argument structure*. Oxford: Oxford University Press.
Croft, W., & Cruse, D. A.(2004). *Cognitive linguistics*. Cambridge, UK: Cambridge University Press.
Dahl, Ö. (1985). *Tense and aspect systems*. Oxford: Basil Blackwell.
Dowty, D. (1979). *Word meaning and Montague grammar*. Dordrecht: Reidel.
Dowty, D. (1991). Thematic proto-roles and argument selection. *Language, 67*,547–619.
Fillmore, C. J. (1982). Frame semantics. In The Linguistic Society of Korea (Ed.), *Linguistics in the morning calm* (pp. 111–137). Seoul: Hanshin.
Fillmore, C. J. (1985). Frames and the semantics of understanding. *Quaderni di semantica, 6*, 222–254.
Goldsmith, J., & Woisetschlaeger, E. (1982). The logic of the English progressive. *Linguistic Inquiry, 13*, 79–89.
Hay, J., Kennedy, C., & Levin, B. (1999). Scalar structure underlies telicity in "degree achievements." *Proceedings of SALT, 9*, 127–144.
Herskovits, A. (1985). Semantics and pragmatics of locative expressions. *Cognitive Science, 9*, 341–378.
Johanson, L. 1996. Terminality operators and their hierarchical status. In B. Devriendt, L. Goossens, & J. van der Auwera (Eds.), *Complex structures: A functionalist perspective* (pp. 229–258). Berlin: Mouton de Gruyter.
Johanson, L. (2000). Viewpoint operators in European languages. In Ö. Dahl (Ed.), *Tense and aspect in the languages of Europe* (pp. 27–187). Berlin: Mouton de Gruyter.
Klein, W. (1994). *Time in language*. London: Routledge.
Langacker, R. W. (1987). *Foundations of cognitive grammar: Vol. 1. Theoretical prerequisites*. Stanford, CA: Stanford University Press.
Luraghi, S. (2003). *On the meaning of prepositions and cases*. Amsterdam: John Benjamins.
Mittwoch, A. (1988). Aspects of English aspect: On the interaction of perfect, progressive and durational phrases. *Linguistics & Philosophy, 11*, 203–254.
Rappaport Hovav, M., & Levin, B. (1998). Building verb meanings. M. Butt & W. Geuder (Eds.), *The projection of arguments: Lexical and compositional factors* (pp. 97–134). Stanford, CA: Center for the Study of Language and Information.
Sasse, H-J. (1991). Aspect and Aktionsart: A reconciliation. In C. Vetters & W. Vandeweghe (Eds.), *Belgian Journal of Linguistics:* Vol. 6. *Perspectives on aspect and Aktionsart* (pp. 31–45). Brussels: Éditions de l'Université de Bruxelles.
Sasse, H-J. (2002). Recent activity in the theory of aspect: Accomplishments, achievements, or just non-progressive state? *Linguistic Typology*, 6, 199–271.
Smith, C. (1991). *The parameter of aspect*. Dordrecht: Kluwer.

Talmy, L. (1976). Semantic causative types. In M. Shibatani (Ed.), *Syntax and semantics: Vol. 6. The grammar of causative constructions* (pp. 43–116). New York: Academic Press.

Talmy, L. (1985). Lexicalization patterns: Semantic structure in lexical forms. In T. Shopen (Ed.), *Language typology and syntactic description: Vol. 3. Grammatical categories and the lexicon* (pp. 57–149). Cambridge, UK: Cambridge University Press.

Talmy, L. (1988). Force dynamics in language and cognition. *Cognitive Science, 12*, 49–100.

Timberlake, A. (1985). The temporal schemata of Russian predicates. In M. S. Flier & R. D. Brecht (Eds.), *Issues in Russian morphosyntax* (pp. 35–57). Columbus, OH: Slavica.

Van Valin, R. D. Jr., & LaPolla, R. J. (1997). *Syntax: Structure, meaning and function*. Cambridge, UK: Cambridge University Press.

Vendler, Z. (1967). Verbs and times. *Linguistics in philosophy*, (pp. 97–121). Ithaca, NY: Cornell University Press.

Personal Tribute

SOONJA CHOI

Working with Melissa has been one of the most fortunate things that has happened in my professional and personal life. She has been a major driving force in my growth over the past 20 years: She has deeply influenced and continues to inspire me in my research interests and approaches. I first met Melissa in late May of 1987 at the Max Planck Institute (MPI) of Psycholinguistics in Nijmegen. I had just finished my doctoral studies at SUNY, Buffalo, and gone to the MPI to work with Melissa to study Korean spatial terms with her. During a conversation we had the first evening, I mentioned to her the Korean verb *kkita* (meaning 'to put something into a "tight fit" relationship'), which one of my Korean child subjects had produced as her first verb (as she was trying to put a video cassette into the cassette slot in a video player). I had been wondering: Why, of all the verbs in Korean, did the child produce this specific verb? Melissa was intrigued by this verb from the first time I mentioned it, and she wanted to understand the meaning of *kkita* 'tight fit' inside out. She knew that the category of *kkita* would be of theoretical importance as it crosscut the categories of *in* and *on* in English. Thus began our many years of collaboration.

In the process of our working together, Melissa has continually brought to the forefront two important things in research: First, to fully understand form–meaning relations one needs to experiment with novel situations that can probe into the essence of meaning. In understanding the meaning of *kkita*, she thought up various situations that all involved tight fit but varied in other features (e.g., tight-fit vertically vs. tight-fit horizontally, tight-fit with solid materials vs. tight-fit with flexible materials). Such thorough investigation with novel situations, in fact, led me (a native speaker of Korean) to better understand the full meaning of the verb. Moreover, this method became the basis of our joint study on spatial terms in English, Korean, and Dutch: We used a variety of toys and objects such as pieces of velcro, hooks, and magnets to elicit children's understanding of spatial terms (Bowerman & Choi, 1994; Bowerman, 1996; Choi, 1997). The second thing that Melissa has always emphasized has been the importance of thinking globally about data: Relate data to "theories." Always think about whether the specific data at hand can be explained by current theories.

Melissa's focus on these two elements in research, her interest in Korean spatial semantics, and her insights about them brought about our 1991 joint paper "Learning to Express Motion Events: Language-Specific Patterns in English and Korean" (Choi & Bowerman, 1991). In that study, we analyzed the morpho-syntactic patterns of Motion events in English and Korean using Talmy's (1985) typological analysis, focusing especially on the way Path is expressed in the two languages. We found that the Korean system had a pattern distinct from English.

In many ways, the present study is an extension of our 1991 paper: The present study investigates linguistic expressions of Cause as well as Path. It expands the linguistic repertoire to four languages to include Japanese and Spanish (in addition to English and Korean). Furthermore, the methodology of the present study is inspired by Melissa's teaching because it uses an elicitation technique to collect data. Melissa, I present to you my findings. You will see in this work that your influence is still evident in my research, and it will always remain so in all of my work to come.

REFERENCES

Bowerman, M. (1996). Learning how to structure space for language: A crosslinguistic perspective. In P. Bloom, M. Peterson, L. Nadel, & M. Garrett (Eds.), *Language and space* (pp. 385–486) Cambridge, MA: MIT Press.

Bowerman, M., & Choi, S. (1994, January). *Linguistic and nonlinguistic determinants of spatial semantic development: A crosslinguistic study of English, Korean, and Dutch.* Paper presented at Boston University Conference on Language Development.

Choi, S. (1997). Language-specific input and early semantic development: Evidence from children learning Korean. In D. I. Slobin (Ed.), *The crosslinguistic study of language acquisition: Vol. 5. Expanding the contexts* (pp. 41–133). Mahwah, NJ: Erlbaum.

Choi, S., & Bowerman, M. (1991). Learning to express motion events in English and Korean: The influence of language-specific lexicalization patterns. *Cognition, 41,* 83–121.

Talmy, L. (1985). Lexicalization patterns: Semantic structure in lexical forms. In T. Shopen (Ed.), *Language typology and syntactic description: Vol. 3. Grammatical categories and the lexicon* (pp. 58–76). Cambridge, MA: Cambridge University Press.

6

Typological Differences in Syntactic Expressions of Path and Causation

SOONJA CHOI
San Diego State University

The overarching goal of the present study is to examine the relation between syntax and semantics in the expression of Motion events. To this end, I have examined the syntactic properties of two semantic components—Path and Cause of Motion—in four languages, English, Japanese, Korean, and Spanish. These languages differ in terms of both general language typology (e.g., word order) and more specifically in their lexicalization patterns of Motion events (S- vs. V-framed languages). The data come from elicited production of Motion event descriptions from adult speakers of the four languages. In the course of the present analysis, I will examine similarities and differences in the way these languages encode Path and Cause of Motion. These crosslinguistic differences can be explained in large part by the lexicalization pattern of the language as defined by Talmy (1985). However, the data will also reveal that some variations exist among the languages of the same lexicalization type. The findings will show that the distinction between S- and V-framed languages forms a continuum rather than a dichotomy.

MOTION EVENTS

In Talmy's analysis, a Motion event is defined as "a situation containing movement of an entity or maintenance of an entity at a stationary location" (1985, p. 60). As in Choi and Bowerman (1991), in the present study I focus on dynamic Motion events in which "directed" or "translative" motion results in change of location.

In describing Motion events, speakers encode four basic components (Talmy, 1985):

Motion: Presence of motion
Figure: The moving object
Ground: The reference object
Path: The course followed by the Figure object with respect to the Ground object.

In addition, speakers can also encode Manner (the manner in which the Figure moves; e.g., *run, walk, slide*), Cause (presence of an agent causing the Figure to move; e.g., *push, kick*) or Deixis (motion toward or away from the speaker). These components are illustrated in the following sentences.

(1) *The mouse*	*ran*		*into*	*the box.*
[Figure]	[Manner + Motion]		[Path]	[Ground]
(2) *John*	*slid(/threw)*	*the mouse*	*into*	*the box.*
	[Manner(/Cause) + Motion]	[Figure]	[Path]	[Ground]

Among these components, Path is the most crucial element (aside from the component of Motion itself). It constitutes the "core schema" of a Motion event (Talmy, 1991) as it encodes the spatial relation that occurs between the Figure and the Ground (e.g., *into*), or characterizes the type of trajectory that the Figure follows with respect to the Ground (e.g., *up*). Because a dynamic Motion event is about movement in space, Path is always present in a Motion event: Without Path there is no Motion event (Slobin, 2004).

Path also plays a critical role in determining the type of "lexicalization" pattern in a language: Language typology concerning the expression of Motion events consists of whether Path is typically encoded in the main verb or in a satellite—i.e., "the grammatical category of any constituent other than a nominal complement that is in a sister relation to the verb root" (Talmy, 1991, p. 486; e.g., particle, affix). Languages that characteristically express Path in particles or affixes are called Satellite-framed languages, whereas those that characteristically express it in the main verb are called Verb-framed languages (Talmy, 1985, 1991). In English, Path is typically encoded in a satellite, such as *into* in (3), but in Spanish it is encoded in the main verb, as in *entró* in (4). (More precisely speaking, *into* in English (e.g., in example 3) consists of a satellite *in* and a preposition *to*.) English is thus an S-framed language, while Spanish is a V-framed language (Talmy, 1985).

(3) English:	*The mouse ran* ***in(to)*** *the box.*				
(4) Spanish:	*El ratón*	***entró***	*en*	*la caja*	*corriendo.*
	'The mouse	entered	in	the box	running.'

S- and V-framed languages are also referred to as Manner- and Path-languages, respectively. The latter pair of terms relates to the type of component the main verb typically expresses. In English the main verb typically encodes Manner or Cause, whereas in Spanish the main verb encodes Path. Thus, in this classification scheme, English is a Manner language and Spanish is a Path language. In this chapter, I will mainly use the terms S- vs. *V-framed languages*, but will also use

Manner vs. *Path languages* when these latter terms seem to clarify the explanations better.

STUDIES ON LEXICALIZATION PATTERNS AND SYNTACTIC EXPRESSIONS OF MOTION EVENTS

Since Talmy's seminal work (1985, 1991) on linguistic typology of Motion event descriptions, a number of crosslinguistic studies have conducted further analyses of the characteristics of the lexicalization patterns. These studies have examined the way the semantic components of Motion events (especially Manner and Path) are grammatically encoded in different languages.

Slobin (1998, 2004) and Berman and Slobin (1994) have conducted extensive crosslinguistic studies on lexicalization patterns with narrative data based on the picture book *Frog, Where Are You?* (Mayer, 1969). They have found that typological differences (S-framed vs. V-framed languages) have ramifications for structural characteristics throughout the narrative. First, S-framed languages allow for detailed description of paths within a single clause since in their grammar it is possible to stack up multiple Path satellites and prepositional phrases onto a single verb (e.g., *the deer threw them* ***off over*** *a cliff* ***into the water***). In contrast, in V-framed languages, such grammatical stacking of paths is not available: One clause can express only one path at a time because Path is expressed in the main verb (e.g., *the deer threw them over, and they fell down*). Thus, in V-framed languages multiple paths do not occur in a single clause. Second, S-framed languages tend toward a greater specification of Manner, because the lexicon provides a large collection of verbs that conflate Manner or Cause with Motion (e.g., *crawl, swoop, tumble; dump, hurl, shove*). In contrast, in V-framed languages, information on Manner or Cause is often not given since it must be described by a separate construction such as a gerundive construction (Berman & Slobin, 1994).

More recently, Slobin (2004) has shown that there is significant variation within a given language type in the degree to which Manner and Path are used in Motion event descriptions. For example, of the two S-framed languages Russian and English, Russian chooses far more Manner verbs than English. Slobin suggests that selection of Manner or Path verbs in Motion event descriptions is influenced not only by the lexicalization pattern of the language but also by language-specific morpho-syntactic properties as well as psycholinguistic and pragmatic factors. For example, when the path (e.g., in the sudden emergence of an owl from a hole in the tree) is the focus of the event, even Manner languages might use a non-Manner expression (e.g., a deictic verb, ***come*** *out*) highlighting the trajectory of the motion.

Other studies have also shown that, although languages can be characterized in terms of being S- or V-framed in a general manner, some languages display unique patterns. Choi and Bowerman (1991) examined lexicalization patterns of English and Korean, particularly in the way the two languages express self-agentive spontaneous motion (e.g., *John* ***went*** *into the room*) and caused motions (e.g., *John* ***put*** *a book into the box*). They observe that English is an S-framed language, whereas Korean is a V-framed language. However, they also observe that the difference between the two languages goes beyond the lexicalization pattern: Whereas English consistently lexicalizes Manner or Cause in the main verb (characteristic of an S-language) for **both** spontaneous and caused motions, Korean uses distinct morpho-syntactic patterns for the two types of motion. In particular, for spontaneous motion, the Path verb in Korean is typically followed by a deictic verb (e.g., *ka* 'go') that informs whether the movement is directed toward or away from the speaker (example 5). In this construction, the deictic verb functions as the main verb. On the other hand, for caused motion, only the Path verb is sufficient, and deictic information is not needed, as shown in (6).

(5) *John-i* *pang* *-ey* *tul* *-e* ***ka*** *-ss* *-ta.*
John-Subj room -Loc enter-Connective go -Past -SE (Sentence-Ending marker)
'John entered (the) room away from the viewer.'

(6) *John-i* *chayk* *-ul* *kapang* *-ey* ***neh*** *-ess* *-ta.*
John-Subj book -DO bag -Loc put.in -Past -SE
'John put the book in (the) bag.'

Systematic variations can occur within a language in what can be encoded in the main verb. Aske (1989) found in Spanish that there is a systematic correspondence between aspectual features and lexicalization pattern. He has shown that although Spanish could largely be characterized as a V-framed/Path language (e.g., *Juan entró a la casa* 'John entered the house'), it systematically chooses a Manner verb as the main verb—a behavior of an S-framed/Manner language—when the motion does not have an endpoint. That is, when the motion is atelic (i.e., the Figure has not reached the goal location) and thus no change of state has occurred, Spanish speakers express Manner in the main verb as in the following example:

(7) *Juan corrió hacia la casa.*
'John ran toward the house.'

STUDIES ON TYPES OF PATH

As Path is an important and necessary element in the expression of Motion events, several studies have examined the semantic and morpho-syntactic aspects of Paths in different languages.

Slobin and Hoiting (1994) examined spatial expressions in Dutch Sign Language and proposed that different paths may have different morphological structures within a language. They show that in Dutch Sign Language a distinction is made based on whether or not the path crosses some kind of boundary. Paths such as 'crossing,' '(going) out,' and 'entering' are good examples of boundary-crossing paths, and signs for these paths are systematically different from signs for nonboundary crossing paths such as 'ascending' and 'descending.' More recently, Slobin (2004) has argued that boundary-crossing verbs essentially express change-of-state, and that these verbs behave differently from other types of Path verbs not only in Dutch Sign Language but also in other languages as well.

Naigles and Terrazas (1998) examined the type of syntactic construction in which Manner vs. Path verbs occur in English and Spanish. (Their study particularly focused on expressions of spontaneous motion.) They point out that there is a systematic correspondence between syntactic constructions and verb types. In English, Manner verbs are consistently produced in intransitive frames with particles (satellites) that express Path (e.g., *Mary ran in(to the house)*), whereas Path verbs such as *enter*, although they occur less frequently in spoken English, tend to be produced in transitive frames (e.g., *Mary entered the house*). In Spanish, Manner verbs are also produced in intransitive frames as in English, but Path verbs are used either in intransitive frames with a 'general' Path preposition *a* (or *de*) or in transitive frames. However, the authors do not provide further analysis on what motivates intransitive and transitive frames for Path verbs in Spanish.

In their insightful analysis, Muehleisen and Imai (1997) showed that among the Path verbs in Japanese, some (e.g., *agaru* 'rise,' *iku* 'go') always occur with intransitive constructions, whereas others (e.g., *wataru* 'cross,' *koeru* 'go.over') occur with transitive constructions. Muehleisen and Imai term the two types of Path verbs Directional Path (DP) verbs and Ground Path (GP) verbs, respectively. They propose that DP verbs differ from GP verbs in two major ways: DP verbs focus on either a starting point or goal but GP verbs focus on "the nature or the shape of the Ground covered in the course of the motion" (p. 331) (i.e., the type of space that the Figure has to traverse to go from the source to goal location). The two types of verb also differ in the degree of transitivity: Whereas DP verbs are low in transitivity, GP verbs are high in transitivity. This is because the Ground nominals of the GP verbs have properties of prototypical patients, as they are directly affected by the agent, and they function as Incremental Themes (Dowty, 1991). This difference in transitivity leads to a systematic correspondence between type of verb and syntactic constructions: DP verbs always occur in intransitive constructions, whereas GP verbs occur in transitive constructions.

SPECIFIC AIMS OF THE PRESENT STUDY

In this study, I take a close look at the syntactic properties of two components of Motion events: Path and Cause. In relation to Path, I examine whether different Path morphemes (particles in S-languages and verbs in V-languages) are associated with different types of syntactic constructions, and whether such associations vary across languages. More specifically, I examine whether there are systematic differences between S- vs. V-framed languages in the way they treat different types of path.

The second part of this chapter concerns the way speakers express the "Cause" component of a Motion event. In previous research, the focus has mostly been on Manner (e.g., how extensively the language encodes Manner in the main verb), and little attention has been given to the Cause aspect of Motion events. However, if one is to investigate syntactic aspects of Motion event descriptions, the encoding of Cause needs to be examined as it relates directly to the issue of transitivity. In this study, I examine the extent to which Cause of motion is highlighted in descriptions of Motion events in different types of language. In particular, I entertain the possibility that there may be typological differences between S-framed languages (e.g., English) which typically express Cause in the main verb and V-framed languages (e.g., Korean) which typically express Path in the main verb. I hypothesize that speakers of S-framed languages will be more sensitive to the causal aspect of a scene (since they encode it in the main verb), and that they will tend to use causative constructions more often than speakers of V-framed languages.

THE STUDY

The present study is part of a larger study that investigates a number of aspects in Motion events (e.g., manner, cause, path, deixis, static vs. dynamic events). Motion events were filmed with real people and objects to elicit naturalistic descriptions from participants. The complete set of stimuli scenes consists of 90 Motion events. In the present study, I examine a subset of stimuli—28 scenes in all—that involve differences in Path of motion and Causation. (The scenes not analyzed in the present study include static Motion events, scenes involving Figure objects of different shapes and sizes, and scenes that differ only in Manner.)

Stimuli Scenes

Table 6.1 lists the 28 scenes along with information about the type of Path and Causation depicted in each scene. The 28 scenes can be classified into five types with regard to causation, as described below:

Spontaneous Motion

Scenes (1) through (21) are all Motion events where the Figure—a person—moves volitionally and spontaneously from one location to another. No causation occurs in these events. These motions differ in path, manner, deixis, or telicity. As shown in Table 6.1, for each type of Path, there were between two and four scenes that differed in one or more features.

Within Spontaneous motion, there were 10 subtypes according to the type of Path expressed:

1. motion *into*—Scenes 1 to 4
2. motion *out of*—Scenes 5 and 6
3. motion *up* (punctual)—Scenes 7 and 8
4. motion *down* (punctual)—Scenes 9 and 10
5. motion *up* (durative)—Scenes 11 and 12
6. motion *down* (durative)—Scenes 13 to 15
7. motion *across* (telic)—Scenes 16 and 17
8. motion *across* (atelic)—Scene 18
9. motion *over*—Scenes 19 and 20
10. no path in the motion—Scene 21

TABLE 6.1 Motion Event Scenes

Scene	Path	Spontaneous vs. caused motion
1. M runs into room (viewer inside the room)	Into	Spontaneous
2. M runs into room (viewer outside)	Into	Spontaneous
3. M walks into room	Into	Spontaneous
4. J hops into room	Into	Spontaneous
5. M runs out of room	Out of	Spontaneous
6. J steps out of room	Out of	Spontaneous
7. J jumps onto chair	Up (punctual)	Spontaneous
8. M steps up onto stool	Up (punctual)	Spontaneous
9. J jumps down from chair	Down (punctual)	Spontaneous
10. M steps down from stool	Down (punctual)	Spontaneous
11. M hops up the stairs	Up (durative)	Spontaneous
12. M walks up the stairs	Up (durative)	Spontaneous
13. M hops down the stairs	Down (durative)	Spontaneous
14. M walks down the stairs (toward viewer)	Down (durative)	Spontaneous
15. M walks down the stairs (away from viewer)	Down (durative)	Spontaneous
16. J runs across the street	Across (telic)	Spontaneous
17. J walks across the street	Across (telic)	Spontaneous
18. J is walking across the street	Across (atelic)	Spontaneous
19. J jumps over bicycle rack	Over	Spontaneous
20. J steps over bicycle rack	Over	Spontaneous
21. M is inside the room, then suddenly outside the room	No Path	Spontaneous
22. J throws keys into basket	Into	Caused (agent visible)
23. J rolls a ball into container	Into	Caused (agent visible)
24. (J) throws keys into basket	Into	Caused (agent not shown)
25. (J) rolls a ball into container	Into	Caused (agent not shown)
26. J runs toward M kicking a ball (viewer is near J)	Toward	Caused and spontaneous
27. J runs toward M kicking a ball (viewer is near M)	Toward	Caused and spontaneous
28. A fan blows and paper falls into basket	Down and Into	Indirect causation

Caused Motion with the Agent Visible In Scenes (22) and (23), the movement of the Figure is externally caused by an agent. The causation is explicitly shown, as each scene clearly shows a person (i.e., agent) causing an inanimate object (i.e., the Figure) to move.

Caused Motion without the Agent Shown In Scenes (24) and (25), the movement of an inanimate object is caused by an agent, but the scene does not show the agent causing it. It only shows the movement of the Figure. For example, in Scene (24), the video clip only shows a ball rolling into a container (i.e., the video part of the agent initially causing the ball to roll has been deleted). In appearance, then, it looks like the Figure is moving by itself.

Spontaneous and Caused Motions Combined In Scenes (26) and (27), both spontaneous and caused motions co-occur in a single event. In both scenes, John is kicking a ball (i.e., caused motion) and running (i.e., spontaneous motion) toward

Mary at the same time. The only difference between the two scenes is the deictic aspect. In Scene (26), John is going away from the viewer/camera toward Mary, and in Scene (27), he is coming toward the viewer/camera, also toward Mary.

Indirect Causation In Scene (28), an electric fan (placed on a table) starts to blow, and a piece of paper that is in front of the fan falls off the table and goes into the waste basket below it. This scene differs from the other caused motions in several ways: The causation is indirect since the causer (i.e., fan) makes no contact with the Figure (i.e., piece of paper) to make the Figure move. Also, the agent (i.e., fan) is an *in*animate object. Moreover, several paths occur in one event: paper blowing *off* the table, falling *downward*, and going *into* the basket.

Data Collection

Speakers of four languages were tested: English, Spanish, Korean, and Japanese. These languages were chosen for the study on the basis of the feasibility of finding participants (and graduate students who could collect data). Among these languages, English is the only Satellite-framed language (S-language) in the sample, where information about Path is encoded in a satellite, namely a particle. The other three languages, Spanish, Korean, and Japanese, are Verb-framed languages (V-language) where Path is encoded in the main verb of the sentence. In both types of languages additional Path information can be provided in adpositional (pre-/postpositional) phrases.

S-framed (Manner/Cause) language	**V-framed (Path) languages**
English	Japanese
	Korean
	Spanish

For each language, 20 native speakers participated in the study. Speakers of English and Korean were recruited in San Diego. All speakers of English acquired the language as their mother tongue, and remained monolingual speakers of English. Speakers of Korean were recruited from the American Language Institute at San Diego State University where English as a Second Language is taught in intensive 10-week courses. The Korean speakers came to the United States within three months before the time of testing. Japanese speakers were recruited and tested in Tokyo, Japan. Spanish speakers were recruited and tested in Tijuana, Mexico. All Korean, Japanese, and Spanish speakers were native speakers of their languages and grew up in monolingual environments. All testing was conducted by an investigator who was fluent in the participant's native language

As mentioned earlier, the 28 scenes were part of a larger study that consisted of a total of 90 scenes. Of the 90 scenes, three were used during the practice session, and the remaining 87 scenes were test scenes. The 87 scenes were divided into two sections (about 44 scenes each). The 28 scenes examined in the present study were interspersed within these scenes: 13 scenes in the first section and 15 scenes in the second section. Each scene was about 8 seconds long and was followed by a 10-second interval. The scenes in each section were sequenced so that any two adjacent scenes varied in at least one aspect of the Motion event (e.g., Path, Manner, Causation). To reduce possible order effects, half of the participants viewed the first section followed by the second, and half viewed them in reverse order. They were given a 10-minute break between the two sections. During this break, the experimenter distracted the participant by conversing about different matters such as the participant's school life.

The testing was conducted individually. The participants were asked to describe the scenes as clearly and briefly as possible, and as they would describe them to a friend during a normal conversation. They were also instructed that if they needed more time to respond, they could ask the experimenter to pause the video. They could also ask the experimenter to replay the scene as many times as they wanted. The participants were also given a chance to redescribe the scene if they thought their first description was not right. However, the data show that self-corrections did not occur very often in the data. Thus, only the first descriptions were taken for analysis.

FINDINGS

Syntactic Encoding of Paths in Spontaneous Motion Events

In this section, the responses for Scenes (1) to (20) are analyzed. For these scenes, the syntactic construction was coded for each type of path. All descriptions were coded as either intransitive or transitive constructions.

Intransitive constructions were those in which the Ground NP was an oblique object (OO) of the main verb. This means that, in English and Spanish, the Ground nominal was the NP complement of a preposition as in the following examples:

English:

(8) *John ran* ***across the street***.

Spanish:

(9) *María entró corriendo* ***al/ hacia el salón***.
'Maria entered running **to the/toward the room**.'

In Japanese and Korean, the Ground NP carried an oblique object marker, such as *-ni* 'at/to' for Japanese, or *–ey* 'at' or *–(u)lo* 'to/toward' for Korean (*-lo* is used when the stem ends with a vowel, and *–ulo* when the stem ends with a consonant.)

Japanese:

(10) *Hanako-san -ga* ***heya -ni*** *hait -te ki -ta.*
Hanako-Miss -Subj. **room -to** enter -Connective come -Past
'Miss Hanako entered and came to (the) room.'

Korean:

(11) *Younghi-ga* ***kyosil -an -ulo*** *tul -e -ass -ta.*
Younghi-Subj **classroom -inside -to** enter -Conn come -Past-SE
'Younghi entered and came to inside (the) room.'

In transitive constructions the noun phrase representing the Ground was a direct object of the main verb. This means that, in English and Spanish, the Ground NP did not accompany any prepositions as in the following examples:

English:
(12) *John crossed* ***the street.***
Spanish:
(13) *María subió* ***las escaleras.***
'Maria ascended **the stairs.**'

In Japanese and Korean, the noun phrase expressing the Ground nominal carried a direct object (DO) marker: *-o* for Japanese and *-(l)ul* for Korean. (*-lul* is used when the stem ends with a vowel, and *–ul* when the stem ends with a consonant.)

Japanese:
(14) *Dansei -ga odandoho -o watat -ta.*
man -Subject **crosswalk -DO** cross -Past
'A man crossed (the) crosswalk.'
Korean:
(15) *Chelswu-ka* ***hweyngtanpoto -lul*** *kenne -ss -ta.*
Chelswu-Subject **crosswalk -DO** cross -Past -SE
'Chelswu crossed (the) crosswalk.'

Table 6.2 summarizes the findings: It shows the average number of responses (per scene) in intransitive sentences for each type of Path for each language. (The maximum number is 20 per scene, since there were 20 participants per language.) The data reveal clear patterns of crosslinguistic similarities and differences in the way the speakers used transitive and intransitive syntactic frames for the scenes. As Table 6.2 indicates, Scenes 1 to 10 show remarkable crosslinguistic similarities: Speakers of all four languages used an intransitive frame. In contrast, Scenes (11) to (20) show a sharp difference between English and the other three languages.

The difference between the two types of language was significant: An ANOVA was conducted with Path type (Scenes 1–10 vs. Scenes 11–20) as the within-subject variable and Language (S- vs. V-language) as the between-subject variable. The dependent variable was the syntactic frame: A score of 1 was given for an intransitive frame, and a score of zero was given for a transitive frame. There was a main effect for Language ($F(3, 76) = 401.74, p<0.0001$). Follow-up analyses (post hoc Tukey tests) show that English was significantly different from Japanese, Korean, and Spanish ($p<0.001$), whereas the latter three languages did not differ. Importantly, the ANOVA also showed an interaction involving Language and Path type ($F(3,76) = 401.74, p<0.0001$). A follow-up analysis shows that the four languages did not differ for Scenes 1–10, but differed significantly for Scenes 11 to 20 ($p<0.001$). (It should be noted that no order or gender effects were found under separate analyses.)

TABLE 6.2 Average Number of **Intransitive** Sentences per Scene Used by Speakers for Different Types of Path

	In/Out Scenes 1-6	Up/Down (Punctual) Scenes 7–10	Up/Down (Durative) Scenes 11–15	Across Scenes 16–18	Over Scenes 19–20
English (N=20)	20	20	20	18	19
Japanese (N=20)	20	20	3	2	0
Korean (N=20)	20	20	2	0	1
Spanish (N=20)	20	20	1	1	2

Note: Decimal points over .5 have been rounded up.

Based on these findings, the kinds of paths I examined in this study can be grouped into two types:

Type I paths (to be called "endpoint" paths): 'into/out of,' punctual 'up/down'
Type II paths (to be called "trajectory" paths): durative 'up/ down,' 'across, over'

Type I paths consist of (going) 'in' and 'out' of an enclosure (e.g., room) (Scenes 1–6), and (going) 'up' and 'down' in one jump or in one step (Scenes 7–10). These 'up' and 'down' motions have a *punctual* aspect in that the motion to the goal is achieved quickly. For these paths speakers of all four languages showed a complete agreement in that all of them used intransitive constructions. That is, speakers of both S- and V-framed languages encoded the Ground as oblique objects of the main verb (see examples 16–23). This was consistent regardless of whether the main verb encoded Path (in examples 18 and 20–23) or Manner (examples 16, 17, and 19). In the case of English and Spanish, the Ground nominal was expressed in a prepositional phrase as in examples (16 to 19) below. In the case of Japanese and Korean, the Ground nominal carried a locative case marker as in examples (20 to 23).

English:
(16) *Mary walked* ***in(to)*** *the room.*
(17) *John jumped* ***onto*** *the chair.*
Spanish:
(18) *María entró corriendo* ***al*** *salón* ***/hacia*** *el salón.*
Maria enter-Past running **to.the** room **towards** the room
'Maria entered the room running.'
(19) *Juan brincó* ***hacia /sobre*** *una silla.*
John jump-Past **towards /on** a chair
'John jumped toward/on a chair.'

Japanese:

(20) *Hanako-san -ga heya* **-ni** *hait -te ki -ta.*
Hanako-Miss- Subj. room **-to** enter -Conn come -Past.
'Miss Hanako entered and came to (the) room toward the viewer.'

(21) *Dansei- ga isu* **-ni** *tobi -agat -ta.*
man- Subj chair **-to** jump -ascend -Past.
'A man jumped up to (the) chair.'

Korean:

(22) *Younghi-ga kyosil -an* **-ulo** *tul -e o -ass -ta.*
Younghi-Subj classroom -inside **-to** enter -Conn come -Past -SE
'Younghi entered and came to inside (the) room.'

(23) *Chelswu-ga uyca -wui* **-lo** *ttwu- -e oll -ass -ta.*
Chelswu-Subj chair -top **-to** jump -Conn ascend -Past -SE
'Chelswu jumped up to top of (the) chair.'

In contrast to the Type I paths, the Type II paths showed a sharp crosslinguistic difference. These paths consist of (going) 'across,' 'over,' and also (going) 'up' and 'down' with a *durative* aspect (Scenes 11–20). The *durative* 'up' and 'down' paths involved making several steps to reach the goal location. For these paths, as shown in Table 6.2, English speakers continued to use intransitive constructions:

English:

(24) *John walked* ***across*** *the street.*

(25) *John jumped/hopped* ***over*** *the bike rack.* (One speaker: *John hurdled the bike rack.*)

(26) *Mary hopped/walked* ***up*** *the stairs.*

In contrast to English, in V-languages intransitive constructions were rare. In fact, speakers of V-languages overwhelmingly used transitive constructions expressing the Ground as a direct object of the main verb (see examples [27] to [35]). In most cases the main verbs were Path verbs, but Manner verbs could also be used as in example (28) in Spanish.

Spanish:

(27) *Juan cruzó /atravezó la calle.*
'Juan crossed /traversed the street.'

(28) *Juan brincó la cerca.*
'Juan jumped the fence.'

(29) *María subió las escaleras.*
'Maria ascended the stairs.'

Japanese:

(30) *Taro-san-ga jitensya -okiba* **-o** *tobi -koe -ta.*
Taro-Mr.-Subj bicycle -depository -DO jump -go.over -Past
'Mr. Taro went over (the) bicycle bar by jumping.'

(31) *Dansei-ga odandoho* **-o** *watat -ta.*
man-Subj crosswalk -DO cross -Past
'A man crossed (the) crosswalk.'

(32) *Hanako-san -ga kaidan* **-o** *nobot -e it -ta.*
Hanako-Miss -Subj staircase -DO ascend -Conn go -Past.
'Miss Hanako ascended (the) staircase away from the viewer.'

Korean:

(33) *Chelswu-ga cacenke -tay* **-lul** *ttwui-e nem -ess -ta.*
Chelswu-Subj bicycle -bar -DO jump-Conn go.over -Past -SE
'Chelswu went.over (the) bicycle bar by jumping.'

(34) *Chelswu-ga hwengtanpoto* **-lul** *kenn-e ka -ss -ta.*
Chelswu-Subj crosswalk -DO cross-Conn go -Past -SE
'Chelswu crossed (the) crosswalk away from the viewer.'

(35) *Younghi-ga keydan* **-ul** *oll -a ka -ss -ta.*
Younghi-Subj staircase -DO ascend -CONN go -Past -SE
'Younghi ascended (the) staircase away from the viewer.'

These findings raise two questions: (1) What is the difference between the Type I and Type II paths? (2) Why do V-languages, but not S-languages, encode the difference?

Difference between Type I and Type II Paths How do the two types of path differ? First, they differ in relation to the semantic roles of the Ground NP. For Type I paths (i.e., 'in/out' and punctual 'up/down'), the Ground is the **goal** or **source** of the motion event. As schematized in the left side of Figure 6.1, the room is the goal (or the "endpoint") in 'John went into the room' and source in 'John went out of the room.' Likewise, the "chair" is the goal in 'John jumped up on the chair.' This is particularly transparent in the prepositions and the locative case markers used by the speakers for Scenes 1 through 10: *to* in English, *hacia* 'toward' in Spanish, *-ni* 'to' in Japanese, and *-lo* 'to' in Korean. I will call these paths "endpoint" paths.

For Type II paths (i.e., 'across' 'over' and durative 'up/down'), however, the Ground does *not* refer to the goal or source, but **the path itself** that the Figure follows to get to the goal location. I will call these paths "trajectory" paths. For these paths, the Ground nominal (e.g., "street" or "fence" in examples (24) and (25)) characterizes the space or barrier (that the Figure has to traverse or overcome) that lies between the source and the goal location. Muehleisen and Imai (1997) present a similar analysis for the Ground nominals for Japanese Path verbs, *wataru* 'cross' and *koeru* 'go.over.' This analysis is schematized in the right side of Figure 6.1. It illustrates that the street or the bicycle rack is something that the Figure has to traverse in order to reach the goal. V-languages encode these entities as core arguments of the main verbs.

It is interesting to note that the determining factor for the use of intransitive and transitive construction does *not* seem to be the verb type, as previous researchers have suggested (Muehleison & Imai, 1997; Naigles & Terrazas, 1998). As has been reviewed above, Muehleison and Imai (1997) argue that there is a systematic correspondence between specific verbs and transitivity: Directional Path verbs (e.g., *agaru* 'rise,' *iku* 'go') always occur with intransitive constructions, whereas Ground Path verbs (e.g., *wataru* 'cross' *koeru* 'go.over') always occur with transitive

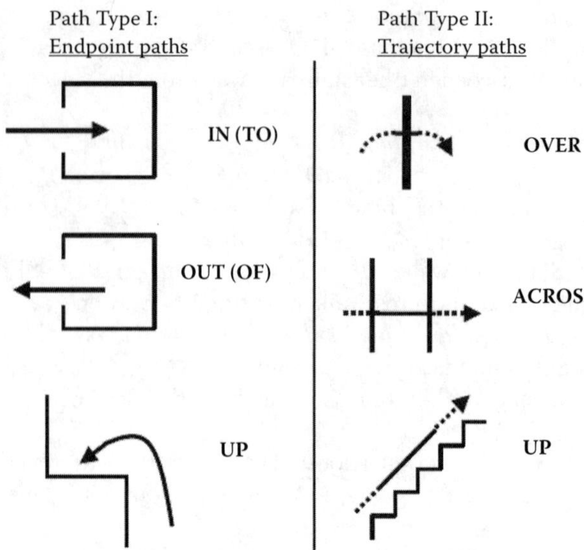

Figure 6.1 Schematic respresentation of two types of Path in spontaneous Motion events.

constructions. Muehleison and Imai's proposal is only partially supported by the present data. In the present data, verbs such as *wataru* 'cross' and *koeru* 'go.over' are indeed consistently used in transitive frames. But, the data also provide critical counterexamples to Muehleison and Imai's claim: Verbs of going up or down are used in *both* intransitive and transitive constructions. For example, Korean participants used the same Path verbs *oll-a-ka* 'go.up,' *nayly-e-ka* 'go.down' in intransitive constructions for Scenes (7) through (10) as well as in transitive constructions for Scenes (11) through (15). This is also the case in our Japanese and Spanish data (e.g., *agaru* 'go.up,' *oriru* 'go.down' in Japanese, and *subir* 'go.up' and *bajar* 'go. down' in Spanish). Based on the data, as has been argued earlier, I propose that the syntactic frame is determined by the type of Path and Ground element rather than the verb type.

The present analysis reveals that the group of morphemes that have been classified collectively as "Paths" are not of uniform nature. Rather, they consist of at least two kinds: Paths that refer to the goal or source of motion, and those that refer to the space traversed by the Figure. These two types of Path result in differential syntactic treatment in V-languages: Endpoint paths occur with an intransitive frame, whereas trajectory paths occur with a transitive frame.

Distinction between "Endpoint" and "Trajectory" Paths in V-Framed Languages Why do V-framed languages differentiate the two types of Path syntactically, whereas S-languages do not? I propose that it is the lexicalization pattern of the V-languages that allows the distinction. In V-languages, Path—the core schema—is expressed by the main verb. This gives speakers flexibility to assign different syntactic and semantic roles for the Ground nominal that follows the main verb. The data reveal that all three V-languages converge on assigning the two types of Ground to different syntactic/semantic roles: direct object when the Ground refers to the path itself but an oblique object when the Ground refers to the goal or source. S-languages do not have such flexibility of making the distinction because they express Path—the core schema—in a satellite. With the satellite being an obligatory element, the resulting syntactic construction is an intransitive frame with the Ground element within a prepositional phrase. Of course, other S-framed languages need to be examined to understand the extent to which this pattern is generalized crosslinguistically.

It should be noted that in English, it is quite possible to express scenes involving trajectory Paths (e.g., 'crossing' and 'going over') with a transitive construction. For example, English speakers can construct transitive sentences by using Path verbs, such as *to cross* in example (36), or perhaps deleting the Path particle as in example (37). In both cases, the Ground nominals are the direct objects of the verbs. These transitive sentences seem to convey a more holistic picture of the event (see Choi & Bowerman, 1991 for further discussion). It is possible that in a different elicitation context (e.g., asking the participant to recall the same scene but as part of a series of Motion events (for example, "John crosses the street and then takes a bus"), English speakers may have responded differently using more transitive constructions.

(36) *John crossed the street.*
(37) *John jumped the bicycle bar.*

But, the fact still remains that given the same context, English speakers overwhelmingly preferred intransitive constructions where speakers of other languages did not (see Table 6.2). This suggests that marking Path in a satellite (e.g., *John went **over** the bar*) is relatively a more productive pattern in English speakers' minds to express events involving trajectory paths.

Syntactic Encoding of Caused Motion: Differences in Perspective

The second inquiry in our study concerns whether speakers of Manner/Cause (S-framed) and Path (V-framed) languages differ in the way they express the causal aspect of a Motion event. Given that S-languages encode Cause (e.g., *push, kick*) in the main verb but V-languages typically encode Path, speakers of the two types of language may differ in the degree of their sensitivity to the Cause components in a Motion event. More specifically, it is possible that speakers of S-languages may be more sensitive to the causal component of a scene and thus may highlight it more than speakers of V-languages. The difference would be reflected in the syntactic frame speakers choose: Emphasis on causal components would lead to more uses of causative/transitive constructions, whereas emphasis on paths/trajectories would lead to more uses of intransitive constructions

One way to test this hypothesis is to present speakers with scenes that would give them a choice about what to highlight in their linguistic expression: either causal or noncausal aspects. For this purpose, scenes were created that varied in the degree of explicitness of causation, as described in the data collection section above ("Caused Motion with the Agent Visible"). Causation is highly explicit in Scenes (22) and (23), as the scenes show the agent causing the Figure to move. But in Scenes (24) to (28), causation is either implicit, as in Scenes 24 to 25, or co-occurs with spontaneous motion, as in Scenes (26) to (28). These scenes offer speakers a choice about the particular perspective they can take and thus about what to highlight in the main clause: highlighting the causation (e.g., *John is kicking a ball*) using a transitive frame or highlighting simply the Figure's motion (e.g., *John is running toward Mary*) in an intransitive frame.

In coding the data, both transitive and passive constructions were coded as causative expression. In Spanish, the *se*-verb constructions, such as those in (38) and (39) below, were coded as passives. (It should be noted that out of the total of 120 responses, there were only five instances of *se*-verb construction.)

(38) *Se avienta una pelota dentro de un envase.*
throws a ball inside of a case.
'(Someone) throws a ball inside of a case.'

(39) *Una pelota se mete a un recipiente.*
A ball clitic put.in to a container.
'A ball goes in a container.'

The data, summarized in Table 6.3, were analyzed in an ANOVA in which Causation Type (Caused motion with agent, Caused motion without agent, Caused and Spontaneous motion) was the within-subject variable, and Language was the between-subject variable. There was a main effect for Language ($F(3,76) = 13.76$, $p<0.01$). Follow-up analyses (post-hoc Tukey tests) show that English differed from all the other three V-languages ($p< 0.01$). Within the V-languages, Spanish differed from Korean ($p = 0.04$) but not from Japanese. Japanese did not differ from either Korean or Spanish. There was also a main effect for Causation type ($F(2,75) = 158.17$, $p<0.0001$). The type of scene with "Caused motion with agent" was significantly different from the other two types ($p<0.01$). More importantly, there was an interaction involving Language and Causation Type. A follow-up analysis shows that the differences across languages lie in the second and third Causation types—that is, Caused motion without agent and Caused and Spontaneous motion ($p<0.01$ for each). Below, I describe the crosslinguistic patterns in more detail.

TABLE 6.3 Average Number of Responses Expressing Causation in the Main Verb (in either **Transitive** or **Passive** Construction)

	Caused motion w/ agent	**Caused motion w/o agent**	**Caused & spontaneous motion**
	Scenes 22-23	**Scenes 24-25**	**Scenes 26-27**
English	20	13	17
Japanese	20	7	6
Korean	20	4	3
Spanish	20	10	8

Caused Motion with the Agent Shown

Scenes (22) and (23) depict caused motions explicitly. For these scenes, all speakers of both S- and V-languages expressed the event in a transitive frame with the agent as the subject of the transitive verb. There were no exceptions.

Caused Motion without the Agent Shown

In Scenes (24) and (25), the motion of the Figure (an inanimate object) is caused by an agent, but the scene does not show the agent. For example, Scene (24) shows the ball rolling into the container on the grass. Similarly, Scene (25) shows keys dropping into a basket. For these scenes, an average of 13 out of 20 (65%) English speakers encoded Causation with either a transitive or a passive construction (e.g., *Someone rolled the ball into the container; The ball was rolled into the container*) (see Table 6.3). Only seven speakers encoded the event with an intransitive construction (e.g., *The ball rolled into the container*). In contrast, half or less than half of the speakers of the Path languages—an average of seven in Japanese (40%), an average of four in Korean (20%), and an average of 10 in Spanish (50%)—used transitive or passive sentence constructions. The preference for an intransitive construction was particularly pronounced in Korean: An average of 16 out of 20 Korean speakers encoded the two scenes with intransitive constructions.

Spontaneous and Caused Motions Combined

In Scenes (26) and (27), both spontaneous and caused motions co-occur in a single event. In Scenes (26) and (27), John is kicking a ball (i.e., caused motion) and running toward Mary (i.e., spontaneous motion) at the same time. Again, in this case, the speaker has a choice about which motion to foreground in the main clause.

In describing these scenes, the English speakers again focused on the causative aspect significantly more often than the speakers of the Path languages. For Scenes (26) and (27), an average of 17 out of 20 English speakers used transitive sentences encoding Cause in the main clause (see example 40). Only three speakers used an intransitive sentence, such as *J is running/coming toward M kicking a ball*, highlighting the spontaneous motion.

English:
(40) *John is kicking a ball to Mary.*

The opposite pattern was shown for the speakers of the three Path languages. Only an average of six Japanese, three Korean, and eight Spanish speakers described the scenes in transitive clauses in the main clause. A majority of these speakers foregrounded the trajectory of the spontaneous motion and expressed the scenes in intransitive constructions expressing Path in the main clause. See the following examples:

Japanese:

(41) *Dansei -ga josei -ni mukatte sakka booru -wa kette -te hashiteiru.*
man -Subj woman -to toward soccer ball -DO kick -Conn run-Progressive
'The man is running toward the woman kicking (a) soccer ball.'

Korean:

(42) *Chelswu-ka chwukgu kong -ul mol- ko yenghi ccok-ulo ka-ss -ta.*
Chelswu-Subj soccer ball -DO kick-by.means.of Yenghi toward go-Past-SE
'Chelswu went toward Yenghi by kicking (a) soccer ball.'

Spanish:

(43) *Juan llega hacia María pateando una pelota.*
Juan arrives toward Maria kicking a ball
'Juan arrives toward Maria kicking a ball.'

It should be noted that five Spanish speakers did not give specific information and simply said *Juan y María están jugando con la pelota*, 'Juan and Maria are playing with a ball,' and did not mention the kicking or the running part. It is not clear why these speakers were non-specific. It may be due to the atelic aspect of the scene.

Indirect Causation

Scene (28) differs from Scenes (24) to (27) in several ways. First, the agent—a fan—is not a prototypical agent, as it is an inanimate object. Second, the causation is indirect, since the fan makes no contact with the Figure (i.e., a crumpled ball of paper) in causing it to move. In fact, in appearance, this event involves two separate events: The fan on a table starts to blow, and the ball of paper (which was in front of the fan and at the edge of the table) falls off the table and goes into a basket. This event offers speakers several choices about which event to highlight in the main clause: the fan blowing, the fan causing the paper to fall, or simply the paper falling off the table. Furthermore, the trajectory of the motion involves several paths: paper going *off* the table, falling *downward*, or going *into* the basket. Speakers may choose to highlight just one or two of these paths.

Chi-square analyses on the use of transitive constructions for the scene show that English differs significantly from Japanese and Korean ($\chi^2(1) = 26.77$ and $\chi^2(1) = 29.56$ respectively, both $p<0.001$) and from Spanish ($\chi^2(1) = 9.46$, $p<0.01$). However, Spanish also differed from Japanese and Korean ($\chi^2(1) = 7.41$ and $\chi^2(1) = 9.47$, respectively, both $p < 0.01$).

There was remarkable agreement among the English speakers, as shown in Table 6.4 (the first column): All 20 speakers used a transitive clause with a Cause verb *blow* expressing the fan as the causer and the paper as the causee. Nineteen of the 20 English speakers described the scene with a single transitive clause: "The fan blew the paper into the basket" expressing the causation as a direct one. Only one speaker in English used a multiple-clause expression: "A fan was used to generate a little wind that would blow the blue piece of paper off of the table and down into the trash can that was below it." This speaker made full use of what S-framed languages can offer—i.e., the possibility of stacking multiple path satellites with one verb, *blow*. However, there was only one speaker who did this.

In contrast to the high uniformity in responses in English, responses of the Japanese, Korean, and Spanish participants were quite diverse. Of the three languages, Japanese and Korean were more similar to each other than they were to Spanish. Only one Japanese and three Korean speakers used a transitive construction for the event of the paper falling with the fan as the agent. All others (i.e., 19 Japanese and 17 Korean speakers) expressed the paper falling event with an intransitive frame. More specifically, as shown in examples (44) and (45), speakers of Japanese and Korean used two or more clauses to describe this event. Typically, these speakers used two separate clauses: one to express that the fan turned on and the other to express the paper falling into the basket.

Japanese:

(44) *Sempuki -ga mawat -te sono -mae -no -gomi -ga shita -no gomi*
fan -Subj turn -Conn it -front -of -garbage-Subj below-of garbage
-bako -ni ochi -mashi -ta.
basket-Loc fall -Polite -Past.
'(The) fan turned on, and (the) garbage in front of it fell to (the) garbage basket.'

Korean:

(45) *Senphwungki-ga tolaka -ni congi -ka hyuci -thong -ulot teleci -ess -ta.*
fan -Subj turn -Conn paper -Subj garbage -can -to fall -Past-SE.
"When (the) fan turned on, (the) paper fell to (the) garbage can."

In Spanish, nine speakers expressed the "paper falling" in a transitive construction with the "fan" as the agent directly causing the falling, as in (46). The remaining 11 speakers in Spanish used intransitive constructions, as shown in (47). Four of the 11 speakers used a periphrastic causative construction with the verb *hacer que* 'make that,' + intransitive clause and conveyed that the causation was indirect as in (48).

Spanish :

(46) *El ventilador empuja un papel hacia un cesto de basura.*
the fan pushes a paper toward a basket of trash.
'The fan pushes a paper towards a trash basket.'

TABLE 6.4 Number of Responses with Transitive Constructions and with Path Specification for the "Paper Falling" Motion Event in Scene 28

	Transitive construction with Cause verb	Expression of 'downward' trajectory	Expression of the dynamic Path 'into'
English	20	1	20
Japanese	1	14	5
Korean	3	12	8
Spanish	9	8	2

(47) *Se prende un abanico y cae un papel sobre la canasta.*
clitic turns.on a fan and falls a paper on the basket
'A fan turns on and a paper falls on the basket.'

Spanish: periphrastic causative

(48) *Está el abanico prendido y hace que el papel caiga sobre una*
is the fan turned.on and makes that the paper fall on a
canasta.
basket
'The fan is on, and it makes the paper fall on a basket.'

Notice that the speakers of the V-languages mentioned the 'fan' turning on. This suggests that the speakers of these languages were aware of the causal role of the fan. They did not convey it explicitly in their grammar, however, and left it up to the listener to make the inference. This is probably because their grammars did not provide them with an easy way of expressing indirect causation in a single clause (see Slobin, 2004 for more discussion on constraints of grammar on speakers' expression of Motion events).

Recall that the scene depicts several paths of the paper's movement: going 'off' the table, falling 'downward,' and going 'into' the basket. The two types of language differed significantly in the kinds of path they expressed in their description. This is shown in Table 6.4. Nineteen of the 20 speakers in English expressed the path 'into' (denoting a change of state) leaving the downward motion unexpressed (see Example 49). Only one speaker expressed both the paths 'into' and 'down' (and also 'off') as in (50).

(49) *The fan blew the paper into the basket.*

(50) *A fan was used to generate a little wind that would blow the blue piece of paper off of the table and down into the trash can that was below it.*

In contrast, a majority of Japanese and Korean speakers focused on downward motion in the main Path verb (e.g., 'fall') as in the above examples (44) and (45), which are repeated here.

Japanese:

(44) *Sempuki -ga mawat-te sono -mae -no -gomi -ga shita -no gomi*
Fan -Subj turn -Conn it -front -of -garbage -Subj below -of garbage
-bak -ni ochi -mashi -ta.
-basket -Loc fall -Polite -Past.
'(The) fan turned on, and (the) garbage in front of it fell to (the) garbage basket.'

Korean:

(45) *Senphwungki-ga tolaka-ni congi -ka hyuci -thong -ulot teleci -ess -ta.*
Fan -Subj turn -Conn paper -Subj garbage-can -to fall -Past-SE.
'When (the) fan turned on, (the) paper fell to (the) garbage can.'

In Spanish, eight speakers used the verb *caer* 'fall' to express the downward motion. No one used the verb *entrar* 'go.in/enter' to express the Path 'into.' Notice also that these speakers used *sobre* 'on.' (One informant later said that *sobre* referred to the resulting state of the paper being on the surface of the bottom of the basket.) The Spanish speakers who used transitive verbs to express causation (e.g., *empujar* 'push,' *aventar* 'throw') used general prepositions *hacia* 'toward,' *a* 'to', or *en* 'in' to express the Path.

The difference between the two paths, *into* and *fall down*, is that *into* expresses change of location, whereas *down* expresses a trajectory. The present data suggest that English speakers foreground the change of state—*into* in this case—whereas speakers of Path languages focus on the trajectory. The crosslinguistic difference was more pronounced between English and Japanese/Korean. The Spanish data were different from both English and Japanese/Korean. More Spanish speakers, expressed Causation than Japanese or Korean speakers did (nine Spanish speakers compared to one Japanese and three Korean speakers), but the number was far fewer than the English speakers (nine Spanish, compared to 20 English speakers). Spanish also differed from Japanese and Korean in the expression of Path: The Spanish speakers did not express the downward trajectory as often as the Japanese or Korean speakers.

Overall, the data show that when the event includes both caused and spontaneous motion, speakers of the two types of language show significant differences. Speakers of S-framed languages have a strong tendency to use transitive constructions expressing Cause in the main clause. (Focus on "change of state" by English speakers (for the "fan and paper" scene) is compatible with their tendency to highlight Cause, in that Cause entails a change.) In contrast, speakers of V-framed languages tend to use intransitive constructions highlighting the Path or trajectory of the motion.

Scene with No Salient Path

The results for Scene (28) above suggest that languages differ in the extent to which they highlight the Cause or Path/trajectory of Motion and that the difference is based on the lexicalization patterns of the languages. This takes us to the last scene to be analyzed in this section, namely Scene (21). In Scene (21), Mary is shown first inside the room (near the door), and next she is outside the room. In this scene, then, the actual process of her going out of the room is not shown. The question here is: To what extent do speakers express the trajectory of the motion?

The participants' responses were categorized in terms of whether they described the event as two separate locative states or one Motion event using a Motion verb such as 'go out' or 'move.' Table 6.5 shows the results: All 20 English speakers, except one (who said "she moved from inside the room to outside the room"), expressed the two states in separate clauses and did not encode the process implicit in the scene, as in example (51).

(51) *She was inside the room, and then outside the room.*

In contrast, several speakers of all three Path languages were quite comfortable in expressing the trajectory that was not explicitly shown. This was again particularly true of Japanese and Korean speakers: Twelve speakers in Japanese and

TABLE 6.5 Number of Responses Expressing Path for Scene 21

	M is inside, then outside	
	Expressing Path 'go out'	**Expressing Motion 'move'**
English	0	1
Japanese	7	5
Korean	9	4
Spanish	4	0

13 speakers of Korean used either the verb 'go' or 'move,' encoding a dynamic trajectory for the scene (see examples 52 and 53).

Japanese:

(52) *Kyoshitsu -no deiriguchi -no temae -ni ita joisei -ga syunkan ido*
classroom -of doorway -of this.side -Loc be woman -Subj instant movement
-de rouka ni deru.
-by corridor -Loc exit.
'A woman who was at this side of (the) doorway of (a) classroom goes out to (the) corridor by instant movement.'

Korean:

(53) *Younghi -ga kyosil pakk -ulo na -o -ass -ta.*
Younghi -Subj classroom outside -to exit -come -Past -SE
'Younghi came out of (the) classroom.'

Spanish speakers showed more English-like behavior than Japanese or Korean: 16 of the 20 Spanish speakers expressed the event as two separate locative states (as in 54), and only four speakers expressed the trajectory with a Motion verb (as in 55).

(54) *Estaba dentro y de pronto estaba fuera.*
'She was inside and suddenly she was outside.'

(55) *María salió del salón de clases.*
'Maria went.out from/left the classroom.'

A one-way ANOVA comparing the four languages (between-subject variable) on whether the speakers expressed the scene as one Motion event or as two separate states (within-subject variable) showed a main effect for Language. Post-hoc Tukey tests showed that English differed significantly from Japanese and Korean ($p<0.001$), but not from Spanish ($p = 0.540$). These data suggest that for many Japanese and Korean speakers, Path is an element that is typically filled in (and inferred) in their linguistic description (and perhaps in their conceptualization of the event), even when they have not actually seen the trajectory in an explicit way. In contrast, English and Spanish speakers focus on change of state in their linguistic description of Motion events and thus do not fill in the Path information if they have not seen it explicitly.

GENERAL DISCUSSION

In this study, I have explored the extent to which S- and V-framed languages (English vs. Japanese, Korean, and Spanish) differ in the way they structure Motion events, particularly in relation to Path and Causation. The data presented here indicate that typological differences in lexicalization patterns lead to systematic differences in the syntactic treatments of those domains.

First, whereas English (an S-framed language) consistently uses an intransitive construction for all types of Path, the three V-framed languages make a syntactic distinction between two types of Path: (1) endpoint paths, 'into,' 'out of,' and punctual 'up/down'; and (2) trajectory paths, 'across,' 'over,' and durative 'up/down.' It is proposed here that the endpoint paths essentially express a change of state (in terms of the spatial relation between the Figure and the Ground element). For this type of paths, completion of the trajectory occurs rather punctually and swiftly, as there is no salient barrier between source and goal. For these paths, all S- and V-framed languages converge on using intransitive clauses with appropriate spatial prepositions or locative markers that refer to the source or goal. In contrast, trajectory paths involve a barrier between source and goal locations. For these paths, the V-framed languages use transitive constructions with the barrier (i.e., Ground nominal) as the direct object (i.e., core argument) of the Motion verb. These findings reveal that Path, which has been classified as a single category, is not of uniform nature. Rather, it consists of different types that may motivate differential syntactic treatments.

Previous studies, e.g., Naigles and Terrazas (1998), Hohenstein, Naigles, and Eisenberg (2004), and Muehleisen and Imai (1997), have proposed that differences in syntactic frames are governed by verb types. Slobin and Hoiting (1994) have also distinguished between boundary-crossing verbs ('enter' and 'cross') and non-boundary-crossing verbs ('ascend,' 'descend,' 'approach,' and 'depart') and have proposed that the distinction has morphological and syntactic consequences. The present data provide only partial support for the claim. First, in support of the claim, my data do show that in V-framed languages, the 'enter' and 'exit' verbs are always realized in intransitive frames and that the 'cross' and 'go.over' verbs are always realized in transitive frames. To this extent, there is a systematic correspondence between the verb type and syntactic frames. However, the 'ascend/descend' verbs provide counterexamples to the claim, as those verbs are used in both syntactic constructions. As I have shown in "Syntactic Encoding of Paths in Spontaneous Motion Events" above, the same verbs (e.g., *ollakata* and *noboru* 'ascend' in Korean and in Japanese, respectively, and *brincar* 'jump' in Spanish) are used in both transitive and intransitive clauses.

It is further proposed here that it is the lexicalization pattern of the V-framed languages that allows differential treatments of syntax for the two types of Path. In V-framed languages the core schema—the Path—is encoded in the main verb, and thus the syntactic role of the Ground can be presented as either oblique or direct object.

The second finding in the present study is the difference between S- and V-framed languages in their expression of complex Motion events. In describing a scene that has multiple components (e.g., both causal and spontaneous motion components), my data show that speakers of Manner/Cause (i.e., S-framed) languages tend to use transitive clauses and highlight the causal aspect of the scene, whereas speakers of Path (i.e., V-framed) languages tend to use intransitive clauses and highlight the trajectory, leaving the causal element in the background (by expressing it in another clause, or not at all). These data suggest that speakers of the two types of language conceptualize Motion event scenes differently at least for the purposes of talking about them. In Slobin and his colleagues' terms, speakers of S- and V-framed languages have different mental images for Motion events (Ozcaliskan & Slobin, 1999). To this extent, the data pose an interesting question about the relationship between language and cognition. For example, do speakers of S-framed languages (more than the speakers of V-framed languages) encode the causal aspect of a Motion event even in a nonverbal situation?

Last, but not least, the present data suggest that the distinction between Manner vs. Path languages does not form a dichotomy but a continuum. I have found that among the Path languages, Japanese and Korean differ from Spanish in that the former show a higher degree of Path language behavior. Conversely, Spanish is more like English. A variation among the languages of the same lexicalization type has been pointed out by Slobin and his colleagues. In their comparison between Turkish and Spanish (both considered to be Path languages), Ozcaliskan and Slobin (1999) found that Turkish speakers were more Path-oriented than Spanish speakers, in that they used more Path verbs in describing events. Japanese and Korean, which are agglutinative languages like Turkish, and are also, like Turkish, SOV languages, also seem to be more Path-oriented than Spanish. Recall that for the "fan and paper" scene (Scene 28), Spanish speakers expressed direct causation significantly more than Japanese and Korean speakers, and for the "no salient Path" scene (Scene 21), they used fewer Path verbs. Further studies need to examine this possibility more systematically.

Finally, although this study did not address the acquisition of these structures, it does raise some important questions for child language research: When and how do children acquire the language-specific patterns? In more specific terms: When and how is the distinction between different types of path made in children? Is the distinction initially made at the lexical level (e.g., semantic distinction between the path morphemes 'into' and 'across') and later at the syntactic level (i.e., syntactic distinction between two types of path in children learning V-languages)? Or is the lexical distinction made through children's early sensitivities to the differences in syntactic frames for the two types of path? Studies by Naigles and her colleagues (Hohenstein, Naigles, & Eisenberg, 2004) would predict that the latter may be the case. Hohenstein et al. (2004) explored the age at which children become sensitive to language-specific lexicalization patterns, particularly in relation to syntactic frames. Their data show that whereas 3½-year-old English and Spanish learners are sensitive to Path-framed and Manner-framed syntax in understanding the meaning of the verb (i.e., when the syntactic frame is Path, children understand the verb to have a Path meaning, but when the frame is Manner, they understand the verb to have a Manner meaning), they are not sensitive to the verb meaning per se when there is no syntactic frame associated with it (i.e., when the verb is presented with no particular syntactic frame—e.g., *they are kradding*). These data would suggest that children develop lexical knowledge through their syntactic analysis of sentence constructions in which the lexical items occur. However, that study was limited to children's understanding of Manner vs. Path meanings of verbs. Further studies are needed to understand the development of different types of paths.

ACKNOWLEDGMENT

I am indebted to Melissa Bowerman for introducing me the topic of Motion events. The data presented here were collected and transcribed in part by my two graduate students, Heather Bentley and Minoru Saito. I thank them also for the many discussion sessions we have had about the data. My deep thanks also go to Ginny Gathercole who gave me valuable comments on an earlier draft.

REFERENCES

Aske, J. (1989). Path predicates in English and Spanish: A closer look. In *Proceedings of the Fifteenth Annual Meeting of the Berkeley Linguistics Society* (pp. 1–14). Berkeley, CA: Berkeley Linguistics Society.

Berman, R., & Slobin, D. I. (1994). *Relating events in narrative: A crosslinguistic developmental study.* Hillsdale, NJ: Erlbaum.

Choi, S., & Bowerman, M. (1991). Learning to express motion events in English and Korean: The influence of language-specific lexicalization patterns. *Cognition, 41,* 83–121.

Dowty, D. R. (1991). Thematic proto-roles and argument selection. *Language, 67,* 547–619.

Hohenstein, J. M., Naigles, L. R., & Eisenberg, A. R. (2004). Keeping verb acquisition in motion: A comparison of English and Spanish. In D. G. Hall & S. Waxman (Eds.), *Weaving a lexicon* (pp. 569–602). Cambridge, MA: MIT Press.

Mayer, M. (1969). *Frog, where are you?* New York: Dial Press.

Muehleisen, V., & Imai, M. (1997). Transitivity and incorporation of ground information in Japanese path verbs. In M. Verspoor, K.D. Lee, & E. Sweetser (Eds.), *Lexical and syntactical constructions and the construction of meaning.* Amsterdam: John Benjamins.

Naigles, L. R., Eisenberg, A. R., Kako, E. T., Highter, M., & McGraw, N. (1998). Speaking of motion: Verb use in English and Spanish. *Language and Cognitive Process, 13,* 521–549.

Naigles, L. R., & Terrazas, P. (1998). Motion-verb generalizations in English and Spanish: Influences of language and syntax. *Psychological Science, 9,* 363–369.

Ozcaliskan, S., & Slobin, D. I. (1999). Learning how to search for the frog: Expression of manner of motion in English, Spanish, and Turkish. In A. Greenhill et al. (Eds.), *The 23rd Proceedings of the Boston University Conference of Language Development* (pp. 541–552).

Slobin, D. I. (1998). *Verbalized events: A dynamic approach to linguistic relativity and determinism.* Paper presented at LAUD-Symposium on "Humboldt and Whorf Revisited," Duisburg, Germany.

Slobin, D. I. (2004). The many ways to search for a frog: Linguistic typology and the expression of motion events. In S. Stromqvist & L. Verhoeven (Eds.), *Relating events in narrative: Vol. 2. Typological and contextual perspectives* (pp. 219–257). Mahwah, NJ: Erlbaum.

Slobin, D. I., & Hoiting, N. (1994). Reference to movement in spoken and signed languages: Typological considerations. In S. Gahl, A. Dolbey, & C. Johnson (Eds.), *Proceedings of the 20th Annual Meeting of the Berkeley Linguistics Society* (pp. 487–505). Berkeley, CA: Berkeley Linguistics Society.

Talmy, L. (1985). Lexicalization patterns: Semantic structure in lexical forms. In T. Shopen (Ed.), *Language typology and syntactic description: Vol. 3. Grammatical categories and the lexicon* (pp. 58–76). Cambridge, UK: Cambridge University Press.

Talmy, L. (1991). Path to realization: A typology of event conflation.In L.A. Sutton & C. Johnson (Eds.), *Proceedings of the 17th Annual Meeting of the Berkeley Linguistics Society* (pp. 480–519). Berkeley, CA: Berkeley Linguistics Society.

Personal Tribute

DAN I. SLOBIN

I first met Melissa through correspondence, in the days long before e-mail. It was 1965, and I had just left Harvard grad school to take up my first (and lifelong) job at Berkeley. She was beginning her studies with Roger Brown and was considering doing an innovative thesis project: investigating acquisition of a language other than English, using the new methods of child language research. She had picked Finnish, and sent me her proposal with a request for advice. I was excited because I had begun to review the published crosslinguistic acquisition literature and felt limited by the general lack of information about non-Indo-European languages, as well as the heavy reliance on diary studies. The next year I dropped in on Roger Brown's research group in the new William James Hall, where I met Melissa, and made various proposals for crosslinguistic research to Brown's group. That was the beginning of a lasting professional and personal friendship. It finally turned out that, with roots in Harvard and Berkeley (where she had grown up), we found ourselves also tied to Holland, and to Nijmegen and Groningen in particular. Melissa found a research home at the Max Planck Institute for Psycholinguistics and a family home with Wijbrandt van Schuur in Nijmegen; I found a half-time family home with my partner, Nini Hoiting, in Groningen—where Wijbrandt is a professor at the University. Over many years, I have had a professional base in Nijmegen, spending sabbaticals and shorter research stays there, and serving on the Scientific Advisory Board (Fachbeirat) for the past dozen years. So, oscillating between Groningen, Nijmegen, and Berkeley, Melissa and I have carried on a running scientific dialog, a sporadic collaboration of her flute and my piano, and a continuing intellectual and personal friendship. Over the years, she patiently weaned me away from my predilection for preestablished starting points in semantic development. She did this by presenting compelling empirical evidence and argumentation, based on crosslinguistic findings that I couldn't resist. We are now both engaged in the search for ways in which the exposure to language guides early development, as well as trying to deal with the challenge of finding natural universal starting points in the light of diversity. I trust that my little contribution to this Festschrift will serve not only as a token of my deep respect for Melissa, but that it will also give the two of us some more questions to ponder together.

7

Relations between Paths of Motion and Paths of Vision

A Crosslinguistic and Developmental Exploration

DAN I. SLOBIN

University of California at Berkeley

The gods…contrived the eyes to give light….The pure fire which is within us…they made to flow through the eyes in a stream smooth and dense….

—Plato, Timaeus (c. 360 BC/1949, p. 27)

…when the eyelids are contracted [the sight] is made to strike in a concentrated way….

—Aristotle, Problems connected with the eyes (31. 7–11, c. 350 BC/1937, p. 189)

We note that the set of prepositions used [with *look* and *see*] is a subset of the prepositions which can be used with an ordinary verb of motion, such as *fly*, to indicate the goal of the motion.

—Gruber (1967, p. 937)

PATHS OF VISION IN LANGUAGE

Whatever the facts of physics and physiology, I feel that I look *out* at the world through my eyes; that I can look *through* the window *over* the treetops *down toward* the city below. The ancient Greeks, too, thought that the eyes send out beams that meet objects and make them visible to us. And linguists, starting at least with Gruber in 1967, have noted that verbs of perception appear in the same syntactic and semantic constructions as verbs of motion. Various terms have been used to designate the imagined "probe" that emanates from the eyes. Gruber suggests that we speak of someone's "gaze" going across a room, just as we speak of a person going across a room. In Talmy's insightful analysis of "fictive motion" he speaks of "the motion of the line of sight that emerges from my eyes" (Talmy, 2000a, p. 110). In a dissertation on English perception verbs, Gisborne (1996) refers to "the path of the gaze" (p. 41) and suggests that the gaze itself is a "hidden theme" (p. 154). Talmy provides an example—*I looked into/toward/past/away from the valley*—and proposes a corresponding image schema:

> Here, the conceptualization appears to be that the Agent subject volitionally projects his line of sight as a Probe from himself as Source along the path specified by the preposition relative to a Reference Object. (Talmy, 2000a, p. 116)

This conceptualization has received explicit formulation in the FrameNet Project of Fillmore and his colleagues (Johnson, Fillmore et al., 2001). Verbs such as *look* fit in the frame PERCEPTION_ACTIVE, which "contains perception words whose Perceivers intentionally direct their attention to some entity or phenomenon in order to have a perceptual experience."[1] The Frame has the following elements that are relevant to the present chapter:

- Perceiver-Agentive — *He looked into the house.*
- Phenomenon — *He looked at the house.*
- Direction — *He looked across the street.*
- Location of Perceiver — *He looked from the balcony.*
- Manner — *He looked carefully.*

In English, at least, various combinations of these elements are possible, such as: *He looked in through the window at her; She looked out from between the curtains.* Directional adverbs can be combined with path phrases—for example, *They looked down/north from the tower toward the sea.* This chapter focuses on the two components that express Path: Direction (way-stations and goal) and Location (source).

This all seems so natural to English speakers that we would be surprised if comparable visual path expressions were found to be lacking in other languages. The ancient Greek idea of emanation or extramission is clearly based on a conceptualization of some visual entity that moves along physical paths. And, indeed,

[1] The following lexemes are listed as fitting this frame: *attend .v, attention .n, eavesdrop .v, feel .v, gaze .n, gaze .v, glance .n, glance .v, listen .v, look .n, look .v, observation .n, observe .v, palpate .v, peek .n, peek .v, peer .v, savor .v, smell .v, sniff .n, sniff .v, spy .v, stare .n, stare .v, taste .n, taste .v, view .v, watch .v.* The present chapter deals only with equivalents of *look .v* in various types of languages.

visual path expressions are widely found across languages.[2] The following examples of expressions that fit the PERCEPTION_ACTIVE frame come from two quite different types of languages, Spanish and Russian, but note that in both languages the constructions in (a) combine a verb of looking with the same path expression that is used in (b) for physical motion.

(1) Spanish:
  a. visual path:
     miraron *hacia* *la* *escalera*
     they:looked toward the staircase
  b. physical path:
     caminaron *hacia* *la* *escalera*
     they:walked toward the staircase

(2) Russian:
  a. visual path:
     starik *vy-* *gljanul* *iz* *okna*
     old.man out- looked from window
  b. physical path:
     ptica *vy-* *letela* *iz* *okna*
     bird out- flew from window

Looking more broadly across languages, the recruitment of path expressions to verbs of looking is widespread and apparently independent of factors of morphological and lexical typology. Table 7.1[3] provides representative examples from a range of languages of different types, underlining expressions of the path 'into the hole' (based on "the frog story"; Berman & Slobin, 1994). The examples present a considerable array of morphosyntactic path constructions: prepositions, particle verbs, serial verbs, verb components, function verbs. The conceptual and linguistic equation of physical and visual paths seems to be universal, although expressed by various linguistic means in languages of different types.

The remainder of this chapter focuses on two major types of languages, categorized by Talmy (1985, 1991) on the basis of their dominant lexicalization pattern for motion events. The classification is based on the preferred means of encoding Path. In one type, *verb-framed*, Path tends to be encoded in the main verb of a clause, using verbs with meanings such as 'enter,' 'exit,' 'ascend,' 'descend.' Verb-framed language groups include Romance, Semitic, and Turkic—represented in the present chapter by Spanish and Turkish. In the other major type,

---

[2] I've supplemented my own observations with helpful responses to queries posted on electronic discussion lists. Such sources are indicated by name and date, without entries in the References. I'm especially grateful to Yo Matsumoto for providing unpublished materials, and to Nikolas Gisborne for providing his unpublished dissertation on English perception verbs (Gisborne, 1996).

[3] The examples in Table 7.1 are drawn from frog story narrations and e-mail correspondence provided by Ayhan Aksu-Koç, Michael Bamberg, Ruth Berman, Lourdes de León, Michael Noonan, Noel Rude, Eva Schultze-Berndt, and Richard Wong. Glosses of grammatical terms can be found in the Appendix.

TABLE 7.1 Examples of Visual Path Expressions in Various Types of Languages*

prepositions: Hebrew (Berman)
ha -yeled mistakel le -tox xor
DEF.ART boy looks to -inside hole
'The boy looks into the hole.'

casemarking: Chantyal [Tibeto-Burman] (Noonan)
mar dula-nɦa-ri pəni kyata-sə sɦya-m
downward hole-INESSIVE also boy-ERGATIVE look.at-NONPAST
'Downward into the hole the boy looks.'

casemarking, prepositions, verb particles: German (Bamberg)
er kuckt in ein loch hin -ein
he looks in INDEF.ART.ACC hole thither -in
'He looks thither into a hole.'

locative nominals (postpositions), casemarking: Turkish (Aksu-Koç)
deliğ -in iç -in -e bak - tı
hole -GEN interior -POSS -DAT look -PAST
'He looked into the hole.'

serial verbs: Cantonese (Wong)
nei5 zong1 jap6 go3 lung1 dou6 aa1
you peek enter CLASSIFIER hole there SENTENCE.FINAL.PARTICLE
'You look into the hole there.'

bipartite verbs: Nez Perce (Rude)
staláhsa 'look up'
steléhnen 'look down'
steléht 'look out'
steylék 'peer in'

directionals (DIR): Tzotzil Mayan (de León)
s-k'el-oj ech'el muyel li tz'i`e
3E-see-PF pass:DIRECTIONAL ascend:DIRECTIONAL ART dog
'The dog is looking away upwards.'

function verbs: Jaminjung [Yirram, N. Australia] (Schultze-Berndt)
ngayirr ganarram jarriny=biyang
peep 3SG:3SG-transfer.away.from.deictic.center hole=FOCUS
'He peeps into the hole.'

* The examples are drawn from frog story narrations and correspondence provided by Ayhan Aksu-Koç, Michael Bamberg, Ruth Berman, Lourdes de León, Michael Noonan, Noel Rude, Eva Schutze-Berndt, and Richard Wong. Glosses of grammatical terms can be found in this chapter's Appendix.

satellite-framed, Path tends to be encoded by elements associated with the main verb, such as verb particles and affixes. The corresponding Path expressions in satellite-framed languages are 'go in/out/up/down.' Satellite-framed language groups include Germanic, Slavic, and Finno-Ugric—represented here by English and Russian.[4]

[4] The last four languages in Table 7.1 represent types that do not readily fit into Talmy's dichotomy (see Slobin, 2004, for a proposal of a third major type: *equipollently framed*). These languages are not considered in the present analysis. However, a recent analysis of visual path expressions in Mandarin (Chu, 2003) indicates that this serial-verb language uses many physical path expressions with verbs of looking, as shown in the examples in Table 7.1; Matsumoto (2001) reports similar use of serial path verbs with a verb of looking in Thai (drawn from Takahashi, 2000).

Although much of the psycholinguistic research in this domain has focused on expressions of Manner of motion in these two language types, it is Path that is at issue in the present cross-typological analysis. In satellite-framed languages with nonbounded verb particles, such as English, a clause with a single verb can present a series of path elements (e.g., *the owl flew down from out of the hole in the tree*). Languages like English and Russian also have a large lexicon of locative prepositions, with various possibilities of combination, such as English *from under* and Russian *iz-pod* 'from-under.' By contrast, in verb-framed languages each change of path requires a separate verb, and combinations are difficult or impossible. In the example given above, one can say that the owl 'descended' (= *down*), that the owl 'exited' (= *out*), or that the owl 'flew'—but these three sorts of information cannot be presented in a single clause. The collection of path markers in noun phrases tends to be limited—a small collection of prepositions in Spanish, with fairly general meanings (e.g., *en* 'in/on'), or a small set of locative nominals in Turkish (e.g., *iç* 'interior,' *üst* 'top') and a binary choice of locative casemarkers: DATIVE (motion toward goal) and ABLATIVE (motion away from goal). Research on path descriptions in novels and elicited narratives (Slobin, 1996b, 1997, 2003) suggests that speakers of satellite-framed languages tend to provide more elaborate path descriptions than speakers of verb-framed languages. This tendency is explored here in the domain of visual paths.

Ongoing research suggests that speakers of these two language types develop different patterns of "thinking for speaking" (Slobin, 1987, 1991, 1996a). Briefly, habitual means for describing physical paths appear to influence mental processes involved in the conceptualization of motion events. Language-specific differences show up in strategies for the presentation of both Path and Manner information in narratives—oral as well as written, produced by children as well as adults (Berman & Slobin, 1994; Slobin, 1996b, 1997). And cognitive effects are found in cross-linguistic studies of mental imagery (Slobin, 2003), memory (Oh, 2003), and learning tasks (Kersten, Meissner, Schwartz, & Rivera, 2003). We also know from the work of Bowerman, Choi, and others that very young children show language-specific conceptual patterns in the domain of space (Bowerman, 1996a, 1996b; Bowerman & Choi, 2001; Choi, 1997; Choi & Bowerman, 1991). Thus, although physical movement must be the same for all people—in terms of perceptual and motor patterns—there is growing evidence that differences on the level of semantics may differentially affect attention to components of motion events.

If these differences carry over into the domain of *visual* motion—that is, a domain of fictive motion—there might be similar differences between verb- and satellite-framed languages in preferred means of encoding visual paths, and consequently, in conceptual representations across languages. On the other hand, verb-framed languages do not provide specialized verbs for visual paths, on a par with 'enter,' 'ascend,' and the like; rather, both types of languages rely on all-purpose perception verbs such as 'look,' combined with various sorts of adjuncts (adpositional phrases and directional adverbs in both language types, plus satellites in satellite-framed languages). It may be, therefore, that the marked differences between the two language types in the domain of physical motion fall away in the domain of visual motion. This chapter is an initial attempt to explore such differences. So far, the only available information comes from data of language production—oral and written texts. The following section explores differences in written materials in two satellite-framed languages, English and Russian, and two verb-framed languages, Spanish and Turkish. The concluding section addresses the same issues in child language, examining transcripts of child-caregiver discourse and elicited oral narratives in the same four languages.

PATHS OF VISION IN ENGLISH

To begin with, consider the English verb *look* and its associated path expressions. The *Oxford English Dictionary* (1994) provides Path as part of the basic meaning of the verb:

I. To direct one's sight.
   1. intr. To give a certain direction to one's sight; to apply one's power of vision; to direct one's eyes upon some object or towards some portion of space.
      a. with phrase or adv. expressing the direction or the intended object of vision.

The basic use of *look*, of course, is in a construction with a generic locative preposition, *look* ***at*** (previously *look* ***upon***). Beyond this core path expression, Branch IV of the OED definition provides numerous "specialized uses with prepositions." Many of them are figurative, but there is a core of visual path expressions across a wide range of prepositions. Some are obsolete, indicating that this is a domain that continues to draw upon directional terms for the expression of visual paths. Table 7.2 lists most of the forms, with an early example of each.

A preliminary search of the British National Corpus (BNC) reveals a much wider range of prepositions and directional adverbs occurring with *look*. The following simple path expressions are found: *about, across, along, among, around, away, back, behind, below, beneath, between, beyond, down, eastward, in, inside, northwards, out, over, past, round, southwards, through, towards, under, underneath, up*.

COMPLEX PATH EXPRESSIONS

The BNC also has numerous examples of complex path expressions, such as *look down into X, look through X into Y,* and *look beyond X then over Y.* Such multisegment paths frequently occur in English descriptions of physical motion, but they are quite rare in some other languages, such as Spanish. This seems to be a general characteristic of satellite-framed languages (e.g., English, German, Russian) in comparison with verb-framed languages (e.g., Spanish, Turkish, Hebrew) (Slobin, 1997). For example, (3) is a sentence from a novel written in English (Anaya, 1972), with a single motion verb, *run*, associated with a complex path: *out–past–towards*. A Spanish translation of this sentence (Anaya, 1992) breaks it into three clauses, each with its own verb and associated preposition: 'exit through'—'pass

TABLE 7.2 Uses of ***look*** with Path Prepositions in the ***Oxford English Dictionary****

† 13. ***look against*** *—. To look at (something dazzling).* Obs.
1598 Shakes. Merry W. *ii. ii. 254 Shee is too bright to be look'd against.*
16. ***look into***—.
b. To direct one's sight to the interior of.
1841 Lane Arab. Nts. I. 99 The fisherman, looking into the lake saw in it fish of different colours.
20. ***look through***—.
a. To direct one's sight through (an aperture, a transparent body, or something having interstices)
1580 Lyly Euphues *(Arb.) 289 Since your eyes are so sharpe, that you cannot onely looke through a milstone, but cleane through the minde.*
21. ***look to***—.
a.To direct a look or glance to. In early use chiefly Sc., equivalent to the mod. look at
c1375 Sc. Leg. Saints *xviii.* (Egipciane) *356 þane stud Þe monk..to Þe erde lukand.*
[then stood the monk…to the earth looking]
22. a. ***look toward(s*** *—.*
a1310 in Wright Lyric P. *69 Ihesu,… With thine suete eyen loke towart me.*
[with thy sweet eyes look toward me]
23. ***look unto*** —. arch. = look to, *in various senses*
1591 Spenser M. Hubberd *292 For ere that unto armesIme betooke, Unto my fathers sheepeIusde to looke.*
30. a. ***look around***. intr. *To look in several directions*
1754 A. *Murphy* Gray's Inn Jrnl. *No. 93 He looked around, and saw a reverend Form advance towards him.*
31. ***look aside***. intr. *To turn aside one's eyes; to look obliquely.*
1855 Browning Andrea del Sarto *147 They pass and look aside.*
32. ***look back***. *intr.*
a. To turn and look at something in the direction from which one is going or from which one's face is turned.
a1586 Sidney Arcadiai(1590) 2 At yonder rising of the ground she turned her selfe, looking backe toward her woonted abode.
33. ***look down.***
a. intr. See simple senses and down adv.
c1375 Sc. Leg. Saints *xxxvii.* (Vincencius) *326 Keparis of Þe presone, Þat thru smal holis lokit done.*
[…that through small holes looked down]
34. ***look downward***. intr. = look down, 33.
1667 Milton P.L. *iii. 722 Look downward on the Globe whose hither side With light from hence, though but reflected, shines.*
35. ***look forth***. intr. *To look out (of a window, etc., on to something). Now arch. and poet.*
1611 Bible Song Sol. *ii. 9 He looketh forth…at the windowe.*
37. ***look in***.
a. See simple senses and in adv.
a1300 Cursor M. *17288 + 188 (Cott.) Iohne…loked in…*
† 38. ***look off.*** *To turn one's eyes away.* Obs.
171011 Swift Jrnl. to Stella *4 Jan., No, no, look off, do not smile at me.*
40. ***look out***.
a. intr. *(See simple senses and out.) To look from within a building or the like to the outside*
1390 Gower Conf. *II. 352 That I be nyhte mai arise, At som wyndowe and loken oute.*
[…at some window and look out]
41. ***look over***.
a. trans. To cast one's eyes over; to scrutinize
1706 Hearne Collect. *8 Mar. (O.H.S.) I. 201 Dr. Kennett..look'd them [MSS.] all over.*
42. ***look round.*** intr.
a. To look about in every direction.

TABLE 7.2 (continued) Uses of ***look*** with Path Prepositions in the ***Oxford English Dictionary****

1526 Tindale Mark *iii. 5 He loked rounde aboute on them angrely.*
43. ***look through****.*
a. trans. *To penetrate with a look or glance*
c1450 Holland Howlat 49, I sawe ane Howlat…Lukand the laike throwe.
[…looking the lake through]
† 44. ***look under****.* intr. *To look down. Obs.*
1700 Dryden Pal. & Arc. *ii. 340 Thus pondering, he looked under with his eyes.*
45. ***look up****.*
a. See simple senses and up adv.; to raise the eyes, turn the face upward.
c1200 Trin. Coll. Hom. *173 Đanne…Þo wreches…lokeð up and dun and al abuten.*
[…looked up and down and all about]

* *For clarification, glosses of path components of older examples are added in square brackets.*

by'—'direct oneself to.' This is required by the fact that Spanish requires each change of path to be expressed by a verb when the change is telic (Aske, 1989), or boundary-crossing (Slobin & Hoiting, 1994), or moving with relation to the earth's gravity (Talmy, 2000b).

(3) **English original**	**Spanish translation**
I ran <u>out</u> the kitchen door,	*<u>Salí</u> por la puerta de la cocina*
	(= I <u>exited</u> the kitchen door)
<u>past</u> the animal pens,	*<u>pasé</u> por los corrales*
	(= <u>passed</u> by the animal pens)
<u>toward</u> Jasón's house.	*y <u>me dirigí</u> a casa de Jasón*
	(= and <u>directed myself</u> to Jasón's house)

Verb-framed languages provide a set of path verbs, whereas satellite-framed languages provide a set of path elements that lie outside of the verb. Accordingly, path elements can be stacked with a single verb in satellite-framed languages, while such stacking is only possible in verb-framed languages under particular circumstances, such as mentioning source, goal, and perhaps a way-station along a path between two points. Thus it is possible in a verb-framed language to "go from X to Y" or even "from X along Y to Z," but not "out of X into Y," where special path verbs are required for each path component.

These facts have been well documented for a number of languages of the two types, beginning with Talmy's original proposal. But there is no obvious reason for similar patterns to be found with regard to verbs of looking, since there is no set of specialized verbs for visual paths, as there is for physical paths—that is, there are no verbs with composite meanings such as 'look + exit.'[5] Furthermore, an act

[5] I have found only one instance of a language that has visual path verbs. Klein (1981) reports that Toba, a Guaykuruan language of Argentina, has a set of vision verbs that, like other path verbs, are inherently marked for directionality, e.g., *âe* 'look outward,' *wa* 'look inward,' *sa:t* 'look up at something moving.' She comments: "…the notion of the direction of the eyes appears to be equivalent in the mind of the native speaker to the notion of direction of a person's legs across space" (p. 234).

of looking doesn't bring about a change of locative state of the fictive agent or of the gaze as an extended entity. That is (at least from the point of view of an English speaker), when I look into another room, my gaze is still anchored at my eyes, and has not left me and achieved a new state of containment on the other side of the threshold. But if my dog goes into that room, he is no longer here at my side, but there, having crossed the boundary. That is, boundary-crossing is a change of state event for physical motion, but not for visual motion. Thus, to put (3) in a visual frame, it should be possible to say the equivalent in Spanish of "I looked out the kitchen door, past the animal pens, towards Jasón's house."

Matsumoto (2001) has explicitly proposed that verb-framed languages should not differ from satellite-framed languages in the domain of visual paths, because they are not constrained by path verbs in this domain. This is also what I had expected, based on the phenomenology of an active perceiver who sends a self-anchored probe out into the world. On the basis of expressions of visual paths ("the fictive motion of emanation") in English, Spanish, Hindi, Japanese, Korean, and Thai, Matsumoto notes that verb-framed languages do not provide a set of distinct visual path verbs comparable to physical path verbs such as 'enter/exit,' 'ascend/descend,' and the like. That is, as noted above, there are no verbs that conflate 'look' with 'in' or 'peer' with 'out.' As a consequence, all types of languages are forced to use path expressions (adpositions, particles, directional adverbs, etc.) in combination with verbs of looking, such as the Spanish example in (1a). Matsumoro concludes:

> The verb-framed nature of verb-framed languages tends to be lost in the description of...fictive motion of emanation. This is partly because of the grammatical difference between adposition/particles and verbs; the latter has an elaborated set of grammatical functions, while the former does not, allowing flexibility in describing...emanation. (Matsumoto, 2001, handout, p. 9)

This is certainly true with regard to the frame element of Direction. In verb-framed languages 'enter' and 'ascend,' for example, require individual path verbs; however, the directions of entering and ascending are readily expressed by a verb of looking plus a directional adverb or a directional phrase, such as the following examples from Spanish and Turkish:

	Spanish	**Turkish**		
look—enter	*mirar adentro*	*içine*	*bakmak*	
	look inside	inside:DAT	look	
	mirar en el agujero	*deliğin*	*içine*	*bakmak*
	look in the hole	hole.POSS	inside:DAT	look
look—ascend	*mirar para arriba*	*yukarı*	*bakmak*	
	look toward up	upwards	look	

No specialized path verb is required (or available), so we might expect that thinking for speaking about physical paths would be irrelevant here. Furthermore, Matsumoto's proposal also suggests that languages of different types should not differ in "flexibility" in describing visual paths. Yet we know that, in the domain of physical motion, languages differ in the range and specificity of path-describing forms, as well as in means for combining individual path segments into complex expressions. In addition, there are strong habits, or stylistic preferences in each language for a particular level of analysis and degree of specificity in describing motion events, and, indeed, events in general. Consider example (3) once again. In English it is common to describe paths with several segments, either with a single verb or with several verbs. The Spanish translation shows that such descriptions, using several verbs, are possible in Spanish, but text analysis (Slobin, 1996b) reveals that extended descriptions of this sort are exceptionally rare. That is, there is a Spanish "narrative style" that prefers to limit the number of Ground elements in path depictions, as well as the number of separate clauses used to describe a trajectory. I have proposed that this style is due to the necessity in Spanish to use separate verbs for individual Path segments, in contrast to the possibility in English of using a series of verb particles and prepositional phrases with a single verb. Although these lexicalization patterns do not apply to the description of visual paths, the narrative habit may still hold sway. Informally, I have ascertained that Spanish speakers do not accept literal Spanish translations of sentences such as *I looked out the kitchen door, past the animal pens, towards Jasón's house*, or *Look through the window past the buildings to the Bay*. That is, they reject the use of the single verb *mirar* 'look' with such series of Path segments. This judgment can be checked by searching for evidence that satellite-framed texts show a greater incidence of complex visual paths than verb-framed texts, even though the constraints on the use of types of path verbs do not apply in this domain. Let us begin with two satellite-framed languages, English and Russian, and go on to two verb-framed languages, Spanish and Turkish.

English

As already noted, complex visual paths occur in English.[6] The constructions are the same as those used in describing physical paths. The analysis makes use of only parts of the FrameNet PERCEPTION_ACTIVE frame. Because the relevant cross-typological issue is the reference to landmarks, I will exclude expressions with *Direction* only and no Ground elements, such as the bare *look up* and its equivalents across languages. In the following discussion, I'll use the term *Ground elements* or *Grounds* to designate only the frame elements *Location of Perceiver* (source) and *Direction* (path) when a specific physical location is mentioned. And I will not count expression of *Phenomenon* (goal), since it does not contribute to the complexity of the visual path—that is, there is always a goal of perception in the examples considered here. Thus, in these terms, there is one Ground element

[6] Examples from English are drawn from the British National Corpus (BNC), newspapers, and novels. Examples from other languages are drawn from various online corpora. There are no numerical findings presented here because of differing sizes of available corpora, ease of searching, and time limitations. Thus these data, while suggestive, can only be considered preliminary.

in *look out of the window* and *look out of the window at her,* and there are two Ground elements in *look out of the window (and) across the garden*. In expressions such as *look toward/to the garden*, I count *garden* as a Ground, because of the choice of the directional *toward/to* rather than the default goal preposition *at,* or equivalent default expressions in the other languages. The role of Ground elements in an extended definition of Path is discussed in detail below in the section "What Constitutes Path Complexity?"

There is no problem for English—in either physical or visual motion descriptions—to include several grounds on the way to a goal, and to include boundary-crossing and gravity-centered segments in a single clause or gapped construction. Consider the following examples in the visual domain:

(4) *Burun looked past Zurachina, out into the courtyard.*
(5) *Isabel…looked over Alida's head and out of the sitting room window…*
(6) *As we look to the left, we look down along the curve of the Orion arm inward toward the center of the spiral and the center of our galaxy.*

Nevertheless, visual path expressions do not match the complexity of physical path expressions. This is because trajectories of gaze are necessarily limited in comparison to trajectories of physical movement: One can only see so far without then moving one's body to see further. I have found no examples of visual paths with more than two Grounds in any language,[7] while paths with more segments and Grounds readily occur in physical path descriptions, where the moving body is not constrained by a fixed length of path. In English, such extended descriptions with a single verb of motion readily include boundary-crossing events, such as (7) with the manner verb *chase* and three Grounds (table, hall, door) and (8), with a vast quantity of Grounds and Path vectors associated with the manner verbs *plunge* and *tilt.*

(7) *She chased him three times around the table, then up through the front hall and out of the door.* (Carson McCullers, *The Member of the Wedding*)
(8) *There is in the Midlands a single-line tramway system which boldly leaves the country town and plunges off into the black, industrial countryside, up hill and down dale, through the long, ugly villages of workmen's houses, over canals and railways, past churches perched high and nobly over the smoke and shadows, through stark, grimy cold little market-places, tilting away in a rush past cinemas and shops down to the hollow where the collieries are, then up again, past a little rural church, under the ash trees, on in a rush to the terminus…* (D. H. Lawrence, *England, My England*).

[7] Example (6) has three Ground references, but two of them refer to the same point: *the center of the spiral* and *the center of our galaxy*. This is the most complex visual path I have found thus far.

To conclude, with regard to English, *look* occurs in the same types of frames as motion verbs like *go*, but with real world constraints on the extent of visual paths in comparison with physical paths.

Russian

There are two verbs of looking in Russian, *smotret'* and *gljanut'*, roughly corresponding to English *look* (ignoring aspectual alternations in Russian).[8] They both indicate the goal of looking with the preposition *na* 'on' plus an accusative noun. In addition, *gljanut'* can occur with Path satellites in the form of prefixes. For example:

(9)	*smotret'/gljanut'*	*v*	*okno*		
	look.INF	in	window.ACC		
(10)	*vy-*	*gljanut'*	*iz*	*okna*	
	out-	look.INF	from	window:GEN	
(11)	*vy-*	*gljanut'*	*iz*	*- za*	*štory*
	out-	look	from	-behind	curtain:GEN

In (11) the path prefix *vy-* 'out' combines with the complex preposition *iz-za* 'from-behind' to depict a path that crosses a boundary ('out') along with specification of the location of the perceiver ('behind curtain'). However, unlike English, I have found no examples of complex paths with two explicit Ground elements. I will return to the issue of complex paths in the section below on "What Constitutes Path Complexity?", after presenting the range of data for the four languages.

Differences in path complexity may be due to an intratypological difference between English and Russian on the morphological level, based on the fact that English satellites are separable verb particles, whereas in Russian they are verb prefixes. Thus it is possible to stack satellites in English, as in Talmy's famous *come right back down out from up in there* (Talmy, 1985, p. 102). Although it is possible to stack prepositional phrases of path in Russian, regardless of boundary crossing, prefixes cannot be stacked. Consider two examples from Dostoevsky's *Brothers Karamazov.* In (12) a single nonprefixed verb carries the moving Figure through several Path segments; however, in (13), as in a verb-framed language, successive verbs have to be introduced in order to carry each new Path prefix.

[8] My choice of verbs of looking in other languages is determined by the FrameNet PERCEPTION_ACTIVE frame. In English, Russian, Spanish, and Turkish, variants of "see" do not completely fit this frame. I have also excluded verbs of manner of looking, such as *peek, peep, peer, glimpse, glare,* and the like, because the goal of this chapter is to broadly explore the range of path expressions rather than distinctions of manner. It is interesting to note, however, that English and Russian seem to have more verbs of manner of looking than Spanish and Turkish, paralleling the differences between satellite- and verb-framed languages with regard to the diversity of manner of physical motion verbs (Slobin, 2003).

(12) *Štabs-kapitan stremitel'no kinulsja čerez seni v izbu k xozjaevam* …
'The junior captain quickly dashed, through the entry-way, into the hut, to the owners…'

(13) …*on obežal bol'šim krjukom, čerez pereulok, dom Fedora Pavloviča, probežal Dmitrovskuju ulicu, perebežal potom mostik i prjamo popal v uedinennyj pereulok* …
'…he ran around in a big detour, through/past the lane, the house of Fyodor Pavlovich, ran along Dmitrovsky Street, then ran across the little bridge and fell directly into the secluded lane…'

Note that the English translation of (13) sounds awkward with the repetitions of *ran around, ran along*, and *ran across*, though the construction is not awkward in Russian. Note, too, that the first instance of *bežal* 'ran,' with the prefix *o*-, carries the figure along in relation to two Grounds, the lane and the house. Examples like (12) and (13) are vanishingly rare in verb-framed languages like Spanish and Turkish; they are found in Russian, but not with the frequency of comparable forms in English. These two Russian scenarios go beyond what can be predicated of visual paths, so it's not clear whether the infrequency of complex visual paths in a (small) Russian sample can be attributed to a narrative style that disfavors highly complex paths in descriptions of physical movement. On the face of it, there should be equivalents of constructions like (5), (6), and (7) in Russian, but I haven't found any yet. In any event, it seems clear that more than satellite-framed typology is at play in influencing the use of path expressions—both physical and visual.

Spanish

In the domain of physical motion, Spanish writers overwhelmingly mention only one Ground, and never mention more than two (Slobin, 1996b). The same is true of visual motion. The vast majority of corpus examples are simple directional expressions, as (14) or (15), though sometimes with a boundary-crossing adverb, as in (16). The only explicit boundary-crossing situation is looking through a window, as in (17).

(14) *Miraron hacia la escalera.*
'They looked toward the staircase.'

(15) *Me mira desde el jardín.*
'She looks at me from the garden.'

(16) *Mira directamente hacia fuera del disco*…
'He looks directly towards outside of the disco…'

(17) a. …*mira por la ventana*…
'she looks through the window…'

b. …*mira a través de las ventanillas del auto* …
'… she looks across/through the windows of the car …'

On the basis of limited evidence, it would appear that Spanish speakers treat visual paths with the same circumspection as physical paths, with the additional possibility of using directional adverbs for boundary-crossing scenarios. I suggested above that it should be possible to say the equivalent in Spanish of "I looked out the kitchen door, past the animal pens, toward Jasón's house." Perhaps it is—but native speakers do not seem to think so, and I have found no such examples in Spanish narratives, written or oral, or in online Spanish corpora from novels and newspapers. Thus it appears that thinking for speaking in Spanish—regardless whether the domain is physical or visual—directs attention only to simple paths and whatever Grounds are necessary to anchor those paths, with little additional elaboration.

Turkish

The situation in Turkish is essentially the same as in Spanish. There are mainly simple directional expressions, as in (18), with occasional mention of source, but no mention of two or more Grounds. Boundary-crossing expressions occur with adverbs (19), mainly with regard to windows (20).

(18) …*çevredeki* *tepeler* -*e doğru* *bak* -*ınca*…
…surrounding hills -DAT directly look -NONFIN…
'…when looking straight at the surrounding hills …'

(19) *Merakla* *kafasını* *uzatıp* *içeriye* *bakıyor*…
curiously head:POSS:ACC extend:NONFIN inwards:DAT looks…
'Curiously, extending his head, he looks inside…'

(20) … *pencere* -*den dışarı* *bak* -*tı*.
… window -ABL outwards look -PAST
'… he looked out from the window.'

Again, as in Spanish, visual paths, like physical paths, are presented with little elaboration. The only feature that is not typical of verb-framing is the use of boundary-crossing adverbials, used in place of the path verbs that are not available for visual descriptions.

FRAMING TYPOLOGY AND VISUAL PATH EXPRESSIONS

What Constitutes Path Complexity?

In order to better understand the differences in path expressions between the satellite- and verb-framed languages in this sample, it is useful to make use of Talmy's Path and Ground properties (Talmy, 2000b, 2000d, 2003, personal communication November 15, 2003). The following components are relevant to visual paths:

- **Vector**: "The Vector comprises the basic types of arrival, traversal, and departure that a Figural schema can execute with respect to a Ground schema" (Talmy, 2000d, p. 53). There is a small, possibly universal set of Vectors of motion, of which the following are applicable to visual paths:

MOVE TO, MOVE FROM, MOVE FROM-TO, MOVE VIA, MOVE ALONG, MOVE ALENGTH.

- **Conformation**: "The Conformation component of the Path is a geometric complex that relates the fundamental Ground schema within a Motion-aspect formula to the schema for a full Ground object" (Talmy, 2000d, p. 54). The relevant Conformations for visual paths are found in the geometry of enclosures, lines, and planes—that is, the configurations that are involved in boundary-crossing (into, out of, across, through).
- **Deixis**: "The Deictic component of Path typically has only the two member notions 'toward the speaker' and 'in a direction other than toward the speaker'" (Talmy, 2000d, p. 56).
- **Earth-Grid Displacement**: This component relates Path directedness to earth-based geometry: up-down, over, north-south-east-west, and other absolute, earth-based coordinates (Talmy, 2000b, pp. 201–203).

Note that these are *concurrent* components of Path. For example, a Figure can move to a point at the interior of an enclosure, down from a point toward the speaker.

With regard to visual paths in the data, all four of the languages under study use variants of 'look' with a single Path component and a Ground object, such as 'look from X' (Vector), 'look across X' (Conformation), and 'look behind X' (Deixis). Furthermore, all four languages can mention two Ground objects if the Vector is MOVE FROM-TO: 'Look from X to Y.' All four languages can also mention one Ground when combining one Vector and one Conformation component, such as 'look into' (MOVE TO + A POINT AT THE INSIDE OF AN ENCLOSURE).

However, this seems to represent the limit of combinatorial possibilities for the two verb-framed languages, as summarized in Table 7.3. The two satellite-framed languages demonstrate more combinatorial possibilities. In both English and Russian, Earth-grid Displacement occurs with a Ground object, such as 'look down at X.' And these satellite-framed languages have a range of more complex combinations.

TABLE 7.3 Degrees of Path Complexity in Satellite- and Verb-Framed Languages

Path Complexity	Satellite-Framed (English, Russian)	Verb-Framed (Spanish, Turkish)
1 Vector + 1 Ground	√	√
1 Conformation + 1 Ground	√	√
1 Deictic + 1 Ground	√	√
Vector FROM-TO + 2 Grounds	√	√
1 Earth-grid + 1 Ground	√	
2 Conformations + 1 Ground	√	
2 Conformations + 2 Grounds	√*	
1 Earth-grid + 1 Conformation + 1 Ground	√	
1 Conformation + 1 Deictic + 1 Ground	√	

**English only*

There are expressions with two Conformation components and one Ground, such as 'look out into.' In the English data there are also combinations of two Conformation components with two Grounds, such as 'look past X into Y.' In both English and Russian there are complex visual Paths with an Earth-grid component and a Conformation component, such as 'look down into,' as well as combinations of Conformation and Deixis, such as 'look out from behind X.'

It is striking that the set of visual paths available to Spanish and Turkish seems to match the set of Path verbs in those languages; for example, 'look into' matches 'enter,' 'look out' matches 'exit,' 'look through' matches 'cross.' Just as these languages cannot combine two verbs in a single phrase, such as 'exit enter,' they cannot express 'look out into' as a complex visual Path. This must remain a tentative and speculative proposal, however, until much more data are systematically examined. The interim conclusion is that in the domain of visual motion—even though visual Path verbs are not available in Spanish and Turkish—the patterns of thinking for speaking about physical Paths carry over into conceptualizations of visual Paths—at least as far as complex paths are concerned. But, as suggested in the next section, there is more to the story.

Conceptualizations of Visual Paths in Verb-Framed Languages: Additional Considerations

After completing the interim summary presented above, I had occasion to present these ideas to linguists who are native speakers of Spanish and French—two Romance verb-framed languages.[9] Their responses suggest that I may have been functioning with a satellite-framed speaker's "thinking for theorizing." Consider a scene from the "frog story" (presented in the section on "Visual Paths in Frog Stories" as part of the discussion of child language). A boy is looking into a hole in a tree. My satellite-framed mental image is a visual path that goes from the boy's eyes into the interior of the hole—that is, a Vector that moves forward and a Conformation component that is at the inside of an enclosure. Romance-language speakers, however, may have a rather different conceptualization. Enrique Palancar, a Spanish cognitive linguist, reports (Palancar, personal communication, November 19, 2002):

> There is no salient container schema in *mirar en el agujero* [= look in the hole]. The phrase is presenting the location where the event occurs.

A French cognitive linguist, Stephane Robert, makes the same observation (Robert, personal communication, November 5, 2002):

> For me, *regarder dans le trou* [= look in the hole] does not express a movement (and therefore does not express a path): It is static. The prepositional

---

[9] Text searches of French revealed uses of the verb *regarder* 'look' that are parallel to the uses of Spanish *mirar* reported above. However, Stephanie Pourcel (personal communication, July 24, 2003) has suggested that spoken French may allow a greater range of complexity in clauses using *regarder*.

> complement governed by the perception verb expresses most of the time the "locus," the region on which the activity of perception is exerted. Surely *regarder dans un trou* for me supposes a movement of the eyes toward the hole, but the path of the gaze is present only as a backgrounded and unspecified component. The path can be inferred, but it is not profiled by the linguistic expression.

It would seem, then, that Spanish and French do not fully adhere to the FrameNet schema of PERCEPTION_ACTION, because the frame element of Direction seems to be absent, or at least not an explicit part of the linguistic expression. That is, the expressions consist of a Perceiver-Agentive along with what might be characterized as a Location of Phenomenon. However, this seeming deviation from the expected crosslinguistic (or universal) pattern of fictive motion may be due to morphological factors, and the languages might provide other construction types that adhere to the FrameNet schema. Note that the locative prepositions in the examples from Palancar and Robert do not distinguish between static location and translocation. That is, prepositions like Spanish *en* and French *dans* only indicate a general locative relation, leaving it to the verbal construction and realworld information to fill in interpretations of location versus motion. Compare, for example, Spanish *estar en el agujero* 'to be.located in the hole' and *meter algo en el agujero* 'insert something in the hole.' It may be that the prepositions have a default interpretation of static location that carries over to visual verbs, contributing to the conceptualizations reported for Spanish and French.

English *in* is similarly vague, though we have recourse to *into* for explicit specification of a motion interpretation. Russian clearly distinguishes the two meanings by casemarking, using the LOCATIVE for static location, e.g., *byt' v duple* 'to be in hole:LOCATIVE,' and the ACCUSATIVE for directed motion, *položit' v duplo* 'put in hole:ACCUSATIVE.' What would happen in a verb-framed language with casemarking? Turkish provides such an example, allowing for the visual path conceptualizations that are available in English and Russian. Compare: *delik-te vardı* 'hole-LOCATIVE was' [= (it) was in the hole] and *deliğ-e koy* 'hole-DATIVE put' [= put (it) into the hole]. In both Russian (satellite-framed) and Turkish (verb-framed) the case used with equivalents of 'look' provides directional meaning in phrases accompanying motion verbs (ACCUSATIVE in Russian, DATIVE in Turkish), indicating that visual paths are conceived of in the same way as paths of physical motion—that is, motion directed toward a goal. David Wilkins (personal communication, November 2, 2002) makes a similar observation about casemarking and visual paths in a very different sort of verb-framed language—the Australian aboriginal language Arrernte. In that language, the verb meaning 'see/look' takes the same case frame as verbs like 'put'—{ERGATIVE, DATIVE, ACCUSATIVE}—using the DATIVE to mark the endpoint of putting an object as well as the endpoint of a path of vision.

I would suggest, then, that the reported conceptualizations for Spanish and French may be based on the absence of some means of grammatically distinguishing static location and direction, rather than on verb-framed typology. In fact, an additional observation indicates that Spanish and French conceptualizations of the verbs *mirar* and *regarder* may not disconfirm the general pattern of fictive motion explored in this chapter. These two languages provide an additional expressive device that seems to be the preferred means of describing visual paths—namely, predicating visual path of a nominal entity meaning 'a gaze' or 'a look': *la mirada* in Spanish and *le regard* in French. That is, a fictive object moves along a path, thus retaining the widespread pattern of fictive motion discussed at the outset of this chapter. These nouns occur with great frequency in text searches—but as representing a fictive object or an object of the agent's manipulation, rather than the movement of the agent. Palancar describes the Spanish pattern as follows (personal communication, November 19, 2002):

> When you want to convey path you use causative motion with nouns that depict gaze—*mirada, vista, vistazo,* etc.—and you make them move. For example [from a Spanish magazine]: *mi mirada recorría el encanto del telón* [= my gaze traveled over the charm of the curtain].

Similarly, Stephane Robert reports for French (personal communication, November 5, 2002):

> If you want to express the path of look, you go more naturally through another construction with a verb of movement combined with the noun *regard: porter ses regards sur* [= carry one's gazes over], *plonger ses regards dans* [= plunge one's gazes in]. These expressions seem to me much more natural for expressing the movement and the path of look.

By means of such constructions, verb-framed languages lacking casemarking still adhere to the FrameNet schema of PERCEPTION_ACTIVE, but using different devices. FrameNet defines Perceiver-Agentive as "the being who performs some action in order to have a perceptual experience." In the case of Spanish and French, the action is to project an object, the "gaze," into space. FrameNet defines Direction as "the path-like expression that describes how the perceiver's attention is directed during the act of perception." The path-like expressions are motion verbs along with prepositional phrases and nouns indicating places.

Again, it remains to more thorough research to determine the range of Path complexity that is possible with these nominal forms in Spanish and French. An example of translation from English to French, discussed in a comparative syntax of the two languages (Guillemin-Flescher, 1981, p. 386) demonstrates the considerable complexity that is available in French when using the noun *regard*:

(21) a. **English Original**. *He looked* at her once hard, his expression empty, and then *beyond* her *out across* the meadow, *beyond* the four oaks and the black distant tree line *into* the vacant sky.

b. **French Translation**. *Impassible, il posa sur elle un seul regard dur que, par delà le pré, les quatre chênes et la noire barrière des arbes à l'horizon, alla se perdre dans la vacuité du ciel d'après midi.*
'Impassive, he placed on her a single hard look which, beyond the meadow, the four oaks and the black tree line at the horizon, went to lose itself in the emptiness of the afternoon sky.'

Note, however, that although the French version presents a fairly complex visual path, the English combination of two Conformation components, *out across*, has disappeared; the French 'look' simply 'goes beyond.' The example suggests that it would be fruitful to analyze 'nominal look' expressions in terms of Talmy's collection of Path components and their combinations.

VISUAL PATHS IN CHILD LANGUAGE

Language-learning children acquire both Path systems in the early years—physical path and visual path expressions. In the following section, we examine CHILDES and frog-story data in the same set of languages. The data indicate that the basic patterns discussed above are in place during the preschool period, with elaboration of the system continuing through childhood. Comparable to developmental investigations of other spatial domains (Bowerman, 1996a, 1996b; Bowerman & Choi, 2001; Choi, 1997; Choi & Bowerman, 1991), children's mastery of language-specific path expressions play an important role in the development of thinking for speaking. As Bowerman (1996a) has pointed out, acquisition of semantic patterns is an important cognitive task in development:

> I have argued that the existence of crosslinguistic variation in the semantic packaging of spatial notions creates a complex learning problem for the child (p. 425).... Regardless of whether the semantic categories of our language play a role in fundamental cognitive activities like perceiving, problem solving, and remembering, we must still *learn* them in order to speak our native language fluently. (p. 404)

Caregiver and Child Speech in English

Conversations between English-speaking caregivers and their preschool-age children contain a variety of path expressions with the verb *look*. Table 7.4 summarizes instances of *look* with a Path expression in the CHILDES corpora of Sachs (Naomi), Brown (Adam, Eve, Sarah), Kuczaj (Walt), Bloom (Allison), Clark (Shem), Howe (several children), and Wells (several children), representing many tens of thousands of utterances in the age range from 18 months to 4 years. However,

TABLE 7.4 Path Expressions with ***look*** in CHILDES Corpora

Path	Caregiver	Child
inside	√	√
inside X	√	
in X	√	√
through X		√
outside	√	√
out X	√	√
under X	√	√
behind X	√	√
up	√	√
down	√	
down through		√

although descriptions of physical motion in these corpora have many paths with multiple components and grounds, in both adult and child speech, the instances with *look* are restricted to a single Path component with no Ground (e.g., *look inside*) or only one Ground (e.g., *look under your chapter*). The only example of a somewhat more elaborated path is a child's description of medical equipment: *You look down through your throat*. Early speech corpora in other languages remain to be examined; however, the frog story corpora (Berman & Slobin, 1994; Strömqvist & Verhoeven, 2004) provide ample data from children of age 3 and older.

Visual Paths in Frog Stories[10]

There are five scenes in *Frog, Where Are You?* (Mayer, 1969) that clearly depict acts of looking.[11] These present a nice variety of visual paths:

1. The boy and the dog look into the jar at their pet frog.
2. The boy looks down into the hole of a ground creature.
3. The boy looks into a deep hole in a tree.
4. The boy and dog look out of a window.
5. The boy and dog look over a log.

In each of the four languages, the basic expressions are in place in the 3- to 4-year-old age group, and clearly productive in the 5- to 6-year-old age group. At the same time, data from each language reveal developing attention to language-specific factors.

Looking in Jars and Holes

- In English, if one says *look in/into/inside* the hole/jar, the feature of containment is highlighted. Young children use these forms for scenes 1–3. In addition, some children seem to pay attention to the directionality and extent of the visual path: The hole in the ground is often marked by *down the hole*, while the hole in the tree is often marked by *through the hole*. This is consistent with adult English-speakers' Path components, as discussed above.
- Russian is similar, with an additional morphological factor. Consider the distinction between PATH-FUNCTION and PLACE-FUNCTION

[10] Frog story data are drawn from unpublished data: English (Renner, Marchman, Wigglesworth: age groups 3, 4, 5, 6, 8, 9, 10), Russian (Slobin, Durova & Yurieva: ages 3, 4, 5, 6, 8, 9), Spanish (Bocaz, Sebastián: ages 3, 4, 5, 9), Turkish (Aksu-Koç, Küntay: ages 3, 4, 5, 7, 9). There are 10 to 12 children in each age group.

[11] I exclude predicates of "looking for" or "searching," because these are ambiguous with regard to the directionality of the visual path and the place where the visual activity takes place. For example, in a scene in which the dog has put his muzzle into the frog's empty jar, the sentence *The dog looked in the jar* could indicate either path or location. This is especially the case in English, where *look* can also mean *look for*. As discussed below, languages with casemarking for allative (path function) and locative (place function) allow for clear marking of this distinction.

(Jackendoff, 1983). Casemarking on Ground nominals distinguishes between directed motion (ACCUSATIVE) and location (LOCATIVE), e.g., *v bank-u* 'in jar-ACC' (= into the jar) versus *v bank-e* 'in jar-LOC' (= located in the jar). Cases are salient noun suffixes and are acquired relatively early in Russian (Gvozdev, 1949; Slobin, 1966). The youngest children use the appropriate preposition, *v* 'in,' and mark the jar or the hole with accusative case, indicating that it is the goal of the visual path. The children provide no further details. However, the casemarking makes it clear that preschoolers conceive of visual paths as directed motion.

- Spanish provides a general locative preposition, *en*, neutral with regard to containment/support and location/direction. This is the only form used for looking in the jar, probably because a jar is a canonical container and nothing more need be specified. Holes allow for more perspectives, and while speakers of all ages use *en* for looking in a hole, there are also attempts to be more specific about entrance into a container. Spanish uses a specialized path verb, *entrar* 'enter,' for such scenes in the realm of physical motion. However, many narrators, beginning in the 3- to 4-year-old age range, use a directional adverb, *adentro* or *para adentro* 'toward inside,' although such boundary-crossing adverbs are dispreferred with verbs of physical motion. In addition, with reference to the tree hole, beginning with age 5 children also use the preposition *por* 'through,' highlighting a visual path that moves some distance into a tunnel-like space, as noted above for English. These preschool productions suggest that—contrary to the intuitions of Palancar—children may conceive of vision as following a path all the way to its goal. That is, the (possibly) universal metaphor seems to be in place for these scenes.
- The Turkish dative, in its directional sense, is neutral with regard to characteristics of the goal object. The language lacks the minimal directional distinction marked by the Spanish prepositions *en* 'in/on' versus *a* 'to.' Thus *deliğ-e bak* 'hole-DAT look' can mean either 'look at the hole' or 'look into the hole.' The choice depends on how one conceives of the default nature of a hole as an object of attention. Precision can be added by a locative nominal (postposition), as shown in Table 1: *deliğ-in iç-in-e bak* 'hole-GEN interior-POSS-DAT look' (= look inside the hole). From the youngest ages, narrators make use of both options for the hole scenes, and there is no further elaboration with age. By contrast, *içine* 'inside' is unfailingly provided in reference to the jar, since the dative alone would have to mean 'look at the jar.' The morphological markers used by Turkish preschoolers seem to show that they have access to the concept of fictive motion in the domain of vision, comparable to the use of casemarkers in Russian.

Looking out of a Window Narrators in all four languages, from the youngest ages, command the basic forms for a path of exiting. Although Spanish and Turkish use a directional verb for physical exiting or traversing a boundary frame, frog story narrators use a basic preposition (Spanish *por* 'through') or casemarker

(Turkish-*TAn* ABLATIVE) for this gaze description. Again, verb-framed characteristics are absent in visual path expressions. In addition, Turkish 5-year-olds often add a directional adverb, as was also found in the adult corpora examined above: *pencere-den dışarı-ya* 'window-ABL outside-DAT' (= from the window outwards). English continues to show its attention to path details: By age 5 narrators frequently say *look out through the window*, in contrast to simply *look out the window*. As in the adult corpora discussed above, English shows greater combinatorial possibilities for Path components.

Looking over a Log This is the most complex visual path in the frog story, and it receives a range of descriptions. Young narrators in all four languages use terms for 'over' or 'behind' in basic visual path clauses. Consistent with the data presented above, English narrators show the most Path elaboration, as in the following examples, with ages in parentheses: *over the other side of the log* (3–4), *over to the other side of the log* (8–10), *around over the log* (adult).

THE DEVELOPMENT OF THINKING FOR SPEAKING

In sum, children easily acquire the use of directional expressions for descriptions of visual paths in these four languages. Spanish- and Turkish-speaking children freely make use of boundary-crossing adverbs to indicate inward or outward gaze direction, although this is not the dominant means of expression with regard to physical paths. Use of directional adverbs for boundary-crossing visual paths in Spanish and Turkish indicates some separation between linguistic expression of the domains of physical and visual motion, with exploration of a somewhat greater range of expressions in the visual domain. English-speaking children, by contrast, often elaborate Paths, adding adverbs of directionality such as *down* and *around*. Note, too, that children learning Russian and Turkish use casemarking to distinguish between the path function and the place function of looking. English- and Spanish-speaking children are often vague about this distinction, suggesting that they do not find it necessary to go beyond the available linguistic means of description.

Crosslinguistic comparisons of child language in a particular domain, such as the use of path constructions to talk about vision, highlight the role of linguistic filtering and packaging of concepts. I offer this small study in response to the challenge that Melissa Bowerman posed to our field two decades ago:

> Only by studying how children approach language systems that differ in their organization of what is, at a deep level, the "same" conceptual material can we begin to discover how language-learners construct a highly structured and language-specific meaning system from their nonlinguistic understanding of daily experience. I hope research of the coming years will pay more attention to this central and fascinating problem of language acquisition. (Bowerman, 1985, p. 1314)

CONCLUSIONS

In conclusion, although visual paths are treated, across languages, as if they were physical paths, the conceptualization of visual path is filtered through language-specific semantic structures and habits of thinking for speaking. Crosslinguistic differences are especially evident with regard to the complexity of visual paths. Speakers of two verb-framed languages, Spanish and Turkish, analyze visual paths into fewer components than speakers of two satellite-framed languages, English and Russian. These differences may be attributable to habits of thinking for speaking that are established for the encoding of physical motion events. Complex paths in such languages require separate path verbs for individual path components, and although there are no visual path verbs in those languages, conceptual patterns may carry over from the domain of physical motion to domains of fictive motion. However, there is some additional evidence that speakers of Spanish (and also French) have recourse to other means of encoding visual paths, using a nominal element meaning 'a look' that can move through space. Therefore a thorough study of conceptual parallels between physical and visual space requires much more detailed examination of the range of available construction types, and in a larger and more systematic data base. However, although much more work is needed before definitive conclusions can be drawn, this preliminary exploration demonstrates a possible universality of conceptions of fictive motion, shaped by linguistic resources and thinking for speaking that vary with language typology.

APPENDIX: GLOSSARY OF GRAMMATICAL ABBREVIATIONS

ACC—accusative
ART—article
DAT—dative
DEF.ART—definite article
GEN—genitive
INDEF.ART—indefinite article
INF— infinitive
NONFIN—nonfinite
POSS—possessive

ACKNOWLEDGMENTS

This chapter is dedicated to Melissa Bowerman, who has always provided me with her vision, wisely pointing to the paths to be followed. The ideas presented here were developed at the Max Planck Institute for Psycholinguistics, Nijmegen, and the University of California, Berkeley (Institute of Cognitive and Brain Sciences,

Institute of Human Development). I thank these institutions for their support, as well as valuable input from colleagues and students. Especially useful suggestions were provided by Colette Grinevald and her students in Lyon, Tatiana Nikitina, Enrique Palancar, Stephanie Pourcel, Stephanie Robert, Len Talmy, Davio Wilkins, and my undergraduate research lab. I am grateful to Ginny Gathercole and an anonymous reviewer for helpful comments on an earlier draft.

REFERENCES

Anaya, R. (1992). *Bless me, Última* (Anon., Trans.). New York: Warner Books. New York: Warner Books. (Original work published 1972)

Aristotle (c. 350 BC/1937). *Problems II: Books XXII–XXXVIII* (H. Rackham, Trans.). Cambridge, MA: Harvard University Press.

Aske, J. (1989). Path predicates in English and Spanish: A closer look. *Proceedings of the Fifteenth Annual Meeting of the Berkeley Linguistics Society* (pp. 1–14). Berkeley, CA: Berkeley Linguistics Society.

Berman, R. A., & Slobin, D. I. (1994). *Relating events in narrative: A crosslinguistic developmental study*. Hillsdale, NJ: Erlbaum.

Bowerman, M. (1985). What shapes children's grammars? In D. I. Slobin (Ed.), *The crosslinguistic study of language acquisition: Vol. 2. Theoretical issues* (pp. 1257–1319). Hillsdale, NJ: Erlbaum.

Bowerman, M. (1996a). Learning how to structure space for language: A crosslinguistic perspective. In P. Bloom, M. A. Peterson, L. Nadel, & M. F. Garrett (Eds.), *Language and space* (pp. 385–436). Cambridge, MA: MIT Press.

Bowerman, M. (1996b). The origins of children's spatial semantic categories: Cognitive versus linguistic determinants. In J. J. Gumperz & S. C. Levinson (Eds.), *Rethinking linguistic relativity* (pp. 145–176). Cambridge, UK: Cambridge University Press.

Bowerman, M., & Choi, S. (2001). Shaping meanings for language: Universal and language-specific in the acquisition of spatial semantic categories. In M. Bowerman & S. C. Levinson (Eds.), *Language acquisition and conceptual development* (pp. 475–511). Cambridge, UK: Cambridge University Press.

Choi, S. (1997). Language-specific input and early semantic development: Evidence from children learning Korean. In D. I. Slobin (Ed.), *The crosslinguistic study of language acquisition: Vol. 5. Expanding the contexts* (pp. 111–133). Mahwah, NJ: Erlbaum.

Choi, S., & Bowerman, M. (1991). Learning to express motion events in English and Korean: The influence of language-specific lexicalization patterns. *Cognition, 41*, 83–121.

Chu, B. (2003). *Paths of vision and paths of motion in Mandarin Chinese*. Unpublished senior honors dissertation, Department of Psychology, University of California, Berkeley.

Gisborne, N. S. (1996). *English perception verbs*. Unpublished doctoral dissertation, University College London.

Gruber, J. S. (1967). Look and see. *Language, 43*, 937–947.

Gvozdev, A. N. (1949). *Formirovanije u rebenka grammatičeskogo stroja russkogo jazyka*. Moscow: Akademija Pedagogičeskix Nauk RSFSR.

Guillemin-Flescher, J. (1981). *Syntaxe comparée du français et de l'anglais: Problèmes de traduction*. Paris: Éditions OPHRYS.

Jackendoff, R. (1983). *Semantics and cognition*. Cambridge, MA: MIT Press.

Johnson, C. R., Fillmore, C. J., Wood, E. J., Ruppenhofer, J., Urban, M., Petruck, M. R. L. et al.. (2001). *The FrameNet Project: Tools for lexicon building* (Version 0.7). http://www.icsi.berkeley.edu/~framenet/book.html

Kersten, A. W., Meissner, C. A. Schwartz, B. L., & Rivera, M. (2003, April). *Differential sensitivity to manner of motion in adult English and Spanish speakers.* Paper presented to Biennial Meeting of the Society for Research in Child Development, Tampa, FL.

Klein, H. E. M. (1981). Location and direction in Toba: Verbal morphology. *International Journal of American Linguistics, 47,* 227–235.

Lawrence, D. H. (1924). *England, my England.* London: Martin Secker.

Matsumoto, Y. (2001, November). *Lexicalization patterns and caused and fictive motion: The case of typological split.* Lecture at SUNY Buffalo, NY.

Mayer, M. (1969). *Frog, where are you?* New York: Dial Press.

McCullers, C. (1946). *The member of the wedding.* Boston: Houghton Mifflin.

Oh, K. (2003). *Language, cognition, and development: Motion events in English and Korean.* Unpublished doctoral dissertation, University of California, Berkeley.

Oxford English Dictionary (2nd ed.). (1994). OED2 on CD-ROM, Version 1.14. Oxford: Oxford University Press.

Plato (c. 350 BC/1949). *Plato's Timaeus* (B. Jowett, Trans.). New York: Liberal Arts Press.

Slobin, D. I. (1966). The acquisition of Russian as a native language. In F. Smith & G. A. Miller (Eds.), *The genesis of language: A psycholinguistic approach* (pp. 129–148). Cambridge, MA: MIT Press.

Slobin, D. I. (1996a). From "thought and language" to "thinking for speaking." In J. J. Gumperz & S. C. Levinson (Eds.), *Rethinking linguistic relativity* (pp. 70–96). Cambridge, UK: Cambridge University Press.

Slobin, D. I. (1996b). Two ways to travel: Verbs of motion in English and Spanish. In M. Shibatani & S. A. Thompson (Eds.), *Grammatical constructions: Their form and meaning* (pp. 195–217). Oxford: Oxford University Press.

Slobin, D. I. (1997). Mind, code, and text. In J. Bybee, J. Haiman, & S. A. Thompson (Eds.), *Essays on language function and language type: Dedicated to T. Givón* (pp. 437–467). Amsterdam/Philadelphia: John Benjamins.

Slobin, D. I. (2000). Verbalized events: A dynamic approach to linguistic relativity and determinism. In S. Niemeier & R. Dirven (Eds.), *Evidence for linguistic relativity* (pp. 107–138). Amsterdam/Philadelphia: John Benjamins.

Slobin, D. I. (2004). The many ways to search for a frog: Linguistic typology and the expression of motion events. In S. Strömqvist & L. Verhoeven (Eds.), *Relating events in narrative: Typological and contextual perspectives* (pp. 219–257). Mahwah, NJ: Erlbaum.

Slobin, D. I., & Hoiting, N. (1994). Reference to movement in spoken and signed languages: Typological considerations. *Proceedings of the Twentieth Annual Meeting of the Berkeley Linguistics Society* (pp. 487–505). Berkeley, CA: Berkeley Linguistics Society.

Strömqvist, S., & Verhoeven, L. (Eds.). (2004), *Relating events in narrative: Typological and contextual perspectives.* Mahwah, NJ: Erlbaum.

Takahashi, K. (2000). *Expressions of emanation fictive motion events in Thai.* Unpublished doctoral dissertation, Chulalongkorn University, Thailand.

Talmy, L. (1991). Path to realization: A typology of event conflation. *Proceedings of the Seventeenth Annual Meeting of the Berkeley Linguistics Society* (pp. 480–519). Berkeley, CA: Berkeley Linguistics Society.

Talmy, L. (1985). Lexicalization patterns. In T. Shopen (Ed.), *Language typology and syntactic description: Vol. 3. Grammatical categories and the lexicon* (pp. 59–149). Cambridge, UK: Cambridge University Press.

Talmy, L. (2000a). Fictive motion in language and "ception." In L. Talmy, *Toward a cognitive semantics: Vol. 1. Concept structuring systems* (pp. 99–178). Cambridge, MA: MIT Press.

Talmy, L. (2000b). How language structures space. In L. Talmy, *Toward a cognitive semantics: Vol. 1. Concept structuring systems* (pp. 176–254). Cambridge, MA: MIT Press.

Talmy, L. (2000c). A typology of event integration. In L. Talmy, *Toward a cognitive semantics: Vol 1. Typology and process in concept structuring* (pp. 213–298).. Cambridge, MA: MIT Press.

Talmy, L. (2000d). Lexicalization patterns. In L. Talmy, *Toward a cognitive semantics: Vol 2. Typology and process in concept structuring* (pp. 21–146). Cambridge, MA: MIT Press.

Talmy, L. (2003). The representation of spatial structure in spoken and signed language. In K. Emmorey (Ed.), *Perspectives on classifier constructions in sign languages* (pp. 169–195). Mahwah, NJ: Erlbaum.

Part IV

Influences on Development

Personal Tribute

RONALD P. SCHAEFER

Mentoring is a complex task at the center of graduate education. Looking back, we have a tendency to measure the professors who guided us by end products—the article published with them, the chapter revised under their editorial guidance, or the book published based on their favorable review.

But there is also mentoring as process. It is the day-in-day-out task of guiding graduate students into a discipline, mentally tracking their progress, and paying attention to their intellectual needs, not only one's own. It is a delicate balance since one must stimulate but not overwhelm. Good, solid mentoring is difficult to sustain. It is an intangible quality, rather like the charisma of politicians: We know it when we experience it, but its definition remains elusive. With this advance warning, I offer my reflections on Melissa Bowerman as mentor.

It had to be good fortune that placed me at the University of Kansas in the mid-1970s. I was a graduate student in the Department of Linguistics, where Melissa had her teaching assignment. A KU graduate recommended Melissa and the department highly and showed me how to convert my Peace Corps experience into a graduate stipend. I took a class with Melissa during my first semester and subsequently registered for independent studies under her direction. In addition, I was able to secure desk space in Varsity House, an old three-story structure on campus that provided various departments common space for faculty and students dedicated to child language development. There were scattered small rooms to accommodate graduate students, creaky stairways, and the inevitable water fountain. Melissa had a top floor office.

Although I entered Melissa's office many times, I remember most vividly leaving it. Typically, I would enter with a book, article, or simply an idea about some aspect of language. But I would leave with a pile of books, a stack of journal articles, or both. Melissa's enthusiasm for language in all its manifestations seemed boundless. It was also contagious. Without apparent effort, Melissa instilled in me a desire to discover more. Often, she would listen to my summation of an article or chapter, and ask a few pertinent questions that would lead me to wonder if I had actually done my reading. Intuitively, Melissa understood the limited conceptual ground I had staked out. Her response was mentoring at its best. She shifted these discussion sessions to a concrete piece of linguistic data she was struggling to understand or some linguistic facts that recently caught her attention. Listening to Melissa intellectually dance around this piece of data, considering it from various theoretical points of view, inevitably moved my own conceptual stakes. From these interactions I discovered how to do linguistics.

Not all mentoring happened in that office. Even chance encounters had that Melissa magic. One evening after a colloquium, Melissa gave me a ride to my car. Our chat about the colloquium topic led to her questions about class work in the department and whether I had yet become immersed in the crosslinguistic studies of Joseph Greenberg. When I indicated my limited exposure, she outlined key ideas undergirding linguistic typology and its implications for child language development. Melissa had other things to do that night: She had a family at home, papers to write, and reviews to complete. Yet, here she was taking her valuable time to lay out for me significant points in the study of linguistic typology. By the time I left the car, the gravitational center of my graduate education had begun to shift.

From my interactions with Melissa, I also learned how to shape my own curiosity about language. As a graduate assistant teaching English as a second language, I pestered my students about verb events in their first language. I would take various objects into class and find out how they combined to realize events comparable to English physical action verbs of cutting and breaking. Some of this comparison benefited the students, but much of it jolted my curiosity about verb events and their components. Melissa encouraged these explorations with articles and books from developmental psychology, linguistics, and anthropology, an interdisciplinary mix characteristic of her advice. Melissa helped me understand that although there were various questions one could ask about verb events, one had to both ask the right question and strive to develop that question until a satisfactory solution emerged. She didn't prejudge what questions should be asked or the theories they came from. And she consistently demonstrated a special sense of patience in sifting through questions implicit in a theoretical framework. It was soon evident that for Melissa all theories could be useful in the march toward understanding the nature of language. My task became clearer: Use theory to assess data and gain insight.

Eventually my curiosity about language and verbs led me to a university position in West Africa and southern Nigeria's serial verb structures. On arrival, I innocently assumed that child language studies could be undertaken by an outsider with knowledge gained from native speakers as well as grammars and dictionaries. However, I quickly confronted the conditions now encapsulated under the heading language endangerment. While my students could collect data from their younger siblings for class projects, most showed a very slippery grasp of their mother tongue. Access to grammars and dictionaries became necessary. But where were they? My subsequent probes revealed that little documentation of individual languages, especially minor vernaculars showing complex tone–morphosyntax interaction, was available. Although I did not realize it at the time, my future path lay before me. I had to start documenting one of these languages, exercising as best I could the disciplined curiosity, sustained patience, and unflappable enthusiasm I had acquired from Melissa.

And to bring this reflection full circle, let me briefly comment on Melissa as silent mentor. As graduate students, we learn how to read book chapters. Gradually, we come to understand that the really crucial information we require from an author is contained in the body of a chapter, in new references at chapter end, or, in rare instances, in footnotes scattered throughout a text. For me, it was always Melissa's footnotes. They provided key distinctions, fundamental insights, and alternative conclusions for consideration. And yes, I confess that some of my products emerged from reading and interpreting those footnotes.

Personal Tribute

MARTHA CRAGO

I came to know Melissa Bowerman in person during the semester that I spent as an invited guest at the Max Planck Institute in Nijmegen. It was a formative period for me, both personally and professionally, and Melissa played a particularly important role in both. I remember well her carefully reasoned and argued comments at the Institute's meetings and speaker events, her meticulous editing of her colleagues' work, her friendly repartee at coffee time, and her personal responsiveness and openness. To this day, whenever we expectedly or unexpectedly cross paths, I marvel at her attentiveness as a listener and her carefully considered replies—which stay with me long after our encounters have ended. This enduring quality has made itself evident to me in another way. In my work as a journal editor, I have noticed that a number of senior colleagues will no longer agree to review articles. This is not true of Melissa. Her willingness to do so is even more remarkable because of the care and attention she dedicates to the task. Her reviews are long, detailed, and most importantly, extremely instructive. The authors profit enormously as do I as an editor and as does our science as a whole. Melissa Bowerman, through her guiding hand, has made a contribution that goes well beyond her own excellent research. Her insights have shaped several generations of researchers and our field as a whole. Language learners and researchers learning about language owe her a debt of gratitude. Thank you, Melissa.

Personal Tribute

EVE V. CLARK

I first met Melissa in 1968 on the campus at the Ohio State University in Columbus as we were walking over to attend a semantics conference there. Since then we have met many, many times, at first mainly at conferences, later spending time together (several years) at the Max Planck Institute for Psycholinguistics, in a friendship that became personal as well as professional. From the start, I have been impressed by Melissa's meticulous analyses of the linguistic claims and theories on which her findings might bear. She has done the field an immense service by analyzing arguments, identifying the logic of their predictions (and their limitations), and evaluating both arguments and predictions against actual data—a model for us all.

Melissa and I collaborated on only one project, and it is the one and only phonology paper either of us will probably ever write. This collaboration allowed us to use data from two of our children who happened to have followed the same strategy in first attempting a tricky problem of articulation (the production of voiced stops in word-final position) and since, at the time, we were living in the Netherlands and California, respectively, we spent many hours on the telephone deciding just how to word our arguments.

Although we have written only one paper together, we have collaborated in thinking about the field and about life for many years. We have also spent many lunchtimes at the Max Planck Institute talking about acquisition, and about space, categories, birds, and dreams. With every discussion, I've come away richer for the experience.

8

What Shapes Children's Language? *Child-Directed Speech, Conventionality, and the Process of Acquisition*

EVE V. CLARK
Stanford University

Adults shape the way children speak by displaying for them the conventional ways of saying things and doing things with language. Not surprisingly, the story of how children engage in learning the conventions of their first language is a complicated one. Conventions govern language use in every community of speakers. Conventions govern the associations of forms and meanings for words and for constructions in a language, and thereby allow speakers to maintain differences in meaning, with consistency, over time. Conventions underlie speakers' choices of words: *squirrel* to designate squirrels in English, *écureuil* to designate squirrels in French; they also underlie choices of constructions as in *He wiped the table clean* with a resultative construction in English, *Il nettoya la table* with a direct causative construction in French. Conventions govern how speakers pronounce words as well, within each community. (There are often quite different conventions from one community to the next on this, even within the same language.) They also govern the patterns of use that speakers favor in a particular community, during a particular era.

The role of conventions in supporting and maintaining languages can be expressed very generally as the principle in (1):

1. *Conventionality*: For certain meanings there is a form that speakers expect to be used in the language community.

One consequence of observing this principle is that if a speaker does not use the expected form (a word, expression, or construction), the addressee will infer that he must have meant something else. This assumption of contrast in meaning is inseparable from speakers' reliance on conventionality in language (see Clark, 1987, 1990, 1993; Clark & Clark, 1979). Consistency of meaning depends on contrasts in meaning within the language. This can be formulated as in (2):

2. *Contrast*: Speakers take every difference in form to mark a difference in meaning.

These two pragmatic principles are observed by adults and children alike. They also play a central role, I argue, in the actual process of acquisition, since acquiring a language effectively demands that children acquire the conventions for using that language.

In this chapter, I take up some of the ways in which adults shape children's language in the early stages of acquisition, and shape it precisely by focusing on the conventions of the language being learned. I begin with David Lewis's classic definition for the notion of *convention* (1969, p. 42):

> A regularity R in the behavior of members of a population P when they are agents in a recurrent situation S is a *convention* if and only if, in any instance of S among members of P,
>
> (1) everyone conforms to R;
> (2) everyone expects everyone else to conform to R;
> (3) everyone prefers to conform to R on condition that the others do,
> since S is a coordination problem and uniform conformity to R is a coordination equilibrium in S.

Conventions, regularities that develop in our behavior, actually govern many kinds of activity. They can hold for just two people (e.g., where to meet my cousin whenever we are both in London at the same time); for larger groups such as club members or an orchestra (e.g., how to carry out a specific activity); for a whole city (e.g., how to celebrate July 14 in Paris), or for a whole country (e.g., what speed to drive cars on highways). Conventions may be initiated by accident (meeting my cousin twice running at Tate Modern), or by explicit agreement among the participants (the coordination of conductor and orchestra members in playing a concerto). Once in place, though, conventions are transmitted to everyone who joins that community. So teenagers who are learning to drive must learn which side of the road to drive on, how to interpret what other drivers are doing, and how to indicate their own intentions. In similar fashion, new members of a choir learn how to follow the directions of the choirmaster. And, of prime importance here, children born into a community learn the language of that community. Effectively, they learn what the conventions for that language are from the speakers who transmit the language to them.

Adults are often the primary source for the language being learned—English, Japanese, Hebrew, Somali, French. And children learn the language of those who speak to them, typically the language of their community. Moreover, in Western cultures, the more adults talk to children, the larger the children's vocabularies by age 5 or 6, and the better they tend to fare in school (e.g., Hart & Risley, 1992, 1995; Hoff-Ginsburg, 1998). Just how much parents talk to their children in Western cultures differs with social class: Middle-class parents treat young children as conversational partners more of the time than lower-class parents do (e.g., Hoff, 2003a, 2003b; Hoff & Naigles, 2002; Huttenlocher et al., 1991) and talk to them more. But cultures do differ in how much adults talk to small children. In many, older siblings are charged with taking care of younger children and so presumably talk to them more than adults would. In those same societies, though, adults may consistently talk *for* young children, modeling what to say when and to whom (e.g., Ochs & Schieffelin, 1984; see also Heath, 1983).

Lastly, although studies of early child-directed speech have focused on adult–child pairs, 2-year-olds appear quite adept at following the conversation when there are three involved, as in family exchanges with a parent and two siblings (e.g., Dunn & Shatz, 1989). And young children can attend fairly early to some overheard speech as well (e.g., Akhtar, Jipson, & Callanan, 2001).

To shape children's language, child-directed speech must present children with consistent information about how different events are represented in that language—in short, what the conventions are. This enables children to learn the appropriate mappings of forms for meanings within each domain—and also to learn what the relevant forms are in the language being learnt (see Bowerman, 1985; Choi & Bowerman, 1991). Adults offer at least two kinds of information as they talk to children. First they offer information about the appropriate terms for things, for relations, and for events. These offers of unfamiliar words don't come unadorned: They are accompanied by a wealth of information that supports and adds to the inferences children can make, in context, about the probable meanings of new words (Clark, 1998, 2002, 2004; Clark & Wong, 2002).

Second, adults provide information about conventional ways to express specific intentions. They frequently check up on just what children mean in the course of conversation, especially when children make errors. This checking up simultaneously establishes what children mean and offers a conventional way to express that meaning in lieu of whatever error(s) the children have made (Clark & Chouinard, 2000, Chouinard & Clark, 2003). Children give evidence of attending to such corrections even when they do not make immediate changes to their own forms. These adult offers present the conventional pronunciations, inflected forms, words, and constructions in direct contrast to the erroneous forms produced by children and designed to express the same meanings. Adult utterances like these therefore provide a source of negative feedback for young children while underlining for them the conventions of the language.

In this chapter I take up these two ways in which adults shape their children's early language: first locally, through their offers of new words and their offers of relations between those words and other terms already familiar to the children, and second, more globally, through their use of reformulations immediately following children's errors. In both situations, adults present children with often extensive information about the conventional forms used to express specific meanings in the language, and they do this in the course of conversation. In each type of exchange, they offer information that shapes children's growing skill in *using* the language being acquired by providing information pertinent to the child's communicative intent.

OFFERS OF UNFAMILIAR WORDS

When adults offer children new words, they typically also provide information about connections between words in the form of relations that help define the place of each word in specific semantic domains. They also offer information about the referents of new words that helps children infer which properties link one word to another and distinguish one word meaning from another.

In making these offers, adults tend to use a small repertoire of fixed frames. These frames are frequent and so should also come to signal the advent of a new word. Among the frames used most commonly in child-directed speech are *This/that is an X, Here's an X, See this X, This is called an X, What's this called?—It's an X, What is he doing?—He's X-ing* (e.g., Clark & Wong, 2002, Masur, 1997). Most direct offers in these frames introduce nouns. Members of other word classes—adjectives, prepositions, and verbs—tend to be introduced indirectly, inside utterances that presuppose that children can work out what the speaker's intended meaning is, even with unfamiliar words.

Consider the typical exchange in (1) where an adult offers a small child a new word. Immediately after the offer, the child takes it up and ratifies it by repeating the new word. In doing this, the child gives some evidence of uptake for the word offered (Clark, 1999, 2002). Consider the exchanges in (1) and (3), together with the inferences they license in (2) and (4), respectively.

(1) D (1;8.2, having his shoes put on; points at some ants on the floor): *Ant. Ant.*
Father (indicating a small beetle nearby): And that's a bug.
D: ***bug***. (Clark, diary data)

The inferences that this child could make about the new word *bug* in this exchange can be characterized in the form of a list, as in (2):

(2) Possible inferences:
New word: BUG
Type: insect
Subtype: differs from ANT?

Adults also make offers where the new word presents an alternative to the term proposed by the child, as in (3).

(3) A (2;4, wanting to have an orange peeled): *Fix it.*
Mother: You want me to peel it?

A: *Uh-huh. **Peel** it.* (Kuczaj, CHILDES)

Here again I list the inferences the child could plausibly make from this exchange, in (4).

(4) Possible inferences
New word: PEEL
Type: action of removing skin/peel from fruit,
Relation to FIX: wrong word? Not the best word? A subordinate word?

Notice that the assignment of the term for picking out an action category is more certain in this case, where the parent has offered an embedded correction in checking on the child's intention, than in (1) where the parent simply offered a new word that the child assumes probably picks out a referent in the same category as the word he has just used. But the relation between *fix* and *peel* has yet to be fully established.

In more sustained exchanges, parents may license successive inferences on the child's part with each further piece of information added after the initial offer of a new word (Clark, 2002), as in (5).

(5) Child (1;8.12, looking at a picture of owls in a new book): *duck duck.*
Mother: yeah those are birds. (looks at the picture) those are called owls. (points at the picture) owls, that's their name. owls. (looks at child)
Child: ***birds.***
Mother: and you know what the owl says? (points at the picture again) The owl goes "hoo, hoo."
Child: ***owl.***
Mother: that's what the owl says.
Child: ***hoo.***
Mother: that's right. (New England corpus, CHILDES)

From the information in the first segment of this exchange, repeated in (6a), the child can assign the new word, *owl*, to a domain, that of birds, but at this point must remain uncertain about how owls might differ from a familiar bird, the duck. The inferences licensed up to this point are listed in (6b).

(6) a. Child (1;8.12, looking at a picture of owls in a new book): *duck duck.*
Mother: yeah those are birds. (looks at the picture) those are called owls.
(points at the picture) owls, that's their name. owls. (looks at child)
Child: ***birds.***

b. Possible inferences:
New word: OWL
Type: bird

In the next segment of this exchange, the mother adds distinguishing information about owls, shown in (7a); the additional inference licensed by this is added in (7b).

(7) a. Mother: and you know what the owl says? (points at the picture again) The owl goes "hoo, hoo."
Child: ***owl***.
b. Possible inferences
New word, OWL
Type: bird;
>>Subtype: owl; referent of OWL differs from DUCK

In the final segment of this exchange, the parent stresses the property that differentiates owls from ducks, and approves the child's uptake of the term for the distinguishing sound, as indicated in (8a). The inferences licensed by this point in the overall exchange are listed in (8b).

(8) a. Mother: that's what the owl says.
Child: ***hoo***.
Mother: that's right.
b. Possible inferences
New word: OWL
Type: bird
Subtype: owl; (differs from duck)
>> Identifying property: sound "hoo"

Notice that by presenting the child with a distinguishing property for owls, as well as the information that they are members of the same superordinate category as ducks, the adult has given the child information about inclusion or superordinate category membership *and* information about how to keep the two subtypes apart. Effectively, whenever adults offer children new words and link them to familiar words, they license further connections within the child's expanding lexicon. Offers of relations between words *anchor* new words to words already known (see also Callanan, 1985, 1990). This is just what the parent did in (5) when she said "Yeah those are birds. They're called owls."

Adults accompany their offers of new words with a variety of meaning relations between words (Clark, 1997; Clark & Wong, 2002). The commonest are listed in (9).

(9) a. Set membership, inclusion (*X is a, is a kind of*)
b. Part of (*X is part of*)
c. Material, substance (*X is made of*)
d. Use, function (*X is for, is used for*)
e. Listing (inclusion in a list of like [sub]kinds: *A, B, C,... X*)
f. Hints (*X looks like*)
g. Alerts (*X looks like...but...*)
h. Definitions (generic)

Some of these relations appear more frequently than others in speech to children under 3. For example, information about set membership and about parts is more frequent than information about material (e.g., Clark & Wong, 2002; Masur, 1997).

Comparisons of some of the relations commonly used when introducing new words suggest that younger children take in the relevant information more readily in some forms than others. In a series of word-learning studies (Clark & McKercher, in preparation), we compared children's uptake of unfamiliar words presented in the context of information about set-membership (*an X is a kind of Y*), in the context of information about use or function (*an X is used for Y*), or simply as part of a list of otherwise familiar objects (*This is an A, a B, a C, and an X*). Children aged 2 to 3 did better with the list-presentations than with presentations giving information about set or function, but older children learned the unfamiliar words equally well in all three conditions.

But even 2-year-olds can make use of information about set-membership as they learn new words. In another study, we taught 2-, 3-, and 4-year-olds pairs of new words in three conditions. In one, teaching of the first word was followed by a single statement of "A Y is a kind of X" just as the second word and its referents were introduced; in the second, there was no connecting relation offered at all, and in the third, the teaching of the first word was followed by a retraction, a repair of the form "I made a mistake, these aren't X's; they're Y's" followed immediately by the teaching of the second word, Y. Nearly all the 2-year-olds took into account the information about set-membership when tested; the same children seldom assumed set-membership when they were not offered the pertinent information. They were, however, well able to deal with the speaker's repair in the third condition: They knew that they didn't know the meaning of X, the first word taught in that pair (Clark & Grossman, 1998). In short, young 2-year-olds make appropriate pragmatic inferences in context when offered unfamiliar words along with added information about how to treat them.

In both offers of words and offers of relations between words, adults present the conventional forms in use in that community to the children they are talking to. That is, they rely on the pragmatic principle of conventionality (Clark, 1990, 1993). This reliance on conventionality necessarily goes hand-in-hand with contrast. For example, the unfamiliar term is frequently juxtaposed to, and thereby contrasted with, other terms already familiar to the child (see also Rogers, 1978; Wilkins, 2002). In addition to offering children unfamiliar words that differ in form from ones the children already know, adults often accompany the new words with critical information for distinguishing one reference-type from another so that children can maintain the contrasts in meaning that are signalled by the different word-forms.

How do these adult offers of words and relations contribute to the actual process of acquisition? First, adult offers appear to flag new information—unfamiliar words and new connections among words—for children to attend to and take up. The fact that children repeat new words they are offered about half the time, and otherwise often make use of them within minutes of being offered them provides direct evidence of their attention to such items in the child-directed speech they hear (Clark, 2007).

Second, adults offer children information about how to link new words to other terms already known. Children can make use of these anchors to connect unfamiliar words to familiar forms and meanings. Such anchors typically help to identify the appropriate semantic field(s) for newly encountered words as well as highlighting characteristic properties or functions. This ensures that children are continually adding to and structuring each semantic domain, connecting the words in each through a growing network of relations.

Third, adult offers of both words and relations add to children's knowledge about the conventional system they are acquiring. Adults offer the conventional words for the objects and events in question, and often do so by contrasting a known word with the new one. In short, they rely on children's ability to use both conventionality and contrast in adding to their lexicon. They do this both for direct offers and for embedded corrections. We will consider some more details of this process—what is involved in the uptake of such information about language by young children—after taking a look at a second source of information about a first language, the information proffered in adult reformulations.

REFORMULATIONS OF ERRONEOUS UTTERANCES

Conventionality and contrast play a fundamental role in the *process* of acquisition. This is particularly clear when one considers how adults respond to children's errors during the earlier stages of acquisition. Although many linguists have long assumed that children receive no negative evidence (e.g., Baker & McCarthy, 1981; see also Bowerman, 1988; Pinker, 1984),[1] adults in fact frequently respond to children's errors with immediate offers of the conventional way to say X. That is, they reword what the child was apparently trying to say, as they check on whether this was what the child had intended. We have called these adult rewordings *reformulations* and argued that these offer one source of negative evidence to children without disrupting the course of the conversation (see Chouinard & Clark, 2003; Clark & Chouinard, 2000).

In a detailed analysis of child errors between ages 2 and 4 in five longitudinal corpora, three from children learning to speak English and two from children learning to speak French, Chouinard and I focused on four issues:

1. How often do adults notice and correct their children's errors?
2. Do adults correct all type of errors—in syntax, phonology, morphology, and the lexicon? And do so equally?

[1] This has long been one of the arguments supporting certain proposals about what must be innate in language acquisition, and often appears alongside claims about poverty of the stimulus and the consequent insufficiency of child-directed speech for learning. For some lucid recent discussion of theoretical problems with the poverty of the stimulus position, see Pullum (1996), and Pullum and Scholz (2002).

3. How do adults make their corrections?
4. Do children attend to the adult corrections they hear?

To answer these questions, we analyzed all the errors made by five children over time, what the adults did in their next turns in the conversational exchange, and how the children followed up on any adult contributions. The data were all drawn from the CHILDES Archive, with three children acquiring English: Abe (transcriptions from 2;4.24 to 3;11.25); Sarah (transcriptions from 2;3.7 to 3;11.29), and Naomi (transcriptions from 2;0.2 to 3;8.19), and two acquiring French: Philippe (transcriptions from 2;1.19 to 3;3.12), and Grégoire (transcriptions from 2;0.5 to 2;5.27) (for further details, see Chouinard & Clark, 2003). In addition to looking at all the *reformulations* adults produced after children had made an error of some kind, we also looked at adult *replays* of conventional utterances from children. In replays, adults repeat just what the child has said, without changes. This allowed us to compare adult responses to erroneous versus conventional forms from children. In what follows, I take up each of our questions in turn.

How Often Do Adults Notice and Correct Their Children's Errors?

For children under age 3, we found that adults offer reformulations of errors between 50% and 70% of the time. This amount of *reformulation*—restatement in conventional form—for errors was compared against how often adults *replay* conventional child utterances, just repeating them verbatim.[2]

At every age, for each child, parental reformulations of erroneous child utterances significantly outnumbered replays of conventional child utterances. This is shown in Figure 8.1 for the data we analyzed from the three children acquiring English. The numbers for replays are probably too high, especially for the youngest age level, since many of the apparent repeats of conventional child utterances are probably reformulations for minor phonological errors (rarely recorded in transcripts) or of utterances said too softly to be fully intelligible.

All five children studied had many of their erroneous utterances reformulated by their adult interlocutors, especially before age 3. For example, between 2;0 and 2;11, Abe had 52% of his erroneous utterances reformulated, Sarah 60%, Naomi 48%, Philippe 64%, and Grégoire 60%. Overall, adults offered reformulations, between age 2;0 and 3;11, for some 44% of erroneous child utterances in English; and in French, between age 2;0 and 3;5, they reformulated 60% of erroneous child utterances. For all five children, adults offered more reformulations the younger the children were and the more errors they were making (see further Chouinard & Clark, 2003).

[2] We computed adult replays of conventional child utterances from samples of 200 utterances drawn from every six-month age slice for each child by first identifying all the conventional (error-free) child utterances in those samples, then tabulating how many of those child utterances were 'replayed' in apparently identical form by the adult in the next turn. These exact repeats of grammatical child forms are *replays* (for further details, see Chouinard & Clark, 2003).

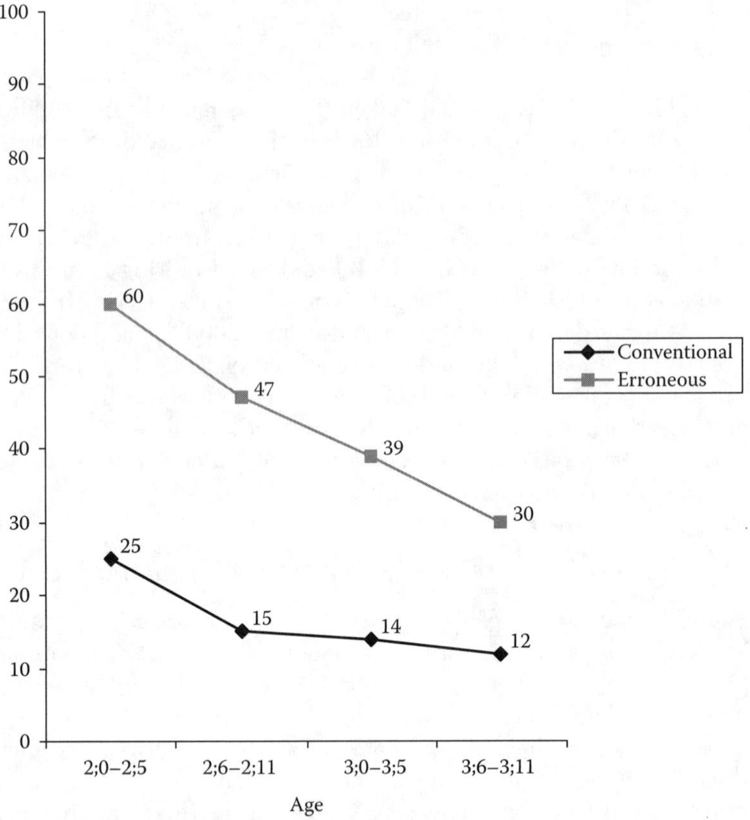

Figure 8.1 Adult reformulations of erroneous child utterances and adult replays of conventional child utterances in English (%).

Do Adults Correct All Types of Errors—In Syntax, Phonology, Morphology, and the Lexicon? And Do So Equally?

Again, the answer here is yes. The adult rates of reformulation were essentially the same for different error-types, for all five corpora we analyzed. This is illustrated in Figures 8.2 and 8.3. Figure 8.2 presents the categorization of reformulations by error-type for Abe, and Figure 8.3 the reformulations by error-type for Sarah. (Phonological information was not recorded in Abe's case, so phonological errors are not included in Figure 8.2.) The general patterns in Figures 8.2 and 8.3 were similar for all five children. Adults reformulated errors of syntax, morphology, lexicon, and phonology. They did so at a very similar rate statistically, at each age-level, regardless of error-type (see further Chouinard & Clark, 2003).

How Do Adults Make Their Corrections?

Adult speakers make use of the normal pragmatic properties of conversational exchange. They rely on children's ability to recognize when adults are either

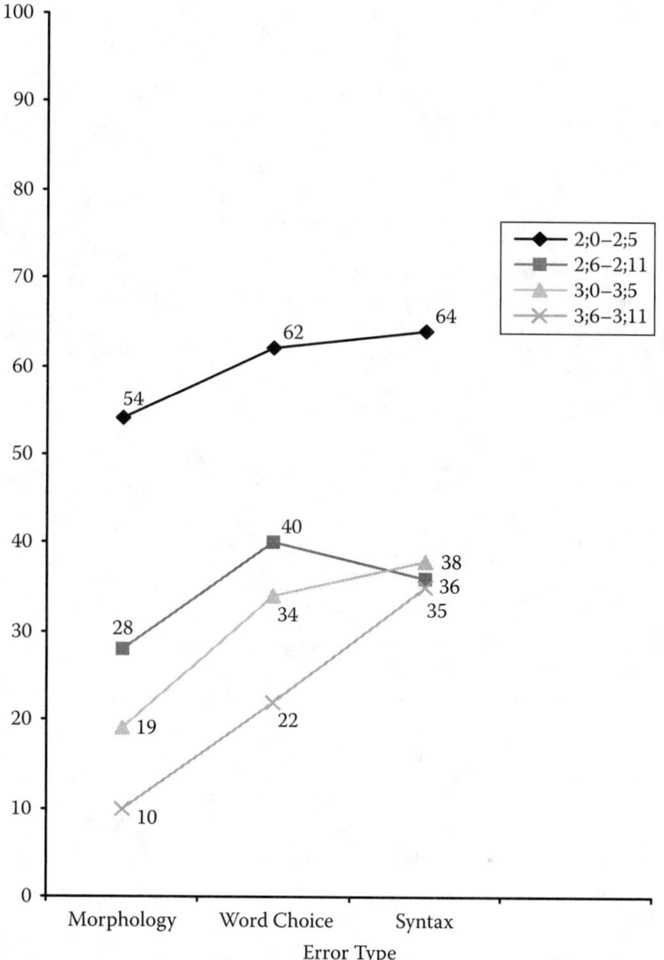

Figure 8.2 Abe's erroneous utterances reformulated for each error type (%).

checking on what the child had intended to say, with a *side sequence* (Jefferson, 1972; Schegloff, 1972), or offering a next-turn repair, with an *embedded correction* (Jefferson, 1982). These two options are illustrated for adult exchanges in (10) and (11), respectively.

(10) <u>A side sequence</u>
Roger: now, —um do you and your husband have a j– car
||Nina: have a car?
||Roger: yeah
Nina: no— (Svartvik & Quirk, 1980, 8.2a, p. 335)

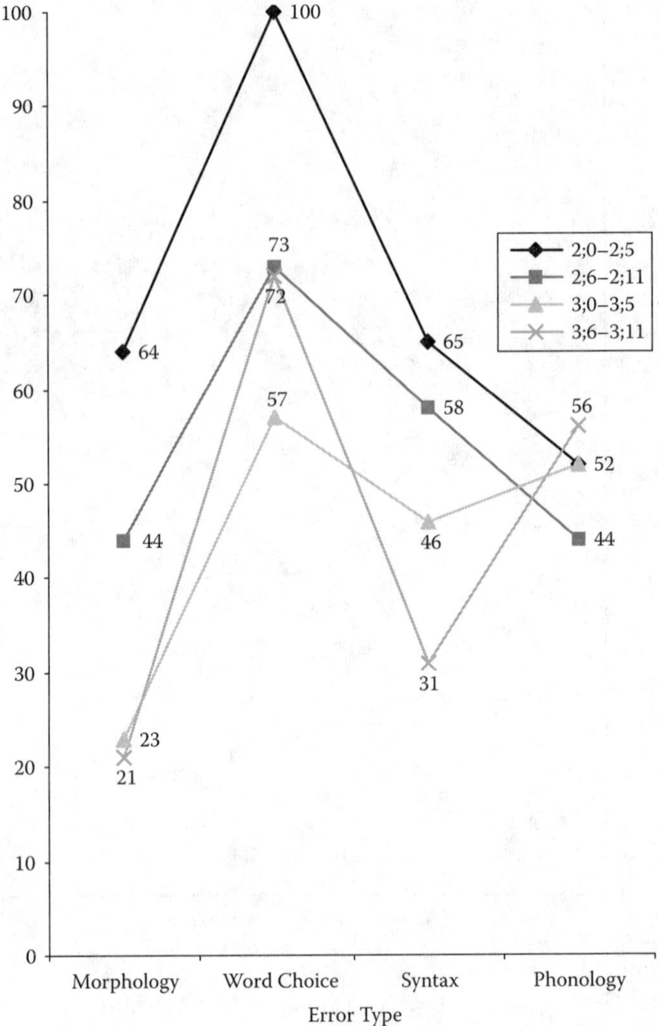

Figure 8.3 Sarah's erroneous utterances reformulated for each error type (%).

Notice that in side sequences, the addressee of the first utterance *checks up* on the speaker's intended meaning (Nina's "have a car?"), and, only once that meaning has been ratified or established (Roger's "yeah"), goes on to answer the original question, as here, or responds in some other way to the utterance that originally prompted the side sequence.

With embedded corrections, the addressee of the initial utterance simply includes the correction in his next turn—in (11), the salesman's *threads*, in lieu of the original *wales*. The correction itself is typically taken up by the other speaker in subsequent turns, especially where the form proposed depends on some specialized knowledge.

(11) An embedded correction
Customer in a hardware store looking for a piece of piping:
Customer: Mm, the *wales* are wider apart than that.
Salesman: Okay, let me see if I can find one with wider *threads*.
(Looks through stock) How's this?
Customer: Nope, the **threads** are even wider than that. (Jefferson, 1982, p. 63)

In our study of adult responses to children's errors, side sequences accounted for 66% of their reformulations overall, with a range from 57% (addressed to Abe) up to 73% (addressed to Philippe). A typical side sequence with a reformulation in response to a child error is shown in (12), where the father's "You want milk?" provides a conventional version of the child's one-word request (*milk*).

(12) Abe (2;6.4): *milk. milk.*
||Father: you want milk?
||Abe: *uh-huh.*
Father: ok, just a second and I'll get you some. (Kuczaj, CHILDES)

After Abe speaks, Abe's father checks on what Abe meant before he responds to the request Abe made, just as in the adult side sequence in (10). The first turn within a side sequence is typically produced with rising intonation, to signal that the speaker is in fact checking on the immediately preceding utterance.

A typical embedded correction offered after a child error is shown in (13), where the adult substitutes the locative phrase "on it" for the child's *mine*.

(13) Abe (2;5.10): *I want butter mine.*
Father: Ok, give it here and I'll put butter on it. (Kuczaj, CHILDES)

Side sequences and embedded corrections together accounted for virtually all the reformulations adults produced. Direct corrections, introduced by forms like "No," "You don't say X...," or "On dit pas ça," were very rare.

In summary, the corrections children receive take the form of offers of a conventional way to say what the child seems to have intended. These reformulations follow immediately on the heels of children's erroneous utterances. For the most part, they function simultaneously to check that the adult is actually interpreting the child's intention correctly and to thereby offer the child a conventional way of expressing that intention.

Do Children Attend to the Adult Corrections They Hear?

Children appear to attend to adult reformulations. The evidence for this comes from their responses in the next turn after a reformulation. For example, some of the time, they take up and repeat the corrected element(s) from the reformulation; they acknowledge adult interpretations with forms like *yeah* or *uh-huh*, and sometimes reject them, with *no*. (When they reject an adult interpretation, they

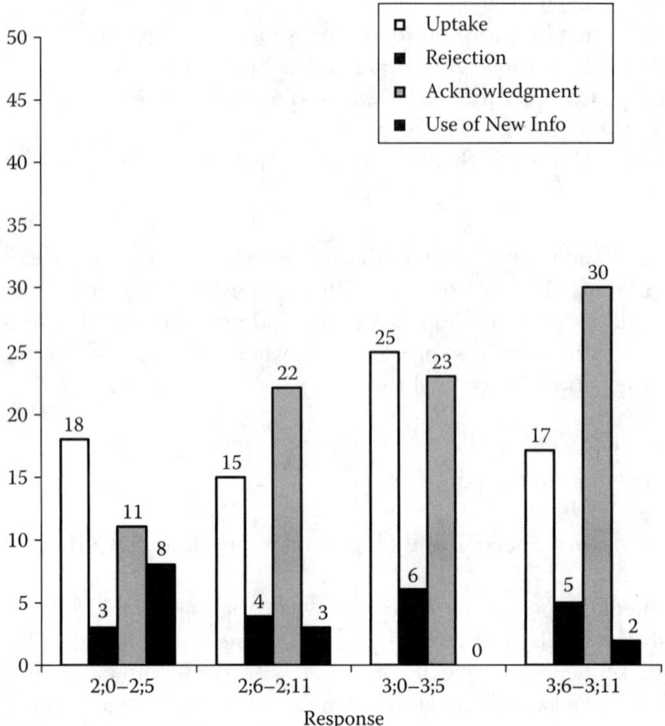

Figure 8.4 Mean percentages for each response type to adult reformulations.

generally try again to say what they intended in some other way.) They also repeat pieces of new information drawn from the adult reformulation, even if not the correction itself. These kinds of follow-ups in the next turn, I argue, all attest to the fact that children listen to and so give evidence of attention to the reformulations adults offer in the course of conversation.

The rest of the time, children simply continue with their next turn in the conversation, maintaining the same topic, and perhaps thereby demonstrating a tacit acceptance of the adult's reformulations.[3] The mean percentages of each response-type from the five children to adult reformulations are illustrated in Figure 8.4. In the first three age levels (from 2;0 to 3;5), the children used immediate uptakes (repeating the correct form from the reformulation) and acknowledgments at similar rates, and then shifted to using a somewhat greater number of acknowledgments. The rates for rejections of the adult interpretation and for uses of some new piece of information from the adult reformulations were consistent, and low, across all four age levels (see further Chouinard & Clark, 2003).

[3] Notice that in adult conversations, continuation on the same topic normally marks acceptance of the information in the preceding turn (see H. Clark 1996; Sacks, Schegloff, & Jefferson 1974).

A typical instance of uptake for a corrected element is given in (14). In this exchange, Abe switched from his initial *mine* to the locative phrase *on it* in the next turn after he heard his father's reformulation (given as an embedded correction):

(14) Abe (2;5.10): *I want butter mine.*
Father: ok give it here and I'll put butter on it.
Abe: *I need butter* ***on it.*** (Kuczaj, CHILDES)

The exchange in (15) illustrates a typical rejection of the father's interpretation in a side sequence where the father was checking on what Abe meant. Once the father got the child's intended meaning right, the new interpretation was acknowledged by Abe with *uh-huh*.

(15) Abe (2;5.7): *the plant didn't cried.*
||Father: the plant cried?
||Abe: ***no.***
Father: oh. the plant didn't cry.
Abe: *uh-huh.* (Kuczaj, CHILDES)

On other occasions, children would repeat a piece of new information (along with the correction itself or along with an acknowledgment of the correction) drawn from the adult's reformulation. This both grounded the new information and, at the same time, showed that the children had been attending to the adult reformulation. These response-types provide explicit evidence that children attend to the reformulations they hear (Chouinard & Clark, 2003). When they do not respond in one of these ways, they simply continue with their next turn in the conversation, a move that, in adults, would be construed as a tacit acceptance of the preceding turn. As Sacks, Schegloff, and Jefferson (1974) pointed out, such moves indicate that the current speaker has passed up any opportunity to repair what has just been said, and has done so because he or she has accepted the utterance as is (see further H. Clark, 1996).

CONTRAST AND CONVENTIONALITY

Reformulations offer children new information about their language, namely the conventional forms that adults would use to express the same intentions and goals children are attempting to express. Because adults use these conventional forms as they check up on their children's intentions, thus making clear that they are expressing the same meaning, children can accept or reject these "checks." When they accept them, children are taking the conventional versions (the adult reformulations) as expressing what they in fact wished to express. But since these conventional versions *contrast* in form with the children's own immediately preceding erroneous utterances, adult reformulations offer them a target form that contains information about what needs to be adjusted or changed in the utterance they used to express that particular intention.

This comparison process consists of the following steps, where *X* stands for the child's erroneous utterance and X^* for the conventional adult version that conveys the same meaning:

1. The child says *X*.
2. The adult checks on the child's intention by reformulating the child's utterance, *X*, in conventional form, X^*, in the next turn.
3. The child compares *X* and X^* and registers any contrast in form between them.
4. The child may then indicate acceptance of X^* by taking up some or all of X^* by acknowledging X^* explicitly; by taking up some other (new) information from the reformulation; or by simply continuing with the exchange.

The responses in (4) provide evidence that children are attending to X^* as a reformulation of *X*. That is, children recognize that X^* expresses the intention they were trying to convey with the erroneous utterance, *X*. It is the contrast between *X* and X^*, both designed to express the same intention (the same meaning) that is critical.[4] Without this, children could not be sure that reformulations were offering negative feedback. With this, reformulations offer timely, informative, and highly focused feedback on specific utterances. In short, they meet the classic criteria for negative feedback.[5]

At the same time, gaining complete mastery of a form takes time. Even when children recognize that a conventional form is conventional, this doesn't guarantee instant changes in children's language. Erroneous forms in production may be so well established for retrieval that they remain the first forms retrieved in production long after children have stored the conventional forms in memory. In fact, learning the correct forms and storing them in memory often takes place long before children manage to retrieve those same conventional forms consistently when they need them in production. In effect, children have to learn to override well-entrenched erroneous forms. Just how much exposure to the conventional form is required before children fully eliminate earlier errors remains unclear. It

---

4 Notice that joint attention does not presuppose either physical copresence or conversational copresence. One can talk about absent or imaginary objects and events (conversational copresence but no physical copresence), and one can draw the attention of another to an object or event through gesture, look, or stance (physical copresence but no conversational copresence). For further discussion, see H. Clark (1996).

5 This also allows children to distinguish reformulations from adult continuations in conversation (see Marcus, 1993). The critical difference lies in whether the adult utterance expresses the same intention, the same meaning as the child's (Chouinard & Clark, 2003).

is also unclear how amount of exposure to conventional forms interacts with how much children already know.[6]

Notice that all these exchanges depend on grounding the information being added. Each participant in an exchange needs to make sure that any new information on offer is taken up by the other, so that, from then on, it counts as part of common ground (H. Clark, 1996). To achieve this, participants must have first established a joint focus of attention where, in the present cases, both adult and child are attending to the same object or event (Clark, 2001; Tomasello, 1995). Grounding depends on more than joint attention, though: The participants in an adult–child conversation typically also rely on physical copresence (the participants and the object or event they are attending to are in the same place) and conversational copresence (both adult and child are talking about the same object or event) as well.[7] When exchanges meet these conditions, the participants can safely assume that the information each conveys is being grounded as they go along. They can make doubly sure of that by taking up new information explicitly by repeating it to mark its uptake, by acknowledging it (with *yeah*, *uh-huh*, or a head nod), and by adding pertinent information on that topic in the next turn.

The grounding that often follows a reformulation is illustrated in the following exchanges, the first about phonology, on the pronunciation of a word, in (16), and the second about morphology, here the agreement of the adjective with the article and the appropriate noun, in (17):

(16) Philippe (2;2.10, of a truck): *il a des neus le camion.*
(Ph. says "neus" for "pneus")
Mother: oui, il a des pneus. pneus.
Philippe: *pneus.* (Suppes & Léveillé, CHILDES)

(17) Philippe (2;1.6, of a small carton of milk) *une petit de lait.*
Mother: Une petite boîte de lait.
Philippe: *petite boîte de lait.* (Suppes & Léveillé, CHILDES)

Grounding, established by the child's uptake of the form introduced by the adult, can also be seen in lexical acquisition, with the child's use of the conventional

---

[6] One could object that the uptake responses, where the child repeats the corrected elements given in the adult reformulation, is simply an instance of priming. But notice that if this is priming, one would predict that children should always respond this way, but they don't. In response to reformulations, they sometimes repeat the element(s) corrected, sometimes simply acknowledge them, sometimes make use of a piece of new information included in the reformulation, and sometimes just continue on the same topic (Figure 8.4). So even if one argued that children's uptakes in the form of repeats have been primed by the adult reformulation, priming *per se* offers no explanation of why children should produce such a repeat on one occasion but not another. At the same time, from a conversational perspective, all these responses to reformulations strongly suggest that children are paying attention to what adults say (Chouinard & Clark, 2003).

[7] Experimental study of initial exposure to a paradigm and the elicitation of child errors, followed by exposure through reformulations to the conventional forms, might begin to offer more precise answers here. See, for example, the studies by Saxton, Kucsar, Marshall, and Rupra (1998).

agentive noun, illustrated in the exchange in (18), and in morphology, with uptake of the preposition *in*, illustrated in (19):

(18) D (2;4.7, reading with his father; naming pictures of different professions)
Father [pointing at someone with a fishing rod]: What about this guy?
D: *A fishing!*
Father: A fisherman.
D: A *fisherman*. (Clark, diary)

(19) Peter (2;0.10): *light there*. [pointing to lamp]
Adult: uhhuh # there's another light.
Peter: *light a hall*. [pointing to overhead light]
Adult: light in the hall.
Peter: *light in a hall*.
Adult: uh-huh # there's a light in the hall. (Bloom, CHILDES)

Notice that in the final utterance in (19), the adult further ratifies the child's uptake. Grounding like this plays the same role in children's acquisition of constructions linked to specific words, illustrated here in the exchanges in (20) and (21):

(20) D (2;8.14, with a toothbrush in his hand): *An' I going to tease.*
Mother [puzzled]: Oh. Oh, you mean you're going to pretend to do your teeth?
D: *Yes.*
<then, as father came by a minute later>
Father: Are you going to do your teeth?
D: *No, I was pretending.* (Clark, diary)

(21) D (2;4.29, as his father picked him up and swung him in his arms near the top of the stairs): *Don't fall me downstairs!*
Father: Oh, I wouldn't drop you downstairs.
D: *Don't drop me downstairs.* (Clark, diary)

In summary, children provide strong evidence of being attentive to adult information about language, whether in the form of offers of new words or more generally in adult reformulations of child errors, in conventional terms, of what the children had intended to say. Children ratify adult offers of new words, and they make use of adult reformulations of child errors (Chouinard & Clark, 2003; Clark, 2001, 2007).

CHILD-DIRECTED SPEECH AND THE PROCESS OF ACQUISITION

Findings like these support the view that child-directed speech plays a critical role in the process of acquisition. This support springs from much more than modifications in the forms of child-directed speech (e.g., Snow & Ferguson, 1977). It springs from adult attention to the meanings carried by expressions and constructions judged to be new to the child on the one hand, and to the conventional ways of conveying specific meanings in the language on the other. In short, in the course of conversation, adults expose children to the language of the community, offering them extensive information about the forms and functions of that language.

Child-directed speech provides children with timely information, pertinent to the occasion, about which words to use, how to pronounce them, and how to inflect them; which constructions to use; which polite forms to choose; and so on. In doing this, adults give children implicit, and sometimes explicit, directions for *using* the linguistic forms they are acquiring (see Clark, 1998; Clark & Grossman, 1998; Clark & Wong, 2002). While not all children receive the same kinds of information, in exactly the same ways as reported here, evidence from a range of cultures suggests that adults and older siblings in many cultures offer children implicit, and sometimes explicit, guidance on what to say when, and to whom. In some cultures, for instance, this guidance takes the form of utterances modeled for the child in context, designed for a specific addressee, and accompanied by an instruction like *Say it* or *Say this* (e.g., Schieffelin, 1979).

However adults go about offering such guidance on usage, they consistently link it to communicative intentions, and to what to say to others in particular settings, on particular occasions. When children's expectations match adult usage, they can consolidate what they have inferred about the conventional usage of the expressions involved. When their expectations are violated, they must adjust to the patterns of use they hear from the adults talking. The same goes for their own usage: When they say something and get the expected result, their assumptions about usage are supported. But when they say something and fail to achieve their goal, they must at some point consider whether what they said may not be the appropriate way to express that intention. Adult reformulations provide an added source of information here, alongside any observations of how others use the language.

In short, speakers—adult and child—appear to act on the general expectation that one uses language for social purposes. To express their intentions is a major goal for children acquiring their first language. Adults do not focus on details of form except where misuses, errors in children's speech, could impede communication by obscuring the child's intentions. This may lead adults to adopt various strategies for ensuring that children express their intentions in a conventional form for the occasion, in that community. One option here is to use reformulations that can both check on what the child intended and offer a conventional model in place of any errors in the child's utterance. Another is to model the appropriate utterance for a specific intention and then ask the child to repeat it (e.g., Schieffelin, 1979). In both instances, children are exposed to conventional ways of expressing specific intentions in the language used by the adults around them.

Children take advantage of information about the language—the appropriate words to use for specific categories of referent, objects and actions; they also attend to other kinds of information that help link unfamiliar words to ones they already know. And they take in information about how to convey their intentions by using conventional pronunciations, word choices, morphological forms, and syntactic constructions. All this information is available in the speech adults address to children as they interact with them, and it is available in adult reformulations when children make errors. Roger Brown presciently observed: "The changes produced in sentences as they move between persons in discourse may be the richest data for the discovery of grammar" (Brown, 1968, p. 288). And even more than that: It is in conversation with others around them that adults shape the language children come to learn.

ACKNOWLEDGMENTS

Preparation of this chapter was supported in part by a grant from the National Science Foundation (SBR97-31781) and by the Center for the Study of Language and Information, Stanford University. It was originally presented at the Symposium in honor of Melissa Bowerman, Max Planck Institute for Psycholinguistics, Nijmegen, NL, April 2002.

REFERENCES

Akhtar, N., Jipson, J., & Callanan, M. (2001). Learning words through overhearing. *Child Development, 72*, 416–430.

Baker, C. L., & McCarthy, J. J. (Eds.). (1979). *The logical problem of language acquisition.* Cambridge, MA: MIT Press.

Bowerman, M. (1985). What shapes children's grammars? In D. I. Slobin (Ed.), *The crosslinguistic study of language acquisition* (Vol. 2, 1257–1319). Hillsdale, NJ: Erlbaum.

Bowerman, M. (1988). The "no negative evidence" problem: How do children avoid constructing an overly general grammar? In J. A. Hawkins (Ed.), *Explaining language universals* (pp. 71–101). Oxford: Blackwell.

Brown, R. (1968). The development of *wh* questions in child speech. *Journal of Verbal Learning & Verbal Behavior, 7*, 279–290.

Callanan, M. A. (1985). How parents label objects for young children: The role of input in the acquisition of category hierarchies. *Child Development, 56*, 508–523.

Callanan, M. A. (1990). Parents' descriptions of objects: Potential data from children's inferences about category principles. *Cognitive Development, 5*, 101–122.

Choi, S., & Bowerman, M. (1991). Learning to express motion events in English and Korean: The influence of language-specific lexicalization patterns. *Cognition, 41*, 83–121.

Chouinard, M. M., & Clark, E. V. (2003). Adult reformulations of child errors as negative evidence. *Journal of Child Language, 30*, 637–669.

Clark, E. V. (1987). The principle of contrast: A constraint on language acquisition. In B. MacWhinney (Ed.), *Mechanisms of language acquisition* (pp. 1–33). Hillsdale, NJ: Erlbaum.

Clark, E. V. (1990). On the pragmatics of contrast. *Journal of Child Language, 17*, 417–431.

Clark, E. V. (1993). *The lexicon in acquisition.* Cambridge, UK: Cambridge University Press.

Clark, E. V. (1997). Conceptual perspective and lexical choice in acquisition. *Cognition, 64*, 1–37.

Clark, E. V. (1998). Lexical structure and pragmatic directions in acquisition. In M. C. Gruber, D. Higgins, K. S. Olson, & T. Wysocki (Eds.), *Papers from the 34th meeting of the Chicago Linguistic Society 1998: The Panels* (pp. 437–446). Chicago: Chicago Linguistic Society.

Clark, E. V. (1999). Acquisition in the course of conversation. [Special Issue] *Studies in Linguistic Sciences*, *29*, 1–18.
Clark, E. V. (2001). Grounding and attention in the acquisition of language. In M. Andronis, C. Ball, H. Elston, & S. Neuvel (Eds.), *Papers from the 37th meeting of the Chicago Linguistic Society* (Vol. 1, pp. 95–116). Chicago: Chicago Linguistic Society.
Clark, E. V. (2002). Making use of pragmatic inferences in the acquisition of meaning. In D. Beaver, S. Kaufmann, B. Clark, & L. Casillas (Eds.), *The construction of meaning* (pp. 45–58). Stanford, CA: CSLI Publications.
Clark, E. V. (2007). Young children's uptake of new words in conversation. *Language in Society*, 157–182.
Clark, E. V., & Chouinard, M. M. 2000. Enoncés enfantins, formules adultes dans l'acquisition du langage. *Langages, 140*, 9–23.
Clark E. V., & Clark, H. H. (1979). When nouns surface as verbs. *Language, 55*, 767–811.
Clark, E. V., & Grossman, J. B. (1998). Pragmatic directions and children's word learning. *Journal of Child Language, 25*, 1–18.
Clark, E. V., & McKercher, D. A. (In preparation). Learning new words: Making use of information about domains, functions, and parts.
Clark, E. V., & Wong, A. D.-W. (2002). Pragmatic directions about language use: Words and word meanings. *Language in Society, 31*, 181–212.
Clark, H. H. (1996). *Using language*. Cambridge, UK: Cambridge University Press.
Dunn, J., & Shatz, M. (1989). Becoming a conversationalist despite (or because of) having a sibling. *Child Development* 60, 388–410.
Hart, B., & Risley, T. R. (1992). American parenting of language-learning children: persisting differences in family–child interactions observed in natural home environments. *Developmental Psychology, 28*, 1096–1105.
Hart, B., & Risley, T. R. (1995). *Meaningful differences in the everyday experience of young American children*. Baltimore, MD: Paul H. Brookes.
Heath, S. B. (1983). *Ways with words*. Cambridge, UK: Cambridge University Press.
Hoff, E. (2003a). The specificity of environmental influence: Socioeconomic status affects early vocabulary development. *Child Development 74*, 1368–1378.
Hoff, E. (2003b). Causes and consequences of SES-relate differences in parent-to-child speech. In M. Bornstein & R. H. Bradley (Eds.), *Socioeconomic status, parenting, and child development* (pp. 147–160). Mahwah, NJ: Erlbaum.
Hoff, E., & Naigles, L. (2002). How children use input to acquire a lexicon. *Child Development, 73*, 418–433.
Hoff-Ginsberg, E. (1998). The relation of birth order and socioeconomic status to children's language experience and language development. *Applied Psycholinguistics, 19*, 603–629.
Huttenlocher, J., Haight, W., Bryk, A., Seltzer, M., & Lyons, T. (1991). Early vocabulary growth: Relation to language input and gender. *Developmental Psychology, 17*, 236–248.
Jefferson, G. (1972). Side sequences. In D. Sudnow (Ed.), *Studies in social interaction* (pp. 294–338). New York: Free Press.
Jefferson, G. (1982). On exposed and embedded correction in conversation. *Studium Linguisticum, 14*, 58–68.
Lewis, D. K. (1969). *Convention: A philosophical study*. Cambridge, MA: Harvard University Press.
Marcus, G. F. (1993). Negative evidence in language acquisition. *Cognition, 46*, 53–85.
Masur, E. F. (1997). Maternal labeling of novel and familiar objects: Implications for children's development of lexical constraints. *Journal of Child Language, 24*, 427–439.

Ochs, E., & Schieffelin, B. B. (1984). Language acquisition and socialization: Three developmental stories. In: R. Schweder & R. Levin (Eds.), *Culture theory: Essays in mind, self and emotion* (pp. 276–320). Cambridge, UK: Cambridge University Press.

Pinker, S. (1984). *Language learnability and language development*. Cambridge, MA: Harvard University Press.

Pullum, G. K. (1996). Learnability, hyperlearning, and the poverty of the stimulus. In J. Johnson, M. L. Juge, & J. L. Moxley (Eds.), *Proceedings of the 22nd Annual Meeting: General Session and Parasession on the Role of Learnability in Grammatical Theory* (pp. 498–513). Berkeley, CA: Berkeley Linguistics Society.

Pullum, G. K., & Scholz, B. C. (2002). Empirical assessment of stimulus poverty arguments. *The Linguistic Review, 19*(1–2), 9–50.

Rogers, D. (1978). Information about word-meaning in the speech of parents to young children. In R. N. Campbell & P. T. Smith (Eds.), *Recent advances in the psychology of language* (pp. 187–198). London: Plenum.

Sacks, H., Schegloff, E. A., & Jefferson, G. (1974). A simplest systematics for the organization of turn-taking in conversation. *Language, 50*, 696–735.

Saxton, M.; Kulcsar, B.; Marshall, G.; & Rupra, M. 1998. Longer-term effects of corrective input: An experimental approach. *Journal of Child Language, 25*, 701–721.

Schegloff, E. A. (1972). Notes on a conversational practice: Formulating place. In D. Sudnow (Ed.), *Studies in conversational interaction* (pp. 75–119). New York: Free Press.

Schieffelin, B. B. (1979). Getting it together: An ethnographic approach to the study of the development of communicative competence. In E. Ochs & B. B. Schieffelin (Eds.), *Developmental pragmatics* (pp. 73–108). New York: Academic Press.

Snow, C. E., & Ferguson, C. A. (Eds.), (1977). *Talking to children: Language input and acquisition*. Cambridge, UK: Cambridge University Press.

Svartvik, J., & Quirk, R. (Eds.). (1980). *A corpus of English conversation*. Lund: Gleerup.

Tomasello, M. (1995). Joint attention as social cognition. In: C. Moore & P. J. Dunham (Eds.), *Joint attention: Its origins and role in development* (pp. 103–130). Hillsdale, NJ: Erlbaum.

Wilkins, D. (2002). *On being "open": An ethno-semantic description of the English verb "open" based on adult–child interactions.* Paper presented at the symposium in honor of Melissa Bowerman, Max Planck Institute for Psycholinguistics, Nijmegen, Netherlands.

Personal Tribute

PING LI

I was very fortunate to work on my doctoral dissertation under Melissa Bowerman's guidance. Much of Melissa's own research has focused on the acquisition of word meaning or the acquisition of form as it is related to meaning. Her insights into language acquisition—in particular, her views on the acquisition of meaning—have greatly influenced my thinking on language and language acquisition. There were at least two important examples from Melissa that became the starting points of my research focus: (1) the cryptotype of *un*-, in which the acquisition of the form depends crucially on the meaning of verbs to which *un*- is attached (see more details in the chapter), and (2) the acquisition of the spatial expressions in Dutch and Korean that correspond to the English prepositions *on* and *in*. In Dutch, the orientation of attachment matters, such that vertical versus horizontal attachments involve the use of different prepositions; in Korean, the degree of fit matters, such that tight-fit versus loose-support situations involve the use of different locative verbs. These two examples highlight the importance of connecting the acquisition of morphology with the acquisition of lexical meaning, and of connecting acquisition theory with crosslinguistic data.

A personal note that I have shared with many colleagues over the years reveals how important Melissa's mentorship has been to me: I remember the time when I first received Melissa's comments on the draft of my dissertation. Her scribbles were all over the pages, with critical but insightful comments—on some pages she wrote even more than I did! One might be discouraged altogether to continue any writing with this quantity of critical comments, but I decided to take up the challenge. Throughout my dissertation period I used Melissa's detailed comments to improve my writing. Melissa stayed up to read and comment on the final draft of my dissertation until 4:00 a.m., so that I could finish the typesetting by 7:30 a.m. A few days later, when the final version came from the print shop, there were still a number of typographical errors (but due to my own oversight, not the printer's). Melissa immediately caught one on the very first page, which read "The expression of time constitutes an indispens*ible* part of language use." Melissa, your scholarship, wisdom, and kindness have been and will continue to be an "indispens*able*" part of my work and my life.

9

Meaning in Acquisition
Semantic Structure, Lexical Organization, and Crosslinguistic Variation

PING LI
The Pennsylvania State University

INTRODUCTION

In this chapter, I examine three problems: the acquisition of tense and aspect, the acquisition of cryptotypes, and the development of lexical structure. The central issue in all three problems is how the child discovers word meanings in a lexical system, and what mechanisms are at work in the process of this discovery. In each case, the problem domain involves the learning of semantic structures that are important for the use of grammatical morphology or lexical categories. In examining these three cases, I argue that structured semantic representations of the lexicon can emerge as a natural outcome of the meaning-form and the meaning-meaning mappings in language acquisition.

Two major perspectives inform the examination of children's development of these structures (and have been key assumptions underlying Bowerman's own work). First, one cannot look at the acquisition of a given set of forms in isolation. In the study of the acquisition of morphology, for example, it is important to examine not only the morphological devices per se, but also the words (particularly verbs) with which these devices are used (Bowerman, 1982, 1983). For example, the acquisition of the prefix *un-* needs to be considered closely with the verbs that can take *un-*. In Whorf's (1956) view, *un-* marks a cryptotype, a covert semantic category that can only be implicitly defined by the devices it goes with. Thus, the understanding of *un-* in child language cannot be complete without a consideration of the cryptotype meanings that are characteristic of the *un*-able verbs. By the same token, the acquisition of tense-aspect suffixes such as *-ing* and *-ed* needs to be considered together with the types of verbs (atelic, telic, result, etc.) to which the suffixes are attached. In the empirical literature there is ample evidence that children pay attention to the inherent meanings of the verbs when they learn to use tense-aspect suffixes (Bloom, Lifter, & Hafitz, 1980; Brown, 1973; Slobin, 1985). In Li and Bowerman (1998) and Li and Shirai (2000), we examined specifically the interaction between grammatical aspect (expressed by morphological markers) and lexical aspect (expressed in inherent meanings of verbs) in both first and second language acquisition, in a systematic attempt to connect morphology and lexical semantics.

A second important perspective championed by Bowerman is that in formulating and testing theories of language acquisition, it is important to examine acquisition data from not only one language (usually English by default), but also from other languages. Crosslinguistic evidence is crucial in many cases because of the language-specific properties associated with individual languages. Often, a given hypothesis appears to be perfect for one language, but it may turn out to be inaccurate or incomplete upon a close look at data from other languages. For example, English uses the prepositions *on* and *in* to express spatial locations of objects in attachment and fitting situations. In Dutch, the orientation of attachment matters, such that vertical versus horizontal attachments involve the use of different prepositions; in Korean, the degree of fit matters, such that tight-fit versus loose-support situations involve the use of different locative verbs. Thus, how English-speaking children learn *on* and *in* will not be sufficiently informative as to how Dutch and Korean children learn the corresponding devices in their languages. A crosslinguistic perspective can be crucial in illuminating the extent to which language-specific input may play a role in shaping children's early grammar (e.g., Bowerman, 1985, 1989, 1996).

This chapter summarizes our research that aims at connecting morphology and lexical semantics and at connecting acquisition theories and crosslinguistic data. The discussion is organized by the three topics that I mentioned, namely, the acquisition of tense and aspect, the acquisition of cryptotypes, and the development of lexical structure. Through careful analysis of crosslinguistic data, as well as connectionist modeling of acquisition, I show that the semantic structure underlying each of these domains emerges from the associations between forms and meanings present in the input.

THE ACQUISITION OF TENSE AND ASPECT

Empirical Observations

The expression of time is one of the central conceptual domains of language, and the acquisition of the ability to talk about time through the use of tense-aspect markers is one of the earliest tasks in language acquisition. In the last 30 years researchers have devoted much attention to the acquisition of tense and aspect in various languages (for general reviews, see Li & Shirai, 2000; Shirai, Slobin & Weist, 1998; Slobin, 1985; Weist, 1986). An early observation of children's acquisition of tense-aspect markers came from Roger Brown (1973). Brown documented two interesting patterns: First, the earliest grammatical device in children's speech, the progressive aspect marker *-ing*, appears virtually always to be used correctly. In particular, children never use *-ing* incorrectly with state verbs; for example, they do not produce overgeneralizations like *knowing* or *wanting*. Second, English-speaking children first use past-tense forms with only a small, semantically coherent set of verbs, including *dropped*, *slipped*, *crashed*, and *broke*, verbs that indicate events that happen instantaneously but lead to clear end results. Some years after Brown's observations, Bloom, Lifter, and Hafitz (1980) provided further evidence that confirmed Brown's analyses (especially the second observation). They found that the inflections used by young English-speaking children correlated with the semantic types of verbs: *-ing* occurred almost exclusively with verbs such as *play*, *ride*, and *write* (durative, nonresultative), whereas past-tense forms occurred predominantly with verbs such as *find*, *fall*, and *break* (punctual, resultative). Together, Brown and Bloom et al.'s data suggested a picture of early "undergeneralization" in the acquisition of inflectional morphology: Rather than using tense-aspect markers with all types of verbs, as adults do, children use them more restrictively. Obviously, this more restrictive use of grammatical morphemes is associated with the inherent semantic differences of the verbs to which the progressive and past-tense forms are attached.

The strong associations between tense-aspect morphemes and verb semantics observed by Brown and Bloom et al. have generated a considerable amount of research. Many studies have examined the acquisition of tense and aspect in other languages, including Chinese (Erbaugh, 1982; Li, 1990; Li & Bowerman, 1998), French (Bronckart & Sinclair, 1973), Italian (Antinucci & Miller, 1976), Polish (Weist, Wysocka, Witkowska-Stadnik, Buczowska, & Konieczna, 1984), Turkish (Aksu, 1978; Aksu-Koç & Slobin, 1985), and other languages (see Li & Shirai, 2000 for a review of relevant crosslinguistic data). In general, data from these studies are robust and consistent with Brown and Bloom et al.'s observations, indicating that the use of imperfective or progressive aspect morphology in children's speech is first associated with atelic, activity verbs, whereas that of perfective aspect/past tense morphemes is associated with telic, resultative verbs.[1]

Subsequent discussions on these empirical data have stimulated intense debates on how children acquire lexical semantics and grammatical morphology and have motivated theoretical accounts of children's semantic and morphological development in general (see Li & Shirai, 2000, for an overview). Here I discuss two major contrasting proposals and then attempt to explain the data from a crosslinguistic developmental perspective.

---

[1] Not all acquisition researchers agree that these association patterns exist crosslinguistically. For example, Weist and his colleagues argued against the proposal of Bloom et al. (1980). They showed that Polish children are able to understand and produce the basic contrast between perfective and imperfective aspect as early as 2;6 (Weist et al., 1984). See Li and Shirai (2000, pp. 40–47) for a discussion of the relevant debate.

Contrasting Perspectives

The major divide in perspectives on the acquisition of tense and aspect falls between formalist-nativist and functionalist-cognitivist approaches. The formalist perspective is strongly associated with a nativist view in the tense-aspect acquisition literature. In its strongest form, Bickerton (1981, 1984) proposed the language bioprogram hypothesis, according to which specific semantic categories and concepts are biologically preprogrammed for the human language learner, and these categories or concepts will naturally unfold in the process of language acquisition. Because the categories and concepts are hard-wired ahead of time, the child simply needs to discover how they are instantiated in specific forms in the language to be learned. Two important innate distinctions in the domain of tense and aspect are between *state* and *process* and between *punctual* and *nonpunctual* categories. Given the innate nature of these distinctions, according to Bickerton, early on in language development *states* will be marked differently from *processes*, and *punctual* situations will be marked differently from *nonpunctual* situations, probably by the use of different tense-aspect markers.[2]

Bickerton first supported his hypothesis with evidence from Creole grammars, arguing that in the absence of relevant input (pidgins, the predecessors of Creoles, do not have tense-aspect markers), first-generation Creole speakers invent tense-aspect systems to mark the bioprogrammed distinctions. Drawing in addition on child language data, he argued that children first use the tense-aspect markers of their language to mark the distinctions between *state* and *process* and between *punctual* and *nonpunctual*. For example, Bickerton used Brown's (1973) observation in support of an innate specification of the distinction between *process* and *state*: Young English-speaking children never overgeneralize the progressive marker *-ing* to state verbs because they are sensitive to the bioprogrammed *state–process* distinction. Similarly, Bickerton argued for the existence of the *punctual–nonpunctual* distinction in the bioprogram, on the basis of interpreting the observations by Antinucci and Miller (1976), Bronckart and Sinclair (1973), and Aksu-Koç and Slobin (1985; originally Slobin & Aksu, 1980) that young children use the past or perfective morphemes to mark punctual events. Thus, although Bickerton's language bioprogram hypothesis originated from studies of Creole languages, many of its arguments rest on interpretations of data in children's acquisition of tense and aspect. Bickerton considered early child languages and Creoles to be ideal cases for observing the bioprogram, because the innate distinctions of the bioprogram are realized in these cases without being

---

[2] A somewhat different, but related view is advocated by Slobin (1985). Slobin proposed the basic child grammar, which contains a prestructured "semantic space" with universal semantic notions or categories. These semantic categories can act strongly to attract the morphological mapping from the input language. *Result* and *Process* are two such semantic categories that have to do with children's acquisition of tense-aspect morphology. However, because the issue of innateness is less fundamental to the basic child grammar than it is to the language bioprogram hypothesis, and because Slobin's (1997) recent reformulation is consistent with a cognitive–functional view, I do not consider the basic child grammar as a formalist–nativist theory in this debate.

contaminated by external factors subject to cultural evolution (e.g., individual linguistic variations that are idiosyncratic).

The language bioprogram hypothesis attempted to explain language acquisition by appealing to innately determined semantic distinctions. A contrasting perspective is the functionalist-cognitivist approach to tense-aspect acquisition, which has had many variants in the literature. One early explanation for the restricted tense-aspect uses in child language drew on the child's purportedly insufficient cognitive ability (Antinucci & Miller, 1976; Bronckart & Sinclair, 1973). Other investigators turned to the "input hypothesis" to explain the early associations between grammatical morphology and lexical aspect (e.g., Stephany, 1981 for Modern Greek; Li, 1990 for child Mandarin; Shirai, 1991 for English). Still others used the "aspect hypothesis" or the "prototype hypothesis" to explain similar patterns in L2 learning (Shirai, 1991; Shirai & Andersen, 1995). More recently, Li and Shirai (2000) presented an integrated view of the functional approach, drawing ideas from both the prototype hypothesis and connectionist networks. They argued that in both L1 and L2, the learner's early associations between lexical meanings of verbs and grammatical morphemes do not indicate innate specifications of semantic categories. Rather, these associations reflect the learner's sensitivity to (and recognition of) the statistical properties of the linguistic input, and in turn, statistical properties in the input may reflect inherent constraints on linguistic communication and event characteristics. The semantic categories believed to be innate can emerge naturally from the learning of the lexical characteristics of verbs in context. Finally, Li and Shirai argued that the associations between grammatical morphology and lexical aspect are probabilistic and not absolute, counter to what nativist proposals would assume. Depending on the structure of the target language, in some cases, learners retreat from the probabilistic associations and develop more flexible patterns of use; in other cases, they hold on to these associations even as they acquire adult patterns of language use.

Resolving the Conflict Crosslinguistically

It has become increasingly clear over the last few years that a strong nativist proposal like Bickerton's cannot account for the large body of crosslinguistic data. Instead, a functional, input-based, probabilistic learning mechanism seems to be most compatible with the way children approach the problem of tense-aspect acquisition. Even Bickerton (1999) himself has significantly weakened the strong predictions of the original language bioprogram hypothesis, assigning an increased role to input language patterns in acquisition. But how does crosslinguistic evidence help in resolving the conflict?

Li and Bowerman (1998) presented crosslinguistic data on the acquisition of aspect in Chinese. In three experiments we showed that young children learning Mandarin Chinese displayed the same type of strong associations between grammatical morphology and lexical aspect as in English and other languages. In particular, children comprehended the progressive marker *zai* better with atelic, activity verbs than with telic verbs, and, conversely, the perfective marker *-le* better with telic verbs than with atelic verbs. Children also produced the imperfective aspect markers *zai* and *-ne* mostly with atelic verbs and rarely with telic verbs, whereas they produced the perfective marker *-le* more frequently with telic verbs than with atelic verbs.

While the Chinese data would seem to be no surprise as compared with data from English and other languages, there were at least two important features that make them special.

1. Unlike English and other Indo-European languages, Mandarin Chinese has a special set of state verbs, the posture verbs, that cannot take the progressive marker *zai* (e.g., *zhan* 'stand,' *zuo* 'sit,' and *tang* 'lie'). Recall that Brown (1973) observed that children do not overgeneralize *-ing* to state verbs in English (posture verbs are not state verbs in English as they are in Chinese), and Bickerton interpreted this as indicative of children's innate sensitivity to the state-process distinction. In child Mandarin, however, children do overgeneralize the progressive marker *zai* to posture state verbs as revealed in our production experiment, and such errors are also observed in children's spontaneous speech. Two lessons can be drawn from this finding.
    a. First, the *state-process* distinction is not a universal semantic primitive as dictated by the language bioprogram hypothesis, and different languages may define the distinction differently. For example, posture verbs are state verbs in Chinese but not in English (in Chinese **ta zai zuo* is ungrammatical while in English *he is sitting there* is perfectly acceptable). The English-speaking child can use *-ing* with *sit* and *stand* to indicate the dynamic aspect of the action, treating sitting and standing as events, while the Chinese-speaking child uses *zai* with *zuo* and *zhan* in Chinese, treating them as states. Comrie (1976) discussed this phenomenon in connection with perception verbs (e.g., *see, hear*): English treats perception verbs as stative and these verbs consequently do not accept progressive marking, while Portuguese treats them as dynamic so they can naturally accept progressive marking.
    b. Even if the state-process distinction is neatly defined by language, children may not observe the distinction in their use of tense-aspect markers. This is consistent with Shirai's (1994) analysis that shows that even in English, children do occasionally generalize *-ing* to state verbs depending on the type of input they receive from maternal speech.
2. A second important feature is that Chinese has a special set of resultative verb compounds (RVCs), such as *ti-dao* 'kick-down,' *qie-kai* 'cut-open,' or *reng-diao* 'throw away,' which are telic verbs that encode a clear end result (Klein, Li, & Hendriks, 2000; Smith, 1997; Tai, 1984). These verbs accept only perfective marking, not progressive marking in Chinese, unlike resultative verbs in English, which can easily take the progressive *-ing* (and so the resultative *-ing* combinations are found in child English). In our study children rarely used the progressive aspect with the RVC verbs, showing that they respected the incompatibility between aspectual

imperfectivity and lexical resultativity from early on. Interestingly, these RVC verbs correspond to a set of verbs that "name events of such brief duration that the event is almost certain to have ended before one can speak" (Brown, 1973, p. 334)—i.e., verbs with which young English-speaking children only use the past-tense forms. Bickerton would have taken the exclusive perfective marking of RVCs as an indication of the *punctual–nonpunctual* distinction, just as he did with the English data. But the crucial evidence from semelfactive verbs (Smith, 1997; e.g., *tiao* 'jump,' *qiao* 'knock,' *ti* 'kick,' which have the punctuality but not the resultativity feature) indicated that it was not punctuality but resultativity that children pay attention to (Li & Bowerman, 1998): With these semelfactive verbs, Chinese-speaking children do use the progressive marker *zai*.

The language-specific properties with RVC verbs in Chinese not only influence the specific patterns of children's acquisition of aspect markers with these verbs, but also speak to several general crosslinguistic differences.

a. First, because the adult language has a constraint on the combination of RVCs with the progressive marker, the picture of lexical aspect and grammatical morphology appears much more absolute than probabilistic, as compared with that in other languages.
b. Second, as compared with children learning other languages, Chinese-speaking children display no developmental transition from prototypical associations (e.g., result verbs with perfective aspect) to nonprototypical associations (e.g., result verbs with imperfective aspect). The prototype hypothesis predicts such transitions as the child's linguistic experience enriches (Shirai & Andersen, 1995). Now, given that the prototypical association between RVCs and perfective marking is preserved in the adult language, there is no reason for children to retreat from this association and move to nonprototypical ones, as they would in other languages where the associations are more flexible.
c. Finally, the combinatorial constraints in adult Chinese might reflect a general constraint on linguistic communication and event characteristics. The prototypical association between RVCs and perfective aspect reflects one of the most natural combinations between verb semantics and grammatical morphology. In Comrie's (1976) view, certain aspect morphemes combine most naturally with certain verb types but not others (the "naturalness of combination" principle). As Brown (1973) had also pointed out, events denoted by verbs like *drop*, *fall*, and *crash* (events expressed by RVCs in Chinese) occur instantaneously; any comment on them will have occurred after their ending. Thus, it is only natural to describe these events with perfective aspect (i.e., to combine *-le* but not *zai* with RVCs in Chinese).

The above crosslinguistic analyses, along with results from studies of other languages indicate that children are highly sensitive to language-specific properties of the input, and are capable of extracting systematic patterns from the input (see Li & Bowerman, 1998; Li & Shirai, 2000 for detailed discussions). Given this, we do not need to presuppose, as nativists do, that certain semantic categories are innately specified and brought to bear on the language acquisition task. Rather, semantic categories can emerge from the learning of the statistical regularities in the input language. But what capacity allows the child to carry out the pattern extraction in learning? Put simply, if input is important to language acquisition, in which way does it play a causal role? I referred earlier to a functional, input-based, and probabilistic learning mechanism that could be responsible for the acquisition task. In the next section, I discuss how such a learning mechanism could work in terms of the operations of connectionist networks.

THE ACQUISITION OF A CRYPTOTYPE

Whorf's Cryptotypes

In one of the classic papers of early cognitive linguistics, Whorf (1956) presented the following puzzle. In English, the reversative prefix *un-* can be used productively with many verbs to indicate the reversal of an action, as in *uncoil, uncover, undress, unfasten, unfold, unlock,* or *untie* (the meaning of reversal can also be expressed by other prefixes such as *dis-* or *de-* in English). However, many seemingly parallel forms are not allowed, such as **unbury, *unfill, *ungrip, *unhang, *unpress, *unspill,* or **unsqueeze.* Why is *un-* prefixation allowed with some verbs but not others?

Whorf's puzzle was deeper than this simple discrepancy. He noted that *un-* is a productive device in English morphology, and that despite the difficulties linguists have in characterizing its use, native speakers do have an intuitive feel for which verbs can be prefixed with *un-* and which cannot. He presented the following thought experiment: If a new verb *flimmick* is coined to mean "to tie a tin can to something," then native speakers are willing to accept the sentence "He unflimmicked the dog" as expressing the reversal of the "flimmicking" action; if *flimmick* means "to take apart," then they will not accept "He unflimmicked the puzzle" as describing the act of putting a puzzle back together. The constrained productivity of *un-* prompted Whorf to conjecture that there is some underlying or covert semantic category, a *cryptotype*, that governs the productive use of *un-*. According to Whorf, cryptotypes only make their presence known by the restrictions they place on the possible combinations of overt forms. When the overt prefix *un-* is combined with the overt verb *tie*, there is a covert cryptotype that licenses the combination *untie*. This same cryptotype also blocks a combination such as **unmove*.

To Whorf, the deep puzzle was that while the use of the prefix *un-* is productive, the cryptotype that governs its productivity is unclear: "We have no single word in the language which can give us a proper clue to this meaning or into which we can compress this meaning; hence the meaning is subtle, intangible, as is typical of cryptotypic meanings" (Whorf, 1956, p. 71). Here we have a case for which language use is conditioned in a principled way, but the principles themselves are not clearly subject to linguistic analysis. At some point Whorf did propose that there was "a covering, enclosing, and surface-attaching meaning" that could be the basis of the cryptotype for *un-*. But this definition was still rather elusive, as it was not clear whether we should view this as a single unit, three separate meanings, or a cluster of related meanings. Subsequent analyses also suggested the existence of other important aspects in the use of *un-* (Clark, Carpenter, & Just, 1995; Marchand, 1969)—for example, that *un-* takes change of state verbs, and that these verbs involve a direct object (so intransitive verbs such as **unswim*, **unplay*, and **unsnore* are ill-formed).

Cryptotypes in Child Language

Whorf's discussion shows clearly how a cryptotype is important to the use of *un-* in adult English. Bowerman was the first to point out that the notion of a cryptotype might also play an important role in child language acquisition.

According to Bowerman (1982, 1983, 1988), children's acquisition of *un-* tends to follow a U-shaped pattern, a pattern found in other areas of morphological acquisition as well, such as the acquisition of the English past tense. Children initially produce *un-* verbs in appropriate contexts, treating *un-* and its base verb as an unanalyzed whole. This initial stage of rote control is analogous to the child's saying *went* without realizing that it is the past-tense form of *go*.

Productivity of *un-* comes at the next stage, when children realize that *un-* is independent of the verb in indicating the reversal of an action. This stage in the acquisition of *un-* begins at around age 3. At this stage, children start to produce overgeneralizations in spontaneous speech such as **unarrange, *unbreak, *unblow, *unbury, *unget, *unhang, *unhate, *unopen, *unpress, *unspill, *unsqueeze*, or **untake* (Bowerman, 1982, 1983). Such overgeneralizations have also been documented by Clark et al. (1995) in both experimental and naturalistic data with children from ages 3 to 5, and were found in the CHILDES database (Li & MacWhinney, 1996). During this period, children also make certain "overmarking" errors. For example, the child might say "unopen" but really only mean to say *open*, or "unloosen" to mean *loosen*. In such cases, the base forms *open* and *loosen* have a reversative meaning that triggers the attachment of the prefix, even when the action of the base meaning is not actually being reversed. These errors are analogous to redundant past-tense marking as in **camed* and redundant plural marking as in **feets*. Finally, at a third stage, overgeneralization and overmarking errors both disappear.

A critical factor that leads to children's overgeneralization of *un-* at the second stage of this U-shaped learning, according to Bowerman (1982), is that children have somehow discovered the inherent meaning common to the verbs that take *un-*. In other words, they have developed what Whorf called the native "intuitive feel" for English verbs with respect to whether they are *un*-able: They have acquired the representation for the *un-* cryptotype. Examining speech errors from a longitudinal dataset, Bowerman further suggested two possible roles for a cryptotype to influence the learning of *un-*: (1) "Generalization via cryptotype": The cryptotype triggers morphological productivity and leads to overgeneralizations. This occurs because, once children have identified the cryptotype, they will overgeneralize *un-* to all verbs that fit the cryptotype, irrespective of whether the adult language actually allows *un-* in these cases (e.g., *squeeze* fits in the cryptotype just as *clench* does, so say "unsqueeze"). (2) "Recovery via cryptotype": The cryptotype helps the child to overcome overgeneralizations made at an earlier stage, if these overgeneralizations involve verbs that fall outside the cryptotype (e.g., *hate* does not fit in the cryptotypic meaning, so stop saying "unhate").

While Bowerman correctly identified the important role of cryptotypes in child language acquisition, one issue remains unclear. According to Whorf, cryptotypes are covert semantic categories that are elusive, subtle, and intangible, and linguists have a hard time to pin down their precise meanings. How then could the child extract the cryptotype and use it as a basis for morphological generalization or recovery, if the *un-* cryptotype is intangible even to linguists like Whorf?

The answers to this question have significant implications for the issue concerning whether language acquisition is a rule-based process or a statistical learning process (Pinker, 1991; Pinker & Prince, 1988; Rumelhart & McClelland, 1986; Seidenberg, 1997). Using the acquisition of the English past tense as an example, researchers have debated whether the acquisition process should be characterized by dual mechanisms (an internalized linguistic rule for regulars and an associative learning process for irregulars) or by a single mechanism (connectionist learning with distributed knowledge representation and adaptive connection weights). Cryptotypes provide another test case for this debate. If the learning of *un-* and its governing cryptotype is a process of rule extraction (category identification), then the overgeneralization errors with *un-* are rule-governed, in the same way as are the overgeneralization errors with *-ed*. However, if the learning of *un-* and the cryptotype is a connectionist statistical process, then the overgeneralization errors are due to the system's computation of relevant semantic features, lexical forms, and prefixation patterns in the form-meaning mapping process.

A Connectionist Model of the un- Cryptotype

Connectionist networks are dynamic learning systems that explore the regularities in the input-output mapping processes through the adjustment of connection weights and the activation of processing units. To answer the above questions, Li (1993) and Li and MacWhinney (1996) built a connectionist model to learn the reversative cryptotype associated with the use of *un-*. Our model was a standard feedforward network consisting of three layers of processing units (input, output, and hidden units). The network was trained with the backpropagation learning algorithm (Rumelhart, Hinton, & Williams, 1986). In our simulations, we used as input to our network 49 verbs that can take *un-*, 19 verbs that can take the competing prefix *dis-*, and 92 randomly selected verbs that can take neither prefix. Each verb was represented by a semantic pattern (a vector) that consisted of 20 semantic features that were selected in an attempt to capture basic linguistic and functional properties inherent in the semantic range of these verbs (see Li, 1993 for details). The task of the network was to take the semantic vectors of verbs as input and map them onto different prefixation patterns in the output: *un-*, *dis-*, or zero.

To analyze how our network developed internal representations, we used the hierarchical cluster analysis (Elman, 1990) to probe into the activation of the hidden units at various points in time during the network's learning. The network received input verbs one by one and determined if each verb should be mapped to *un-*, *dis-*, or no prefix. Each time the network received some feedback as to whether the mapping was correct. After learning, the averaged representations of the verbs at the hidden-unit level were clustered. Figure 9.1 presents a snapshot of the network's hidden-unit representations when the network had learned 50 verbs cumulatively. This graph shows two general clusters: one for the *un-* verbs, and the other for the zero verbs, verbs that cannot be prefixed with *un-* or *dis-*. Our interpretation of these clusters is that the network has acquired a distinct representation for the *un-* verbs by identifying the relevant semantic features shared by these verbs, and this representation corresponds most closely to Whorf's *un-* cryptotype. For example, most of the verbs in the *un-* cluster share the meaning of binding or locking: *bind, chain, fasten, hitch, hook, latch,* etc. Not all meanings relevant to the cryptotype are identified at this early stage in Figure 9.1. For example, the verbs *ravel* and *coil* were correctly categorized into the *un-* cluster, but the verb *roll* was incorrectly classified into the zero-verb cluster.

Note that our network received no discrete label of the semantic category associated with *un-* (the labels in Figure 9.1 were there simply to indicate which prefix the verb is supposed to take), nor was there a single categorical feature that tells which verb should take which prefix (hence Whorf's problem). All that the network received was the semantic feature information distributed across input patterns. Over time, however, the network was able to identify the regularities that hold between distributed semantic patterns and patterns of prefixation, and developed a structured representation that corresponded to Whorf's cryptotype. The cryptotype representations in the network thus emerged as a function of the network's learning of the association between form and meaning, not as a property that was given ad hoc to the network by the modeler.

Our simulation results provide support for Bowerman's (1982) hypothesized role of cryptotypes in inducing overgeneralizations. In Bowerman's data, most of the errors fell within the realm of Whorf's cryptotype (e.g., *squeeze* is similar to *clench*, so *squeeze* can also take *un-*). In Clark et al.'s (1995) data, the child's innovative uses of *un-* also respected the cryptotype from the beginning: They matched the semantic characteristics of the cryptotype even when the conventional meanings of the verb in the adult language did not. For example, **unbuild* was used to describe the action of detaching Lego-blocks, **undisappear* was used to describe the releasing of the child's thumbs from inside his fists.[3] Our simulations also indicate how the network generalized *un-* on the basis of the cryptotype. In Figure 9.1,

[3] Diary notes of my daughter's speech also include similar uses: "unbuild the snowman" was used to refer to the detachment of decorative pieces from the snowman, and "untape" to refer to the removal of scotch tape from a piece of paper (age of child was 6;9).

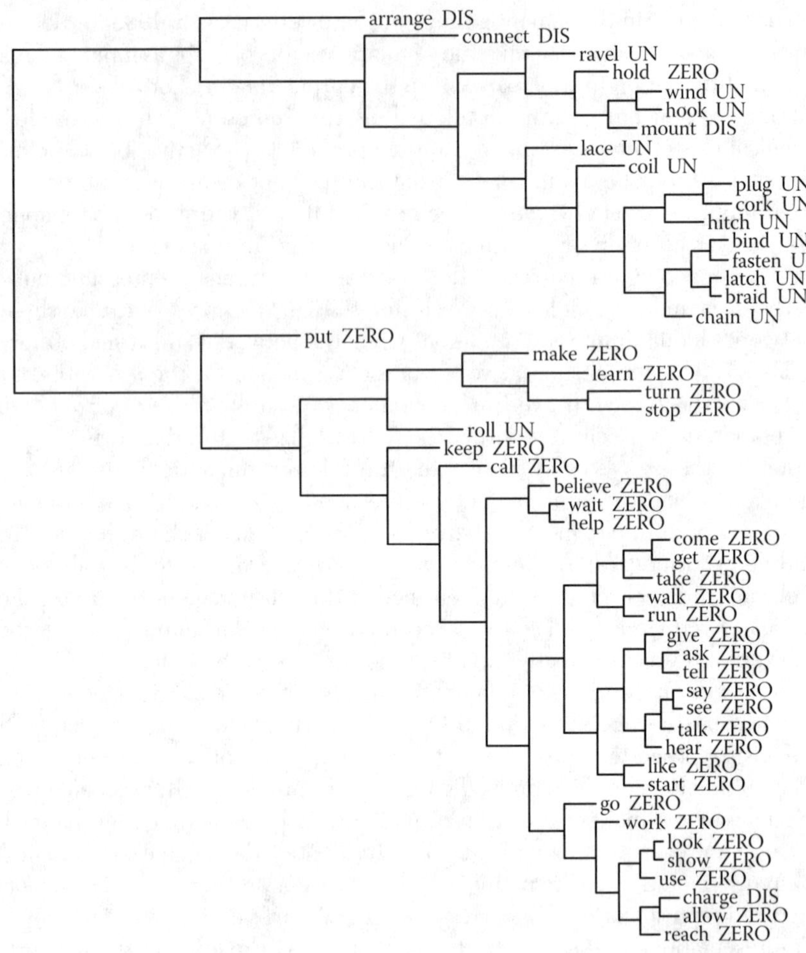

Figure 9.1 A hierarchical cluster analysis of the network's hidden-unit representations at the 50-word stage. The similarity function is determined by the Euclidean distances of the items on the cluster tree. The capitalized marker after each verb indicates the prefixation pattern of the verb, but the network did not receive these labels during training.

the network included both *hold* and *mount* (which should not take *un-*) in the *un-* category. These verbs were included apparently because of their semantic similarity with members of the cryptotype (e.g., *bind, chain, fasten, hitch, hook, latch*). Examining *hold* and *mount* in the network output patterns, we found that *un-* was overgeneralized to these verbs at the end of the 50-word stage. Similar errors produced by the network included **unbury, *uncapture, *unfill, *unfreeze, *ungrip, *unhold, *unloosen, *unmelt, *unpeel,*unplant, *unpress, *unsplit, *unsqueeze, *unstrip, *untack,* and **untighten.* In contrast to these cases, the network produced few errors that constitute flagrant violations of the cryptotype; hence there was no basis for the model to verify Bowerman's (1982) second hypothesis that the cryptotype can serve to eliminate overgeneralizations. Thus, in our simulations, overgeneralizations went hand-in-hand with the network's representation of the cryptotype. This is clearly another case (in addition to tense-aspect acquisition discussed earlier) where the understanding of morphological behavior requires the examination of the semantic structure of the words with which the grammatical morphemes are used.

Implications of the Connectionist Model

A connectionist perspective as described above provides us with a natural way of capturing Whorf's insights into cryptotypes as well as a formal mechanism to mimic their acquisition. In our view, there can be several "mini-cryptotypes," each of which represents some underlying semantic features that work together as interactive "gangs" (McClelland & Rumelhart, 1981). For example, "enclosing" verbs, such as *coil, curl, fold, reel, roll, screw, twist,* and *wind*, all seem to share a meaning of circular movement. Similarly, "attaching" verbs, such as *clasp, fasten, hook, link, plug,* and *tie,* all involve hand movements. Still another cluster of verbs such as *cover, dress, mask, pack, veil,* and *wrap* forms the "covering" mini-cryptotype. These mini-cryptotypes or mini-gangs interact collaboratively to support the formation of the larger cryptotype that licenses the use of *un-* in terms of summed activation in a connectionist network.

Note that the mini-gangs collaborate rather than compete because their members are closely related by the overlap of semantic features. For example, the verb *screw* in *unscrew* may be viewed as having both a meaning of circular movement and a meaning of binding or locking, *zip* in *unzip* may be viewed as sharing both the "binding/locking" meaning and the "covering" meaning, and both *screw* and *zip* involve hand movements. Moreover, a feature may also vary in the strength with which it is represented in different verbs. For example, circular movement is an essential part of the meaning of *screw*, but less so for *wrap* (one can wrap a small ball with a tissue paper without turning around either the object or the wrapping paper). In this way, the meaning of the *un-* cryptotype constitutes a complex semantic network, in which verbs can differ in (1) how many features are relevant to each verb, (2) how strongly each feature is activated in the representation, and (3) how strongly features overlap with each other across category membership (all true with the input to our network). It is these complex relationships that give rise to the meaning of the cryptotype. It is also these complex relationships that gave trouble to traditional rule-based linguistic analyses (hence Whorf's statement regarding the elusive and intangible character of its semantic content).

While these complex structural properties render a symbolic analysis less effective if not impossible, they are accessible to native intuition, according to Whorf. Native intuitions are clearly implicit representations of the complex semantic relationships among verbs and morphological markers, and connectionist networks provide a formal mechanism to capture these intuitions through weighted connections, distributed representations, and statistical learning. In our simulations, the network was able to explore and identify these relationships through the input-output mapping process. The network computed the combinatorial constraints on the co-occurrences of the prefix *un-* and the distributed semantic features of verbs. The result of this process was that new representations that developed at the hidden layer of the network differed from each other in the number of features they shared and in the strengths with which the features were activated, as revealed in Figure 9.1.

Our network's behavior suggests that children, in learning to use the reversative prefix *un-*, may also abstract the semantic regularities from the *un-* verbs through combinatory restrictions that the prefix places on these verbs. In this perspective, children's learning of *un-* is not the learning of a symbolic rule for the use of the prefix with a class of verbs, but rather the accumulation of the connection strength that holds between a particular prefix and a set of weighted semantic features in verbs. The learner groups together those verbs that share the largest number of features and take the same prefixation patterns. Over time, the verbs gradually form coherent classes, with respect to both meaning and prefixation. This learning process can best be described as a statistical procedure in which the child implicitly tallies and registers the frequencies of co-occurrences of distributed semantic features, lexical items, and morphological markers. Not surprisingly, the same process would apply equally well to the acquisition of lexical aspect categories and tense-aspect morphology (see Li & Shirai, 2000 for an analysis; Zhao & Li, in press, for a recent connectionist formalization).

The formation of a cryptotype as in the case of *un-* is not an isolated linguistic phenomenon. It can be observed in many domains in which the problem is primarily semantically motivated. For example, the use of classifiers is one of the hardest problems for second language learners of Chinese, as well as a major challenge for linguistic description (cf. Chao, 1968; Lakoff, 1987). Each noun in Chinese has to be preceded by a classifier that categorizes the object of the noun in terms of its shape, orientation, dimension, texture, countability, and animacy. The appropriate use of classifiers by native speakers is largely automatic, yet it is difficult for linguists to come up with a clear description of rules that govern their use (Erbaugh, 2006). We can probably assume that native speakers have acquired a representation that is cryptotype-like, in which multiple semantic features connected in a network jointly support the use of classifiers.

In short, our connectionist model provides significant insights into the understanding of Whorf's cryptotype—in particular, the understanding of complex structural relationships in lexical semantics and the role of a structured semantic representation in the overgeneralization of morphology in language acquisition. Our model demonstrates how cryptotype representations can emerge in connectionist networks as a natural result of the meaning-form mapping processes. These findings help us to better understand the processes underlying important phenomena such as U-shaped behavior in language acquisition.

LEXICAL ORGANIZATION IN DEVELOPMENT

Lexical Categories and Lexical Organization

The previous discussion examined two morphological cases, tense-aspect suffixes and reversative prefixes, and in both cases our focus has been on the emergence of the corresponding lexical semantic categories associated with the uses of the morphology. But lexical categories develop over time in children, and the structural relationships between words can change as learning progresses. In a seminal paper on the acquisition of word meaning, Bowerman (1978) discussed the issue of semantic organization in child language (the essence of the issue was reflected clearly in the title: "Systematizing Semantic Knowledge: Changes over Time in the Child's Organization of Word Meaning"). Bowerman's discussion focused on reorganization (see also Bowerman, 1982): Reorganization in the child's mental lexicon occurs when word pairs that are apparently not initially recognized as semantically related move closer together in meaning. The reorganization is often signaled by speech errors, where semantically similar words compete for selection in production in particular speech contexts—for example, substitutions of *put* for *give* ("put me the bread") or *fall* for *drop* ("I falled it").

Such a reorganization view has important implications for current theories of the mental lexicon. It suggests that we need to take a developmental, dynamic perspective on the lexical system (with respect to both semantic and grammatical properties of the lexicon). A popular trend in cognitive neuroscience today is the attempt to localize various "lexicon modules" in the brain. Using neuroimaging techniques, researchers have identified specific areas in the brain that respond to different lexical categories, such as nouns and verbs, concrete words and abstract words, content words and function words, and words for animals, persons, and tools (e.g., Caramazza & Hillis, 1991; Damasio, Grabowski, Tranel, Hichwa, & Damasio, 1996, Pulvermueller, 1999). The underlying hypothesis is that different linguistic categories are subserved by different neural substrates, thus supporting the modularity of the mind/brain hypothesis (Fodor, 1983). Neuroscience research in this direction, along with its companion theory of modularity in psychology and philosophy, echoes a long historical tradition in brain localization (Bates, 1999; Gardner, 1986; Uttal, 2001). A fundamental problem with this approach, however, is that it ignores the fact that lexical modules, if they exist, need not be in the brain from the beginning. By assigning an undue weight to a static structure that is "in there," it fails to address the origin of the representation of linguistic categories in the brain.

Taking a developmental, dynamic perspective on this issue, research in my lab attempts to (1) identify crosslinguistic differences in lexical organization and, (2) capture structured, localized, representations of lexical categories as a function of learning and development. First, to identify crosslinguistic differences, in a recent neuroimaging study we found that Mandarin speakers show no distinct neural responses to nouns and verbs in Chinese (both the frontal and the temporal regions were activated by both nouns and verbs), in contrast to findings that distinct cortical regions are involved with nouns versus verbs in other languages (Li,

Jin, & Tan, 2004). Second, assuming that these distinct lexical modules do exist in other languages, we have attempted to describe how they could emerge from the learner's organization and reorganization in response to characteristics of the learning environment, in both monolingual and bilingual contexts (see Hernandez, Li, & MacWhinney 2005, for a review; Chan et al., in press for the neural representation of nouns and verbs in bilinguals). To this end, we have developed DevLex, a self-organizing connectionist model of the development of the lexicon. Our model is designed to achieve two goals at the same time: to model the acquisition of lexical organization as a developmental process in child language, and to examine the emergence of categorical representations in our network as a possible explanation of neural representations.

The DevLex Model

Current connectionist models of language acquisition have focused on the examination of phonological patterns rather than meaning structure of words, on the use of artificially generated input rather than realistic linguistic data, and on the use of supervised learning algorithms rather than unsupervised learning (see Li, 2003 for discussion). These limitations led us to consider a model that deals with the acquisition of semantics, with exposure to realistic child-directed parental input, and in self-organizing neural networks with unsupervised learning. Our primary concern has been the development of a psycholinguistically plausible model that can handle realistic linguistic data in the domain of lexical acquisition.

Like most previous connectionist models of language acquisition, the *un*-model I presented earlier was based on the back-propagation learning algorithm. Although significant progress has been made with models based on back-propagation, such models have serious limitations with regard to their neural and psychological plausibility as models of human learning. In particular, "back-propagation networks" are known to suffer from catastrophic forgetting (inability to remember old information with new learning), from scalability (inability to handle realistic, large-scale problems), and above all, from error-driven learning, which adjusts weights according to the error signals from the discrepancy between desired and actual outputs. Some of these problems become most transparent in the context of language acquisition. For example, it would take a strong argument if one claimed that the feedback process used in back-propagation resembles processes of child language learning. Children do not receive constant feedback about what is incorrect in their speech, nor do they get the kind of error corrections on a word-by-word basis that is provided to the network (cf. the "no negative evidence problem" in language acquisition; Baker, 1979; Bowerman, 1988). Instead, much of language acquisition in the natural setting, especially the organization of the mental lexicon, is a self-organizing process that proceeds without explicit teaching.

The DevLex model (Li, Farkas, & MacWhinney, 2004; Li, Zhao, & MacWhinney, 2007) is a type of self-organizing neural network. In contrast to networks with back-propagation learning, self-organizing networks do not require the presence of an explicit teaching signal; learning is achieved entirely by the system's self-organization in response to the input. Self-organization in these networks

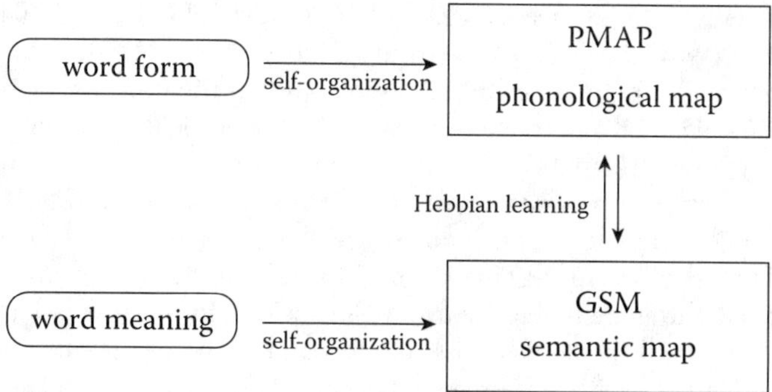

Figure 9.2 DevLex: A self-organizing neural network model of the development of the lexicon.

typically occurs in a two-dimensional map—a self-organizing map (SOM; Kohonen, 1982, 2001). Each processing unit in the network is a location on the map that can uniquely represent one or several input patterns. At the beginning of learning, an input pattern randomly activates a set of units that surround the best matching unit (the "winner"). Once these units become active in response to a given input, the weights of the winner and those of its neighboring units are adjusted such that they become more similar to the input, and these units will therefore respond to the same or similar inputs more strongly the next time. This process continues until all the inputs can elicit specific response patterns in the network. As a result of this self-organizing process, the network gradually develops concentrated areas of units on the map (the "activity bubbles") that capture input similarities, and the statistical structures implicit in the high-dimensional space of the input are preserved on the 2-D space in the map.

The self-organizing process and its representation have clear implications for language acquisition: The formation of activity bubbles may capture critical processes for the emergence of semantic categories in children's acquisition of the lexicon. In particular, the network organizes information first in large areas of the map and gradually zeros in onto smaller areas; this zeroing-in is a process from diffuse patterns to focused ones, as a function of the network's continuous adaptation to the input structure. This process allows us to model the emergence of linguistic categories as a gradual process of lexical development. It also has the potential of explaining language disorders that result from the breakdown of focused activation or the inability to form focused representations (Miikkulainen, 1997; Spitzer, 1999).

Figure 9.2 presents a diagrammatic sketch of the DevLex model (for technical details, see Farkas & Li, 2002a; Li, Farkas, & MacWhinney, 2004; see also Li, Zhao, & MacWhinney, 2007 for DevLex-II, an extension of the original DevLex model). It consists of a lexical (phonological) map that processes phonological information of words (PMAP), and a growing semantic map that processes semantic information (GSM). An important feature of the model is that the GSM network can automatically extract semantic and grammatical features of each word by computing the transitional probabilities of co-occurring words in speech context (Farkas & Li, 2001). The size of GSM can also grow along with a growing lexicon in incremental vocabulary learning (Farkas & Li, 2002b; Li et al., 2004). GSM is connected to PMAP via Hebbian learning (Hebb, 1949), according to which the associative strength between two units is increased if the units are both active at the same time. Upon training of the network, a phonological representation of the word is presented to the network, and simultaneously, the semantic representation of the same word is also presented to the network. Through self-organization the network forms an activity on the phonological map in response to the phonological input, and an activity on the semantic map in response to the semantic input. At the same time, through Hebbian learning the network forms associations between the two maps for all the active units that respond to the input. The combination of Hebbian learning with self-organization in this way can account for the process of how the learner establishes relationships between semantic features, lexical forms, and morphological markers, on the basis of how often they co-occur and how strongly they are coactivated in the representation.

DevLex based on the above characteristics (1) allows us to track the development of the lexicon clearly as an emergent property in the network's self-organization (from diffuse to focused patterns or from incomplete to complete associative links), (2) allows us to model one-to-many or many-to-many associations between forms and meanings in the development of the lexicon and morphology, and (3) provides us with a set of biologically plausible and computationally relevant principles to study language acquisition—biologically plausible because the human cerebral cortex can be considered as essentially a self-organizing map (or multiple maps) that compresses information on a 2-D space (Kohonen, 2001; Spitzer, 1999), and computationally relevant because language acquisition in the natural setting (especially organization and reorganization of the lexicon) is largely a self-organizing process (MacWhinney, 1998, 2001). In what follows, I focus on the model's first property, that is, how it is able to model the development of lexical organization. Other aspects of the model, including simulations of the acquisition of cryptotypes and tense-aspect markers and an account of the vocabulary spurt, can be found in Li (2003), Li et al. (2004), and Li et al. (2007).

Lexical Organization in Development

Because DevLex was designed to model a realistic lexicon, we used two sets of child language corpora as the basis of our modeling: the vocabulary from the MacArthur-Bates Communicative Development Inventories (the CDI; Dale & Fenson, 1996) and the parental speech from the CHILDES database (MacWhinney, 2000). From CDI's Toddler List (680 words) we extracted 500 words, excluding homographs, word phrases, and onomatopoeias in the original list. The 500 words were sorted according to their order of acquisition, determined by the CDI lexical norms at the 30th month. In the CDI, early words can be divided into four major categories: (1) nouns, including animals, body, clothing, food, household, outside, people, rooms, toys, and vehicles; (2) verbs; (3) adjectives; and (4) closed-class words, including auxiliary verbs, connecting words, prepositions, pronouns, quantifiers, and question words.

To represent these 500 words as input to DevLex, we first produced the CHILDES parental corpus, which contains the speech transcripts from child-directed adult speech in the CHILDES database (Li, Burgess, & Lund, 2000). Next we presented the sentences (word by word) in the parental corpus to the growing semantic map (GSM). The GSM then computed the lexical co-occurrence statistics for each of the 500 words in terms of the transitional probabilities of successive words, and used these statistics as values in a vector to represent word meaning. One might wonder how much these co-occurrence statistics can capture the semantic as well as the grammatical information of words, but a series of previous experiments indicate the validity of this method in representing the meaning of words (Li, Burgess, & Lind, 2000; Li, Farkas, & MacWhinney, 2004; Farkas & Li, 2001, 2002a, 2000b). To model lexical organization over time, we divided the 500 words into 10 growth stages, each comprising 50 words (cumulatively). Thus, lexical representations may vary (become enriched) from stage to stage, as more and more words are added into the target lexicon.

Figure 9.3 presents snapshots of the GSM at four different stages of learning in the network. These snapshots illustrate the process of lexical organization and reorganization in the network, as a result of the growing lexicon and the development of enriched lexical representations over time. In particular, one can see how the major categories of nouns, verbs, adjectives, and closed-class items start to form coherent classes. At the beginning of learning (stage 1), due to a strong bias in favor of nouns in the CDI vocabulary (and perhaps in child English in general), nouns spread all over the map. A few verbs present in the lexicon are scattered but have not formed any compact clusters. As learning progresses, more verbs, adjectives, and closed-class words enter the vocabulary, and the noun area starts to give way to words in other categories. The developing categories are also clearly reflected in the formation of smaller clusters over several areas on the map—for example, verbs at stage 2. More important for our discussion here, these results not only show the development of major grammatical categories, but also the emergence of semantic categories within the major categories. Most noticeably, within the boundary of nouns a number of compact clusters emerge toward the end of learning. For example, words representing animals, people, household items, food, and body parts (the CDI semantic subcategories) are correspondingly clustered within the nearest neighborhoods on the map. By contrast, the clustering of semantic categories for these words is much less clear at the early stages (i.e., words that belong to the same category are spread farther apart on the map). These results illustrate clearly how lexical organization may change and develop over time, with respect to both grammatical and semantic features of words.

Implications of the Model

As mentioned earlier, DevLex is designed to achieve two goals: to model the acquisition of lexical organization as a developmental process in child language and to examine the emergence of categorical representations in the brain.

With respect to the first goal, our hypothesis is that there are inherent statistical (e.g., distributional) differences between nouns, verbs, adjectives, and closed-class

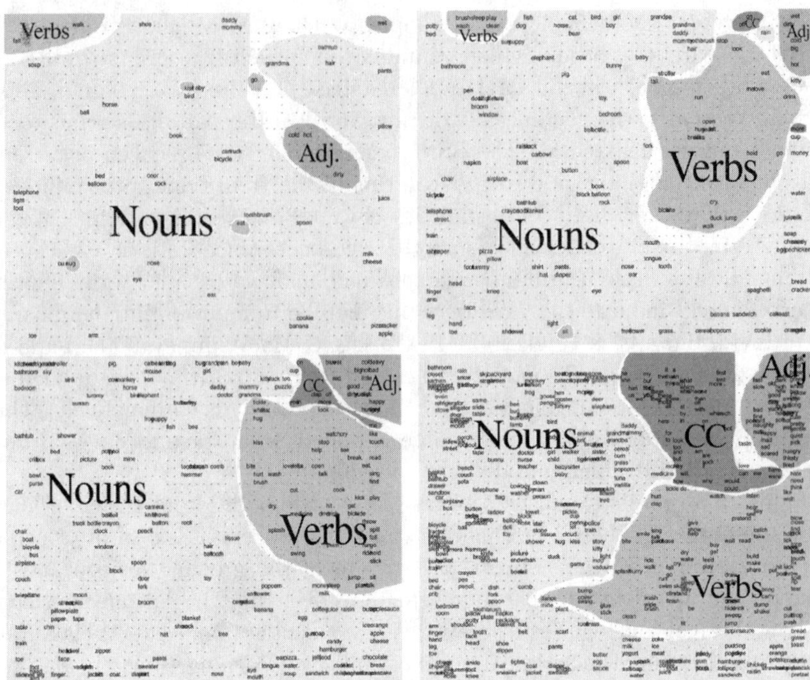

Figure 9.3 Snapshots of GSM at the end of different stages of development: stage 1 (50 words—upper left), 3 (150 words—upper right), 5 (250 words—lower left) and 10 (all 500 words—lower right). The sequence of images illustrates the nature of changes underlying the developmental process, as a result of a developing vocabulary and the changing/enriched word representations. GSM clearly separates the four major categories (and the semantic subcategories within each category) toward the final stage. Because of the large number of words involved in each map, the individual words are not legible in this figure. (Reprinted from *Trends in Cognitive Sciences*, Vol. 9, Hernandez, A., Li, P., & MacWhinney, B: *The emergence of computing modules in bilingualism*, pp. 220–225, Copyright (2005), with permission from Elsevier.)

words in English and that the network can identify these differences through the analysis of lexical co-occurrences. Traditional linguistic analyses (e.g., structuralism) already had ample evidence on the distributional differences between lexical categories (de Saussure, 1916). The question for acquisitionists is how the child can make use of these statistical differences in learning the functions of words, and how this learning can result in different organizational patterns over time.

The DexLex model shows the developmental pathways to lexical representation and organization, in that early on the category memberships are rather diffuse and distributed, and later on with learning, they become more focused and localized. This development from diffuse to focused patterns is consistent with recent findings by Schlaggar et al. (2002) showing that children and adults display different patterns of neural activities in language processing. For children, the activation pattern is diffuse and unfocused, whereas for adults, the activation pattern is more focused, and dedicated to specific cortical regions. Note that this early-diffuse-late-focused pattern is not an artifact of the modulation of the network's training parameters—critical parameters such as learning rate and network size were kept constant across stages in our simulations. Our simulation results also match up with Bowerman's (1978) analyses of the organization and reorganization of the lexicon in development: Many words that are far apart on the map at an earlier stage become grouped together at a later stage. This type of reorganization, within and across categories, clearly serves to structure lexical domains as a whole (Carey, 1978). In addition, according to Bowerman (1978), such reorganization is often signaled by speech errors, where semantically similar words compete for selection in production. In a separate study where production was modeled in DevLex, we found that the organizational structure of the categories has a significant impact on the number of naming errors as well as word confusions in the network (Farkas & Li, 2002b).

With respect to the second goal, our model shows that a developmental connectionist perspective can yield significant insights into the nature and origin of categorical representation in the brain. Cognitive neuroscientists have identified various "brain centers" of language for nouns, verbs, tools, fruits, animals, and so on. An important assumption in many of their studies is that the brain is a highly modularized system, with different cognitive functions localized to different cerebral regions, perhaps from the beginning (the classical "modularity of mind" hypothesis; Fodor, 1983). The ability of DevLex to represent major linguistic categories distinctively without distinct representational modules attests further to the process of "emergent organization" through which localized representations or modules can arise as a function of the developmental processes during ontogenesis, confirming Elizabeth Bates' motto "modules are made, not born" (see Hernandez et al., 2005 for a discussion). Our model shows how the organization of local maps can give rise to emergent categories across stages of learning, with substantial early plasticity and early competition for the organization and reorganization of category members. In our model, the GSM has no pool of units dedicated to any specific category at the outset of learning, but as it progresses through learning, certain groups of units start to develop sensitivity to only the same kinds of words that form coherent categories.

Although there is an obvious difference between "neuronal" activities in our model and neural activities in the brain, DevLex can illustrate the functional mechanisms for the emergence of categorical representations through learning and development. In the spirit of Bowerman's research philosophy, one can often find alternative explanations to a strong brain localizer's account. For example, Farah (1994) pointed out that the well-known deficit with some patients at processing closed-class words might be due to speech stress patterns that differentiate closed-class words from open-class words—that is, patients have trouble dealing with certain words because of the unstressed pattern and short duration, as if damage occurs only to the closed-class words. Similarly, Shi (2006) pointed out that newborn infants are able to categorically discriminate lexical content words from grammatical function words on the basis of multiple acoustic and phonological cues. Functional mechanisms offered by connectionist models such as DevLex are consistent with such explanations, but are often at odds with brain localization accounts in current cognitive neuroscience.

CONCLUSIONS

In this chapter I have discussed the acquisition of word meaning in three domains: tense-aspect acquisition, cryptotype formation, and lexical organization. I have attempted to show that the semantic structure of the lexicon, whether it be overt or covert, can emerge from the interaction between the learner and the linguistic input in the form-meaning mapping process, and we need no a priori assumptions about the innate status or the symbolic nature of semantic categories in the learner's representational system.

The search for meaning is characteristic of children's early lexical and morphological development. It is also characteristic of Bowerman's research emphasis. The three examples that I have discussed here illustrate the importance of semantic learning, the role of linguistic input, and the role of crosslinguistic data, all of which have been carefully examined by Bowerman. In my discussion, I have highlighted how connectionist networks can help us understand the acquisition of lexical semantic representations—in particular, how semantic representations may emerge through the statistical analysis of the linguistic input. Thus, before attributing semantic representations in children as "pre-linguistic" or innate, it is better to first consider mechanisms of learning and the learning environment as potential sources of solution (consistent with Bowerman's approach in "considering the alternatives first"). Our discussions show that the linguistic input contains rich information that the child can exploit in the acquisition of the lexicon, and that modular lexical categories that have often been considered innate (e.g., Bickerton, 1981) may emerge from the learning of statistical properties in language use. Clearly, the data-rich, highly consistent, and statistically regular input in the child's learning environment is at odds with the "poverty of stimulus" hypothesis that the child is exposed to error-laden, random, and inconsistent input. The view that children are statistical learners for language is gaining popularity in recent years since the publication of a number of important volumes and articles (e.g., Elman et al., 1996; MacWhinney, 1998; Saffran, Aslin, & Newport, 1996).

Current debates in cognitive science and cognitive neuroscience revolve around the issue of the nature of linguistic representation. Models based on classical linguistic theories construe linguistic representations in terms of rules in symbol systems. A child is said to have internalized a general rule in her mental representation, "adding *-ed* to make the past tense," at some stage of language acquisition. This kind of description seems intuitively clear, and the rules offer great descriptive power. However, connectionist models provide alternative explanations to this perspective, explanations that place strong emphasis on the statistical learning processes that lead to rule-like behaviors. These models are especially suited for solving problems with which traditional symbolic analyses have difficulty, such as the cryptotype problem discussed here that was once thought "subtle" and "intangible" by Whorf. The distributed representations and adaptive weights used in connectionist models provide mechanisms to capture the complex semantic relationships among words and between words and their morphological markers.

In sum, my conclusion is that structured semantic representations can emerge through statistical computations of the various constraints among lexical items, semantic features, and morphological markers, and the development and organization of the representations are due to basic probabilistic procedures of the sort embodied in connectionist networks in the learning of form-to-form and form-to-meaning mappings. We only need to make a few simple assumptions for this type of probabilistic procedures to work for young children—for example, a working memory that can hold items in sequence and the ability to track distributional regularities (e.g., co-occurrences) in the sequence. Such abilities, as recent studies of statistical learning in infants have revealed, seem to be readily available to the young child at a very early stage (Saffran, Aslin, & Newport, 1996; Saffran, Newport, Aslin, Tunick, & Barrueco, 1997).

ACKNOWLEDGMENTS

Preparation of this article was supported by grants from the National Science Foundation (#BCS-9975249 and #BCS-0131829). I would like to thank Elizabeth Bates, Melissa Bowerman, Brian MacWhinney, and Risto Miikkulainen for their comments and insights on the ideas presented here.

REFERENCES

Aksu, A. (1978). Aspect and modality in the child's acquisition of the Turkish past tense. Unpublished doctoral dissertation, Department of Psychology, University of California, Berkeley.

Aksu-Koç, A., & Slobin, D. (1985). The acquisition of Turkish. In D. Slobin (Ed.), *The crosslinguistic study of language acquisition* (Vol. 1, pp. 839–878). Hillsdale, NJ: Erlbaum.

Antinucci, F., & Miller, R. (1976). How children talk about what happened. *Journal of Child Language, 3*, 167–189.

Baker, C. (1979). Syntactic theory and the projection problem. *Linguistic Inquiry, 10*, 533–581.

Bates, E. (1999). Plasticity, localization and language development. In S. Broman & J. M. Fletcher (Eds.), *The changing nervous system: Neurobehavioral consequences of early brain disorders* (pp. 214–253). New York: Oxford University Press.

Bickerton, D. (1981). *Roots of language*. Ann Arbor, MI: Karoma.

Bickerton, D. (1984). The language bioprogram hypothesis. *Behavioral and Brain Sciences, 7*, 173–188.

Bickerton, D. (1999). Creole languages, the language bioprogram hypothesis, and language acquisition. In W. C. Ritchie & T. K. Bhatia (Eds.), *Handbook of child language acquisition*. San Diego, CA: Academic Press.

Bloom, L., Lifter, K., & Hafitz, J. (1980). Semantics of verbs and the development of verb inflection in child language. *Language, 56*, 386–412.

Bowerman, M. (1978). Systematizing semantic knowledge: Changes over time in the child's organization of word meaning. *Child Development, 49*, 977–987.

Bowerman, M. (1982). Reorganizational processes in lexical and syntactic development. In E. Wanner & L. Gleitman (Eds.), *Language acquisition: The state of the art* (pp. 319–346). Cambridge, UK: Cambridge University Press.

Bowerman, M. (1983). Hidden meanings: The role of covert conceptual structures in children's development of language. In D. Rogers & J. Sloboda (Eds.), *The acquisition of symbolic skills* (pp. 445–470). New York: Plenum.

Bowerman, M. (1985). What shapes children's grammars? In D. Slobin (Ed.), *The crosslinguistic study of language acquisition* (Vol. 2, pp. 1257–1319). Hillsdale, NJ: Erlbaum.

Bowerman, M. (1988). The "no negative evidence" problem: How do children avoid constructing an overly general grammar? In J. Hawkins (Ed.), *Explaining language universals* (pp. 73–101). New York: Blackwell.

Bowerman, M. (1989). Learning a semantic system: What role do cognitive predispositions play? In M. Rice & R. L. Schiefelbusch (Eds.), *The teachability of language* (pp. 133–169). Baltimore, MD: Paul H. Brookes.

Bowerman, M. (1996). Learning how to structure space for language: A crosslinguistic perspective. In P. Bloom, M. Peterson, L. Nadel, & M. Garrett (Eds.), *Language and space* (pp. 385–436). Cambridge, MA: MIT Press.

Bronckart, J., & Sinclair, H. (1973). Time, tense and aspect. *Cognition, 2*, 107–130.

Brown, R. (1973). *A first language*. Cambridge, MA: Harvard University Press.

Caramazza, A., & Hillis, A. E. (1991). Lexical organization of nouns and verbs in the brain. *Nature, 349*, 788–790.

Carey, S. (1978). The child as word learner. In M. Halle, G. Miller, & J. Bresnan (Eds.), *Linguistic theory and psychological reality* (pp. 264–293). Cambridge, MA: MIT Press.

Chan, A.. Luke, K., Li, P., Li, G., Yip, V., Weekes, B. et al. (in press). Neural correlates of nouns and verbs in early bilinguals. *Annals of the New York Academy of Sciences.*

Chao, Y.-R. (1968). *A grammar of spoken Chinese.* Berkeley: University of California Press.

Clark, E., Carpenter, K., & Deutsch, W. (1995). Reference states and reversals: Undoing actions with verbs. *Journal of Child Language, 22*, 633–662.

Comrie, B. (1976). *Aspect: An introduction to the study of verbal aspect and related problems.* Cambridge, UK: Cambridge University Press.

Dale, P. S., & Fenson, L. (1996). Lexical development norms for young children. *Behavior Research Methods, Instruments, & Computers, 28*, 125–127 (Information about CDI is available at http://www.sci.sdsu.edu/cdi/#lexnorms).

Damasio, H., Grabowski, T., Tranel, D., Hichwa, R., & Damasio, A. (1996). A neural basis for lexical retrieval. *Nature, 380*, 499–505.

Elman, J. (1990). Finding structure in time. *Cognitive Science, 14*, 179–211.

Elman, J., Bates, A., Johnson, A., Karmiloff-Smith, A., Parisi, D., & Plunkett, K. (1996). *Rethinking innateness: A connectionist perspective on development.* Cambridge, MA: MIT Press.

Erbaugh, M. (1982). *Coming to order: Natural selection and the origin of syntax in the Mandarin speaking child.* Unpublished doctoral dissertation, University of California, Berkeley.

Erbaugh, M. (2006). Chinese classifiers: Their use and acquisition. In P. Li, L. Tan, E. Bates, & O. Tzeng (Eds.), *Handbook of East Asian psycholinguistics: Vol.1. Chinese* (pp. 39–51). Cambridge, UK: Cambridge University Press.

Farah, M. (1994). Neuropsychological inference with an interactive brain: A critique of the "locality" assumption. *Behavioral and Brain Sciences, 17*, 43–104.

Farkas, I., & Li, P. (2001). A self-organizing neural network model of the acquisition of word meaning. In E. M. Altmann, A. Cleeremans, C. D. Schunn, & W. D. Gray (Eds.), *Proceedings of the Fourth International Conference on Cognitive Modeling* (pp. 67–72). Mahwah, NJ: Erlbaum.

Farkas, I., & Li, P. (2002a). Modeling the development of lexicon with a growing self-organizing map. In H. J. Caulfield et al. (Eds.), *Proceedings of the 6th Joint Conference on Information Sciences* (pp. 553–556). JCIS/Association for Intelligent Machinery, Inc.

Farkas, I., & Li, P. (2002b). DevLex: A self-organizing neural network of the development of lexicon. In *Proceedings of the International Conference on Neural Information Processing.*

Fodor, J. (1983). *The modularity of mind.* Cambridge, MA: MIT Press

Gardner, H. (1986). *The mind's new science: A history of the cognitive revolution.* New York: Basic Books.

Hebb, D. (1949). *The organization of behavior: A neuropsychological theory.* New York, New York: Wiley.

Hernandez, A., Li, P., & MacWhinney, B. (2005). The emergence of competing modules in bilingualism. *Trends in Cognitive Sciences, 9,* 220–225.

Klein, W., Li, P., & Hendriks, H. (2000). Aspect and assertion in Mandarin Chinese. *Natural Language and Linguistic Theory, 18,* 723–770.

Kohonen, T. (1982). Self-organized formation of topologically correct feature maps. *Biological Cybernetics, 43,* 59–69.

Kohonen, T. (2001). *The self-organizing maps* (3rd ed.). Berlin: Springer.

Lakoff, G. (1987). *Women, fire, and dangerous things.* Chicago: University of Chicago Press.

Li, P. (1990). *Aspect and aktionsart in child Mandarin.* Unpublished doctoral dissertation, Leiden University, the Netherlands.

Li, P. (1993). Cryptotypes, form-meaning mappings, and overgeneralizations. In E. V. Clark (Ed.), *The Proceedings of the 24th Child Language Research Forum* (pp. 162–178). Stanford, CA: Center for the Study of Language and Information, Stanford University.

Li, P. (2003). Language acquisition in a self-organising neural network model. In P. Quinlan (Ed.), *Connectionist models of development: Developmental processes in real and artificial neural networks* (pp. 115–149). Hove, UK & New York: Psychology Press.

Li, P., & Bowerman, M. (1998). The acquisition of lexical and grammatical aspect in Chinese. *First Language, 18,* 311–350.

Li, P., Burgess, C., & Lund, K. (2000). The acquisition of word meaning through global lexical co-occurrences. In E. Clark (Ed.), *Proceedings of the Thirtieth Stanford Child Language Research Forum* (pp. 167–178). New York: Cambridge University Press.

Li, P., Farkas, I., & MacWhinney, B. (2004). Early lexical development in a self-organizing neural network. *Neural Networks, 17,* 1345–1362.

Li, P., Jin, Z., & Tan, L. (2004). Neural representations of nouns and verbs in Chinese: An fMRI study. *NeuroImage, 21,* 1533–1541.

Li, P., & MacWhinney, B. (1996). Cryptotype, overgeneralization, and competition: A connectionist model of the learning of English reversive prefixes. *Connection Science, 8,* 3–30.

Li, P., & Shirai, Y. (2000). *The acquisition of lexical and grammatical aspect.* Berlin & New York: Mouton de Gruyter.

Li, P., Zhao, X., & MacWhinney, B. (2007). Dynamic self-organization and early lexical development in children. *Cognitive Science, 31,* 531–612.

MacWhinney, B. (1998). Models of the emergence of language. *Annual Review of Psychology, 49,* 199–227.

MacWhinney, B. (2000). *The CHILDES project: Tools for analyzing talk.* Hillsdale, NJ: Erlbaum.

MacWhinney, B. (2001). Lexicalist connectionism. In P. Broeder & J. M. Murre (Eds.), *Models of language acquisition: Inductive and deductive approaches* (pp. 9–32). Oxford: Oxford University Press.

Marchand, H. (1969). *The categories and types of present-day English word-formation: A synchronic-diachronic approach.* Munich: C. H. Beck'sche Verlagsbuchhandlung.

McClelland, J., & Rumelhart, D. (1981). An interactive activation model of context effects in letter perception: Part 1. An account of the basic findings. *Psychological Review, 88,* 375–402.

Miikkulainen, R. (1997). Dyslexic and category-specific aphasic impairments in a self-organizing feature map model of the lexicon. *Brain and Language, 59,* 334–366.

Pinker, S. (1991). Rules of language. *Science, 253,* 530–535.

Pinker, S., & Prince, A. (1988). On language and connectionism: Analysis of a parallel distributed processing model of language acquisition. *Cognition, 28,* 73–193.

Pulvermueller, F. (1999). Words in the brain's language. *Behavioral and Brain Sciences, 22,* 253–336.

Rumelhart, D., Hinton, G., & Williams, R. (1986). Learning internal representations by error propagation. In D. Rumelhart, J. McClelland, & the PDP Research Group (Eds.), *Parallel distributed processing: Explorations in the microstructures of cognition* (Vol. 1, pp. 318–362). Cambridge, MA: MIT Press.

Rumelhart, D. & McClelland, J. (1986). On learning the past tenses of English verbs. In J. McClelland, D. Rumelhart, & the PDP research group (Eds.), *Parallel distributed processing: Explorations in the microstructure of cognition* (Vol. 2, pp. 216–271). Cambridge, MA: MIT Press.

Saffran, J., Aslin, R., & Newport, E. (1996). Statistical learning by 8-month-old infants. *Science, 274,* 1926–1928.

Saffran, J., Newport, E., Aslin, R., Tunick, R., & Barrueco, S. (1997). Incidental language learning: Listening (and learning) out of the corner of your ear. *Psychological Science, 8,* 101–105.

Saussure, F. de. (1916). *Cours de linguistique générale.* Paris: Payot. (English translation: *A course in general linguistics.* New York: Philosophical Library; Chinese translation: *Putong Yuyanxue Daolun.* Beijing: Peking University Press).

Schlaggar, B., Brown, T., Lugar, H., Visscher, K., Miezin, F., & Petersen, S. (2002). Functional neuroanatomical differences between adults and school-age children in the processing of single words. *Science, 296,* 1476–1479.

Seidenberg, M. (1997). Language acquisition and use: Learning and applying probabilistic constraints. *Science, 275,* 1599–1603.

Shi, R. (2006). Basic syntactic categories in early language development. In P. Li, L. Tan, E. Bates, & O. Tzeng (Eds.), *Handbook of East Asian psycholinguistics: Vol.1. Chinese* (pp. 90–102). Cambridge, UK: Cambridge University Press.

Shirai, Y. (1991). *Primacy of aspect in language acquisition: Simplified input and prototype.* Unpublished doctoral dissertation, University of California, Los Angeles.

Shirai, Y. (1994). On the overgeneralization of progressive marking on stative verbs: Bioprogram or input? *First Language, 14,* 67–82.

Shirai, Y., & Andersen, R. (1995). The acquisition of tense-aspect morphology: A prototype account. *Language, 71,* 743–762.

Shirai, Y., Slobin, D., & Weist, R. (1998). Introduction: The acquisition of tense/aspect morphology. *First Language, 18,* 245–253.

Slobin, D. (1985). Crosslinguistic evidence for the language-making capacity. In D. Slobin (Ed.), *The crosslinguistic study of language acquisition* (Vol. 2, pp. 1158–1249). Hillsdale, NJ: Erlbaum.

Smith, C. (1997). *The parameter of aspect* (2nd ed). Dordrecht: Kluwer.

Spitzer, M. (1999). *The mind within the net: Models of learning, thinking, and acting.* Cambridge, MA: MIT Press.

Stephany, U. (1981). Verbal grammar in modern Greek early child language. In P. S. Dale & D. Ingram (Eds.), *Child language: An international perspective.* Baltimore, MD: University Park Press.

Tai, J. (1984). Verbs and times in Chinese: Vendler's four categories. In *Papers from the parasession on lexical semantics of the Chicago Linguistic Society* (pp. 289–296).

Uttal, W. (2001). *The new phrenology: The limits of localizing cognitive processes in the brain.* Cambridge, MA: MIT Press.

Weist, R. (1986). Tense and aspect: Temporal systems in child language. In P. Fletcher & M. Garman (Eds.), *Language acquisition.* Cambridge, UK: Cambridge University Press.

Weist, R., Wysocka, H., Witkowska-Stadnik, K., Buczowska, E., & Konieczna, E. (1984). The defective tense hypothesis: On the emergence of tense and aspect in child Polish. *Journal of Child Language, 11*, 347–374.

Whorf, B. (1956). Thinking in primitive communities. In J. B. Carroll (Ed.), *Language, thought, and reality.* Cambridge, MA: MIT Press. (Original work published 1936)

Zhao, X., & Li, P. (in press). The acquisition of lexical and grammatical aspect in a developmental lexicon model. *Linguistics.*

Personal Tribute

MABEL RICE

Melissa Bowerman was my teacher and mentor during my doctoral studies. If I remember correctly, I formally enrolled in three courses that she taught, and there probably were independent study enrollments to cover the time she devoted to my dissertation project. Most important, however, were the many occasions on which she devoted time to substantive conversations with me about the many questions and observations I wanted to discuss with her regarding children's language acquisition. In retrospect, I am deeply impressed by her ability to convey respect for what surely were naïve and poorly formed contributions on my part.

I recall a formative discussion in which I shared with her my hope that my studies of normative language acquisition would provide benchmarks to help identify children who deviate from the expected course of acquisition. My recollection is that she was somewhat horrified that I had such an unrealistic expectation. She helped me apprehend that it is the nature of the questions asked of the available literature that determine the nature of the answers to be discovered. Simply put, my questions were not the questions of scholars of children's language acquisition, in the general sense, although relevance was surely to be found in their questions and contributions. She encouraged me to seek answers to my questions, in effect, to assume ownership and responsibility for the search for answers. It is my pleasure to honor her guidance with my chapter in this volume, as a form of interim report of how the search for answers to my questions has fared in the elapsed time since her tactful and generous guidance.

There is something like a full circle of influence operating here. As Professor Bowerman notes (1988), her interest in normal language acquisition was sparked by conversations with a speech pathologist who "described a child in her clinic who, despite apparently normal intelligence, had not progressed beyond the most rudimentary syntax" (1988, p. 23). Bowerman regarded training in speech pathology as a rather circuitous route to learning about normal acquisition, and chose a more direct route of studies with Roger Brown. When I met her, I was trained in speech/language pathology, so the direct route to normal acquisition studies was not a viable option. As it turned out, although my path has been more circuitous nevertheless it seems to have returned to some of the basic issues and questions that guided the work of Bowerman, Brown, and many others.

Professor Bowerman's style of scholarship and teaching made a lasting imprint on me. I recall well the symposium at the Society for Research on Child Development conference held in Boston, 1981, in which Roger Brown introduced several of his graduates who spoke on the topic of "The Development of Language and Language Researchers: Whatever Happened to Linguistic Theory" (cf. Kessel, 1988, p. 2). In his introduction of Bowerman, Brown characterized her as the "Jane Austen of language acquisition scholars." As I remember it, he made reference to her precision, her astute and detailed observations, her tight line of argumentation, her patience and persistence, and her deceptively gentle style, all of which in combination could deliver a devastating and decisive critique of a misguided hypothesis. He may also have noted that she was fearless, in that she applied this scholarly approach to all ideas and models, regardless of the levels of popular acceptance or the acclaim of their proponents. These characterizations rang true to me, as I thought of how she had demonstrated those qualities in her teaching and mentorship. She provided a powerful and pure model of the highest standards of scholarship, in which ideas matter and should hold up to serious scrutiny. I took her example as one to aim for, even if such expectations are only intermittently possible to achieve.

For her paper in honor of Roger Brown, Bowerman quoted Brown and Bellugi (1964) as the original source of the fundamental issue that motivated her scholarship: "The discovery of latent structure is the greatest of the processes involved in language acquisition, and the most difficult to understand" (p. 315). Upon rereading Bowerman's paper, I am struck by the realization that the issue has been at the core of much of my work as well, even if it might not have always been obvious as my program of investigation unfolded. In retrospect, this is not surprising, given Bowerman's powerful impact as teacher and mentor and the many ways in which her example has influenced intellectual inquiry.

REFERENCES

Bowerman, M. (1988). Inducing the latent structure of language. In F. S. Kessel, *The development of language and language researchers: Essays in honor of Roger Brown* (pp. 23–50). Hillsdale, N.J. Erlbaum.

Brown, R., & Bellugi, U. (1964). Three processes in the child's acquisition of syntax. In E. H. Lenneberg (Ed.), *New directions in the study of language*. Cambridge, MA: MIT Press.

Kessel, F. (1988). On words and people: An introduction to this collection. In F. S. Kessel (Ed.), *The development of language and language researchers: Essays in honor of Roger Brown* (pp. 1–8). Hillsdale, NJ: Erlbaum.

10

Language Acquisition Lessons from Children with Specific Language Impairment

Revisiting the Discovery of Latent Structures

MABEL L. RICE
University of Kansas

The central theme of this chapter is drawn from Melissa Bowerman's paper in honor of Roger Brown (Bowerman, 1988), in which she quoted Brown and Bellugi (1964) as the original source of the fundamental issue that motivated her scholarship: "The discovery of latent structure is the greatest of the processes involved in language acquisition, and the most difficult to understand" (p. 315). As a student of Bowerman's, I was well tutored in the significance of the latent structure issue for theories of children's language acquisition.

Much of my scholarship has focused on children with language impairments and a search for the ways in which their language acquisition mechanisms are weak or show a deficit, in order to enhance the identification of affected children and the development of effective intervention programs. The focus on the limitations of language acquisition mechanisms can obscure the ways in which affected children also demonstrate robust language acquisition mechanisms that seem to parallel those of unaffected children. My intent here is to honor Bowerman's formative influence on my scholarship by broadening the perspective on children's language impairments with consideration of the fundamental issue she introduced to me.

In this chapter I evaluate the nature of the language impairments of children with Specific Language Impairment (SLI) in terms of the "discovery of latent structures," with an eye toward the relevance of the work for enhancing our understanding of the underpinnings of language acquisition of children in general. In so doing, I draw heavily on my own work, as well as that of my contemporary colleagues. I begin with a brief description of the condition of SLI. The main structure that follows is one frequently used by Bowerman in her writing—namely, first laying out a phenomenon and an explanatory model or perspective, and then evaluating the model via the pros and cons drawn from available evidence. The long-standing prevailing model posits that the language problems of children with SLI are attributable to problems with the discovery of latent language structures. In closing I will argue that children with SLI are surprisingly like unaffected children, in spite of some striking and powerful deficits in language acquisition, deficits that persist for a long time. This apparent discrepancy between what they can and cannot do poses strong challenges to generic one-size-fits-all-dimensions-of-language accounts of language acquisition and more specifically language impairments associated with SLI.

SPECIFIC LANGUAGE IMPAIRMENT IN CHILDREN

Specific Language Impairment (SLI) is a disorder in which children perform below age expectations on language measures despite having adequate cognitive and sensory skills for language development. SLI is usually diagnosed according to a set of inclusionary and exclusionary criteria. Children are included if their performance on an omnibus language measure is at least one standard deviation below age expectations (a level approximately equivalent to the 15th percentile of the normative distribution). Children are excluded if their nonverbal intelligence is below age expectations, or if they have hearing loss, clinical levels of neurological impairment, or a diagnosis of psychiatric impairment such as autism. It is estimated that approximately 7% of children aged 5 to 6 years can be classified as SLI (Tomblin, Records et al., 1997).

Recent epidemiological investigation has established that in the general population speech impairments are orthogonal to language impairments (Shriberg, Tomblin, & McSweeny, 1999). Because children with speech impairments are more likely to be identified for clinical services and children with SLI who participate in experimental studies are often recruited out of clinical caseloads, an overlap of speech and language impairment is often reported for children who participate in scientific studies. Thus it is important to keep in mind that although sampling confounds may exist in much of the literature, in the general population language impairments are essentially independent of speech impairments.

There is now an extensive literature that is largely devoted to the determination of the nature of the language impairments of children with SLI, the extent to which related cognitive and social abilities are also affected, and the identification of possible etiological factors (cf. Leonard, 1998). With regard to the nature of the language impairments, it has been very helpful to keep in mind two different benchmarks for characterizing the language systems of affected children. One benchmark is the expectation relative to a child's chronological age, which is the reference level for clinical diagnosis. The second benchmark is the performance of younger children at equivalent levels of language acquisition, often indexed by mean length of utterance (MLU). There is strong reason to believe that children with SLI are delayed in the onset of their language acquisition. A long-standing question is whether their language impairment is a matter of general language delay, in which case their language systems should be highly similar to those of younger children. In this scenario, the language of affected children would be generally immature and expected to synchronize across linguistic dimensions in the same way as the language of younger children. An alternative is a delay-with-disruption model (Rice, 2003, 2004a, 2004b, 2007). This model captures the fact that some elements of affected children's grammars are less developed than expected, even relative to younger control children. In effect, while many elements are delayed, some elements are even weaker than a general delay would predict. The point to highlight here is that age defines a "delay," wherein general immaturity is a unifying construct, whereas a "disruption" involves areas of weakness that are unsynchronized within an immature grammar.

The nature of the underlying factors that account for the language impairments of SLI has been a topic of lively debate. The major views can be categorized in two ways. One approach targets a breakdown in learning processes, broadly conceived. In recent models this perspective focuses on putative limitations of memory, input processing, or general cognitive mechanisms (cf. Leonard, 1998). Another approach places emphasis on domain-specific limitations inherent in the underlying linguistic representations. Under this perspective, language acquisition mechanisms (and, presumably, breakdowns in those mechanisms) can be relatively independent of general learning mechanisms. A final general observation is that genetic models are under current investigation. Evidence in support of genetic contributions is accumulating and attracting widespread support, although precise genetic sources for language impairments have yet to be identified (Fisher, 2005; Rice & Smolik, 2007; Rice, Warren & Betz, 2005; Smith & Morris, 2005). Although the genetics initiative was first resisted by advocates of the general learning breakdown approach (see critique by Conti-Ramsden, 1997 and reply by Rice, 1997; Snow, 1996), it is now embraced by most scholars as consistent with either general learning deficits or language-specific deficits. In today's scholarship, a possible inherited contribution to language impairment is best regarded as compatible with either perspective. Under the general learning perspective, general learning mechanisms that guide language acquisition could be weakened as a consequence of genetic variations (cf. Plomin, 1999; Plomin & Kovas, 2005), whereas under the language domain mechanism model more specific processes relatively targeted to language acquisition could be under genetic control (cf. Fisher, 2005).

Bowerman's fine-grained and rigorous approach to unpacking a linguistic phenomenon could be fruitful for clarifying some of the issues involved in an explanation of the underpinnings of the language impairments of SLI. In this spirit, I explore a relatively unacknowledged conundrum inherent in the available evidence. I frame the issue in terms of the problem of "the discovery of latent structure," as the bedrock process of language acquisition and therefore of prime suspicion as the source of impairment in SLI. I examine available evidence to see the extent to which children with SLI are able to discover latent structures, and when they apparently do not, and the import of a side-by-side consideration of such evidence.

EVIDENCE THAT SUGGESTS POSSIBLE PROBLEMS WITH THE DISCOVERY OF LATENT STRUCTURES

Much of the literature describing the language of children with SLI has focused on the ways in which these children's language systems are not as expected for age or language-equivalent levels of performance. In effect, we have wanted to know what is underdeveloped in the language systems of affected children. There has been considerable progress in this regard within the last decade. For a comprehensive review, see Leonard (1998). For this discussion three linguistic phenomena provide useful examples: vocabulary development, morphosyntax, and overregularizations.

Delayed Vocabulary Acquisition

One of the hallmark characteristics of children subsequently diagnosed as SLI is late onset of first words, a condition referred to as Late Talking (LT) (cf. Ellis Weismer, 2007; Rice, Taylor, & Zubrick, in press; Rescorla, 2002; Zubrick, Taylor, Rice, & Slegers, 2007). Although only a minority of LT children ultimately are diagnosed as SLI (25% is a likely estimate; Paul, 1996), it is thought that most if not all children with SLI are slow in language emergence. Definitive estimates require an epidemiological prospective study of young children, an expensive undertaking which has yet to be done.

Growth data are available, however, for clinically ascertained children with SLI at 5 years of age with delays in vocabulary development. These data document that the delays persist for years. See Figure 10.1 for the general pattern of the growth trajectories. This figure shows longitudinal outcomes on the raw scores of the Peabody Picture Vocabulary Test-Revised (Dunn & Dunn, 1981) for a group of children with SLI and a younger control group, both of whom are participants in an ongoing longitudinal investigation. Graphed in Figure 10.1 are data for three years with 4 data points, once annually, per group, covering an age span of approximately 3 to 8 years of age. The two groups were at equivalent levels of MLU at the start of the longitudinal study (see Rice, Redmond, & Hoffman, 2006 for details). It is important to highlight that although the groups were equated at the outset on MLU, there was no initial matching on the basis of PPVT-R raw score.

There are several points of interest. One is that the affected children's mean level of performance on the vocabulary assessment is equivalent at the outset to the mean of the MLU-equivalent group who were two years younger, on average. Second, the two groups of children maintained a general equivalency of both PPVT-R raw scores and MLU levels throughout the four times of measurement. Third, within each group the vocabulary and MLU levels followed similar, predominantly linear trajectories. The main point here is that the affected children with initial vocabulary delays maintain levels of performance below their age peers

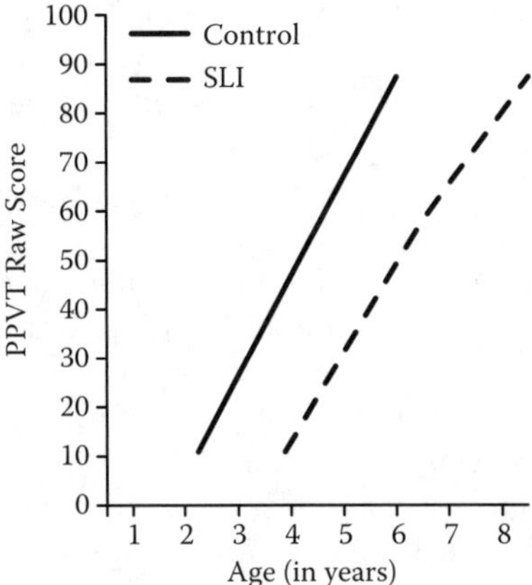

Figure 10.1 Growth of vocabulary in children with SLI and MLU-matched control children.

between ages 5 and 8 years, at levels equivalent to children two years younger. Furthermore, ongoing assessments underway in my lab show the delay to persist well into adolescence.

The implication is that the cluster of abilities needed to figure out the meanings of novel words is not as effective in affected children as in age controls, and is instead more commensurate with younger children. This is also confirmed in a series of experimental studies of word acquisition. Rice, Oetting, Marquis, Bode, and Pae (1994) found that affected children and younger MLU controls needed high frequency input of novel words in order to store them in memory; Oetting (1999) found that 6-year-old affected children used cues to interpret verb meaning as well as younger MLU equivalent controls, but they were less able to retain new verbs than the younger group. Other studies report mixed outcomes for the SLI/MLU groups comparison (cf. Hoff-Ginsberg, Kelly, & Buhr, 1996; O'Hara & Johnston, 1997; Van der Lely, 1994), which Oetting (1999) suggests may be attributable to task differences and memory demands. Although some relatively subtle differences between groups have been reported, overall in the area of lexical acquisition the general picture seems more compatible with a delay model than for a delay-with-disruption model. Especially when we consider longitudinal growth trajectories, there are strong parallels between affected children and younger language-equivalent controls. In each of the groups, vocabulary acquisition and MLU are synchronized over time, although both of these domains are delayed in the affected group relative to their age peers.

Morphosyntax and Finiteness

The picture shifts when we consider the morphosyntactic domain of finiteness marking. For some time verb morphology was known to be a weak element for children with SLI, although morphology was widely viewed as a problem of lexical stem + affix, and surface characteristics of morphology, such as perceptual salience, were accorded a strong role in accounting for affected children's limitations (cf. Leonard, 1998). Recent advances in linguistic theory (cf. Pollock, 1989) have clarified the close relationship between morphology and syntax, in models of verb movement, universal grammar, and projected clausal sites for moved elements. These distinctions have allowed for a more precise characterization of the nature of language impairments.

Finiteness is a central property that involves *tense* and *agreement* features on verbs in main clauses, features that interact with syntactic requirements of clause structures. In current theories of the adult grammar (cf. Haegemann, 1994) it is hypothesized that features such as *tense* and *agreement* are tightly interrelated in the syntax of clause structure, and that the structural clausal configuration of phrases and sites for finiteness marking are part of an architecture that underlies the movement rules. Note that the term *tense* is used in two ways: It can refer to the semantics of reference to temporal dimensions (as in "present" vs. "past" tense), and it also has a second sense of a required grammatical property which is not so tightly linked to temporal dimensions (e.g., the need to insert auxiliary *DO* in questions). In order to highlight this second sense, sometimes I have used the term *grammatical tense marking* to describe the deficit in SLI children (Rice, Tomblin, Hoffman, Richman, & Marquis, 2004).

"Agreement" involves person and number marking on nouns, markings which are "copied over" onto verbs, where they do not add additional meanings to the verbs. Most of the literature summarized here has focused on subject–verb agreement, although agreement within noun phrases is also of interest. In this framework, tense and agreement features are distinguished from other properties of the underlying syntax.

Pollock (1989) initially worked out how this system is manifest in English grammar in terms of tense and agreement marking and related morphosyntactic properties. Finiteness is marked by the following morphemes: third person singular present tense *-s*, as in *Patsy runs home every day*; past tense *-ed*, as in *Patsy walked/ran home yesterday*; copula or auxiliary *BE*, as in *Patsy is happy* or *Patsy is running*; and auxiliary *DO*, as in *Does Patsy like to run*? In a simple clause there is only one site for finiteness marking, and no more than one finiteness marker can appear, as shown in the following examples where an asterisk is inserted to indicate ungrammatical clauses: **Runs Patsy home every day*; **Does Patsy likes to run*?; **Patsy is runs home every day*; **Does Patsy is happy*? Note that the set of morphemes is not limited to verbal affixes but instead includes irregular stem-internal morphophonological variants and free-standing morphemes as well. Subject–verb agreement requires agreement of the person/number features on the noun and verb. These sentences violate that requirement: **Patsy are happy*; **I runs home every day*.

This perspective brings several advantages to studies of children's grammars. One is a finer set of distinctions to evaluate underlying similarities and differences relative to the adult grammar. Shütze (2004, p. 355) noted: "…it is possible for children with normal syntactic structures to sound very unlike adults, because in their lexicon certain morphemes either are missing or have incorrect features associated with them." In many languages children show an acquisition period in which they produce infinitival forms of verbs where finite forms are required in the adult grammar (cf. Guasti, 2002 for an extensive review). At the same time, young English-speaking children produce uninflected verbal forms or omitted forms, such as "*Patsy go home" and "*Patsy happy." With Pollock's (1989) study as precedent, Wexler (1992) noted the parallels between English and other languages, such that the uninflected verbal forms of English in children's grammars were the English versions of the infinitival forms evident in children's grammars in non-English languages such as French and German.

Wexler launched a program of investigation with his interpretation of these phenomena as an *optional infinitive stage* (Wexler, 1994, 1996), which was later revised to an *agreement tense omission model* (ATOM) (Schütze & Wexler, 1996; Wexler, Schütze, & Rice, 1998) and then to a *unique checking constraint model* (Wexler, 1998) as the theory evolved to account for a wider range of phenomena across languages. The basic claims about finiteness in English-speaking children, however, remained the same as the theory evolved. The fundamental notion is that, in some languages, young children go through a period in which they seem to treat finiteness marking as optional, although it is obligatory in the adult grammar. At the same time they know many other properties of clausal construction. In the normative literature, the phenomenon is now widely attested, with ongoing discussion and debate about the nature of the underlying linguistic representations, the reasons why this period is evident in some but not all languages, and the way in which finiteness is linked to other properties of the grammar.

The theory was extended to children with SLI in the prediction that their long delay in the acquisition of verbal morphology is an extension of a phase that is part of younger children's grammatical development (Rice, Wexler, & Cleave, 1995). This was regarded as an enriched *extended development model* (Rice & Wexler, 1996), which recognizes the many ways in which the language of children with SLI is similar to younger unaffected children, but with a greatly protracted period of incomplete acquisition of finiteness marking.

This led to a program of longitudinal investigation of finiteness marking in English-speaking children with SLI, across the set of morphemes involved. The children who participated in the longitudinal study of MLU and receptive vocabulary described above also received tasks to measure finiteness marking. Unlike the outcomes for MLU and receptive vocabulary, the results revealed multiple ways in which the affected group did not perform as well as the younger MLU comparison group. Each of the target morphemes showed such a deficit at almost each and every measurement point. Further, the set of morphemes showed strong associations among the items, supporting the prediction that the deficits were attributable to the shared linguistic property of finiteness in spite of differences in surface forms. Finally, the difference was evident across tasks: Spontaneous language samples, elicited production tasks, and grammatical judgment tasks yielded the same pattern of outcome (see Rice, Wexler, & Hershberger, 1998 for the detailed report).

A generalized growth curve for the two groups representing the findings is presented in Figure 10.2, measured as a percentage of finiteness marking in obligatory contexts, collapsed across the individual morphemes, for production data. The

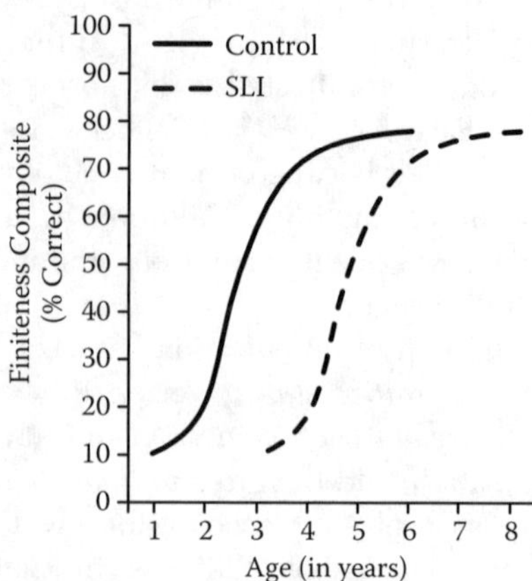

Figure 10.2 Growth of finiteness in children with SLI and MLU-matched control children.

actual ages of measurement are approximately 3 to 6 years for the control group, and 5 to 8 years for the affected group, with projections in this figure for the lower ends of the curves (cf., Rice, Wexler & Hershberger, 1998). Note that the two curves, although similar in growth trajectory, are farther apart than the curves in Figure 10.1, corresponding to the greater lag in finiteness growth relative to the MLU comparison group than for lexical acquisition.

The conclusion is that finiteness acquisition by children with SLI shows a delay-with-disruption, in which this dimension of morphosyntax is so protracted in acquisition that it is, in effect, out of synchrony with the other indicators of language growth, MLU and lexical development. This is the one dimension of language acquisition in which there is consistent and reliable replication of the finding that there is a disrupted element relative to a general language delay. This outcome is reported across different labs (cf. Bedore & Leonard, 1998; Conti-Ramsden, Botting, & Faragher, 2001; Eadie, Fey, Douglas, & Parsons, 2002; Grela & Leonard, 2000; Joseph, Serratrice, & Conti-Ramsden, 2002; Leonard, Eyer, Bedore, & Grela, 1997; Marchman, Wulfeck, & Ellis Weismer, 1999; Oetting & Horohov, 1997). It is widely accepted as a strong candidate as a clinical marker of the condition of SLI (cf. Tager-Flusberg & Cooper, 1999), especially for children in the 4- to 8-year-old age range, as documented by a standardized assessment instrument (Rice & Wexler, 2001). Thus, the empirical phenomenon is well established, although there is a lively and flourishing dialog about the interpretation. One caveat is that a finiteness marker does not necessarily imply that it is the only possible such grammatical marker (cf. van der Lely's 1998 claim of a condition described as "grammatical SLI," thought to be a subset of the generic SLI clinical group characterized by other syntactic limitations), although other possible markers would lead to different predictions for certain elements of grammar.

The major point here is that affected children are obviously quite limited in their ability to discover the latent structure of language that guides finiteness marking. They behave as if they accept a grammar that allows these morphemes to be optional instead of obligatory, a devastatingly inept inference given the structural demands of English.

Although English is the language for which there is the most extensive evidence, the phenomenon is apparent in other languages as well, depending upon the way in which finiteness is expressed in the language. This includes German (cf. Rice, Noll, & Grimm, 1997), and Swedish (Leonard, Hansson, Nettelbladt, & Deevy, 2004), but may be evident only in very young Spanish-speaking children (Torrens & Wexler, 2001) given the early acquisition of finiteness by unaffected Spanish-speaking children (Gathercole, Sebastián, & Soto, 2002). Perhaps most compelling is the evidence from bilingual French/English-speaking children with SLI (Paradis, Crago, Genesee, & Rice, 2003). The study of bilingual children offers the powerful experimental advantage of controlling the variance attributable to individual differences, because the two languages are observed within the same child. French and English offer interesting comparisons because young French-speaking children acquire the grammatical tense marking system at younger ages than do English-speaking children, roughly around 2- to 2½ years in French compared to around 4 years in English. This difference is attributed to differential properties of the morphophonological and morphosyntactic systems of the two languages (cf. Wexler, 2003, who hypothesizes that the differences involve null subjects and operations requiring tense and agreement properties), although the details remain to be worked out and the interpretations are debated. Of interest here, the affected bilingual children at 7 years of age show the expected gap between tense-marking and non-tense-marking morphology in both English and French, although the tense-marking structures appear early on in unaffected French-speaking children. Thus, irrespective of surface differences in how the tense-marking system appears in French versus English, affected children show limited ability to discover the underlying structures.

Late Onset of Morphological Overregularizations

Beginning with the signal study of Jean Berko Gleason (Berko, 1958), children's overregularization of irregular past tense verbs has been taken as indicative of their ability to induce latent structures that guide the phonological expression of morphological forms. An example would be children's use of "falled" instead of "fell." Evidence is available, from the same children reported in Figures 10.1 and 10.2 above, showing that children with SLI are less likely to generate overregularization errors than the younger control children for the period of 5 to 6 years; but when they begin to increase their rate they subsequently follow a trajectory of overregularization rates similar to the younger children (see Figure 9 of Rice, Wexler, Marquis, & Hershberger, 2000, p. 1139). Further evidence for delayed overregularization of irregular past tense forms exists for a large epidemiologically ascertained sample of children with SLI, age control children, and a group of children with language impairments and borderline nonverbal intelligence (Rice, Tomblin, Hoffman, Richman, Zhang, & Marquis, 2004). Finally, studies of overregularization of plural morphology (e.g., "mouses") found that the children with SLI performed at levels below age peers, although commensurate with the younger controls (Oetting & Rice, 1993; Rice & Oetting, 1993). Overall, the delayed onset of overregularizations is consistent with the possibility that children with SLI are limited in their discovery of the latent structure of morphophonological rules.

RELATED DEFICITS POINTING TOWARD PROBLEMS WITH THE DISCOVERY OF LATENT STRUCTURES

The evidence summarized in the previous section is but a part of the broader literature that documents the dimensions in which language acquisition is not robust in children with SLI. The likelihood that the language weaknesses are attributable to weaknesses in general learning mechanisms is a widely held assumption that is strengthened further by evidence showing performance below age expectations in related abilities. I summarize three areas here.

Possible Memory Deficits

The memory requirements for young children's language acquisition are surely complex, and there is no one widely accepted unifying model. This situation has posed challenges for attempts to link memory deficits to the language impairments of children with SLI. A number of investigations have explored the domain with a number of different tasks. The outcomes differ with regard to the robustness of group differences between affected and unaffected children, the extent to which the results have been replicated across studies and labs, and the coherence of the line of interpretation. One task, involving nonword repetition, stands out above others with replicated findings of group differences between affected children and their age peers (cf. Bishop, North, & Donlan, 1996; Conti-Ramsden 2003; Dollaghan and Campbell, 1998; Gathercole and Baddeley, 1990). Tager-Flusberg and Cooper (1999) identified nonword repetition, as well as tense-marking, as a candidate for a clinical marker of SLI. There are two general findings: Affected children are less able to repeat nonwords of longer lengths (3 to 5 syllables) than are their age peers, and performance on nonword repetition tasks tends to be correlated with language tasks, particularly vocabulary tasks. On the face of it, these outcomes could be regarded as a deficit in memory likely to be affecting their language acquisition, given the similar memory demands inherent in language acquisition.

There is a lively debate, however, about the interpretation of the evidence and whether poor verbal memory plays a causal role in language impairment. A recent special issue of the journal *Applied Psycholinguistics* features a keynote article by Gathercole (2006), who lays out a causal role for temporary phonological storage deficits. But she also notes the likely role of multiple contributing factors.

Her paper is followed by 14 commentaries, many of them critical in nature. For example, Bishop (2006) argues that phonological short-term memory does not play an independent causal role in syntax impairment, based in part on her findings from a twin study showing that the inherited contributions to performance on nonword repetition tasks and language tasks come from different sources. Other complicating evidence includes recent factor analytic studies that yield contradictory outcomes about the pattern of associations between nonword repetition and language tasks (cf. Colledge et al., 2002; Tomblin, Zhang, Catts, Ellis Weismer, & Weiss, 2004; Viding et al., 2003).

Other complications appear with regard to possible speech production limitations in samples of affected children. Recall the earlier conclusion that in epidemiologically ascertained samples the overlap of clinically significant speech problems and language impairments is minimal, but in clinically ascertained samples the co-occurrence of speech and language impairments is a potential issue and not always well documented. This is relevant to the nonword repetition tasks, because a correct response requires correct repetition of the phonemes. Corrections or adjustments for speech accuracy are seldom reported. As Gathercole (2006, pp. 531–532) acknowledges, low performance on nonword repetition tasks would be expected for children with speech/motor impairments. In the current literature this is a potential confound of unknown extent and may contribute to some of the differences across studies. She argues, however, that individual variation in speech skills cannot explain the consistent patterns of association of nonword repetition performance and language acquisition. The conclusion here is that although the interpretation of low performance on nonword repetition tasks remains to be fully worked out, the replicated finding of group differences is widely taken to be consistent with a memory limitation that creates problems for the ability of affected children to induce latent language structures.

Auditory/Input Processing Deficits

A great deal of research attention has focused on the possibility that children with SLI have difficulties with processing auditory information, a difficulty that contributes to their language weaknesses. Early on, this line of investigation focused on aspects of the speech stream which is rapidly changing and brief in duration (c.f. Tallal & Piercy, 1973; Tallal, Stark, Kallman, & Mellits, 1981). More recently, Tallal (2000) has argued that auditory processing difficulties interfere with encoding and producing speech, and ultimately lead to expressive and receptive language problems, as well as problems with literacy. This causal claim has been challenged by Bishop et al. (1999), among others, who concluded from their empirical study that there was "no evidence that auditory deficits are a necessary or sufficient cause of language impairments" (p. 1295).

Another approach to input processing limitations has been proposed by Leonard (cf. Leonard, 1989, 1998; Leonard, McGregor, & Allen, 1992). His approach is known as the surface account, which proposes that children with SLI have processing deficits in the form of reduced speed of processing. This account has focused on the tendency, particularly of English-speaking children, to omit final consonants such as the -*s* in third person singular present tense (e.g., *she talks*). The surface account posits that such processing demands interact with the demands of discovering the grammatical functions of such forms, and as a result create particular difficulty for affected children. Under this model, affected children can perceive the acoustic properties, but they cannot overcome the limits of processing demands when they must simultaneously form grammatical categories. This model, too, has been of considerable debate. For example, Evans, Viele, Kass, and Tang (2002) report that the expected deficits in speech perception abilities of affected children were evident in synthetic but not natural speech, and the children's use of inflectional morphology in obligatory contexts was not correlated with their perception abilities. On the other hand, Montgomery and Leonard (1998) provide evidence supporting the surface account.

These two examples do not exhaust the current perspectives on how weaknesses in auditory processing mechanisms are implicated in the language impairments of children with SLI. What the various models share is the assumption that a fundamental source of the weakness in language acquisition is to be found at the initial point of input processing, at a step early in the process of inducing the latent structures of language. Differing perspectives focus on different places or in different steps along the way to linguistic induction in the input processing where weaknesses are thought to be operative.

Generalized Slowing

Other explanatory models have turned attention to more general limitations in nonverbal cognitive capacities that are proposed as the source of the problems in linguistic induction. A well formulated candidate of this perspective is the generalized slowing model put forth by Kail (1994). This model posits a generalized slowing of processing that affects linguistic and nonlinguistic tasks. Specific problems with language, such as the grammatical tense marker, are interpreted as localized consequences of more generalized, limited time-dependent linguistic input processing. Miller, Kail, Leonard, and Tomblin (2001) reported that SLI children and language-impaired children with below-normal nonverbal IQ levels—termed Nonspecific Language Impaired (NLI)—performed more slowly than age peers. They attributed the lower language performance of the NLI group to a deficit in speed of processing. This model, however, was not supported in a study of grammatical tense marking with the same sample of children. Rice, Tomblin et al. (2004) found lower performance on the grammatical tense marker for the SLI children relative to age controls, and the NLI children relative to the SLI group, but also reported results for a group of children with low nonverbal IQ (referred to as Low Cognition, at levels equivalent to the NLI group) who did not have deficits in the grammatical tense marker but instead performed at levels equivalent to the age controls. Performance IQ was not associated with tense-marking in the SLI or the Low Cognition group, and accounted for only a small amount of variance (about 6%) in the age controls and the NLI group. The general slowing account has also been challenged on methodological grounds (Windsor, Milbrath, Carney, &

Rakowski, 2001) and on findings that processing speed is not related to the severity of language impairment (Lahey, Edwards, & Munson, 2001).

A broader version of this perspective, evident in twin studies, is that language impairments are attributable to a general cognitive limitation, which is manifest in closely associated language and nonverbal ability, an association which shares a common genetic factor (Viding et al., 2003). As noted above, the lack of an association of nonverbal intelligence and performance on the grammatical tense marker is inconsistent with the general deficit view (cf. Rice et al., 2004), although a general cognitive deficit model seems to have widespread appeal.

Overall, a pattern of low performance of affected children, relative to age peers, on nonword repetition tasks, auditory processing tasks, and latency measures on cognitive tasks collectively contributes to the impression that affected children lack fundamental processing or cognitive mechanisms needed for the discovery of latent language structures. At the same time, there are significant caveats to this generalization. There are nontrivial methodological challenges to be overcome, as well.

COUNTEREVIDENCE OF ROBUST DISCOVERY OF LATENT STRUCTURES

Although attention has rightfully focused on the weaknesses in the linguistic systems in affected children and related abilities, this focus has deflected serious attention from the ways in which children with SLI indicate that they can and do discover abstract latent linguistic structures. Here I limit the observations to linguistic phenomena for which young affected children are surprisingly like their age peers, which sets a very high standard for considering the robustness of their acquisition mechanisms.

Some Elements of Morphology Are Robust

By 5 years of age, children with SLI are quite accurate in their use of plural *-s*. For example, Rice and Wexler (1996) found average plural use for the affected group to be 88%, which did not differ from the age control group. This finding is interesting because there are many similarities between the regular plural affixation and third person singular present *-s* on verbs, in that they share similar phonetic properties, involve affixation to lexical stems, show allophonic variants within class, require coordination of number marking in subject/verb contexts, and are constrained to particular lexical classes. Yet plurals are mastered at the same time that third person singular present *-s* is likely to be omitted (approximately 30% use in obligatory contexts as reported by Rice & Wexler, 1996; approximately 42% in the larger normative sample in Rice & Wexler, 2001). At the level of discovery mechanisms related to the likelihood of use in obligatory contexts, the conclusion is that such mechanisms are working quite well in one area of morphology but are strikingly weak in another.

A related example concerns past tense morphology versus participial morphology. This is evident in contexts such as *the boy kicked the ball* versus *the ball was kicked*, where the surface morphology of the main verb *kicked* is the same although the underlying grammatical structures are different. Redmond (2003) found that 6-year-old affected children performed at high levels on participial *-ed* (all but one child were 100% accurate) at the same time as they were likely to omit past tense *-ed* (on average, 56% use in obligatory contexts). The affected children did not differ from age controls on participles but differed from both age and language-matched controls on past tense morphology. Thus, discovery works for obligatory use of participles but not for past tense.

This conclusion is modulated somewhat by the finding of Leonard et al. (2003) who examined participial use in longer, full passive utterances (e.g., *the frog got kissed by the kitty*) in a sentence completion task. Their affected children were younger than those of Redmond (2003), from 4;5 to 6;10. The affected children performed better on participles (approximately 55%) than on regular past tense (approximately 30%), although at lower levels than unaffected language or age controls (approximately 80% on participles for the younger controls and approximately 95% for the older controls). One possibility is that the different outcomes between the two studies are attributable to different ages of affected children, in which case the younger SLI children may still be in the discovery phase for participles, which is nevertheless more robust than for past tense. Another possibility is that the task demands of Leonard et al. (2003) introduced other performance factors that diminished the performance of the affected group to a greater degree than that of controls (cf. Redmond 2003 for discussion of full vs. truncated passives, among other issues).

Observations from French-speaking children provide further evidence of selective robustness of morphological acquisition for affected children. Jakubowicz, Nash, Rigaut, and Gérard (1998) reported that French-speaking children with SLI (ages 5;7 to 13 years) had high levels of accuracy in obligatory contexts for *la* and *le* as determiners, but their performance was much lower (and lower than the control group) when the same forms were pronoun clitics. Thus, young affected children acquiring French show robust acquisition of determiners but not clitics, even though the surface forms are the same.

Avoidance of Overt Errors

There is convergence across studies that children with SLI show strong avoidance of plausible errors of usage, even for the forms that are difficult for them. Let us begin with the forms they seem to do well on. Perhaps they achieve high levels of usage by relying on simplified rules, or they are likely to misuse the forms at the same time that they use the forms in obligatory contexts. With regard to plurals, Rice and Oetting (1993) examined lexical productivity (the extent to which children used different words with the plural affix), contrastivity (contrastive marking of singulars and plurals), and morphological productivity (overregularizations). They report that the affected children showed robust use of plurals under each of these criteria. Further, Oetting and Rice (1993) report that in a study of noun compounding, 5-year-old affected children did not differ from age peers—like them, they compounded regular plural nouns ("rat eaters") differently from irregulars ("mice-eater"). Thus, they showed "a productive and differentiated plural marking system that is sufficiently robust to guide word formation processes" (p. 1245).

Let us now turn to the morphemes that are weak in English for affected children, focusing on the grammatical tense-marking morphemes of past tense, third person singular present *-s*, copula *BE*, and auxiliaries *BE* and *DO*. Recall the earlier observation that affected children distinguish past tense and participle functions (Leonard et al., 2003; Redmond, 2003), indicating that they distinguish the syntactic functions of similar surface morphology even when one of the morphological applications (i.e., past tense) is weak. So we can see that they are clearly drawing upon syntactic knowledge that coexists with morphosyntactic weaknesses.

A further way to investigate possible weaknesses is to examine other possible errors of usage. If the children are having problems discovering the latent properties of weak morphemes, we could expect them to make overt errors in spontaneous or elicited utterances. Yet the overwhelming conclusion from years of explicit data coding in my lab and in the labs of other investigators is that children with SLI are very unlikely to commit such errors of use. For example, Rice and Wexler (1996) report that when SLI children do use an inflected form,

> ...the surface form of the morpheme is almost always correctly applied to the stem (in the case of an affix) or the correct form is chosen (in the case of suppletive forms such as for the *BE* paradigm) in the contexts where it is allowed by the adult grammar, and the choice of form corresponds to that required by the person and number marking on the subject. SLI children are unlikely to say "*they runs" or "*they am happy" or "*I is happy" or "*he is not want the cookie." This phenomenon shows that the children are able to enter the correct surface forms into their mental representations and to fit them into a paradigm of person and number distinctions. (p. 1253)

In the same study, although the SLI group was more likely to omit determiners (e.g., *a*, *an*, or *the*) than language equivalent controls were, they did not generate overt errors such as "*the runs" or "*boy the runs" but instead their errors were confined, with rare exceptions, to omissions.

Grammaticality judgment data confirm that children with SLI are sensitive to subject/verb agreement violations, such as *he are mad* at the same time as they are likely to omit copula or auxiliary *BE*. Rice, Wexler, and Redmond (1999) report that sensitivity to agreement violations are significantly better than sensitivity to omitted *BE*. Extensive data collection with elicitation of *BE* and *DO* questions documents only rare occurrences of confusion of forms of *BE* and *DO*; errors such as "*Is he want a cookie?" or "*Do they sleeping" are almost entirely avoided. Other possible errors, such as confusion of licensed sites for finiteness marking, are also avoided; errors such as "*he not is happy" or "*likes he the dog?" do not occur. Errors representing an insertion of regular past tense or third person singular present tense affixes into infinitival verb phrases, such as "you made him walked/

walks," appear rarely in either spontaneous or elicited productions (Redmond & Rice, 2001; Rice, unpublished data reported in Redmond, 1997; Rice, Wexler, & Cleave, 1995; Rice & Wexler, 1996).

Avoidance of errors is also apparent in the verb argument structures generated by young children with SLI. In an extensive study of 5,486 spontaneous utterances of three affected boys (approximately 4 years of age), Rice and Bode (1993) report some kind of error of lexical verb choice in only 2% of the utterances produced by the subjects. This 2% constituted all instances of non-adult-like lexical verb use. Further, most of these errors were in the use of the most frequently occurring verbs, such as "you get in that guy and it'll work" (meaning "you push that guy…") or "I'm going underhand" (meaning "I'm throwing underhand"). Verbs like *get* and *go*, referred to by Rice and Bode (1993) as "general all purpose" verbs, have very elastic semantic properties and were scored quite strictly in the analyses (i.e., we scored as an error anything that did not meet a dictionary definition, although some of the uses are quite likely to appear in adult utterances as well), so the low percentage of error in verb choice is all the more striking. As indicated by the examples, verb-argument structure was maintained despite incorrect verb choice. The overarching conclusion is that in the naturalistic setting in which the children's utterances were recorded (a preschool classroom, where the children were interacting with peers), there was a remarkably robust ability to generate well-formed clausal structures with regard to verb argument structures. Although these youngsters had the typical general lexical delays and problems with tense-marking, they seemed to have discovered much of the fundamental latent structure for the expression of meanings via clausal constituents.

A recent experimental elicitation study of *Wh*-questions also shows some rather solid performance by 5-year-old children with SLI (Deevy & Leonard, 2004). Questions of the form, *Who is washing the dog*? (requiring no movement of clausal constituents) and *Who is the dog washing*? (requiring movement of the object *wh*- word to the sentence-initial position) were well comprehended by the affected children (at 88% and 86% correct, respectively), who did not differ from lexically matched children about one year younger. When the sentence length was increased (e.g., *Who is washing the happy brown dog*? and *Who is the happy brown dog washing*?) the affected children's performance remained high for subject questions (89%) but decreased for object questions (77%), a decrease that was not observed for the control children. This was taken to indicate that the affected children's knowledge of clausal movement was evident but could be affected by increased linguistic processing demands. I include the study in this section as an indication of the affected children's knowledge of the underlying latent structures involved in question formulation at the relatively young age of 5 years.

Bilingual Children with SLI Do Not Show a Bilingualism Effect Relative to Monolingual Children with SLI

To return to the study of Paradis et al. (2003), it is relevant to note here that on both morphemes that mark grammatical tense and on control morphemes affected children who are bilingual in French/English perform at levels equivalent to monolingual French- or English-speaking children with SLI. Thus, there is no apparent penalty or decrement attributable to the demands of acquiring two languages simultaneously. Not only can affected children discover the latent structures of their native language when exposed to a single language; apparently they can also do so under the increased demands of exposure to multiple languages. The symptoms are language-specific, but the performance levels are commensurate whether under monolingual or bilingual acquisition circumstances (cf. Genesee, Paradis, & Crago, 2004).

THE LOGICAL PROBLEM: HOW TO RECONCILE LATENT STRUCTURES OF LANGUAGE WITH WEAKENED ACQUISITION MECHANISMS?

The puzzle here is how to reconcile the fact that affected children are able to discover many of the fundamental latent structures of language at the same time as they show general language delays and selective disruptions in their grammatical systems. Although these youngsters are very likely to omit third person singular present *-s* from obligatory contexts, they have robust use of plural *-s*, clearly showing that they can discover (1) the mechanisms for morphological paradigm building, (2) the noun class of lexical items that take regular plural affixation, and (3) even rules for noun compounding. Likewise, affected youngsters are likely to omit forms of *BE* and *DO* at the same time as they avoid errors of use in the forms. Error avoidance, combined with the types of structures that the children attempt, reveals that they have a wealth of knowledge, (1) that *BE* is linked to progressive lexical verbs or to predicate adjectives, (2) that it appears in certain slots in clause structure, (3) that it must be marked for person and number agreement with the subject if in the matrix verb slot but if it follows *to* or a modal such as *gonna* in a verbal complement position it appears in the infinitival form, and (4) that it cannot appear with finite forms of *DO* in the same matrix clause. Also, they know many things about *DO*: (1) that it is linked to lexical verbs but not predicate adjectives or progressives; (2) that it must be inserted prior to negative forms in clauses, after WH forms in questions, but at the beginning of *Yes/No* questions; (3) that it must be conjugated for third person singular present tense subjects; and (4) that it cannot appear with finite forms of *BE* in the same matrix clauses.

Affected children know that past tense morphology cannot be applied to nonpast contexts; that there is site licensing for tense marking (errors such as "*he made him ate" or "*he made him walked" are rare); and although the surface morphology is homophonous with participial morphology, the two functions are distinct—past tense morphology is much more likely to be omitted in past tense contexts than in participial contexts.

Affected children know fundamental properties of argument structure and movement rules by 5 years of age, although this is a period when they are likely to omit grammatical tense markers at a high rate. They produce thousands of well-formed utterances, with a rate of 2% of overt errors of verb choice in which their novel verb uses nevertheless are likely to honor argument structure requirements. They differentiate subject versus object-movement questions.

These examples, among others, suggest very strongly that children with SLI have access to mechanisms that allow them to discover important latent structures of their native language. So are these youngsters very limited in language acquisition, or are they very robust? Are their grammatical weaknesses due to limited abilities to discover latent structures, and, if so, why are significant latent structures nevertheless spared? How do they come to know what they know about language if their underlying acquisition system is generally weak? This would be tantamount to a flawed software program that nevertheless functions as efficiently as a well designed one. Somehow affected children would have to be able to solve the language discovery problems in spite of a limited system, in which case an argument could be made that they were even better at language acquisition than their unaffected peers were.

Consider that the ways in which unaffected children are able to discover latent structures of language are not yet well understood, some 40 years after Brown and Bellugi's elegant formulation of the problem. Much has been made of the richness of the cognitive abilities that unaffected children bring to the task, and indeed that the task demands a wide range of cognitive skills. These include auditory perceptual abilities at an early age, parsing of linguistic input, memory for linguistic input, algorithms for deducing grammatical regularities, co-occurrences and recurrences, ability to carry out simultaneous calculations, and the integration of perceptual and conceptual input. Presumably each and every one of these aptitudes, as well as others, is called upon for language acquisition, and therefore would be a possible point of breakdown for the language impairments of children with SLI. Given that there is not yet a fully satisfactory explanation of how unaffected children accomplish the discovery process, with robust auditory, perceptual, and processing abilities to bring to bear on the task, one can only imagine the complexities of trying to account for how affected children manage the task with putatively impaired or sluggish mechanisms of any one or any combination of these—of auditory perceptual abilities at an early age; of abilities to parse linguistic input; of memory for linguistic input; of algorithms for deducing grammatical regularities, co-occurrences, and recurrences; of an ability to carry out simultaneous calculations or the integration of perceptual and conceptual input; or any other such limitations. Only three such possible limitations have been discussed above—i.e., auditory processing deficits, memory deficits, and/or general slowing/cognitive function deficits. The challenge is overwhelming, I believe, for a full account of how the children with SLI manage to discover so much of the latent structure of language with such fundamental deficiencies, because such deficiencies surely would mislead them in multiple ways as they entertain all possible alternatives suggested by a faulty acquisition system. As noted above, if language acquisition requires cognitive software to manage the task, then the affected children would be operating with a program with multiple bugs, and yet this program would nevertheless function as efficiently as a well designed one in many respects. This is surely an implausible scenario.

LESSONS TO BE LEARNED FROM SLI: MULTIPLE LINGUISTIC DIMENSIONS WITH DIFFERENTIATED TIMING MECHANISMS

One of the fundamental ways in which the language acquisition of children with SLI is different from that of unaffected children is that it is very protracted. This allows for a close observation of relative weaknesses and strengths in the emerging language structures. The rapid growth of language in unaffected children, in contrast, can create the strong impression, and empirical evidence, of an overarching discovery mechanism that amalgamates the linguistic dimensions discernible in adult linguistic systems. Under the perspective of such a discovery mechanism, language acquisition can be regarded as growth in a relatively unitary construct with collinear dimensions (Plomin, 1999; Plomin & Kovas, 2005). In contrast, documentation of the linguistic strengths as well as weaknesses of children with SLI strongly suggests that multiple, discernibly distinct linguistic dimensions are involved. Unlike typically developing children, children with SLI show that in certain ways morphosyntax can be disrupted—i.e., be out of synchrony with the rest of the linguistic system. This is the case even though much of the necessary infrastructure of morphosyntax is known (such as the architecture of clause structure with designated sites for finiteness, the phonetic properties of surface morphology, and related principles of constituent movement). General cognitive mechanisms, such as verbal memory, auditory processing, and speed of processing show a complex relationship to the discovery of latent linguistic structure. It is clear that such mechanisms can support the ways in which affected children show linguistic competency, and in these ways their presence in affected children appears to be at a level at which language acquisition could normally be expected to occur. Yet such apparent sufficiency is not enough to ensure uniformly robust language acquisition, because the affected children display selective linguistic weaknesses as well as general delays in language onset.

Further indication of differentiated linguistic dimensionality is evident in the growth patterns of affected and unaffected children. The parallels between affected and unaffected children become even more striking when we consider the timing mechanisms inherent in growth data. As demonstrated in Figures 10.1 and 10.2, growth varies depending upon the linguistic domain: linear for receptive vocabulary in the 3- to 8-year period, and nonlinear (with quadratic elements) for grammatical tense marking in the same age period.

For the linear trajectory of lexical acquisition, the affected youngsters follow the same linear path as the unaffected children, just offset by two years. Note that this holds even though the life experiences, amount of exposure to native language, and cognitive and social achievements of the two groups of children are quite different. One implication of the same linear path is that the affected children do not "catch up" at some later time, an observation becoming more and more apparent as longitudinal investigations continue. The second implication is that the beginning of language acquisition, that is, the intercept for the growth curves, is delayed for affected children. As noted earlier, there is strong reason to suspect that children with SLI are among the Late Talker group of children at 2 years of age, although not all Late Talkers become SLI.

For the nonlinear trajectory of finiteness marking, the affected youngsters also follow the same path (although offset to a level below that of MLU-equivalent children and therefore not fully synchronized with the rest of the language system). In this case the path is more complex. Growth does not show a consistent rate but instead has points of change in the rate, where the acceleration increases toward the expected levels of near 100% use in obligatory contexts. There is also strong suggestion that the affected group of children may be more likely to plateau at a level of performance somewhat below that of unaffected children, as if the initial weakness in the grammatical system persists to prevent a fully robust end state. Note that the points of acceleration change—i.e., the places of curvature in the growth trajectory are benchmarked to elapsed time in the growth trajectory, not a particular age level. This is particularly striking given that the children's educational experiences, language exposure, social and cognitive development are also underway during this time and play out at different levels in the two groups. Nevertheless, it is as if the template for change in finiteness marking or the discovery mechanism is shared, although the onset of the mechanisms is timed differently.

Thus, this growth-timed perspective emphasizes the significant roles of onset, slope, and points of change in acceleration as vital elements in our understanding of the nature of language impairment. Growth is not the same across all elements of language, yet growth is parallel for affected and unaffected children. Of great clinical importance is the fact that because growth is parallel, the affected children are not able to "catch up" or "outgrow" the condition. Note that this "catch-up" model is actually a complex one in that there would have to be some way for the affected children to grow at a rate faster than unaffected children in order to close the gap. There is no evidence that such an accelerated rate comes into play.

Elsewhere, I have argued that the parallels in timing mechanisms, across the different linguistic dimensions, for affected and unaffected children, can be accounted for by strong underlying maturational timing mechanisms that include linguistic-specific elements (Rice, 2003, 2004a, 2004b, 2007, in press). Just as developmental mechanisms in other cortico-neurological domains are tied to inherited timing mechanisms (cf. Fisher, 2005), it is plausible that inherited timing mechanisms are also operative in the higher cognitive processes involved in language acquisition.

Maturational models have been out of favor since earlier writings on the topic of language impairment by Lenneberg (1967). Wexler (2003) has updated Lenneberg's perspective in the Unique Checking Constraint (UCC) model of optional infinitives. This model is based on checking theory of tense and agreement features in the functional projections of underlying syntactic representations. The UCC model is formulated to capture the ways in which crosslinguistic similarities and differences are expected for this period of grammatical weakness. Essentially, the notion is that young children call upon a single-checking operation for an early period of time, which can serve them well if their native language requires only a single-checking mechanism (such as Italian) but can pose difficulties if their native language requires two checking operations, as is the case for English. In this case, children must resolve the single-checking default in order to move into the adult system, a resolution that requires additional time to put into place. Under this model, the affected children would be in an Extended Unique Checking Constraint (EUCC) for a much longer period, and may not completely resolve this limitation. At the same time, many other properties of their linguistic infrastructure would be sound, allowing them to avoid grammatical errors in ways consistent with the evidence described above.

With regard to the discovery of latent linguistic structure, the EUCC/EOI perspective brings a mixed view of facilitative and inhibiting mechanisms involved in language acquisition. On the one hand, children can draw upon a small set of grammatical principles to facilitate linguistic discovery, and on the other hand child-specific assumptions can be inconsistent with the discovery requirements for a particular language, such as English. Affected children can call upon many of the discovery mechanisms that they share with unaffected children to bring about change in their linguistic systems in the same way as unaffected children.

As a recently developed theory of children's grammatical development, the OI/UCC model is under extensive investigation. The idea of an EOI/EUCC period is even more recent, and the necessary empirical investigations are really just beginning. Although initial outcomes are strongly supportive, many details remain to be worked out. The scope of the model does not include all the symptoms of SLI, but to date it has been very helpful in the identification of a reliable and theoretically interpretable clinical marker for the condition (cf. Rice & Wexler, 2001). The model does not rule out other possible areas of grammatical disruption in affected children, nor possible (but as yet undiscovered) ways in which the language impairments of SLI are similar to or different from other conditions of language impairment (cf. Rice & Warren, 2004).

The EOI/EUCC perspective does, however, bring to the table a model that is mindful of linguistic details, linguistic coherence and continuity with the adult grammatical system, as well as the developmental trajectory as children move from an immature to a mature grammatical system. Although the technical properties of this model and subsequent models are expected to evolve and change, we can now see that any fully successful model of SLI must account for (1) robust as well as weak mechanisms for latent linguistic structure discovery, (2) strong parallels in growth trajectories of affected and unaffected children, and (3) delays as well as selective disruptions that interact with particular linguistic properties.

CONCLUDING COMMENTS

Revisiting the broad theme of children's ability to discover latent linguistic structures in terms of what we have learned about children with SLI has pointed again toward the need for precise attention to linguistic particulars and careful consideration of the ways in which language changes over time in young children. I believe these themes are key components of the legacy of Melissa Bowerman, who taught her students to respect these realities, and who demonstrated in her own work how to apply them to the deep puzzles of children's language acquisition. It has been my privilege to explore them in children with language impairments.

ACKNOWLEDGMENT

Preparation of this chapter was supported by the Merrill Advanced Studies Center at the University of Kansas and grants from the National Institutes of Health to the University of Kansas through the Center for Biobehavioral Neurosciences in Communication Disorders (P30DC005803) and the Mental Retardation and Developmental Disabilities Research Center (P30HD002528), R01DC001803, and R01DC005226.

REFERENCES

Bedore, L. M., & Leonard, L. B. (1998). Specific language impairment and grammatical morphology: A discriminant function analysis. *Journal of Speech, Language, and Hearing Research*, *41*, 1185–1192.

Berko, J. (1958). The child's learning of English morphology. *Word*, *14*, 150–177.

Bishop, D. V. M. (2006). Beyond words: Phonological short-term memory and syntactic impairment in specific language impairment. *Applied Psycholinguistics*, *27*, 545–547.

Bishop, D. V. M., Carlyon, R. P., Deeks, J. M. & Bishop, S. J. (1999). Auditory temporal processing impairment: Neither necessary nor sufficient for causing language impairment in children. *Journal of Speech, Language & Hearing Research*, *42*, 1295–1310.

Bishop, D. V. M., North, T., & Donlan, C. (1996). Nonword repetition as a behavioral marker for inherited language impairment: Evidence from a twin study. *Journal of Child Psychology and Psychiatry*, *37*, 391–403

Bowerman, M. (1988). Inducing the latent structure of language. In F. S. Kessel, *The development of language and language researchers: Essays in honor of Roger Brown* (pp. 23–50). Hillsdale, N.J. Erlbaum.

Brown, R., & Bellugi, U. (1964). Three processes in the child's acquisition of syntax. In E. H. Lenneberg (Ed.), *New directions in the study of language*. Cambridge, MA: MIT Press.

Colledge, E., Bishop, D. V. M., Koeppen-Schomerus, G., Price, T. S., Happé, F. G. E., Eley, T. C. et al. (2002). The structure of language abilities at 4 years: A twin study. *Developmental Psychology*, *38*, 749–757.

Conti-Ramsden, G. (1997). Genes, language and Specific Language Impairment (SLI). First Language, *17*, 321–332.

Conti-Ramsden, G. (2003). Processing and linguistic markers in young children with specific language impairment (SLI). *Journal of Speech, Language, & Hearing Research, 46*, 1029–1037.

Conti-Ramsden, G. & Botting, N. (1999). Classification of children with SLI: Longitudinal considerations. *Journal of Speech, Language, Hearing Research, 42*, 1195–1204.

Conti-Ramsden, G., Botting, N., & Faragher, B. (2001). Psycholinguistic markers for specific language impairment. *Journal of Child Psychology and Psychiatry, 42*, 741–748.

Deevy, P., & Leonard, L. B. (2004). The comprehension of *Wh*-questions in children with Specific Language Impairment. *Journal of Speech, Language, and Hearing Research, 47*, 802–815.

Dollaghan, C. A., & Campbell, T. F. (1998). Nonword repetition and child language impairment. *Journal of Speech, Language, & Hearing Research, 41*, 1136–1146.

Dollaghan, C. A., Campbell, T. F., Paradise, J. L., Feldman, H. M., Janosky, J. E., Pitcairn, D. N. et al. (1999). Maternal education and measures of early speech and language. *Journal of Speech, Language, Hearing Research, 42*, 1432–1443.

Dunn, L. M., & Dunn, L. M. (1981). *Peabody picture vocabulary test-Revised.* Circle Pines, MN: American Guidance Service.

Eadie, P. A., Fey, M. E., Douglas, J. M., & Parsons, C. L. (2002). Profiles of grammatical morphology and sentence imitation in children with specific language impairment and Down syndrome. *Journal of Speech, Language, and Hearing Research, 45*, 720–732.

Ellis Weismer, S. (2007). Typical talkers, late talkers, and children with specific language impairment: A language endowment spectrum? In R. Paul (Ed.), *The influence of developmental perspectives on research and practice in communication disorders: A festschrift for Robin S. Chapman.* Mahwah, NJ: Erlbaum.

Evans, J. L., Viele, K., Kass, R. E., & Tang, F. (2002). Grammatical morphology and perception of synthetic and natural speech in children with specific language impairments. *Journal of Speech, Language, Hearing Research, 45*, 494–504.

Fisher, S. (2005). Dissection of molecular mechanisms underlying speech and language disorders. *Applied Psycholinguistics, 26*, 111–128.

Gathercole, S. E. (2006). Nonword repetition and word learning: The nature of the relationship. *Applied Psycholinguistics, 27*, 513–544.

Gathercole, S. E., & Baddeley, A. D. (1990). Phonological memory deficits in language disordered children: Is there a causal connection? *Journal of Memory and Language, 29*, 336–360.

Gathercole, V. C. M., Sebastián, E., & Soto, P. (2002). The emergence of linguistic person in Spanish-speaking children. *Language Learning, 52*, 679–722.

Genesee, F., Paradis, & Crago, M. B. (2004). *Dual language development and disorders: A handbook on bilingualism and second language learning.* Baltimore, MD: Brookes. Grela, B., & Leonard, L. B. (2000). The influence of argument structure complexity on the use of auxiliary verbs by children with SLI. *Journal of Speech, Language, and Hearing Research, 43*, 1115–1125.

Guasti, M. T. (2002). *Language acquistion: the growth of grammar.* Cambridge, MA: MIT Press.

Haegemann, L. (1994) *Introduction to government and binding theory* (2nd ed.). Cambridge, MA: Blackwell.

Hoff-Ginsberg, E., Kelly, D., & Buhr, J. (1996). Syntactic bootstrapping by children with SLI: Implications for a theory of specific language impairment. *Proceedings of the 20th Annual Boston University Conference on Language Development* (pp. 329–339). Somerville, MA: Cascadilla Press.

Jakubowicz, C., Nash, L., Rigaut, C., & Gérard, C. (1998). Determiners and clitic pronouns in French-speaking children with SLI. *Language Acquisition, 7*, 113–160.

Joseph, K. L., Serratrice, L., & Conti-Ramsden, G. (2002). Development of copula and auxiliary BE in children with specific language impairment and younger unaffected controls. *First Language, 22*, 137–172.

Kail, R. (1994). A method of studying the generalized slowing hypothesis in children with specific language impairment. *Journal of Speech and Hearing Research, 37*, 418–421.

Lahey, M., Edwards, J., & Munson, B. (2001). Is processing speed related to severity of language impairment? *Journal of Speech, Language, Hearing Research, 44*, 1354–1361.

Lenneberg, E. (1967). *Biological foundations of language*. New York: Wiley.

Leonard, L. B. (1989). Language learnability and specific language impairment in children. *Applied Psycholinguistics, 10*, 179–202.

Leonard, L. B. (1998). *Children with specific language impairment*. Cambridge, MA: MIT Press.

Leonard, L. B., Deevy, P., Miller, C. A., Rauf, L, Charest, M., & Kurz, R. (2003). Surface forms and grammatical functions: Past tense and passive participle use by children with SLI. *Journal of Speech, Language & Hearing Research, 46*, 43–55.

Leonard, L. B., Eyer, J., Bedore, L., & Grela, B. (1997) Three accounts of the grammatical morpheme difficulties of English-speaking children with specific language impairment. *Journal of Speech, Language, and Hearing Research, 40*, 741–753.

Leonard, L. B., Hansson, K., Nettelbladt, U., & Deevy, P. (2004). Specific language impairment in children: A comparison of English and Swedish. *Language Acquisition, 12*, 219–246.

Leonard, L. McGregor, K., & Allen, G. (1992). Grammatical morphology and speech perception in children with specific language impairment. *Journal of Speech and Hearing Research, 35*, 1076–1085.

Marchman, V. A., Wulfeck, B., & Ellis Weismer, S. (1999). Morphological productivity in children with normal language and SLI: A study of the English past tense. *Journal of Speech, Language, and Hearing Research, 42*, 206–219.

Miller, C. A., Kail, R., Leonard, L. B., & Tomblin, J. B. (2001). Speed of processing in children with specific language impairment. *Journal of Speech, Language, and Hearing Research, 44*, 416–433.

Montgomery, J. W., & Leonard, L. B. (1998). Real-time inflectional processing by children with specific language impairment: Effects of phonetic substance. *Journal of Speech, Language, and Hearing Research, 49*, 1238–1256.

Oetting, J. B. (1999) Children with SLI use argument structure cues to learn verbs. *Journal of Speech, Language, and Hearing Research, 42*, 1261–1274.

Oetting, J. B., & Horohov, J. E. (1997). Past-tense marking by children with and without specific language impairment. *Journal of Speech, Language, and Hearing Research, 40*, 62–74.

Oetting J. B., & Rice, M. L. (1993). Plural acquisition in children with specific language impairment. *Journal of Speech, Language & Hearing Research, 36*, 1236–1248.

O'Hara, M., & Johnston, J. (1997). Syntactic bootstrapping in children with SLI. *European Journal of Disorders of Communication, 32*, 189–205.

Paradis, J., Crago, M., Genesee, F., & Rice, M. L. (2003). French-English bilingual children with SLI: How do they compare with their monolingual peers? *Journal of Speech, Language, and Hearing Research, 46*, 113–127.

Paul, R. (1996). Clinical implication of the natural history of slow expressive language development. *American Journal of Speech-Language Pathology, 5*, 5–21.

Plomin, R. (1999). Genetics and general cognitive ability. *Nature, 402*, C25–C29.

Plomin, R., & Kovas, Y. (2005). Generalist genes and learning disabilities. *Psychological Bulletin, 131*, 592–617.

Pollock, J. (1989). Verb movement, universal grammar, and the structure of IP. *Linguistic Inquiry, 20*, 365–424.

Purnell, B. (2003). To every thing there is a season. *Science, 301*, 325.

Redmond, S. M. (1997). *A grammatical analysis of irregular past tense in school age children with and without histories of specific language impairment.* Unpublished doctoral dissertation, University of Kansas, Lawrence, KS.

Redmond, S. M. (2003). Children's production of the affix *-ed* in past tense and past participle contexts. *Journal of Speech, Language, Hearing Research, 46*, 1095–1109.

Redmond, S. M., & Rice, M. L. (2001). Detection of irregular verb violations by children with and without SLI. *Journal of Speech, Language, Hearing Research, 44*, 655–669.

Rescorla, L. (2002). Language and reading outcomes to age 9 in late-talking toddlers, *Journal of Speech, Language and Hearing Research, 45*, 360–371.

Rice, M. L. (1997). Response to reviewer's comments on *Towards a Genetics of Language. First Language, 17*, 333–340.

Rice, M. L. (2003). A unified model of specific and general language delay: Grammatical tense as a clinical marker of unexpected variation. In Y. Levy & J. Schaeffer (Eds.), *Language competence across populations: Toward a definition of specific language impairment* (pp. 63–95). Mahwah, NJ: Erlbaum.

Rice, M. L. (2004a). Growth models of developmental language disorders. In M. L. Rice & S. F. Warren (Eds.), *Developmental language disorders: From phenotypes to etiologies* (pp. 207–240). Mahwah, NJ: Erlbaum.

Rice, M. L. (2004b). Language growth of children with SLI and unaffected children: Timing mechanisms and linguistic distinctions. In A. Brugos, L. Micciulla, & C. Smith (Eds.), *Proceedings of the 28th Annual Boston University Conference on Language Development.* Somerville, MA: Cascadilla Press.

Rice, M. L. (2007). Children with Specific Language Impairment: Bridging the genetic and developmental perspectives. In E. Hoff & M. Shatz (Eds.), *Blackwell handbook of language development* (pp. 411–431). Malden, MA: Blackwell.

Rice, M. L. (in press). How different is disordered language? In J. Colombo, P. McCardle, & L. Freund (Eds.), *Infant pathways to language: Methods, models, and research directions.* Mahwah, NJ: Erlbaum.

Rice, M. L., & Bode, J. (1993). Gaps in the verb lexicons of children with specific language impairment. *First Language, 13*, 113–131.

Rice, M. L., Noll, K. R., & Grimm, H. (1997). An extended optional infinitive stage in German-speaking children with Specific Language Impairment. *Language Acquisition, 6*, 255–295.

Rice, M. L., & Oetting, J. B. (1993). Morphological deficits of children with SLI: Evaluation of number marking and agreement. *Journal of Speech, Language, & Hearing Research, 36*, 1239–1257.

Rice, M. L. Oetting, J. B., Marquis, J., Bode, J., & Pae, S. (1994). Frequency of input effects on word comprehension of children with specific language impairment. *Journal of Speech, Language, & Hearing Research, 37*, 106–122.

Rice, M. L., Redmond, S. M., & Hoffman, L. (2006). MLU in children with SLI and younger control children shows concurrent validity, stable and parallel growth trajectories. *Journal of Speech, Language & Hearing Research, 49*, 793–808.

Rice, M. L., & Smolik, F. (2007). Genotypes of language disorders: Clinical conditions, phenotypes, and genes. In M. G. Gaskell (Ed.), *The Oxford handbook of psycholinguistics (pp. 685–700). Oxford:* Oxford University Press.

Rice, M. L., Taylor, C., & Zubrick, S. R. (in press). Language outcomes of 7-year-old children with or without a history of late language emergence at 24-months. *Journal of Speech, Language, & Hearing Research.*

Rice, M. L., Tomblin, J. B., Hoffman, L.M., Richman, W. A., & Marquis, J. (2004). Grammatical tense deficits in children with SLI and nonspecific language impairment: Relationships with nonverbal IQ over time. *Journal of Speech, Language, and Hearing Research, 47,* 816–834.

Rice, M. L., & Warren, S. F. (Eds.). (2004). *Developmental language disorders: From phenotypes to etiologies.* Mahwah, NJ: Erlbaum.

Rice, M. L., Warren, S. F., & Betz, S. K. (2005). Language symptoms of developmental language disorders: An overview of autism, Down syndrome, fragile X, specific language impairment, and Williams syndrome. *Applied Psycholinguistics, 26,* 7–28.

Rice, M. L., & Wexler, K. (1996). Toward tense as a clinical marker of specific language impairment in English-speaking children. *Journal of Speech and Hearing Research, 39,* 1239–1257.

Rice, M. L., & Wexler, K. (2001). *Rice/Wexler test of early grammatical impairment.* San Antonio, TX: The Psychological Corporation.

Rice, M. L., Wexler, K., & Cleave, P. L. (1995). Specific language impairment as a period of extended optional infinitive. *Journal of Speech, Language, and Hearing Research, 38,* 1239–1257.

Rice, M. L., Wexler, K., & Hershberger, S. (1998). Tense over time: The longitudinal course of tense acquisition in children with specific language impairment. *Journal of Speech, Language, and Hearing Research, 41,* 1412–1431.

Rice, M. L., Wexler, K., Marquis, J., & Hershberger, S. (2000). Acquisition of irregular past tense by children with SLI. *Journal of Speech, Language, and Hearing Research, 43,* 1126–1145.

Rice, M. L., Wexler, K., & Redmond, S. M. (1999). Grammaticality judgments of an extended optional infinitive grammar: Evidence from English-speaking children with specific language impairment. *Journal of Speech, Language, and Hearing Research, 42,* 943–961.

Schütze, C. T. (2004). Morphosyntax and syntax. In R. D. Kent (Ed.), *The MIT encyclopedia of communication disorders* (pp. 354–358). Cambridge, MA: MIT Press.

Schütze, C. T., & Wexler, K. (1996). Subject case licensing and English root infinitives. In A. Stringfellow, D. Cahana-Amitay, E. Hughes, & A. Zukowski (Eds.), *BUCLD 20 proceedings.* Somerville, MA: Cascadilla Press.

Shriberg, L. D., Tomblin, J. B., & McSweeny, J. L. (1999). Prevalence of speech delay in 6-year-old children and comorbidity with language impairment. *Journal of Speech, Language, and Hearing Research, 42,* 1461–1481.

Smith, S. D., & Morris, C. A. (2005). Planning studies of etiology. *Applied Psycholinguistics, 26,* 97–110.

Snow, C. E. (1996). Toward a rational empiricism: Why interactionism is not behaviorism any more than biology is genetics. In M. L. Rice (Ed.), *Toward a genetics of language.* Mahwah, NJ: Erlbaum.

Tager-Flusberg, H., & Cooper, J. (1999). Present and future possibilities for defining a phenotype for specific language impairment. *Journal of Speech, Language, and Hearing Research, 42,* 1275–1278.

Tallal, P. (2000). Experimental studies of language learning impairments: From research to remediation. In D. V. M. Bishop & L. B. Leonard (Eds.), *Speech and language impairments in children* (pp 131–156). Hove, UK: Psychology Press.

Tallal, P., & Piercy, M. (1973). Defects of nonverbal auditory perception in children with developmental aphasia. *Nature, 241,* 468–469.

Tallal, P., Stark, R., Kallman, C., & Mellits, D. (1981). A reexamination of some nonverbal perceptual abilities of language impaired and normal children as a function of age and sensory modality. *Journal of Speech, Language & Hearing Research, 24,* 351–357.

Tomblin, J. B., Records, N. L., Buckwalter, P., Zhang, X, Smith, E. & O'Brien, M. (1997). The prevalence of specific language impairment in kindergarten children. *Journal of Speech, Language & Hearing Research, 40,* 1245–1260

Tomblin, J. B., Zhang, X., Buckwalter, P., & O'Brien, M. (2003). The stability of primary language disorder: Four years after kindergarten diagnosis. *Journal of Speech, Language & Hearing Research, 46,* 1283–1296.

Tomblin, J. B., Zhang, X., Catts, H., Ellis Weismer, S., & Weiss, A. (2004). Dimensions of individual differences in communication skills among primary grade children. In M. L. Rice & S. F. Warren (Eds.), *Developmental language disorders: From phenotypes to etiologies* (pp. 53–76). Mahwah, NJ: Erlbaum.

Torrens, V., & Wexler, K. (2001). Language delay in the acquisition of Castillian and Catalán. *Aloma, 9,* 131–148.

Van der Lely, H. (1994). Canonical linking rules: Forward versus reverse linking in normally developing and specifically language-impaired children. *Cognition, 51,* 29–72.

Van der Lely, H. J. K. (1998). SLI in children: Movement, economy, and deficits in the computational-syntax system. *Language Acquisition,* 7(2–4), 161–192.

Viding, E., Price, T. S., Spinath, F. M., Bishop, D. V. M., Dale, P. S., & Plomin, R. (2003). Genetic and environmental mediation of the relationship between language and nonverbal impairment in 4-year-old twins. *Journal of Speech, Language & Hearing Research, 46,* 1271–1282.

Wexler, K. (1992) *Optional infinitives, head movement and the economy of derivation in child grammar* (Occasional paper No. 45). Cambridge, MA: Center for Cognitive Science, MIT.

Wexler, K. (1994). Optional infinitives, head movement and the economy of derivations. In D. Lightfoot & N. Hornstein (Eds.), *Verb movement* (pp. 305–350). Cambridge, UK: Cambridge University Press.

Wexler, K. (1996). The development of inflection in a biologically based theory of language acquisition. In M. L. Rice (Ed.), *Toward a genetics of language* (pp. 113–144). Mahwah, NJ: Erlbaum.

Wexler, K. (1998). Very early parameter setting and the unique checking constraint: A new explanation of the optional infinitive stage. *Lingua, 106,* 23–79.

Wexler, K. (2003). Lenneberg's dream: Learning, normal language development and specific language impairment. In Y. Levy & J. Schaeffer (Eds.), *Language competence across populations: Towards a definition of specific language impairment* (pp. 11–61). Mahwah, NJ: Erlbaum.

Wexler, K., Schütze, C. T., & Rice, M. L. (1998) Subject case in children with SLI and unaffected controls: Evidence for the Agr/Tns Omission model. *Language Acquisition, 7,* 317–344.

Windsor, J. Milbraith, R. L., Carney, E. J., & Rakowshi, S. E. (2001). General slowing in language impairment: Methodological considerations in testing the hypothesis. *Journal of Speech, Language & Hearing Research, 44,* 446–461.

Zubrick, S., Taylor, K., Rice, M. L., & Slegers, D. (2007). An epidemiological study of late-talking 24-month-old children: Prevalence and predictors. *Journal of Speech, Language, & Hearing Research, 50,* 1562–1592.

Personal Tribute

VIRGINIA C. MUELLER GATHERCOLE

For John Cleese, it was "Geoffrey Bartlett,"
for Anita Roddick "Betty Springer,"
for Jeremy Paxman "George Sayer,"
for Ben Elton "Gordon Valance,"
for Bob Hoskins "Di Jones,"
for Joanna Lumley "Sister Dilys Dodd,"
for Stephen Hawking "Mr. Todda,"
for Tony Blair "Eric Anderson."

For me, it was Melissa Bowerman.

"No one forgets a good teacher."

Adapted from ad, Training and Development Agency for Schools, U.K., 1998[1]

Chapter 11 is a labor of love. It reports data from two people who are dear to my heart—my daughter, Rachel, and her daughter, Sadie. It involves something of a collaboration with my daughter; this might have been unthinkable when I was first collecting data from her and my son when they were small. Furthermore, it is written in honor of Melissa Bowerman; it has brought me back to work that I initiated when I was working under Melissa on my doctoral dissertation, as her first PhD student, way back when.

The prospect of returning to take a much closer look at the development of the structures reported here, with naturalistic data collected from children, has been on my agenda all these years since I first studied under Melissa, and snippets of which have been the topic of study in a variety of studies I have conducted since then.

[1] I am grateful to Annabell Norden, Account Manager, DDB London, for providing me with a copy of the ad.

When considering what was most appropriate for a Festschrift in Melissa's honor, I kept coming back to this topic. This work helps to "close the circle" somewhat of work I began at that time, and it encapsulates many of the things I've learned from Melissa—both during the time when I was a graduate student working under her and in the many years since then. I offer this chapter in full celebration of those things that Melissa has represented for me and for our field in general.

Just to highlight some of the very important things Melissa represents and has taught me—and those in the field of child language—both explicitly and by example:

- Listen to the child. Listening to the child means listening to the data that come from children.
- Let the data speak for themselves. Melissa always stressed that the truth will eventually find its way to the surface if one pays attention to the data. I hope that this chapter helps to confirm that conviction.
- The story is probably a complex one. To arrive at psychologically real descriptions of the child's acquisition of any structure, one must examine as many of the aspects of those structures as possible. This chapter is an attempt to bring together a whole range of related structures in a way that might reveal how their development is interrelated in the process of acquisition.
- Take advantage of the fact that languages are different. What children acquire similarly across languages and what they acquire differently can go a long way toward illuminating what is universal and what is language-specific about language learning.
- Consider alternative explanations for the phenomena found. If there is one thing I feel Melissa's own work champions, it is approaching child language phenomena with a completely open mind concerning their theoretical implications and delving deeply into whether the implications of distinct theories are upheld by the data.

These all have to do with what Melissa has taught me about being a responsible, truth-seeking psycholinguist working on child language acquisition. More important than these elements, though, I have learned immeasurable lessons from Melissa regarding academic professionalism. Apart from Melissa's obvious respect for the data and complete honesty in accurately representing what they show, I know of very few people of Melissa's stature as an academic who have influenced so many people's thought and who is yet so humble and unassuming about this. While someone else might aggressively push his or her own position, Melissa quietly considers the other's position, weighing the evidence, and incorporating any positive aspects of that position into her own thinking. Her respect for the child language data is paralleled by her respect for other researchers working in the field.

But probably most important of all, Melissa has been an extraordinary model as a human being. I have been continually inspired by and in awe of Melissa's ability to apply the same patience and regard for others in her personal life that she shows in her professional life. I have been astounded on many occasions by the good faith

Melissa has shown toward others and by her total self-assurance and selflessness, even at times when others would have given up. If I could achieve even only a small percentage of the level of fortitude that Melissa has shown in her personal life, this would indeed be the best lesson I will have learned from her.

Melissa, thank you. This chapter is for you.

REFERENCE

Training and Development Agency for Schools. (1998). Ad in campaign "No one forgets a good teacher." London.

11

"It Was So Much Fun. It Was 20 Fun!"[1]

Cognitive and Linguistic Invitations to the Development of Scalar Predicates

VIRGINIA C. MUELLER GATHERCOLE

Bangor University

with contributions from RACHEL GATHERCOLE

> The choices that speakers make as they piece together sentences from the lexical, syntactic, and morphological resources of their language are not carried out independently of one another.... Learning how to coordinate the components of grammar is an important aspect of first-language development.... (Bowerman, 1981, p. 179)

How do children develop complex linguistic systems that necessarily involve multiple concurrent developments in semantic, syntactic, and cognitive realms? Research is often of necessity restricted to examining developments within one realm or another (e.g., syntactic, semantic, or cognitive),[2]

[1] Sadie 3;4.8 (see text for further details on this utterance).

[2] I am using the terms *semantic* and *cognitive* throughout fairly narrowly: *semantic* to refer to meaning that gets encoded in language, and *cognitive* to conceptual understanding of the world irrespective of how and whether those concepts get encoded in the language. The two are inextricably linked, of course, but are not one and the same; for example, young infants learning both Korean and English may well understand (i.e., cognitively) that spatial relations between objects may involve tight fit, as opposed to loose fit (Choi, 2006; Casasola, Wilbourn, & Yang, 2006), but Korean-speaking children need to learn as well that this notion gets encoded semantically in Korean, while English-speaking children learn it is irrelevant to English semantic structure (Choi, 2006).

or within a small set of linguistic structures within a given domain (e.g., tense or inflectional elements, active vs. passive sentences, word meaning, development of one word (*more, big*) or a few related words (e.g., *more* and *less*; *more* and *-er*; *all, every, some*). We do not often get many glimpses of real-language data that allow us to see how the acquisition of multiple sets of constructs interact over time. Bowerman's work has provided some of the most valuable insights into such interaction, showing how distinct structures influence each other when they begin to "bump up against each other's territories" (Bowerman, 1978, p. 391; Bowerman, 1982). Her ground-breaking work on late-emerging errors in a number of realms (e.g., spatial and temporal terms, causative verbs, Figure–Ground expressions, and verb–argument structure) has provided countless new insights into the ways in which the child goes about constructing a grammar that encompasses a wide range of substructures. That work has provided some of the impetus behind much current theorizing on language development positing that children establish systems on the basis of networks in interaction, or dynamical systems. These theories suggest that the more children learn, the more their knowledge in one realm will begin to influence their knowledge in another (Elman, 1998; Gershkoff-Stowe & Thelen, 2004; Smith, 1999). The purpose of this chapter is to examine closely another wide range of structures in order to gauge the extent to which their acquisition hinges on such interaction between structures, and on interaction between syntactic, semantic, and cognitive factors. The data are interpreted as indicating that such interactions occur at multiple levels throughout the development of the forms in question.

The structures of interest here are a complex set of English constructions that broadly involve quantification and the specification of degree. These are related in the adult language through common syntactic patterns as well as related semantic content. The question addressed here is how the development of these constructs proceeds in the English-speaking child. Of critical interest are several major questions:

To what extent do children approach these structures on the basis of broad syntactic categories and structures? That is, does knowledge of syntactic structure guide children's acquisition of these forms, or do the syntactic structures emerge out of the children's experience with the forms?

Are the developments in the syntactic and semantic (and cognitive) realms autonomous, or do developments in one area influence developments in another?

Do children follow a common trajectory in the development of these systems, or is the developmental path followed idiosyncratic and distinct across children?

Does language lead cognitive development, cognitive development lead language, or a mixture of these two?

An examination of spontaneous speech data from two children will reveal that the process of learning is long and drawn out, involving considerable early lexically specific knowledge that evolves through small, repeated steps involving the child's discovery of syntactic and semantic linkages, into a complex network of structures.

The structures to be examined are primarily those shown in (1) (related forms will be included as relevant). These involve degree markers such as *too, -er, -est, enough,* and the first *as* in constructs with adjectival and nominal heads, as in (1a) and (1b), as well as standard markers, which introduce standards of comparison, such as the last *as* in (1ai) and (1bi) and *than* in (1av) and (1bv).

(1) a. As:
- i. *J is as happy (as T).*
- ii. *J is too happy (for his own good/to Y).*
- iii. *J is that happy.*
- iv. *J is so happy [that….]*
- v. *J is happier (than a lark/than S). J is more intelligent (than…)*
- vi. *J is the happiest (of all/in the world). J is the most intelligent….*
- vii. *J is happy enough (to Y/for Y).*

b. Ns:
- i. *J has as much bread/as many meatballs (as T).*
- ii. *J has too much bread/too many meatballs (for his own good).*
- iii. *J has that much bread/that many meatballs.*
- iv. *J has so much bread/so many meatballs [that…]*
- v. *J has more bread/more meatballs (than T).*
- vi. *J has the most bread/the most meatballs (of all/in the whole class).*
- vii. *J has enough bread/enough meatballs (to Y/ for Y).*

Such structures are relevant to the questions above for a number of reasons. First, they involve a whole set of structures that are interlinked. By examining their development, we can explore the extent to which a child builds up a system, rather than (or in addition to) storing individual constructions, and we might discover the point at which such a system might emerge.

Second, the structures are complex, both syntactically and semantically, as outlined below. An examination of their acquisition by children can therefore provide some insight into how children tackle complex constructs with complex interrelations.

Third, they involve individual lexical items that themselves show a range of lexical complexity. Many of the lexical items are polysemous or homophonous (e.g., *as* [*J is as tall as H; J cried as he entered the room; J works as a plumber*], *too* [*J is too tall; M is tall, too*], *so* [*J is so happy; J sat down so he could rest, and Mary did so too*]). Many of them show syntactic co-occurrence or agreement patterns; for example, *-er* must take standard marker *than*; degree marker *as* requires standard marker *as*; and so forth.

Fourth, discovering how these develop across time could provide a possible window into the relationship between syntactic, semantic, and cognitive development. The semantic content of these structures is closely tied with certain cognitive concepts (e.g., they involve comparison across instances or items, assessment of relative degrees of the presence of a property or item, assessment of the serial order of the presence of such a property, and so forth). They may thus provide substantial information on the relationship between language and cognition and possible insights into how and when language might "lead" cognition, and how and when cognition might "lead" language.

Fifth, examining such a broad range of structures in several children's development may provide a possible window into universals and individual differences across children in the course of development.

In what follows, I will first review some of the relevant properties of the syntactic and semantic makeup of these structures, in order that we can then examine the syntactic and semantic development in children. It will become clear, even with this rather cursory overview, that these structures involve complex and sometimes unpredictable relations, both at the syntactic and semantic levels. The syntactic complexities involve orders of constituents within phrases, co-occurrence restrictions both within local forms and between elements and their complement types, and lexically specific idiosyncratic patterns of usage; the semantic complexities involve the polysemy of many forms, restrictions on semantic modification, and relative levels of semantic complexity across forms. I will go into considerable detail regarding the syntactic and semantic patterns observed in adult English, to provide the reader with a taste of the complex nature of this set of structures, and to help the reader gain an appreciation of the enormity of the task faced by the young language-learning child.

Following the initial layout of these structures, I will then outline some of what is already known about the acquisition of such structures. This will then be followed with the data from the children reported on here and an assessment of the relevance of those data to theories of acquisition in general.

SYNTACTIC CONSIDERATIONS

Local Form

One could briefly describe the shared syntactic makeup of these structures as involving degree markers, as in (2a), and quantifiers, as in (2b).

(2) a. Degree markers: *as, too, that, so, -er, -est, how*
    b. Quantifiers: *much, many, little, few, enough*

With adjectives, the degree markers occur immediately before the adjective in most cases: *as happy, too happy, that happy, so happy, how happy*, as in (3a), but the bound forms *-er* and *-est* attach as suffixes to many adjectives (*happier, happiest*).

With nouns, the degree markers alone cannot occur immediately preceding the noun, but must occur with a quantifier, as in (3b): *as much bread, too much bread, that much bread, so little bread, how little bread*. Mass nouns select *much* and *little* as quantifiers, count nouns select *many* and *few* (*as many meatballs, too few meatballs*, etc.).

The bound forms *-er* and *-est* can overtly attach to the quantifier *few* (*fewer, fewest*), but suppletive forms *more* and *most* are used instead of *much-er, many-*

er, much-est, many-est. Similarly, suppletive forms *less* and *least* occur instead of *little-er* and *little-est*.[3]

The quantifier *enough* can occur with adjectives, but must occur after them (*happy enough*), as well as with (both mass and count) nouns (*enough bread, enough meatballs*), as in (3c). *Enough* cannot occur with any of the degree markers: **so enough bread, *that happy enough*.

(3) a. *as/too/so happy*
b. *as much/too little/so much bread* [Mass N]
as many/too few/so few meatballs [Count N]
c. *happy enough*
enough bread
enough meatballs

Finally, while many adjectives (mostly single syllable, and two-syllable forms ending in an unstressed vowel (*happy*), /ər/, or syllabic /l/, plus a few idiosyncratic forms (e.g., *quiet*) (Quirk & Greenbaum, 1973)) show suffix *-er* and *-est* for the comparative and superlative; longer adjectives (other two-syllable forms and longer forms) take *more* and *most*: *more intelligent, the most interesting*.

The precise syntactic structure of these forms is hotly debated. Disagreements concern, among others, the status of the degree markers: Are they specifiers of APs, as in (4) (e.g., White, 1998); modifiers of As, as in (5) (Bresnan, 1973); DP heads, as in (6) (Corver, 1990; White, 1998), etc.? Is *more* of the Q (Corver, 1997b) or Deg (Rijkhoek, 1998) category, and are *enough, much*, etc., Q heads (Corver, 1997b) or adjuncts (Doetjes, 1997, Doetjes, Nelleman, & Van de Koot 1998)? Also in dispute is the number of distinct structural types involved (e.g., Bresnan, 1973: one; Corver, 1997b: two; Kennedy & McNally, 2005: three), related to the questions of whether the adjectival modifiers and the nominal modifiers derive from the same or different structures and whether the degree markers are of the same or different syntactic classes (Deg vs. Q). (For a sample of alternative treatments, see, e.g., Bowers, 1970; Bresnan, 1973; Corver, 1997a, 1997b; Doetjes, 1997; Doetjes, Neeleman, & Van de Koot, 1998; Hackl, 2001; Huckin, 1977; Huddleston, 1967; Keenan, 1987; Kennedy, 2000; Kennedy & McNally, 2005; Liao, 2005; Matushansky, 2002; Napoli, 1983; Pinkham, 1985; Rayner & Banks, 1990; Rijkhoek, 1998; White, 1998). (See Androutsopoulou and Español-Echevarría [2006] for a comparison of English with another language, Spanish.)

These considerations are well beyond the scope of this chapter. However, they highlight the intricate nature of the syntax of even the local constructs and should alert us to potential key questions regarding acquisition: Does a given modifier (e.g., *so*) emerge with adjectives and nouns at the same time, and do children treat its use with adjectives and nouns in the same way? Do all, or even a subset, of the modifiers develop concurrently, indicating a shared syntactic source, or do they develop separately?

---

3 The forms *littler* and *littlest* occur as the comparative and superlative forms of the adjective *little*, of course, but not as the comparative and superlative of the quantifier *little*.

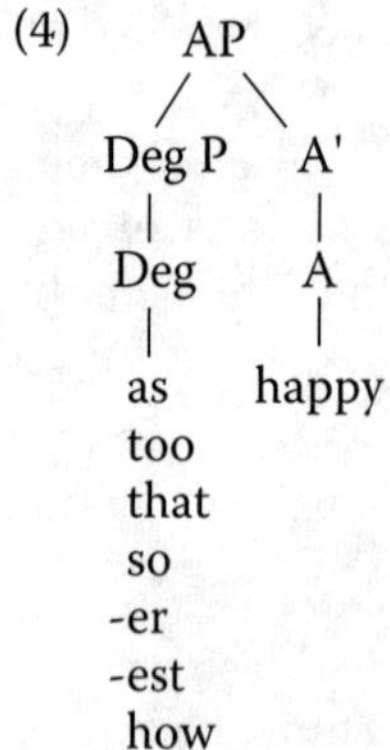

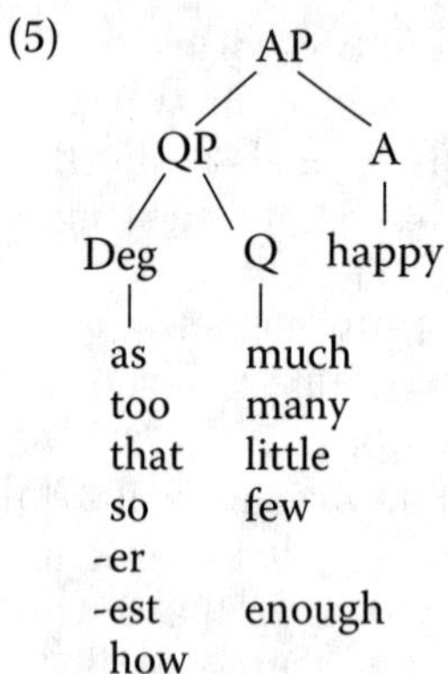

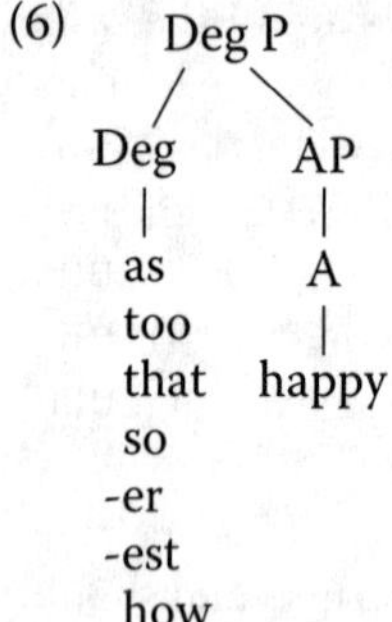

Elaborated Forms

Beyond these local/immediate patterns, one key feature of these constructs in English is the ability to "stack" or employ "multiple modification" with these phrases. Thus, one can use phrases such as *much, so much, as much* in conjunction with Degs *too* and *-er* as in (7):

(7) a. Adjectives:
J is much too courageous for...
J is so much happier than T
J is as much more courageous than T as B is.
b. Nouns:
M has much more courage than A.
M has so much more courage than A.
M has that many too many meatballs.
M has many too many friends.

Again, researchers have disagreed on the best syntactic analysis of such structures in the adult language, primarily according to whether local degree modifiers are viewed as specifiers of AP, in which case, the structure might be, for example [$_{AP}$ [$_{DegP}$ [$_{DP}$ so much] more] courageous] (Bresnan, 1973); or as DP heads, in which case, the structure might be [$_{DegP}$[$_{DP}$ so much] [$_{DegP}$ more [$_{AP}$ courageous]]] (White, 1998).

Despite the differences in analyses, some important aspects of the behavior of these structures are relevant to any analysis. For the purposes of exposition, I will not make any assumptions regarding the internal structure of these constructs and will use "Deg" and "Q" for the elements in each of the two "modifiers" in the sequence, so each multiple modification can be described as involving a sequence Deg_1 - Q_1 - Deg_2 - Q_2 [with or without one or more elements in this sequence as null elements].

Some important co-occurrence restrictions apply to the multiple modification of forms:

First, the first modifier must have a nonempty Q_1. One cannot say, for example, **so more courageous*, **so happier*, **so more courage*, but must say *so much more courageous, so much happier, so much more courage.*

Second, Deg_2 must be nonempty. One cannot say, for example, **so much ____ much courage*, **this much____ much courage*, **that much ____ happy* but can say, e.g., *so much more courage, this much too much courage, that much happier.* This implies that *enough* cannot occur as Q_2, which is the case: **so much enough courage.*

Third, the only degree markers that can occur as Deg_2 are *-er* and *too*: *so much happier, this much too much milk* are possible, but not **so much as much courage*, **so much as courageous*, **this much enough milk*. This appears to be related to the semantics of *-er* and *too*, described below.

Finally, multiple modification is not restricted to these forms. Other quantifiers and terms expressing quantities besides *much, many, few,* and *little* can occur in initial position, as in (8):

(8) *J gave us two gallons too much water.*
J has five dollars too much.
There are tons more people here than we thought.
J is five inches taller than M.
This dress is a (little) bit too short.
It is way too short.
It is a lot shorter than hers.

(See Kennedy and McNally [2005] for a proposed syntactic and semantic analysis of the full set of forms into three types.)

Status of **Very**

One word that participates in many of these constructions is *very*. The syntactic status of *very* is unclear (e.g., Androutsopoulou & Español-Echevarría, 2006; Bresnan, 1973). In some ways, *very* acts similar to the Deg markers above, in that it can combine with adjectives and quantifiers, as in (9a) and can combine with a Q_1 *much/many* to act as a modifier of a Deg_2 - Q_2 structure, as in (9b).

(9) a. *very happy*
very much bread/very many meatballs
b. *very much bigger*
very much more intelligent
very much too big
very much more N
very many more N

Compare (9) with the forms in (10) with the semantically similar forms *really* (and *real* in colloquial American English), which are not allowed in many of these structures. Note also that the acceptable forms—10d, 10f, 10h—take on the meaning "truly much bigger," and so on, not "very much bigger."

(10) a. *really/real happy*
b. **really/ *real much/many N*
c. **[really/real much] bigger*
d. *really [much bigger]*
e. *?[really much] too big*
f. *really [much too big]*
g. *?[really much/many] more N*
h. *really [much/many more N]*

On the other hand, *very* is unlike the Deg markers in that it can modify a second Deg_2, *-est*, without an intervening Q_1, as in (11a) (and 11b?), and it can occur in combination with an immediately preceding Deg_1 without *much* intervening, as in (11c). However, even its acceptability modifying *-est* is restricted: It is (marginally?) acceptable with *most* in adjectival phrases (11b), but not in nominal phrases (11d).

(11) a. *the very biggest/ *the very much biggest*
b. *? the very most intelligent*
c. *so very big/ *so much very big*
d. **? the very most bread/ *? the very most meatballs*

These idiosyncratic properties of *very* appear related to and grounded in its source meaning, "true," coming from Old French *verai* (F *vrai*) (*Cassell's Concise*

Dictionary, 1997; see Slobin, 1997, for similar relic semantics invading the use of indirect and direct object markers in Chinese and Persian.) Indeed, in earlier times, English allowed *verier* and *veriest*, but these are now obsolete. It is also of note that there are some polysemous uses of *very* that also reflect and derive from this earlier meaning; see (12).

(12) Polysemous uses of *very*:
  a. *the very end; the very top; the very bottom* [= absolute]
  b. *her very own; the very same day* [= absolutely, exactly]
  c. *the very thought, the very idea* [= mere?]

Order of Constituents within NPs

When an NP contains both a nominal Det (*a, the*) and an adjectival phrase containing a degree marker, the order of constituents depends on whether the Deg form is bound (*-er, -est*) or free (*too, so, as, this, that*). If Deg is free (and, therefore, precedes the adjective), the nominal Det must occur between the A and the N, as in (13). (Note that in this regard *very* does not act like a free Deg; see (14).)

(13) a. **a too happy N*
  b. *too happy a N*

  c. **an as happy N as....*
  d. *as happy a N as...*

  e. **a that happy N*
  f. *that happy a N*

  g. **a so happy N*
  h. *so happy a N*

(14) a. *a very happy N*
  b. **very happy a N*

Also note that an alternative to *so A a N*, as in (13h), is *such a A N*, as in (15) (see Bresnan, 1973):[4]

(15) *such a happy N*

When Deg is *-er* and *-est*, however, both orders are used, but acceptability depends on whether the *-er* and *-est* have been suffixed to the following adjective or occur in the suppletive forms *more* and *most*, and on the desired meaning. In (16), for example, the order in (16b), (16f), and (16h) appear archaic or obsolete, but in (16d), the comparable order appears acceptable. In (16g), *the most handsome N*

---

[4] Note that if constructions like that in (15) are viewed as deriving from *a so much happy N*, with a rule that *so + much* → *such*, there is a problem in that this rule could not apply to comparable phrases such as *so much rice* and *so many things*, as these do not mean the same as *such rice* and *such things* (Bresnan, 1973).

has a superlative meaning, whereas *a most handsome N* has an "intensifier" meaning (= "a very handsome N"). In contrast, in (16h), only the form with *a* is even marginally acceptable, and it carries the meaning of intensification; the form with *the* appears unacceptable.

(16) *I never saw...*
  a. *a happier N*
  b. Archaic?: *happier a N*
  c. *a more handsome N*
  d. *more handsome a N*

  He is...
  e. *the happiest N*
  f. *?*happiest the N*
  g. *a/the most handsome N*
  h. Archaic?: *most handsome a/*the N*

Long Distance Co-Occurrence Limitations

Complement Types One key aspect of the syntax of these forms is the co-occurrence restrictions on the forms that complements must take for certain structures. The degree markers *as*, *-er*, *-est*, *too*, and *enough* all take strictly constrained standard markers and complement types. With degree markers *as* and *-er*, the standard markers are strictly *as* and *than*, respectively:[5]

(17) a. *T is as happy as J.*
  b. *T is as happy *like/*than/*from/*to/*that/*when/*of J.*
  c. *T is happier than J.*
  d. *T is happier *from/*to/*of/*in J.*

With *-est*, *too*, and *enough*, wider options of complement types are available, although still restricted:

(18) a. *T is the happiest in the world/of all/ (out) of that group.*
  b. *T is the happiest *from/*than them.*
  c. *T is too short to play that part/for that part.*
  d. *T is too short *of/*in/*than X.*
  e. *T is tall enough to play that part/for that part.*
  f. *T is tall enough *of/*in/*than X.*

The degree markers *so* and *how* do not usually occur with complements (but see, e.g., *T is so happy that he can't stop smiling*). Nor does the degree marker *that*; this is because *that* itself expresses the standard of comparison. Thus, *T is that tall* is equivalent to *T is as tall as that.*

---

[5] In the case of *as...as*, it is of note that the degree marker *as* can be omitted in some contexts, such as more archaic uses (*Its fleece was white as snow*, *He came in quiet as a mouse*) and some more colloquial and idiomatic speech (*He's blind as a bat*).

Obligatoriness of Complements For most of these forms, in principle, the complement/standard of comparison is not obligatory. If a complement is not specified, the standard of comparison is understood from the discourse or context of the utterance. Thus, given the appropriate contexts, one can say: *This is just as tall/taller/the tallest/too tall/tall enough.*

Nevertheless, an initial examination of real language use reveals important differences in the occurrence of complements across structures: A good, and pertinent, example is a comparison of *as…as* and *-er…than* constructions.

To gauge the occurrence of complements with these two structures, two types of data were consulted: first, a set of written texts, and, second, a collection of Kuczaj's Abe transcripts from CHILDES (http://childes.psy.cmu.edu). The data show that degree marker *as* is invariably accompanied by standard marker *as* and that *-er* is much less reliably linked with *than*.

Written Texts: A search in three written texts (Oller & Eilers, 2002; Schwartz, 2003, n.d.) involving eight different writers and a total of 99,241 words, reveals the following:

For *as…as*: Out of 510 total uses of (any meaning of) *as*, only 5.3% (N = 27) involved the degree marker *as*. But within these 27, fully 92% (i.e., 25) involved overt specification of the standard of comparison with *as*…. The remaining two occurrences were both of the type *as A or A-er than* (e.g., "as large or larger than…"), where the use of *than* precluded the use of *as*. In addition, there were other uses of *as* showing distinct semantic usage, see below, as well as two occurrences of *as much as + Number*, three occurrences of *as long as* to mean "providing/provided," and 30 occurrences of *as well as* (plus 12 occurrences of *as well*). Thus, when degree marker *as* does occur, it seems to be highly linked overtly with its standard marker *as*.

For *-er…than*: There were 402 total occurrences of *-er* forms with comparative import in these written texts. (This leaves out idiomatic or frozen phrases such as adverbial *further, the latter, no longer* (time), and so forth.) Of the 402 *-er* comparatives, 160 involved *better, fewer,* and *significantly* A-*er*, mostly used in reporting of statistical results in which one or other group was reported as performing "better" or "significantly higher/lower" than another group. Since the occurrence of these forms in these academic texts may inflate the patterns artificially and could skew the general distribution of the use of *than* phrases, the remaining 242 occurrences were examined without these. The remaining 242 occurrences of *-er* forms show 31.8% of the constructions including a *than* phrase, and 68.2% without. Thus, the link between *-er* and its standard marker *than* appears less strong than that between degree marker *as* and its standard marker *as*.

Furthermore, the occurrence of the *than* phrase appears to be related to the overall structure of the sentence. When the *-er* phrases occurred with *than,* only 33.8% of the sentences showed the comparative as a noun modifier (i.e., 66.2% were like *larger than X*, not *larger N than X*). In contrast, when the *-er* phrase occurred without *than*…, fully 78.2% of the sentences showed the A-*er* modifying a noun (e.g., *larger N*). This difference is likely related to differences in the informational structure of the discourse in the two cases.

It is also worth noting that both *A-er*...*than* and *A-er* without *than* showed similar numbers (16 vs. 15, i.e., 20.8% of constructs with *than* vs. 9.1% of constructs without *than*, respectively) of constructs involving qualification of the *A-er* form through modification by *much, a lot, slightly, somewhat*, etc. (e.g., "much stronger than," "slightly smaller than," "considerably weaker than," "notably smaller").

Adult Speech to Children: These glances at the usage of forms by adults in written texts suggest that children may be confronted by a number of different patterns of co-occurrence of usage across what may be deceptively similar constructions. In order to gauge whether these patterns hold also in adults' speech to children, a collection of Kuczaj's Abe files on CHILDES (http://childes.psy.cmu.edu) were examined.

For *as...as*: To examine the use of *as*...*as* by adults, the first and last 50 Abe files (files 1–50 and 161–210) were examined. In all 100 transcripts, Abe's mother and father showed a total of 32 utterances in which (all meanings of) *as* was used. Out of these 32, 4 involved *as* as a standard marker occurring with *same* ("same... as"). Of the remaining 28, 26 (92.9%) involved the degree marker *as* (as opposed to other semantic uses of *as*), a proportion of usage that is much higher than for the adult written uses of degree marker *as*.[6] (Of these 26 utterances, 23 (88.5%) also included the standard marker *as*. Of these 23, 13 were *as soon as*, 4 were *as big as*, 2 *as far as*, 2 *as many as*, and 1 each of *as long as* and *as good as*. The three that did not include standard marker *as* were all within the scope of negation—*not as bright in here, not as annoying, not quite as wobbly*.)

This high proportion of occurrence of the standard marker *as* is in line with the high occurrence in the adult written texts, indicating a reliable occurrence of standard marker *as* whenever degree marker *as* is used. Interestingly, on one occasion when Abe used degree marker *as* without the standard of comparison (in Abe 23), and another when Abe similarly used *same* (in Abe 180), his parents questioned him: "as much money as what?" "the same as what?"—suggesting the adults' expectation that degree *as* is accompanied by a standard of comparison introduced by *as*.

For *-er...than*: Adults' use of *-er* forms in speech to children was similarly examined in the first 50 Abe files. In those files, Abe's mother and father and one other adult used 57 comparative forms. Of those, 55 (96.5%) occurred without an accompanying *than* phrase. One of the two that did occur with *than* was used in reaction to Abe's "huh?" when the mother first used *A-er* without *than*; the other was used by the father in addressing the mother, not Abe. Among the 55 *-er* forms without *than*, 26 (47.3%) were uses of *later*, 14 (25.5%) were uses of *better*, all but twice in conjunction with a verb (*like it, taste, make it, shows up, set, look, feel, aim, work, looks*). Only two out of all 57 utterances contained a modified noun (e.g., "better idea"), one of these in imitation of Abe ("bigger shoes").[7]

---

6 The remaining two uses of *as* were: "We want them to do as they want to do" and "as a matter of fact."

7 See Alrenga (2005) for a discussion of the occurrence of weak and strong nominal determiners in attributive comparative constructions, in which a comparative adjective occurs pronominally.

It is also interesting to note that the only uses of *A-er* involving multiple modification in speech directed to Abe involved *a little ((tiny) bit) A-er*, which occurred in 6 of the 55 utterances (10.9%) without *than* phrases. There was also one use of *a lot older than*, but this was directed by the father to the mother. Finally, there was a relatively high number of noncomparative uses of *better* (9 uses) as a quasi-modal, as in his father's "we better run fast if we see any ghosts # huh?" (Abe 46).[8]

These data on *-er* indicate that the link between *-er* and *than* in adults' speech to children is much more tenuous than in the written adult texts, which also showed a less reliable link between *-er* and *than* than between *as* and *as*. This suggests that the link of *-er* with *than* may lack "validity" (in the Competition Model sense [MacWhinney, 1987; McDonald, 1989]) for children. At the same time, the qualification of *A-er* with multiple modification may be fairly similar in incidence to comparable forms in adult language to adults (here, use in about 10% of *-er* forms that occurred without *than* phrases).

We will see below in the data from Sadie and Rachel that these differences between such constructs as *as…as* and *-er…than* may have significant consequences in children's acquisition of these forms.

Challenges for the Child

These syntactic considerations highlight a number of aspects that may pose challenges for children. These include:

- Differences between adjectival and nominal structures in the overt use of a quantifier after Deg modifiers (*so happy, *so much happy, *so bread, so much bread*): Do children show evidence at any point of treating these as having either separate or common source structure?
- Suppletive forms (*less, least, more, most*): At what point do children realize that these express comparative and superlative notions and are related to *-er* and *-est*?
- Idiosyncrasies of the placement and use of *very*: Do children treat *very* like the Deg markers?
- Polysemy of *very* (and others, see below)
- Local distributional restrictions:
  - Distributional restrictions concerning mass/count forms (*much, many*, etc.)
  - Distribution of *-er* versus *more* as comparative markers on adjectives.

  How and when do children link these? Or do they?

---

[8] In Abe's speech across these transcripts, he used comparative-looking forms 46 times, all but once with just three forms, *better, bigger*, and *later*: He used Modal *better* 9 times, *later (on)* 10 times, *better* with a verb 9 times (6 of these: *feel better*), *bigger* 10 times, mostly (80%) with *grow* ("grow bigger," "grow bigger and bigger," "grow bigger and biggest" [also "grow big and big"]). He used *bigger N* 7 times, and *bluer* (with uncertain semantic content) once.

- Long distance distributional restrictions:
  - Co-occurrence restrictions, e.g., between *-er* and *than* and between *as* and *as*: At what point do children observe these?
- Degree of obligatoriness of standard of comparison: Does the highly reliable and available link in *as...as*, for example, make *as...as* easier to learn than the largely unavailable link between *-er* and *than*?
- Form of multiple modification:
  - Must have a nonempty Q_1
  - Restricted to modification of *-er* and *too* as Deg_2

  When do children begin multiple modification, and do they observe these restrictions?
- Order of constituents:
  - *A enough* vs. *enough N*
  - Order within NPs with nominal determiners (*so great a man* vs. *such a great man; too great a man* vs. *a very great man*; etc.)

  When do children observe these?

We will see that all of these syntactic matters come to bear and pose their own challenges in children's development of these forms.[9] While it is impossible to address all of them thoroughly within the scope of this chapter, the longitudinal data presented will help provide some insights into their answers.

SEMANTIC CONSIDERATIONS

An examination of the semantic content of these forms provides another window into the challenges faced by the child in acquiring these forms. I will discuss the major semantic notions encoded through these forms; examine the complexities involved with the encoding of these notions, their polysemous character, and their relationship with cognitive concepts; and return again to the challenges these pose for children acquiring these forms.

Meanings Encoded

INTENSIFICATION

Modifiers of Adjectives or Quantifiers: First, a wide collection of these forms, as well as others, are used to express INTENSIFICATION,[10] or to express "very X" (or

[9] There are, of course, many other matters relevant to the acquisition of the syntax of comparatives, which will not be covered here. These include, for example, the syntax and semantics of post- and prenominal comparatives (*She met a dancer younger than Mary; She met a younger dancer than Mary*) (e.g., Lechner, 2000); comparative correlatives (*The more you eat, the fatter you get*; e.g., den Dikken, 2005).

[10] SMALL CAPS will be used throughout to represent semantic concepts.

a similar paraphrasable notion involving "very"). These include all of the fairly standard degree-marking forms in (19), used to modify adjectives and quantifiers, as well as more colloquial forms such as those in (20) (which have often evolved by semantic bleaching from other meanings).

(19) *so* ____
very ____
really ____
real ____
quite ____

reduplication ("a big big X," "a little little X," "itsy bitsy spider")
lengthening ("a biiiiig X," "a liiiiiittle X")

(20) *great* ____ ("great big"; selects for *big*? Probably a variant of reduplication, given "big" meaning of *great*— "The Great Lakes")
all ____ (as in "all dirty," "all clean," "all messy," where *all* is not interpreted as a quantifier but as an intensifier)
pitch ____ ("pitch black"; selects for *black, dark*; from original meaning, "as black/dark as pitch")
damn/darn ____ ("a damn/darn good read")
stone ____ ("stone cold"; selects for *cold*; but see: "I'm stone in love with you" [Stylistics])

The meaning INTENSIFICATION is also often expressed on adjectives and quantifiers with the noninterrogative uses of *how*, as in (21).

(21) "How sweet it is to be loved by you." [sung by James Taylor/Carole King, lyrics and music by Holland, Dozier, & Holland]
"I just called to say I love you. I just called to say how much I care. I do. (…) And I mean it from the bottom of my heart." [composed and sung by Stevie Wonder]

This use of *how* is quite common in parents' speech to children, as in the following casually overheard examples:[11]

(22) [Dad to child, about 3 1/2—Dad bringing pizza to table in airport:]
Dad: Look **how big** this pizza is!

[11] Note: Throughout the text, and in all tables, cited forms shown in bold are the target forms. Underlining of cited forms indicates stress.

[M, F, and child (boy, about 3) have walked out to end of pier]
M: Do you see **how far out** we are!
Boy: How? [with falling intonation][12]

Finally, while the marker *-est* has as its central use the marking of the superlative (below), it is also used, in a semantically bleached fashion, to express intensification, as in (23).

(23) *This dress is made of the finest silk.* [to mean "very fine silk," not necessarily the absolute best]
She is a/the most intelligent person! [to mean "really intelligent," not necessarily the most intelligent]
This is the best ice cream! [to mean "really good," not necessarily the best]

Multiple Modification: The meaning INTENSIFICATION is also expressed through quantifiers and other forms modifying a degree marker, Deg_2, as in (24).

(24) *a lot* ____ ("a lot bigger"; selects for *-er*; cannot be used with the other Deg_2 form, *too*— *a lot too big)
much ____ ("much bigger," "much too big," "much more," "much too many"; can be used with either Deg_2 form, *-er* or *too*)

---

[12]The response of this child, using *How?* with falling intonation and without the modified adjective, instead of the appropriate *How far?* suggests that the child does not treat *how far* as a constituent. This type of query is common among young children. Other examples from my son, Jaime, are the following:

(i) (J 3;9.2)
M: How old is Amy today?
J: **How** [with falling intonation]?
M: Four.
J: Why?
M: 'Cause it's her birthday.
J: Is she a mommy?
M: No—she's not as big as her mommy, is she?
J: What's her mommy?
M: How old is her mommy [checking that is what J meant]?
[J nods].
M: Twenty-nine.
J: And what is Rachel?
[J answers own question by holding up one finger].
M: One.
J: What is Julio? [re: boy living in apt downstairs]
M: How old is Julio?
J: **How** [with falling intonation]?
M: Two.

(ii) (J 3;9.11)
J: Cows have three feet.
M: Uh-uh. [="no"]. How many do they have?
J: **How** [with falling intonation]?
M: Four feet.

way ____ ("way bigger," "way too big," "way more," "way too much/many"; can be used with either Deg_2 form, *-er* or *too*)

EXTREME ENDS Another group of forms express the placement of a property or quantity at (the absolute) extreme ends of a scale—that is, encoding that the item in question exemplifies the property in question more than any other item it is being compared with. As noted by Ultan (1972), these express "absolute disparity" (shown through the occurrence of *the* as the accompanying article). These include *-est* and its suppletive variants, as in (25).

(25) ____ *-est* ["biggest," "most intelligent," etc.]
best [= good + -est]
worst [= bad + -est]

The proper identification of X as the entity with the highest degree of presence of some property entails (at least an implicit) comparison of the level of the property in that entity with every other entity. In this regard, the superlative is similar in use to words like *favorite, top, bottom, first, last.* This makes a superlative, in the adult language, a "specialized" comparative, and this is reflected in the fact that across languages, superlatives are generally more marked than comparatives (Ultan, 1972) (e.g., superlative degree markers are often derived from comparative markers in languages, but not vice-versa). However, because superlatives usually refer to items that show extreme presence of a property, the more complex processing involved in multiple comparisons may be "bypassed" at least sometimes when superlatives are used, which may lead ultimately to a simpler processing than for comparatives. This simpler processing results in the common evolution across languages of the superlative form into a form used for INTENSIFICATION, as in (23) above (Ultan, 1972).

RELATIVE POSITION ON A SCALE A number of these forms express the relative position of an entity along a scale or property in relation to either some explicitly specified standard of comparison or one that is implicitly understood from the context. These include *-er, too, enough,* and *as*. The comparative expresses the relative position of an entity or property X in relation to a standard of comparison, Y, along a scale. Explicit comparatives thus

> Establish an ordering between objects *x* and *y* with respect to gradable property *g* using special morphology whose conventional meaning has the consequence that the degree to which *x* is *g* exceeds the degree to which *y* is *g*. (Kennedy, 2005, p. 7)[13]

[13] Note that all gradable predicates, including comparatives "...map objects onto abstract representations of measurement (SCALES) formalized as sets of values (DEGREES) ordered along some dimension (HEIGHT, LENGTH, WEIGHT, etc.)" (Kennedy 2005: 2).

The forms *too X* and *X enough* express the surpassing of an upper limit on a desired range or the surpassing of a lower limit on a desired range, respectively.

The meanings of the negative forms of these constructs are fairly straightforward for *-er* and *enough*: *not…X-er* denies that the item in question surpasses the standard of comparison (and is, therefore, either equal to it or below it in the presence of the property in question); *not…enough* denies that the item in question has passed the lower limit into the desired range of a property.

However, for *too X*, the negative has two separate interpretations. When *too X* is accompanied by a complement, or one is understood from the context—"J is not too old to play Peter Pan"—or when the negation is denying a prior assertion—"J is too old; No, he's not too old"—the interpretation is one in which *not…too X* denies the surpassing of an upper limit on a desired range. However, when *not…too X* is not accompanied by a *to X* or *for X* complement expression, as in (26), the negative form is ambiguous. It often does not mean the denial of a surpassing of an upper limit, but is rather the equivalent of the negation of *very X*, with the resulting meaning "not very X."[14]

(26) *T is not too bright.*
I don't have too many cards left.

The equative form, *as…as*, expresses that X reaches the same level as another entity Y along some scale. An important characteristic of the semantics of *as…as*, as for all scalar predicates (Gazdar, 1979; Horn, 2004; Levinson, 2000) is that it only asserts a lower limit (Horn, 1972), not an upper limit. Note, for example, that *as…as* is not equivalent to *the same…as* in (27) to (32). While in (27), the two appear more or less synonymous, this is not true for the others. In (28), (a) indicates that J is shorter than T, while (b) does not carry that implication. In (29), (a) suggests that J has just made it to T's height, while (b) is more likely to be a sarcastic quip that J and T are not the same height at all. A form like (30a) usually means that J is shorter than T, while (30b) means simply that the two are different heights (and J may be taller). And the forms in (31a) and (32a) are perfectly acceptable, while those in (31b) and (32b) are marginally acceptable, if acceptable at all.

---

[14] I am focusing primarily on internal negation, rather than external negation. Internal negation refers to the normal uses of negation, in which an expression is embedded under a negative term. External negation refers to negation that applies to the choice of expression; it questions the appropriateness of that expression over another. As examples, (iii) presents examples of internal negation, (iv) examples of external negation.

(iii) a. Today's not a cold day. [i.e., it's warm]
b. I don't have any sisters. [i.e., I have no female siblings]
c. Bryn Terfel didn't sing last night. [i.e., no melodious sounds came from his mouth]
d. This window isn't too big. [i.e., it's not very big]

(iv) a. Today's not a **cold** day, it's freezing.
b. I don't have **any** sisters; I have extra special sisters.
c. Bryn Terfel didn't **sing** last night; he warbled like the angels.
d. This window isn't **too** big; it fits the opening exactly.

(27) a. *J is as tall as T.*
b. *J is the same height as T.*

(28) a. *J is almost as tall as T.*
b. *J is almost the same height as T.*

(29) a. *J is hardly as tall as T.*
b. *J is hardly the same height as T.*

(30) a. *J is not as tall as T.*
b. *J is not the same height as T.*

(31) a. *J is as tall as T, if not taller.*
b. *? *J is the same height as T, if not a greater height.*

(32) a. *J is at least as tall as T.*
b. *? *J is at least the same height as T.*

The reason for this discrepancy is that *as…as* asserts meeting the lower limit of a range on a scale (Horn, 1972), with that lower limit specified by the standard of comparison ("T"). This implies a direction on the scale, going from the lower levels to the higher levels. The use of *as…as* conversationally implicates "not more than Y," but this implicature can be overridden, as in (31) and (32), or as in "I'm certainly/at least as old as you (if not older, in fact older….)" (Horn, 1972). I shall return to this below.

One final form that should be mentioned in relation to relative position on a scale is the interrogative use of *how*. *How X* ("How many do you want?" "How blue are his eyes?" "How deep is your love?") questions the relative position of an entity along some property or quantity—thus, asking where along a scale this particular item falls. Some noninterrogative uses also relate to the relative position on a scale, as in, *Let's see how many beads we have*, or *The inspector wants to know how clean the restaurant is*. This scalar use of *how*, questioning the relative placement of some item along the scale in question, stands alongside the intensifier use discussed in relation to (21) and (22) above.

Complexities Involved

Polysemy of Forms One notable aspect of these forms is that they frequently exemplify polysemous uses.[15] Take, for example, *as*. In addition to its equative/degree marking use, *as* has a number of other meanings. Some of these uses are quite frequent, as exemplified by the written texts examined above: Out of 510 uses of *as* in the written texts, we find the following distribution of uses:

as = degree marker (discussed above): 5.3%
as = "like"/"same as": *as it is in Grade 5*; *as in Miami* [16.1%]

[15]They can also exemplify homonymic uses—e.g., *-er* of the comparative vs. agentive *-er*. But most of the uses discussed here are taken to be cases of polysemy, unless otherwise noted, so I will use the term *polysemy* throughout.

as = "categorized as": *he worked as a chef; regarded as prestigious; treated as a variable* [32.2%]
as = "according to": *as measured by, as explained by* [10.8%]
as = "during" or "because": *as he was leaving; as she had heard the news* [10.4%]

In addition, there are many idiomatic and semi-idiomatic uses, including *as well (as)* [8.2%]; *(such) as* [5.9%]; *as a result (of)* [1.8%]; *as a whole* [1.6%]; *as opposed to* [1.9%]; and, less frequently, *as much as + Number, as long as* [= "provided"], *as follows, as an example, as a consequence of, as compared to/with, as if, as such, as to/for* [= "about"], *insofar as, as of* [these latter uses about 5.9% all together]).

Many of the other forms are similarly polysemous: e.g., *so* [intensifier (*so big*), "thus" (*it was dark, so she turned on the light*), place holder (*he did so*), etc.],[16] *too* [affirmative *too big* versus negative *not too big*; (homonymic?) conjunction *too*; etc.], and *very*, mentioned above. (This is also true of some of the other relevant forms as well; e.g., *some*—see below.) It is not known to what extent such polysemy may affect acquisition. Do all children acquire the same meanings for a form in the same order (i.e., for the same submeanings first, second, etc.)? Does acquisition of one meaning deter the acquisition of another for the same form? Does polysemous use make the meaning of a form opaque? For example, is it harder for English-speaking children to learn the superlative meaning of *-est* than the comparative meaning of *-er* because of the polysemous use of *-est* for both the superlative and intensification? Is it harder for Spanish-speaking children to discover the comparative meaning of *más—más grande* 'bigger,' than it is for English-speaking children to discover the comparative meaning of *-er* because of the frequent polysemous use of *más* as an intensifier in constructs such as *¡Qué niño más grande!* 'What a big boy!'

Semantic Modification Given the semantic content of these forms, we can return to a consideration of those Deg forms that allow for multiple modification. It will be recalled that only *-er* and *too* can occur as Deg_2, allowing modification such as *so much bigger, a lot taller, way too tall*, and so forth. We can now relate this to the semantics of these forms: The two forms *-er* and *too* express the relative position of an item on some scale, either in relation to a standard of comparison (in the case of *-er*) or in relation to some desired range on a scale (in the case of *too*). The multiple modification allowed with them expresses the quantification of

[16] Out of 85 uses of *so* in the written texts discussed earlier, the following meanings were in evidence:
so = intensifier [23.5%]
so = "thus": *it was dark outside, so she entered the house* [28.2%]
so = "in order that": *he coughed so she would know he was there* [9.4%]
so = place holder : *do/did/done so; and so on; especially so; and so forth* [25.9%]
so = "also," "and": *...and so did she* [3.5%]
and many idiomatic uses [about 9.4%], such as *so far* [= "up to now"], *or so* [= "more or less"/"something like that"], *so* = "in this way" ["so selected"], *so much/many X* [= "a certain amount/number of X"], *even so*.

the distance of the item being compared from that standard of comparison or the desired upper limit—*much taller, this much too tall.*

It is not surprising, perhaps, that multiple modification is not allowed, then, in cases in which other semantic notions do not involve such a comparison—as in the cases of those expressing INTENSIFICATION or EXTREME ENDS. However, there are some other forms that, like *-er* and *too*, express relative position on a scale, but that nevertheless do not allow expression of modification through multiple modifications. In particular, one cannot use multiple modification with *as* or with *enough*: **T is this much as tall as J*, **T is way tall enough for the part*, **T is as much tall enough for the part as J is.*

Another semantic anomaly concerns limitations on the choice of forms as Deg_1 - Q_1 modifiers that can occur with the two possible Deg_2 forms: While *-er* and *too* can both appear as Deg_2 with many forms (*much bigger, much too big; 5 feet bigger, 5 feet too big*), not all constructs are equally acceptable with *-er* and *too* as Deg_2 (*a lot bigger,* **a lot too big, so much bigger,* *?*so much too big*).

These anomalies can be seen as gaps in the system, insofar as not every Deg_2 element meeting the semantic requirements for multiple modification is acceptable within the adult system. How do such gaps affect the acquisition of these forms? Does the semantics of multiple modification guide syntactic development, or vice-versa (or is there an interaction of the two)? If semantics guides development, we might expect that when children first begin using multiple modification, they will use it for *-er* and *too*, but also overgeneralize it (only) to *as* and *enough* (*this (much) as big, so (much) big enough*). If syntax guides semantics, we might expect children to use multiple modification initially with Deg_2 - Q_2 forms that express wider notions than allowed semantically—producing, for example, *this (much) so big, so (much) biggest.*

Semantic/Cognitive Complexity? Finally, it appears that the semantic content of the forms in question can be ranked or compared in terms of the cognitive complexity that may be associated with understanding their full import.

Some forms—the intensifiers—express the presence of a property in one item. Others entail the assessment and comparison of the same property in two or more referents (*X-er, X-est* [in its full superlative meaning]). In terms of cumulative cognitive complexity, we can expect the latter types to be more complex than the former:

Intensification: Judge extent of A in X.
Comparative and Superlative: Judge extent of A in X and of A in Y, and compare those extents.

Still other forms (*too, enough*) demand the assessment of a property in some entity and a comparison of that extent to some desired range, whether that desired range is explicitly or implicitly specified. Again, in terms of cumulative cognitive complexity, we can expect these to be more complex than those expressing a simple specification of the extent of A in X:

Intensification: Judge extent of A in X.
Too and *enough*: Judge extent of A in X, and compare this with the limits on a desired range of that property A.

Finally, some of these expressions entail a direction of the range of a property on a scale. Thus, *-er, as, enough*, for example, express the assertion of meeting or surpassing some limit from below that limit. Their negation expresses that they have not met or have not surpassed that limit, again coming from the lower end of the scale upward. Thus, *J isn't taller than M* does not usually mean that J is shorter, just that he is either the same height or shorter; *J isn't as tall as M* does not usually mean that J might be taller than M, just usually that he is shorter; and so forth. Cognitively, the understanding of such forms, including the representation of a directional scale, is necessarily more complex than understanding forms that do not imply a direction on a scale and only specify whether a given point on a scale is met (e.g., *the same X, not the same X*).

Furthermore, these forms that involve an upward perspective on a scale generally carry the conversational implicature that a higher level on the scale does not apply. Thus, for example, *J is as tall as M* generally implies that J is not taller than M. This implicature is a default interpretation of scalar predicates and is not an absolute, as the implicature can be denied—*J is [at least] as tall as M; in fact, he's about a foot taller* (see Papafragou, 2003b; Papafragou & Musolino, 2003 for discussions). One can predict that the complex pragmatic signals that govern the licensing or denial of the implicature may demand cognitive abilities that go beyond the assertional aspects of these structures and will need to build on such understanding. As such, the child's facility with the pragmatics of implicature can be expected to be acquired after the semantic aspects of reference are in place.

Challenges for the Child These semantic aspects, like the syntactic aspects above, highlight some of the major challenges facing children acquiring the meanings of these constructs. These include:

- Many of the lexical items are polysemous: *very* (intensification, absolute, etc.), *-est* (superlative/extreme ends, intensification), *as, so, too X* vs. *not too X*, and so forth. How does the child discover the meanings associated with such forms, and does their polysemous nature affect acquisition?
- There are restrictions on semantic modification in multiple modification:
  - Only some Deg_2 meanings are modifiable through multiple modification— these have to do with relative position on a scale (*-er, too*); but not all forms expressing relative position on a scale can be modified in this way (e.g., *as, enough*, even *-est*). Do children attempt to express multiple modification for such forms?
  - While *-er* and *too* can both appear as Deg_2 with many Deg_1 - Q_1 forms, not all Deg - Q options are equally acceptable with *-er* and *too* as Deg_2. Again, do such gaps in the system pose significant challenges for children?

- Semantic/cognitive complexity:
  - While some forms entail the assessment of the presence of a property in one item (e.g., intensifiers— *very X, so X*), others entail the assessment and comparison of the same property in two or more referents (*X-er, X-est, as X as*).
  - Some forms (*too X, X enough*) entail the assessment of the presence of a property for some (often unexpressed) desired purpose, which entails a desired range of the property.
  - The proper use of some forms requires an understanding that their use implies a direction on the scale (e.g., *as X as, X enough*).
  - The proper interpretation of such forms further requires an understanding and control of the conversational implicatures associated with their use (i.e., understanding that a default interpretation implies that a stronger predicate on the same scale does not apply, but also that such an implicature can be modified—denied or asserted explicitly).[17]

  Do these differences in semantic/cognitive complexity affect the development of these forms in children's speech—especially their order of acquisition and any immature uses?

As with the syntactic complexities, all of these semantic factors play roles in the development of these forms. While it is, again, impossible to address all of these questions thoroughly here, the data presented will provide some insights into possible answers.

SNAPSHOT OF ACQUISITION FROM PREVIOUS RESEARCH

A great deal of work has focused on children's acquisition of some aspects of these structures. Most prominent among these is work on the acquisition of the comparative and superlative and work on the acquisition of the mass/count distinction; some recent work has also begun to address the acquisition of conversational implicature. There are also some suggestions of how children develop the syntax of multiply modified constructs. I will briefly outline some of this background literature before turning to the data at hand.

Comparative, Superlative, and Related Forms

There is a considerable body of literature suggesting that children's very early uses of several of these forms, in particular *A-er, too A, A-est*, express simply "X" or "very X" (Carey, 1978b; Clark, 1970; Donaldson & Wales, 1970; Ehri, 1976;

[17] Even beyond this, children will have to learn the direction of the implications attached to scalar predicates, as they do not always involve upward inferences, but sometimes downward orientation, as, for example, with *barely* (Horn, 1997).

Gathercole, 1979b, 1983; Townsend, 1976). Some examples of such "absolute" or "intensive" uses from my own data are as in (33).

(33) J 3;3 Put it **too close**. [requesting candy be moved closer]

R 3;6 I'm **too high**, Daddy [standing on table to reach light switch, can barely reach; proud of how high she is]

R 3;6 Don't make this **tighter**. It's **tighter**! [trying to open jar lid; finds she can't open it]

MO 3;0 **Too many** ronis. [re: macaroni on his plate. MO then proceeds to eat all his macaroni and go get and eat another helping] (Gathercole, 1979b, p. 312).

Saul 3;3.26 You can carry me 'cause you're **too heavy**.... [i.e., "you're very strong"] I'm little and you're heavy.

Saul 4;3.15
Saul: Sadie's sweet, and I'm sweeter than her, and you're sweeter than me, and Daddy's sweeter than you.
M: Wow! I just thought we were all sweet.
Saul: We are! Didn't you hear what I was saying? We're all **sweeter**!

At the same time, it is clear that these forms don't quite mean "X," "very X" for the child—at least their use is not limited to such meanings. In fact, their use appears to be based on either stored prototypical uses of these forms or stored haphazard examples (Gathercole, 1979b, 1983). This is because at the same time as children are using *X-er, X-est,* and *too X* for "(very) X," they also use the forms appropriately (see (34)), and for other uses that appear to have their source in the correct uses—e.g., using the comparative to compare two things that are alike or different (see (35)).

(34) R 3;6
R: Are you done?
M: Mhm. I'm in the clean plate club.
R: Then I eat slower. I'm little. You're **bigger than me**, right?

J: 3;9 [carrying large coloring book:]
This is **too big for my pocket**, right? My pocket's for little things, right? My fireman's little. It's little for my pocket, right? My hand's little for my pocket, right? [fireman = 1½ in. peg doll]

(35) R 3;6.14 [R comparing lengths of two sticks in picture—refers to the same two sticks with:]
shorter [vs.] longest; **longer** [vs.] **shorter**

R: 3;6.29 [R asking to have crackers after supper; none in sight:]
Two big ones. Two **bigger** ones. Two big ones.

R: 3;7.1 I don't get **better** gloves, but you do. [When asked further, R asserted that mine were better because they're black.]

I have argued (Gathercole, 1979b, 1983) that the range of usage for these forms arises through complexive extensions of the forms from the prototypical or stored examples of usage. That is, the child picks up early uses of these forms in appropriate contexts, but then extends their use to contexts that share only a subset of the characteristics of those appropriate contexts (Bowerman, 1978; Carey, 1978a).

The ability to use comparatives beyond absolute or intensive uses develops during the preschool years, and perhaps well into the school age years (Ehri & Ammon, 1974; Gobbo & Agnoli, 1985; Kallio, 1988). Their interpretation by young children is complicated by the child's developing understanding of the adjectives on which they are built. The fact that some adjectives themselves involve relative degrees of the presence of properties (*big*, *tall*, etc.), and that their application depends on the type of referent (cf. *big ant* vs. *big elephant*) (see, e.g., Kennedy 2005), as well as the fact that some adjectives refer to positive ends of scales (e.g., unmarked adjectives, like *big*, *tall*) while others to negative ends (e.g., marked adjectives like *little*, *short*) affect the relative ease with which the structures built on them are acquired (Ehri & Ammon, 1974; Gobbo & Agnoli, 1985; Nelson & Benedict, 1974; Ryalls, 2000; Syrett, Bradley, Kennedy, & Lidz, 2005).

Among the relevant research is work suggesting a strong link between the development of linguistic forms like the comparative and the development of cognitive skills such as seriation and conservation (e.g., Ehri, 1976; Shaffer & Ehri, 1980). Given the semantic notions encoded through the structures of interest here, we might predict that we will find similar links between linguistic and cognitive development with even a broader range of these structures.

Acquisition of ***More*** *and* ***Less***

A great deal of research has also focused on the acquisition of just the two words *more* and *less* (see review in Gathercole, 1979a). It is clear that children's understanding and usage of these words develop over a long stretch of time before all of the meanings and uses are incorporated into children's linguistic system. The initial uses of *more*, in the one- and two-word periods, tend to be for "recurrence" [*more bottle*, *more tickle*, etc.] (Bloom, 1970, 1973). Children's understanding of *more* as referring to the greater of two amounts begins to take hold around 3½ years of age, and may go through a period in which *more* means "additional amount" in the same referent (Gitterman & Johnston, 1983; Hudson, Guthrie, & Santilli, 1982). But children's full appreciation that *more* can refer to the greater of two distinct amounts, and to a difference *either* in mass or in number does not develop fully until around 5 years of age (Gathercole, 1985b, 1986) or later (e.g., Arendasy, Sommer, Ponocny, 2005) (see example of the conflict this can pose for children in (36)). Children's understanding of *less* appears to come in only after they have gained a relatively full understanding of *more* (around age 4½ to 5 years) and can appreciate the relationship between *more* and *less* (Carey, 1978b; Gathercole, 1979a; Gordon, 1978).

(36) Saul 4;11.12

S: You have 10 fingers and I have 10.
M: So who has more?
S: You.
M: I have more?
S: Yes, because yours are bigger. I mean just look at them!

Children's use of *more* as a marker for comparative forms of adjectives (*more interesting, more difficult*) also takes a long time to develop. Children's abilities with this use of *more* appear to come in at around 4½ years of age, long after extensive use of the *-er* marking for comparatives (Gathercole, 1985b). It is also at about this age that children begin using extensive double marking on adjectives ("more bigger"), suggesting that they have brought the two modifiers together semantically and/or syntactically—they have come to "bump up against each other's territories," in Bowerman's sense (1978, p. 391).

Mass and Count

The development of the linguistic mass–count distinction has also been the subject of extensive research (e.g., Gathercole, 1985a, 1986; Gordon, 1982; Soja, Carey, & Spelke, 1991). There is a wide range of constructs that participate in the mass–count distinction in English (e.g., *a/some,* categorization of nouns into one group or another, *much/many, more* for comparative of *much* vs. for comparative of *many*). Children's development across these forms again appears to be protracted and to come in piece by piece. Thus, children learn early that *a X* refers to a (single) object, while *some X* refers to a substance (Gathercole, Cramer, Somerville, & Jansen op de Haar, 1995; Soja, 1992; Soja et al., 1991). Children learn early that some nouns can be quantified by numbers, while others cannot (Gordon, 1982, 1988; see Bloom, 1994; Carey, 1994 for discussion). But children take a very long time to sort out where *much* has to be used and where *many* is used (Gathercole, 1985a, 1986). We will see below that this may have to do in part with the distinct developmental trajectories for *much* and *many*.

Qs and Numbers

There is a considerable body of research on children's understanding of quantifiers, especially in relation to universal quantification (*all, every, each*), but also *some, many, most,* and to the scope of operators, beginning with work by Donaldson and colleagues in the 1970s (e.g., Donaldson & McGarrigle, 1973) and continuing through to the present (see reviews in Brooks, Braine, Jia, & Dias, 2001; Drozd, 2001). Without going into details of this work, it is worth noting here that the quantifiers themselves and their semantic interpretations are fraught with complexities (e.g., Horn, 1997, 2000 for the interpretation of *all, some, every,* and *any*) and that the interpretation of quantifiers is highly influenced at young ages by contextual factors, including nonlinguistic factors (Brooks, Braine, Jia, & Dias 2001; Drozd 1996), linguistic factors (Brooks et al., 2001; Philip, 1995; Takahashi, 1991), and pragmatic factors (Brinkman, Drozd, & Krämer 1996; Crain et al., 1996). Furthermore, their semantics is developing co-temporaneously with the development of number concepts, which may be related (see debate in Bloom & Wynn, 1997; Briars & Siegler, 1984; Carey, 2001, 2004; Cordes & Gelman, 2005; Fuson, 1988; Gelman & Butterworth, 2005; Hurewitz, Papafragou, Gleitman, & Gelman, 2006; Mix, Huttenlocher, & Levine, 2002; Pollmann, 2003; Rips, Asmuth, & Bloomfield, 2006; Sarnecka & Gelman, 2004).

Apart from this possible relationship, the conceptual underpinnings of numbers and their acquisition may be relevant to the structures examined here, and to their acquisition. Of note is the set of concepts that Gelman and colleagues (e.g., Gelman, 1978; Gelman & Gallistel, 1978, Gelman, Meck, & Merkin, 1986; Greeno, Riley, & Gelman, 1984) have proposed are essential to the understanding of number. They have outlined five distinct principles:

1. *One-to-One Principle*: Each item in an array receives one and only one "tick." This involves *partitioning*, grouping the items into those that have been counted and those that have not, and *tagging*, assigning distinct tags to the items that have been ticked.
2. *Stable-Ordering Principle*: The tags assigned to items in an array are produced in a stable, repeatable order.
3. *Cardinal Principle*: The final tag assigned has special significance—it labels the quantity of the array.
4. *Abstraction Principle*: Any type of items can be counted.
5. *Order-Irrelevance Principle*: It does not matter which order items are counted in; one will still end up with the same cardinal number.

These principles are relevant in that they indicate—especially Principles 2 and 3—that central to the acquisition of number is the understanding that numbers lie along and represent distinct points on a scale. The timing of the acquisition of these principles is also relevant: Gelman argues that children observe the first three principles, at least with small numbers (up to three), by age 3 (Gelman, 1978, p. 235), and with sets up to size seven by age 5 (Gelman, 1978, p. 233; see also Gelman, 1993). Understanding of number is not complete, however, by age 5; it continues to develop beyond these ages (Gelman, 1978, p. 239; Skwarchuk & Anglin, 2002; Sophian & McCorgray, 1994).

As scalar predicates involve "domains that are partially ordered according to some property that permits grading" (Matushansky, 2002, p. 244), the conceptual basis underpinning Gelman's Principles 2 and 3 is also relevant to scalar predicates. To what extent do the development of numbers and (other) scalar predicates go hand in hand? The data below will suggest that children's understanding of the scalarity of predicates may be facilitated through their understanding of number. (See Carey (2001, 2004) for a somewhat different perspective.)

Scalarity and Conversational Implicature

A number of studies have also begun examining children's understanding of conversational implicatures associated with scalar predicates. Several studies have reported that preschoolers and school-age children are insensitive to such conversational implicatures. That is, children do not infer from the use of a scalar predicate lower on a scale (e.g., *some*) that a predicate higher on the scale (*all*) does not apply. For example, Noveck (2001) found that children aged 7 to 9 treated *might* as compatible with *must*, and children aged 8 to 10 treated *some* as compatible with *all*; Hurewitz, Papafragou, Gleitman, and Gelman (2006) and Papafragou and Musolino (2003) found that 3-, 4-, and 5-year-olds interpreted *some* as meaning "at least some, possibly all" (Hurewitz et al. 2006, p. 88); Papafragou (2003b) and Papafragou and Musolino (2003) found that Greek 5-year-olds failed to interpret the words for 'begin,' 'start,' and 'half' as implicating 'not finish' and 'not all'; Papafragou and Schwarz (2006) report similar findings for 4-, 7-, and 10-year-old children's interpretation of *most*.[18] (See also Chierchia, Crain, Guasti, Gualmini, & Meroni, 2001; Gualmini, Crain, Meroni, Chierchia, & Guasti, 2001; Lidz & Musolino, 2002.)

However, there are some qualifications to this insensitivity. First, it depends on the predicate involved. Papafragou (2003a, 2003b), Papafragou and Musolino (2003), and Papafragou and Schwarz (2006) report that 5-year-olds were more successful in interpreting *half, two*, and *three* as implicating "not all" than in interpreting *begin, start* as "not finish" and than treating *most* as "not all." (These researchers have argued that there may be some difference in implicature interpretations for numbers (or their vagueness) in comparison with other types of scalar predicates at these ages.) In addition, contextual factors influence interpretations (Musolino, 2004; Papafragou, 2003a, 2003b, 2006; Papafragou & Musolino, 2003, Papafragou & Tantalou, 2004).

It may be of significance that many of these studies involve the quantifier *some*, in its use in contrast to *all*. One important aspect of *some* is that it is polysemous: The quantifier *some*, as in (37), is different from the determiner *some*, as in (38) (Lyons, 1977).

(37) A: *Did all your family go to the party?*
B: *Well, some went.*

(38) A: *Who came to the door?*
B: *Some children selling chocolate bars.*

In the first, *some* the quantifier lies on a scale with *all* at the extreme end. This quantifier *some* is often used in a partitive construction: *some of my family went.* As a scalar form, this quantifier *some* conversationally implicates "not all." In the second case, *some* acts as the plural equivalent of singular *a*—*a child came selling chocolate bars.* This *some* is not the quantifier but an indefinite determiner. This

---

[18] These authors note, importantly, that their youngest group, 4-year-olds, had not yet acquired the semantics of the two quantifiers studied, *half* and *most*.

some does not usually occur in a partitive constructions. Critically, determiner *some* does not carry any conversational implicature about set size.

Most of the studies examining children's interpretation of implicatures with *some* have assumed that children are treating *some* as the quantifier *some*. However, they may have been interpreting it as determiner *some*, which is perfectly compatible with an "all" reading. This polysemy of *some* raises questions regarding the interpretation of results concerning children's understanding of conversational implicature. Are we sure that children know the (relevant) meanings of the forms tested? What evidence is there regarding children's acquisition of conversational implicature in the case of forms whose semantic content we know that children understand? The data below suggest that the acquisition of scalar predicates and their conversational implicature entails several distinct components of development—acquiring the semantics of the form, placement of the form on the appropriate scale with competing terms, and viewing the scale in the proper (upward) direction. I will argue that these all must be in place before the conversational implicatures can be understood.

Multiple Modification

Not much is known about how children develop the whole system of degree-marking elements, including multiple modification. In an initial examination of this issue, I analyzed data from 12 children who were observed in groups of four children of the same age on four occasions (Gathercole, 1979b, CHILDES data bank). From this cross-section of data, it appeared that children seem initially to use a given Deg either only with A or only with or as Q, not both. It is only with time that children learn to extend the use of each Deg to use with the other form (Gathercole, 1979b).

The data from this cross-section of children revealed the following pattern:

a. Initially (around 3 to 4½ years of age), the Degs were restricted as follows:
   very, so, how, as/ ___ A
   more, this, that, enough, much, most/ with or as Q

b. At an intermediate age (around 4½ to 5½), children began associating forms initially restricted to use with As to use with Qs: *very, so, how/* ___ Q

c. At a still more advanced age (around 5½ to 6½), forms initially restricted to use with or as Qs migrated to use with As: *more, this, that, enough, much/* ___ A

However, it should be noted that the numbers of occurrences of these forms overall were small, so any conclusions drawn from that initial set of data had to be tentative. But we will see parallel developments in the data below.

What We Do Not Know

Beyond these, there is little known about a number of issues related to the acquisition of these forms:

- Beyond the study mentioned above, little is known about the acquisition of multiple modification.
- Little is known about the development *within* each structure. How do uses of each form—*very, too, as, than, more, many*, etc.—change with time and experience?
- Little is known about how development *across* the whole range of structures evolves. How do the developments of *as…as, -er…than, X enough, too X* interact?
- Not much is known about individual differences in the acquisition of these forms across children.
- Further work is needed regarding the acquisition of language versus the acquisition of cognitive understanding.
- Very little is known still about children's understanding of scalar predicates, such as *as…as, too X, X enough,* especially in relation to the understanding that they involve the assertion of meeting a lower limit and viewing the scale from below upward.

The research reported here was conducted with the hope of helping to answer some of these open questions. In particular, the data can provide further insight into the developments of individual lexical structures; into the development of links between structures and of the whole linguistic system; into the influences of cognitive, semantic, and syntactic aspects on the course of acquisition; and into the range of individual differences and range of commonalities in the acquisition of these structures.

METHOD

The data reported here come primarily from two children—my daughter, Rachel, and her daughter, Sadie. These data are supplemented, where appropriate, with data from my son, Jaime, and Rachel's son, Saul, and with occasional data from other children. The data from my own and Rachel's children consist primarily of error[19] and nonerror data collected by myself, for both Rachel and Sadie (and Jaime and Saul), and by Rachel, for Sadie (and Saul).

[19] Please note: The term *error* is used here to refer to uses by children that deviate from the adult norm. I do not mean to imply that these forms are "errors" in any sense with regard to the child's own developing system, nor that the "errors" constitute a regression or lapse on the child's part. Indeed, as we will see, the "errors" are usually indicative of children's linguistic advances (see, e.g., Bowerman 1982).

For the data from Rachel (and Jaime), any errors uttered, regardless of type of error (i.e., even outside the structures of interest here), were collected, by writing down the utterances and as much of the conversational exchange as possible immediately following the utterance. Because utterances containing errors in one realm include correct forms in another, the data include both correct and incorrect utterances involving the structures of interest here. For data from Sadie (and Saul), both errors and correct uses of the structures of interest here were targeted, similarly by writing down the utterances and as much of the conversational exchange as possible immediately following the utterances. In the case of Sadie (as well as Saul), Rachel spent virtually 24 hours a day, 7 days a week with her, so the data can be considered extremely representative.

The data reported here span primarily the ages from birth until 4;0 for Sadie and from 1;0 to 6;00 for Rachel. The data from Sadie and Rachel will first be laid out separately. This will be followed by a summary of the shared aspects of development in the two children and the differences between them.

The immediate goals in the examination of the data from these children were the following:

1. To trace each child's development of the full range of structures of interest here.
2. To uncover commonalities and differences across the development of the structures and across the children.
3. To examine how and if children develop a full system. What are the roles of form, of semantic content, of cognitive underpinnings, of syntactic complexity?

In all of what follows, key criteria for judging the child's knowledge of the structures in question involved (1) the order and timing of emergence of forms, (2) the contexts of utterances, (3) the nature of errors, and (4) gaps or missed opportunities in the child's interpretation of others' uses of forms or in their own use of forms available in their own repertoire.

The data are then examined in the Discussion with regard to the larger questions posed at the outset:

- To what extent do children approach these structures on the basis of broad syntactic categories and structures? That is, does knowledge of syntactic structure guide children's acquisition of these forms, or do the syntactic structures emerge out of the children's experience with the forms?
- Are the developments in the syntactic and semantic (and cognitive) realms autonomous, or do developments in one area influence developments in another?
- Do children follow a common trajectory in the development of these systems, or is the developmental path followed idiosyncratic and distinct across children?
- Does language lead cognitive development, cognitive development lead language, or a mixture of these two?

SADIE

The data from Sadie are taken from approximately 900 utterances and exchanges containing relevant forms between birth and 4;0. The examination of the data will focus on three major types of developments: developments with adjectives, developments with quantifiers, and developments with phrases and their elaboration in multiple modification.

Earliest Ages: By 1;7.6

By the age of 1;7, Sadie had 176 words, and she was beginning to produce two-word utterances. By this time, her vocabulary included the following adjectives and quantifiers (exhaustive list):

Adjectives

stinky
naked [in relation to self, when she had diaper off]
heavy
yucky
wet
tired
ready

Quantifiers

more [when requesting more of something]
first
two [Note: up until 1;8, used for anything more than one— "lots," plural?]

Earliest Ages: 1;7–3;0

In the following period, Sadie's development was as follows:

Adjectives Sadie begins to use modifiers of adjectives during this period:

Ages 1;8–2;2: INTENSIFICATION Her earliest modification of adjectives consists of the use of *so, very, quite, all, really*, and reduplication of *very* and *really,* all used to express INTENSIFICATION (see Table 11.1A). In addition to these forms, she uses *-er* once, in *later* (reminiscent of the *later* frequently used by Abe's parents, above), and *too A* several times, in apparently appropriate contexts (see Table 11.1B). Later misuses of *too X*, however, suggest perhaps that these earliest uses ("too big," "too tired") are "rote learned" or prototypical uses learned in context, as suggested in Gathercole (1983).

Ages 2;4–3;0: Later Modification for INTENSIFICATION By 2;4, Sadie continues to express INTENSIFICATION through these early means. She also begins adding other intensifying modifiers to her repertoire, such as *way, freezing, heck-out*, and, notably, *how*. The use of these forms goes beyond acceptable use in adult speech, as in "heck-out dirty water," "freezing tired" (see Table 11.1C).

At this same time, she also begins to generalize the use of reduplication for intensification beyond *very* and *really* to adjectives themselves, to verbs, and to adverbials, as in "this large, large thing," "waiting and waiting and waiting and waiting and waiting," "I've been waiting for a while and a while." Further, she also begins using other lexical forms expressing intensification, such as *love*, *full*, and *like crazy* (see Table 11.1C).

The expansion of intensification beyond adult usage in these multiple ways suggests that Sadie has discovered that INTENSIFICATION is a notion that can be expressed, and she draws on multiple sources in the input to be able to express this notion.

Ages 2;3–2;6: EXTREME ENDS: At this same time, Sadie begins to use multiple lexical forms to express extreme ends. These include *favorite, first, last, best* (see Table 11.1D).

Ages 2;4–2;6: LIKE: Similarly, during this time, Sadie begins to use lexical forms to express "likeness." These include *same, match, like*, as well as *this A* ("this big"—"big like this"), as in Table 11.1D.

Ages: 2;4–3;0: *Comparative Forms -er and than*: At this age, Sadie also begins using the modifier *-er* as well as the standard marker *than*, as shown in Tables 11.1E and 11.1F. Some of the uses of these forms appear appropriate semantically, but some are clearly inappropriate. For example, at 2;5.10, in reference to sockets in the wall, Sadie says that she herself is "…very little **than** these. [R: What's very little than those?] Me! I'm very little **than** these"; she appears to mean "little like these." She does not appear to respect the link between *-er* and *than*, as the latter appears often with simple adjective forms or forms with other modifiers—"very little than," "so fast than," "perfect than." At least sometimes, *than* in such forms appears to mean "like" (see also Gathercole, 1979b, 1983). The emergence of these comparative forms (*-er* and *than*), and their use for likeness/comparisons at the same time as the emergence of lexical forms to mean "like" (*same, match*, etc.) suggests that their use coincides with a discovery of the fact that LIKENESS can be encoded semantically.

Quantifiers

Ages 1;8–2;2: By 2;2, Sadie uses a number of quantifiers, *a lot, a little bit*, in addition to the earlier *first, two, more*. See Table 11.2A.

Q Modification: X + *more*: The very earliest instances of any type of Q modification occur with *more*, beginning around 1;11: *a lot more, a little bit more, no more, any more.* Note that these are all appropriate in form (see Table 11.2B).

Ages 2;2–2;6: At a slightly later age (about 2;4), Sadie begins using *all* and *a few*, in addition to the earlier Qs (see Table 11.2C). Note that the earliest use of *few* does not respect mass/count co-occurrence restrictions: "That's a few toilet paper." (2;4.22)

TABLE 11.1 Adjectives Sadie 1;7–3;0

Table 11.1A Early Adjective Modification—INTENSIFICATION

so

S: **So funny!**
M: What's so funny?
S: That box. 1;11.29

very

F: Don't touch that. [re: something hot in kitchen]
S: Hot.
F: Yes, it's hot.
S: **Very hot.**
F: Yes.
S: ***Very very hot.*** 1;8.14

Very very very hot. [re: pancakes] 1;8.15
Very very heavy. [S trying to pick up phone book. Can't pick it up.] 1;9.10
Put it [re: cup] on your big hand. I'm gonna put Kaysie's cup on **my very big little hand.** 2;1.17

quite

It's **quite hurting**. [describing a hurt she has] 2;1.27

all

All clean! [during bath] 1;9.22

Reduplication of *very, really*

That hurts **very very hurting.** 2;1.9

M: Do you like wrestling?
S: Yes. But it hurts me **very very very bad**.
M: Then why do you like it?
S: Because right now! 2;1.12

I like to eat **really really really really really spicy** sausage! 2;1.28

Table 11.1B Early Adjective Modification, Beyond INTENSIFICATION

-er

S: Can I eat this?
M: No.
S: Can I eat it **later**? 2;0.1

too

Too big. [re: something that doesn't fit] 1;9.13

Saul: Hey, Sadie, do you want a bite of ice cream?
Sadie: No thanks. I'm **too tired** to bite ice cream. 2;0.17

I'm **too tired** to play cups. 2;0.29

Table 11.1C Later Expressions of INTENSIFICATION

Continued use of above forms

I closed it. It's **very hard** to open. [re: a book that snaps shut with a snap] 2;5.6
Very scary. 2;5.10
Toasted bagels are **so good**! 2;5.15
That pencil you're sharpening is **so small**! 2;5.15
I was **very fast**. [re: her running] I got **so fast** than Saul! 2;6.4
I'm **all filthed** with milk. (i.e., dirty with spilled milk—"all filthy") 2;9.18

Table 11.1C (continued) Later Expressions of INTENSIFICATION

Additional modifiers for INTENSIFICATION

The cows are **way far** than me. [i.e., far away from me] 2;4.29

S: I'm gonna be **a great big grown-up!**
M: When?
S: When I turn six! 2;5.12

They kept going and going and going until they were **freezing tired**. [i.e., as in "freezing cold"] 3;0.11
That is **heck-out dirty** water! 2;9.18
Look **how tall** I am! [Sad standing on an upside-down bowl] 2;5.15
I want you to watch me **how fast** I can go! I **jump and jump how fast** I can go! 2;6.5

Reduplication of *very, really* and beyond

Look! Big! [re: a French fry] **Very very long!** 2;4.26
Saul **waited and waited and waited** for bagels! And I was hungry. And Daddy bought bagels for us! Two bagels. [F had bought two bags of six bagels.] And **more and more and more bagels**. They might be **really really yummy**. They smell yummy. 2;5.3
I've been **waiting and waiting and waiting and waiting and waiting** to read this book for a while! I've been waiting **for a while and a while!** 2;4.10
Look at **this large, large thing.** [re: a one inch by one inch piece of onion in her soup] 2;4.24
Hey, Saul! Look! A **little tiny** baby pencil! [re: a colored pencil that has been worn down because of use] 2;4.25
I do this **every every** time. [re: roll the toilet paper a certain way] Why do you do that **every every** time? [re: M rinsing her mouth every time she brushes her teeth] 2;4.26
[Sad has been waiting for F to get up and read her books. Sad sees F:] Oh! I was **asking and asking** to read those books for a while! 2;5.4

S: Did you hear that noise?
M: Yep, I sure did.
S: Do you want to **hear it and hear it and hear it** again? 2;5.6

They kept **going and going and going** until they were freezing tired. [i.e., as in "freezing cold"] 3;0.11

Other INTENSIFICATION

I'm going to make you a beautiful castle. Do you **love** castles? 2;5.12
Look at my rocks **full** of the net. [carrying fishing net full of pebbles] [Said several times.] [i.e., "my net full of rocks"] 2;6.9

M: Sadie, you're taking the cake! [i.e., getting lots of pairs in Memory game]
S: Yeah! Actually, it's cards.
[later:]
S: I think I'm going to **clean up the cake**! [i.e., win all the pairs in Memory] 2;10.5

Achoo! Whew! I blessed **like crazy**! [i.e., "I sneezed …"] 3;0.14*

[*Note: Sadie used *bless* often to mean "sneeze." Note that this means that she has interpreted "bless you" as involving "you" as the post-verbal (!) subject.]

Table 11.1D Other Notions Expressed

EXTREME ENDS

This is my **favorite** song! 2;3.6

[Sad is taking pieces of toilet paper off roll]
M: No more toilet paper.
S: One more **last**, please? 2;4.20

M: Do you want me to help you write more sentences?
S: Yeah. I want to erase it **first.** 2;4.17

M: I'm going to make you a taco salad.
S: A taco salad! Mmm! That's my **best!** I want a taco salad! 2;4.19

Table 11.1D (continued) Other Notions Expressed

My **favorite** candy is tic tacs. 2;5.19

M: Put away the balloons now, please.
S: I want one **last**.
M: Nope, no more.
S: Okay. 2;5.28

I have one **last** of this. I want you to have it. 2;6.4

LIKE

S: Can I do the napkins?
M: Yes. Pick three that are the same as each other.
S: [Sad holding up two:] Are these **sames**? 2;4.2

These are **same**! [re: a racket and its reflection in the glass door] 2;4.24
I'm a kitty and a dog **same** times. [i.e., at the same time] 2;4.26

[M has given Sad more water in her cup than usual.]
S: What full water!
M: Are you saying that because there's so much in the cup?
S: Yeah. I almost got two cups…at the **same** time!
M: Two cups in one cup? 2;5.9

S: I want to hear "So-so," Mommy.
M: You want to hear "So-so"?
S: It's a CD song **like** I once heared.
M: I'm sorry, I don't know what song it is.
S: It's a CD song. 2;4.25

S: Will you read me this book?
M: That book is scary.
S: Oh. Is it Daddy's?
M: No, it's for kids, but it's for big kids.
S: For not my **matching** baby? Big little **matching** baby? Very scary. [appears to mean "not for a baby like me, a big little baby like me?"] 2;5.10

S: They have "Green Eggs and Ham" **like** we have "Green Eggs and Ham"! [re: the book] We **match**!
M: You and Andrea?
S: You and Andrea. [re: Andrea is the mother of some friends of Saul and Sadie's] 2;5.14

I want a piece of cheese. **This big** of cheese! [showing M with her fingers] 2;5.16

Table 11.1E Use of Comparative Form *-er*

I don't like peanut butter on top of my jelly, but I like jelly **better** than peanut butter. 2;4.13

S: Can I have some of yours? [re: fruit leather; Sad and M each have a fruit leather of different flavors]
M: Some of mine?
S: It's even **better**. [i.e., even better than mine] 2;4.25

I'm gonna go it **faster** than I can go **it faster**! Because I can go **it faster**! [making rocking horse go faster—means "I'm gonna make it go really fast like I can make it go fast"?] 2;6.4

Table 11.1F Standard Marker *than*

I don't like peanut butter on top of my jelly, but I like jelly better **than** peanut butter. 2;4.13
The cows are way far **than** me. [i.e., far away from me] 2;4.29

Table 11.1F (continued) Standard Marker *than*

S: ...very little **than** these.
M: What's very little than those?
S: Me! I'm very little **than** these.
[re: sockets in the wall—appears to mean "I'm very little like these"] 2;5.10

This is more lighty **than** the kitchen's more lighty. [i.e., brighter] 2;5.20

I was very fast. [re: her running] I got so fast **than** Saul! [means "faster than Saul"? "very fast like Saul"?] 2;6.4

I'm gonna go it faster **than** I can go it faster! Because I can go it faster! [making rocking horse go faster—means "I'm gonna make it go really fast like I can make it go fast"?] 2;6.4

M: The one in your hand is perfect. Use that one. [re: spatula in S's hand]
S: But that's perfect **than** this one. ["that"=a different spatula—it's "more perfect" than the first?] 2;9.23

Q Modification: Q + Q: In this period, starting around 2;3, Sadie extends modification of *more* to not only the appropriately formed "a lot more," "a little bit more," "no more," and "any more," but also to "yes more," "one more," and "some more."[20] She also begins other (inappropriately formed) Q + Q combinations, "a little bit some," "a lot of three" (see Tables 11.2D and 11.2E).

Q Modification: Deg + much: At precisely the same time (2;3), Sadie begins using the quantifier *much*, always occurring with some Deg modifier—*very much, how much, so much* (and at least once, *a much*); see Table 11.2E. Note that these are the first uses of *very, so, how* in relation to a quantifier; these were previously restricted to use with adjectives. Since these early uses of *much* always occur with Degs that largely carry the same semantic import of INTENSIFICATION as they had already expressed with adjectives, these structures may serve to "invite" the child to broaden the structural options within these constructs, bringing Degs previously linked only with As into Q expressions. (Note also that this step in development is consistent with step (b) discussed in the introduction in relation to the data from the cross-section of children in Gathercole (1979b).)

Q+A/Deg: Around 2;5 or 2;6, slightly (about two months) after the introduction of new quantifiers modifying *more*, of some Q + Q forms, and of some Degs linked with *much*, Sadie starts using some Qs, previously occurring as isolated Qs, as modifiers in adjectival constructions, and as modifiers of Degs in other (verb) constructions: "a-little-bit-loose diaper," "all that fast," "a lot salty pretzels," "somewhat better," "a lot similar," "a lot so love you" (see Table 11.2F). (Again note that this is parallel to the sequence observed in Gathercole (1979b).)

[20]Rachel, at a similar age, similarly made a connection between *no* and *yes* in adjective modification:

(v) R: That's **no good**.
M: That's no good?
R: That's **yes good**.
[R pointing to light in study—changed her mind.] 2;8.5

TABLE 11.2 Quantifiers Sadie 1;7–3;0

1;7 - 2;2

Table 11.2A Early Uses of Qs

more

more cheese [requesting more] 1;9.22
more. more water. [wanting M to turn water back on so she can get more water on her toothbrush] 1;9.28

M: I will read these books to you.
Sadie: Read myself.
[S sits down with books to read through herself.]
[S telling story to herself:]
S: Winnie plays ball. Winnie wakes up. Annie wakes up. Winnie's happy. Annie…Mommy... Daddy fell. Uh-oh! Annie let her out. Mommy, Annie, Daddy... Winnie barks **more**. Barks **a lot more**. Winnie plays ball. Hu-Dokey ate it. ["Hu-Dokey" = "Hunky Dorey"] Winnie barks **more** 1;11.28

(I want) **more** of your cereals! 2;1.5
I want **more** eggs. I want **more** big eggs. [i.e., I want another big bite of eggs] 2;1.14
I want **more** bite. I want **more** bites of your eggs. Give me some bites. I'm gonna feed me bites. [=I'm going to feed myself bites] 2;1.14

a lot (of)

Saul: What is Sadie doing [re: with the toilet paper] ?
Sadie: Wiping myself!
Sadie: **A lot**! [admiring the toilet paper she has put in the toilet] 2;0.6

Saul: What do you want, Sadie?
Sadie: I want a bananas. I want bananas.
Saul: How many?
Sadie: Just one two three four five!
[Saul gives Sadie bananas]:
Saul: What do you want now, Sadie?
Sadie: Maybe **a lot** of prunes! 2;1.16

Feed me **a lot** of bites. [M feeds Sad a tiny bite of cereal.] No! Not that little. 2;1.23

a little bit (of)

Can I drink **this a little bit** of milk? [i.e., this (a little bit of milk)] 2;2.4

Table 11.2B Modification of Q *more*

[S telling story to herself:] Winnie plays ball. Winnie wakes up. Annie wakes up. Winnie's happy. Annie…Mommy... Daddy fell. Uh-oh! Annie let her out. Mommy, Annie, Daddy... Winnie barks **more**. Barks **a lot more**. Winnie plays ball. Hu-Dokey ate it. ["Hu-Dokey" = "Hunky Dorey"] Winnie barks **more** 1;11.28

S: 'Nother one.
M: No.
S: **No more pieces**? 2;0.6

M: Can I have the rest of your cereal or are you going to eat it?
S: Mommy's eating it. I'm drinking your milk. Mmm! That's good milk. You try it.
[M drinks some.]
S: It's all gone?
M: No.
S: There's **a little bit more**? 2;1.5

I cannot wear these **any more**. 2;1.21
I'm gonna not bite you **any more**. 2;1.28

TABLE 11.2 (continued) Quantifiers Sadie 1;7–3;0

2;2–2;6

Table 11.2C Later Uses of Qs

a lot (of)

I ate **a lot** of crackers! 2;3.22
There's a squirrel! In some leaves! A **lot** of leaves! 2;4.15

M: Do you want to make another one? [re: S's on paper]
S: Yeah. **A lot** of them! 2;4.17

[Sad carrying pile of books:]
S: Would you read me these books?
F: I'll read one or two of them.
S: No, would you read **a lot** of them! Read all of them! 2;4.17

all (of)

[Sad carrying pile of books:]
S: Would you read me these books?
F: I'll read one or two of them.
S: No, would you read a lot of them! Read **all** of them! 2;4.17

a few

M: Uh-oh, there's no toilet paper left.
S: [Sad pointing to almost empty roll:] That's **a few** toilet paper....There's other toilet paper in the other bathroom.
M: Let's go get some of that.
S: So it doesn't keep wasting. 2;4.22

Table 11.2D Modification of *more*

I want **yes more** baguette. I want **yes more** cheese! I forgot I already had baguette! 2;3.7
Some are fixed and some are broken. [re: bubbles to pop in bubble wrap] Let me see **some more** bubbles 2;4.11

[Sadie is taking pieces of toilet paper off roll]
M: No more toilet paper.
S: **One more** last, please? 2;4.20

M: That's the last one (re: piece of silverware to put in the dishwasher)
S: Is there **no more**?
M: Yes, there's no more.
S: [Sadie pointing to empty detergent container/receptacle in dishwasher:] There's **no more**. 2;4.17

I want water! [i.e., to drink] [Sadie holding up almost empty water jug:] Is there **no more** water? 2;4.17

[Sadie has just eaten sliced-up pieces of kiwi] Zach, is there **any more** kiwi? 2;4.17
I don't want **any more** deviled eggs. 2;5.6

S: Daddy's not sleeping!
M: No, he's not, is he?
S: Did Daddy sleep?
M: Yes.
S: Did Saul sleep?
M: Yes.
S: Did I sleep?
M: Yep.
S: Did not anybody sleeped **any more**? [i.e., is nobody still asleep?]
M: Everybody's awake!
[re: In morning, when Sad awoke to discover F and Saul awake in the living room. She is confused as to whether anybody has slept, and whether everyone is now awake.] 2;5.8

Table 11.2D (continued) Modification of *more*

There is **no more** bag of cups! 2;5.14
No more room. [re: paper with stickers] **No more** room. **Yes more** room. [deciding there's room after all] 2;6.9

Table 11.2E Other Q Modification

Q modifying Q

Sadie:	May I share-chair-io, Saul? [i.e., may I share your chair--with hi-ho the dairy-oh song]
Saul:	Sure.
Sadie:	Can I draw?
Saul:	Yes, at your drawing station.
Sadie:	All right. I'm gonna be back soon to share-chair-io.
Saul:	Okay.
Sadie:	May I borrow a pencil, Saul?
Saul:	Sure.
Sadie:	Okay. I'm gonna borrow two pencils. But not three pencils.
Saul:	It's okay, Sadie. You can borrow three pencils.
Sadie:	Okay. Can I borrow **a lot of three** pencils?
Saul:	You can borrow as many as you want.
Sadie:	Okay! These are a lot! Can I borrow my crayons?
Saul:	Of course, Sadie. They're your crayons!
Sadie:	Okay. 2;3.12

I need **a little bit some** space. [Sad about to set rocks out on seat of chair.] 2;6.9

Modification of *much*

I don't like rocks **very much**. 2;3.3
[to Saul:] **How much** I love you! Look **how much** I love you! 2;4.27
Oh, **how much** I love you, Saul! 2;4.27
Woah! I have **so much** balls! [Sad carrying five or six balls] 2;5.7

S:	This is **a <u>much</u>** applesauce.
M:	This is what?
S:	Much applesauce. 2;5.7

I liked and loved Saul's castle **<u>very much</u>**. 2;5.12
I do**n't** like it **very much**. 2;6.4
That's **<u>so</u> much** I want. [F has just put pile of rice on Sad's plate] [means "the (large) amount I want"?] 2;6.9
I petted Cumquat **so much** days. [re: dog named Cumquat, i.e., so many days] 2;6.9
I like the purple dress **not very much** as that. [means she likes the purple dress more] 2;10.4

Table 11.2F Q Modifying A/Deg

I **a lot so** love you. 2;5.19
A nice, new, clean, **a-little-bit-loose** diaper. 2;5.23
I can go **all that fast**. [re: riding on a play horse] 2;6.4
They're **a lot salty** pretzels. 2;6.9
My toe is looking **somewhat better**. [re: a wound that is healing] 2;9.17
P and Ds look **a lot similar**. 2;11.21

Summary, Early Uses, Sadie

We can summarize these early developments as follows:

- *Semantic encoding*: The semantics expressed through these early morphological forms for modification primarily revolve around the notions of INTENSIFICATION, EXTREME ENDS, and LIKENESS.
- *Form*:
  - Forms of As: The early modification of Adjectives is primarily carried out with intensifiers, including *so, very, real(ly), -er,* and reduplication.
  - Forms of Qs: *much* enters Sadie's speech always linked with a Deg modifier; these constructs might be considered the germ of Deg + Q forms, but in which the only Q participating is *much*.
  - Elaborated Q forms:
    - Beginning expression of modification of Qs:
      Sadie begins (around 2;0) with some appropriately formed X + *more* constructs: *a little bit, a lot, no + more*
    - Elaboration of X + *more:*
      - These early uses are followed approximately three months later (around 2;3) by the extension of these forms in two ways:
        - First, Sadie introduces related forms into the pre-*more* slot: *some, any, yes + more.*
        - Second, she introduces other Qs into the slot occupied by *more*: *a little bit, a lot of / __some, 3.*
      - It is exactly at this same time that Sadie begins using expressions containing a Deg and *much*: *so, very, how + much.*
  - Further elaboration of forms:
    - Approximately two months later (around 2;5), she introduces some Quantifier modifiers into adjectival phrases: *a little bit, a lot, all, somewhat/*__(Deg) A. In some cases, the Q occurs directly before an A ("a little bit loose," "a lot salty," "a lot similar"), in other cases, the Q occurs before a Deg + A ("all that fast," "somewhat better"). (In one case, Sadie uses Q + Deg + Verb: "I **a lot so** love you.")

I have expressed these developments in terms of "Deg," "Q," and "A," but it is likely that Sadie did not initially have such broad categories. The evidence supporting this is twofold: first, her initial usage of a number of forms was clearly restricted, and, second, subsequent stages can be seen as clearly emergent from earlier stages.

First, her initial uses of any modification of these forms were limited to the use of intensifiers (*so, very, quite, really, all*) with adjectives, on the one hand, and the forms *any, no, a lot,* and *a little bit* with *more,* on the other. The first step beyond these initially restricted forms is that the presence of (legitimate/heard) X + *more* in her speech appears to have opened up a "slot" to be filled preceding *more*; this slot was then filled with other forms related to those already filling that slot (e.g., *no more* → *yes more; a lot more, a little bit more* → *some more, one more*). This in turn seems to have opened up the possibility of inserting elements similar in meaning to *more* (*some*, 3) into the same position as *more*, leading to expansion to "a little bit some," and so forth (see Drozd, 2002 for an alternative view).

Similarly, the introduction of Deg-like elements into quantifier modification was initially restricted to cases of *much* modification. The fact that the form *much* entered Sadie's speech at exactly the same time as the introduction of *yes more, a little bit some*, and the like, and that it was always accompanied by an intensifier (of the Deg variety) also suggest that these may all have taken a form modifier + Q. (And note that the modifiers expressed a variety of notions, suggesting that this abstract modifier + Q form had a syntactic, not a semantic, base.) The subsequent (and fairly rapid) expansion to the use of *a little bit, a lot* as modifiers of adjectives suggests the beginning of the emergence of a modifier + modified structure at that point (although subsequent developments, to be outlined below for 3;0 to 4;0, indicate that she has not yet arrived at a fully general structure). The concurrent flowering of means of expressing other types of modification—additional lexical intensifiers for adjectives, such as *way* A, *freezing* A, *heck-out* A, as well as a proliferation of reduplication on As, Qs, and Vs—at exactly this same time supports this suggestion.

Thus, the early germs of the emergence of these structures appear to have come from two source routes: Intensifier + Adjective, on the one hand, and Modifier + *more* on the other. These separate routes become linked through (a) the expansion of X + *more* in two ways— through elaboration of what "X" can be and through extension to quantifiers like *more*—and (b) the introduction of Deg + *much* structures, involving Deg forms already being used in A modification. These together seem to lead to the expansion to a broader structure involving *a lot, a little bit, very, how, so* + X, where X is indiscriminately a quantifier, an adjective, or another modifier.

What Is Missing in This Early Period? The forms that are missing from Sadie's speech during this early period are as instructive as those that are present. Up to age 3;0, the following elements seem lacking:

1. Despite some limited very early uses, there is overall little use of *too* X, *-er, this* X, and *that* X, and no uses of *as…as* or *enough* in these A and Q constructions. Note that all of these involve, in adult usage, the expression of the presence of a property or quantity along a scale.
2. There are occasional instances in which Sadie either misses opportunities to use one of these forms or misinterprets others' use of them or other scalar expressions (see, for example, Table 11.3A). In one case, she misses the opportunity to use *too* A and uses A alone ["It was dirty to eat"]; in other cases she misinterprets her mother's use of *as* A *as, too much*, and *until*, which expresses a point on a scale of an imaginary time line. For example, on one occasion, when her mother is pretending to be Ernie,

Ernie says, "It's twice as big as I am!" and Sadie responds "No, you're little."

3. During this period, she is developing a rudimentary understanding of the numbers *one* and *two* (Table 11.3B), but her understanding beyond this is limited, and she shows confusion of the link between numbers versus names in relation to questions regarding age and name (see Table 11.3C).
4. There is no evidence of respect for a mass/count distinction in the use of *much* and *few*; for example, there are many co-occurrence restriction errors, such as "I have so much balls!" "I petted Cumquat so much days," "That's a few toilet paper."
5. Despite ending this period with structures allowing for a quantifier modifying an A ("a lot salty pretzels"), there are no instances of *more* used in A modification during this period.

Intermediate Ages: By 3;0–4;0

INTENSIFICATION During the next period, Sadie shows continued use of forms for INTENSIFICATION, and she adds *quite* as a modifier (see Tables 11.4A and 11.4B). But she also increases her use of *so* for intensification with verbs (seen already once at 2;5.19: "I a lot so love you") as well ("I so need...") (see Table 11.4C).[21] She also adds to her repertoire new lexical items expressing INTENSIFICATION, such as *galore*, used to modify a verb ("Mommy, he's been drawing **galore**!") and *gallon* (to mean "lots"; see Table 11.4D). Beyond this expansion of the expression of INTENSIFICATION, we see several new developments in Sadie's use of the relevant forms.

Adjectives First, with Adjectives, she continues using forms that have already entered her speech (*-er*), but now with more appropriate meanings, and begins using new modifiers that encode meanings beyond INTENSIFICATION. These forms include *how, too, -est, as...as,* and *enough* (see Table 11.5). However, in many cases, the forms are still used inappropriately; for example, Sadie associates *how old* with the spelling of her name: "**How old** I am is S-A-D-I-E. My name is S-A-D-I-E," and her use of *too old* occurs sometimes where *very old* appears intended.

On other occasions, the forms appear to be used with appropriate semantic content; for example, Sadie's use of the superlative. Note that the superlative is used with double marking on a number of occasions (see below), and the superlative is used with the standard markers *out of the world* and *of the world.*

Of particular note are the forms that for the adult encode specification of a property along some scale— particularly *too, enough,* and *as...as.* While on a few occasions their use appears inappropriate and perhaps even involving the wrong

[21] It is interesting that it is the Deg *so* that is brought into these verbal constructions. There may be some influence of the fact that there is a homophonous/polysemous form *so* that is used with verbs in, for example, *and so does she*, etc.

TABLE 11.3 Missing Sadie 1;7–3;0

Table 11.3A Missed Opportunities for Use of Modifiers or Misinterpretations of Another's Utterance

[M and S playing; M pretending to be "Ernie" (= "Little Buddy"):]
S: I not eated my sandwich, Little Buddy.
Ernie: Why not?
S: It was **dirty to eat**, Little Buddy.
{missing "too..." ; i.e., "it was too dirty..."] 2;1.27

[M "talking for" Ernie, a doll that is about 5 inches tall:]
Ernie: I can't write anything with that pen. It's **twice as big as I am**!
S: **No, you're little.**
E: I know.
S: I'm little too.
[S has misinterpreted Ernie's utterance as saying that Ernie is big.] 2;4.17

M: There's **too much** stuff on the counter, isn't there?
S: Yeah! There's **many** stuff, like ___ and ___ and ___ and ___.... 3;1.30

S: You might have to help me. [re: putting blocks into a tub]
M: Actually, we'll have to wait **until Daddy says the tub is (clean and) ready for us to use.**
S: Okay. **Until the tub's clean**, you might have to help me. **[means "...when..."; not scalar]** 2;9.18

Table 11.3B Number Concepts

M: How many kisses do you have for me?
S: **Two** kisses!
[S sometimes says "Three kisses"] 1;9.22

Sadie: May I share-chair-io, Saul? [i.e., may I share your chair—with hi-ho the dairy-oh song]
Saul: Sure.
Sadie: Can I draw?
Saul: Yes, at your drawing station.
Sadie: All right. I'm gonna be back soon to share-chair-io.
Saul: Okay.
Sadie: May I borrow a pencil, Saul?
Saul: Sure.
Sadie: Okay. I'm gonna borrow two pencils. But not three pencils.
Saul: It's okay, Sadie. You can borrow three pencils.
Sadie: Okay. Can I borrow **a lot of three pencils**?
Saul: You can borrow as many as you want.
Sadie: Okay! These are **a lot**! Can I borrow my crayons?
Saul: Of course, Sadie. They're your crayons!
Sadie: Okay. 2;3.12

Sadie: I'm back to share-chair-io. Can I draw on your paper?
Saul: No, but you can draw at your drawing station.
Sadie: Okay. Can I borrow **one of your pencils**?
Saul: Yes.
Sadie: Okay. I'm gonna borrow **two**. And a marker. 2;3.12

Table 11.3B (continued) Number Concepts

I'm gonna borrow **one** of these. 2;3.12

Saul:	Take one of these cushions.
Sadie:	**One** of these cushions?
Saul	Yeah. Any cushion. 2;4.13

[Sadie is taking pieces of toilet paper off roll]

M:	No more toilet paper.
S:	**One** more last, please? 2;4.20

There's **one** chair. There's not **two** chairs! [i.e., like there usually are] 2;4.20

Saul waited and waited and waited for bagels! And I was hungry. And Daddy bought bagels for us! **<u>Two</u>** bagels. [F had bought two bags of six bagels.] And more and more and more bagels. They might be really really yummy. They smell yummy. 2;5.3

I have a crayon! And I have **two** bagels! Peanut butter on my bagel and no peanut butter on my bagel. Just nothing—only bread! [One half-bagel is plain and one half-bagel has peanut butter on it,] 2;5.4

[M has given Sadie more water in her cup than usual.]

S:	What full water!
M:	Are you saying that because there's so much in the cup?
S:	Yeah. I almost got **<u>two</u>** cups…at the same time!
M:	Two cups in one cup? 2;5.9

M:	Put away the balloons now, please.
S:	I want **one** last.
M:	Nope, no more.
S:	Okay. 2;5.28

I have **one** last of this. I want you to have it. 2;6.4

I'm carrying **both** of us! [Sad coming into room carrying Ernie doll and Barney doll--both of them] 2;1.17 [cf: 1;11.28: Look at us! [re: pair of shoes in picture]]

That is **both** mine and Saul's. 2;2.15

Table 11.3C Immature Number Concepts

[M and Sadie playing. M pretending to be "Elmo":]

S:	I'm two.
E:	Wow! Elmo is excited to hear that!
S:	Guess what.
E:	What?
S:	'Sat thing? [="what's that thing?"] Guess what, Elmo.
E:	What?
S:	Saul's name.
E:	I don't know. **What is Saul's name**?
S:	**Six, seven, eight**. [Saul is 6.]
E:	Oh.
S:	I'm two. 2;0.0

F:	Did we see that one time or two times? [re: Bojangles restaurant]
S:	**Eleven** times! [comment: it was actually twice.] 2;4.24

There's **one two three four five** soap! [Sad counting pieces of soap in bathtub; but there are only three in reality] 2;5.3

I'm gonna be a grown-up when I get **six**. [Her brother is 6.] 2;5.4

TABLE 11.4 Sadie 3;0–4;0 Continued Use of Forms for INTENSIFICATION

Table 11.4A Adjectives (& Adverbs)

This is {my/like/a} ice skating (rink). It moves me **very well**. *[Sad sliding feet along bathtub top.] 3;9.24

I have something **very cool**. [re: new swimming pool she's getting for her birthday; squirts water up through middle] 3;11.30

Actually, even though I'm 3 1/2, I'm **quite little**. 3;9.27

Table 11.4B Quantifiers

so

[V sent Sad package full of hair clips at Halloween time. Sad mentioning how much fun it was to open up the package:] It was **so much fun**. It was 20 fun! [Sadie then counts to 20, showing how long it takes to get to 20.] It takes a long time to get to 20. 3;4.8

Reduplication of Q

V:	[on phone] Did you put up a Christmas tree?
S:	No. We put a tree in the house.
V:	Did you decorate it yet?
S:	It has **lots and lots** of lights. 3;5.26

Table 11.4C Beyond As and Qs

so / ___ V

Oh! I **so need** to poop! 3;1.21

S:	I **so wish** we could get that thing out of my butt!
M:	The poop?
S:	Yeah! 3;1.21

I **so missed** you, Saul! 3;1.22

Table 11.4D Additional Lexical Items for INTENSIFICATION

[Saul has drawings lying all over the table.] Mommy, he's been drawing **galore**! 3;8.4

[Sadie on toilet:] I think I'm gonna use up a **gallon** of that toilet paper! 4;2.2

* This is a nice utterance to add to Melissa's causative verb error repertoire: i.e., it CAUSES me to MOVE very well.

direction on a scale ("I'm tired enough…means I'm not too tired"), on others, they seem quite appropriate; for example, "If I was brave enough for me to get buy-en…" [i.e., "If I was brave enough to let myself get bought…."]; "Is everybody as tired as I am?"

Quantifiers

Q: First, two new quantifiers enter Sadie's speech early in her fourth year—*many* and *enough*—and *a little* is now in evidence alongside *a little bit* (see Table 11.6A). Her use of *many* clearly does not respect mass/count co-occurrence restrictions ("many stuff"). Her use of *enough* appears appropriate. Interestingly, all uses of *enough*, either as a Q or with an A, occur with a complement, "for…" or "to …."

Deg + Q: We saw that up until 3;0, the only Deg + Q combinations were ones involving *much* modified by intensifiers *how, very,* and *so.* Table 11.6B shows Sadie's further development of Deg + Q expressions. First, Table 11.6B1 shows her further use of Deg + *much*: her use of *how much* goes beyond intensification; she also adds *too* and *as* as Deg modifiers of *much* during this period—both of these

TABLE 11.5 Adjectives Sadie 3;0–4;0

Table 11.5A Initial Uses of Forms Beyond INTENSIFICATION

how

How old I am is S-A-D-I-E. My name is S-A-D-I-E. 3;2.14

-er

Doesn't it look **even nicer** this way? [Sad taking egg out of second pot of dye] 3;9.26

M: Sadie, you get to pick which one [bowl of rice] you want.
Sadie: I'm gonna have the a **lotter** one.
M: The a lotter one?
Sadie: The **lotter** one. The **fuller** one. 3;11.25

too

When I get **too big** for it, and it gets **too small** for me, I could ride any of those. But I could get a new one. [re: rocking horse: "when I get too big for it….I couldn't ride any of those…"] 3;7.30

[Sad had taken a break from shucking 4 ears of corn; is now ready to help out again:]
S: I'm tired enough to do some corn.
V: You're tired enough?
S: Yeah. That means I'm **not too tired.**
[use of "not too tired" appears appropriate; use of "tired enough" appears to specify wrong direction on scale?] 3;9.24

Saul to M: I can't believe you're 30!
Sadie: Yeah, and she's **not too old**!
M: Too old for what?
Sadie: You know, to walk and stuff!
[Sadie appears to mean something like "not very old."] 3;9.25

F: Are you in your pajamas?
Saul and Sadie: Yeah!
F: Are you two ready to spin?
Sadie: I'm **not too ready**! 3;10.14

-est

[Sad had been talking about which superheroes she liked most.]
M: Superman is the best one?
S: Mm hmm. [="yes"] But Superman is **my bestest**. 3;7.27

[Sad has just put on a sparkly head band]
V: The sparkly girl!
S: **Most sparkliest** out of the world! 3;9.24

V: That's a pretty necklace, Sadie.
S: I'm **fanciest** of the world. 3;9.24

enough

[Sad had taken a break from shucking 4 ears of corn]
S: I'm **tired enough** to do some corn.
V: You're tired enough?
S: Yeah. That means I'm not too tired. 3;9.24

[Sad put price tag on belly. V told her she cost 50 cents. She said she couldn't be bought because she came out of Mommy's tummy.] If I was **brave enough** for me to get buy-en…. [=…for me to get bought… i.e., "If I was brave enough to let myself be sold"] 3;9.25

as…as

Is everybody **as tired as** I am? I'm 150 tired…I'm 199 tired. 3;9.22

modifiers that in the adult language express specification on a scale. (Note that her use of *as* occurs with complement *as*—both here and in the case of the use of *as* with an adjective.)

We also see for the first time, from 3;8 on, uses of *much* without a Deg—in all cases, "(not) much of (a) N." Sadie also begins during this time to use other Quantifiers with Deg modifiers—"quite a little," "quite a bit," "-er + a lot" (see Table 11.6B2). And in one case (Table 11.6B3), we see her struggling to put together the appropriate Deg + Q expression—"too little," but she finally gives up and substitutes "not enough."

Q + (Deg) A: We saw in the previous period for Sadie the beginning of constructions involving Q + (Deg) + A (e.g., "a little bit loose"). The Qs that previously occurred in such constructs were appropriate for English: *a little bit, all, a lot, somewhat.* During this next period, we see further use of Q + A and Q + Deg + A, first with filling in more Qs from this same set—*any, some* (Table 11.6C1, 11.6C2):

Q + A: "a bit spicy," "any spicy," "little bit tie-dyed," "some good,"
Q + Deg + A: "any too tight,"

but also Qs from a distinct set, that of numbers (Table 11.6C3):

Q + A: "20 fun!" "150 tired," "199 tired," "20 hundred and 750 lucky."

Other Q/Deg combinations*:* We also see during this time a proliferation of other Q and Deg combinations (see Table 11.6D):

Deg + Deg +Q: "**quitest bit**"
Deg + Deg + A: "**very too** small"
Q + Q: "Not even 2. Not even 3. Not even 4. Not even **5....bit**."
Q + Q + Deg + A: "**once less** brav**er**"
Q + Q + Deg + Deg + A: "**much lesser** brav**er**"

These combinations suggest that Sadie has discovered that there are multiple ways in which Degs and Qs can be combined, and she extends the combinations indiscriminately, as far as form is concerned. (They do, however, seem to be constrained semantically—whenever a Deg_2 is modified, it appears to express *too*, *-er*, or *-est*.) There is no evidence of her establishing any internal phrase structure to these combinations; rather, they appear to be placed together by concatenation. Sadie's response to her father with isolated "How?" in the following supports this suggestion (see note 12):

(39) F: Do you know how many times he asked a $64,000 question?
S: **How?** [with falling intonation] 3;9.23

It is worth commenting as well that it is during this time that Sadie uses Double Marking on superlative forms and comparative forms—*most sparkliest, less braver, lesser braver.* These may be produced, at least in part, as a result of these developments allowing liberal concatenation of Q and Deg forms.

Development of Scalarity During this year of development, we can see that scalar expressions have been seeping into Sadie's speech, but they are not always

TABLE 11.6 Quantifiers Sadie 3;0–4;0

Table 11.6A Additional Qs

many

M: There's too much stuff on the counter, isn't there?
S: Yeah! There's **many stuff**, like ___ and ___ and ___ and ___... 3;1.30

enough

[Sadie explaining to V on phone that there was not enough snow to make a snowman or snowballs-- there was too little snow:] 'Cause there was too-- there was only a little bit. There was too-- There was **not enough** snow to make snow balls. 3;5.18

a little (of)

S: I'm going to pour myself **a little** of water.
M: You're going to pour yourself a little of water?
S: I'm going to pour myself **a little bit** of water. I'm going to pour myself **a little** water. 3;6.10

Table 11.6B1 Deg + Q

Deg + *much*

how

How much are you tired? [to F, then to M] 3;9.21

F: Do you know how many times he asked a 64,000 dollar question?
S: **How**? [with falling intonation] 3;9.23

too

M: There's **too much stuff** on the counter, isn't there?
S: Yeah! There's **many stuff**, like ___ and ___ and ___ and ___.;.. 3;1.30 [Sadie misinterprets M's "too much stuff" as "a lot of stuff".]

Look…it's **too much**. [re: water] He's barely sinking in it… [i.e., he's practically drowning or sinking in the water; barely means "almost"] 3;10.24

as…as

I'm gonna get **as much stuff as** I can. 3;2.3

0 + *much*

S: We have quite a little soap.
M: We have quite a little soap?
S: Yeah. Like we have **not much of soap**. 3;8.2

That wasn't **much of a sneeze**. That was **much of a cough**! 3;10.12

Table 11.6B2 Deg + Q, other Qs

quite + a little, quite + a bit

S: We have **quite a little soap**.
M: We have quite a little soap?
S: Yeah. Like we have not much of soap. 3;8.2

[S telling V on phone that Saul has built a maze. V has asked S if it's hard to find the way through:] It's **quite a bit** of dead ends. And you know what **quite a bit** means! 4;0.3

-er + a lot

M: Sadie, you get to pick which one [bowl of rice] you want.
S: I'm gonna have the **a lotter** one.
M: The a lotter one?
S: The **lotter** one. The fuller one. 3;11.25

TABLE 11.6 (continued) Quantifiers Sadie 3;0–4;0

Table 11.6B3 Missing: *too/ ___ little*

[Sadie explaining to V on phone that there was not enough snow to make a snowman or snowballs—there was too little snow:] 'Cause there was **too**—there was only a little bit. There was **too**—There was not enough snow to make snow balls. [wanted to say "too little snow"] 3;5.18

Table 11.6C Q + (Deg) + A

Table 11.6C1 Q + A

Is it **a bit spicy**? Is it **any spicy**? [re: food V has made, Thai food—S wants to know if it's spicy before she tries it] 3;9.22

I like my **little bit tie-dyed** paper towel. [Sadie holding up paper towel which had been used to tie-dye eggs] 3;9.26

That's **some good**. [re: color of egg—dying eggs for Easter] 3;9.26

It doesn't look **<u>any</u> green**. [Sadie making sure some food isn't moldy] 3;9.27

It doesn't feel **any cold** or **any hot**; it just feels <u>normal</u>. <u>Just right</u>. [re: temperature outside] 3;9.28

Table 11.6C2 Q + Deg + A

They're **any too tight** to put on myself. [re: clothes] 3;9.26

Table 11.6C3 Number + A

[V sent Sadie package full of hair clips at Halloween time. Sadie mentioning how much fun it was to open up the package:] It was so much fun. It was **<u>20</u> fun**! 1, 2, 3, 4, 5, 6, 7, 8, 9, 10, 11, 12, 13, 14, 15, 16, 17, 18, 19, 20. It takes a long time to get to 20. 3;4.8

Is everybody as tired as I am? I'm **150 tired**…I'm **199 tired**. 3;9.22

You're very lucky. You're **20 hundred and 750 lucky**. 3;9.24

Table 11.6D Other Deg/Q Combinations

<u>Deg + Deg + Q</u>

F: Is this your egg in the blue?
S: Yes.
F: Are you sure?
S: I'm sure **the <u>quite</u>st bit**. 3;9.26

<u>Deg + Deg + A</u>

[Sadie holding little pretzel up on nose] How do you like my glasses? **<u>Very</u> too small** for me! 3;9.25

<u>Q + Q</u>

[V and Sadie discussing how Sadie was "lost" at a park one time:]
V: But Sadie wasn't worried. Not one teensy bit.
S: **Not even 2. Not even 3. Not even 4. Not even 5…bit**. 3;9.24

<u>Q + Q + Deg + A</u>

I'm like **once less braver** than Saul. I'm much lesser braver than Saul. I'm much less braver than Saul. 3;11.27

<u>Q + Q + Deg + Deg + A</u>

I'm like once less braver than Saul. I'm **much lesser braver** than Saul. I'm much less braver than Saul. 3;11.27

TABLE 11.7 Immature Scalar Understanding

By then, my hair was always hanging in my eyes. [i.e., before V sent S package full of barrettes] 3;9.23	
[V and S talking on phone and mentioning that V is going to be visiting S's house soon—will be there for S's M's 30th b-day and for Easter]	
V:	I haven't been there for a long time.
S:	Yeah. **Until** Easter! [pauses as if trying to rephrase:] And you weren't here when Easter came.
V:	What?
S:	I'm sure you weren't here when Easter came.
V:	No, I wasn't.
S:	And me and Saul hid eggs. 3;7.0
Remember that time…I think you were not in our house **by then**. 3;9.23	
S:	I can **barely** jump off of roller coasters. I can't really.
V:	Does barely mean you can or you can't?
S:	Barely means "half way". 3;9.21
[Saul going across swing set that has various swings on it without touching ground. Sadie is on a horse swing at the end where he is headed. Saul wants her to get off.]	
Saul:	Sadie, can you get off?
Sadie:	OK. You're **barely** there. [Saul is on 3rd-last item--2 away from Sadie] 3;9.21
You're **barely** done, Grandma Ginny! [i.e., almost done, getting dressed] 3;9.23	
Look. . .it's too much [i.e., water]. He's **barely** sinking in it. . . (i.e., he's practically/almost drowning or sinking in the water) 3;10.24	

used appropriately with scalar import. When they are not used for scalar meanings, they are sometimes used to express INTENSIFICATION, as in her utterance "she's not too old" to mean "not very old," sometimes to express the wrong direction on the scale, as in "I'm tired enough to do some corn" to express that she could now continue helping with shucking corn (Table 11.5A).

There is supporting evidence outside of these structures that Sadie's understanding of scalarity is still immature. Some examples are shown in Table 11.7, involving the use of *by then*, *barely*, *until*, and *catch up with*. All of these in the adult usage encode positioning on a scale, viewed from a lower level upward, and Sadie's usage lacks this scalar meaning. She uses *by then* to mean "at that time," *barely* to mean (perhaps) "half way," *until* to mean "at" [point in time], "when."[22] For example:

(40) **By then**, my hair was always hanging in my eyes.
[i.e., before V sent S package full of barrettes] 3;9.23

[22]We will see similar examples from Rachel later. But examples from other children using *until* to mean "when" or "at" are:

(vi) You have to see it **till** it's done. [J putting together train tracks.] (J 3;10.6)

(vii) Aunt Virginia got up **till** ten o'clock. No, Aunt Virginia got up **till** eleven o'clock. (Laura 5;3)

(41) [V and S talking on phone and mentioning that V is going to be visiting S's house soon—will be there for S's M's 30th birthday and for Easter, a holiday for which V has not previously been present.]
V: I haven't been there for a long time.
S: Yeah. **Until** Easter! [pauses as if trying to rephrase:] And you weren't here when Easter came.
V: What?
S: I'm sure you weren't here when Easter came.
V: No, I wasn't.
S: And me and Saul hid eggs.
3;7.0 [S appears to mean "At Easter"— i.e., you haven't been here at Easter time.]

One interesting development, noted above, is the introduction of numbers into the constructs of interest. We have seen in Table 11.6C3 that numbers are introduced as modifiers of adjectives, in positions where other quantifiers would occur.[23] However, there is further evidence beyond these that there may be an association of scalar expressions with number. Forms such as *very* A, *how much*..., and *as X as* are often tied with numbers, often outlandishly high numbers; for example, "You're very lucky. You're **20 hundred and 750 lucky**" (3;9.24). See further examples in Table 11.8. It is as if Sadie's growing understanding of number and relative size related to number is tied integrally with her growing understanding of these scalar

[23]The introduction of numbers into such adjectival modification (and quantifier phrases), or to more generally express scalar concepts, is not uncommon among English-speaking children. Two examples come from a (nonlinguist) colleague of mine who protested, when I showed him some of the utterances I was analyzing, that these children must be somehow unusual. The very next two days he sent me two examples from his own son, E:

(viii) [E had done something wrong.]
F: How much remorse do you have?
E: **Five remorse**. (E 3;6.3)

(ix) [E was talking about how BIG a building in the distance was. His father asked him how big it was, and first he used his hands to show it. Then his father asked him to use words to describe how big it was and he said:]
It's **a millions big**. (E 3;6.4)

Further examples will be given below from Rachel. Some examples from Saul are the following:

(x) I like it **30 bits**! (Saul, 4;9.28) [cf.: I don't like it one bit!]

(xi) She is **infinity nice** Grandma! (Saul, 5;4.29)

And some examples from adults:

In the film *What a Girl Wants* the mother and daughter say:

(xii) [Mother to daughter:] I love you **a million** Swedish fish.
[Daughter to mother:] I love you **a million** red M&Ms.

In an interview with Jonathan Aitken on June 27, 2004, on BBC2 radio, the interviewer asks if Jonathan Aitken thinks he has a lot in common with Richard Nixon. He says,

(xiii) Actually, he was a much greater politician than me by **many hundreds of miles**.

Finally, a caller on BBC2's "Sunday Love Songs" asks that a song be dedicated to his loved one:

(xiv) We love you **infinity plus one**.

TABLE 11.8 Association of Scalarity with Number

M: Sadie, do you know how much I love you?
S: **An a million dollars**! 2;9.23

[V sent Sad package full of hair clips at Halloween time. Sad mentioning how much fun it was to open up the package:] It was so much fun. It was **20 fun**! 1, 2, 3, 4, 5, 6, 7, 8, 9, 10, 11, 12, 13, 14, 15, 16, 17, 18, 19, 20. It takes a long time to get to 20. 3;4.8
That doesn't make **any sense**. Not **one single** {sent/cent}. 3;8.24
Is everybody as tired as I am? I'm **150 tired**...I'm **199 tired**. 3;9.22
You're very lucky. You're **20 hundred and 750 lucky**. 3;9.24

[V and Sad discussing how Sadie was "lost" at a park one time:]
V: But Sadie wasn't worried. Not one teensy bit.
S: **Not even 2. Not even 3. Not even 4. Not even 5...bit**. 3;9.24

Actually, even though I'm **3 1/2**, I'm quite little. 3;9.27
I'm like **once** less braver than Saul. I'm much lesser braver than Saul. I'm much less braver than Saul. 3;11.27

predicates. In one telling occasion, Sadie even makes this association explicit, taking the time to count from 1 to 20 to exemplify how vast 20 is, and, hence, how vast the "fun" is that she wants to express:

(42) [V sent Sadie package full of hair clips. Sadie mentioning how much fun it was to open up the package:]
Sadie: It was so much fun. It was **20 fun**! 1, 2, 3, 4, 5, 6, 7, 8, 9, 10, 11, 12, 13, 14, 15, 16, 17, 18, 19, 20. It takes a long time to get to 20. 3;4.8.

The question arises as to why numbers are brought into these structures. From the acquisition of number literature, we can surmise that this is a critical period in children's developing understanding of number. The fact that Sadie can count well—at least clearly up to 20—and that she associates the counting with the amount of time it takes to get through that counting suggests that her understanding of number—at least with regard to cardinality and the stable ordering principle—is fairly well formed. So several possible explanations for this development present themselves:

First, it is possible that the central understanding of scales—especially the stable ordering principle—comes through an understanding of number and perhaps through the understanding that a number represents a position in a sequence (Gelman et al., 1986; see introduction). The introduction of numbers into these adjectival structures may be an attempt to gain a firm grasp of scalarity through a metaphorical extension of the number scale to nonnumerical quantities.

A second possibility, however, is that numbers are brought into these structures as a result of bringing other quantifiers—*a little bit, all, a lot, any*—into adjectival phrases. The introduction of numbers may be a simple overextension of that development. It may be that the language is "inviting" the child to make such an extension.

A third possibility, of course, is that both of these may be operating. It may be that the language invites the child to introduce numbers into adjectival scalar expressions, and that children's growing understanding of number goes hand in hand with their growing understanding of nonnumerical scales.

Summary, Intermediate Uses, Sadie

We can summarize these intermediate developments as follows:

- *Semantic Encoding*: The semantics expressed during this period still involve INTENSIFICATION, EXTREME ENDS, and LIKENESS, but Sadie now also begins to use expressions that go beyond these. However, there appears to be quite a bit of instability in the semantics associated with the forms that in the adult language encode scalarity. Scalar modifiers are sometimes used appropriately, sometimes in an immature fashion. In addition, Sadie begins making explicit remarks linking numbers with scalarity. This suggests that the understanding of scalar predicates may be facilitated by this association with number, or alternatively that number is introduced into adjectival constructs on the basis of linguistic overgeneralization, or perhaps some composite of these—that the development of the understanding and formation of scalar predicates evolves hand in hand with an understanding of number relations.
- *Forms*:
    - Forms of As: The modification of adjectives during this period expands to include *quite*, *how* beyond INTENSIFICATION, *too*, and *enough*, plus use of superlative forms.
    - Forms of Qs: *enough* enters as well as a quantifier; *many* and *most* enter, but the latter is only used in Double Marking of the superlative. Also, *much,* previously tied with Deg modifiers, is used for the first time without a Deg during this period.
    - Elaborated Q forms:
        - Deg + Q: Previously, Sadie used Deg + *much*, and we see this extended in two ways:
            - First, Sadie adds additional Deg forms to those she uses with *much*: *how* with nonintensification meaning, *too*, and *as…as*.
            - Second, she uses other Deg + Q combinations more extensively: *quite a lot, quite a bit, the a lotter* [= (*-er* + *a lot*)] *one.*
        - Q + (Deg) A: Previously, Sadie had some expressions in which *a little bit, a lot, somewhat,* and *all that* preceded adjectives.
            - She now adds *a bit, any*, and *some* as preadjectival forms, plus uses *any too* A.
            - Furthermore, she begins using other non-Q quantifiers—numbers—as adjectival modifiers: *20 fun, 10 tired,* etc.

- Other Q and Deg combinations: During this time, Sadie also continues to form apparently indiscriminate combinations of Qs and Degs, including:
  - Deg + Deg + Q: "quitest bit"
  - Deg + Deg + A: "very too small"
  - Q + Q: "Not even 2. Not even 3. Not even 4. Not even 5….bit."
  - Q + Q + Deg + A: "once less braver," "much lesser braver"

The Deg, Q, and A combinations Sadie uses are still apparently combined without any clear overarching syntactic structure (although there may be the constraint that the only Deg_2's that can be modified are *too*, *-er*, and *-est*).

Finally, it is worth noting that all uses of *enough* and *as* during this period occur with explicit complements (*enough…for*, *as…as*).

What Is Missing During This Intermediate Period? While Sadie has begun using scalar markers (comparative, *as…as*, *too X*, *enough*), their use is not always appropriate—instead of expressing scalarity, they are sometimes used immaturely. Scalar uses are still relatively rare, and immature, during this period.

There is still no evidence of respecting a mass/count distinction in the quantifiers.

And there is still no evidence of the use of *more* in A modification.[24]

Finally, there is an apparent lack of any imposition of phrase-structure onto these multiply modified forms as they enter Sadie's speech. Instead, their collocation appears governed more, initially, by lexically specific formulas, which, with time, get expanded to a fuller set of possibilities that appear constructed on the basis of concatenation.

RACHEL

The data from Rachel are from birth until approximately 6;0. The data consist of approximately 3,000 utterances involving relevant structures, collected on the spot in normal conversational interactions.

---

[24]There is only one early use of *more* with a possible adjective, *lighty*, but it is not clear what word class *lighty* is:

(xv) This is more lighty **than** the kitchen's more lighty. [i.e., brighter] 2;5.20

At a somewhat later age, beyond those examined here, we begin to see double marking of comparatives, in which *more* is used with *A-er*, in Sadie's speech:

(xvi) I want to get **some more higher**. [F lifting Sadie up on his lap.] (4;7.9)

(xvii) [Sadie trying to throw a bag into the garbage and coming up short:]
I should throw it **more harder** next time. [S throws it again] That was even worse! (4;6.16)

Earliest Ages: Up to 3;0

Let us first look at Rachel's use of adjectival and quantifier forms during the earliest period, up to 3;0.

Adjectives As with Sadie, the earliest modified adjectival forms appear on the whole to express INTENSIFICATION. These include uses of reduplication and *really* (although *really* may instead, or in part, be connected with the expression of reality) (see examples in Table 11.9A). In contrast to Sadie, Rachel used *-er* and *-est* quite extensively for absolute uses (to mean "X") and for INTENSIFICATION; see further examples in Table 11.9A.

Like Sadie, Rachel also talked about EXTREME ENDS, using lexical forms like *first* and *favorite*, and she used *same* to express LIKENESS (see Tables 11.9B and 11.9C). She also showed early attention to expressing CONTRAST, as in Table 11.9D, mostly with contrasting use of lexical opposites: *little* vs. *up*; *little* vs. *long*.

Finally, at this early age, Rachel also used *too*, but mostly in the expressions *too late* and *too heavy*, used extensively to express impossible situations, or "can't" (or in one case, the last example, possibly "can"). See examples in Table 11.9E.

TABLE 11.9 Adjectives Rachel Up to 3;0

Table 11.9A Early Adjective Modification—INTENSIFICATION

Reduplication

Look, he has **long, long, long, long** feet. [R looking at ad for panty hose--only legs showing.] 2;7.10

really

I'm not **a really monster**. 2;10.15

***-er* used for "X" or "very X"**

Not **too faster** [R closed refrigerator door fast.] 2;2.23
Look—I'm **bigger than** Jaime. I'm tallest than Jaime. I'm **taller**. [R standing on tip-toes. J is two years older. Appears that R probably means "big like."] 2;9.3
My hand's **taller than** yours. [R holding her arm out next to M's. Her arm's "longer than"? "the same length as"? M's.] 2;9.3

R: I'm not **stronger** to do that.
J: If you were stronger, you could do it, Rachel.
[Re: cracking walnuts. R trying, but not able to crack them. J is 5;1.] 2;9.27

I'm the **stronger** one who can lick this. [R licking pie turner.] 2;10.7
See. I was **stronger** to put that comb up. [R has put comb up on chest of drawers.] 2;10.13

than* without *-er

That's **orange than** my room. [R pointing to a card that is about the same shade of orange as the wall in R's room. Means "orange like"?] 2;10.0

***-est* used for "X" or "very X"**

Look at that towel. It's **highest**. [re: towel hanging from shower door bar. No other towels in vicinity.] 2;7.25
I got the **prettiest** that you got. [context not clear] 2;8.9
Look—I'm bigger than Jaime. I'm **tallest** (than) Jaime. I'm taller. [R standing on tip-toes.] 2;9.3

TABLE 11.9 (continued) Adjectives Rachel Up to 3;0

Table 11.9B Early expression of EXTREME ENDS

[ə̃ mɪwk fəəts] [="[I want] milk **first**"] 1;10.15

[M asking if R's favorite food is hot dogs.]
M: Rachel's favorite?
R: [ãĩn] **favorite**. 2;1.22

Table 11.9C Expression of LIKE

These are the **same** ones, right? [re: R's pockets on her pants are the same. [i.e., match]] 2;10.27

Table 11.9D CONTRAST

My other fork's dirty—'cause I need to use this one. [i.e., "…so…"] 2;7.16
She's little, and she's up. [1st "she"=doll without legs—little; 2nd "she"=doll with legs—up; R standing them both by potty she's sitting on.] 2;7.23
[aĩ] little before you. [i.e., "I'm littler than you"] 2;8.4
[R referred to baby potty as:] "little potty" [and then the toilet as] "up potty." 2;8.13
That's my little finger. That's my little finger, and that's my up finger. 2;8.13

F: She's only little. [re: R]
R: And you guys are long. 2;10.4

Mommy, yours is little and mine is long. [M's cereal and R's cereal boxes standing on table—R's is taller than M's.] 2;10.19

Table 11.9E Immature Uses of *too A*

Earliest uses, with *late* and *heavy* for "can't"

too late [used for impossible situations, e.g., R had brought M a right shoe to put on her left foot. M told her it wouldn't fit. R responds with "too late."] 1;11.16
that **too late** 2;0.13

M: You put on your socks.
R: I [nasalized: [aĩ]] **too heavy** [i.e., to put socks on--means "I can't"; R wanting M to put socks on her.] 2;6.27

You're **too heavy**. [M carrying R to get PJ's; R has to bend far down to reach them. i.e., M "can't"?] 2;7.16
I need to throw them in, don't my. 'Cause I'm **too heavy** for them. [R threw PJ's into crib. i.e., "I can"?] 2;8.11

Uncertain meaning—"so X"?

Not **too faster** [R closed refrigerator door fast.] 2;2.23

Quantifiers As in Sadie's case, one of the earliest quantifier forms to be used is *more*, initially used for requesting recurrence. But toward the end of this period, just before turning 3, Rachel seems to take *more* to mean something like "amount" (see Table 11.10A).

In addition, Rachel used *many* and *much* early, but both of these were highly restricted. First, *many* was used only in relation to age: "This is the many I'm gonna be. I'm gonna be three in a minute" (2;11.6; more below on this). And in the case of *much*, as with Sadie, the earliest use was tied with a Deg, in Rachel's case *too* (see Tables 11.10B and 11.10C).

Finally, as in Sadie's case, we see the early use of some modifiers with *more* in Rachel's speech, at 2;7: *any more* and *no more*.

TABLE 11.10 Quantifiers Rachel Up to 3;0

Table 11.10A Early Uses of *more*—Recurrence, Amount

more [used when bringing toys to MOT; going to get more]. 1;6.27
more [R looking at empty glass in bathroom - wanting water]. 1;6.11
mo poon [Imitation] [R picking up spoons off floor; R repeated "more spoons."] 1;6.13
mo mo ba ba [i.e., "more bottle"] [R holding out bottle for more milk.] 1;7.6
oh **mo** down [R dropped toy cat, then dropped bottle.] 1;8.6
/ay gat may luwdo/ ["I got my noodle"] [R holding noodle.] /**mor** nuwdoz/ ["more noodles"] [R wanting more noodles.] 2;0.8
/**mor** mɛəd/ [= "more bread"]. 2;1
[aĩə̃] **more** cracker of Jaime's. [i.e., "I want more cracker of Jaime's"] [R wants more of the kind of crackers that J is eating—J's kind.] 2;2.30
It's long sugar. Long **more** sugar. [R had taken a heaping teaspoon of sugar for cereal. Means something like "a huge amount of sugar"] 2;9.11
I sleeped a long **more**. [i.e., "…a long amount," "… a long time"] 2;10.13

Table 11.10B *many* [Connected with AGE]

This is **the many** I'm gonna be. I'm gonna be three in a minute. [R holding up three fingers; i.e. "I'm gonna be three soon."] 2;11.6

Table 11.10C *much*

There was **too much** toys in my purse. [R's purse is full of toys; toy "Cookie Monster" fell out.] 2;11. 21

Table 11.10D X + *more*

R:	**Any more**! Mommy **any more.**
M:	Any more what, Rachel?
R:	I don't want **any more**. No more. **No more** milk. 2;7.10

Summary, Early Uses, Rachel

These developments are entirely consistent with those we observed early on for Sadie.

- *Semantic Encoding*: The semantics expressed through these early morphological forms for modification primarily revolve around the notions of INTENSIFICATION, EXTREME ENDS, and LIKENESS. Rachel adds as well the notion of CONTRAST, the flip side of the coin to LIKENESS.
- *Forms:*
    - Forms of As: The early modification of Adjectives primarily is carried out with reduplication and suffixes. While Sadie at these ages primarily used pre-adjectival forms *so*, *very*, *real(ly)*, and reduplication for the purposes of expressing intensification, Rachel used reduplication and the suffixes *-er*, *-est*.

      Rachel also used the forms *too late* and *too heavy* extensively. However, their semantics was related to impossible situations or the expression of "can't." They in no way carried the semantic import that these would have in adult speech.

- Forms of Qs: Rachel, like Sadie, used *more* early on for recurrence, but then later for "amount." Rachel, like Sadie, used *much* fairly early, but, also like Sadie, *much* was linked with a Deg modifying it.
  In addition to these quantifiers, Rachel used *many*, but only in relation to age.
- Elaborated Q forms:
  - Beginning expression of modification of Qs:
    Rachel begins (around 2;7) with some appropriately formed X + *more* constructs: *any, no + more.*
  - It is slightly later (2;11) that we have evidence of the first expression containing a Deg and *much*: *too + much.*

As in the case of Sadie, I have expressed these developments in terms of "Deg," "Q," and "A," but there is no evidence that Rachel had any broad categories governing these forms as she was expanding these possibilities. Instead, there is clear evidence of early limited knowledge; for example, restriction of *too* for adjective modification to *late* and *heavy*; early restricted modification of *more*, with *any* and *no*; restriction of *much* to use with a Degree marker, *too*; and the early use of *many* restricted to age.

What Is Missing in This Early Period? The forms that are missing from Rachel's speech during this early period are as instructive as those that are present. Up to age 3;0, the following elements seem lacking:

1. Despite prolific inappropriate early uses of *-er, -est,* and *too*, there is little evidence of appropriate semantics associated with these forms. Furthermore, like Sadie at this age, there is no use of *as...as, enough, that X, this X* in these A and Q constructions. Note again that all of these involve the expression of the presence of a property or quantity along a scale.
2. It is worthy of note that Rachel's use of *than* is not restricted to use with *-er,* but is also used with bare adjectives; for example, "That's orange than my room" (2;10.0). Furthermore, the standard of comparison with *-er* is not always introduced with *than*, but sometimes with other, inappropriate standard markers—"stronger...to do that," "the stronger one who can lick this," "stronger to put that comb up." This indicates that Rachel has not yet grasped the necessary link between *-er* and *than*. In addition, the meaning of *than* seems to be taken as "like" in many cases.
3. As in Sadie's case, there is no evidence of respect for a mass/count distinction in the use of *much*; for example, her one attested use of *much* is in the utterance, "There was too much toys...."

Intermediate Ages: 3;0–4;0

INTENSIFICATION, LIKENESS, CONTRAST, etc. During the next period, Rachel shows continued use of forms for INTENSIFICATION, adding several new modifiers to her repertoire, especially in the first half of this year. These include *very* and *real*, in addition to continuing use of reduplication, *-er*, and *-est* to express INTENSIFICATION. She also adds *enough* and *too*. The last of these now occurs with spatial adjectives, and not just in *too late* and *too heavy*. But these early expanded uses of *too A* appear to be largely for INTENSIFICATION (see Table 11.11A).

We also see continued expression of LIKENESS and CONTRAST, as shown in Table 11.11B and 11.11C. And we see continued use, at least in the first few months, of *too heavy* to mean "can't," shown in Table 11.11D.

Beyond these forms and uses, we see several new developments in Rachel's use of the relevant forms:

Adjectives First, with the forms already in her speech—especially *-er* and *-est*, she begins showing apparently appropriate uses; they seem to start coming in for *-er* around 3;5 or 3;6 and for *-est* around 3;8; see examples in Table 11.11E. It is of note that for both *-er* and *-est*, when Rachel uses a standard of comparison at these later ages, she uses an appropriate form: *than* with *-er*, and *in the whole wide world* or *that we never ever saw* with *-est*.[25]

In the case of *too*, around 3;3, Rachel begins using *too* with adjectives other than *late* and *heavy*, and, as already noted, at first the dominant meaning seems to be in relation to INTENSIFICATION, as in the examples in Table 11.11A. Around 3;6, however, there are some possibly appropriate uses of *too A* emerging (see Table 11.11E).

Also at approximately the same age, Rachel begins using *how* with *old* (and only *old*), for the specification of age. Finally, we see an initial attempt at using *as*, shown in Table 11.11E, but the form is inappropriate—*as bigger than*—and the semantic import is very unclear ("as big as," "bigger than," "big like"?).

Before leaving the adjectival forms, there is further evidence in the first half of this year that Rachel has trouble interpreting the linguistic forms that have scalar meanings. Some examples are evident in the examples in Table 11.11; for example, the exchange at 3;6:

(43) R: Can you reach it?
M: No.
R: Are you **too little**?
M: Yeah.
R: Are you **too big**? You're not **too little**! Look at you.
[R wanting R or M to get pitcher up high on cabinet. First *too little* appropriate. Second *too little* as if R has heard what she has said, and reinterprets it as "very little."] 3;6.30

Other examples come from Rachel's interpretation of spatial scalar adjectives; for example, on one occasion we were playing with eight graduated rings, and we began talking about which ring(s) were *biggest*, *largest*, *smallest*, and so forth:

[25] I will not concern myself here with the negative in *that we never ever saw*, even though it is interesting in that it is consistent with the form that would be expected in some languages other than English; for example, Spanish: *Es lo más grande que nunca he visto* 'It is the biggest that I have never seen.'

TABLE 11.11 Adjectives Rachel 3;0–4;0

Table 11.11A Continued Modifications Expressing INTENSIFICATION

very

I'm gonna be **very short** with my beans. 3;5.8

Reduplication

It's gonna be for a **long, long** time. [i.e., R's going to take a long time to finish cereal.] 3;4.26
You know what I like...**real real**?...Milk. 3;6.17
Here's a **long, long**, **longer** noodle. [R placing noodle out straight on table. No comparison apparent.] 3;7.19

real

You know what I like...**real real**?...Milk. 3;6.17
The milk goes out **real** fast, doesn't it. [R talking about milk when poured from pitcher....“comes out”...Pitcher just standing on table in front of R.] 3;8.7

X-*er* used for “X” or “very X”

R: His hat's **bigger**.
M: It's bigger than what?
R: His hat's **bigger than** my coats.
[R referring to inflated Santa Claus's hat. Santa is standing in R's room, and his hat reaches as high as the coats that are hanging in her closet. R apparently means something like “big (high) like my coats.”] 3;0.19

R: My shoes are **littler than** my feet.
M: Are they gonna fit your feet?
R: Yeah.
[In discussion, R kept to her contention that her shoes were “littler than” her feet and would fit her feet. Apparently means “little like” her feet.] 3;1.28

I'm **as bigger than** her. [R standing up to compare herself with photo of herself. Meaning might be “I'm the same size as her” or “I'm bigger than her.”] 3;4.26
I get the **littler** spoon. [R went and got one of the baby spoons out of the drawer; R setting table, or about to eat.] 3;5.0
Don't make this **tighter**. [R trying to open pickle jar lid. She finds she can't open it.] It's **tighter**! 3;6.14
Hey! I got two **prettier** shirts! [R has taken one of her favorite shirts out of her drawer to put it on. When asked about “two” R referred to a shirt that she wore home from school, after getting her other clothes wet at school.] 3;6.23
Two big ones. Two **bigger** ones. Two big ones. [R asking to have crackers after supper; none in sight.] 3;6.29
I don't get **better** gloves, but you do. [As M gets out R's and M's gloves. When questioned, R asserts that M's are black, makes no reference to her own.] 3;7

X-*est* used for “X” or “very X”

If we have a **biggest** mouth, we have to put a **biggest** popsicle in it. [M getting popsicles out for children.] 3;2.28

***too* X used for “X” “very X”**

Put that in my place ‘cause it's **too little**. [R getting out spoons for dinner. Handing M a very little spoon that she chose for her own use.] 3;3.14
Your hands are **too big**. [context?] 3;6
I'm **too high**, Daddy. [R standing on table to turn light on, can barely reach light switch; proud of how high she is.] 3;6.6

Table 11.11A (continued) Continued Modifications Expressing INTENSIFICATION

J: Look how long our train is.
R It's **too long**, right?
[Both J and R eager to make the train they are putting together as long as possible.] 3;6.8

Look how high it is. **Too high**. **Too high** means too tall. 3;6.23

enough

R: We came home **fast enough**.
F: Fast enough for what?
R: We came home in the car **fast enough**.
[R doesn't understand why F asked her the question; rephrases her statement.] 3;7.15

Table 11.11B Continued Expression of LIKE

same

R: Big swimming suit is the **same** and big undershirt is the **same**.
M: The same as what?
R: They're **the same together... They're the same**.
[R apparently referring to the fact that swimming suit and undershirt have **same** kind of straps.] 3;6.21

They're both the **same** amount. They're half. They fit. They both fit. They're the **same** amount. [R holding two lids of same size of her toy dishes together—inside to inside.] 3;6.23

R: C'mere—I got **the same socks**.
M: What do you mean "you got the same socks"?
R: I got two socks.
[i.e., two socks that match; R found pair of socks in drawer to put on.] 3;6.23

Table 11.11C Continued Expression of CONTRAST

M: They're too little. [re: pair of shoes R has outgrown.]
R: When I grow **big**, then I can have them on....Do shoes grow? 3;4.28

...when I grow **back** to a baby **down**. [...then R will go on an airplane again. R & M had been talking about the fact that R had gone on an airplane when she was a baby.] 3;5.2

Jasmine's **the little** Amy's dog. Jasmine's **the little** dog that's Amy's. [Amy has 2 dogs; Jasmine is the smaller of the 2.] 3;5.11

[F asked R if there were two Terry's at R's school, and R said "yes," then:]
R: **One is different, and one isn't**.
M Which one is different?
R: Terry L___ is different.
[Terry L taught there last year, not this year.—R perhaps referring to this.] 3;7.18

Table 11.11D Continued Use of *too heavy* for "can't"

M: You're not too heavy for me.
R: I'm **too heavy** to pick you up. [i.e., "I can't pick you up."] 3;0.25

M: Only daddy can go up there.
R: I'm **too heavy**.
[R wanting to climb on piano to get to attic.] 3;2 to 3;4

TABLE 11.11 (continued) Adjectives Rachel 3;0–4;0

Table 11.11E Beyond INTENSIFICATION

***-er* possibly used appropriately**

M: That dress is too big.
R: I'll get a **littler** one. ["little" "littler" "very little"]
[M dressing R.] 3;1.28

You're **prettier** than me, 'cause I smile **not harder** than you. [R referring to the fact that M hadn't bought R's school pictures because R wasn't smiling in the picture. Second clause means either "I don't smile hard like you" or "I smile less hard than you".] 3;5.5

[R and M eating. M has cleaned the plate; R still has food on hers.]
R: Are you done?
M: Mhm. I'm in the clean plate club. [At school, children who finish their food are in a "clean plate club."]
R: Then I eat **slower**. I'm little. You're **bigger than** me, right? 3;6.29

When the water gets **littler**, then I don't need to be careful of the glass. [R then pours out some water]. The water got **littler**. 3;6.30

***-est* used for Superlative**

Look what sharpest knife this is. It's the **sharpest** knife **in the whole wide world**. 3;8.4
I want yellow. 'Cause yellow's my **best**. I like yellow **best**. [R picking yellow gingerbread man out of four men in game.] 3;8.13
Some people say "**favorest**," right? Not **favorest**. Yeah, **favorest**. 3;11.0

M: What did you see at the museum, Rachel?
R: The **biggest** dinosaur **that we never ever saw**.
[R, J, and F just got back from natural history museum.] 3;11.4

I'll still be a big kid—a big kid **in the whole wide world**. [R standing on toes with hands way up high.] 3;11.17

***too* used appropriately**

R: Can you reach it?
M No.
R: Are you **too little**?
M: Yeah.
R: Are you **too big**? You're not **too little**! Look at you.
[R wanting R or M to get pitcher up high on cabinet. First *too little* appropriate. Second *too little* as if R has heard what she has said, reinterprets it as "very little."] 3;6.30

I'm **too big**…to drop through that hole—to drop through my pretend babies' hole. [R holding hands together, interlacing fingers except pinkies, with which she is forming a "hole."] 3;6.30
This is real soft to carry for me. I'm **too tired** to carry this. 4;0.12

***how* / ____ *old* connected with AGE**

I'm gonna tell them **how old** they are. "**How old** are you guys?" [R pretending to talk to her aunt and uncle on telephone.] 3;7.28

as

I'm **as bigger than** her. [R standing up to compare herself with photo of herself. Meaning might be "I'm the same size as her" or "I'm bigger than her."] 3;4.26

(44) [R and M are playing with eight graduated rings; M puts them in a line from largest to smallest:]
M: Which is the biggest?
R: This the biggest [picking the biggest].
R: These three are the biggest [pointing to three largest]. These are the littlest [picking up the other five]…. Which is the largest?
M: Which?
R: **I don't know.**
[M separates rings, spreads them around randomly.]
M: Which one's the smallest?
R: That's the tiniest [pointing to littlest].
M: Which is largest?
[R chooses third smallest]
R: Let's see if it fits on there…. [setting that ring on other, larger ring; etc.]
[M tells R to put tiny toy baby bottle on "biggest" ring; R places it on biggest; M tells R to put bottle on "smallest" ring; R places it on second smallest; then:]
R: Do you want me to put it on the tiniest?
[R then puts bottle on smallest ring.]
[M places rings in line.]
R: All those are larger [re: biggest six rings]. Those two are smaller [re: smallest two rings].
M: Which one's littler than this [M pointing to fourth smallest ring, in line]?
R: These are littler [pointing to smallest three].
M: Which one's bigger than this [M pointing to same fourth smallest ring]?
R: These are bigger [pointing to largest four rings].
M: **Which one's littler than this** [pointing to third largest ring]**?**
R: **That's big!**
R: These are **littler** [pointing to smallest three], and these are **bigger** [pointing to other five].
M: Which one's the **largest**?
[R points to **third largest**]. 3;6.30

It seems that Rachel is, first, more or less overlooking the *-er* and *-est* endings on the adjectives and seems to be trying to understand the adjectives *tiny, small, little, large, big.* She seems to be attempting to locate these adjectives in a line from *tiniest*, at the extreme end, to *smallest* to *largest* to *biggest*, with *littlest* somewhere in between. But her difficulty in applying a scalar distribution of the terms, attempting to fit them into a sequence (to which they do not fit) appears to leave her stumped. The application of each term and where it fits relative to the others, especially in combination with *-er* and *-est*, poses a tricky challenge when scalarity and the meanings of *-er* and *-est* are still somewhat shaky.

On another occasion, at 3;8.27, Rachel corrects my choice of *little* to *tiny*:

(45) [M and R are doing a puzzle. M tells R to look for a piece with brown, blue,...:]
M: ...and a little bit of yellow.
R: a **tiny** yellow, you mean.

Quantifiers Earlier, before 3;0, Rachel already had *more* in her speech, but, as noted, she seemed to use *more* to mean something like "amount." By 3;11, Rachel's use of *more* seems to refer appropriately to comparative amount (see Table 11.12A).

Between 3;0 and 4;0, there are also uses of *a lot*, *much*, and *most* (see Table 11.12B). Both *a lot* and *much* are inappropriately linked with *than*. Both combinations appear to be used with a comparative import ("more...than") at a time when *more* was being used for some less mature meaning ("some"). There are also a few late use of *most* (note, not as an adjectival modifier).

Quantifier Modification Rachel continues to modify *more* with *any* (see Table 11.12C). The primary uses of *much* and *many* occur with modifiers—*too much/too many*, *that much*, and *how many* (Table 11.12C). While the semantics of *too many* is not clear, the semantics of *too much* and *that much* appear to be appropriate, and these occur at about the same time as the appropriate uses of A-*er*, A-*est*, and *too* A also begin to occur. The use of *how many* (as was the case for *the many* and *how A—how old*) encodes reference to age.[26]

What Is Missing? As in Sadie's case, with regard to form, there is very little (or in some cases, no) use of a number of forms: *as...as*, *enough*, *that* X, and *this* X. Unlike Sadie, Rachel does use many early *-er*, *-est*, and *too* A forms, but mostly with meanings of INTENSIFICATION until around 3;6, when more appropriate uses appear to be emerging. Rachel does not use *very* A or *how* X very much, except for the use of *how* X in a couple of references to age with "how old" and "how many."

As noted above, Rachel's inappropriate uses of these forms are missing notions of scalarity; for example, in her use of *fast enough*, in (46), she appears to mean "very fast":

[26]This association of *many* and *how many* with age is not unusual. Some examples from other children:

(xviii) ...what old will I be? **How many** will I be when it be's my birthday?... I'll be **this many** when it's my birthday [holding up five fingers]. Because that means older. (Jaime 4;0.23)

(xix) Tracey (3 yrs): That's **how many** I am. [holding up three fingers]
Jaime (7;4.1): "Here's how much I am," she should have said.

TABLE 11.12 Quantifiers Rachel 3;0–4;0

Table 11.12A *more*

more time today, right? [R drinking tea w/ spoon; M isn't? R had commented that we can drink tea w/ spoon. meaning not clear.] 3;6.21
Can I touch the table **any more**? [R asking if she can touch table which M had painted yesterday, so yesterday R couldn't touch it 'cause it was wet.] 3;7.9
This one gots **more**—most. [R holding two packs of paper, one thin, one fat.] 3;11.0

Table 11.12B Other Quantifiers

a lot

I want **a lot** of noodles **than** this. [i.e., "...more..." M had put some noodles on R's plate.] 3;2.19

much

Daddy gots **much** milk **than** me....Daddy gets **too much**. 3;6.21

most

They were **most** bad and not **most** good. [R's dolls have to sit on chairs because they were naughty; i.e. they were "mostly bad."] 3;9.2
This one gots more—**most**. [R holding two packs of paper, one thin, one fat.] 3;11.0

Table 11.12C Modification of Qs

more

Can I touch the table **any more**? [R asking if she can touch table which M painted yesterday, so yesterday R couldn't touch it 'cause it was wet.] 3;7.9

much

Daddy gots **much** milk **than** me....Daddy gets **too much**. 3;6.21
Are my gonna carry **that much** plates? It's **too much**. It's **too much** plates. One, two, three, four, five. Five plates. 3;9.16
Three things. My tummy can't take **that much** things. [i.e., cookies, crackers, candy.] 3;10.10

many

And there was a little boy that told me **how many** I am. [i.e., "...that asked me how old I am"] 3;0.26
(There's) **too many** people (in the swimming pool). [R pretending cheerios in milk are people; not clear if means "a lot."] 3;6.21

(46) R: We came home **fast enough**.
F: Fast enough for what?
R: We came home in the car **fast enough**.
[R doesn't understand why F asked her the question; rephrases her statement.] 3;7.15

As in Sadie's case, there are indications outside of these forms—for example, in the realm of time expressions—that support the claim that Rachel lacks an appreciation of scalarity:

(47) R: (When we got our clothes off) we'll **still** be cold.
M: Are you cold now, Rachel?
R: No, 'cause I got my PJ's on.
[means "we'll be cold then"] [R's interpretation is not scalar, but punctual] 3;8.28

TABLE 11.13 Problems with Scalarity

R: (When we got our clothes off) we'll **still** be cold.
M: Are you cold now, Rachel?
R: No, 'cause I got my PJ's on.
[means "we'll be cold then"] [R's interpretation is not scalar, but punctual] 3;8.28

You get it **until** I get my clothes. [F should get tea for R after she gets her clothes on. R means "you get it…when…I get my clothes"] [R's interpretation is not scalar, but punctual] 2;10.24

He's gonna get up **till** night-time. [J going to take a nap—idea: will sleep a long time—will get up "at" night-time.] [not scalar, but punctual] 3; 5.12

I won't eat it **until** I don't have any salt on it. [R won't eat supper till she can put salt on it. "I will eat it …when…"?] 3;7.7

No wonder we can have a birthday **till** Christmas. [R was asking M when her, J's, M's birthdays were. M's birthday is on Christmas day. [till = …"at"…?] not scalar] 3;8.5

(48) He's gonna get up **till** nighttime. [J going to take a nap—idea: will sleep a long time—will get up "at" night-time.] [not scalar] 3;5.12

See further examples with *until* and *still* in Table 11.13. Both *still* and *until,* in their appropriate adult usage, encode a relation between positions on a time scale viewed from below upwards until a cut-off point; that is, both scalarity and direction on the scale are encoded. Rachel uses *still* and *until* with a punctual import, to mean something more like "when" or "then."

Summary, Intermediate Uses, Rachel

During the first half of this year, Rachel's understanding of the comparative and the superlative appears to be still very immature, with uses for "X" and "very X." Around halfway through this year, nonintensifying uses of these forms and of *how, too,* and *enough* also begin to emerge. But Rachel's understanding of scalarity is still immature.

With regard to form, at about the same time as appropriate semantics for *A-er* and *too X* begin to emerge, Rachel seems to more consistently link *-er* with *than* complements. During this period, *much* also enters her speech as the second element in *too much* and *that much.*

Subsequent Advances: 4;0–5;0

Adjectives

INTENSIFICATION: During the next period, first, Rachel shows continued use and expansion of forms for INTENSIFICATION. This includes reduplication, *very, real(ly)* [and *real* is also used for "authentic"], *so,* and *pretty.* These are shown in Table 11.14A. During this time, around 4;6, another use of *very,* to mean "absolute" becomes very prominent, as seen in Table 11.14B. And her use of *how* with adjectives also expands beyond exclusive use with *old.* The semantic import of these utterances is sometimes not clear. But at least some of the uses appear to be for INTENSIFICATION.

(49) Look **how big** I got this. [R pulled off big lump of shell from Easter egg; she apparently means something like "Look what a big piece came off."] 4;11.12

At other times, the import seems to be more scalar. This seems most evident in utterances like the following at 4;11, in which she is comparing bigness in two things, implying some placement of the two relative to each other on a scale.

(50) R: Look **how bigger** the ladder is from you.
M: What?
R: Look **how big** the ladder is from you.
[R and M in back yard; ladder taller than M.] 4;11.4

***A-er*:** Her use of *A-er* during this time confirms semantic solidification prior to 4;0. There is no evidence of further uses of *A-er* to mean "A" or "very A" (see Table 11.14D, which shows unmodified uses of *A-er*). Her knowledge that *-er* is linked with *than*, when a standard of comparison is expressed, also continues to show solidification by this time; she no longer uses alternative standard markers with the comparative.

Interestingly, at 4;9.24 Rachel produces one use of *less A* ("less cold"), shown in Table 11.14E. But we will see below, in the next period, a serious struggle with the expressions of forms encoding negative ends or direction on a scale.

***A-est*:** She also uses *A-est* extensively during this period. Uses of *A-est* that are not modified are shown in Table 11.14F. As is true for the uses of *A-er*, the semantics of *A-est* shows solidification also prior to 4;0, with no further uses to mean "A" or "very A."

It is worth noting, before going into further modifications of the adjectival forms, a few developments in relation to the form of the simple superlative. First, Rachel shows some clear struggling with the form of the superlative: While in the adult language, the superlative virtually always occurs with *the*, Rachel sometimes uses *my*, sometimes *the* before *A-est*. This is perhaps a carry-over from *my favorite* [*favorite* has been in Rachel's speech from the earliest stages], as well as her clear association of *favorite* with *best*, as in:

(51) I'll tell you what's **my best** Kool Aid—pink. [F, M, J, R talking about "Country Time" lemonade being like yellow Kool-Aid.] 4;4.27

What is **your best book** of mine? [= "what book of mine is your favorite?"] 4;10.25

Purple is Nicole's favorite color—**best** color. 4;10.26

Daddy, here is **my best** part—"21 on none." [in book—21 people on no bike.] 4;11.4

That's **my best** song in the whole wide world. 4;11.14

R: That's **my best** thing.
M: That's your best thing?
R: Uhu. [= yes] ... I mean that's <u>**the**</u> [= /ðə/] **best** thing. 4;11.19

Oh, that's **my best** part! [R in kitchen—hears song on Sesame Street that she likes; then runs into living room to watch; song: "People in Your Neighborhood"] 5;0.11

(Note her self-correction to *the* in the second-to-last example.) She even uses *best* as the degree marker at this same time:

(52) R: Wonder Woman is **the best great** of all.
J: No, Green Goblin.
R: Green Goblin is **the best great** of all.
[R and J playing wrestling; R is W.W., J is G.G.] 4;9.29

She also shows some overextensions to *marveloust, differentest* (and *favorest* just prior to this period, at 3;11). And toward the end of this period, around 4;10 onward, she shows double marking (*the most A-est*) on superlatives (Table 11.14G).

The second aspect of the form of the superlative that is developing during this time is the standard of comparison. For Rachel, the clear favorite form is *in the (whole wide) world*, as shown in the examples in Table 11.14H. But, like her early use, around age 3, of *than* phrases outside of *A-er* phrases, Rachel's use of *in the (whole wide) world* at this age, at age 4½ to 5, extends beyond the superlative (and takes on a superlative type import in those phrases). Furthermore, she eventually turns this expression into *world's*, used preadjectivally as a superlative marker, also shown in Table 11.14H—e.g., in:

(53) The greatest **world's** mommy. [R being affectionate.] 4;11.0

This association of *in the world* with *world's* is quite explicit in the following utterance:

(54) [R is reporting to M a dream she had:]
R: [R says she dreamt about:] the **world('s)** stealer.
M: Does he steal the world, Rachel?
R: No, he steals everything he finds. 4;11.17

Finally, during this time, we also see greater use of scalar modifiers. She uses *too A/enough A*, shown in Table 11.14I, even in self-correction from what appears to be an initial use of *too A* to mean "very A" to a more appropriate *A enough*. There are many more occurrences of *as A as*, shown in Table 11.14J. It is clear that the semantics of these uses of *as…as* is deficient, however. In most cases, Rachel appears to mean "the same X as," so *as big as* means "the same size as," and so

TABLE 11.14 Adjectives Rachel 4;0-5;0

Table 11.14A For INTENSIFICATION:

Reduplication

There's a **big, big, big, long** dinosaur. [R drew a tall, skinny ghost-like shape.] 4;6.7

R: They're way so down ....
M: What?
R: I mean they're way so far down they look like **tiny, tiny** ants.
[R looking at people outside 4th floor window, down on ground through window.] 5;0.24

That is a busy street—**busy, busy, busy** street. [re: main street through town] 5;0.30

very

R: That's littler and that's taller. [re: two glasses almost exactly same height, but very different in diameter; first = juice glass, second = mug]
[M writes this down; R then asked M what she wrote and M read it; R corrects:]
R: **very tall**.
M: And is that very little?
R: Yea, and that's **very taller**. Look how big that is. Can you see how tall it is? 4;6.25

M: Why don't you use one of your purses for your crayons?
R: No, I have a **very better** idea.
[R collecting up crayons; R then goes to get one of her dishes to put crayons in.] 4;11.3

Ronald McDonald is littler than Saasha—**very littler**. [re: R.McD. hand puppet] 4;11.6

real

M: They don't like babies at my school.
R: Unless they're **real ones** that belong to mommies and daddies.
[R asking M if M will take her doll baby to university.] 4;10.8

R: Keep your foot hard to the ground.
M: What?
R: Keep it to the ground **real hard**.
[R wants to "crack" M's toes; M has to hold foot back.] 5;0.23

really

The jug **is really filled** with milk. 4;11.29

so

Yea, because I was **so busy**. Except I'm gonna be so busier this time. [J wants to lie in M's bed w/ M for nap, then told R she could, since she hadn't done it on a previous occasion.] 4;9.0

pretty

This is **pretty hard** to show up. [R trying to write her name on book; the name is hard to see.] 4;10.16

Table 11.14B *very* for "absolute"

The **very next** top drawer. I mean, the very third drawer. [R telling M that she found item she was looking for in 3rd from top drawer in kitchen] 4;6.24

I can even do the **very back** one. [R snapping PJ top to bottom—there is 1 snap in the middle of the back.] 4;9.18

J: Rachel, where's your PJ drawer?
R: On the **very bottom**.
[J putting R's PJ's away; J doesn't know which drawer to use.] 4;10.4

Table 11.14B (continued) *very* for "absolute"

R: What day's just before—the **very before** Easter?
M: What?
R: What day's right before Easter? 4;11.0

You made me have to do the **very rest**. [M waited for R to let M wash R's face; R washed all dirt off and M told R M didn't need to wipe R's face since it was all clean; then R wiped forehead and said above.] 4;11.26

That's because the blocks were at the way—on the **very bottom**. [re: R moved top toy bins to get to bottom one which had blocks in it --was way at the bottom.] 5;0.18

Table 11.14C *how*

Do you wanna see **how big** their fingers are? [i.e. the "daddy" forks—the tongs of big forks.] 4;3.13

R: That's littler and that's taller. [re: two glasses almost exactly same height, but very different in diameter; first = juice glass, second = mug]
[M writes this down; R then asked M what she wrote and M read it; R corrects:]
R: <u>very</u> tall.
M: And is that very little?
R: Yea, and that's very taller. Look **how big** that is. Can you see **how tall** it is? 4;6.25

R: Look **how bigger** the ladder is from you.
M: What?
R: Look **how big** the ladder is from you.
[R and M in back yard; ladder taller than M] 4;11.4

Look **how big** I got this. [R pulled off big lump of shell from Easter egg; she apparently means something like "look what a big piece came off."] 4;11.12

Look **how big** daddy gave me a bowl. Look **how big** of a bowl daddy gave me. [re: bowl for egg shells.] 4;11.12

R: Look **how big** my mouth is.
F: Wow, what if I fell in there?
R: You wouldn't, because it's not so little ... I mean, so big.
[R showing F her mouth with it wide open.] 5;0.6

Table 11.14D *A-er*

M: Who's bigger than me, Rachel?
R: Daddy.
M: Who's littler than me?
R: Jaime.
M: Who's the littlest, Rachel?
R: Jaime and me. 4;0.7

[A girl and a boy on Sesame Street help each other put smocks on. The girl is shorter than the boy.]
The little girl is **littler**, just like me…[R looks at J] is **littler than** Jaime! 4;4.6

F: Whose sandwich is this?
R: Ann said she'd leave it for me unless I want it **later**. [i.e., "…in case I want it later"]
[F has found sandwich in the refrigerator.] 4;8.6

I'm **bigger than** anyone in the world. [R standing on table.] 4;10.6
Higher, higher. [i.e., louder, music on radio; R wants M to turn up radio.] 4;10.15
(Do you know why I got back here?) Because it's **the warmer** place. [R behind sofa] 4;10.27

Table 11.14D (continued) *A-er*

J: I like 'em better.
R: He said "I like 'em better."
F: What's he supposed to say?
R: I like 'em **better than** that. (4;11.7)

This can't be coffee 'cause it tastes so good—how'd they take the **better** taste—the best taste out. [R singing commercial; real words: "How'd they take the bitter taste out?"] 4;11.9

It helps your bones get strong/**stronger** unless the hammer's too heavy for you. [re: milk. J had said milk was good for nails (referring to fingernails); R picks up on this, thinking he was referring to nails for hammering. She means "It helps your bones get strong/stronger in case the hammer's too heavy for you."] 4;11.18

Table 11.14E *less A*

Sherbet is **less cold than** this snow ice cream. [R thinks snow ice cream is colder.] 4;9.24

Table 11.14F *A-est*

Black is **my terriblest** color. 4;1.0

R: I wish I was Jaime.
M: Why?
R: 'Cause Jaime gets to do **the funnest than** me.
[R, M, J talking about J's tumbling class and R doing dancing class] 4;1.24

R: Which finger do you think **is the heaviest** for this?
M: I don't know.
R: This finger.
[R holding small piece of curled crayon paper in 1 hand, picks it up by inserting ring finger of other hand and lifting it w/ it wrapped around finger. "heavy" = "strong"?] 4;2.18

I'll tell you what's **my best** Kool-Aid—pink. [F, M, J, and R talking about "Country Time" lemonade being like yellow Kool-Aid.] 4;4.27

Mommy, here's some paper unless you hear someone say **the darndest**. [R handing M pack of 3 X 5's. We call these utterances "the darndest things." R means "… in case you hear…"] 4;8.26

I like those **best** the same amount. [in book, it says to circle the box you think is the prettiest; R first circled 1 box, then decided she liked another just as much.] 4;8.30

I'll tell you which one of those toothbrushes are **smallest**. [R and J in bathroom.] 4;9;21

Whoever be's **the quietest** gets the prize. [R and J playing wrestling; M in audience.] 4;9.29

OK—here's the prizes for whoever be's **the quietest**. [R bringing prizes after wrestling match between R and J.] 4;9.29

(Don't let anybody see the prizes) until they be **the quietest** and we give it to 'em. 4;9.29

... give to **the most best** person that be's **quietest**. 4;9.29

R: Wonder Woman is **the best great** of all.
J: No, Green Goblin.
R: Green Goblin is **the best great** of all.
[R and J playing wrestling; R is W.W., J is G.G.] 4;9.29

My pants are **the wettest** I have on. [R has just taken off long pants which got all wet from melting snow.] 4;10.10

Are red or yellow apples **the juiciest**? [R has just gotten red apple out for herself; M eating yellow apple.] 4;10.12

R: Put those over there unless someone can't reach it.
[R telling F to put cheerios in middle of table. F then read above out loud.]
R: <u>That</u> isn't **a darndest thing**! 4;10.14

Table 11.14F (continued) *A-est*

I don't like anybody 'cept you **the best**. [R to M; R mad at J and F.] 4;10.15
The marvelousт mommy in the world. [R thinking out loud.] 4;10.18
What is **your best book** of mine? [= "what book of mine is your favorite?"] 4;10.25
Purple is Nicole's favorite color—**best** color. 4;10.26
This one is the different of all. This is **the differentest** I ever had. [R just got new purse in mail.] 4;10.27
The greatest world's mommy. [R being affectionate.] 4;11.0
I'll get you something unless somebody says some **darndest** things. [R handing M pad of paper.] 4;11.3
Daddy, here is **my best** part—"twenty one on none." [in book—21 people on no bike.] 4;11.4
That's **my best** song in the whole wide world. 4;11.14

R: That's **my best** thing.
M: That's your best thing?
R: Uhu. [= "yes"] ... I mean that's **<u>the</u> [= /ðə/] best** thing. 4;11.19

Oh, that's **my best** part! [R in kitchen -- hears song on Sesame Street that she likes; then runs into living room to watch; song: "People in Your Neighborhood"] 5;0.11

Table 11.14G Double Marking: *the most A-est*

... give to **the most best** person that be's quietest. 4;9.29
I told you it would be **the most funniest** world's champion. [R and J playing wrestling.] 4;9.29
The most biggest one is that. [R pointing to biggest leaf on rubber plant; R, J, and F discussing its new leaves, etc.] 4;11.9
Here comes **the most beautifulest** thing. [M putting J's cover on his bed, as M makes bed.] 4;11.11

Table 11.14H *...in the (whole wide) world*

<u>*A-est* ____ :</u>

The marvelousт mommy **in the world**. [R thinking out loud.] 4;10.18
That's my best song **in the whole wide world**. 4;11.14

<u>A ___ or other context:</u>

I wish my tummy was empty of everything **in the world**. 4;8.28
I like both of you **in the whole wide world**. [R to F and M.] 4;11.1

<u>in the world → *the world's*:</u>

I told you it would be the most funniest **world's** champion. [R and J playing wrestling.] 4;9.29
The greatest **world's** mommy. [R being affectionate.] 4;11.0

[R is reporting to M a dream she had:]
R: (I dreamt about) the **world('s)** stealer.
M: Does he steal the world, Rachel?
R: No, he steals everything he finds. 4;11.17

Table 11.14I *too A/A enough*

I was **too strong** to open it. I was **strong enough** to open it. 4;2.7
She [re: R's doll] said she's sweating **too hot**. 4;10.27

Table 11.14J *as A as*

They're about **as old as** me—five. [= "they're about the same age as me"; R pretending cheerios are kids; R is four; M then asks R if she's five; R says "no, they are."] [not scalar; wrong direction on scale?] 4;4.11.
Except they're not **as big as** each other. [R, J, F saying that two girls down the street are twins, then above (the girls are not really twins).] 4;6.5

Table 11.14J (continued) *as A as*

As long as I move the table over here. [= "as soon as..."; R asked for milk; M told her to come in kitchen; R wants her table in living room] [cf. "long" for time?—as long as it takes me to…] 4;8.25

Maybe that's **as far as** he can throw. [M found newspaper up by front door; paperboy usually throws paper onto front lawn, nearer street; M said boy put it by the door, then above.] [has wrong implicature—no further than that] 4;8.28

That's about **as warm**—that's about **so warm that** we could go to the lake. [R had called time and temp.; temp. is 64°.] [means "warm enough"] [stops w/ **as**…, since she'd have to continue with **as** …?] 4;11.25

M: Are you **as cold as** I am, Rachel?
R: No, I'm colder, **not as cold**!
[re: a chilly morning] 5;0.25

Table 11.14K *that A*

How could it be **that little** when it's mommy's. [F holding up R's coat asked "Is this yours or is it mommy's?" R means "...if it's mommy's."] 4;11.3

[R asked M to open her bedroom door at bed time, after M put R to sleep; M opened door a little, and R said:] I don't mean **that far.** [R then got up and opened the door even more. Wrong direction on scale] 5;0.8

forth. This indicates that she is not using *as…as* strictly as a scalar predicate, with a direction from below upward on the scale, but more as indicating a point on a scale. And many of her utterances clearly lack the appropriate semantics that such a scalar understanding would entail. For example, on one occasion, I had found our newspaper up right by our front door, not where the paperboy usually threw our paper—onto the front lawn, nearer the street. I made a comment about the fact that the boy put our newspaper by the door, and Rachel says:

(55) Maybe that's **as far as** he can throw. 4;8.28

This use of *as…as* is odd, because it does not carry the normal implicature "up to that point and no further." Rachel seems to be saying "Maybe he can throw that distance."

The same can be said for her uses of *that* A at the same time (see Table 11.14K). She uses *not that far*, for example, to mean "not that distance," lacking the scalar encoding of movement up the scale. Thus, her statement at 5;0.8, when she chides me for the amount that I have left her bedroom door open, does not carry the appropriate implicature, and entails the wrong direction on the scale:

(56) [R asked M to open her bedroom door at bedtime, after M put R to sleep;
M opened door a little, and R said:]
I don't mean **that far**.
[R then got up and opened the door even more.] 5;0.8

Finally, it is of note that Rachel's uses of *as…as*, like Sadie's at an earlier age, invariably have both the appropriate degree marker and the standard marker, linked from the start (more on this below).

These developments with adjectives reveal the following advances during this period:

- First, R's use of the comparative appears to be semantically correct by age 4.
- R's use of the superlative appears to be semantically correct by this same age.
- R's realization that the simple *-er* comparative is linked with the standard marker *than* appears to be solidified by this period.
- R's formation of the simple *-est* superlative, however, appears to be in a protracted period of transition during which she has not settled on the correct degree marker, alternating *-est* with *best*, and using *the* and *my*. She also uses *in the (whole wide) world* as the dominant standard of comparison, and she has a period during which this phrase alternates with preadjectival *world's*.
- In addition to these developments within simple comparative and superlative forms, Rachel begins during this time to use *how* with spatial adjectives, sometimes to encode INTENSIFICATION, and sometimes apparently with a scalar sense. She also uses A *enough* in an appropriate sense.
- Finally, she begins using the scalar modifier *as…as*, but semantically, it appears to mean "the same … as," rather than to be strictly scalar. That is, the interpretation has to do with a more punctual assessment of the degree of presence of a property, and to lack a scalar interpretation of asserting a lower limit, moving from low on the scale upwards. The use of these forms, thus, lacks in many cases the appropriate semantics and implicature for these expressions.

Quantifiers

Q: There are very few cases of isolated quantifiers in the data, as most quantifiers during this period are used in combination with other modifiers (see Table 11.15A).

Q + *more*: In the previous periods, Rachel used *any more* and *no more*; here she adds other quantifiers preceding *more*: *three more, a lot more* (see Table 11.15B).

X/Deg? + *much (many)*: Rachel also was already using *too much* and *that much*, and she continues to do so, and she adds other modifiers to the repertoire preceding *much* (and occasionally *many*): *so, how, as* (see Table 11.15C).

As much/many (as) is of particular note: At the same time as Rachel begins using *as…as* with adjectives, Rachel begins using *as…(as)* with *much* and *many*, indicating a shared syntactic/semantic source. Examples are given in Table 11.15D. While the adjectival forms showed a link between the use of both the degree marker and the standard marker *as* from 4;4, the quantifier forms show consistent use of both markers from just before 4;10. She corrects herself at 4;9.30 from "get as many glasses out you want" to "get as many glasses out as you want." This may be one case in which there is evidence of transferring what has been learned in one domain (*as…as* with As) to another domain (*as…as* with Qs).

With regard to semantic content, many of these utterances, just as those for *as A as* and *that* A, still reveal an immature understanding of the scalar semantics associated with these forms. For example, Rachel uses *that much* for the wrong direction on the scale at 4;10.25:

(57) How come you have **that much** and I don't? [to F, who had almost finished his bowl of cereal; R had just started hers.] 4:10.25

At the same time, she shows, as Sadie did, an emergent association of scalarity with number, as in:

(58) You know **how many** times I love you? I love you **one hundred times**. 4;10.7

[R comparing amount she's sweating and amount she's tired:]
I'm **sweating three times**, and I'm **tired two times**.
[i.e., sweating at a value of 3 and tired at a value of 2.] 4;11.25

Interestingly, the adult form in the first of the utterances in (58) would have used *how much*. Utterances in, for example, Table 11.15C make it clear that Rachel still does not respect the mass/count distinction for *much* and *many*, usually overusing *much* where *many* should be used. But Rachel's choice of *many* in this utterance, which was previously associated with numbers connected with age, and her association of the magnitude of her feeling with a (high) number (… *one hundred times*), is consistent with Sadie's association of scalarity with numbers, as in the examples in Table 11.15H. We will see more of this in Rachel's data for 5;0 to 6;0 below.

X + A-er: Around 4;6, Rachel begins placing modifiers in front of *A-er*: This includes *even, enough, more, so, much, very,* and *how*. Initially, there is one occurrence of *too much A-er* alternating with *much too A-er* (see Table 11.15E). There are several important aspects concerning these structures:

- All of the modifiers are placed before *A-er*, even *enough*: *enough closer*.
- They seem to emerge fairly co-temporaneously, indicating a probable comparable construction governing them. That is, there is no evidence for any difference in Rachel's composing of, for example, *much + A-er* and that of *how + A-er, even + A-er, so + A-er, very + A-er*.
- This is despite the fact that she has had for some time already in her speech forms like *too much* and *that much*. So, the potential to form expressions such as *too much bigger* and *that much bigger* was clearly available in her repertoire, but the fact that she did not produce such combinations supports the likelihood that she had a simple rule at this time of concatenation: *X + A-er*.
- And, finally, the elements that fall into the category of pre-*A-er* options include *more*. These are the first occurrences of double marking of the

TABLE 11.15 Quantifiers Rachel 4;0–5;0

Table 11.15A Q

a lot

A row of O's. When there's **a lot** of O's, you can call it a "row of O's" [R seeing "92,000,000" in phone book.] 4;1.10

more

Ann's came **more than** Janet. [i.e., as babysitter; R says she said "Ann" not "Ann's."] 5;0.5

most

R:	There's **most** girl babies **than** boy babies.
M:	What?
R:	There's **most** girl babies in the world **than** boy babies.

[needs "more," not "most"] 4;11.25

Table 11.15B X + *more*

We better be (finished) hanging all our stuff for Halloween until it's **three more** days. 4;6.14
I need **a lot more** bites ... more than eleven ... to do all of it. [M told R to eat 11 more bites of her supper; she at first said that would be all the rest of the food...] 4;7.1

Table 11.15C X + *much/many*

I can hold **this much** in one blow. [R holding bunch of cookie cutters—"at one time"; J and R picked up "in one blow" from "Seven at a Blow."] 4;2.8
Look **how much** shells you got. [R to F; F eating nuts, putting shells on plate.] 4;8.4
Mommy, look **how much** checkers I got. [R w/ checker game, collected lots of checkers by jumping; R playing w/ herself.] 4;8.11
They have **so much** colors. They have **so much** colors from the paint. [R looking at tree ornamemts she made and painted at school.] 4;8.20
Mommy, now there's **so much** people. [in auditorium, waiting for show] 4;8.25
Look **how much** E's I got. [R playing Scrabble (Juniors).] 4;8.26
You're gonna have to put it on unless I put **too much**. [salt on zucchini; "in case I (would) put too much."] 4;8.28
It [re: house] has **so much** windows. 4;9.1
First I gotta count **how much** there are. [R wants to count beads on necklace.] 4;9.28
Let me see **how much** necklaces I have. I have one, two, three, four—[R thinking of the necklaces she has.] 4;9.29
Mommy, do you know **how much** you should give me? [M tearing pieces of tape off roll for R to use; R goes to see how many she needs] 4;9.30
You know **how many** times I love you? I love you one hundred times. 4;10.7
I wanna see **how much** things—no, **how much** pieces....[R cutting cheese into pieces.] 4;10.8
...'cause I drank **so much** things and ate **so much** things. [That's why R has to go potty.] 4;10.23
How come you have **that much** and I don't? [to F, who had almost finished his bowl of cereal; R had just started hers.] [wrong direction on scale] 4:10.25
You cut this part of my bangs **too much** [= "too short"]. 4;11.20
I'm not so hungry for soup—soup is **too much**. [R wanting cracker for snack, not hungry enough for soup she left from lunch.] 5;0.20

Table 11.15D *as + much/many (+ as)*

That's **as much** I took. [J putting ketchup on his plate—as much as R took.] 4;6.27
Can I taste **as many** cookies I want? [re: Xmas cookies.] 4;8.4
Daddy, get **as many** glasses out you want. [F did not understand and R repeated:] Daddy, get **as many** glasses out **as** you want. 4;9.30
You can have **as many** pieces **as** you want. [R offered F some of apple she has cut up.] 4;10.12
That's **as much as** I could only get out. [R getting grapefruit out of skin—having a hard time; "I could only get out that little" R showing M how little there is in bowl. wrong direction on scale? problem of scope?] 4;11.25

Table 11.15D (continued) *as + much/many (+ as)*

F: They're **as much** Henderson's and mine **as** anybody else's.
R: **Much** Hendersons! There's only one Henderson.
[misunderstood "as much…as"; also, her link of *much* with *Hendersons* reveals lack of respect of mass/count distributional restrictions—*much* + singular] 5;0.26

[R says she wants to give M...]
As many hugs and kisses you are ... **as many** years old you are.
[R was going to say "as many hugs and kisses you are old," but then put in "…as" and got convoluted] 5;0.27

Table 11.15E X + *A-er*

Angie's **much too bigger than** me. I'll tell you who's **too much bigger than** me. You're **much too bigger than** me. 4;6.10
Why didn't you get **enough closer** to the door? [R asking M why M didn't answer R knocking on front door; M told R that M didn't hear her knocking.] 4;6.16

R: I did it **even bigger than** that.
M: I know, and I want you to do it smaller.
R: I mean I did it littler.
[R picking up glob of cranberry littler than F said she had.] 4;7.20

That chair's **more funner than** any other chair. [first double marking. AFTER other *X + A-er* forms] 4;8.2
This feels **more better** up here. [R feeling velvet on top part of chair.] 4;8.25
Yea, because I was so busy. Except I'm gonna be **so busier** this time. [J wants to lie in M's bed w/ M, then told R she could, since she hadn't done it the last time.] 4;9.0
There, I made the hole **much bigger**. [R made opening to cheerios package bigger.] 4;10.20

M: Why don't you use one of your purses for your crayons?
R: No, I have a **very better** idea.
[R collecting up crayons; R then goes to get one of her dishes to put crayons in.] 4;11.3

R: Look **how bigger** the ladder is **from** you.
M: What?
R: Look how big the ladder is from you.
[R and M in back yard; ladder taller than M.] 4;11.4

Ronald McDonald is **littler than** Saasha—**very littler**. [R.McD. hand puppet.] 4;11.6
Scoot the chair **more farther**. [R wants M to scoot chair closer to cabinet so she can reach can opener; R on chair.] 4;11.19
Hail! That would be **even badder than** hard snow. [i.e., if it fell on umbrella.] 5;0.29

Table 11.15F *even/much more A-er*

I have something that's **even more better**. [To J; J and R playing in R's room.] 4;10.15
I'll have to get **much more bigger** before I can wear his yellow raincoat. [i.e., J's raincoat.] 4;10.25
I'll have to grow **much more bigger** until I can wear this. 4;10.25
The kid's **much more older than** the baby. [R said she's going to take her kid for a ride; F asked her if the kid was the same as her baby, which R had previously said had died today.] 4;10.26
I'm **much more bigger than** my door. 4;11.15
This is **even more better than** D.Q. [R eating ice cream cone from supermarket; D.Q. = Dairy Queen.] 5;0.27
A snake would be **much more bigger than** that was. [re: Play-Do mold for a worm: R couldn't remember if it was a worm or a snake, decided it was a worm.] 5;0.28

TABLE 11.15 (continued) Quantifiers Rachel 4;0–5;0

Table 11.15G Problems with Scalarity

We better be (finished) hanging all our stuff for Halloween **until** it's three more days. 4;6.14
I'm [=/ãĩn/] just gonna get one out **until** I'm [ãĩn] done eatin' this one. [R getting nut out of bowl and setting it on table to wait till she's done eating the one she's just started; i.e., "...for when..."] 4;8.5

Table 11.15H Association of Scalarity with Number

You know **how many times** I love you? I love you **one hundred times**. 4;10.7
[R comparing amount she's sweating and amount she's tired:]
I'm sweating **three times**, and I'm tired **two times**.
[i.e., sweating at a value of 3 and tired at a value of 2.] 4;11.25

comparative in Rachel's speech. It is not clear if there is any possibility that *more A-er* forms prompted her to expand to a larger rule of *X + A-er*, or whether *more A-er* simply fell into line along with other *X + A-er* constructs. The timing of the emergence of *more A-er*, however, suggests that it is simply one type of the *X + A-er* constructs, as the first examples of doubly marked comparatives appeared about two months after the first *X + A-er* constructions.

- The conclusion that the doubly marked comparatives grew, at least in part, out of the availability of *X + A-er* constructs is supported with the subsequent development of these constructs, below, as well as the timing of the doubly marked superlative constructs, which emerged approximately two months after the doubly marked comparative forms. Thus, *X + A-er* forms emerged around 4;6, doubly marked comparatives emerged around 4;8 (possibly as a development of the *X+A-er* forms), and doubly marked superlatives emerged around 4;10 (Table 11.14G).

***even/much more A-er*:** About half a month after the emergence of doubly marked superlatives, and after the *X + A-er* forms had been in Rachel's speech for about four months, she began to produce constructs of the form *even/much more A-er* (Table 11.15F). There are a number of important aspects of these structures:

- First, the initial modifier always occurs with *more A-er*, never simply *A-er*, and never with any of the other *X + A-er* forms in Rachel's speech (e.g., never *much so bigger, much very bigger*, etc.).
- Second, the initial modifiers in evidence were only *even* and *much*. Again, while Rachel clearly had forms like *too much* and *that much* in her repertoire, she did not produce forms like *how much better, that much closer, too much bigger*, or even *that much more bigger.*

More Elaborated Structures There is also evidence during this time that Rachel begins to develop longer structures involving these forms:

Standard of comparison: First, as we have seen, Rachel appears to have established prior to this age that when the standard of comparison is expressed with the comparative, *than* is used. With *as*, she seems to link the degree marker *as* from the beginning of its use with the standard marker *as*. Moreover, she seems to conclude by 4;10 that the standard of comparison is *required* in such *as…as* constructs. At 4;9.30, she corrects her own utterance from one without the standard marker to one with the standard marker *as*. Interestingly, it is at exactly this same time that Rachel corrects her (older) brother's use of a comparative without a standard of comparison:

(59) J: I like 'em better.
R: He said "I like 'em better." [as if "catching" a mistake]
F: What's he supposed to say?
R: I like 'em **better than** that. 4;11.7

If indeed she did conclude that the standard marker *as* (or by extension, *than*) was required, this would be a case of a child drawing up a structure on the basis of positive evidence only. Recall from the examination of the written texts and of Abe's corpora that there is a probable high frequency of co-occurrence between degree marker *as* and standard marker *as* in input to children.

Nominal heads: It is at this time that we also see attempts at constructing more elaborate structures, and Rachel's attempts help highlight some important issues these present.

First, we begin to see problems with constructs that include a nominal head—for example,

(60) Look **how big** Daddy gave me **a bowl**. Look **how big of a bowl** Daddy gave me. 4;11.12

The appearance of such structures and a closer examination of all of the utterances up to this point reveal a striking fact: Prior to 4;11, the only constructs involving elaborated adjectival forms modifying noun heads are of two types:

First, there are a few forms that would be considered outside of the system in question in the adult language and are often immature sounding:

- Reduplicated forms, such as "There's a **big, big, big, long** dinosaur." [R, 4;6.7]
- Forms with *real(ly)*, when these mean "authentic," such as in (61), and forms in which *very* is used to mean "absolute," such as in (62).

(61) I'm not **a really monster**. 2;10.15

M: They don't like babies at my school.
R: Unless they're **real ones** that belong to mommies and daddies.
[R asking M if M will take her doll baby to university.] 4;10.8

(62) R: The **very next top drawer**. I mean, the **very third drawer**.
[R telling M that she found rope lighter in 3rd from top drawer in kitchen] 4;6.24

R: I can even do the **very back one.**
[R snapping PJ top to bottom—there is 1 snap in the middle of the back.] 4;9.18

The second and only other type of structure in which Rachel uses adjectival forms with noun heads prior to 4;11 is superlative structures, such as the following:

(63) Look **what sharpest knife** this is. It's **the sharpest knife** in the whole wide world. 3;8.4

M: What did you see at the museum, Rachel?
R: **The biggest dinosaur** that we never ever saw.
[R, J, and F just got back from natural history museum.] 3;11.4

Black is **my terriblest color**. 4;1.0

I'll tell you what's **my best Kool Aid**—pink. [F, M, J, R talking about "Country Time" lemonade being like yellow Kool-Aid.] 4;4.27

...give to **the most best person** that be's quietest. 4;9.29

The marveloust mommy in the world. [R thinking out loud.] 4;10.18

What is **your best book** of mine? [= "What book of mine is your favorite?"] 4;10.25

As we've already noted, Rachel vacillates in such forms in her choice of determiner, mostly between *the* and a possessive form. And even in such superlative structures, a noun is sometimes curiously missing:

(64) Mommy, here's some paper unless you hear someone say **the darndest**. [R handing M pack of 3 × 5's. We always call these utterances "the darndest things."] 4;8.26

My pants are **the wettest** I have on. [R has just taken off long pants which got all wet from melting snow.] 4;10.10

The first of these is especially odd, since in the family we always referred to these expressions as "the darndest things" (from the old Art Linkletter TV program, on which he had a segment called "Kids Say the Darndest Things" in which he interviewed young children).

Beyond these two types of structures, for all other structures in which elaborated adjectival forms (i.e., other than simple adjectives) occurred, virtually not a single utterance before 4;11 allowed the adjectival form to occur with a nominal head. This includes utterances involving *A-er, too* A, *so* A, *real(ly)* A (for intensification), *pretty* A, *how* A, and *X* + *A-er.*

I say "virtually" because at the earliest uses of *A-er,* in the first half of the year when Rachel was 3, she did use *A-er* forms with nominal heads, as in:

(65) Hey! I got two **prettier shirts**! [R has taken one of her favorite shirts out of her drawer to put it on. When asked about "two" R referred to a shirt that she wore home from school, after getting her other clothes wet at school.] 3;6.23

Two big ones. Two **bigger ones**. Two big ones. [R asking to have crackers after supper; none in sight.] 3;6.29

I don't get **better gloves**, but you do. [As M gets out R's and M's gloves. When questioned, R asserts that M's are black, makes no reference to her own.] 3;7

M: That dress is too big.
R: I'll get a **littler one.** ["little" "littler" "very little"]
[M dressing R.] 3;1.28

It may be highly significant that, as noted above, at this early stage Rachel seems to be using these forms semantically as noncomparative forms, almost like alternants of simple *A* forms.

Then at 4;11, we begin to see uses of these comparative forms with noun heads:

(66) (Do you know why I got back here?) Because it's **the warmer place.** [R behind sofa.] 4;10.27

M: Why don't you use one of your purses for your crayons?
R: No, I have **a very better idea.**
[R collecting up crayons; R then goes to get one of her dishes to put crayons in.] 4;11.3

This can't be coffee 'cause it tastes so good—how'd they take **the better taste**—the best taste out. [R singing commercial; real words: "How'd they take the bitter taste out?"] 4;11.9

And it is at exactly this same time that we see Rachel's self-correction from using a possessive determiner for a superlative form to using the definite determiner *the*:

(67) R: That's **my best** thing.
M: That's your best thing?
R: Uhu. [= yes]...I mean that's **<u>the</u> [= /ðə/] best** thing. 4;11.19

These developments are highly suggestive that it is not until this time that Rachel begins to construct the more complex phrase structure patterns that will allow for adjectival forms involving degree-marked adjectives within nominal phrases. Whether the late establishment of more complex syntactic structures of this type is due to the fact that the emergence of such constructs is contingent on the prior working out of simpler syntactic details (e.g., the appropriate degree and standard markers, co-occurrence patterns) or is related to the relatively infrequent occurrence of such forms in the input (as judged by the Abe corpora—only 2 out of 57 utterances had comparatives with nominal heads—see the introduction) is a question that will have to await further study.

Clausal Complements: It is also at the end of this period that we see Rachel begin to attempt complex clausal complements of these structures, such as the following:

(68) [R says she wants to give M...]
as many hugs and kisses you are...**as many years old** you are.
[appears she was going to say "as many hugs and kisses you are old," but then put in "...as" and got convoluted] 5;0.27

There has to be **as many people**... [R hesitates and says she does not know how to say it, then:]
There has to be **as many people**...um...**that as many words** there are. 5;2.15

It may well be that she has been "pushed" into working out these structures, at least in part, as a consequence of her conclusion that the standard of comparison in *as...as* structures must be explicit.

Interpretation of Scalar Forms: As noted, Rachel continues to show immature understanding of scalarity in her uses of *as much* and *that much*. And we similarly see continued misuse of scalar temporal forms like *until*, as in the following (see Table 11.15G):

(69) I'm [= /ãĩn/] just gonna get one out **until** I'm [= /ãĩn/] done eatin' this one. [R getting nut out of bowl and setting it on table to wait till she's done eating the one she's just started; that is, "...for when..."] 4;8.5

Again, she seems to use *until* as if it means "for when," not as encoding position on a temporal scale viewed from below upward.

Summary, Subsequent Advances, Rachel

This period seems to be an important period in Rachel's development of these forms. There are significant advances concerning the semantics of the forms, as well as in their syntactic form.

Semantics First, from the beginning of this period, we have confirmation of Rachel's correct semantic interpretation prior to 4;0 for both the comparative and the superlative. She no longer uses either of them to mean "X" or "very X."

She also begins to use *too, enough, how,* and *as*, sometimes for emergent encoding of scalarity. *How*, previously used only in *how old* and *how many*, both in relation to age, is now associated with other spatial adjectives and with *much*. However, her understanding/encoding of scalarity is immature during this period, showing no evidence of an understanding that scalar predicates involve an assertion concerning upward values on a scale.

Finally, *many*, previously linked with age (and, therefore, number) appears more broadly linked with number here, as in her utterance: "You know how many times I love you? I love you one hundred times." 4;10.7

Syntax The syntactic developments during this period appear equally significant. First, her knowledge that *X-er* requires *than* as a standard marker, along with her association from the beginning of degree marker *as* with the standard marker *as*, are important advances. These long-distance links, and especially her evident conclusion that the standard of comparison is required, especially with *as*, may be responsible for prompting her to pay attention to complement clauses and to attempt longer structures involving clausal complements.

At the same time, she is still unsure of the expression of the standard of comparison for superlatives, and is not even sure of its placement pre- or postadjectivally: "the…in the world" vs. "the world's….". It is possible that the preadjectival uses were promoted by expressions such as "world champion boxer."

(70) I told you it would be **the most funniest** world's champion. [R and J playing wrestling.] 4;9.29

Two other very important developments took place during this period: One was the introduction, fairly early in this period, of modifiers before *A-er* constructs: *too, so, very, how, even, much,* and *more.* Notably, many of these—but, crucially, not all of them—had already been used before *much* in Rachel's speech: *too, so, very, how*—but not *even, much, more.* This suggests that, even though Rachel had developed constructs allowing X + *much* in her speech, this development of X + *A-er* was not exactly the same development or a straightforward outgrowth from it. However, both of them constitute significant steps in the formation of syntactic constructs governing the formation of degree-marking and multiply modified structures—Deg modification of *much* and *many*, and Deg/Q modification (albeit incorrectly formed) of modified adjectival forms (albeit only *A-er*). The latter also allowed for the introduction of *more* into *A-er* constructs, resulting in the first doubly marked comparative forms, and, by extension, the first association of *more* with adjectives.

A second important development that occurred somewhat later in this period (around 4;11) was the introduction of modified adjectival phrases into nominal constructs. Prior to this period, these had largely occurred as free-standing adjectival phrases, except in the case of superlative constructs.

Finally, near the very end of this period, we see Rachel's initial attempts at expressing much more complex constructs involving clausal standards of comparison. However, her attempts are largely unsuccessful.

Even Greater Advances: 5;0–6;0

During the next year, we see expansion of these developments, as well as some important developments in new directions.

Continuation of Forms Already In Evidence First we see continued use of forms already in evidence. These include modification of As with *very*, *real(ly)*, *so*, and reduplication for INTENSIFICATION (see Table 11.16A). Rachel also continues using *very* for "absolute," *real(ly)* for "authentic," *too* A, A *enough*, *as* A *as*, *this* A, *how* A, A*-er*, and A*-est* (see Table 11.16B). Note that overextensions of *-er* and *-est* continue [*beautifuler* (5;8.22), *nakeder* (6;4.21), *goodest* (5;3), *favoritest* (5;5), *marevloust* (5;5), *beautifulest* (5;6), *specialest* (5;7)], as do doubly marked superlatives [*the most strongest* (5;1), *the most prettiest* (5;2), *the most beautifulest* (5;2)].

She also continues to use forms such as *any/seven + more*, X (*this, that, so, very, too, as, how*) + *much*, X (*how, more, even*) + A*-er* (see Table 11.16C). There is also continued prolific use of *much more* A*-er* (Table 11.16D).

And we see expanded attempts at constructing structures with modified adjectives in structures with nominal heads, shown in Table 11.16E. Many of these attempts result in non-adult-like forms, revealing their immature status in Rachel's system: *the closest one sitting to her* for "the one sitting closest to her," *a too big hand* for "too big a hand," *so greasy of meat* for "such greasy meat." It is of note that *such* emerges at this time, and Rachel seems to struggle regarding the placement of articles relative to these modifiers and nouns and regarding the choice between *so* and *such* ("It's such yukky under there").[27] Her utterance involving "peace and quiet" highlights the difficulty of the choice: It is not only a case of word order (*such a long beard* vs. *so long a beard*; *what a long beard* vs. *how long a beard*), but also a problem of identifying the word class (adjective or noun) of the modified word (*so quiet*, *so peaceful*, but *such peace* (and, in fact, *such quiet* is possible)).

(71) R: It's **so quiet**, mommy; it's **so peace and quiet**, isn't it? Isn't it?
M: What?
R: It's **so peace and quiet**.
[re: J has just turned off the television.] 5;7.3

Similarly, attempts at constructing structures in which the standard of comparison is expressed through a clausal complement continue to pose difficulties (see Table 11.16 F).

Some Further Developments

Semantics During this period, Rachel shows great attention and attempts at encoding negation and references to negative ends of scales. But her attempts show she was clearly struggling: For negative comparative and superlative adjectives, she

[27] Similar errors occurred in Sadie's speech in the year following those examined here for her:
(xx) "Why do you have **such big of a cape**, Batman?" said Robin. [Sadie making up a Batman and Robin puppet show] (Sadie 4;10.8)

TABLE 11.16 Rachel 5;0–6;0, Continued Development of Forms Already in Evidence

Table 11.16A A Modification for INTENSIFICATION

very

You can't see the steam **very well** because it looks so much like the air. 5;5.26

real(ly)

I should've gave you the flourescent crayons. They're **really neat**. [R had given M regular box of crayons.] 6;0.14

But it was **real low**, so I couldn't reach. Was their pool lower than the Municipal Pool? [R remembering when she went to the Bowermans' pool last summer; their pool has no shallow water; *low* = "deep"] 6;1.15

People would think it was **real real hot** for the winter, to be the winter [re: 60 degrees in winter; i.e., if this were the winter]. 6;4.1

so

I can't carry 'em **so heavy**. [M has asked R to take 3 pillows at school back to place where they belong; R trying to carry them, finding it a little difficult.] 5;1.29

R: It's the only thing I painted **so long**. [R going to get a picture she painted.]
[later:]
M: What does this mean, what you said before, "It's the only thing I painted so long"?
R: **So far.** I said **so far**. 5;4.8

It's been **so soft** that I haven't even been knowing that it was there. [R has sore on heel.] 5;4.15

Mommy, that was **so fun** playing 5;4.17

R: It's **so quiet**, mommy; it's **so peace and quiet**, isn't it? Isn't it?
M: What [w/ rising intonation—i.e., I didn't hear you] ?
R: It's **so peace and quiet.**
[re: J has just turned off the television.] 5;7.3

Reduplication:

The stars are **tiny tiny tiny**. But the balloon got tinier than the stars. The balloon got tiny until it disappeared. [re: a helium balloon that escaped] 5;3.21

Table 11.16B Use of Modifiers Beyond INTENSIFICATION

***very* for "absolute"**

You can do it in your **very own** yard if you want. [re: camping--M had mentioned that you can't camp in public parks] 5;2.4

***real(ly)* for "authentic," "true/truly"**

A **real** witch would be much more bigger than that was. [re: puppet witch in Hansel and Gretel show]. 5;5.25

I think I'll just cut it unless he **really** wants to see. [F asked R to show him her preschool's way of cutting bananas; F changed his mind; then R decided to cut it anyway; *unless* = "in case."] 5;6.10

too A

Not too much, not **too small**, not too much. Not too much, not **too little**, not too much. [R singing made-up song.] 5;1.4

Oh, oh, we've waiten **too long**. [R holding R's pants up to F; joking that "F's grown too big."] 5;5.8

A enough

They're pretty for the secret club; they're **pretty enough** for the secret club. [R about to put mukluks on to go play. correct use?] 5;2.22

Table 11.16B (continued) Use of Modifiers Beyond INTENSIFICATION

The Osh-Kosh-B'Gosh ones are **cool enough** for a day like today. [R dressing for a hot day; Osh-Kosh B'Gosh pants have been turned into shorts, and will be cool. right direction on scale] 5;2.1

Do you think this hole is **small enough** for this? [context?] 5;7.28

R: They're biggest.
F: What do you mean?
R: They're all big. They're **big enough** to sew.
[F had told R that some pants that were torn should be thrown out rather than fixed; pants are R's; R means they still fit her, so why not fix them.] 6;1.17

as…as

R: Do you know how high he made the motorcycle jump?
M: No.
R: **As high as** birds fly.
[re: acrobat on TV circus] 5;1.28

R: I'm not gonna go **as far as** I can't reach.
M: You mean reach the bottom?
R: I'm not gonna go farther than I can't reach.
[re: swimming; R won't go in water that's too deep. means "I'm not gonna go farther than where I can reach/so far that I can't reach the bottom"] 5;2.19

Ice and ice-cream are both **as cold as** each other. 5;3.3

Five is just **as old as** I am. [pointing to five leaves on a plant she had drawn] 5;5.14

Are you **as tired**—Are you **as waked up as** I am? 5;6.1

On the box it says "makes you clean **as fun as** getting dirty." On the box it says "helps you get clean **as fun as** getting dirty." [re: box of bubble bath; really says "Makes getting clean almost as much fun as getting dirty."] 5;7.19

He's almost tall **as** the ceiling. [R telling friend T about adult, A]. [first use of "as…as" without first "as" ?] 5;8.2

how A

R: **How long** is a week till we next go to school? [Today is Saturday.]
F: I have a question for you. How long is a piece of string?
R: They're all a different size. 5;5.14

It's not thick; it's fat! See **how fat** it is? [R protested when F said the slice of cheese on her cracker was thick.] 5;8.30

A-er

England is **farther than** Chicago. 5;1.21

Ultra Brite toothpaste is **better than** any other toothpaste in the world. [R had seen ad for Crest or some toothpaste on TV; went to bathroom, saw we had U.B. there.] 5;1.28

Baby cats get **tireder than** the daddy cats. 5;2.26

They look **oranger** when they're cooked. [re: baked beans; R had said she likes them better uncooked.] 5;3.0

The stars are tiny tiny tiny. But the balloon got **tinier than** the stars. The balloon got tiny until it disappeared. [re: a helium balloon that escaped] 5;3.21

I should have did the "e" **littler**. [re: R doesn't have room on card for "r" of "Jennifer."] 5;4.5

R: See, at least that's **littler than** the others.
M: It is?
R: Yea—**bigger**.
[re: large brown bowl; M had asked R to find a big brown bowl for salad.] 5;4.26

Table 11.16B (continued) Use of Modifiers Beyond INTENSIFICATION

And I might even get the thing **lower**. [re: tomorrow R might get hole in sand, in tire hole, deeper.] 5;6.10

R: Nobody likes 'em **better**!
M: Than you?
R: Than anyone!
[J had said he probably likes the cupcakes he and R are eating "better" because he ate his fast and R's still eating hers; J obviously means "better than R," but R doesn't react as if this is what he meant.] 5;6.12

No, out there's **the better** [R pointing to front yard]. [re: Out front is better than back yard for Secret Club; M had suggested using back yard.] 5;6.20

R: You're **bigger**.
F: Bigger than what?
R: **Bigger**. Big of all.
[R talking in sleep.] 5;7.2

R: Stephanie was **the prettier than** Mary.
M: What?
R: Stephanie was **the prettier than** Mary. 5;7.15

The pointier it gets, **the bigger** it gets. [re: candy cane, as she licks it. 5;8.11
beautifuler. 5;8.22

A-est

That's **my best one**. That's **the best one**. That's **the one I like best**. [re: board game; Peanut Butter and Jelly game. R correcting self from "my best…" to "the best…"] 5;1.15
Do you wanna know who swam **the best** out of Matthew and Blake? 5;2.8
I get the special spoon....well, this is **the specialest** because .... [re: pretty little baby spoon]. 5;3.23
You wanna see **the goodest** one I made? [re: R has made some "prints" with a toy "printer" and ink pad] 5;3.27
Who's your **favoritest** clown?... Ronald, Ronald McDonald. [R singing; repeats many times.] 5;5.6

R: Who's **the marveloust** cat in the world?
M: What? [not knowing if there's a /t/ at end]
[R repeats above 2 times].
M: What?
R: Who's the best (marveloust) cat in the world?
[M asks R to say it slowly].
[R says slowly 3 times, last time:]
R: Who is the **mar—ve—lous—t** cat in the world? 5;5.17

They were both funny, except one was **the funniest**. [The librarian read 2 stories to the kids at the library at school today.] 5;5.28
Mommy, choose **your nicest** picture. You choose just ten **nicest** pictures. [R laying all the pictures she has drawn down on the floor.] 5;6.0
I don't like yukky Kleenexes on **my beautifulest** puzzle in the world...which is that, which that is. [R has just handed 2 Kleenexes to M; R cleaning R's room; Kleenexes had been on R's puzzle.] 5;6.14

Table 11.16B (continued) Use of Modifiers Beyond INTENSIFICATION

That was **my favoritest** Halloween thing. [re: witch dress that M has just taken out of wash.] 5;7.1
... **your specialest day** on Christmas. You're the only one who has a **specialest, specialest, specialest** day on Christmas. [to M, whose b-day is on Xmas.] 5;7.18
The marveloust mommy in the world. 5;10.18
Which is **the littlest**? [re: two pieces of pizza on supper table] 5;11.4
It is **the best** number. [Of 11 and 19; R has just said that in TV book it says Ses. St. is on 11 and 19; R about to turn on TV] 5;11.19
I get **the tallest** one. [re: of two candles] 5;11.27

Double Marking: *most ...-est*

[R and M playing: R in blue]
M: [pretending to be a witch:] I like girls with dark blue clothes on, 'cause they're the most delicious.
R: They're **the most strongest**. [R pulling M off chair.] 5;1.9

When I pat your hand, it means you're **the most prettiest** girl in the world. 5;2.30
When I lick your hand, it means you're **the most beautifulest** girl—lady in the whole wide world. 5;2.30

Table 11.16C Continued Use of Q Forms

a lot

M: Remember those ducks at Sunshine Acres [= name of school]?
[R nods, and eyes get big]
R: They've grown up **a lot** so they had to take 'em to the teacher's farm....
[R had been acting like a duck; R hasn't been to S.A. for about 1 ½ months.] 5;1.30

more

I like to look down **more** than I like to look up—I mean sideways. 5;2.4
If daddy haven't come out—If daddy didn't come out, I could have been the waiter **more**. 5;2.10
Nobody can take **more** than that! Unless they have a bigger glass. [re: amount of liquid R has poured into her glass] 5;3.1

a little bit

Every time I drink **a little bit of milk** my ear has a funny feel. 5;9.23

most

I want all colors and **most** pinks. I want **most** strawberry. [re: Neopolitan ice cream: "…mostly…"] 5;3.23
You're the **most** writer-downer. [to M, re: writing down "darndest things"]. 5;3.25

R: I love you, daddy, but I love mommy **most**.
M: Most of who?
R: You and daddy. 5;6.28

X + *more*

My pants are choking me. [i.e., they are "too tight" around waste.] Just so it doesn't choke me **any more**. [as M opens button to take pants off.] 5;4.17

Table 11.16C (continued) Continued Use of Q Forms

Number + more

How much do I need? **Seven more**? [re: bites] 5;4.29

X + much

this much

It makes it be more weight with **this much** people in it. [re: car's weight w/ 8 people in it. note: not "heavier"] 5;1.18
I don't think I can take much sugar on **this much** cereal. [R has very little cereal in bowl. [first "not…much" OK; second "this much"—this amount—wrong direction; should be "this little"] 5;2.24
Do you wanna see how much pictures I've made? [M nods. R goes to get pile of pictures.] **This much.** Do you want to see what they all are? 5;4.24

that much

That's too much. It won't take **that much**. [R had asked M how many bites she had left to eat; M said 9, then above; R thinks there isn't enough food for 9 bitefuls.] 5;2.2
I was waiting about **that much**. I was waiting **that much**. [R holding arms apart-i.e., "that long"; R waited for M at Community Building after art class.] 6;0.14
Why would the stars be out when the sun is **that {much/far/high} up**? 6;2.19
But you could never get **that much** logs! [re: 30 logs for building a sandbox] 6;3.27

so much

If you didn't give me **so much** noodles .... [i.e., "I wish you hadn't given me so many noodles"] 5;1.30

R: Maybe you should have gave me less strawberries, 'cause with **so much** strawberries…I would take a longer time to finish eating…strawberries.
M: Longer than what?
R: Longer than I would have to sit up at the table than, …I don't know. 5;2.3

Mommy, how come I have to hold **so much** things? Two in each hand? [R holding 2 cleaning tools in each hand.] 5;3.8
There's **not so much** people in the lake this time, 'cause it's not such a cold day. [re: cheerios in bowl of cereal, R pretending they are people in a lake; "…'cause it is such a cold day"?] 5;3.9
People are giving me **so much** favors. [i.e., asking her to do so many favors; J and M asking R to get toy men for swimming pool and book off floor, respectively.] 5;4.2
Do you know why I'm using **so much** things? [R playing with all her blocks and prickle sticks.] 5;4.2
There's **so much** Jeff's! [R has just read that book R and M are going to read is by Jeffrey—; R comments on Daddy (Geoff) and Jeff at school.] 5;5.12
How come it's freezing **so much**? [re: frozen bread "how come… so frozen"] 5;5.16
You can't see the steam very well because it looks **so much** like the air. 5;5.26
There's **so much** nice things in here. [re: in bowl of Halloween candy.] 5;6.19
(One day I forgot to get the things out of my mailbox at Kindergarten and Raintree) and today I got **so much** things. [J has marveled at how many things R has brought home from school today; asked R where she got so much work.] 5;7.3
That's **not so much** words as him. 5;7.13
I have**n't** got **so much** left that I can't—that I can hardly get it. [re: little amount of cereal left; = "I've got so little left ..."] 5;10.7
Look at all those toys. You never saw **so much** toys at Grandma's house! 6;5.14

very much

I've certainly not seen **very much** cats around. 5;6.25

Table 11.16C (continued) Continued Use of Q Forms

R: Look, there's not **very much** left. [re: number of balloons in bag to blow up for party]
F: Many.
R: I can say "much" if I want. 5;8.23

too much

Not **too much**, not too small, not **too much**. Not **too much**, not too little, not **too much**. [R singing made-up song.] 5;1.4

R Too many windows are open.
F: There's only two open [or so].
R: I know. That's **too much**! 5;1.6

Too much. [R had asked M how many bites were left on R's plate for R to eat; M held up 4 fingers for number of bites left; R said "too much" for 4 and 3, agreed that she would need 2 more bites to finish.] 5;1.28

That's **too much**. It won't take that much. [R had asked M how many bites she had left to eat; M said 9, then above; R thinks there isn't enough food for 9 bitefuls.] 5;2.2

R: Five is **too much**.... Five isn't too much, but it's just the opposite of **too much**.
M: What is the opposite of too much?
R: I don't know.
[means "…too little…"] 5;4.15

You put **too much** pictures for me. [R looking at "baby R" photo book.] 5;4.29

There's **too much** different stories—too many, I mean. 5;5.15

R: I got **too much** peach.
M: You got too many peaches?
R: Yeah, I got **too much** peach.
[R sticks with "much" + sing N] 6;4.16

M: Aren't you gonna write (th)em down, Rach?
R: There's **too much** numbers.
[R adding on calculator.] 6;4.20

R: Do you want **too much** on it, like this? [re: mustard on sandwich]
M: What, Rach?
R: Is this enough? 6;5.8

I thought I was writing **too much** "I-s". 6;5.18

as much

F: [to J:] You must've read that about fifteen times, Jaime.
R: He hasn't read it **as much times as** me. 5;1.19

It's **not as much as** I wanted. [R complaining that M put too much cheese on her food; wrong direction on scale] 5;2.19

M: One or two? [offering cookies to R]
R: **As much as** I can have. 5;3.23

Mommy, I got just **as much as** I want. [R has poured cheerios into bowl; proud of herself that she only put the right amount in bowl.] 5;4.8

how much

Mommy, do ya wanna see **how much** things I have? [R w/ bag of things she made in R's and J's "fun club."] 5;1.2

Table 11.16C (continued) Continued Use of Q Forms

R:	**How much** do you want? Two? [getting cookies for F]
F:	How many do I want [correcting R].
R:	Yea [= "yes"], how many. 5;1.4

Look **how much** rocks we have. [R and friends M & S each making piles of leaves, rocks, etc.] 5;1.7

[R first asks M if we can weigh fan; M says "no"; then:]

R:	Can we inch it?
M:	What?
R:	Can we use the ruler to see **how much** it...weighs...inches...**how much** it is? 5;1.7

Look **how much** O's that is. [re: on Mother Gooooose book.] 5;1.11

How much people is there in the house? **How much** people are there in the house? How many people are there in the house? **How much** people is there in the house? [R correcting herself, not sure which form to use. ["much…is," "many..are…"] 5;1.18

How much boxes of presents is there? [R has wrapped toys in boxes for Scott's "1/2 b-day party."] 5;1.18

R:	**How much** {was/were} the balloons we got for my birthday?
M:	What?
R:	**How much** inches were the balloons we got for my birthday?

[We had bought 4-ft. long balloons for R's birthday.] 5;1.27

R:	**How much** can we have? [re: pieces of choc. candy out of box]
M:	1.
R:	2?
M:	1. 5;2.6
R:	I don't care how many ....
M:	You don't care how many?
R:	I don't care **how much**—.
M:	Which?
R:	**How much** and many. Both.

[re: cents—to "pay" for milk R gave M.] 5;2.12

See **how much** bubbles! [R splashing in tub.] 5;2.17

Look **how much** people are comin' in one car. Look **how much** people there are in the car. [re: cheerios on R's spoon; R pretending bowl is lake, spoon is car, cheerios are people going to swim in lake; common fantasy of R's.] 5;3.9

Do you wanna see **how much** pictures I've made? [M nods. R goes to get pile of pictures.] This much. Do you want to see what they all are? 5;4.24

How much do I need? Seven more? [re: bites remaining] 5;4.29

R:	**How much** do you think I should take?
M:	How much? [absent-mindedly]
R:	Yea, **how much.** How many. 5;5.6

Look **how much** are left from yesterday. [R pulling bowl of nuts towards her.] 5;7.9

When I counted those, **how much** were there? [re: Xmas lights; F has just said there were 100 lights.] 5;7.13

Look **how much** words, and on this one look **how much** letters. [re: message R has written] 5;8.2

Mommy, look **how much** things I'm giving Matthew. [R has just made "presents" for M] 5;8.30

R:	How many are there? [re: cheerios in bowl]
M:	Why don't you say "how much are there"?
R:	I could say "**how much** <u>is</u> there"!
M:	What could you say that for?
R:	Cream ... orange juice ... ice cream ... belly buttons, in the whole world.
M:	What else could you say "how many are there" for?
R:	Fingers—5...hands--6...cheerios—I bet 10,000...Rachels-- 3. 5;9.18

Table 11.16C (continued) Continued Use of Q Forms

How much apples are there !? [R seeing lots of apples in refrigerator] 6;1.19
I'm gonna see **how much** you measure. [R holding stick over friend A as A stands against a tree.] 6;5.7
Look **how much** costumes we have for Halloween. 6;5.22

X + A-er

R: Can I see **how bigger** he is?
J (7;9.20): [measuring with hand] I'm this bigger. I'm this much bigger.
[J measuring self to R] 5;6.11

I like red **more better**. [re: 3 pieces of Santa Claus cookie; red and white icing and raisins.] 5;8.8
Lift me up more carefully—**more bigger**. [F lifting R up on his lap; R standing; up high.] 5;9.16
Onions are...kinda like **more flatter** pickles. [re: i.e., not like bean sprouts.] 5;9.18
But I like it **more better** with ice cream—I mean icing. [re: home-made cookies.] 5;9.30
Mommy, **how higher** is the water at the diving board **than** you? 6;1.20
Mine was gigantic—**even giganticer than** Jaime's. [re: balloons.] 6;2.12

Table 11.16D Continued Use of *much more A-er*

even/much more A-er

[Big fan is making a lot of noise:]
R: The other fan is much...
F: quieter.
R: Yes, **much more quieter than** this one. 5;1.11

That is **much more thinner than** ours was. [R to friend M, re: bird feather M has; few days earlier J and R had found feather on our front lawn.] 5;1.18
Much more littler. [context?] 5;2.25
One for grass is **much** **more bigger**. [re: scissors; M had told J he shouldn't have used the pinking shears for cutting grass because they're not for grass.] 5;3.8
It was **much more louder**. [re: an ambulance R saw a different day had siren on] 5;4.17
A real witch would be **much more bigger than** that was. [re: puppet witch in Hansel and Gretel show]. 5;5.25
My pinky's **much more bigger than** this. [R's pinky under magnifying glass is much bigger than pinky away from magnifying glass.] 5;6.4
Before they were **much more longer than** this. [re: mukluks; R having trouble getting them on; her feet have grown.] 5;6.15
... but it's **much more colder**. [re: baby pool at Aunt Betty's, compared to big pool (which was warm when we went swimming in it); R had said that she'd like to go visit Betty again to go in the pools again.] 5;7.0
That's **much more smoother**. [R has stuck her finger under the curling iron sprung holder lengthwise; previously had finger under it crosswise.] 5;7.5

M: Do you know this one, Rach?
R: Yes, that's **much more louder.** This is **much more louder**.
[re: Xmas carol on record.] 5;7.13

Table 11.16E Modified A + N

-er, so, -est, too

Nobody can take more than that! Unless they have **a bigger glass**. [re: amount of liquid R has poured into her glass] 5;3.1
I'm **the closest one** sitting to her [sitting closest to M; R sitting next to M's place at table: "..the one sitting closest to her"] 5;8.4

Table 11.16E (continued) Modified A + N

Don't give me **so greasy meat**. [I think R said this without *of*, but not absolutely sure. Then R repeated:] Don't give me **so greasy of meat**. 5;8.29
What is **your best food** that you can put on sandwiches [to M]? 5;9.0
Mommy, you're **a so funny girl**. 5;9.12
You have **a too big hand**. [M's hand can't fit through hole in R's pants.] 5;10.24

such (a) A N / what A a N

F: We'll go to the lake tomorrow unless it's not such nice weather.
R: We <u>can</u> go if it's **such nice weather**.
[F means "unless the weather's not nice"; today is a nice day. R understood F as "if it's not such nice weather"—then uses "if" herself] 5;1.3

I wanna show you **what big a heap** I got. [R sweeping floor; heap of dirt. Note: cf. "how big a heap" vs. "what a big heap"] 5;3.8
There's not so much people in the lake this time, 'cause it's not **such a cold day**. [re: cheerios in bowl of cereal, pretending they are people in a lake; "...'cause it is such a cold day"?] 5;3.9
You know what? Nathan doesn't believe out of Santa Claus.... He should believe Santa Claus, because who would have **such a long beard**?...Because who would have a suit like that? 5;4.12

such A

It's **such yukky** under there. [re: under kitchen table—R had gone under and is now out.] 5;4.13
My legs are **such tired**! [re: after sitting on toilet for long time.] 5;4.16

Table 11.16F Attempts at Expressing the Standard of Comparison through a Clausal Complement

R: Maybe you should have gave me less strawberries, 'cause with so much strawberries...I would take a longer time to finish eating...strawberries.
M: Longer than what?
R: **Longer than I would have to sit up at the table than, ...I don't know**. 5;2.3

There has to be as many people…[R says she doesn't know how to say it, then:] There has to be as many people ... um ... **that as many** words there are. 5;2.15

uses *not farther* to mean "less far," *the non-pointiest* to mean "the least pointy," *the last oldest* to mean "the youngest" (see Tables 11.17A, 11.17B).[28]

For the quantifiers *little* and *the least*, she uses constructions like *the opposite* with the positive quantifier; or *the most littlest*; or *non-* with the positive quantifier, *non-most* (Table 11.17C):

(72) R: Five isn't too much, but it's the **opposite of too much**.
M: What is the opposite of too much?
R: I don't know. 5;4.15

One has the most; one has **the most littlest**…. This is the one that has the **non-most**. (re: milk in glasses) 5;6.27

[28] An example from Jaime:
(xxi) [J has on baseball uniform PJ's. M suggested he could wear them for Halloween. Jaime protests:]
It's **not gooder** than any costume. [means "It's less good than any costume"] (5;9.22)

For the quantifier *less*, in addition to occasional uses of *less*, she draws on spatial terms and on her long-standing association of age with number and uses *lower, under, thinner,* and *younger* to encode negative amount (see Table 11.17C). These developments appear to indicate that Rachel has now linked the two ends of a scale. She may now be seeing both ends as lying on one scale rather than as two separate properties.

Finally, it is at this time that we see her first use of the quantifier *much* without a Deg, in a negative context (Table 11.17C):

(73) I don't think I can take **much** sugar on this much cereal. [R has very little cereal in bowl. [first "not...much" OK; second "this much"—this amount—wrong direction; should be "this little"] 5;2.24

Syntax In the previous period, we saw Rachel using the forms X + *more*, Degs *this, how, so, too, that* + *much* (and *as/how* + *many*), forms of X + *A-er*, and *even/much more A-er*. During this new period, she expands on these forms in a number of ways.

much more A-er* → *more A First, for the first time, we see Rachel use *more* as an A modifier without *much* and without *-er*; for example, *more safe, more bad:*

(74) Jaime says the ladder's **more safe** the way he has it. 5;2.30

Further examples are shown in Table 11.18A. It is of note that that *most* does not occur as a superlative marker without *-est* for the first time until a year later: "Jaime told me his **most favorite** book was One Hundred Folk Tales." 6;1.4

Deg + *much* → Deg + *many*; differentiation of *much* and *many* In addition, while *many* previously occurred only with *as* and *how*, it now occurs, and quite prolifically, with all of the Degs that were previously used with *much* (see Table 11.18B). It is of note that Rachel often self-corrects her choice of *much* versus *many*. By 5;6 or so, she seems to have a fairly clear grasp of the association of *many* with certain (countable) items and *much* with certain (uncountable) items, although the association is not perfect:

(75) R: **How many** are there? [re: Cheerios in bowl]
M: Why don't you say "how much are there"?
R: I could say "how much <u>is</u> there"!
M: What could you say that for?
R: Cream...orange juice...ice cream...belly buttons, in the whole world.
M: What else could you say "how many are there" for?
R: Fingers—5...hands—6...cheerios—I bet 10,000...Rachels—3. 5;9.18

Of further note is that by now the previously used forms "How many" and "How old" for age have now merged into "How many years old...":

TABLE 11.17 Rachel 5;0–6;0 New Developments, Negation and Negative Ends of Scales

Table 11.17A Negative comparative A

Topeka is**n't farther than** Kansas City. [M asks R if K.C. is farther than Top. to clarify and R says "yes." R means "Top is less far than KC." Problem with direction on scale? "Not farther than" is not same as "less far than"; "not farther than" denies passing limit of distance set by KC] 5;2.13

R: I'm not gonna go as far as I can't reach.
M: You mean reach the bottom?
R: I'm **not** gonna go **farther than** I can't reach.
[re: swimming; R won't go in water that's too deep. means "I'm not gonna go farther than where I can reach the bottom"—negation of Stand of Comparison with *than*] 5;2.19

Table 11.17B Negative superlative A

That's the pointiest one. Now I'm gonna find **the non-pointiest one**. That's **the non-pointiest one**. [re: candy corns; R first had pointy one, then one with the top half broken off.] 5;6.14
Jim's the tallest one of all, and Fran's **the tallest littlest one**,.... [R has 3 things standing up—Jim (fork), Fran (magic marker), Scott (marker cap).] 5;7.12

R: The first oldest is Brian Q____. The **last oldest** is Timmy. [re: boys in class]
F: Do you mean the youngest?
R: Yes. 6;0.4

Table 11.17C Negative Q

="little"

R: Five is too much.... Five isn't too much, but it's just **the opposite of too much**.
M: What is the opposite of too much?
R: I don't know.
[means "…too little…"] 5;4.15

I have**n't** got **so much** left that I can't—that I can hardly get it. [re: little amount of cereal left; = "I've got so little left ..."] 5;10.7

="the least"

[R and Aunt Fran looking at R's Star Record Book; R has gotten stars for doing different tasks well; Fran asks R: "which one has **the least** stars?" (i.e., which line); R points to line with <u>most</u> stars. When Fran tells her that's not correct, that it has the most, then R chooses the line with the least.] 5;1.17
One has the most; one has **the most littlest**.... This is the one that has **the non-most**. [re: levels of milk in glasses] 5;6.27

= "less"

Was that **lower than** a minute? [R had told M to wait a minute before doing something, or M had told R to wait a minute before she would do something; then M ready to do that thing; i.e., "was that less than a minute?"] 5;1.7
That was **<u>lower</u> than** ten. [re: R ate fewer than 10 bites and she was finished w/ her food; M had told R that she should eat 10 more bites; it took R about 6 bites to clean her plate. ["lower than" = "less than"] 5.1.26

Table 11.17C (continued) Negative Q

R: Maybe you should have gave me **less** strawberries, 'cause with so much strawberries...I would take a longer time to finish eating...strawberries.
M: Longer than what?
R: Longer than I would have to sit up at the table than,...I don't know 5;2.3

Ten or **under** ten. [i.e., that's how many bites she wants to have of beans off plate. [means "less than 10"—at same time as having trouble with "least"—non-most/most littlest] 5;6.28
I want **younger than** this. [re: amount of noodles on her plate. i.e., "…less…"] 6;0.14
Fifteen! **Lower than** fifteen! [R, M, and friend F talking about school J and R had gone to in Chicago; M asked R how many kids were there; F asked if there were 15.] 6;1.12

R: Mommy, are the morning and afternoon the same amount of day?
M: Mhm.
R: Oh, I thought the afternoon was **bigger and older**, and [? I thought] the morning was **littler and thinner—and younger**. 6;1.20

not…much
I do**n't** think I can take **much** sugar on this much cereal. [R has very little cereal in bowl. first "not…much" OK; second "this much"—this amount—wrong direction; should be "this little"] 5;2.24

(76) **How many years old** is Eva? **How many years old** is Christy? [M, J, & R in car on way to Eva and Christy's house] 5;1.28

This development, crucially, comes at the same time as, for the first time, Rachel begins using a full Deg-Q form (*how many*) as a modifier of *more* (where previously, the modifiers were unanalyzed forms *a lot*, *a little bit*, numbers).

(77) **How many more** bites? How bites? **How more** bites? **How more** bites? **How many more** bites? [R fooling; protested when M went to get paper, and said it has to be last line above.] 5;1.30

Mommy, **how many more** bites? [R eating lunch] 5;2.14

It is noteworthy that (a) the vacillation in the first of these examples is indicative of the tenuous nature of this construct for Rachel at this point, and (b) these developments coincide with indications that Rachel has gained some clarity with regard to the differential meaning of *many* and *much*.

X + *A-er* / *most* + *A-est* → X + *A-est* During this period we also see expansion of quantifier phrases in a number of ways. First, where previously, the only modified A form that allowed modifiers was *A-er*, plus the doubly marked superlative, Rachel now begins using modifiers (*very*, *really*, *so*, and even *more*) with *A-est* as well. Examples are shown in Table 11.18C.

much more A-er → much too A-er → much too A We also see the constructs involving *even/much* with *more A-er* evolving in a number of ways. First, Rachel allows *too* in place of *more*, yielding *much too A-er*, which eventually gives way to *much too* A (see Table 11.18D).

even/much more A-er → a lot/one more A-er Second, Rachel begins to allow *a lot* or a number before *more A-er*. Recall that earlier Rachel had already been using for some time forms such as *one more* and *a lot more*; so this expansion seems to be an incorporation of those forms into the *much more A-er* construct (see Table 11.18E).

All of these developments take place mostly during the first half of this year. However, we see a very important change at around 5;11 that is connected with these *a lot/one more A-er* constructions. Prior to this time, it is impossible to tell whether the syntactic organization of these forms is [much [more A-er]], [a lot [more A-er]], with *more* acting as a double marker for the comparative, or [[much more] A-er], [[a lot more] A-er], with the modifier forming a constituent with *more*. At 5;11, we begin to see some clear cases in which the structure takes the latter form. First, there are utterances such as the later two in Table 11.18E:

(78) You're **one more older than** her. [To F; about M; J had asked M, then F, what year they were born.] 5;11.25 Note: [[one more] older], not [one [more older]]

He has **a whole bunch more littler** circles. [i.e., than R or than he has big circles. R saying J has design drawing set that has big circle and a lot of little circles. R has own in hand, could only find a medium size circle of her own design set.] 6;3.27 [Note: [a whole bunch more] [littler circles]]

This coincides with the emergence of measure phrases modifying *A-er* and *as* A (Table 11.18F), as in (79), as well as of a quantifier modifying a Q other than *more*: *much + much*, as in (80).

(79) Daddy's arms are **two arms longer** than {mine/my arms}.
[R wearing F's sweater] 5;11.16

I'm **one step later** than you.
[R following M to car; R wants to give M good-bye kiss before M leaves.] 6;3.30

It was a big name.... It's **twice as big as** "Gathercole." [re: tumbling teacher's name] 5;11.14

(80) I get **much much** lots of water. I get **much much** of water. I get whole bunches of water....I get lots and lots of water. [R in bathtub] 5;11.24

TABLE 11.18 Rachel 5;0–6;0 New Developments, Qs

Table 11.18A *more A*

?? It makes it be **more weight** with this much people in it. [re: car's weight w/ 8 people in it. note: not "heavier"] 5;1.18

Jaime says the ladder's **more safe** the way he has it. [re: ladder to swing set. [first *more A* without *-er* on adjective] 5;2.30

All the bad babies, when I spank 'em, they be **more bad**. [R discussing her "bad babies"; said she has on occasion spanked them; M asked if they behaved after R spanked them. [note: not "more badder"]] 5;8.3

I'm away from you. I'm **more close** to you. I'm **more close** to you now. 5;9.1

Lift me up **more carefully**—more bigger. [F lifting R up on his lap; R standing; up high.] 5;9.16

Table 11.18B Expansion of X + *many*

too many

R Too many windows are open.
F: There's only two open.
R: I know. That's too much! 5;1.6

R	**Too many** windows are open.
F:	There's only two open.
R:	I know. That's too much! 5;1.6

There's too much different stories—**too many**, I mean. 5;5.15

There's **too many** people at Aunt Rainie's. [= "...so many people..." at Xmas supper; M and F ask R many questions like why she thinks there are too many; gives no reason.] 5;7.18

R:	I got too much peach.
M:	You got too many peaches?
R:	Yeah, I got too much peach. [R sticks with "much" + sing N] 6;4.16

as many

I can't make just **as many** flowers. [R drawing picture like one she says she made before; picture had flowers on it; I think she means she can't make exactly the same number of flowers.] 5;1.15

There has to be **as many** people…[R says she doesn't know how to say it, then:] There has to be **as many** people ... um ... that **as many** words there are. 5;2.15

Can I choose as much—**as many as** I want? [re: marshmallows] 5;4.29

[R asks M how many dollars she has left, at store]

M:	Four.
R:	That's under—that's almost **as many as** I am—five. 5;5.16

We'd just use **as many** candles that would make a three. [re: for M's birthday—for "3" of "31".] 5;8.4

I got about **as many** you need. I got six. [M needs five magic markers.] 6;3.6

this many

I'm **this many** years old. I'm **this many** years old. I'm **this many** years old. I'm **this many** years old. I'm **this many** years old. [R holding up first 1, then 2, then 3, then 4, then 5 fingers; R to Aunt Fran, sort of teasing; previously, it was always "the many" or "how many" w/o "years old"] 5;1.15

that many

F:	They were doing that at the Topeka Zoo, weren't they, Rachel?
R:	[nods] But not with **that many** elephants!

[There were 2 at T. Zoo, 4 on TV—doing trick where 1 elephant is bridge, others walk under] 5;1.28

how many [previously connected with AGE]

R:	How much do you want? Two? [R getting cookies for F]
F:	How many do I want [correcting R].
R:	Yea [= "yes"], **how many**. 5;1.4

Table 11.18B (continued) Expansion of X + *many*

How much people is there in the house? How much people are there in the house? **How many** people are there in the house? How much people is there in the house? [R correcting herself, not sure which form to use. ["much…is," "many..are…"] 5;1.18

How many years old is Eva? **How many** years old is Christy? [M, J, & R in car on way to Eva and Christy's house] 5;1.28

How many more bites? How bites? **How more** bites? **How more** bites? **How many more** bites? [R fooling; protested when M went to get paper, and said it has to be last line above.] 5;1.30

R: I don't care **how many**....
M: You don't care how many?
R: I don't care how much—.
M: Which?
R: How much and many. Both.
[re: cents—to "pay" for milk R gave M] 5;2.12

Mommy, **how many more bites**? [R eating lunch] 5;2.14

R: **How many** bites?
M: Mm—thirteen.
R: Too much .... Has to be ten or under ten.
[re: bites left to eat at supper] 5;4.29

R: How much do you think I should take?
M: How much? [absent-mindedly]
R: Yea, how much. **How many**. 5;5.6

There's too much different stories—**too many**, I mean. 5;5.15

R: **How many** holes are there?
M: You mean to hang the toothbrushes?
R: No, not to hang 'em. To put the toothbrushes through. 5;6.2

[M tests R's judgements on some N's on whether you should say "How much X" or "How many X": **How much**: paint (N offered by R), cake, milk (N offered by R), pie; **How many**: teeth, plates, cake plates, children, pieces of pie, costumes, leafs. 5;6.15

How many rides...? [re: at Maple Leaf Festival; how many rides does each one get?] 5;6.15

J (8;0.9): How much peanut butter balls did you have?
F: How much!?
R: **Many**!
F: [to J] You mean "how many"?
J: Mhm [as if to say, "Sure, why do you ask?"]. 5;9.0

R: **How many** are there? [re: cheerios in bowl]
M: Why don't you say "how much are there"?
R: I could say "how much is there"!
M: What could you say that for?
R: Cream...orange juice...ice cream...belly buttons, in the whole world.
M: What else could you say "how many are there" for?
R: Fingers—5...hands—6...cheerios—I bet 10,000...Rachels—3. 5;9.18

Table 11.18B (continued) Expansion of X + *many*

[written note from R to M:]
"To mom. I love you! **How many** pages have you made now? Answer [followed by arrow pointing down on the page, showing where M should answer]. Love, Rachel" 6;2.14

Table 11.18C Expansion of X + ***A-er*** → X + ***A-est***

[R had asked M to pick favorite ("best") picture of bear drawn by R and two friends, M & S:] I mean your **very, very, very, very, very, very, very, very best** one. 5;1.1

[R, M, and Aunt Fran all playing ABC game; players must choose red, blue, or yellow cards to play; R asks them what color they "like best," then "just like," then: last utterance not necessarily distinct from "like best"; R just wants a final decision, I think.] What is your **really best** one? 5;1.18

That's not a bad record. Only "Santa" is the very last one. On the tape it's the **very middlest** one. [re: new Xmas record, "Santa Claus is coming to town". R doesn't like having to wait until the last song to hear it; prefers the tape.] 5;7.13

R: Mommy, you're **so the cutest**.
M: Hm? What does that mean?
R: You're the cutest in the whole world. 5;7. 29

That's **more best**. That's best of all of 'em. [re: a particularly good place for sledding.] 5;8.24

Table 11.18D *much more A-er* → *much too A-er*

[R said that only little people could ride in the stroller where little friend H was riding; then:]
M: I'm as little as H_!
R: [ʔə̃ ʔə̃].
R: H___'s **much too smaller**.
[Note: "too" not scalar] 5;1.1

[R said section of orange she had cut was "too big."]
M: Rach, how would you say it if it was really, really too big.
R: "**much too big**." I wouldn't say it like this, "too too too big." [2 times] I would say "it was **much too big**." 5;7.13

Table 11.18E *much more A-er* → *a lot/one more A-er*

Thanks. This [re: robe] makes me **a lot more cooler.** [M has just put it on? taken it off? exchanged what she had on for the robe? on Rachel.] 5;7.13

You're **one more older than** her. [To F; about M; J had asked M, then F, what year they were born.] 5;11.25 [Note: [[one more] older], not [one [more older]].]

He has a **whole bunch more littler** circles. [i.e., than R or than he has big circles. R saying J has design drawing set that has big circle and a lot of little circles. R has own in hand, could only find a medium size circle of her own design set.] 6;3.27 [Note: [[a whole bunch more] [littler circles]].]

Table 11.18F Emergence of Measure + A-*er*, Measure + *as* A, Q + Q

Daddy's arms are **two arms longer** than {mine / my arms}. [R wearing F's sweater] 5;11.16

I'm **one step later** than you. [R following M to car; R wants to give M good-by kiss before M leaves.] 6;3.30

It was a big name....It's **twice as big** as "Gathercole." [re: tumbling teacher's name]. 5;11.14

I get **much much lots** of water. I get **much much** of water. I get whole bunches of water....I get lots and lots of water. [R in bathtub] 5;11.24

And a few months later, we see the first occurrence of a full Deg-Q form (*as much*) modifying *A-er*:

(81) She's just **as much older** than me (as) I'm older than you. [re: friend; "...as I am you."] (6;1.4)

But the system is far from sorted, as we see continued errors beyond these dates; for example, just a few days later, Rachel says:

(82) Mommy, **how higher** is the water at the diving board than you? [i.e., how much deeper is the water than you are tall] (6;1.19)

Scalarity During this year, we still see continued errors in the use of scalar expressions. The primary difficulty now appears to be one of appreciating the importance of the direction on the scale (see Table 11.19A). At the same time, Rachel still uses *catch up* as a nonscalar predicate to mean something more like "beat," as in Table 11.19B.

At the same time, we see further attempts at the expression of scalarity that appear more appropriate, as in Table 11.19C. It appears that by the middle of this year, Rachel is developing a more sophisticated appreciation of scale. And this appears in part to be promoted by the use of spatial imagery (see Table 11.19D). Also, as noted above, Rachel's attention to negative ends of scales is posited to be related to her growing appreciation of scales and her linking of the two ends of scales.

Summary, Even Greater Advances, Rachel

During this period, we see several significant advances. First, Rachel appears to have linked the two ends of scales, as evidenced in her attempts at expressing negation and negative ends of scales, with both adjectives and quantifiers, and her grasping at terms for the negative ends ("non-most"). This development may be an outgrowth, at least in part, of her previous developing awareness of scalarity, as well as a co-temporaneous expression of scalarity through spatial imagery. She may now be able to lay multiple levels of presence of a property along a single scale.

She also appears to have come to an appreciation of the mass/count difference between *much* and *many*. This coincides with a proliferation of the use of *many* in her speech.

In relation to syntax, Rachel appears to be working on the syntax of degree-marked and quantified phrases with nominal heads and of clausal complements, although she seems to have not yet worked these out. And she seems to come to more all-encompassing structure(s) for such phrases, leading to Q-A (*more* A), Deg-Q (*how many*), Deg-Q-Q (*how many more*), Q-Deg-A (*much too* A) and Measure word-Q/Deg-A (*one more older*; *two arms longer*) forms. (It is not until later that we see Deg-Q-Deg-A (*as much older*) forms, however.)

TABLE 11.19 Scalarity

Table 11.19A Direction on Scale

too, as

R: It may be **too late**, 'cause they may still be in bed.
M: It may be too late?
R: It may be **too early** because they may be—they may still be in bed.
[R wanted to go play with neighbors M and S early in the a.m.; M told R to wait a bit till later; M probably said something about M & S might still be in bed. [first "too late" wrong direction on scale] 5;1.18

It's **not as much as** I wanted. [R complaining that M put <u>too much</u> cheese on her food. [wrong direction on scale] 5;2.19

I don't think I can take much sugar on **this much** cereal. [R has very little cereal in bowl. [first "not…much" OK; second "this much"—this amount—wrong direction; should be "this little"] 5;2.24

I got about **as many** you need. I got six. [M needs five magic markers.] 6;3.6

[R holding up piece of bread, M having told her to put back end piece because it was too small.]
R: This is **as small as** they come.
M: What do you mean? Is that the biggest piece you can find or not?
R: Yeah, it's the biggest piece.
[wrong direction on scale] 6;3.29

until

How do we call her **until** that tower's finished? [re: calling her grandmother in England from the US; we had been discussing how a new microwave tower they've been building will facilitate overseas calls.] 5;0.2

R: Now it's real long ago that you've cut it.
M: What?
R: Now it's real long ago **till** you cut it.
[M has made a remark about how happy she is she cut R's hair; R told M not to talk about it, since it's so long since she cut it; M cut R's hair about a month ago.] 5;5.7

Table 11.19B Non-Scalar Uses of *catch up with*

Daddy **caught up with** all three of us, cause he was done before us. ["beat?" "catch up" demands sense of scale—moving up on scale; lacking in R's understanding?] 5;1.7

[R is <u>ahead</u> of M: R pretending M is girl, R is mother.]
R: I'm **catching up with** you, little girl.
M: What does that mean, Rach?
R: It means I'm getting closer to the place I'm going. Oh, I'm **catching up with you**, that's for sure.
[Not clear; *catch up* appears to mean "beat"] 5;4.17

I was tryin' to **catch up with** daddy, so you didn't know he was here in the first place. [R was trying to rush ahead of F to get up to M at her office before him; she was trying to "beat daddy, so that…".] 6;4.1

TABLE 11.19 (continued) Scalarity

Table 11.19C Expression of Scalarity

It'll be long since now **until** your birthday comes. [R to friend T. [scale of time]] 5;8.2
[R explaining how a boy who was 6 differed in age from her and Jaime: He was…] The **second** age as me, and the **first** age...I mean, the **second** age from me, and the **first** age from Jaime. 5;4.26

Table 11.19D Scalarity Linked with Spatial Imagery

Was that **lower** than a minute? [R had told M to wait a minute before doing something, or M had told R to wait a minute before she would do something; then M ready to do that thing; i.e., "was that less than a minute?"] 5;1.7
Ten or **under** ten. [i.e., that's how many bites she wants to have of beans off plate. Means "less than 10"—at same time as having trouble with "least"—non-most/most littlest] 5;6.28
I was waiting about that much. I was waiting that much. [R **holding arms apart**—i.e., "that long"; R waited for M at Community Building after art class.] 6;0.14
Fifteen! **Lower** than fifteen! [R, M, and friend F talking about school J and R had gone to in Chicago; M asked R how many kids were there; F asked if there were 15.] 6;1.12
(I want something we haven't had) for a real, real, real long time—like **about from the hallway to that side of the garage**. 6;1.4

What Is Missing? One aspect of these forms that children must still sort out is which adjectives go with *-er* and which with *more* in comparatives:

(83) Mine was gigantic—even **giganticer** than Jaime's. [re: balloons] (R 6;2.12)

J: The least you could do is be **more quiet**.
F: Why didn't you say "**quieter**"?
J: Because "be **more quieter**" wouldn't make sense. (J 7;6.17)

[Family is riding overnight in car to Chicago. J has just woken up. Beginning to dawn.]
J: It's becoming **more light**, everybody.
M: What?
J: It's becoming **lighter**. (J 7;7.3)

I found two really interesting ones. One is **interestinger** than the other. Which one do you want to see—the **interestinger** one? (Saul 5;2.4)

Only if I had kept these stamps in a **secreter** place. [J regretting that he hadn't put his stamps in a more secret place than he had. Means "If only...."] (J 7;7.29)

You feel much **uneasier**—much **more uneasier** in an elevator with a wheelchair. (J 14;1.9)

This is complicated by the fact that the choice is not strictly lexically based, but is dependent on the overall structure. Thus, for example, *He is bigger than he is tall* does not mean the same as *He is more big than he is tall.* Utterances from children such as the following reveal that sorting this out is not unproblematic:

(84) I'm strong and I'm brave. But I'm braver than I am strong. [means "I'm brave more than I'm strong" or "I'm more brave than I am strong"?] (Saul 6;3.29)

Syntactically, Rachel appears to be on the brink of sorting out fully the syntax of degree and quantifier phrases. However, many of the problematic forms (*much more A-er*, Degs with *A-er* without an intervening *much*, Deg + *much* + A, and *so* vs *such*) hang on in children's speech beyond these ages, indicating that the process of sorting the whole set of structures out fully is protracted beyond these ages.

COMBINED SUMMARY, BOTH SADIE AND RACHEL

What aspects of development are common to Sadie and Rachel, and where does their development differ? The following summary is provided in an attempt to clarify the commonalities and the differences in the developmental trajectories followed by Sadie and Rachel.

Semantics

Semantic Development Before 3;0 With regard to the semantics of their expressions, both Sadie and Rachel begin early on, before age 3;0, to use modifiers to express INTENSIFICATION. For Sadie, the forms used were generally preadjectival modifiers, *so, very, quite, all, really*, and reduplication of *very* and *really* (and occasionally *-er*). After initial appropriate use, Sadie showed extensive overgeneralization of the expression of INTENSIFICATION outside the acceptable adult norms; for example, to *way/freezing/heck-out* A, reduplication of verbs and adverbs. Rachel also used *really* and reduplication of the adjective itself, but she also used the suffixes *-er* and *-est* prolifically for this meaning.

Both children also used forms before 3;0 to express EXTREME ENDS and LIKE. Sadie often used *match*, Rachel used *same* to express LIKENESS. Both children often used *than* to mean "like." For Sadie, the expression of these notions seems to have come in after the expression of INTENSIFICATION. For Rachel, the timing appears to have been more co-temporaneous. Rachel also expressed CONTRAST during this period.

During this early period, neither child expressed notions associated with *as… as, enough*, or *too*. If they used these forms at all, they were used immaturely (e.g., Rachel's use of *too late* and *too heavy* for "can't").

Semantic Development 3;0–4;0 During the next year, both children continued prolific expression of INTENSIFICATION, adding forms used to express this notion. Sadie added *quite* as a modifier, and she extended the use of *so* and *galore* to use with verbs. Rachel added *very* and *real* as intensifiers.

Both children also began during this time to add the forms *as…as, A enough*, and *too* A to their repertoires, and Sadie added *how* and *-er*. (However, Rachel only used *how* with *old* during this period.) While these forms seem to have been used occasionally in appropriate contexts, with possible appropriate import, on the whole they revealed immature use. Both children showed a clear lack of understanding of the scalar nature of these, that they entail specification on a scale viewed from below going upward on the scale. They often used them instead for more "punctual" readings. This absence of a scalar usage is also evident in both children's use of *until* and *catch up with*, and in Sadie's use of *barely*.

Evidence of consistently appropriate semantic usage of the comparative appears at around 3;6 in Rachel's speech, followed by appropriate use of the superlative around 3;8. Appropriate uses of *too* A appear around this same time. With this consolidation of the semantics of the comparative and the superlative, not only is the usage of *-er* and *-est* appropriate, but when *-er* is accompanied by a standard of comparison, it is appropriately introduced by *than*. Rachel's use of *as...as* continues to show problems with scalarity, however.

Semantic Development 4;0–5;0 Rachel continues to expand on the expressions used for INTENSIFICATION, now adding *so* and *pretty* for adjective modification. She also now uses *how* for this purpose, as well as for nonintensive meaning.

Her uses from 4;0 on show confirmation of solidification of the semantics for A-*er* and A-*est*, with no further misuses for less mature meanings. However, while the use of *than* is by now established as accompanying *-er*, the form of the superlative is more tenuous. Rachel begins alternating *-est* with *best*, she vacillates between *the* and *my* as the determiner accompanying the superlative, and she shows variable use of *of all*, *in the world*, and *world's* as the standard of comparison.

Rachel also begins to use *very* quite a lot for "absolute," modifying expressions of EXTREME ENDS. She also shows greater use of *as* A *as* (and *that* A), although she still uses this as marking a point on a scale (as if it means "the same as"), rather than as encoding a point on a scale as seen from below upward.

Semantic Development 5;0–6;0 Finally, during the final year examined, Rachel shows heightened attention to negative poles of scales. She often uses the positive-pole term with *opposite* or *non-* to refer to the negative pole. This is interpreted as an indication that she has now realized that the positive and negative ends of the scales lie along the same scale.

Her usage of the scalar forms *too* A and *as* A *as* appear to be developing, with a greater appreciation of the scalar nature of these predicates. However, she still makes errors in giving these forms nonscalar readings.

Forms

Forms Before 3;0 Prior to age 3, both children used *more* as one of their earliest quantifiers, with immature meaning, alongside a few free-standing others such as *two*, *first*. Both children's first steps to more complex expressions involved adding *any more* and *no more* to their repertoires. For Rachel, prior to age 3, the next development was to add *many* to refer to age ("the many") and the occasional *too much* (with uncertain semantic import).

For Sadie, there was further development prior to age 3: First, she also added the quantifiers *a lot* and *a little bit* to her lexicon. Subsequent to these, she added *all* and *a few*, and she expanded the modifiers occurring with *more* to *yes more, one more, some more,* and she added other quantifiers that allowed modification: *a little bit some, a lot of three.* At approximately the same time, she added Deg + *much* (*very, how,* and *so* + *much*, all used for INTENSIFICATION) to her repertoire, with *much* never appearing without such a Deg marker.

Subsequently, about two months later, Sadie began using some of the Qs in her speech as Adjective or Deg modifiers; for example, *a little bit loose, a lot salty, a lot so love you, all that fast, somewhat better.*

Forms 3;0–4;0 In the next year, Rachel began using *more* for amount, and she added the Qs *a lot, much, most* to her repertoire. These were occasionally linked with *than,* expressing "like." She also continued using *any more,* but expanded her use of Deg + Q to *too/that much* and *how many* (for age only). Rachel appears to have been somewhat behind Sadie in her development of the forms of these structures at a comparable age.

For Sadie, developments were more extensive regarding forms at this age. First, she added *many* and *enough* to her Qs, and she began using *how/too/as much* beyond INTENSIFICATION. By 3;8, the first use of *much* without a Deg word was observed.

During this time, there also seems to have been in Sadie's speech an explosion of Deg and Q and A combinations, apparently quite indiscriminate in syntactic form. These included Deg + Q ("quite a bit," "quite a lot," "the a lotter"), Q-A ("a bit spicy," "any spicy"), Q-Deg-A ("any too tight"), Deg-Deg-Q ("quitest bit"), Deg-Deg-A ("very too small"), Q-Q ("5…bit"), Q-Q-Deg-A ("once less braver," "much less braver"). However, while these appear to have been indiscriminate in <u>form</u>, when they involved multiple modification, they seem to have involved the semantic modification of *-er, too,* and *-est*; that is, the second Deg_2 appears to always have been *too, -er,* or *-est.*

Finally, Sadie also began using numbers as A modifiers ("150 tired") at this same time. These are likely to have been related to the other Q-A forms, but it is hypothesized that the introduction of numbers into these constructs may signal an important role for numbers in children's developing understanding of scalarity.

Forms 4;0–5;0 Rachel's early development during this year was similar to Sadie's in the previous year in many respects: She expands on modification with *more—three more, a lot more,* and she expands on Degs used with *much*—not only *too/that much,* but also *so/how/as much.*

Beyond this, like Sadie, Rachel expands the forms of the constructs. Unlike Sadie, however, her expansion of the forms in question appears to have progressed through the development of *X-A-er* in her speech, around 4;6. This expands, first, at around 4;8 to *more A-er,* and at around 4;10 to *most A-est.* About half a month later, *even/much more A-er* emerged.

There appear to have been several important steps for Rachel during this year in the development of the syntactic form of these constructs. First, the development of *as…as* appears important. *As much* emerged at the same time as *as* A, indicating a shared source. But *as* A was accompanied early on, from 4;4, with the standard marker *as*; this close link was not the case with *as much* until about 4;10, when Rachel seems to have come to the conclusion that the standard of comparison was required. This tight link between Deg *as* and standard marker *as* appears to have been transferred over to *-er* and its association with *than*, which she explicitly links.

Furthermore, these developments appear potentially linked with Rachel's new attention to clausal complements of these forms. It was hypothesized that Rachel's conclusion that the standard of comparison was required with *as…as* and possibly *-er…than* constructs may have forced her to attempt the expression of complex clausal standards of comparison in these structures.

In addition, the more elaborated, multiply modified forms developing during this time seem to be related to the development of more complex local syntactic structures. This includes the development of constructs with nominal heads, in which the degree phrases are incorporated into constructs involving nominal determiners and nouns. Rachel's difficulties with these constructs reveal that this was a far from straightforward task.

Finally, like Sadie at one year younger, Rachel at this age, around 4;10, seems to have associated scalarity with number. While Sadie brought number into A modification, Rachel seems to use numbers more adverbially, as in "I'm sweating three times, and I'm tired two times."

Forms 5;0–6;0 During this year, Rachel appears to develop a refined set of structures out of the forms that were developing during the previous year. First, *more* A emerges for the first time, likely a development from *much more* A-*er*. Deg + *many* emerges, comparable to the previously available Deg + *much*, and this development seems to coincide with a developing understanding of the differential mass/count status of *much* and *many*. Similarly, X + A-*est* appears to emerge out of X + A-*er* (perhaps in combination with *most* A-*est*); *much too* A and *a lot/one more* A-*er* emerge from *even/much more* A-*er*.

OVERALL DISCUSSION

What do these data ultimately reveal concerning the acquisition of language, in particular language involving a complex set of interrelated forms and meanings? First, they reveal a complex interweaving of cognitive, semantic, and syntactic factors that contribute to the timing and sequence of acquisition.

Cognitive and Semantic Development

Encodable Notions First, on a cognitive and semantic level, it appears that certain concepts are "accessible" early to children; others appear more inaccessible and do not come in until later. Among the relatively accessible notions are

INTENSIFICATION and LIKENESS. Comparison of the relative presence of a property in two or more individuals appears more complex and less accessible to young children. Thus, the early uses of forms in children's speech tend to be associated with meanings of INTENSIFICATION and LIKENESS. If in the adult language a given form expresses scalarity, that form, if used by children, will tend to be misused for one of these simpler notions.

This cognitive/semantic factor interacts with factors related to the form of the linguistic input. There are many ways to express INTENSIFICATION and LIKENESS in English, and different children appear to "grab" different expressions and run with them. Sadie used a lot of preadjectival forms (*very*, *so*, etc.) to express INTENSIFICATION; Rachel tended to use suffixal forms (*-er*, *-est*). Sadie used *match* quite a bit to express LIKENESS; Rachel used *same(s)*. Beyond the data examined here, my son, Jaime, used *as* quite a bit for LIKENESS, which he picked up through his fondness for books ("Its fleece was white as snow"); see (85). Melissa Bowerman's daughter Christy, on the other hand, used *so* (as in "so is she") for LIKENESS; see (86).[29]

(85) ...but she's not big **as** her brother so she can't say "thank you" **as** her brother, right? (J 3;9.25)

It's pink **as** your shirt. The balloon's pink like your PJ's. (J 4;1.4)

(86) I want ice cream **so** boy. (= "I want ice cream like the boy has." As M & C pass boy eating ice cream.) (C 2 yrs.)

I have ə go potty ... **so** Mark. (= "...like Mark." C at home, but Mark goes potty when she is at his house every day.) (C 2 yrs.)

Each child seems to have drawn on his or her linguistic experience to express this commonly understood notion of LIKENESS.

Development of Scalarity The lack of accessibility of notions of scalarity is associated early on with misuse of a variety of expressions. This includes early use of, e.g., *A-er*, *A-est*, and *too* A for "A" or "very A," as well as misuse and misunderstanding of *as X as*, *that X* in an immature fashion, to mean "the same X as." This usage shows a lack of appreciation of the fact that scalar predicates involve a direction on a scale, asserting a lower limit on the scale in the affirmative, denying the meeting of that lower limit in the negative.

Problems with scalarity also affect forms that go well beyond the forms of primary interest here, spilling over to all other scalar expressions, including those involving time (*until*, *still*) and notions like "catching up." Children's early misuses of these forms treat them as if they express more punctual notions like "when," "at that time," and "beat."

The growing understanding of scalarity associated with these linguistic forms seems to emerge in two ways. First, children begin to explicitly associate the magnitude of a property they are expressing with numbers. It is possible that this devel-

[29] I am grateful to Melissa Bowerman for these data.

opment has its source in the child's growing understanding of number or in the child's growing command of these linguistic structures themselves. The former case would mean that as children are beginning to understand number and scalarity outside of these expressions, they then bring that understanding into these expressions as a consequence, to help them gain a greater scalar command of those expressions. Another possibility, however, is that the linguistic forms themselves invite children to think of them as directly involving number themselves.

There are several ways in which language may be providing such an invitation, in that many associated constructs contain quantifier and number-related forms; for example,

(87) ***no*** *more,* ***some*** *more,* ***one*** *more*
more *delicious*
(not) ***one*** *bit*
any *more,* ***any*** *X-er,* ***any*** *good*
a bit*,* ***a bit*** *more,* ***a bit*** *A*
twice *as X*
five *times X-er*
lots *X-er*
much *X-er*

The data here make it clear that children pick up on such associations and try to generalize from them:

(88) I want **yes more baguette**. I want **yes more cheese!** I forgot I already <u>had</u> baguette! (Sadie 2;3.7)

That doesn't make **<u>any</u> sense**. Not **one single** /sɛnt/ [= {sent?/cent?}] (Sadie 3;8.24)

Is it **a bit spicy**? Is it **any spicy**? [re: food V has made, Thai food—S wants to know if it's spicy before she tries it] (Sadie 3;9.22)

[V and Sad discussing how Sadie was "lost" at a park one time:]
V: But Sadie wasn't worried. Not **one teensy bit**.
Sadie: **Not even 2. Not even 3. Not even 4. Not even 5…bit.** 3;9.24

I like it **30 bits**! (Saul 4;9.28)

[Rachel comparing amount she's sweating and amount she's tired:]
I'm sweating **three times**, and I'm tired **two times**.
[i.e., sweating at a value of 3 and tired at a value of 2.] (Rachel 4;11.25)

I'm like **once** less braver than Saul. (Sadie 3;11.27)

The direction of influence may, of course, go both ways, and is at this point unclear; this can only be answered through further research.

At the same time, Rachel's growing understanding of scalarity associated with these linguistic forms seems to emerge in a second way, in her focus on negation and on negative ends of scales. Her focus on negative ends and her expression of those ends often with the positive-pole forms ("nonmost," "the opposite of too much," etc.) suggest a linking of the two ends of the scale into a single scale. Rachel's utterances expressing scalarity seem to also draw on spatial metaphors, such as in the use of *lower* and *under* for "less than." However, these may simply be attempts at expressing negative ends of scales when the appropriate lexical items are not readily available, as she also draws on, for example, *younger, thinner,* and *older* for such purposes.

Scalar Predicates and Conversational Implicature If these analyses are correct, they suggest that the acquisition of scalar predicates involves several separate developments in the semantics of the forms, and is not simply a matter of coming to understand the conversational implicatures associated with them. We can discern five developments necessary for coming to understand the relevant forms:

1. First, the child must gain an appreciation of something of the core meaning associated with the form in question. Thus, learning *too* involves going beyond initial uses limited to, for example, *heavy* or *late* with an immature semantic content, to understanding that it involves whether there is a fit for some purpose. Learning *more* involves going beyond use for recurrence, or for "amount," to knowing it expresses relative amount. Learning *some* entails learning two meanings: the determiner meaning, used as a plural equivalent of *a* with count nouns, and as a singular determiner with mass nouns; and the quantifier meaning, which contrasts with *all*. Learning *as...as* or *-er...than* entails learning that a comparison of two things is involved. This may be easier with *as...as* than with *-er...than* if, like Rachel, most children link degree marker *as* from the beginning with standard marker *as* (while the link of *-er* with *than* takes longer). The explicit link with a standard of comparison may make it clear from the beginning that degree marker *as* entails such a comparison. And so on.

2. Learning the core meaning also entails understanding that the application of scalar predicates is usually context-dependent for application. What is *bigger* in one context might be *smaller* in another context. What is *too big* in one context can be *too small* in another. It has long been recognized that certain adjectives like *big* demand reference to the context for proper interpretation, but the same applies to quantifiers and scalar forms (Moxey & Sanford, 1993; Papafragou & Schwarz, 2006).

3. Third, the acquisition of these forms entails their placement on a scale along with other terms. Knowledge of the forms entails, as with numbers, knowing their relative positions and their order on such a scale. Thus, for example, knowing *big* entails knowing where it lies on a scale relative to *huge, small, large, tiny,* and so forth. Knowing *A-er* entails knowing how it relates to *as A as, A-est,* etc. Knowing quantifier *some* entails knowing that it encodes a quantity on the same scale as *all.*

4. Knowing the placement or point on a scale where a given scalar predicate falls does not necessarily mean that one also understands that the use of the term asserts the lower limit, and that the scale is viewed from below upward. The acquisition of these forms involves acquiring this as well as the first three elements.

So, for example, a child may understand that *as…as* has to do with the specification of two entities at the same point on a scale (elements 1 to 3), but not that it asserts the meeting of a lower limit at that point. Not until a child understands this will he or she be able to adequately use and understand, among other things, negation of scalar predicates—e.g., that *A is not as X as B* means "A is less X than B," not "A is either less or more X than B."

5. And, finally, the acquisition of scalar predicates entails understanding the pragmatic implicatures involved and controlling the linguistic devices that confirm or deny such implicatures. Among these understandings is knowing that the default pragmatic implicature is that a higher/stronger term is not applicable. Thus, to say *A is as X as B* usually, as a default, invites the inference that "A is not X-er than B."

Much of the work to date on the acquisition of scalar predicates has focused on the child's knowledge of the pragmatic implicatures associated with the forms in question, element 5. However, equally important is ascertaining whether the child has the first four elements in place; without them, the child will not have the option of applying or denying implicatures. Many of the studies in the literature have found that children are more likely to associate implicatures with numbers than with nonnumerical scalar predicates. However, in most of those studies, the question of whether the child even understands or knows the meaning of the non-numerical form in question or its scalar nature has not even arisen. A child cannot interpret *some* in relation to *all* if the child only knows the determiner meaning of *some*; similarly, a child cannot interpret *most* as implicating *all* or *not all* if he or she does not know what *most* means or primarily knows *most* as a (double) marker for superlative adjectives.

Later Semantic Developments Have Their Roots in Earlier Semantic Developments The data here suggest that each predicate will have its own history of development and its own status vis-à-vis the child's knowledge of its scalarity. These forms undergo critical and important changes in the child's use and understanding at the ages studied here, up through age 6, and beyond. The present data suggest that the earliest that any of these forms have scalar-like semantics (i.e., in relation to elements 1 to 3 above) is around 4 years of age, and that understanding may even come in quite a bit later. Understanding that such forms assert a lower bound, item 4, comes in even later.

Furthermore, the history of a form in a given child's usage will affect her understanding of that form at a later point in development. Thus, for example, Rachel's use of *many* was linked from the start with number through her use of *the many* and *how many* in relation to age. This early link with number may mean that whatever scalarity she learned to associate with number may have accrued fairly automatically as well to *many*. In contrast, a form like *some*, which may well be learned early as a determiner before it is used as a quantifier, may retain some of an early association with unspecified sets when children begin to understand its use as a quantifier; as a result, it may not be surprising that children interpret *some* as including reference to a whole set. This contrasts further with a form like *as…as*, which, according to the data here, is probably never taken by the child as allowing application beyond the point at which the standard of comparison lies. That is, it is unlikely, given the data here, that children go through any early stage (comparable to those reported for *some* when children allow it to refer to "all") at which they interpret *A is as X as B* as allowing for A to be "X-er" than B.

Recall that children's insensitivity shown toward conversational implicatures in previous studies has been attenuated if the relevant contextual support has been made available, and has varied from predicate to predicate. I would suggest that one of the reasons that children's honouring of conversational implicature varies from predicate to predicate and from study to study has had to do with items 1 to 4 above: First, children will have varying degrees of knowledge of the semantics of the terms themselves (1 above); for example, they will know what some of the words "mean" and others they will not know; they may know one use of a word (e.g., *some* as a determiner), but not another (*some* as a quantifier). Second, children initially fail to appreciate the scalar nature of the predicates (3 above); for example, knowing the "meaning" of quantifier *some* does not necessarily mean knowing where *some* lies on a scale relative to *all* on the same scale. Third, children do not appreciate until late that scalar predicates entail a direction on the scale (element 4). Until these four components of knowledge are in place, it is unlikely that children can come to the critical knowledge that scalar predicates involve default conversational implicatures.

Syntactic Development: Limited Formulas

What do these data reveal about the syntactic contributions to the development of these forms? First, it is apparent that children begin with highly restricted formulas; for example, *no more, any more*; *this many, how many* [for age only]; reduplication restricted to *very very* and *really really*; *much* occurring always preceded by *too*; and so forth. These gradually, bit by bit, piece by piece, get expanded to broader constructions, sometimes extending beyond the adult possibilities. Thus, for example, *no more, any more* get expanded to *some more, one more,* and even *yes more*; *this many* and *how many* may be to extended to *how old*, and then eventually to *how* A. *Very very* A, *really really* A might get extended to reduplication of adjectives themselves, and then to reduplication of any type of word, including verbs. *Too much, that much* might extend to any degree marker + *much*. *A little bit more, a lot more, one more, some more* might extend to *a little bit some, one…2…3…4…5 bit*. As Deg + *much* brings in Degs initially associated with As (e.g., *very, so*), the link between quantifiers and adjectives is opened up, then allowing modifiers used with Qs to subsequently move into A modification (*a bit* A, *any* A, *some* A, etc.).

There are moments when we can observe general insights on the child's part—but these are usually, at least during the earlier stages, relevant to a small subset of the system. For example, Sadie's transfer of Degs initially associated with As to *much* seems to have occurred in one step, not each Deg at separate moments. Rachel's acquisition of *as…as* for both As and *much* at the same time is indicative of these developments having a common source. And Rachel's later use of *many* as a quantifier with Degs, just as she had used *much* with them, coincides with her understanding of the mass/count distinction between *much* and *many*: It is as if this latter insight allowed the extension of what had been learned with *much* to *many*. But these are all "small" insights, applying to a relatively restricted set of structures, and do not appear to reflect a more global understanding of the syntactic makeup governing the whole set of structures.

Indeed, there is little evidence prior to the later stages (around 4;10 for Rachel) that the children had broad syntactic categories governing these constructs or guiding their acquisition. Indeed, there is some evidence against that possibility. First, there are several cases in which it is clear that a child had certain forms available but did not bring these into other constructs when the option became available; for example, even though Rachel had Deg + *much* constructs available to her, she did not use Deg modifiers of *much* when she first began producing *much more A-er* forms; that is, she did not produce forms like *so much more A-er, that much more A-er,* and the like. Likewise, even though Rachel had by now introduced X + *A-er* forms into her speech, with X coming from a wide range of modifiers (*very, how, so,* etc.), when *much more A-er* emerged, she did not produce any forms like *much so A-er* or *much very A-er.*

Second, there is no evidence of any broad understanding of constituent phrase structure governing the children's early usage. As just mentioned, in some cases, the children had full phrases available for combining, for example, quantifier elements and adjectival elements (*too much + more A-er*), but they did not draw on these available forms when first combining *much* with *more A-er.* There is also evidence that children did not treat forms that in the adult language are constituents as indivisible units, but rather treated the subcomponents as free-standing elements. These children, as others, often use *How* with falling intonation in answer to adults' questions like "Do you see how far out we are?" in places where *How far, How old,* or *How big,* etc., should be used.

The first evidence of the establishment of some broad overall structure governing the syntax of these forms appears around 4;10, when Rachel begins using modified adjectival forms in conjunction with nominal heads, uses more complex degree-phrase and quantifier forms (e.g., as evidenced in her new "how many years old" construct), and begins using complex clausal complements.

Later Syntactic Developments Have Roots in Earlier Syntactic Developments As was the case with semantics, it is quite apparent that at every step, the children are drawing on what they have already learned to build up new structures; later developments are rooted in earlier developments. The links that children form early on between forms and their meanings, for example, seem to stay tied with those forms for a long time. Thus, for example, Rachel's association of *many* with age, and, in turn, age with number, seems to have been an anchor that helped to keep *many* associated with number throughout, and, further, seems to be associated with her later use of *younger* and *older* for "less" and "more." Similarly, Rachel's early use of *very* concentrated on the "absolute" sense, so the link of *very* with superlatives ("very best") seems a natural outgrowth of this and may have played some role in her expansion of X + *A-er* to X + *A-est* constructs. Rachel's preference for *in the world* as a standard of comparison for

X-est, combined with her exposure to *world champion*, together seem to have led to her attempts at marking the superlative with *world's*. Sadie's early association of the word *how* in A modification with INTENSIFICATION may have made the later leap to use of *how* with *much* for a similar notion a natural outgrowth. Similarly, Sadie's early use of *all* with As for intensification may have paved the way for its use with Deg_2s (*all that fast*) for a similar meaning.

One very interesting place where this type of association may have had a critical impact on syntactic development was in Rachel's association of standard marker *as* with degree marker *as*. She appears to have concluded at one point that the standard of comparison was required when the degree marker *as* was used. (And she explicitly states that *than* is required with the comparative, although she does not religiously follow this herself.) This development is interesting in two ways. First, it means that Rachel has drawn a conclusion about structure on the basis of positive evidence alone. We know from the examination of the Kuczaj data, above, that in adult speech to children, degree marker *as* is invariably accompanied by standard marker *as*.

Second, this conclusion on Rachel's part appears quite likely to have forced her to pay attention to the structure of complement clauses. If the *as* standard marker introduced a clause, she had to find a way to say it, as in her utterance at 5;2:

(89) There has to be as many people…[R says she doesn't know how to say it, then:] There has to be **as many** people…um…**that as many** words there are. 5;2.15

CONCLUSION

The data and analyses presented here provide insight into one area of language that involves a complex set of semantically and syntactically related forms. The data from Sadie and Rachel suggest that the acquisition of such forms is a long drawn-out process in which multiple developments are occurring side by side across structures.

At the outset, several questions were raised concerning aspects of development related to these particular forms. Let us return to these to reflect on how these data shed light on them:

(1) Little is known regarding the acquisition of multiple modification:

These data indicate that children work out the structure of multiple modification piece by piece, drawing on prior-learned constructs at every step.

(2) Little is known about the development *within* each structure (how do uses of each form—*very, too, as, than, more, many*, etc.—change with time and experience?):

These data suggest both piecemeal learning (e.g., the semantics of Rachel's use of *too* in *too heavy* and *too late* was not linked with the subsequent semantics of *too* in *too A* constructions) and the development of networks of linked constructs (e.g., Rachel's early use of *how* and *many* were linked with age and number, and this early connection seems to have supported subsequent developments for these forms; in Sadie's speech, the entry of Deg forms initially associated with As (*very, how, so*) into constructs with *much* may have provided an impetus for further linking of A and Q structures). Both children's early use of *than* for "like" seems to have been influenced by notions that were cognitively and semantically accessible, but its semantic development appears to have been related in time to its growing syntactic ties with the comparative.

(3) Little is known about how development <u>across</u> the whole range of structures evolves; for example, how do the developments of *as…as, -er…than, X enough, too X* interact?

Again, while the data here indicate much early piecemeal learning, they also suggest that linkages across forms occasionally push the child along. As noted, for example, it appears that Rachel's apparent conclusion that degree marker *as* must be accompanied by standard marker *as* spilled over into her understanding of the structure of comparatives, and these in turn affected her attention to the expression of clausal complements.

(4) Not much is known about individual differences in the acquisition of these forms across children.

These data suggest some commonalities in development across children, some idiosyncracies. Some commonalities appear to be that children attempt to express certain concepts (INTENSIFICATION, EXTREME ENDS) earlier than others (SCALAR POSITION), and that children's syntactic development of these forms may be anchored primarily around certain forms (*more, A-er,* and *much*) and developments associated with them. Children differ, however, in which exact forms they pick up to express the notions in question (e.g., *very* vs. *so* vs. *-er* vs. *-est* vs. reduplication for INTENSIFICATION) and how they go about expanding the modification of As and Qs. For example, in Sadie's case, she developed a syntactically indiscriminate combining of Deg and Q forms; in Rachel's case, she progressed through the expansion of *X + A-er, much more A-er,* and Deg + *much* forms.

(5) Further work is needed regarding the acquisition of language versus the acquisition of cognitive understanding.

While this study did not examine this question directly, it has provided indirect evidence that certain cognitive concepts seem more easily accessible to children than others, and this affects their early use of forms that in the adult language are linked with the less accessible forms. Thus, scalarity is relatively inaccessible early on, so younger children use language that expresses scalar notions (*as…as*, *enough*, *until*, *catch up with*, etc.) for nonscalar meanings.

(6) Very little is known about children's understanding of scalar predicates.

These data suggest that children initially misuse and misinterpret scalar predicates. It also suggests that the development of scalar predicates involves several components in development, and that the semantic appreciation of scalarity may go hand in hand with the child's developing understanding of number.

Among the broader questions posed here were the following:

(7) To what extent do children approach these structures on the basis of broad syntactic categories and structures? That is, does knowledge of syntactic structure guide children's acquisition of these forms, or do the syntactic structures emerge out of the children's experience with the forms?

It is clear that these children are not guided by broad syntactic structures in the development of these forms. Rather, the data here clearly point to the development of syntactic structures in a piecemeal fashion, and syntactic structures eventually emerge as a product of development.

(8) Are the developments in the syntactic and semantic (and cognitive) realms autonomous, or do developments in one area influence developments in another?

The answer to this question is mixed. On the one hand, there is clear interaction:

(a) Children's early limited cognitive understanding leads them to attach accessible notions (INTENSIFICATION, EXTREME ENDS) to forms, both appropriately (*very* A, *so* A) and inappropriately (A-*er*, A-*est*).
(b) Children's immature understanding of A-*er* leads to immature understanding and use of *than*, and figuring out the meaning of *than* seems to coincide with figuring out that -*er* requires *than* as standard marker.
(c) Determining the meaning of the superlative appears linked with its association with *in the world* or *out of the world*; the meaning of degree marker *as* is tied with its high occurrence with standard marker *as*.
(d) A child's early association of a given meaning with a form (e.g., *many* with age, and, hence, number) can carry over into later developments (the correct association of *many* with countable entities when it is later used appropriately as a quantifier).
(e) Overextensions of semantic notions can lead to inappropriate syntactic structures (e.g., Sadie's expansion of INTENSIFICATION to verbs—"he's drawing galore").
(f) The development of multiple modification appears to have been anchored around A-*er* (Rachel) or A-*er*, *too* A, A-*est* (Sadie). It is

not clear whether this is because the children discovered a semantic property—e.g., that the notion expressed by *A-er* can be modified semantically— or is an outgrowth of the addition of syntactic patterns to their speech (e.g., *very bigger, that bigger*).

If the former was the case, this would mean that semantics led syntactic development. However, it would be hard to explain (a) why neither child used multiple modification with *as* and *enough* (see introduction) and (b) why Rachel's initial steps revolved only around *A-er.*

If the latter was the case, it would mean that both children took small, conservative syntactic steps in developing these forms, which ultimately would involve both syntactic and semantic structure.

At the same time, semantic and syntactic developments for a structure are not necessarily tied.

(g) Take, for example, the case of the comparative vs. the superlative. Since the superlative *A-est* is related to the expression of EXTREME ENDS, a notion that is fairly accessible to children, its semantic use is appropriate fairly early, even while *A-er* is being used immaturely. However, in syntactic development, the development of the comparative seems to generally precede/lead the development of the superlative: The association of *than* with *-er* becomes solidified earlier than the association of *in the world* with *-est*; the introduction of quantifier modifiers (*much*) into A constructs is tied with the comparative (e.g., *much more A-er*) more than with the superlative.

(h) Developments regarding the form of degree phrases appear to occur largely independent of their meaning, as the child discovers commonalities across forms (e.g., between Deg + A and Deg + *much*).

(9) Do children follow a common trajectory in the development of these systems, or is the developmental path followed idiosyncratic and distinct across children?

With regard to semantic development, both Sadie and Rachel seem to have expanded their repertoire of messages from initial notions of INTENSIFICATION, EXTREME ENDS, LIKE, through comparative and superlative notions, through to scalar notions encoded through *as*...*as* and *enough*.

However, the data here indicate also that not all children will necessarily follow the same steps in their choice of initial limited formulas, nor in the expansion of these initially limited formulas. For example, in Sadie's case, the introduction of Q modifiers into A structures and of A modifiers into Q structures led to syntactically quite indiscriminate combining of Deg and Q patterns. In Rachel's case, on the other hand, the introduction of multiple modification, for As, revolved around modification of *A-er* constructs and the introduction of *much more A-er,* and for Qs, around Deg + *much* constructs. The difference between the two children may have stemmed from the early differences in their attention to premodifiers of As (Sadie's preference) vs. postmodifiers (Rachel's preference). That is, Sadie's early attention to X + A forms may have influenced her later development of pre-modifiers of bare As and Qs, while Rachel's early attention to *X-er* and *X-est* forms may have influenced her later syntactic expansion, based on *A-er*, to X + *A-er* forms.

(10) Does language lead cognitive development, cognitive development lead language, or a mixture of these two?

Again, the answer appears mixed:

On the one hand, the common semantic trajectory shared by Sadie and Rachel seems to have its roots in cognitive accessibility of the notions encoded.

At the same time, these data open the possibility, at least, that it is children's understanding of scalarity associated with number and the introduction of numbers syntactically into these scalar predicate expressions that may facilitate children's developing understanding of the concepts underlying these scalar predicates.

As stated at the outset, this research was conducted with the hope of helping to answer some of these open questions, and of providing further insight into the developments of individual lexical structures; into the development of links between structures and of the whole linguistic system; into the influences of cognitive, semantic, and syntactic aspects on the course of acquisition; and into the range of individual differences and range of commonalities in the acquisition of these structures. With the help of Sadie and Rachel, I hope that this chapter provides food for thought on the answers to these questions.

ACKNOWLEDGMENTS

I am very grateful to Ken Drozd, Julian Pine, and Nick Sobin for helpful comments on a previous version of this chapter.

REFERENCES

Alrenga, P. (2005, January 8). Specificity condition effects in the English attributive comparative construction. Paper presented at the LSA Annual Meeting, Oakland, CA.

Androutsopoulou, A., & Español-Echevarría, M. (2006). Much-support and unpronounced much. *Proceedings of the 2006 Annual Conference of the Canadian Linguistic Association*.

Arendasy, M., Sommer, M., & Ponocny, I. (2005). Psychometric approaches help resolve competing cognitive models: When less is more than it seems. *Cognition and Instruction* 23(4), 503–521.

Bloom, L. M. (1970). *Language development: Form and function in emerging grammars*. Cambridge, MA: MIT Press.

Bloom, L. M. (1973). *One word at a time: The use of single word utterances before syntax.* The Hague: Mouton.

Bloom, P. (1994). Syntax-semantics mappings as an explanation for some transitions in language development. In Y. Levy (Ed.), *Other children, other languages: Issues in the theory of language acquisition* (pp. 41–75). Hillsdale, NJ: Erlbaum.

Bloom, P., & Wynn, K. (1997). Linguistic cues in the acquisition of number words. *Journal of Child Language 24,* 511–533.

Bowerman, M.. (1978). The acquisition of word meaning: An investigation into some current conflicts. In N. Waterson & C. Snow (Eds.), *The development of communication* (pp. 263–287). New York: Wiley.

Bowerman, M. (1981). The child's expression of meaning: Expanding relationships among lexicon, syntax, and morphology. In H. Winitz (Ed.), *Native language and foreign language acquisition* (pp. 172–189). New York: The New York Academy of Sciences.

Bowerman, M. (1982). Starting to talk worse: Clues to language acquisition from children's late speech errors. In S. Strauss & R. Stavy (Eds.), *U-shaped behavioral growth* (pp. 101–146). New York: Academic Press.

Bowers, J. (1970). Adjectives and adverbs in English. Distributed by Indiana University Linguistics Club.

Bresnan, J. (1973). Syntax of the comparative clause construction in English. *Linguistic Inquiry, 4*(3), 275–344.

Briars, D. J., & Siegler, R. S. (1984). A featural analysis of preschoolers' counting knowledge. *Developmental Psychology, 20,* 607–618.

Brinkman, U., Drozd, K. F., & Krämer, I. (1996). Physical individuation as a prerequisite for children's symmetrical interpretations. In A. Stringfellow, D. Cahana-Amitay, E. Hughes, & A. Zukowski (Eds.), *Proceedings of the 20th annual Boston University conference on language development* (pp. 99–110). Somerville, MA: Cascadilla Press.

Brooks, P. J., Braine, M. D. S., Jia, X., & Dias, M. (2001). Early representations for *all, each,* and their counterparts in Mandarin Chinese and Portuguese. In M. Bowerman & S. C. Levinson (Eds.), *Language acquisition and conceptual development* (pp. 316–339). Cambridge, UK: Cambridge University Press.

Carey, S. E. (1978a). The child as word learner. In M. Halle, J. Bresnan, & G. Miller (Eds.), *Linguistic theory and psychological reality* (pp. 269–293). Cambridge, MA: MIT Press.

Carey, S. E. (1978b). Less may never mean more. In R. N. Campbell & P. Smith (Eds.), *Recent advances in the psychology of language* (pp. 109–132). New York: Plenum.

Carey, S. (1994). Does learning a language require the child to reconceptualize the world? In L. Gleitman & B. Landau (Eds.), *The acquisition of the lexicon* (pp. 143–167). Cambridge, MA: MIT Press.

Carey, S. (2001). Bridging the gap between cognition and developmental neuroscience: A case study of the representation of number. In C.A. Nelson & M. Luciana (Eds.), *The handbook of developmental cognitive neuroscience* (pp. 415–432). Cambridge, MA: MIT Press.

Carey, S. (2004). Bootstrapping and the origins of concepts. *Daedalus, 133*(1), 59–68.

Casasola, M., Wilbourn, M. P., & Yang, S. (2006). Can English-learning toddlers acquire and generalize a novel spatial word? *First Language, 26*(2), 187–205.

Cassell's concise dictionary. (1997). London: Cassell.

Chierchia, G., Crain, S., Guasti, M. T., Gualmini, A., & Meroni, L. (2001). The acquisition of disjunction: Evidence for a grammatical view of scalar implicatures. In A. H. J. Do, L. Dominguez, & A. Johansen (Eds.), *Proceedings of the 25th annual Boston University conference on language development* (pp. 157–168). Somerville, MA: Cascadilla Press.

Choi, S. (2006). Influence of language-specific input on spatial cognition: Categories of containment. *First Language, 26*(2), 207–232.

Clark, H. H. (1970). The primitive nature of children's relational concepts. In J. R. Hayes (Ed.), *Cognition and the development of language* (pp. 269–278). New York: Wiley.

Cordes, S., & Gelman, R. (2005). The young numerical mind: When does it count? In J. I. D. Campbell (Ed.), *Handbook of mathematical cognition* (pp. 127–142). New York: Psychology Press.

Corver, N. (1990). The syntax of left branch extractions. Unpublished doctoral dissertation, Katholieke Universiteit, Brabant.

Corver, N. (1997a). Much-support as a last resort. *Linguistic Inquiry, 28*, 119–164.

Corver, N. (1997b). The internal syntax of the Dutch extended adjectival projection. *Natural Language and Linguistic Theory, 15*, 289–368.

Crain, S., Thornton, R., Boster, C., Conway, L., Lillo-Martin, D., & Woodams, E. (1996). Quantification without qualification. *Language Acquisition, 5*, 83–153.

den Dikken, M. (2005). Comparative correlatives comparatively. *Linguistic Inquiry, 36* (4): 497–532.

Doetjes, J. (1997). *Quantifiers and selection: On the distribution of quantifying expressions in French, Dutch, and English*. The Hague: Holland Academic Graphics.

Doetjes, J., Neeleman, A., & Van de Koot, H. (1998). *Degree expressions and the autonomy of syntax*. (Working Papers in Linguistics 10). London: University College London.

Donaldson, M., & McGarrigle, J. (1973). Some clues to the nature of semantic development. *Journal of Child Language, 1*, 185–194.

Donaldson, M., & Wales, R. (1970). On the acquisition of some relational terms. In J. R. Hayes (Ed.), *Cognition and the development of language* (pp. 235–268). New York: Wiley.

Drozd, K. F. (1996). Quantifier interpretation errors as errors of distributive scope. In A. Stringfellow, D. Cahana-Amitay, E. Hughes, & A. Zukowski (Eds.), *Proceedings of the 20th annual Boston conference on language development* (pp. 177–188). Somerville, MA: Cascadilla Press.

Drozd, K. (2001). Children's weak interpretations of universally quantified questions. In M. Bowerman & S. C. Levinson (Eds.), *Language acquisition and conceptual development* (pp. 340–376). Cambridge, UK: Cambridge University Press.

Drozd, K. (2002). Negative DPs and elliptical negation in child English. *Language Acquisition, 10*(2), 77–122.

Ehri, L. C. (1976). Comprehension and production of adjectives and seriation. *Journal of Child Language, 3*, 369–384.

Ehri, L. C., & Ammon, P. R. (1974). Children's comprehension of comparative sentence transformations. *Child Development 45*(2), 512–516.

Elman, J. L. (1998). Connectionism, artificial life, and dynamical systems: New approaches to old questions. In W. Bechtel & G. Graham (Eds.), *A companion to cognitive science* (pp. 488–505). Oxford: Blackwell.

Fuson, K. (1988). *Children's counting and concepts of number*. New York: Springer-Verlag.

Gathercole, V. C. (1979a). The acquisition of *more* and *less*: A critical review. In G. Gathercole & K. Godden (Eds.), *Kansas Papers in Linguistics, 4*(2), 99–128.

Gathercole, V. C. (1979b). Birdies like birdseed the bester than buns: A study of relational comparatives and their acquisition. Unpublished doctoral dissertation, University of Kansas.

Gathercole, V. C. (1983). Haphazard examples, prototype theory, and the acquisition of comparatives. *First Language, 4*, 169–196.

Gathercole, V. C. (1985a). "He has too much hard questions": The acquisition of the linguistic mass-count distinction in *much* and *many*. *Journal of Child Language, 12*, 395–415.

Gathercole, V. C. (1985b). More and more and more about *more*. *Journal of Experimental Child Psychology, 40*, 73–104.

Gathercole, V. C. (1986). Evaluating competing linguistic theories with child language data: The case of the mass-count distinction. *Linguistics and Philosophy, 9*, 151–190.

Gathercole, V., Cramer, L., Somerville, S., & Jansen op de Haar, M. (1995). Ontological categories and function: Acquisition of new names. *Cognitive Development, 10*, 225–251.

Gazdar, G. (1979). *Pragmatics: Implicature, presupposition, and logical form*. New York: Academic Press.

Gelman, R. (1978). Counting in the preschooler: What does and does not develop? In R. S. Siegler (Ed.), *Children's thinking: What develops?* (pp. 213–241). Hillsdale, NJ: Erlbaum.

Gelman, R. (1993). A rational-constructivist account of early learning about numbers and objects. *The Psychology of Learning and Motivation, 30*, 61–96.

Gelman, R., & Butterworth, B. (2005). Number and language: How are they related? *Trends in Cognitive Science, 9*(1), 6–10.

Gelman, R., & Gallistel, C. R. (1978). *The child's understanding of number.* Cambridge, MA: Harvard University Press.

Gelman, R., Meck, E., & Merkin, S. (1986). Young children's numerical competence. *Cognitive Development, 1*, 1–29.

Gershkoff-Stowe, L., & Thelen, E. (2004). U-shaped changes in behavior: A dynamic systems perspective. *Journal of Cognition and Development, 5*(1), 11–36.

Gitterman, D., & Johnston, J. R. (1983). Talking about comparisons: A study of young children's comparative adjective usage. *Journal of Child Language, 10*, 605–621.

Gobbo, C., & Agnoli, F. (1985). Comprehension of two types of negative comparisons in children. *Journal of Psycholinguistic Research, 14* (3), 301–316.

Gordon, P. (1978). Partial lexical entry and the semantic development of more and less. Unpublished manuscript, University of Stirling.

Gordon, P. (1982). The acquisition of syntactic categories: The case of the count/mass distinction. Unpublished doctoral dissertation, Massachusetts Institute of Technology, Cambridge, MA.

Gordon, P. (1988). Count/mass category acquisition: Distributional distinctions in children's speech. *Journal of Child Language, 15*, 109–128.

Greeno, J. G., Riley, M. S., & Gelman, R. (1984). Conceptual competence and children's counting. *Cognitive Psychology, 16*, 94–134.

Gualmini, A., Crain, S., Meroni, L., Chierchia, G., & Guasti, M. T. (2001). At the semantics/pragmatics interface in child language. In R. Hastings, B. Jackson & Z. Zvolenszky (Eds.), *Proceedings of SALT* 11. Ithaca, NY: Cornell University.

Hackl, M. (2001). Comparative quantifiers and plural prediction. In K. Megerdoomian & L. A. Bare-el (Eds.), *WCCFL 20 Proceedings* (pp. 234–247). Somerville, MA: Cascadilla Press.

Horn, L. (1972). On the semantic properties of logical operators in English. Doctoral dissertation, University of California, Los Angeles. (Distributed by Indiana University Linguistics Club, 1976).

Horn, L. (1997). Negative polarity and the dynamics of vertical inference. In D. Forget et al. (Eds.), *Syntax and semantics* (pp. 157–182). Amsterdam: John Benjamins.

Horn, L. (2000). Any and ever: Free choice and free relatives. In *Proceedings of the 15th annual conference of the Israeli Association for Theoretical Linguistics* (pp. 71–111).

Horn, L. (2004). Implicature. In L. Horn & G. Ward (eds.), *The handbook of pragmatics* (pp. 3–28). Oxford: Blackwell.

Huckin, T. N. (1977). The nonglobality of *-er* suppletion. *Linguistic Analysis, 3*, 217–226.

Huddleston, R. (1967). More on the English comparative. *Journal of Linguistics, 3*, 91–102.

Hudson, L. M., Guthrie, K. H., & Santilli, N. R. (1982). The use of linguistic and non-linguistic strategies in kindergarteners' interpretations of more and less. *Journal of Child Language, 9*, 125–138.

Hurewitz, F., Papafragou, A., Gleitman, L., & Gelman, R. (2006). Asymmetries in the acquisition of numbers and quantifiers. *Language Learning and Development, 2*(2), 77–96.

Kallio, K. D. (1988). Developmental differences in the comprehension of simple and compound comparative relations. *Child Development* 59(2), 397–410.

Keenan, E. (1987). Multiply-headed noun phrases, *Linguistic Inquiry, 18*(3), 481–490.

Kennedy, C. (2000). Comparative (sub)deletion and ranked, violable constraints in syntax, *The Proceedings of NELS 30*. Amherst, MA: GSLA Publications.

Kennedy, C. (2005, November 10). Parameters of comparison. Paper presented at Cornell University.

Kennedy, C., & McNally, L. (2005). The syntax and semantics of multiple degree modification in English. In S. Müller (Ed.), *Proceedings of the HPSG05 conference* (pp. 178–191). Stanford, CA: CSLI Publications.

Lechner, W. (2000, April 16-18). A derivational head-raising analysis of comparatives. Paper presented at 23rd GLOW Colloquium, Vitoria-Gasteiz.

Levinson, S. (2000). *Presumptive meanings*. Cambridge, MA: MIT Press.

Liao, Wei-wen. (2005). The comparative construction and the *wh*- movement. *USTWPL, 1*, 187–204.

Lidz, J., & Musolino, J. (2002). Children's command of quantification. *Cognition 84*(2), 113–154.

Lyons, J. (1977). *Semantics* (Vol. 2). Cambridge, UK: Cambridge University Press.

MacWhinney, B. (1987). The competition model. In B. MacWhinney (Ed.), *Mechanisms of language acquisition* (pp. 249–308). Hillsdale, NJ: Erlbaum.

Matushansky, O. (2002). Tipping the scales: The syntax of scalarity in the complement of *seem*. *Syntax, 5*(3), 219–276.

McDonald, J. (1989). The acquisition of cue-category mappings. In B. MacWhinney & E. Bates (Eds.), *The crosslinguistic study of sentence processing* (pp. 375–396). Cambridge, UK: Cambridge University Press.

Mix, K. S., Huttenlocher, J., & Levine, S. C. (2002). Multiple cues for quantification in infancy: Is number one of them? *Psychological Bulletin, 128*(2), 278–294.

Moxey, L., & Sanford, A. (1993). *Communicating quantities: A psychological perspective.* Hillsdale, NJ: Erlbaum,

Musolino, J. (2004). The semantics and acquisition of number words: Integrating linguistic and developmental perspectives. *Cognition, 93*, 1–41.

Napoli, D. (1983). Comparative ellipsis: A phrase structure analysis. *Linguistic Inquiry, 14*, 675–694.

Nelson, K., & Benedict, H.. (1974). The comprehension of relative, absolute, and contrastive adjectives by young children. *Journal of Psycholinguistic Research, 3*(4), 333–342.

Noveck, I. (2001). When children are more logical than adults: Experimental investigations of scalar implicature. *Cognition, 78*, 165–188.

Oller, D. K., & Eilers, R. E. (Eds.). (2002). *Language and literacy in bilingual children.* Clevedon, UK: Multilingual Matters.

Papafragou, A. (2003a). Aspectuality and scalar structure. *Proceedings of the 27th Annual Boston University Conference on Language Development.* Somerville, MA: Cascadilla Press.

Papafragou A. (2003b). Scalar implicatures in language acquisition: Some evidence from Modern Greek. Proceedings from the 38th annual meeting of the Chicago Linguistics Society. Chicago: University of Chicago Press.

Papafragou, A. (2006). From scalar semantics to implicature: Children's interpretation of aspectuals. *Journal of Child Language, 33*, 721–757.

Papafragou, A., & Musolino, J. (2003). Scalar implicatures: Experiments at the semantics-pragmatics interface. *Cognition, 86*, 253–282.

Papafragou, A., & Schwarz, N. (2006). *Most* wanted. *Language Acquisition, 13*, 207–251.

Papafragou, A., & Tantalou, N. (2004). Children's computation of implicatures. *Language Acquisition, 12*, 71–82.

Philip, W. (1995). *Event quantification in the acquisition of universal quantification.* Amherst, MA: GLSA.

Pinkham, J. (1985). *The formation of comparative clauses in French and English.* New York: Garland.

Pollmann, T.. (2003). Some principles involved in the acquisition of number words. *Language Acquisition, 11*(1), 1–31.

Quirk, R., & Greenbaum, S. (1973). *A concise grammar of contemporary English.* New York: Harcourt Brace Jovanovich.

Rayner, M., & Banks, A. (1990). An implementable semantics for comparative constructions. *Computational Linguistic, 16*(2), 86–112.

Rijkhoek, P. D. (1998). On degree phrases and result clauses. Unpublished doctoral dissertation, University of Groningen.

Rips, L. J., Asmuth, J., & Bloomfield, A. (2006). Giving the boot to the bootstrap: How not to learn the natural numbers. *Cognition, 101*(3), B51–B60.

Ryalls, B.O. (2000). Dimensional adjectives: Factors affecting children's ability to compare objects using novel words. *Journal of Experimental Child Psychology, 76*(1), 26–49.

Sarnecka, B. W., & Gelman, S. A. (2004). Six does not just mean a lot: Preschoolers see number words as specific. *Cognition, 92*, 329–352.

Schwartz, R. A. (2003). *The 1950s: An eyewitness history.* New York: Facts on File.

Schwartz, R. A. (n.d.). The literary election. Unpublished manuscript.

Shaffer, T. M., & Ehri, L. C. (1980). Seriators' and non-seriators' comprehension of comparative adjective forms. *Journal of Psycholinguistic Research* 9, 187–204.

Skwarchuk, Sheri-Lynn, & Anglin, J. M. (2002). Children's acquisition of the English cardinal number words: A special case of vocabulary development. *Journal of Educational Psychology, 94*(1), 107–125.

Slobin, D. I. (1997). The origins of grammaticizable notions: Beyond the individual mind. In D. I. Slobin (Ed.), *The crosslinguistic study of language acquisition: Vol. 5. Expanding the contexts* (pp. 265–323). Mahwah, NJ: Erlbaum.

Smith, L. B. (1999). Children's noun learning: How general learning processes make specialized learning mechanisms. In B. MacWhinney (Ed.), *The emergence of language* (pp. 277–303). Mahwah, NJ: Erlbaum.

Soja, N. N. (1992). Inferences about the meanings of nouns: The relationship between perception and syntax. *Cognitive Development*, 7, 29–45.

Soja, N. N., Carey, S., & Spelke, E. S. (1991). Ontological categories guide young children's inductions of word meaning: Object terms and substance terms, *Cognition, 38*, 179–211.

Sophian, C., & McCorgray, P. (1994). Part-whole knowledge and early arithmetic problem solving. *Cognition and Instruction, 12*(1), 3–33.

Syrett, K., Bradley, E., Kennedy, C., & Lidz, J. (2005). Shifting standards: Children's understanding of gradable adjectives. GALANA.

Takahashi, M. (1991). Children's interpretation of sentences containing *every*. In T. L. Maxfield & B. Plunkett (Eds.), *University of Massachusetts occasional papers: Special edition: Papers in the acquisition of WH* (pp. 303–329). Amherst, MA: GLSA Publications.

Townsend, D. J. (1976). Do children interpret "marked" comparative adjectives as their opposites? *Journal of Child Language, 3*, 385–396.

Ultan, R. (1972). Some features of basic comparative constructions. *Working Papers on Language Universals, 9*, 117–162.

White, J. R. (1998). Syntax-LF mapping and the internal structure of comparatives. *UCL Working Papers in Linguistics, 10*, 1–21.

Author Index

A

B

C

D

E

F

G

L

M

N

O

P

Q

R

S

Subject Index

D

E

F

G

H

I

J

K

L

M

N

O

P

Q

R

S